D1560749

Over the last thirty years, scholars have begun to explore the implications of an ancient Jewish and Christian tradition that referred to the "Minor Prophets" as "the Twelve," "the Twelve Prophets," or the "Book of the Twelve." Scholarly work on the Book of the Twelve in the last quarter century has focused on two issues: (1) examining how the Book of the Twelve came to be recorded on a single scroll and (2) isolating unifying elements that transcend the individual writings and take on new significance when the Book of the Twelve becomes a single collection. Nogalski's comprehensive commentary offers an overview of the ancient traditions concerning the Book of the Twelve that lays the foundation for understanding these recent developments.

---

Jim Nogalski has worked longer and deeper on the "Minor Prophets" than anyone else. He has brought to his study energy, attentiveness, and expertise. He is a trail-blazer in canonical interpretation and here uses his sense of the final form of the text as a basis for a rich, reliable, and probing commentary. He shows how these mostly neglected "books" matter decisively for the full range of biblical faith.

—WALTER BRUEGGEMANN
*Columbia Theological Seminary*

A notable achievement! At once both sober and daring, Nogalski's commentary builds upon scholarly work of the past thirty years in order to treat the Minor Prophets as a . . . single literary work, which is how they were once understood and transmitted . . . . But he also reorients and advances the discussion in the process, not least by patiently bringing the Book of the Twelve into productive theological conversation with pressing issues of our day.

—STEPHEN B. CHAPMAN
*Associate Professor of Old Testament, Duke University*

---

The Smyth & Helwys Bible Commentary series brings insightful commentary to bear on the lives of contemporary Christians. Using a multimedia format, the volumes employ a stunning array of art, maps, and drawings to illustrate the insights of the Bible. It is built upon the idea that meaningful Bible study can occur when the insights of contemporary biblical scholars blend with sensitivity to the needs of students of Scripture. In addition, the CD-ROM, which offers powerful searching and research tools, pairs the text with a digital resource that is a distinctive feature of this series.

# THE BOOK OF THE TWELVE
# HOSEA–JONAH

Smyth & Helwys Bible Commentary: The Book of the Twelve: Hosea–Jonah

Publication Staff

President & CEO
*Cecil P. Staton*

Publisher & Executive Vice President
*Lex Horton*

Vice President, Production
*Keith Gammons*

Book Editor
*Leslie Andres*

Graphic Designers
*Daniel Emerson*
*Dave Jones*

Assistant Editors
*Rachel Stancil Greco*
*Kelley F. Land*

Smyth & Helwys Publishing, Inc.
6316 Peake Road
Macon, Georgia 31210-3960
1-800-747-3016
© 2011 by Smyth & Helwys Publishing
All rights reserved.
Printed in the United States of America.

The paper used in this publication meets the minimum
requirements of American National Standard for Information
Sciences—Permanence of Paper for Printed Library Materials.
ANSI Z39.48–1984 (alk. paper)

*Library of Congress Cataloging-in-Publication Data*

Nogalski, James.
The Book of the Twelve: Hosea–Jonah / by James D. Nogalski.
p. cm.—(The Smyth & Helwys Bible commentary ; v. 18a)
Includes bibliographical references and index.
ISBN 978-1-57312-075-3 (hardback : alk. paper)
1. Bible. O.T. Minor Prophets—Commentaries. I. Title.
BS1560.N64 2011
224'.07—dc23

2011018092

SMYTH & HELWYS BIBLE COMMENTARY

# THE BOOK OF THE TWELVE
# HOSEA–JONAH

## JAMES D. NOGALSKI

PUBLISHING INCORPORATED · MACON, GEORGIA

# DEDICATION

To Melanie, Megan, and Toni;
the women who make my life meaningful.

# CONTENTS

# JOEL

# AMOS

# OBADIAH

# JONAH

# ABBREVIATIONS USED IN THIS COMMENTARY

Books of the Old Testament, Apocrypha, and New Testament are generally abbreviated in the Sidebars, parenthetical references, and notes according to the following system.

*The Old Testament*

| | |
|---|---|
| Genesis | Gen |
| Exodus | Exod |
| Leviticus | Lev |
| Numbers | Num |
| Deuteronomy | Deut |
| Joshua | Josh |
| Judges | Judg |
| Ruth | Ruth |
| 1–2 Samuel | 1–2 Sam |
| 1–2 Kings | 1–2 Kgs |
| 1–2 Chronicles | 1–2 Chr |
| Ezra | Ezra |
| Nehemiah | Neh |
| Esther | Esth |
| Job | Job |
| Psalm (Psalms) | Ps (Pss) |
| Proverbs | Prov |
| Ecclesiastes | Eccl |
|   or Qoheleth | Qoh |
| Song of Solomon | Song |
|   or Song of Songs | Song |
|   or Canticles | Cant |
| Isaiah | Isa |
| Jeremiah | Jer |
| Lamentations | Lam |
| Ezekiel | Ezek |
| Daniel | Dan |
| Hosea | Hos |
| Joel | Joel |
| Amos | Amos |
| Obadiah | Obad |
| Jonah | Jonah |
| Micah | Mic |

| | |
|---|---|
| Nahum | Nah |
| Habakkuk | Hab |
| Zephaniah | Zeph |
| Haggai | Hag |
| Zechariah | Zech |
| Malachi | Mal |

*The Apocrypha*

| | |
|---|---|
| 1–2 Esdras | 1–2 Esdr |
| Tobit | Tob |
| Judith | Jdt |
| Additions to Esther | Add Esth |
| Wisdom of Solomon | Wis |
| Ecclesiasticus or the Wisdom of Jesus Son of Sirach | Sir |
| Baruch | Bar |
| Epistle (or Letter) of Jeremiah | Ep Jer |
| Prayer of Azariah and the Song of the Three | Pr Azar |
| Daniel and Susanna | Sus |
| Daniel, Bel, and the Dragon | Bel |
| Prayer of Manasseh | Pr Man |
| 1–4 Maccabees | 1–4 Macc |

*The New Testament*

| | |
|---|---|
| Matthew | Matt |
| Mark | Mark |
| Luke | Luke |
| John | John |
| Acts | Acts |
| Romans | Rom |
| 1–2 Corinthians | 1–2 Cor |
| Galatians | Gal |
| Ephesians | Eph |
| Philippians | Phil |
| Colossians | Col |
| 1–2 Thessalonians | 1–2 Thess |
| 1–2 Timothy | 1–2 Tim |
| Titus | Titus |
| Philemon | Phlm |
| Hebrews | Heb |
| James | Jas |
| 1–2 Peter | 1–2 Pet |
| 1–2–3 John | 1–2–3 John |
| Jude | Jude |
| Revelation | Rev |

Other commonly used abbreviations include:

| | |
|---|---|
| * | A standard symbol in redactional studies signaling "part of the verse or passage." Details regarding the specific portion of the verse represented by the * are treated in the commentary proper |
| 2fs | second person feminine, singular |
| 2ms | second person masculine, singular |
| 2mp | second person masculine, plural |
| 3mp | third person masculine, plural |
| AD | *Anno Domini* ("in the year of the Lord") (also commonly referred to as CE = the Common Era) |
| BC | Before Christ (also commonly referred to as BCE = Before the Common Era) |
| C. | century |
| c. | *circa* (around "that time") |
| cf. | *confer* (compare) |
| ch. | chapter |
| chs. | chapters |
| d. | died |
| ed. | edition or edited by or editor |
| eds. | editors |
| e.g. | *exempli gratia* (for example) |
| et al. | *et alii* (and others) |
| f./ff. | and the following one(s) |
| gen. ed. | general editor |
| Gk. | Greek |
| Heb. | Hebrew |
| ibid. | *ibidem* (in the same place) |
| i.e. | *id est* (that is) |
| LCL | Loeb Classical Library |
| lit. | literally |
| MT | Masoretic Text |
| n.d. | no date |
| rev. and exp. ed. | revised and expanded edition |
| sg. | singular |
| trans. | translated by or translator(s) |
| vol(s). | volume(s) |
| v. | verse |
| vv. | verses |

Selected additional written works cited by abbreviations include the following. A complete listing of abbreviations can be referenced in *The SBL Handbook of Style* (Peabody MA: Hendrickson, 1999):

| | |
|---|---|
| AB | Anchor Bible |
| *ABD* | *Anchor Bible Dictionary* |
| ACCS | Ancient Christian Commentary on Scripture |
| *ANF* | *Ante-Nicene Fathers* |
| ANTC | Abingdon New Testament Commentaries |
| BA | *Biblical Archaeologist* |
| BAR | *Biblical Archaeology Review* |
| *CBQ* | *Catholic Biblical Quarterly* |
| *HALOT* | *The Hebrew and Aramaic Lexicon of the Old Testament* |
| *HAL* | *Hebräisches und aramäisches Lexikon zum Alten Testament* |
| *HTR* | *Harvard Theological Review* |
| *HUCA* | *Hebrew Union College Annual* |
| ICC | International Critical Commentary |
| *IDB* | *Interpreters Dictionary of the Bible* |
| *JBL* | *Journal of Biblical Literature* |
| *JSJ* | *Journal for the Study of Judaism in the Persian, Hellenistic, and Roman Periods* |
| *JSNT* | *Journal for the Study of the New Testament* |
| *JSOT* | *Journal for the Study of the Old Testament* |
| KJV | King James Version |
| LXX | Septuagint = Greek Translation of Hebrew Bible |
| *MDB* | *Mercer Dictionary of the Bible* |
| MT | Masoretic Text |
| NASB | New American Standard Bible |
| NEB | New English Bible |
| NICNT | New International Commentary on the New Testament |
| NIV | New International Version |
| *NovT* | *Novum Testamentum* |
| NRSV | New Revised Standard Version |
| *NTS* | *New Testament Studies* |
| *OGIS* | *Orientis graeci inscriptiones selectae* |
| OTL | Old Testament Library |
| *PRSt* | *Perspectives in Religious Studies* |
| *RevExp* | *Review and Expositor* |
| RSV | Revised Standard Version |
| *SBLSP* | *Society of Biblical Literature Seminar Papers* |
| SP | Sacra pagina |
| *TDNT* | *Theological Dictionary of the New Testament* |
| TEV | Today's English Version |
| WBC | Word Biblical Commentary |

# AUTHOR'S PREFACE

To borrow the words of Malachi, this commentary has become my own "book of remembrance." Prophetic books are often characterized as focusing upon the enemies, and some might wonder, in the application of these texts, who the enemies are today. But this commentary, like the prophetic books themselves, was composed for the faithful, not the hostile.

My teachers gave me more than facts. Each taught me many things in the classroom, but they impressed me more as I learned about them outside the classroom. Karen Joines showed me what it means, and what it can cost, to think outside the box. Page Kelley showed me how teaching is as much about investing in the lives of students as it is in conveying information. J. J. Owens taught me how to love learning and started my interest in the Book of the Twelve. Hans Mallau taught me that patience and passion are not mutually exclusive. Odil Hannes Steck taught me to love the details and the importance of method. These teachers changed my life in ways I can never repay.

My pastors have served as models of people who genuinely want to teach as they preach. I thought of them frequently as I tried to connect prophetic texts to the life of the community today. These pastors did not always know that I was watching them for ideas and inspiration because I was not always in the pew of their churches weekly. Diane Pomeroy and Dorisanne Cooper have led their churches to think more deeply about what it means to be a community of believers committed to social justice. Marvin Wiley, Clinton Feemster, and James Smith taught me about what it means to lead African-American communities in a complex world. Les Holland and Tony Tench taught me to stay committed and engaged in the life of the congregation.

My colleagues and my students have given me encouragement at many points. Several groups of students got more than they bargained for as they came along for the ride while I wrote sections of this commentary; they took classes on prophetic books about which I was writing. I thank them for their patience and their encouragement. Gerald L. Keown has been a great friend and mentor. He has listened patiently as some of my ideas took shape, and his life has had a profound impact upon mine. Conversation partners have been many through the years, but none have had a more sustained influence than the friendship and professional engagement of the core of scholars who have been exploring the Book of the Twelve in the Society of Biblical Literature since 1993. Two of these, in particular, I need to mention by name: Paul Redditt and Aaron Schart. They have pushed me, encouraged me, and shared the same journey on trying to understand how the Book of the Twelve came to be. Finally, I want to express sincere gratitude to Roy Garton, to Anna Sieges, and to the Religion Department of Baylor University for helping bring this work to a close. Baylor has provided me with time to write as well as students to teach. Roy Garton's careful reading of this manuscript eliminated dozens of errors, provided fresh insight, and helped me clarify my thoughts. Anna Sieges helped to finalize the manuscript and prepare the indexes. Her positive attitude helped move the projects along in a timely manner.

My family has been patient with me during the many long hours of work on this commentary. My daughters, Megan and Toni, remind me what is at stake in trying to think about the big issues for this generation. My wife, Melanie, has been on this journey from the beginning. She has encouraged me beyond measure. She has listened to my thoughts and provided feedback all along the way. She has given me ideas and wisely kept me from using others. She has always been my partner in crime, but her ability to see people for who they are and who they can become has provided me with hope and gratitude time and again.

Finally, I want to thank my editors, Sam Balentine and Paul Redditt, whose careful reading of the manuscript has added immeasurably to its clarity. Sam's patient prodding helped move the commentary along even while demanding I take the time necessary to produce a volume that deals with roughly a third of the number of "books" in the Old Testament. The staff members at Smyth & Helwys also deserve recognition for the valuable assistance they provide to this volume and to this entire series. A great deal of credit goes to Scott Nash, Keith Gammons, Leslie Andres, and others whose careful reading caught numerous errors, made probing suggestions, and generally improved the finished product in ways that are not apparent to the readers. None of us realized what a daunting task this would be when we began.

*James D. Nogalski*
*April 2011*

# SERIES PREFACE

The *Smyth & Helwys Bible Commentary* is a visually stimulating and user-friendly series that is as close to multimedia in print as possible. Written by accomplished scholars with all students of Scripture in mind, the primary goal of the *Smyth & Helwys Bible Commentary* is to make available serious, credible biblical scholarship in an accessible and less intimidating format.

Far too many Bible commentaries fall short of bridging the gap between the insights of biblical scholars and the needs of students of God's written word. In an unprecedented way, the *Smyth & Helwys Bible Commentary* brings insightful commentary to bear on the lives of contemporary Christians. Using a multimedia format, the volumes employ a stunning array of art, photographs, maps, and drawings to illustrate the truths of the Bible for a visual generation of believers.

The *Smyth & Helwys Bible Commentary* is built upon the idea that meaningful Bible study can occur when the insights of contemporary biblical scholars blend with sensitivity to the needs of lifelong students of Scripture. Some persons within local faith communities, however, struggle with potentially informative biblical scholarship for several reasons. Oftentimes, such scholarship is cast in technical language easily grasped by other scholars, but not by the general reader. For example, lengthy, technical discussions on every detail of a particular scriptural text can hinder the quest for a clear grasp of the whole. Also, the format for presenting scholarly insights has often been confusing to the general reader, rendering the work less than helpful. Unfortunately, responses to the hurdles of reading extensive commentaries have led some publishers to produce works for a general readership that merely skim the surface of the rich resources of biblical scholarship. This commentary series incorporates works of fine art in an accurate and scholarly manner, yet the format remains "user-friendly." An important facet is the presentation and explanation of images of art, which interpret the biblical material or illustrate how the biblical material has been understood and interpreted in the past. A visual generation of believers deserves a commentary series that contains not only the all-important textual commentary on Scripture, but images, photographs, maps, works of fine art, and drawings that bring the text to life.

The *Smyth & Helwys Bible Commentary* makes serious, credible biblical scholarship more accessible to a wider audience. Writers and editors alike present information in ways that encourage readers to gain a better understanding of the Bible. The editorial board has worked to develop a format that is useful and usable, informative and pleasing to the eye. Our writers are reputable scholars who participate in the community of faith and sense a calling to communicate the results of their scholarship to their faith community.

The *Smyth & Helwys Bible Commentary* addresses Christians and the larger church. While both respect for and sensitivity to the needs and contributions of other faith communities are reflected in the work of the series authors, the authors speak primarily to Christians. Thus the reader can note a confessional tone throughout the volumes. No particular "confession of faith" guides the authors, and diverse perspectives are observed in the various volumes. Each writer, though, brings to the biblical text the best scholarly tools available and expresses the results of their studies in commentary and visuals that assist readers seeking a word from the Lord for the church.

To accomplish this goal, writers in this series have drawn from numerous streams in the rich tradition of biblical interpretation. The basic focus is the biblical text itself, and considerable attention is given to the wording and structure of texts. Each particular text, however, is also considered in the light of the entire canon of Christian Scriptures. Beyond this, attention is given to the cultural context of the biblical writings. Information from archaeology, ancient history, geography, comparative literature, history of religions, politics, sociology, and even economics is used to illuminate the culture of the people who produced the Bible. In addition, the writers have drawn from the history of interpretation, not only as it is found in traditional commentary on the Bible but also in literature, theater, church history, and the visual arts. Finally, the *Commentary* on Scripture is joined with *Connections* to the world of the contemporary church. Here again, the writers draw on scholarship in many fields as well as relevant issues in the popular culture.

This wealth of information might easily overwhelm a reader if not presented in a "user-friendly" format. Thus the heavier discussions of detail and the treatments of other helpful topics are presented in special-interest boxes, or Sidebars, clearly connected to the passages under discussion so as not to interrupt the flow of the basic interpretation. The result is a commentary on Scripture that focuses on the theological significance of a text while also offering the reader a rich array of additional information related to the text and its interpretation.

An accompanying CD-ROM offers powerful searching and research tools. The commentary text, Sidebars, and visuals are all reproduced on a CD that is fully indexed and searchable. Pairing a text version with a digital resource is a distinctive feature of the *Smyth & Helwys Bible Commentary.*

Combining credible biblical scholarship, user-friendly study features, and sensitivity to the needs of a visually oriented generation of believers creates a unique and unprecedented type of commentary series. With insight from many of today's finest biblical scholars and a stunning visual format, it is our hope that the *Smyth & Helwys Bible Commentary* will be a welcome addition to the personal libraries of all students of Scripture.

*The Editors*

# HOW TO USE
# THIS COMMENTARY

The *Smyth & Helwys Bible Commentary* is written by accomplished biblical scholars with a wide array of readers in mind. Whether engaged in the study of Scripture in a church setting or in a college or seminary classroom, all students of the Bible will find a number of useful features throughout the commentary that are helpful for interpreting the Bible.

## Basic Design of the Volumes

Each volume features an Introduction to a particular book of the Bible, providing a brief guide to information that is necessary for reading and interpreting the text: the historical setting, literary design, and theological significance. Each Introduction also includes a comprehensive outline of the particular book under study.

Each chapter of the commentary investigates the text according to logical divisions in a particular book of the Bible. Sometimes these divisions follow the traditional chapter segmentation, while at other times the textual units consist of sections of chapters or portions of more than one chapter. The divisions reflect the literary structure of a book and offer a guide for selecting passages that are useful in preaching and teaching.

An accompanying CD-ROM offers powerful searching and research tools. The commentary text, Sidebars, and visuals are all reproduced on a CD that is fully indexed and searchable. Pairing a text version with a digital resource also allows unprecedented flexibility and freedom for the reader. Carry the text version to locations you most enjoy doing research while knowing that the CD offers a portable alternative for travel from the office, church, classroom, and your home.

## Commentary and Connections

As each chapter explores a textual unit, the discussion centers around two basic sections: *Commentary* and *Connections*. The analysis of a passage, including the details of its language, the history reflected in the text, and the literary forms found in the text, are the main focus of the *Commentary* section. The primary concern of the *Commentary* section is to explore the theological issues presented by the Scripture passage. *Connections* presents potential applications of the insights provided in the *Commentary* section. The *Connections* portion of each chapter considers what issues are relevant for teaching and suggests useful methods and resources. *Connections* also identifies themes suitable for sermon planning and suggests helpful approaches for preaching on the Scripture text.

### Sidebars

The *Smyth & Helwys Bible Commentary* provides a unique hyperlink format that quickly guides the reader to additional insights. Since other more technical or supplementary information is vital for understanding a text and its implications, the volumes feature distinctive Sidebars, or special-interest boxes, that provide a wealth of information on such matters as:

- Historical information (such as chronological charts, lists of kings or rulers, maps, descriptions of monetary systems, descriptions of special groups, descriptions of archaeological sites or geographical settings).

- Graphic outlines of literary structure (including such items as poetry, chiasm, repetition, epistolary form).

- Definition or brief discussions of technical or theological terms and issues.

- Insightful quotations that are not integrated into the running text but are relevant to the passage under discussion.

- Notes on the history of interpretation (Augustine on the Good Samaritan, Luther on James, Stendahl on Romans, etc.).

- Line drawings, photographs, and other illustrations relevant for understanding the historical context or interpretive significance of the text.

- Presentation and discussion of works of fine art that have interpreted a Scripture passage.

Each Sidebar is printed in color and is referenced at the appropriate place in the *Commentary* or *Connections* section with a color-coded title that directs the reader to the relevant Sidebar. In addition, helpful icons appear in the Sidebars, which provide the reader with visual cues to the type of material that is explained in each Sidebar. Throughout the commentary, these four distinct hyperlinks provide useful links in an easily recognizable design.

## AΩ

### Alpha & Omega Language

This icon identifies the information as a language-based tool that offers further exploration of the Scripture selection. This could include syntactical information, word studies, popular or additional uses of the word(s) in question, additional contexts in which the term appears, and the history of the term's translation. All non-English terms are transliterated into the appropriate English characters.

### Culture/Context

This icon introduces further comment on contextual or cultural details that shed light on the Scripture selection. Describing the place and time to which a Scripture passage refers is often vital to the task of biblical interpretation. Sidebar items introduced with this icon could include geographical, historical, political, social, topographical, or economic information. Here, the reader may find an excerpt of an ancient text or inscription that sheds light on the text. Or one may find a description of some element of ancient religion such as Baalism in Canaan or the Hero cult in the Mystery Religions of the Greco-Roman world.

### Interpretation

Sidebars that appear under this icon serve a general interpretive function in terms of both historical and contemporary renderings. Under this heading, the reader might find a selection from classic or contemporary literature that illuminates the Scripture text or a significant quotation from a famous sermon that addresses the passage. Insights are drawn from various sources, including literature, worship, theater, church history, and sociology.

## Additional Resources Study

Here, the reader finds a convenient list of useful resources for further investigation of the selected Scripture text, including books, journals, websites, special collections, organizations, and societies. Specialized discussions of works not often associated with biblical studies may also appear here.

## Additional Features

Each volume also includes a basic Bibliography on the biblical book under study. Other bibliographies on selected issues are often included that point the reader to other helpful resources.

Notes at the end of each chapter provide full documentation of sources used and contain additional discussions of related matters.

Abbreviations used in each volume are explained in a list of abbreviations found after the Table of Contents.

Readers of the *Smyth & Helwys Bible Commentary* can regularly visit the Internet support site for news, information, updates, and enhancements to the series at **www.helwys.com/commentary**.

Several thorough indexes enable the reader to locate information quickly. These indexes include:

- An *Index of Sidebars* groups content from the special-interest boxes by category (maps, fine art, photographs, drawings, etc.).

- An *Index of Scriptures* lists citations to particular biblical texts.

- An *Index of Topics* lists alphabetically the major subjects, names, topics, and locations referenced or discussed in the volume.

- An *Index of Modern Authors* organizes contemporary authors whose works are cited in the volume.

# INTRODUCTION TO THE BOOK OF THE TWELVE

Over the last thirty years, scholars have begun to explore the implications of an ancient Jewish and Christian tradition that referred to the "Minor Prophets" as "the Twelve," "the Twelve Prophets," or the "Book of the Twelve." Scholarly work on the Book of the Twelve in the last quarter century has focused on two issues in particular: (1) developing models regarding how the Book of the Twelve came to be recorded on a single scroll and (2) isolating unifying elements that transcend the individual writings (including catchwords, themes, and motifs) and take on new significance when the Book of the Twelve becomes a single collection rather than twelve distinct writings. An overview of the ancient traditions concerning the Book of the Twelve will lay the foundation for understanding these recent developments.

## Historical Traditions

Ancient traditions referred to the scroll upon which Hosea–Malachi were transmitted as one of the four scrolls containing the Latter Prophets (Isaiah, Jeremiah, Ezekiel, and the Twelve). These four prophetic scrolls, along with the four Former Prophets (Joshua, Judges, Samuel, and Kings) formed the Nebi'im, the prophetic writings in the Hebrew canon. In terms of the content and significance of these ancient traditions, the implications become clear: by 200 BCE the Twelve was written on a single scroll and, significantly, counted as a single book.

The earliest reference to the Twelve Prophets as a corpus appears in Sirach, a book of the Apocrypha composed around 180 BCE and translated by his grandson who also added a prologue to the beginning. Both this prologue and the end of Sirach contain points of reference for understanding the development of the Hebrew canon. The prologue begins, "many great teachings have been given to us through the Law and the Prophets and the others that followed them . . . ." Despite a few recent objections, this statement has been interpreted as a sign of a developing sense of canon in the early second century BCE, which recognized both the Torah (Law) and the Nebi'im (Prophets) as two groups of writings that held special significance for the Jewish community.[1] At the end of Sirach (44–49), one finds an extended poetic composition recounting the exploits of the ancestors whose stories appear in the biblical narratives. Within this poetic material, the author refers to the two heroic kings of Judah who saved Jerusalem (Hezekiah in 48:17-22 and Josiah in 49:1-3) followed by references to prophets in the Nebi'im. The recollections of Hezekiah are followed by a passage on the prophet Isaiah (48:23-25) while the references to Josiah are followed by references to Jeremiah (49:6-7), Ezekiel (49:8), and the bones of the Twelve Prophets (49:10) who comforted the people and gave them hope. Clearly, this section of the Hymn of the Fathers refers to the canonical books, and does so in the order in which they would come to be transmitted.

Two writings from the first century CE confirm that the Book of the Twelve was counted as one book. Josephus (*Ag. Ap.* 1.40) and 4 Ezra 14 refer to the number of canonical writings as 22 and 24 respectively. These numbers seem odd to modern readers who think of 39 Old Testament books, but when one realizes that prior to the Middle Ages Jewish tradition did not subdivide Samuel, Kings, or Chronicles into two books, and that it counted the Book of the Twelve as one book, then one actually can understand these numbers as close to the current number of writings in the canon.[2]

Jewish traditions also presume the transmission of a unified corpus of the Twelve. In the Babylonian Talmud, Baba Batra 13b-15a treats the Twelve collectively (14b) in terms of its order in the Nebi'im. It also allows fewer lines between the writings of the Book of the Twelve than between other books (13a). The Masoretic notes lining the margin of the Leningrad Codex, which forms the basis of most printed Hebrew Bibles because it represents the oldest complete manuscript, also testifies to the treatment of the Book of the Twelve as a single corpus. The end of Malachi contains Masoretic notes regarding the total number of verses in the Twelve, and Micah 3:12 contains a note in the margin designating this verse as the midpoint of the Twelve.

Jerome's (347–420 CE) Prologue to the Twelve Prophets in the Vulgate references the tradition that "the Twelve is one book."[3] Further, he also reports a hermeneutic for reading the Twelve when he indicates that the six undated writings should be read as coming from the time of the last king mentioned. One can surmise with some level of probability that Jerome was reporting traditions at this point that he had learned from the rabbis who taught him Hebrew.

Jerome's contemporary, Augustine (354–430 CE), by contrast, had more effect on Christianity's relegation of the Book of the Twelve to the margins of prophetic literature. His reference to the collection as the Minor Prophets emphasized the smaller size of the individual writings, which likely had the unintended consequence of lessening their significance.

The implications for this brief overview are clear. Both Jewish and Christian traditions from 200 BCE to the Middle Ages indicate that the Twelve Prophets were considered as a single collection of prophetic writings that were counted as a single book. Jerome, probably reflecting Jewish tradition, implies that this book should also be read sequentially. Unfortunately, neither Christian nor Jewish hermeneutical practices of the time dealt much with reading prophetic books as books, so evidence for doing as Jerome suggests rarely appears.[4]

## The Sequence of the Writings

While the continuing transmission of the Twelve Prophets on a single scroll indicates the collection had an established identity as a group by the beginning of the second century BCE, the order in which these writings appear within the corpus is not completely uniform. Two sequences have wide attestation, that of the MT and several strands of the LXX.[5] The order of the first six writings in the MT and the LXX varies, though the last six appear in precisely the same order. [MT and LXX Orders] Substantial, though not universal, agreement exists that the MT reflects the original order of the writings.[6] Two reasons account for this opinion. First, elsewhere, the LXX reorders other books according to a sense of chronology. For example, Ruth, Chronicles,

### MT and LXX Orders

The order of the first six writings of the Book of the Twelve differs between the Masoretic Text and the primary order attested in the Septuagint (LXX): When considered from the question of priority, the likelihood is that the LXX order derives from a decision to change the MT order. The LXX elsewhere reflects the rearrangement of books by placing them in their "historical" location (e.g., moving Ruth so it appears after Judges rather than near the end of the canon in the MT order). By simply bringing the three eighth-century prophets (Hosea, Amos, and Micah) together, and keeping them in the same order, one can easily see that the other three (undated) writings that follow still reflect the MT order of Joel, Obadiah, and Jonah.

| MT | LXX |
|---|---|
| Hosea* | Hosea* |
| Joel | Amos* |
| Amos* | Micah* |
| Obadiah | Joel |
| Jonah | Obadiah |
| Micah* | Jonah |

\* Superscriptions mention eighth-century kings

Ezra, and Nehemiah all appear among the Writings (*Ketubim*) in the Hebrew canon, but are moved to different locations in the LXX. Ruth is placed after Judges because Ruth 1:1 sets the book "in the time when the Judges judged." Chronicles essentially covers the same material as Samuel and Kings, so Chronicles is placed after Kings. Ezra and Nehemiah preceded Chronicles in the *Ketubim*, but they are placed after Chronicles in the LXX because they pick up where Chronicles ends.

Second, given this tendency, the LXX can be simply explained as deriving from the MT order. Three writings in the Book of the Twelve contain references to eighth-century kings (Hosea, Amos, Micah). In the MT, these three writings are separated, but in the LXX, they appear adjacent to one another (presumably they were rearranged because of their overlapping chronology), but otherwise Hosea, Amos, and Micah appear in the same sequence as in the MT. Further, the other three writings that now appear sequentially in the LXX (Joel, Obadiah, Jonah) still appear in the same order as they did in the MT. For these reasons, it appears far more likely that the LXX order derives from the MT than the other way around.

Additionally, catchword connections between the writings of the Book of the Twelve appear far more prominently in the MT.[7] Quite consistently, concluding passages in the writings comprising the Book of the Twelve exhibit significant clusters of words that reappear at the beginning of the next writing in ways that suggest these catchword connections were heightened and/or created by editing one book in light of another. The effect of these catchwords serves as an invitation to read the two passages, and the two writings, in tandem with one another. This third reason, then, leads to a discussion of extensive scholarly treatments in the last thirty years that finally began to take seriously the implications of reading the Book of the Twelve as a single corpus rather than twelve completely independent writings.

## Recent Studies

Since 1979, a number of works have appeared dealing with literary and historical issues surrounding the topic.[8] This work on the Book of the Twelve in recent years has resulted in several models regarding how and when the writings entered the developing corpus. There is no space in this commentary to explore adequately the complexity and relative merits of the various models. Nevertheless, more agreement exists on some issues than on others regarding the history of the developing corpus. For this reason, a brief summary of points of agreement and disagreement may help the reader of this commentary to place these discussions in context.

### Current State of Redactional Discussions

Relatively widespread is the idea that the Book of the Twelve was preceded by two multivolume collections that each experienced editorial changes in light of their respective writings: the Book of Four and the Haggai/Zechariah 1–8 corpus. The Book of Four refers to Hosea, Amos, Micah, and Zephaniah as an edited collection whose common editing reflects concerns of the exilic and early postexilic period, probably from a group living within Judah. Patterned references to kings in the superscriptions of these four writings provide the chronological framework upon which much of the Twelve rests. [Kings in Superscriptions] In most models, Hosea and Amos circulated together even earlier. This group of four functions together to provide a prophetic rationale for the destruction of Israel and Judah, particularly as recounted in the book of Kings. Hosea and Amos focus on the northern kingdom with occasional

---

**Kings in Superscriptions**

Five kings are mentioned in the superscriptions of Hosea, Amos, and Micah in a manner that suggests these writings have been linked together editorially.

| Hosea 1:1 | Amos 1:1 | Micah 1:1 | Zephaniah 1:1 |
|---|---|---|---|
| Uzziah (Judah) (786–746) | Uzziah (Judah) | | |
| Jotham (Judah) (756–741) | | Jotham (Judah) | (Hezekiah mentioned) |
| Ahaz (Judah) (741–725) | | Ahaz (Judah) | |
| Hezekiah (Judah) (725–696) | | Hezekiah (Judah) | |
| Jeroboam (Israel) (786–746) | Jeroboam (Israel) | | Josiah (Judah) (639–608) |

The superscription in Hosea list all five kings, but names the four kings of Judah sequentially before listing Jeroboam, king of Israel, last—the only king of Israel mentioned even though there were kings of Israel ruling during the reigns of Jotham, Ahaz, and Hezekiah. By contrast, Amos 1:1 lists only Uzziah king of Judah and Jeroboam king of Israel, two kings who were roughly contemporary with one another. Mic 1:1 lists the same three kings of Judah who appear in Hos 1:1 as the second, third, and fourth kings mentioned. However, the internal evidence of Micah provides no solid indication of texts unequivocally related to the time of Jotham or Ahaz (see the commentary on Mic 1–3), suggesting that Mic 1:1 shows more interest in coordinating a time frame with Hosea and Amos than with reflecting the life of the prophet. Zeph 1:1 jumps from the reign of Hezekiah to Josiah, leaving a gap of nearly 60 years, conveniently ignoring Manasseh (696–641) and Amon (641–640), the two kings of Judah who are categorically denounced in negative terms (2 Kgs 21:2, 10-12, 20-23). Nevertheless, this chronological gap is effectively closed by tracing the genealogy of the prophet Zephaniah back and unprecedented four generations in order to link him to King Hezekiah (see the discussion of Zeph 1:1).

notes regarding Judah, while Micah and Zephaniah pick up with the destruction of the northern kingdom and focus on the anticipated destruction of Jerusalem. Further, the structure of the collections of these four writings creates a pattern whereby first Israel and then Judah are presented with choices regarding their fate, though neither responds positively to those choices. Hosea continually alternates messages of judgment with words of hope for Israel, while Amos begins with the assumption that Israel will not change, so that the message of judgment is never really in doubt. Micah begins with a warning to Judah and Jerusalem not to be like Israel, and then proceeds to alternate words of judgment and words of hope, much like Hosea. Zephaniah, like Amos, leaves no doubt that judgment is coming, but Zephaniah's words of judgment, like Micah's, are directed toward Judah and Jerusalem. Both Amos and Zephaniah receive eschatological expansions at the end of their respective writings dealing with the restoration of the kingdom. Micah also contains eschatological material, especially in the promise sections, dealing with the same themes.

Haggai and Zechariah 1–8 constitute a second group of writings that seem to have existed independently as an edited collection of two before being added to the Book of Four. These two writings focus on the same time frame using similar chronological formulae, and both deal extensively with the question of the reconstruction of the temple and its implications.

Less clarity has been achieved regarding when the remaining six writings entered the corpus. Here the various redactional models still present a rather dizzying array of possibilities for reconstructing the order(s) in which these six writings arose and/or were incorporated into the Book of the Twelve. What does seem clear from these discussions is that four of the six (Nahum, Habakkuk, Jonah, and Malachi) play directly off the chronological movement created by the superscriptions of the six writings dated to the reigns of particular kings.

The last king mentioned in Micah (Hezekiah) and the king mentioned in Zephaniah (Josiah) leaves a gap of sixty to eighty eventful years of the seventh century unaccounted for. During this period, Assyria de facto controlled Judah economically and militarily before Assyria was destroyed in 612 BCE. Soon thereafter, Babylon would defeat Egypt and become the de facto ruling power in Judah following the battle of Carchemish in 605. It is surely no accident that Nahum follows Micah and deals with the imminent downfall of Assyria, while Habakkuk begins with the same prophetic denunciations of society that appear at the beginning of Micah 7, and then pronounces YHWH's decision to send Babylon to punish Judah. Nahum and Habakkuk thus effectively fill the chronological gap between Micah and Zephaniah. Redactionally, theophanic hymns added to the beginning of Nahum and the end of Habakkuk both emphasize the role of YHWH in overthrowing enemy nations.

Jonah is largely viewed as a latecomer to the collection. The story stands out dramatically from the other prophetic writings for several reasons, both formal and thematic. Nevertheless, Jonah's position in the MT reflects a chronological awareness. Jonah, according to 2 Kings 24:15, was a prophet of the northern kingdom during the reign of Jeroboam II, the last king mentioned in the superscription of Amos. Since the first king mentioned in Micah, Jotham, comes after Jeroboam, the book of Jonah must come after Amos and before Micah if it is to observe the chronology implied in the Book of the Twelve.

The fourth undated writing that owes its location to chronological considerations is Malachi, the final writing within the Book of the Twelve. Its reference to the ruler using the Persian word for governor provides strong evidence that Malachi reflects the Persian period setting. The fact that the temple in Malachi appears to be fully functional means that Malachi cannot precede either Haggai or Zechariah, both of whom presume the temple is not yet completely built. Thus, ten of the twelve writings owe their position, in some way, to a chronological arrangement that unfolds across the writings.

The locations of the other two writings, Joel and Obadiah, are closely associated with adjacent writings by thematic and linguistic elements. This commentary treats both writings as composite productions of preexisting source material that have been joined together in light of their respective positions in the Book of the Twelve.

Joel functions as the literary anchor for the entire corpus. Joel begins with an extended call to repentance, precisely the way that Hosea ends; and it concludes with an eschatological portrayal of judgment against the nations, while Amos begins with an extended pronouncement of judgment against the nations. The fact that Joel

3:16, 18 (MT 4:16, 18) contain quotes from Amos 1:2 and 9:13 means that the end of Joel effectively cites the beginning and end of Amos.

Obadiah deals with the fate of Edom in ways that parallel the structure and theme of Amos 9, a passage that deals with the destruction of Israel. From a Judean perspective, the destruction of Israel and Edom plays off the fate of their respective ancestors, Jacob and Esau. The intricacy of the connections of Joel and Obadiah to their contexts suggests that their final form owes much to their literary locations in the Book of the Twelve.

For these reasons, there is little doubt that the six undated writings have undergone editing based upon their locations in the Book of the Twelve. What continues to be debated is the extent and sequence of the editorial adaptations by which the six undated writings, and Zechariah 9–14, were incorporated into the larger collection. These debates have yet to achieve consensus. For example, several of the redactional models argue that Malachi originally followed Zechariah 8, while chapters 9–14 were inserted later. Others argue that Zechariah 9–14 were added following Zechariah 8, while Malachi was added later. Debates about the book of Joel center largely on the time elapsed between the constituent parts and whether these components entered in a single compositional act or whether Joel developed in stages (and if so, which of these stages involved an orientation for the Book of the Twelve). So, investigations into the editing the Book of the Twelve have made much progress, but they still require more work to resolve these issues with some degree of consensus.

### Current State of the Literary Analysis

Synchronic studies on the Book of the Twelve have also developed during the same time, without necessarily assuming a diachronic model for the common transmission lying behind the final form of these

**Choir of Prophets**

Fra Angelico (1387–1455). *Choir of Prophets.* Duomo, Orvieto, Italy. (Credit: Alinari/Art Resource, NY)

Fra Angelico placed the company of Old Testament prophets to the left of Christ in this work that adorns the ceiling of the Chapel of St. Brizio in the Duomo, Orvieto, Italy. The Minor Prophets and Daniel sit in successive tiers above and behind Isaiah, Jeremiah, and Ezekiel, with the entire body making up a tribunal of judgment.

texts. [Synchronic and Diachronic] Before turning to the recurring themes, a few words about the nature of this prophetic book are in order.

*The Nature of the Book.* The Book of the Twelve unfolds as a compendium of prophetic speeches and stories delivered ostensibly by prophets from the eighth century until well into the Persian period. These twelve writings thus cover a 300- to 400-year span, and most of the writings within the Book of the Twelve exhibit signs that they circulated as independent collections before being incorporated into a developing multivolume corpus. But what is this corpus attempting to do? Brief mention of two texts (Neh 9:32 and Mal 3:16-18), one inside the Book of the Twelve and one outside, provides a necessary perspective for understanding the Book of the Twelve from two directions: (1) as a book design to be studied alongside the story of Israel and Judah, providing a rationale for Assyrian, Babylonian, and Persian occupation of YHWH's land, and (2) as a book designed to provide instruction for the faithful.

Nehemiah 9:32 offers insight into an important concept that helps to explain why the prophetic books (Isaiah, Jeremiah, Ezekiel, and the Book of the Twelve) begin only with the eighth century, even though prophets appear in the narratives of the Torah and Joshua through Kings long before the eighth century. Nehemiah 9 presents an episode from the postexilic period when Ezra stands before the people, on a platform made by the Levites (9:4), and begins to teach them about the history of YHWH's people. His interpretation of this history, beginning in 9:6, recounts the outline of a continuing canonical narrative. This narrative runs from Abraham (9:7-8), through the exodus and the wilderness (9:9-23), the conquest (9:24-25), and the judges and kings (9:26-31). It continually emphasizes YHWH's compassion and the people's stubbornness. At that point, Ezra petitions YHWH in 9:32 to change the fate of the people ("Do not treat lightly the hardships that have come upon us . . ."). This petition recognizes YHWH's justice (see 9:33), but asks YHWH to take into account that the punishment has already lasted "from the time of the kings of Assyria until today." In other words, it is not just the exile and the destruction of Jerusalem that are depicted as YHWH's punishment, but the time of Assyrian, Babylonian, and Persian occupation that runs from the eighth century to the Persian period.

**Synchronic and Diachronic**

In biblical studies these two terms now largely refer to various methodologies and their approach to the question of how a text came into its present form. Synchronic methods do not concern themselves with a text's history or prehistory. They look only at the final form of the text. Diachronic methods, by contrast, evaluate texts, in part, by asking questions designed to determine a text's history.

This is precisely the time frame covered by the Book of the Twelve and Isaiah. [The Time Frame of the Latter Prophets] Jeremiah and Ezekiel deal with the end of the seventh and the beginning of the sixth centuries. This time frame is thus covered by the prophetic writings, and they illustrate the reasons for YHWH's punishment, YHWH's attempts to bring Israel and Judah back to YHWH, and YHWH's continuing acts of judgment and deliverance.

---

**The Time Frame of the Latter Prophets**

 The four Latter Prophets, in their most common order, represent a collection whose chronological perspective pivots around the destruction of Jerusalem, as indicated in the following chart.

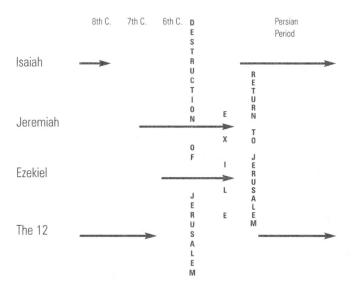

Both Isaiah and the Twelve span the time from the eighth century to the Persian period. Significantly, both books skip the destruction of Jerusalem entirely. They either look forward to it or they look back upon it, but they do not describe it. For example, Isaiah subtly anticipates Jerusalem's destruction by Babylon with the account of Hezekiah's showing off of Jerusalem's wealth to the Babylonians (Isa 39:1-8) which concludes a four-chapter block of texts (36–39) that also appear in 2 Kings (18–20). These texts, whose literary setting is the eighth century, come just prior to Isaiah 40, which begins with the announcement that Jerusalem's punishment is over. In the Twelve, a similar jump occurs when Zephaniah, set in the time of the seventh-century king Josiah, pronounces the coming destruction of Jerusalem (chs. 1–2) that will ultimately lead to Jerusalem's restoration (ch. 3). The next book, Haggai, picks up with the people back in the land and the prophet's challenge to rebuild the temple. In chronological terms, Isaiah jumps from 700 (just after Sennacherib's siege) to around 539 (the reign of Cyrus) while the Twelve jumps from the time of Josiah (640–609) to 520. Ezekiel begins after the first deportation (597 BCE) but ends with a vision of the restored temple (40–48). Jeremiah begins in Josiah's thirteenth year (1:2), or 627 BCE, and ends with a parallel from 2 Kgs 24:18–25:21, 27-30, noting Zedekiah's reign and Jerusalem's destruction (Jer 52:1-30) and Jehoiachin's release in 560 BCE (Jer 52:31-34). Thus, Ezekiel and Jeremiah cover the destruction and exile, with Jeremiah starting a bit earlier. Isaiah and the Twelve cover the same time frame as one another (including skipping the time frame covered by Jeremiah and Ezekiel). Yet, one corpus covers from the eighth century to the Persian period using the voice of one named prophet (Isaiah) while the other corpus uses twelve prophetic figures to accomplish the same task.

The end of Malachi (3:16-18) refers to a Book of Remembrance that was written to give guidance to those fearing YHWH. Often misinterpreted as a book containing the names of the faithful, this Book of Remembrance in actuality is presented as a book for the faithful to help them remember YHWH and to discern between the righteous and the wicked before the coming day of YHWH. This book is precisely the model of the Book of the Twelve in which twelve prophetic writings take the reader from the eighth century to the Persian period, documenting YHWH's accusations, punishments, deliverance, and hopes for the people of Judah and Israel.

*Recurring Themes and Motifs.* At least four recurring themes and related motifs have been isolated in a wide array of essays and monographs.[9] They include the day of YHWH, fertility of the land, the fate of God's people, and the theodicy problem.

1. Perhaps the most notable recurring theme, the overwhelming majority of references to the "day of YHWH" in the Hebrew Bible appears in the Book of the Twelve. The day of YHWH, however, can also be elicited with other terms, such as a day of affliction or a day of darkness. Further, claims about what will happen on this impending day do not reflect a single, imposed ideology. Instead, this recurring imagery creates a tapestry of expectations for the imminent and distant future as one reads through the Book of the Twelve. This day of YHWH refers to a point of divine intervention, but each reference must be evaluated in its context to understand the time frame, the targets, and the means YHWH will utilize on the coming day. The time frame can be imminent, requiring an immediate response (e.g., Joel 2:1-11, 12-17), or it can be distant, instilling hope that things may change (e.g., Joel 3:1-21 [MT 4:1-21]). The target can be YHWH's people (in the form of Judah, Jerusalem, Israel, or Samaria) or various foreign nations (Edom in Obadiah, Assyria in Nahum, Babylon in Habakkuk 3, or the nations as a group in Zechariah 14). The means by which YHWH intervenes on this day can include YHWH's role as heavenly judge in Joel 3, or as the commander of the heavenly host as in Joel 2:1-11. It can also imply YHWH's use of an earthly nation such as Assyria in Micah 7 or Babylon in Habakkuk 3. This motif does have climactic passages in the Book of the Twelve. Joel's presentation of the day of YHWH that threatens first Judah, then the nations, seems paradigmatic for the

corpus. Zephaniah 1:1-18 depicts the imminent destruction of Jerusalem using a cluster of phrases for the day of YHWH that appear elsewhere in the corpus. Zechariah 14 offers a composite collection of images and expectations for the judgment of the nations on the day of YHWH. Malachi 3 ends the Book of the Twelve with the expectation of the coming day of YHWH that will be used to purify God's people, separating the righteous from the wicked. On the one hand, this variety of expectations strongly suggests the use of divergent source material; on the other, the prominence and in some cases the interplay of these day of YHWH passages with other texts in the corpus suggest this perspective characterizes the Book of the Twelve in ways that are distinct from the other three prophetic books.

2. The second recurring theme, the fertility of the land, plays a significant role in the Book of the Twelve on several levels. This motif is first encountered in the judgment and promise metaphors of Hosea 2. Hosea 2 portrays YHWH's wife as a harlot motivated by the produce of the land. Here, the harlotry serves as metaphor for idolatry, and the wife serves as metaphor for the land. As a result of her actions, YHWH withholds the grain, wine, and oil (2:8 [MT 2:10]) in an attempt to get her to recognize that these gifts come from YHWH, not Baal. This judgment material turns to promise as YHWH isolates his wife in the wilderness, seeking to restore their relationship (2:16-20 [MT 2:18-22]). Then YHWH will answer the earth and restore the grain, wine, and oil (2:21-23 [MT 2:23-25]). The promise material in Hosea's concluding call to repentance includes promises for the olive tree (14:6 [MT 14:7]), the grain, and the vine (14:7 [MT 14:8]). These promises parallel the elements whose restoration 2:21-23 anticipates since the oil comes from the olive tree, and wine comes from the vine. These changes will come about only if the people repent.

Juxtaposed to this promise, the book of Joel opens with the land of Judah in utter devastation, leading Joel to issue a call to repentance. At the core of Joel's description of the land lie several forms of devastation that have cut off the grain, wine, vine, oil, and other agricultural products. In the background of these images, one hears the covenant curses of Deuteronomy (see especially 28:51). The threats in Joel include a series of locust plagues, enemy attack, and drought (some of which take up the language of Hosea 2). The infertility of the land causes the prophet to call the people to repentance (2:12-17) in the hopes that YHWH will restore the land's fertility by restoring the grain, wine, and oil (2:18-19; see also 2:21-22, 24) and removing the foreign army (2:20; see also 2:25). Despite the two promises of Hosea 14:4-7 and Joel 2:18-25, neither of these calls to repentance actually reports that the people repent. The promises are thus contingent upon how people the people respond, but the response of the people is not narrated.

Having discerned a pattern of judgment and promise using the fertility of the land, the reader of the Twelve becomes sensitive to the places in the corpus where this language reappears. When it does reappear, it does so in two ways. When speaking of invading armies or pestilence, the reader finds language associated with the locusts of Joel (see Amos 4:9; Nah 3:15-17; Hab 1:9; Mal 3:11). When focusing upon the fate of the people, the reader finds variations of the constellation of grain, wine, vine, and oil serving to underscore the threat against or promise to the people (see Amos 4:6-12; 9:13-15; Mic 6:15; Hab 3:17; Hag 2:17-19; Mal 3:10-11).

3. The third recurring theme concerns the fate of God's people. It is closely related to and often intertwined with language about the fertility of the land, but it also includes political and eschatological perspectives. The fate of the people is at issue in both of the preexisting corpora.

In the Book of Four (Hosea, Amos, Micah, and Zephaniah), the fate of God's people concerns punishment and restoration of Israel and Judah. Hosea and Amos essentially explain the downfall of the northern kingdom with illustrations of Israel's cultic and political shortcomings. Micah begins by applying the lessons of Samaria's destruction to Judah and Jerusalem (1:2-7) before outlining the prospects for judgment and deliverance in the remainder of the book. Zephaniah, like Amos, presumes judgment is unavoidable, but Zephaniah deals with the judgment of Judah and Jerusalem in this context rather than the northern kingdom. All four of these writings also contain promissory material for Israel and Judah. Amos, Micah, and Zephaniah in particular conclude with promises that represent exilic and postexilic eschatological perspectives.

Haggai and Zechariah 1–8 illustrate the positive outcomes for the people when they begin to return to YHWH. The temple is rebuilt because Haggai confronts the priest, the governor, and the people with the need to express their commitment to YHWH. Zechariah begins with an account of the repentance of the people

(1:2-6) followed by the prophet's vision to restore Jerusalem and punish the nations (see 1:14-17). By the end of this collection, it is clear that things have begun to change for the better but that consistency will be required if the full measure of restoration is to come about (8:9-12).

The remaining six writings and Zechariah 9–14 deal with the fate of the people in various ways. Joel offers a paradigm that functions, in many ways, for the entire corpus of the Twelve. A call to repentance goes out amid the devastation of the land and the impending day of YHWH because repentance represents the only hope for restoration. Once Judah and Jerusalem repent, the day of YHWH against the nations can begin. Obadiah anticipates that, like the northern kingdom, Edom will also be punished and this punishment will inaugurate the day of YHWH against the nations. Nahum and Habakkuk offer both the anticipation of judgment against YHWH's people and their ultimate deliverance. Nahum does so by celebrating YHWH's decision to overthrow Assyria, while Habakkuk anticipates both the arrival and the destruction of Babylon. Zechariah 9–14 explores various eschatological scenarios for Ephraim (9–11) and for Judah (9; 12–14) with a particular emphasis upon the coming day of YHWH. Malachi challenges cultic abuse by both the people and the priests as the harbinger of the coming day of YHWH wherein the righteous within Judah will be purified while the wicked will be punished. One cannot hope to escape the day of YHWH—only to survive it by God's grace.

4. The fourth recurring theme concerns theodicy. The major texts exploring this issue appear within the first seven writings. Specifically, four of these writings (Joel, Micah, Nahum, and Jonah) develop aspects of YHWH's compassion and judgment through citations of Exodus 34:6-7. Joel 2:13-14 draws upon Exodus 34:6, dealing with the compassion of YHWH toward YHWH's people, while Joel 3:19-21 (MT 4:19-21) alludes to Exodus 34:7 to affirm YHWH's eventual punishment of the wicked. The same dual emphasis reappears in the corpus at the end of Micah and the beginning of Nahum where Micah 7:18-20 draws upon Exodus 34:6 to plead for YHWH's compassion, while Nahum 1:3 draws upon Exodus 34:6-7 to affirm YHWH's punishment of the wicked.

Going beyond this duality, the narrative in Jonah plays upon Joel's version of Exodus 34:6-7, complicating the issue on at least two levels theologically. By stressing YHWH's compassionate character, Jonah 4:2 accuses YHWH, through the discontent of the prophet, of being too soft. For the character of Jonah, YHWH's propensity for compassion gets in the way of justice. Further, to make matters worse, YHWH exercises this compassion upon the nations (illustrated by YHWH's failure to punish Nineveh) as well as YHWH's own people. By satirizing Jonah's myopic view, of course, the story of Jonah challenges particularistic attitudes that do not take account of YHWH's salvific work in the world.

The theme of theodicy also comes into play in a series of four texts related to the mockery of Judah by the nations; two of these texts anticipate judgment in the form of becoming a mockery among the nations, while the other two promise to remove this burden. These texts include Joel 2:17, 19; Micah 6:16; and Zephaniah 3:18. Once again, Joel has a pair of texts with this motif. Joel 2:17 offers a petition that YHWH's people not become a byword among the nations, while 2:19 appears as a promise from YHWH that if the people do repent, YHWH will no longer make them a byword among the nations. Micah 6:16 condemns Judah for behaving like the northern kingdom with the result that they will become a mockery, but Zephaniah 3:18 offers a promise from YHWH that Zion will no longer be a mockery.

The final disputation in Malachi raises the issue of theodicy one last time in the Book of the Twelve when YHWH confronts the people for questioning his justice and his presence (3:13-15). In response, YHWH affirms that the wicked will perish on the day of YHWH, while the righteous who are prepared will survive that day (3:19-21 [MT 4:1-3]).

In the end, the effect of these theodicy texts reinforces the image of YHWH as a just deity who tempers judgment with compassion, but whose compassion has limits. YHWH's compassion extends beyond the borders of Judah to powerful foreign empires (so Jonah), but these empires will also be judged when they abandon YHWH's righteousness (so Nahum). YHWH's own people also become the subject of judgment, but time and again YHWH shows compassion by removing that judgment. At the end of Malachi, the threat of judgment for the wicked on the day of YHWH affirms a basic response to the theodicy problem. Namely, the wicked prosper only for a time because they will be judged by YHWH at a time of YHWH's choosing. The role of the righteous is to remain faithful in order to endure the coming day of YHWH. Toward this end, a book of remembrance is provided to the faithful to help them discern between the righteous and the wicked.

These four recurring motifs create an intriguing web of connections. A case can be made that many of these links were intentionally created in the process of compiling and editing the writings within the Twelve. Cumulatively, especially given the early traditions that the Twelve was a single scroll, these recurring motifs put the Book of the Twelve on a par with the other three scrolls of the Latter Prophets (Isaiah, Jeremiah, and Ezekiel). At some point, one needs to ask about the role of the entire corpus for creating meaning, not merely the individual passages. In the case of the Twelve, the web of motifs invites questions and leads to theological reflection. The links often assume one knows the story of Judah and Israel as told in the Torah and the Former Prophets. As one reflects upon these connections, one also cannot help pondering how one sees one's own story politically, ecclesiologically, and personally in comparison to the message of the Twelve.

# NOTES

1. Recent work has demonstrated that the term "prophets" in the next three centuries does not always refer to the second portion of the canon, but in my opinion, this variety does not affect how the term is understood in the prologue of Sirach because of the so-called "Hymn of the Fathers" in chapters 44–50.

2. The five books of the Torah followed by the eight books in the Nebi'im (Joshua, Judges, Samuel, Kings, Isaiah, Jeremiah, Ezekiel, and the Book of the Twelve) totaled 13 books for the first two parts of the canon. Twelve writings make up the Ketubim, ultimately providing for 25 books in the canon. Josephus's number of 22 books probably means he did not accept some of these writings as authoritative. Some combination of Esther (because it never mentions God), Song of Songs (because of the explicit sexual imagery), and Ecclesiastes (because of the theological difficulties it creates) would be the most likely candidates for exclusion in Josephus's number. The reference to 24 books in 4 Ezra 14 means that the author omitted one book, or counted Ezra/Nehemiah as a single book.

3. *Biblia Sacra Vulgata*, vol. 2 (Stuttgart: Würtembergische Bibelanstalt, 1969) 1374.

4. That such sequential reading did take place can be deduced, for example, from rabbinic traditions concerning Nahum and Jonah. See Beate Ego, "The Repentance of Nineveh in the Story of Jonah and Nahum's Prophecy of the City's Destruction— A Coherent Reading of the Book of the Twelve as Reflected in the Aggada," in *Thematic Threads in the Book of the Twelve* (ed. Paul L. Redditt and Aaron Schart; BZAW 325; Berlin: de Gruyter, 2003) 155–64.

5. A third order appears in one Qumran manuscript wherein Jonah appears at the end of the corpus following Malachi. See Russell Earl Fuller, "The Form and Formation of the Book of the Twelve: The Evidence from the Judean Desert," 86–101, in *Forming Prophetic Literature: Essays on Isaiah and the Twelve in Honour of John D. W. Watts* (ed. Paul R. House and James W. Watts; JSOTSup 235; Sheffield Academic Press, 1996) 9–496. The canonical implications for this one manuscript, however, are minimal. See O. H. Steck, "Zur Abfolge Maleachi—Jona in 4Q76 (4QXlla)," *ZAW* 108 (1996): 249–53.

6. More work needs to be done concerning the Septuagint version of the Book of the Twelve, but only a small minority has suggested the LXX order is older. See, for example, Barry Alan Jones, *The Formation of the Book of the Twelve: A Study in Text and Canon* (SBLDS 149; Atlanta: Scholars Press, 1995) 43–78. See also the work of Sweeney, who explores how the different orders change the focus of the two collections: Marvin A. Sweeney, "Sequence and Interpretation in the Book of the Twelve," in *Reading and Hearing the Book of the Twelve* (ed. James D. Nogalski and Marvin A. Sweeney; SBLSymS 15; Atlanta: Society of Biblical Literature, 2000) 49–64.

7. See James D. Nogalski, *Literary Precursors to the Book of the Twelve* (BZAW 217; Berlin: De Gruyter, 1993) and James D. Nogalski, *Redactional Processes in the Book of the Twelve* (BZAW 218; Berlin: De Gruyter, 1993).

8. A thorough online bibliography on the topic has been maintained by Aaron Schart and can be consulted (http://www.uni-due.de/Ev-Theologie/twelve/12b_bib.htm).

9. These four areas are explored more thoroughly than can be done here in the spring 2007 issue of the journal *Interpretation*, a volume devoted entirely to literary and theological readings of the Book of the Twelve.

# BIBLIOGRAPHY

Barton, John. "The Day of Yahweh in the Minor Prophets." In *Biblical and Near Eastern Essays: Studies in Honour of Kevin J. Cathcart*, edited by Carmel McCarthy, 68–79. Journal for the Study of the Old Testament: Supplement Series 375. London: T & T Clark International, 2004.

Beck, Martin. *Der "Tag YHWHs" im Dodekapropheton: Studien im Spannungsfeld von Traditions-und Redaktionsgeschichte*. Beihefte zur Zeitschrift für die alttestamentliche Wissenschaft 356. Berlin: de Gruyter, 2005.

Bosshard-Nepustil, Erich. *Rezeptionen von Jesaja 1-39 im Zwoelfprophetenbuch: Untersuchungen zur literarischen Verbindung von Prophetenbuechern in babylonischer und persischer Zeit*. Orbis Biblicus et Orientalis 154. Freiburg, Switzerland: Universitaetsverlag, 1997.

Coggins, Richard J. "The Minor Prophets–One Book or Twelve?" In *Crossing the Boundaries: Essays in Biblical Interpretation in Honour of Michael D. Goulder*, edited by S. E. Porter, P. Joyce, and D. E. Orton, 57–68. Biblical Interpretation Series 8. Leiden: Brill, 1994.

House, Paul R. *The Unity of the Twelve*. Journal for the Study of the Old Testament: Supplement Series 77. Sheffield: Sheffield Academic Press, 1990.

House, Paul R., and James W. Watts, editors. *Forming Prophetic Literature: Essays on Isaiah and the Twelve in Honour of John D. W. Watts*. Journal for the Study of the Old Testament: Supplement Series 235. Sheffield Academic Press, 1996.

Jones, Barry Alan. *The Formation of the Book of the Twelve: A Study in Text and Canon*. Society of Biblical Literature Dissertation Series 149. Atlanta: Scholars Press, 1995.

Nogalski, James D. *Literary Precursors to the Book of the Twelve*. Beihefte zur Zeitschrift für die alttestamentliche Wissenschaft 217. Berlin: de Gruyter, 1993.

———. *Redactional Processes in the Book of the Twelve*. Beihefte zur Zeitschrift für die alttestamentliche Wissenschaft 218. Berlin: de Gruyter, 1993.

Nogalski, James D., and Marvin A. Sweeney, editors. *Reading and Hearing the Book of the Twelve*. Society of Biblical Literature Symposium Series 15. Atlanta: Society of Biblical Literature, 2000.

Redditt, Paul L. and Schart, Aaron, editors. *Thematic Threads in the Book of the Twelve*. Beihefte zur Zeitschrift für die alttestamentliche Wissenschaft 325. Berlin: de Gruyter, 2003.

Roth, Martin. *Israel und die Völker im Zwölfprophetenbuch: Eine Untersuchung zu den Büchern Joel, Jona, Micha und Nahum*. Forschungen zur Religion und Literatur des Alten und Neuen Testaments 210. Göttingen: Vandenhoeck & Ruprecht, 2005.

Schart, Aaron. *Die Entstehung des Zwoelfprophetenbuchs: Neubearbeitungen von Amos im Rahmen schriftenuebergreifender Redaktionsprozesse*. Beihefte zur Zeitschrift für die alttestamentliche Wissenschaft 260. Berlin: de Gruyter, 1998.

Schwesig, Paul-Gerhard. *Die Rolle der Tag-JHWHs-Dichtungen im Dodekapropheton*. Beihefte zur Zeitschrift für die alttestamentliche Wissenschaft 366. Berlin: de Gruyter, 2006.

Scoralick, Ruth. *Gottes Güte und Gottes Zorn: die Gottesprädikationen in Exodus 34,6f und ihre intertextuellen Beziehungen zum Zwölfprophetenbuch.* Herders biblische Studien 33. Freiburg, Germany: Herder, 2002.

Sweeney, Marvin A. "Sequence and Interpretation in the Book of the Twelve." In *Reading and Hearing the Book of the Twelve*, edited by James D. Nogalski and Marvin A. Sweeney, 49–64. Society of Biblical Literature Symposium Series 15. Atlanta: Society of Biblical Literature, 2000.

———. *The Twelve Prophets.* Edited by David W. Cotter. 2 volumes. Berit Olam. Collegeville: Liturgical Press, 2000.

Van Leeuwen, Raymond C. "Scribal Wisdom and Theodicy in the Book of the Twelve." In *Search of Wisdom: Essays in Memory of John G. Gammie*, edited by Leo G. Perdue, Bernard Scott, and William Wiseman, 31–49. Louisville: Westminster John Knox, 1993.

Wöhrle, Jakob. *Der Abschluss des Zwölfprophetenbuches: Buchübergreifende Redaktionsprozesse in den späten Sammlungen.* Beihefte zur Zeitschrift für die alttestamentliche Wissenschaft 389. Berlin: de Gruyter, 2008.

———. *Die frühen Sammlungen des Zwölfprophetenbuches. Entstehung und Komposition.* Beihefte zur Zeitschrift für die alttestamentliche Wissenschaft 360. Berlin: de Gruyter, 2006.

Wolfe, Rolland Emerson. *The Editing of the Book of the Twelve: A Study of Secondary Material in the Minor Prophets.* Ph.D. dissertation, Harvard, 1933.

Zenger, Erich, editor. *"Wort JHWHs, das geschah . . ." (Hos 1,1): Studien zum Zwölfprophetenbuch.* Herders Biblische Studien 35. Freiburg: Herder, 2002.

# HOSEA

# INTRODUCTION TO THE BOOK OF HOSEA

## Dating the Prophet and the Book

The book of Hosea largely deals with the northern kingdom of Israel. Only one other canonical prophetic writing, Amos, directs its message specifically to the northern kingdom. Unlike Amos, who came from the southern town Tekoa, 10 miles south of Jerusalem, it is widely believed that Hosea came from the north. [Hosea in Jewish Tradition] Scholars believe that Hosea preached later than Amos by fifteen to twenty years, even though the book of Hosea precedes Amos in the Book of the Twelve.

Apart from the name of his father mentioned in 1:1 and the accounts of his marriage to a prostitute with whom he had three children, no explicit biographical information appears in Hosea. Even the widely accepted idea of Hosea's northern origin derives from the focus on Ephraim (a name used to refer to the central part of the northern kingdom) in the book.

The lack of biographical data notwithstanding, eighth-century events play a role in several speeches. The substance of some of these speeches may even be contemporary with the events themselves. Knowledge of events surrounding the Syro-Ephraimite War, for instance, forms the backdrop for several passages (5:10-11, 13; 7:7). Nevertheless, later perspectives also shape the book. For example, in Hosea 13 eighth-century events form the subject of later reflection. Specifically, the deportation of King Hoshea and the destruction of Samaria form part of the retrospective in the Hosea 13:1-2, 10-11, but these references also utilize traditions from the Pentateuch and the Former Prophets in ways that suggest an awareness of a developing canon in the exilic period and beyond.

The five kings mentioned in Hosea 1:1 frame a significant period in the history of Judah and Israel. The relationship between Judah and Israel degenerated after the death of Jeroboam and Uzziah around 746 BCE, culminating in the Syro-Ephraimite War (734–732 BCE) in which aggression by Syria and Israel ("Ephraim") against

## Hosea in Jewish Tradition

The interpretive legends (*haggadah*) concerning Hosea in rabbinic sources reflect several distinct interests: the prophet's Reubenite ancestry and prophetic preeminence; the prophet's pious encounters with YHWH; and the prophet's death. Hosea's father, Beeri (*bĕ'ērî*), is equated with the Reubenite Beerah (*bĕ'ērâ*) mentioned in 1 Chr 5:6. This Reubenite association allows two predictions ostensibly delivered to Reuben in a midrash to the Jacob and Joseph stories. In the first, Reuben, son of Leah and Jacob, repents of his jealousy of Rachel's relationship with Jacob following Rachel's death. In response, God promises Reuben that Hosea would be the first to call Israel to repent (Ginzberg, 416). The second prediction concerning Hosea derives from Reuben's actions in stopping Joseph's brothers from killing him (Gen 37:21-22). According to this tradition, Reuben returned to look for Joseph after his brothers threw him in a pit, but Reuben was unable to get there in time to release Joseph (Ginzberg, 416). Nevertheless, God rewards Reuben since "God not only rewards for good deeds, but for good intentions as well." God tells Reuben, "Since you were the first to try to restore a child to its father, so Hosea, one of your descendants, will be the first to try to lead Israel back to its heavenly father." Both predictions offer explanations for Hosea's preeminence as the first prophet based upon a particular understanding of Hos 1:2 (see discussion of "first" in Hos 1:2).

Characterizations of Hosea in rabbinic sources, however, are less flattering than one might presume (Ginzberg, 4:260–61). Hosea's marriage results from a lesson God chose to teach the prophet. God spoke about Israel's sin,

anticipating that Hosea would defend his own people. Instead, Hosea essentially tells God to do away with them: "O, Lord of the world, the universe belongs to you. Instead of Israel, choose another people from among the nations of the earth." Taken by surprise, God commands Hosea to take a wife of ill repute. After she bears several children with Hosea, God asks him why he does not dismiss his wife since Hosea cannot be sure of her fidelity. Hosea replies that he cannot dismiss her because she has born him children, so God drives home the point by saying, "Then how can I separate myself from Israel, from my children, the children of my elect, Abraham, Isaac, and Jacob?" Hosea asks God to forgive him, but God admonishes Hosea to "pray for the welfare of Israel, for you are the reason I issued three decrees against them." Presumably, these three decrees refer to the three judgments based on the names of the children (Hos 1:4-5, 6-7, 8-9).

The third stream of Hoseanic traditions relates a story about the death of Hosea (Ginzberg, 4:261). According to this tradition, Hosea died in Babylon after prophesying for ninety years. On his deathbed, Hosea asked that his corpse be placed on a camel and sent back to Israel. Where the camel stopped would become the place to bury Hosea. The camel, on its own, went without disturbance from Babylon to Palestine and stopped in Zefat (Safed) north of the Sea of Galilee.

Louis Ginzberg, *The Legends of the Jews*, vols. 1 and 4 (Philadelphia: The Jewish Publication Society of America, 1947).

Judah forced Judah's king to turn to Assyria for military aid. (See [Syro-Ephramite War].) With Assyrian help, Judah survived but was forced to pay such heavy tribute to Assyria that it soon crippled Judah's economy. However, within three decades, Judah, under the leadership of King Hezekiah, attempted to rid itself from the Assyrian burden by also refusing to pay this tribute. The consequences were nearly disastrous for Jerusalem since most of Judah was lost to Assyrian military incursion, and Jerusalem barely survived the siege of Sennacherib in 701.

Overall, the situation presumed in many of the speeches in Hosea portrays a society in chaos, especially when compared with the more stable economic and political picture in Amos. Hosea accuses priests of conspiring with thieves to rob those on the way to worship (6:9). The cavalcade of kings caused by assassinations and usurpations created an unstable political environment. Kings were threatened from within the royal household (7:5-7) and from outside the country (8:4-10; 10:6-7, 14-15; 11:5-6). Lax ethical standards were a hallmark of the society in the descriptions of the prophet (4:1-3; 10:13). However, the most stinging denunciations condemned the illicit practices of the worship of other gods. Virtually every chapter in Hosea 4–10 contains condemnations of Israel's abandonment of true YHWH worship by those worshiping Baal and those worshiping idols. Many of these confrontations also show affinities with the religious practices of the northern kingdom as described in the book of Kings.

Dating the book of Hosea is a complicated task because it has a long history of transmission and redaction, with the latter stages presuming exilic and postexilic settings in places. At least three kinds of later material have entered the book. First, beginning with Hosea 1:1, later perspectives shape the structure and message of the book. Specifically, Hosea 1:1 places the work of the prophet into the reigns of five kings, the last of whom (Hezekiah) undoubtedly continued to rule after the death of the prophet. Second, in several places in Hosea, the message of the prophet has been applied to the kingdom of Judah (1:1, 7, 11; 4:15; 5:5, 10-14; 6:11; 8:14; 10:11; 11:12; 12:2), even though the book was originally addressed

**Idols of Deities**

The worship of deities other than YHWH in the eighth and seventh centuries in Judah and Israel is well established by figurines and shrines such as these.

Four Astarte figurines, supporting their breasts with hands. Israelite, from Lachish and Ein Shemesh. Terracotta, pillar-type, 1000–600 BCE. Iron Age. Israel Museum (IDAM), Jerusalem, Israel. (Credit: Erich Lessing/Art Resource, NY)

**Judah and Israel**

The kingdoms of Judah and Israel resulted from the split after Solomon's reign according to biblical accounts. Judah (the southern kingdom) was ruled continuously by descendants of David, while Israel (the northern kingdom) did not come from a single family. The map below offers a rough approximation of the borders of these kingdoms.

### Hosea 12–13 and Canonical Traditions

Hos 12–13 contains significant intertextual material in the form of allusions to Israel's narrative traditions and formulations that reappear in elsewhere in Hosea, as well as Amos and Micah. See discussions of these texts in the commentary proper.

| Hosea | Other Texts |
|---|---|
| 12:3-4 | Jacob Story |
| 12:3a | Gen 25:24-26 |
| 12:3b | Gen 32:22-32 |
| 12:4 | Gen 33 |
| | |
| 12:6-7 | Amos 8:5; Mic 6:8, 11 |
| | |
| 12:12-13 | Gen 28–29 |
| 12:13 | Moses |
| | |
| 13 | Hosea, Amos, Micah texts |
| 13:6 | Exodus and Entering Land |
| 13:11 | 1 Sam 8 |

### Deuteronomy, Deuteronomic, and Deuteronomistic

Following standard practice, this commentary uses "Deuteronomy" to refer to the biblical book, while the adjective "Deuteronomic" refers to characteristics of that book. By contrast, "Deuteronomistic" refers to characteristics (usually editorial or theooogical) of *other* books that share some level of ideology and/or phraseology with Deuteronomy. The Deuteronomistic History refers to the books of Joshua, Judges, 1–2 Samuel, and 1–2 Kings. These books tell the story of Judah and Israel in the land based, in part, upon prominent emphases in Deuteronomy.

For further reading, see Steven L. McKenzie, "Deuteronomistic History," *New Interpreter's Dictionary of the Bible* 2:106–108.

to the northern kingdom of Israel. While some of these statements are more integral to their contexts than others, most reflect a tendency to make sure Judah hears the same warning as Ephraim, and some of these texts also suggest a hope for a restored Davidic kingdom (1:7, 11). Third, the use of intertextual traditions in Hosea 12–14 may be more aware of the developing Hebrew canon than is often acknowledged. [Hosea 12–13 and Canonical Traditions] The use of material from the Pentateuch and the Deuteronomistic History in Hosea 12–13 likely reflects the interests of those responsible for telling the story of Israel and Judah.[1] [Deuteronomy, Deuteronomic, and Deuteronomistic] In all likelihood, the editorial interests of Hosea, Amos, Micah, and Zephaniah correlate those prophetic messages with the stories of Judah and Israel as a warning that God would discipline God's people if they did not change their behavior.

## Literary Form, Structure, and Unity of Hosea

The structure of the book of Hosea alternates between judgment and promise. Each of the first three chapters offers an extended marriage metaphor and transitions from judgment to promise by the end of the chapter. Chapter 1 begins with the birth narratives of the children of the prophet and the prostitute, where the children's names first convey a message of judgment before becoming symbols of hope at the end of the chapter (1:10–2:1 [MT 2:1-3]). Hosea 2 conveys an extended metaphor depicting the land as the personified wife of YHWH, the wounded husband. The husband's actions are confrontational at first but lead to a message of hope (2:16-23 [MT 2:18-25]). Hosea 3 presents, in autobiographical style, an account of the prophet's marriage to an adulteress in a manner that symbolizes YHWH's pain as caused by Israel. Israel's rejection causes YHWH to threaten exile before conveying a message of hope for the restoration of the Davidic kingdom (3:5). Thus, three times in rapid succession a marriage metaphor seeks to equate prostitution and adultery with the abandonment of YHWH by the people of Israel. Yet each passage ends in hope.

The remainder of the book divides into two sections of extended judgment (Hos 4–10; 12–13) followed by powerful passages of hope (Hos 11, 14). Chapters 4–11 largely consist of accusations, judgment speeches, and warnings (Hos 4–10), followed by a message of promise (Hos 11). The judgment orientation in 4–10 is broken only by the implicit call to repentance in 6:1-3. This section contains a much higher percentage of judgment material than chapters 1–3, but this material serves the purpose of its compilers to accentuate the pervasiveness of idolatry, ethical impropriety, and political stupidity. Hosea 11 presents a soliloquy that depicts YHWH as a grieving father who refuses to give up on his wayward son. Chapters 12–14 rely heavily on biblical traditions from the Pentateuch and the Deuteronomistic History to demonstrate Israel's long-standing rebellion against YHWH (12–13), before concluding with an open-ended call to repentance containing a contingent promise of restoration (14).

The effect of this alternation of judgment and promise throughout the book is twofold. First, the dominance of the judgment sayings comes through pointedly. Judgment begins the book, and it makes up the bulk of each section, driving home the seriousness of the message. Second, deliberate inclusion of a message of hope in each section underscores the image of a God who does not desire to punish God's people. As a result, (1) the names of the children change from symbols of judgment to symbols of hope in Hosea 1–3; (2) the adulterous relationship of the mother in Hosea 2–3 also moves from judgment to hope; (3) the soliloquy of Hosea 11 conveys the anguish and suffering experienced by YHWH when considering punishment of a recalcitrant child; and (4) Hosea 14 ends the book with a final call to repentance, even after Hosea 12–13 has demonstrated how unlikely it is that Ephraim will listen. God has a hard time giving up on God's children. Thus, the book of Hosea is largely a book of admonition and choice for the people of Israel.

## The Message of Hosea

The message of Hosea revolves around three topics: love, fidelity, and failure. Periodically, Hosea portrays God's *love* in direct statements, but it appears primarily in the relational metaphors of YHWH as husband and father. In addition, a constellation of words like "pity" and "compassion" undergirds the affirmation of YHWH as a loving God. Closely related to this theme is the lack of reciprocation from God's people.

The book of Hosea contains three direct statements regarding YHWH's *love* for the people (3:1; 11:1; 14:4), but all three underscore the problem of Israel's rejection of God's love. First, in 3:1, YHWH commands the prophet to love an adulteress as YHWH has loved Israel, thereby comparing Israel's love to that of an adulteress. Second, Hosea 11:1 depicts God's love for Ephraim as a young child, but Ephraim rebelled against God's love. Finally, Hosea 14:4 (MT 14:5) speaks of God's love in the context of a promise of what YHWH will do should the people repent.

In addition to direct statements about divine love, the verb "love" in Hosea more frequently conveys rejection in that Israel loves other gods rather than YHWH (2:7, 10, 12, 13 [MT 2:9, 12, 14, 15]; 4:18; 9:1, 10, 15; 10:11; 12:8). The ironic twist involving the verb "love" subtly emphasizes one of the major theological points of the book: namely, Israel threatens to destroy its relationship with YHWH by its continual rejection of YHWH's love and compassion. This rejection plays a prominent role in the metaphors of God as husband and father as well.

God's love is also conveyed through the metaphor of YHWH as husband. Chapters 1 and 3 tell the story of the prophet's marriage to a prostitute/adulteress as a means of drawing an analogy to the way Israel has treated God's love. Hosea 2, by contrast, utilizes the relationship of the land and YHWH in an extended marriage metaphor where YHWH is the husband and the land is the wife/mother. By implication, Hosea 2 functions as the hermeneutical cipher for Hosea 1–3, interpreting the symbolic action of the prophet marrying a prostitute as an analogy for the relationship between YHWH and Israel. The wife in Hosea 2 takes other lovers, thereby shunning and ignoring her husband. In response, the husband threatens, cajoles, and pleads with his wife in an attempt to win her back. The end of the chapter anticipates that the wife will come to her senses following a time of punishment involving humiliation and exile, and thus usher in a new period of fertility and commitment.

The portrayal of YHWH as father in Hosea takes place in direct and indirect ways. The names of the children in Hosea 1 draw an indirect analogy to God as the father of the people Israel, especially the daughter (not pitied; Lo-Ruhamah) and the second son (not my people; Lo-Ammi). Hosea 11, by contrast, portrays God explicitly as the father of Ephraim. In this scenario, YHWH recounts YHWH's own suffering as a grieving father whose son continually rejects the tender love of the father.

The book of Hosea also deals with the issue of *fidelity* from two perspectives: the fidelity of YHWH to Israel and Israel's lack of fidelity to YHWH. Fidelity implies that the actions of covenant partners are consistent with the expectations of their covenant. YHWH's faithful actions toward Israel are sometimes recounted (2:8 [MT 2:10]; 11:1-2; 13:4-6; 14:4-7 [MT 14:5-8]), but more often presumed. By contrast, YHWH's fidelity to Israel is not in dispute, despite YHWH's threat to end the long-standing relationship with Israel. In Hosea, YHWH reminisces about the distant past when Israel showed promise (2:15; 11:3-4), but Israel has displayed its guilt for so long, and its guilt covers so much of its society, that only God's grace and compassion have allowed it to survive. In short, while God has kept God's side of the covenant, Israel continually shows it lacks the capacity for fidelity (4:1; 5:7; 6:7; 14:4 [MT 14:5]).

Fidelity to YHWH has been broken by Israel and/or Judah (cf. Hos 4:15; 5:5, 10-15; 6:11; 8:14; 10:11; 12:2), and the prophet calls them to change their behavior. Thematically, the breaking of the first and second commandments comes into play throughout the book. Specific allusions appear periodically to these two commands (2:5, 12; 3:1; 10:2; 13:4) and others (4:2). Anti-idolatry polemic becomes a recurring topic (4:17; 8:4-6; 10:5-6; 11:2; 13:2; 14:8). Specifically, Anti-Baal polemic is a major motif in direct and subtle ways: 2:8, 13, 16, 17 (MT 2:10, 15, 18, 19); 11:2; 13:1. In addition, many of the harlotry references (4:10, 12, 15; 5:3-4; 6:10; 9:11) clearly function as accusations of false worship because of the metaphors in Hosea 1–3. Thus, the accusations of wrongdoing (especially in Hosea 4–10) are not delivered in a vacuum, but function as examples of how Israel has broken faith in its relationship to YHWH. The same can be said for the marriage metaphors as well. The words of judgment and warning regarding Israel's infidelity are painstakingly obvious, and their harshness is even clearer when dealing with the political and religious leadership of Israel.

Israel's *failure* to keep the covenant constitutes a third topic in Hosea. Hosea blames the breakdown on the failure of Israel's kings to rely on YHWH and the failure of Israel's priests to teach the knowledge of YHWH. In Hosea, the behavior of kings exacerbates the problems, but Hosea also presumes that kingship in general carries too many temptations to rely upon human power rather than depend upon YHWH. Human power is subject to corruption. Several passages in Hosea condemn the action of Israel's kings (5:1-2; 7:3), warn of the imminent end to kings or kingship in Israel (3:4; 7:5-7; 8:4; 10:15), and presume the loss of a king (10:3, 7; 13:10-11) or the impending rule of foreign kings (5:13-14; 8:10; 10:6; 11:5). In addition, occasional texts posit that the restoration of kingship in Israel will take place in the future, but only through a descendant of David, that is, a king of Judah (1:11; 3:4-5), a perspective that connects with editorial concerns in Amos (9:11-12) and Micah (5:2-5).

As with the kings, Hosea also admonishes the priests in the strongest terms, for they had failed to teach the people in the knowledge of God (4:4-6) and failed to conduct sacrifices properly (5:1-4; 6:4-6). They not only failed to lead by example but they also joined in the culture of corruption (6:9) when they encouraged the people to sin in order to benefit from the sacrifice (4:8). As a result, the cultic center of Bethel was to be destroyed along with the political center of Samaria (5:8; 10:5; 13:16 [MT 14:1]). In the end, the punishment of the people largely results from the failed policies of leaders who could not see past their own selfish interests.

## Hosea and the Twelve

It is no longer adequate to treat Hosea in isolation from the other writings in the Twelve. Recent work (especially that of Schart and Jeremias) explores the interrelationship between Hosea and Amos.[2] The role that Hosea plays in the rest of the Book of the Twelve has also begun receiving attention. While Hosea's role plays out most clearly in the group of four writings whose combination likely began the multivolume corpus that would lead to the Twelve, it also continues to shape the reading of the corpus as a whole.

Within the group of four writings (Hosea, Amos, Micah, and Zephaniah), Hosea leads to Amos theologically. The prophet Amos preached before the prophet Hosea, but the various orders of the Book of the Twelve put the writing associated with the name Hosea first (see the "The Sequence of the Writings" in the introduction to the Book of the Twelve in this commentary). Hosea's position as the first writing has structural and linguistic rationale. Structurally, the fate of the northern kingdom (its destruction by the Assyrians) remains an open issue in Hosea from the first to the last chapter. The alternating structure of judgment and salvation in Hosea, combined especially with the concluding call to repentance in Hosea 14, leaves open the possibility that Israel/Ephraim may yet come to its senses and return to the path of YHWH. By contrast, the book of Amos presumes judgment is inevitable, and only the end of the book (9:7-10, 11-15) explores any possibilities for Israel's future *after* its destruction. This line regarding Israel's fate is presumed at the beginning of Micah where, much like 2 Kings 17, the destruction of Samaria is used as a paradigm by which to warn Jerusalem. Micah and Zephaniah repeat the same theological structure as Hosea and Amos, but they focus on Judah.

Linguistically, the superscription of Hosea 1:1 mentions all five kings who reappear in Amos and Micah (see discussion of Hos 1:1), which provides the chronological framework of the Book of Four and the preexilic section of the Book of the Twelve.[3] Hosea's accusations against YHWH's people are laid out clearly, and these accusations are assumed in Joel to apply to the people of Judah as well. Joel also takes up Hosea in other ways that apply Hosea to Jerusalem and Judah within an eschatological framework. Joel focuses on the fertility of the land, the repentance of the people, and the coming day of judgment, but much of the imagery draws upon and extends specific images from Hosea. In this sense, the position of Hosea continues to influence the reading of the Book of the Twelve. In so doing, Joel extends these images into a paradigm of history that anticipates the coming days of YHWH, and in part does so through its adaptation of forms, concepts, and allusions to Hosea (see the discussion of Joel and the Twelve).

Finally, Hosea introduces several recurring motifs that will reappear or be developed through the Book of the Twelve. These motifs all appear in Hosea 1–3 and include the land and its fertility; the fate of Israel and Judah; the patience of YHWH and its limits (a concept that lays the groundwork for development of allusions to Exod 34:6-7); idolatry; the need for repentance; the love of YHWH; the day of YHWH's intervention; and the use of other biblical traditions. Periodically, imagery and citations from Hosea reenter the Book of the Twelve as the objects of literary allusions (see specific discussions of Joel 1:8-10, 17, 19; Zech 13:9; and Mal 1:2).

# NOTES

1. Recent scholarship has become increasingly skeptical of dating written sources for the Pentateuch prior to the time of the exile. See Konrad Schmid, *Genesis and the Moses Story: Israel's Dual Origins in the Hebrew Bible* (trans. James D. Nogalski; Winona Lake: Eisenbrauns, 2010) 1–49. The Deuteronomistic History likely took shape between the finding of the book of the law in the reign of Josiah (622 BCE) and the release of Jehoiachin from prison in Baylon in 560 BCE, which is referenced at the end of the book of Kings (2 Kgs 25:27-30). See Thomas Römer, *The So-called Deuteronomistic History: A Sociological, Historical and Literary Introduction* (New York: T & T Clark, 2007) 1–43.

2. Aaron Schart, *Die Entstehung des Zwölfprophetenbuchs: Neubearbeitungen von Amos im Rahmen schriftenübergreifender Redaktionsprozesse* (BZAW 260; Berlin: Walter de Gruyter, 1998); Jörg Jeremias, "Die Anfänge des Dodekapropheton: Hosea und Amos," in *Hosea und Amos: Studien zu den Anfängen des Dodekapropheton* (FAT 13; Tübingen: Mohr, 1996) 34–54.

3. See "Current State of Redactional Discussions" in the introduction to the Book of the Twelve at the beginning of this commentary.

# OUTLINE OF HOSEA

I. Hosea 1:1-11 (MT 1:1–2:2): Children of Judgment and Promise
    A. 1:1: The Superscription
    B. 1:2-5: God Sows Judgment
    C. 1:6-7: YHWH Withdraws Compassion
    D. 1:8-9: God Disowns a People
    E. 1:10-11 (MT 2:1-2): YHWH Changes His Mind
II. Hosea 2:1-23 (MT 2:3-25): Judgment and Promise for YHWH's Wife
    A. 2:1-4 (MT 2:3-6): Children, Contend with Your Mother

# CHILDREN OF JUDGMENT AND PROMISE

## Hosea 1:1-11 (MT 1:1–2:2)

### COMMENTARY

Hosea begins with three extended passages that rely upon marriage metaphors to accentuate problems in the relationship between God and Israel (1:1-11 [MT 1:1–2:2]; 2:1-23 [MT 2:3–2:25]; 3:1-5). Each passage presents a message whose pronouncements move from judgment to promise. Moreover, each of these extended metaphors exhibits characteristics that distinguish it from the others, but each passage also contains elements that overlap with the other sections. This first sign-event (1:1-11 [MT 1:1–2:2]) presents the marriage metaphor within a third person report of the prophet's marriage to a "wife of whoredom" (1:2) and the birth of their three children. In the second unit YHWH speaks about his own wife who "has played the whore" (2:5 [MT 2:7]). In the third section, the prophet speaks about his wife "who has a lover and is an adulteress" (3:1).

Hosea 1:1-11 falls into five sections: the superscription to the book (1:1), three sign-events of judgment on the three children (1:2-5, 6-7, 8-9), and a promissory summation (1:10-11 [MT 2:1-2]). The voice of a narrator recounts the sign-events and introduces YHWH's speeches (1:2, 4, 5, 9). The sign-event for each child follows a similar pattern: "Name him/her/him . . . X . . . ," which announces a symbolic name, followed by a brief explanation of the name. The hand of an editor appears in 1:1 where the superscription introduces the book of Hosea, not just the first chapter. This editorial perspective displays an interest in relating the message of Hosea to a Judean setting, though most of the material in Hosea addresses the northern kingdom of Israel. One detects similar Judean interests in the expansions to the formulaic explanations of the names of the children (1:7, 11). The message of the chapter moves from judgment to deliverance, a movement that typifies the structural elements of Hosea.

## YHWH

AΩ The four letters represent the name of God in Hebrew and, if spoken, are usually pronounced Yahweh. Out of respect, the name YHWH is not usually pronounced in Jewish contexts. Instead, one speaks *Adonai* (which means Lord) or *Ha-Shem* (which means "the name"). YHWH is translated as "the Lord" in English Bibles, but this practice masks the personal nature of YHWH as a name.

## The Superscription, 1:1

Hosea 1:1 functions as a superscription to the book. It affirms YHWH as the source of the prophet's message, identifies the prophet Hosea, and sets the message of that prophet in a particular time frame. In addition, this superscription functions as one of four related superscriptions that help provide the chronological schema for much of the Book of the Twelve.

The book of Hosea begins with a typically prophetic formula: "The word of YHWH came to . . . ." [YHWH] This phrase claims YHWH as the source of the message. The phrase "word of YHWH" appears overwhelmingly in prophetic contexts (either in prophetic books or as speeches by prophets in narrative texts), and variations of this phrase open many of the prophetic books.

The prophet Hosea (whose name means salvation) is mentioned by name three times in Hosea 1:1-2 but nowhere else in the Hebrew Bible. By listing the father's name, the editor avoids any confusion over the prophet's identity, since Hosea was a relatively common name in the biblical narratives.[1]

The prophet's father, Beeri, is not mentioned elsewhere in the Bible, but Jewish traditions associate Beeri (*bĕʾērî*) with the Reubenite Beerah (*bĕʾērâ*) mentioned in 1 Chronicles 5:6 (see [Hosea in Jewish Tradition]). Modern scholarship, however, tends to treat the prophet Hosea as Ephraimite because that is the location of the prophet's ministry.[2]

The remainder of the superscription sets the book in a chronological framework by listing five kings during whose reigns Hosea purportedly preached in the latter half of the eighth century. This list of

### Hosea and the Delphic Sibyl

Bernardino Pinturicchio (1454–1513). *Amos and the European Sibyl*. Appartamento Borgia, Vatican Palace, Vatican State. (Credit: Scala/Art Resource, NY)

In the Renaissance, Hebrew prophets were sometimes paired with Sibyls (Latin for *prophetess*). Michelangelo depicts twelve Old Testament prophets along with five pagan Sibyls in the Sistine Chapel. Above, the work of Pinturicchio (1454–1513) combines the prophet Hosea with the Sibyl of Delphi. The Sibyls were famous in the ancient world for their oracular powers.

five kings is unique among the prophetic writings, and the way the list unfolds indicates that the editor intended to link Hosea, Amos, Micah, and Zephaniah. [Chronological Framework] Hosea 1:1 references the kings of the southern kingdom while the book as a whole concentrates on the northern kingdom. It lists four Judean kings first but only lists Jeroboam II from Israel, even though six kings

**Chronological Framework**

| Southern Kings | Hosea 1:1 | Amos 1:1 | Micah 1:1 | Zephaniah 1:1 |
|---|---|---|---|---|
| | Uzziah | Uzziah | | |
| | Jotham | ___ | Jotham | |
| | Ahaz | ___ | Ahaz | |
| | Hezekiah | ___ | Hezekiah | (Hezekiah) |
| | Jeroboam | Jeroboam | | |
| | | | | Josiah |

Uzziah (786–746); Jotham (756–741); Ahaz (742–725); Hezekiah (725–696); Jeroboam II (786–746); Josiah (639–608)

subsequently ruled Israel. This link to other writings in the Twelve creates a sense of continuity, inviting the reader to keep the chronological setting in mind while reading.

## God Sows Judgment, 1:2-5

This first unit consists of narration interspersed with YHWH speeches. A narrator tells the reader what happens (1:2a, 3-4aa), while YHWH's speeches (1:2b, 4ab-5) interpret the action. These two elements react to one another and cannot be separated.

The opening phrase of 1:2 creates translation difficulties. The NRSV treats Hosea 1:2a as a commissioning statement describing God's initial message to Hosea: "When the LORD first spoke to Hosea." Another interpretation treats the phrase as a superscription to 1:2-9: "The beginning of the LORD's speaking through Hosea." Both options present syntactical problems, but the latter is easier to explain in light of the MT, since it would only involve re-pointing a single Hebrew vowel.[3] Apparently, this phrase also influenced ancient scholars to interpret Hosea as the first prophet when they interpreted the phrase to mean "the LORD spoke first to Hosea" (see [Hosea in Jewish Tradition]). Hosea 1:1 provides a superscription for the book, so a second superscription is unnecessary, but it probably provides a window into the compilation process of Hosea. The introductory line (1:2a) suggests that 1:2-9 circulated independ-

## The Narrative Framework of Hosea 1:2-9

Hos 1:2-9 exhibits a narrative framework that consists of (a) narrative transition, (b) introduction of YHWH's speech, (c) YHWH's command to the prophet, (d) a rationale for the command introduced by "for," and (e) an extended explanation. The first speech sets the stage for the sign-events of the births of the children.

| Speech 1 (1:2b) | Speech 2 (1:3-5) | Speech 3 (1:6-7) | Speech 4 (1:8-9) |
|---|---|---|---|
| | (a) So he went and took Gomer . . . and she conceived and bore him a son | (a) She conceived again and bore a daughter. | (a) When she had weaned Lo-ruhamah, she conceived and bore a son. |
| (b) And YHWH said to Hosea, | (b) and YHWH said to him | (b) Then YHWH said to him, | (b) Then YHWH said |
| (c) Go, take for yourself a wife of whoredom and children of whoredom | (c) Name him Jezreel | (c) Name her Lo-ruhamah | (c) Name him Lo-ammi |
| (d) for the land commits great whoredom by forsaking the Lord. | (d) for in a little while I will punish the house of Jehu for the blood of Jezreel, and I will put an end to the kingdom of the house of Israel. | (d) for I will no longer have pity on the house of Israel or forgive them. | (d) for you are not my people and I am not your God. |
| | (e) On that day I will break the bow of Israel in the valley of Jezreel. | (e) but I will have pity on the house of Judah, and I will save them by the LORD their God; I will not save them by bow, or by sword, or by war, or by horses, or by horsemen. | |

---

ently of 1:1 and that whoever incorporated the unit also incorporated its introduction.

Hosea 1:2b begins the first of four YHWH speeches (1:2, 4, 6, 9) where the narrator explicitly indicates that YHWH speaks to the prophet. [The Narrative Framework of Hosea 1:2-9] This first speech commissions the prophet to do something shocking: create a family with a prostitute. The law condemned the practice of harlotry as abhorrent to YHWH (Lev 19:29; 21:7-14 [for priests]; 21:9, 14; Deut 22:21; 23:17-18). Legal material also uses "prostitution" as a powerful symbol to refer to idolatry (Exod 34:15-16; Lev 17:7; 20:5-6; Num 15:39; 25:1; Deut 31:16). [Meanings of "Prostitute"]

Just beneath the surface of this command to the prophet lies the implication that the prophet will learn what betrayal feels like to

---

**Meanings of "Prostitute"**

AΩ Connotations of the word "prostitute" in a modern context are not identical with those in the ancient world. The Hebrew root *znh* originally referred to any "unregulated, illicit sexual behavior between man and woman." The assumption was that a woman did not have sex outside of marriage. The term is sometimes translated merely as "fornication" for this reason, but males are not typically associated with this root. Modern usage limits the word "prostitute" to one who has sex for money, but that is not really the issue in Hosea. In Hosea, the assumption of the metaphor is that a woman can only "belong" to one man (either her husband or her father). In the case of Hosea 2 the woman symbolizes the land, so the root *"znh"* castigates the woman for *seeking* lovers other than her husband, YHWH (see 2:7). She credits these "lovers" with providing her with gifts (2:5 [MT 2:7]) that in reality came from YHWH (2:8 [MT 2:10]). Her "whoredom" (NRSV) is thus really adultery, but in Hosea it is also used symbolically to condemn Israel's worship of deities other than YHWH, especially fertility deities like Baal. In the case of Hosea 1, the "wife of whoredom" for the prophet also symbolizes the land (1:2), and its shock value lies not only in the assumption that it refers to a woman who purposefully violates her relationship with her husband, but in using this metaphor to refer to the land, it symbolizes the people and thus also accuses men of spiritual adultery. Recent authors have raised serious questions about the problematic nature of this metaphor. For example, see Peggy L. Day, "A Prostitute unlike Women: Whoring as Metaphoric Vehicle for Foreign Alliances," in *Israel's Prophets and Israel's Past: Essays on the Relationship of Prophetic Texts and Israelite history in Honor of John H. Hayes* (Library of Hebrew Bible/OTS 446; New York: T & T Clark, 2006) 167–73; and Renita J. Weems, *Battered Love: Marriage, Sex, and Violence in the Hebrew Prophets* (OBT; Minneapolis: Fortress, 1995).

J. Kühlewein, *"znh,"* Theological Lexicon of the Old Testament (ed. Ernst Jenni and Claus Westermann; trans. Mark E. Biddle) 1:389.

---

YHWH. YHWH commands the prophet to take a family of whoredom for himself, "*for the land commits great whoredom by forsaking the LORD.*" It is as though YHWH says, "You do this and see how you like it." The first speech thus depicts YHWH acting from a sense of pain to communicate the depths of the betrayal implicit in Israel's idolatrous behavior.

The narrator's voice resumes in Hosea 1:3 with a report that Hosea did what YHWH told him to do—Hosea married and had a child. The narrator then identifies Hosea's wife as Gomer, daughter of Diblaim. Only this verse mentions Hosea's wife by name. The name "Gomer" appears elsewhere only as a man's name (Gen 10:2-3 [= 1 Chr 1:5-6]; Ezek 38:6), and her father's name, "Diblaim," appears nowhere else in the Old Testament. Immediately after learning the identity of Hosea's spouse, the narrator uses a common idiom to tell the reader that "she conceived and bore a son."[4]

Hosea 1:4 begins with the narrator's introduction of YHWH's next speech, the first of three speeches by which YHWH tells the prophet what to name a child and why (see also 1:6, 9). All three speeches begin with a similar naming formula: a command (name him/her "X" . . .) followed by an explanation (for . . .).

Following this formula, YHWH speaks a three-part pronouncement in 1:4-5 playing off the name of the first child. "Jezreel"

**Plain of Jezreel**

The spacious Jezreel Valley spreads out to the north and east from Mount Carmel, providing convenient passage for international travelers in ancient times. The fertile alluvial soil makes this the country's breadbasket as well. The Bible speaks of the gathering of armies in this valley at the place of Armageddon.

(Credit: Todd Bolen/BiblePlaces.com)

means "God sows" and evokes positive images of a fertile region by that name. Hosea 1:4 juxtaposes the name against a message of imminent judgment. [The Names of the Prophet's Children] First, the pronouncement announces judgment on the house, or dynasty, of Jehu for the bloodshed of Jezreel, an allusion to Jehu's annihilation of Ahab's descendants in 2 Kings 10.[5] Interpreters generally relate this pronouncement to the end of Jehu's dynasty, which occurred with the death of Jeroboam's son Zechariah. [Kings of the Northern Kingdom from Jehu to Hosea]

Second, the pronouncement extends the judgment to the entire nation by announcing that YHWH will "put an end to the

**The Names of the Prophet's Children**

AΩ *Jezreel.* The name of oldest son manifests a double word play. First, Jezreel elicits associations with the town of that name. In biblical narratives, Jezreel is portrayed as the winter capital during the reign of Ahab (c. 875–854). It plays a central role in the story of Ahab's downfall and is the site of Jezebel's death (2 Kgs 9:30-37) and Jehu's orchestrated massacre of the sons and supporters of Ahab that allowed Jehu to solidify his control of Israel (2 Kgs 10:1-11). The Jezreel valley refers to the valley near the town in the northwest mountains of Israel. Hos 1:4 evokes Jezreel to reference Jehu's actions there. Second, the name Jezreel means "God sows." The town was originally named Jezreel as a statement of fertility, but Hos 1:4-5 reverses this affirmation by pronouncing judgment, implying that God "sows" judgment. As with the other children's names, this message of judgment is reversed twice (1:10-11 [MT 2:1-2]; 2:22-23 [MT 2:24-25]). In 1:11 (MT 2:1), allusions to Israel and Judah "rising from the land" on the "day of Jezreel" convert the message of judgment to one of harvest and regeneration. Hos 2:23 (MT 2:25) also reverses the judgment of Jezreel (cf. 2:22) when YHWH says, "*I will sow* her for myself in the land."

*Lo-ruhamah.* This compound name combines two Hebrew words (*lô'* and *ruḥâmâh*), with the first meaning "not" and the second meaning "pitied." The idea implied by the word "pitied" is broader than can be captured in a

single English word. This word "pity" does not conjure up the image of an emotional response to someone who is in dire straits. Rather, pity implies mercy and compassion in the face of expected punishment. The verb often appears in contexts of God (as judge) withholding punishment of the guilty. In these contexts, the word could just as easily be translated "spared" (e.g., Deut 13:18; 30:3; 2 Kgs 13:23). In Hosea 1:6-8, the word implies YHWH will not spare Israel from punishment. An editor has added a clarification that YHWH will spare Judah (1:7a). The judgment on Israel proclaimed in the explanation of this name appears again in YHWH's speech about the mother (2:6). However, the judgment is twice reversed in chapter 2 using word plays (2:1, 23 [MT 2:3, 25]). Lo-ruhamah (not-pitied) is called Ruhamah (pitied) in 2:1, and in 2:23 YHWH promises to spare her: "I will pity 'not-pitied.'" A final allusion to this name appears in the call to repentance in Hos 14:3 (MT 14:4).

*Lo-ammi.* This name means "not my people," and it shockingly connotes YHWH's intention to disinherit the people of Israel. With the name of the first child, YHWH announces he will punish Israel. With the pronouncement of the second child, YHWH announces he will not spare Israel. With the final child, YHWH announces his intention to disown his people. As with the other children's names, this judgment is reversed in subsequent passages (1:10, 2:1, 23 [MT 2:1, 3, 25]).

kingdom of the house of Israel." While the first portion of the judgment can be interpreted to happen *relatively* quickly, the northern kingdom existed for more than twenty years after Jeroboam's death, and included six more kings. Thus, 1:4 presents a message of judgment with short-term and long-term implications for the northern kingdom. While the end of Jehu's dynasty occurs with the murder of Jeroboam's son, Zechariah, in 746 BCE, the end of the northern kingdom does not occur until 722 BCE.

| Kings of the Northern Kingdom from Jehu to Hosea | |
| --- | --- |
| **Jehu's Dynasty** | **Remaining Kings** |
| Jehu (845–817) | Shallum (746) |
| Jehoahaz (817–801) | Menahem (746–736) |
| Joaz (801–786) | Pekaiah (736–734) |
| Jeroboam II (786–746) | Pekah (734–732) |
| Zechariah (746) | Hosea (732–723) |

Hosea 1:5 concludes YHWH's judgment with a third statement related to the birth of Jezreel: "On that day I will break the bow of Israel in the valley of Jezreel." A significant number of scholars see this verse as an addition to the original oracle because the formula, "on that day," appears three other times in Hosea in redactional contexts (2:18, 20, 23). Hosea 1:5 also presumes that the valley of Jezreel is a place of punishment rather than a symbol for the reason for punishment. At any rate, 1:5 builds upon the immediate context.

The phrase "break the bow of" signifies the elimination of military power (cf. Jer 49:35; see also Hos 2:20; Pss 46:10; 76:4). In a certain sense 1:5 continues the last line of 1:4, although the elimination of military power appears anticlimactic following the elimination of the entire kingdom. The Jezreel valley was important for producing grain for the entire region, and reference to it as the place of defeat evokes images of Tiglath-pileser III's conquest of the valley of Jezreel in 733, an event that marks the beginning of Assyria's overthrow of Israel.

## YHWH Withdraws Compassion, 1:6-7

The narrator's voice resumes in 1:6 by recounting that Gomer conceived and bore another child, this time a daughter. The narrator introduces YHWH's second naming formula (see 1:4), commanding the prophet to call his daughter "Lo-ruhamah." This name means "not pitied" (see [The Names of the Prophet's Children]), and YHWH's speech utilizes word plays to pronounce a message of judgment using the verbal root *rḥm* (pity): ". . . For I will no longer *pity* the house of Israel or spare them." The implication is clear.

## Judah in Hosea and in the Book of the Twelve

Much has been written about why Judah is mentioned so frequently in Hosea, since the prophet was from the northern kingdom (specific references to Judah in Hosea appear in 1:1, 7, 11 [MT 2:2]; 4:15; 5:5, 10, 12, 13, 14; 6:4, 11; 8:14; 10:11; 11:12 [MT 12:1], 12:2 [MT 12:3]). The dominant explanations of many of the references to Judah, though not all, have contended that the tradents of the book (i.e., those responsible for its transmission) were forced to flee the northern kingdom following Samaria's destruction in 722. Consequently, and over time, these tradents updated the message of the book to make sure it applied to their new context. This updating does not merely offer words of comfort to Judah. Rather, Judah is held to the same standard as Israel, so that after Hosea 5, statements specifically concerning Judah also reflect an increasingly dire fate for Judah, though they leave open the possibility that Judah may yet change its behavior.

As one reads through the Book of the Twelve, however, it becomes increasingly clear in the messages of Joel, Amos, and Micah that Judah will be punished like Israel for its refusal to return to YHWH. Judah, however, receives a chance to learn from the mistake of Israel. Nevertheless, at the pivotal moments of choice (cf. especially Mic 1:1-9), Judah does not change and ultimately learns that Jerusalem will be destroyed (cf. Hab 1:5-12; Zeph 1:4-18). Even so, these messages of judgment are tempered with words of deliverance (cf. Hab 3; Zeph 3:14-20). Most of these promises, however, presume that the deliverance will come only after YHWH punishes Judah.

See Jörg Jeremias, "The Interrelationship between Amos and Hosea," in *Forming Prophetic Literature: Essays on Isaiah and the Twelve in Honor of John D. W. Watts* (ed. James W. Watts and Paul R. House; JSOTSup 235; Sheffield: Sheffield Academic Press, 1996) 171–86; and Lothar Ruppert, "Erwägungen zur Kompositions-und Redaktionsgeschichte von Hosea 1-3," *BZ* 26 (1982): 208–23.

YHWH has shown compassion in the past but will not continue to do so. This verse offers a subtle reminder that although the book of Hosea has just begun, the relationship between Israel and YHWH has a long history that includes numerous points at which YHWH has demonstrated compassion.

Hosea 1:7 contrasts the fate of Judah with the fate of Israel. Hosea 1:6 announces an end to YHWH's compassion on Israel, while 1:7 proclaims YHWH's deliverance of Israel's neighbors to the south: "But the house of Judah I will pity, and I will save them . . . ." Much has been written about how the book of Hosea has been updated to include a message for Judah. With 1:7, the reader confronts for the first time the book's explicit distinction between Israel, who will be judged, and Judah, who will be spared.[6] This contrast of fates does not always appear in Hosea, but it raises important issues to bear in mind while reading texts related to Judah in Hosea and in the Book of the Twelve. [Judah in Hosea and in the Book of the Twelve]

## God Disowns a People, 1:8-9

As in 1:3 and 1:6, the narrator transitions to the next scene by providing new information and introducing a speech in which YHWH names the child. In 1:8, the narrator tells the reader that Gomer weaned Lo-ruhamah and immediately conceived and bore a second son. In 1:9, for the third time YHWH names the prophet's child with a name symbolizing judgment. YHWH calls the third child Lo-ammi, which means "Not-my-People" in Hebrew. This pronouncement challenges one of Israel's cherished traditions—YHWH's selection of Israel for a covenant relationship.

When explaining the meaning of this child's name (". . . for you are not my people and I am not your god"), YHWH threatens to rescind a concept closely connected to Israel's national narrative about the escape from Egyptian slavery, and in a real sense threatens Israel's very existence. ["My People"]

Thus, the names of the children in Hosea 1:2-9 symbolize YHWH's anger with Israel by conveying YHWH's judgment, lack of compassion, and disinheritance. Yet, the story does not end here. In a move that typifies the organization of the prophetic message in Hosea, the next verses abruptly change the thrust of the message to announce that YHWH will not abandon his promises to this people.

**"My People"**

Exod 6:7 offers a classic statement of the relationship between God and Israel that is closely associated with exodus traditions: "I will take you as my people, and I will be your God. You shall know that I am the Lord your God, who has freed you from the burdens of the Egyptians." This sentiment lies at the core of Israel's religious identity, and appears in a number of texts across the Hebrew canon (e.g., Jer 7:22-23; 11:4; 30:22; 31:33; Ezek 36:28; Lev 26:12-13; Ps 81:8-10). Burnett refers to this idea as "relational reciprocity," in which the divine (superior) partner takes on a people to provide welfare and protection. In the ancient world, threatening the removal of this patronage was to threaten a country's ability to endure.

See Joel S. Burnett, *Where Is God? Divine Absence in the Hebrew Bible* (Minneapolis: Fortress, 2010) 14–15.

## YHWH Changes YHWH's Mind, 1:10-11 (MT 2:1-2)

Formally, the speaker of the previous speech continues in 1:10-11, but the message of 1:10-11 (MT 2:1-2) contrasts dramatically with the message of 1:2-9, suggesting that these verses reflect a different agenda if not a different hand. The verses certainly derive from their context, as is evident from the transitional conjunction at the beginning of the verse and the word play on the names of two of the prophet's children. However, rather than continuing a message of impending judgment, 1:10-11 unexpectedly offer a message of hope. These verses do more than just jolt the reader with an unexpected promise; they also recall the promises given to the patriarchs, and they explicitly reverse the message of the preceding verses by alluding to the children's names as signs of restoration. In so doing, 1:10-11 forces the reader to confront one of the major theological dilemmas of Hosea: reconciling judgment with hope.

Hosea 1:10 (MT 2:1) begins with a promise that recalls the language of one of the ancestral promises: "Yet the number of the people of Israel shall be like the sand of the sea, which can be neither measured nor numbered" (cf. Gen 22:17; 32:12 [MT 32:13]). This promise raises interesting questions. Would not most of Hosea's informed readers have expected this promise to have been fulfilled long ago? If so, then why is this promise set in the future? The answer comes by recognizing that Hosea 1:10 demonstrates awareness of its context. It surprisingly offers a message of promise to Israel, but 1:10 implies that this promise will only take effect *after* the judgment pronounced in the preceding verses. This perspective becomes clear in 1:10b where YHWH's speech alludes explicitly to Hosea 1:8: "And in the place where it was said to them, 'You are not my people,' it shall be said to them 'Children of the living God.'" Thus, Hosea 1:10b promises a restoration of the relationship that YHWH had disavowed in 1:8.

Hosea 1:11 (MT 2:2) continues the promise of the previous verse, and it relies on a wordplay from the preceding context by referring to the name of the first child, Jezreel. However, while Hosea 1:4-5 used Jezreel as a symbolic name to pronounce judgment, Hosea 1:11 (MT 2:2) reconfigures Jezreel as a symbol of political reunification and restoration. Hosea 1:11 promises that Israel and Judah will join together, appoint a single leader, and take possession of the land.[7] Hosea 1:11 presumes precisely the same dynamics as 1:10, alluding to another text to convey a promise that makes sense only after judgment has occurred. It is difficult to see how a promise to possess the land would make sense unless they had already lost the land. The setting for this promise is difficult to determine, but likely stems from the hand of a Judean redactor, since the idea of restoration under a single king has much in common with other prophetic texts whose Judean provenance is more readily apparent. It may very well come from the same hand of an exilic redactor who added similar ideas to the end of Amos (see Amos 9:11-15).

# CONNECTIONS

Hosea 1:1-11 presents contrasting messages from the mouth of YHWH. Judgment comes not once but three times in the form of the symbolic names of the prophet's children. YHWH predicts Israel's end (1:4-5), withholds pity (1:6-7), and disowns his people (1:8-9). However, just as one begins to develop a picture of YHWH as a God who will have nothing to do with Israel, 1:10-11 brings words of promise and comfort to the very people whom YHWH had written off in the preceding verses. How does one reconcile this bifurcated message, or this picture of God who both condemns and saves?

Often, biblical interpretation requires filling in the gaps where the text lacks explicit information. In Hosea 1:1-11 (MT 1:1–2:2), the road to explaining sayings of both judgment and hope involves context, editorial techniques, and listening carefully to what the text does say. First, one must bear in mind the context of these passages as one interprets the change in tenor. The text itself forces the attentive reader to see the contradiction between the judgment and hope of the preceding verses by reversing the symbolism of the children's names (1:10, 11). However, Hosea 1:10 also alludes to ancestral promises from Genesis in a manner that reminds the reader that YHWH's relationship with Israel has a long history and that ultimately YHWH will not renege on his promises. Thus, the context casts the message of judgment against the backdrop of YHWH's longstanding history of acting on Israel's behalf.

Second, prophetic literature of the Hebrew Bible does not stem from the hand of a lone individual sitting down to write a "book" in a single setting. The prophetic books as we have them derive from persons well versed in the practice of compiling, placing, and updating the message of prophets into complex anthologies that usually build upon core collections of sayings, poems, or speeches. One of the techniques for structuring these messages has long been recognized by scholars: the practice of juxtaposing conflicting sayings by placing them next to one another as a means of communicating truth. [Paradoxical Truth] Prophetic writings in the Hebrew Bible are often shaped by the movement from judgment to promise. Those who collected and commented upon prophetic sayings often placed the judgment sayings at the beginning of a book, followed by oracles against the nations and then salvation sayings. This paradigm played a major role in the structuring of Ezekiel and Jeremiah (especially the LXX version). Hosea uses the tension between these two elements throughout the book. Frequent changes from judgment to salvation appear in chapters 1–3, and this variation continues in 4–14, where the intervals increase between sayings of judgment and deliverance.

**Paradoxical Truth**

Paradoxical truth derives from two seemingly contradictory statements, both of which are believed to be true. The purpose of these contrasting statements is to force readers/hearers to wrestle with both claims and to discern for themselves which one takes prominence in a given situation. For specific examples of how this technique can be seen in other texts of the Hebrew Bible, cf. Prov 26:4 with 26:5; 17:27 with 17:28; and Amos 9:8a with 9:8b.

For an extensive treatment of how paradox, or polarity, plays a major role in Christian theology, see Frank Stagg, *Polarities of Human Existence* (rev. ed.; Macon: Smyth & Helwys, 1994).

Third, as is often the case, a message of hope does not remove the consequences of judgment. Rather, it offers hope after judgment. Hosea 1:11 (MT 2:2) promises a time when Judah and Israel will be gathered under a single leader. This promise is tinged with subtle indications that trouble still lies ahead. In order for this promise to occur, Israel and/or Judah would have to be scattered before they could be gathered together. In context, this gathering implies that the promise would occur after the events anticipated in 1:4-5, 6-7. Thus, the promise of gathering does not revoke the coming judgment. It *presumes* the judgment will occur, but offers hope that YHWH has not utterly abandoned Israel, despite the fact that the last two judgment symbols say that YHWH will abandon Israel by showing no compassion (1:6-7) and disowning them (1:8-9).

More complicated is the question of how, or whether, the promise of Hosea 1:10-11 (MT 2:1-2) was fulfilled. Israel was never officially reunited under a single king. Judah survived, but only during the reign of Josiah (639–608 BCE) over a century after Samaria's destruction did Judah make any real effort to unite the territories of the two kingdoms. That attempt did not succeed. The question of how Old Testament prophecy is fulfilled is complex.[8] One is forced to ask whether this promise was ever fulfilled, or whether one must look for clues within the corpus to explain the relationship of the promises to the historical entities of Israel and Judah. At the very least, one is forced to take a much broader perspective than merely the lifetime of the prophet.[9]

What does this tension mean for the modern community of faith? First, in order to appropriate this alternating message of judgment and hope for today, one has to come to grips with the role of Scripture as testimony about God rather than dictation from God. These prophetic messages were recorded because they represented the faith affirmations of ancient communities of faith. They were preserved because subsequent generations perceived to them to be true statements of their experience with God. These texts attest to that experience; they do not function as some kind of eternal code pointing to some secret manifestation of events in our time. Second, one has to interpret individual passages in light of the entire writing. In the case of Hosea, those responsible for compiling the sayings as we have them have gone to considerable lengths to preserve both words of judgment and words of hope, often in close proximity to one another. Surely, they did not understand these messages as being identical with one another, but they probably did not understand these two perspectives as antithetical to one another either. Rather, these two perspectives related closely to expectations regarding the nature of the divine-human covenant itself. Promises of protection, and covenantal terms, were issued by the superior covenant partner (either the deity or the conquering human king) on the assumption that fidelity to the covenant was maintained by the inferior party. In this respect, consequences are implicit for those who have broken the stipulations of the covenant. Such covenant concepts virtually require some understanding of punishment as the consequence for breaking faith with YHWH. Third, the collection process incorporated both judgment and hope because the covenant relationship was deemed as ongoing. Consequently, certainly by the later stages of the collection and editing process, those who compiled Hosea and the other writings would have been keenly aware that while the judgment sayings of the collection could be seen as "fulfilled" in a real sense, the same could not be said of the promises. The tensions between these promises and their fulfillment, however, did not cause the compilers to abandon hope or to eliminate the promises from the collection. Rather, these promises called them to recommit to the covenant. Fourth, those responsible for collecting the words of Hosea and the other prophets did not believe that the implications of the message ceased with the death of the prophet or the prophet's generation. Passages such as Hosea 14:9 (MT 14:10) indicate that the compilers of the text expected the reader to interpret the message as an admonition to remain faithful to God.

The specifics of what that process means for individuals and for later communities of faith derives from engagement with the text, one's theological tradition, and one's cultural context. Each generation of believers finds itself faced with choices regarding how to speak about God and how people of faith should demonstrate their commitment. To adopt biblical metaphors blindly and literally is to short-circuit the process of theological engagement. Whatever the promise of a reconstitution of the Davidic kingdom meant when it was originally incorporated in Hosea 1:11, to conceive it today in literal terms represents, at best, a shortsighted misappropriation of the power of this promise. The appointment of a new king did not solve the problems of ancient Israel or Judah any more than polit-

ical power alone will resolve the world's problems in our generation. Hope, by contrast, that people of faith can positively
influence life in this world because of their commitment can and
should motivate today's believers to live a life of hope and commitment to the God they serve.

# NOTES

1. Four other Hoseas appear in biblical material: Hosea, son of Nun (Num 13:8, 16; Deut 32:44), whose name is changed to Joshua by Moses; Hosea, son of Elah (2 Kgs 15:30; 17:1-6; 18:1, 9, 10), who was the last king of Israel (732–724); Hosea, son of Azaziah, the chief officer of the Ephraimites in the time of David (1 Chr 27:20); and Hosea, one of the chiefs of the people in the time of Nehemiah (Neh 10:23 [MT 10:24]).

2. For example, see Hans Walter Wolff, *Hosea* (Hermeneia; Philadelphia: Fortress Press, 1974) xxii; or James L. Mays, *Hosea* (OTL; London: SCM Press, 1969) 1.

3. Proponents of the second interpretation note that the unusual form of the first word, literally meaning "the beginning of," introduces a verbal phrase ("YHWH spoke through Hosea . . .") that makes little sense unless one modifies the Hebrew text. The construct form requires that a noun or an infinitive follow. However, in the MT a finite verb comes next (*dibber*). This finite verb form requires only vowel points be changed to create an expected form: *dabber* needs one vowel change to read, "the beginning of the Lord's speaking through Hosea", and *dĕbbar* requires two changes to convey, "the beginning of the word of the Lord through Hosea." By contrast, the expected form of the NRSV interpretation would require changing the consonantal text.

4. The combination of the words "conceived" and "bore" appears at least 23 times in the Old Testament: Gen 4:1, 17; 21:2; 29:32, 33, 34, 35; 30:5, 7, 17, 19, 23; 38:3, 4; Exod 2:2; 1Sam 1:20; 2:21; 2Kgs 4:17; Isa 8:3; Hos 1:3, 6, 8; 1 Chr 7:23.

5. The judgment on the house of Jehu for the "bloodshed of Jezreel" presupposes a different attitude toward Jehu's actions against the descendants of Ahab than the attitude of the narrator of those events in 2 Kgs 10.Whereas Hos 1:4 refers to Jehu's action as "bloodshed," 2 Kgs 10 portrays these actions as divinely mandated punishment of Ahab (note especially the relatively positive evaluation of Jehu in 2 Kgs 10:30, along with a promise that Jehu's dynasty will last four generations).

6. See especially Jörg Jeremias, "The Interrelationship between Amos and Hosea," in *Forming Prophetic Literature: Essays on Isaiah and the Twelve in Honor of John D. W. Watts* (ed. James W. Watts and Paul R. House; JSOTSup 235; Sheffield: Sheffield Academic Press, 1996) 171–86.

7. The NRSV translates the Hebrew phrase *wĕ'ālû min-hā'āreṣ* as an idiom meaning "take possession of the land" in the sense of revolt rather than a literal, but more ambiguous, rendering: "They will go up from the land."

8. J. J. M. Roberts, "A Christian Perspective on Prophetic Prediction," *Int* 33 (1979): 240–53.

9. See the discussion of the metahistorical perspective and its effect on the reader of prophetic books in Odil Hannes Steck, *The Prophetic Books and Their Theological Witness* (trans. James D. Nogalski; St. Louis: Chalice Press, 2000) 43–65.

# JUDGMENT AND PROMISE FOR YHWH'S WIFE

## Hosea 2:1-23 (MT 2:3-25)

### COMMENTARY

In this chapter, the reader enters a new metaphorical world even though these verses continue to use a marriage metaphor. Chapter 1 used the marriage of the prophet, Gomer, and their children to proclaim a message of judgment and promise, but Hosea 2:1-23 (MT 2:3-25) personifies the land as the wife of YHWH. Hosea 2:1-23 (MT 2:3-25) forms a type of divine monologue that consistently portrays YHWH as speaker in the roles of a wounded husband, a prosecuting attorney laying out the case against his wife, and a judge who is both harsh and lenient in handing out sentences. Despite these changes in metaphor, the reader finds several clear allusions to the preceding chapter that reflect knowledge of the literary context. This chapter is framed by references to the children from Hosea 1. The children are addressed directly by YHWH in 2:1-2 (MT 2:3-4), and explicit word plays presuppose the names of the children in 2:21-23 (MT 2:23-25).

Hosea 2:1-23 (MT 2:3-25) contains six interrelated sections, forming an intricate web of interrelated warnings, accusations, judgments, and promises. The first section has YHWH calling on children to contend with their mother, lest YHWH punish her by stripping her and banishing her to the wilderness to die of thirst (2:1-4 [MT 2:3-6]). The next two sections display patterns typical of judgment oracles where accusations of infidelity lead to divine judgment of the personified land (2:5-6, 7-9 [MT 2:7-8, 9-11]). The last three sections of the chapter begin with temporal markers regarding the present and the future. First, Hosea 2:10-15 (MT 2:12-17) prepares a transition to promissory material by pronouncing judgments that cause this woman to cease her illicit behavior, to recognize that YHWH has her best interest at heart, and to return to the commit-

### Hosea and Family

This Reformation-era woodcut depicts Hosea, Gomer, and three children. The image invites interpretation: Is Hosea gesturing caringly toward the children who surround their mother as his face is turned toward the voice of God, or is he pointing *at* them, suggesting they are an example of the fate of whoredom?

Friedrich Peypus (1485–1534), printer. *Hosea and Family*. Woodcut. (Credit: Pitts Theology Library. Emory University. Atlanta GA)

ment of her youth. Then, Hosea 2:16-20 (MT 2:18-22) anticipates a future when YHWH reconciles with his wife, and finally Hosea 2:21-23 (MT 2:23-25) announces that the land, in that time, will again yield produce and its children will become signs of restoration.

## Children, Contend with Your Mother, 2:1-4 (MT 2:3-6)

Several markers in Hosea 2:1-4 suggest that Hosea 2:1 (MT 2:3) begins something new, yet these verses also have ties to the immediately preceding context. Thus, these verses exhibit a shift in perspective with a change to plural forms in the commands ("say" and "plead"), the suffixes ("your"), and the objects in 2:1-2 ("brothers" and "sisters").[1] If one takes these markers seriously, then YHWH addresses one group about another group: "Say (pl.) to your (pl.) brothers (pl.), Ammi, and to your (pl.) sisters (pl.), Ruhamah. Plead (pl.) with your (pl.) mother, plead—for she is not my wife, and I am not her husband" (Hos 2:1-2 [MT 2:3-4]). The identity of these groups must be inferred. References to the children's names from Hosea 1 assume knowledge of the preceding context, but this same context eliminates the children themselves as potential addressees. Because Hosea 1 narrated the birth of two boys and *one* girl, the reference to sisters (pl.) indicates a larger group is intended than just the three children from chapter 1. As Hosea 2 unfolds, the metaphorical understanding of the children and the mother becomes clearer. The children are the people as a whole, while the mother is a personification of the land. This personification draws from ancient Near Eastern concepts of cities personified as the wife of the deity. [Cities Personified] In the Hebrew Bible, these concepts appear most frequently in texts where Lady Zion (= Jerusalem) is personified as the wife of YHWH.

Hosea 2:1 (MT 2:3) begins this unit positively by alluding to the names of two children from Hosea 1 in forms that evoke the promises begun in 1:10-11 (MT 2:1-2). Instead of "Not-Pitied" (1:6-7)

## Cities Personified

The ancient Near Eastern world was largely polytheistic. Local gods often played protective roles, and cities, especially prominent regional centers, were often conceptualized as either deities in their own right or consorts of the local deity. In Western Semitic regions, including Judah and Israel, cities were treated as feminine entities (semantically and conceptually), though they were not always treated as deities. Not surprisingly, poetic and prophetic texts in the Hebrew Bible draw upon these traditions to personify Lady Zion as wife when talking about Jerusalem's relationship to YHWH. Often, these texts portray the people of the city as her children. Sometimes, these texts point to the special status of Zion as YHWH's chosen (e.g., Ezek 16:1-14; Isa 60:1-22). They may portray Jerusalem as an unfaithful wife using the marriage metaphor to express religious infidelity (e.g., Ezek 16:15-19; see also Jer 3:1-3, which use similar language for the land personified). These texts blend images of the city with the personification of YHWH's wife (cf. Isa 54:5) who decorates her walls (cf. Isa 54:11-12) and whose children are her inhabitants (cf. Isa 54:13). The former image does not appear in Hos 2, while the latter is present in several places. In all likelihood, Hos 2 conceptualizes YHWH's wife as the land personified, even while drawing upon the consort tradition used in conjunction with capital cities.

For more detailed reading on the role of Lady Zion as YHWH's consort and mother of Jerusalem's children, and the ancient Near Eastern background of the personified city, see Mark E. Biddle, "The Figure of Lady Jerusalem: Identification, Deification and Personification of Cities in the Ancient Near East," in *The Biblical Canon in Comparative Perspective* (ed. B. Batto et al.; Scripture in Context 4; Lewiston NY: Mellen Press, 1991) 173–94; Julie Galambush, *Jerusalem in the Book of Ezekiel: The City as Yahweh's Wife* (SBLDS 130; Atlanta: Scholars Press, 1992)]; John J. Schmitt, "The Motherhood of God and Zion as Mother," RB 92 (1985): 557–69; Aloysius Fitzgerald, "The Mythological Background for the Presentation of Jerusalem as a Queen and False Worship as Adultery in the OT," *CBQ* 34 (1972): 403–16; Christl M. Maier, *Daughter Zion, Mother Zion: Gender, Space, and the Sacred in Ancient Israel* (Minneapolis: Fortress, 2008).

See the discussions in [Jerusalem Personified] in the introduction to Micah and [Lady Zion] in Zeph 3:14-20 in James D. Nogalski, *The Book of the Twelve: Micah–Malachi* (Smyth & Helwys Bible Commentary Series).

and "Not-My-People" (1:8-9), YHWH calls them "My-People" and "Pitied." Hosea 2:1-2 presumes the judgment represented by these children has been reversed, just as 1:11 had done for Jezreel. Hosea 2:1 presumes acceptance and compassion from YHWH for the people who formerly stood under judgment. However, the message of acceptance is short lived.

Hosea 2:2 (MT 2:4) dramatically reverts to a message of confrontation, although the subject of the confrontation shifts from the children to the mother. The people addressed with words of comfort in the previous verse are now told to confront their mother. The language of 2:2 evokes images of YHWH in the role of prosecuting attorney and plaintiff in which he calls upon the children to join him in suit against their mother. First, the phrase "contend with . . ." is a legal term of accusation.[2] Further, the formulaic statement of rejection ("She is not my wife and I am not her husband") sounds like a divorce decree that could be spoken when a husband gives his wife a certificate of divorce (cf. Deut 24:1, 3). However, the rhetorical goal of YHWH's speech is the return of his wife, not the desire to send her away (2:6). The second half of 2:2 provides the accusation: she has been unfaithful to YHWH.

The consequences of infidelity become the focus of Hosea 2:3-4 (MT 2:5-6). While 2:2 called upon her to cease her infidelity, 2:3 provides five statements graphically detailing YHWH's punishment. The first two statements maintain the personification of the husband/wife metaphor. YHWH threatens to humiliate her ("lest I strip her naked and expose her as in the day of her birth"). The remaining three statements in 2:3 (MT 2:5), however, illustrate that the object of this extended metaphor is not the wife of the prophet but that YHWH threatens to punish the land: "and I will make her like a wilderness, and turn her into a parched land, and kill her with thirst."

Hosea 2:4 (MT 2:6) expresses the implications of YHWH's punishment for the wife/land as they relate to her children: YHWH will not have pity on her or her children. This verse plays on the name of the daughter, Lo-Ruhamah, from chapter 1, but its message of judgment on the children contradicts the message of acceptance in Hosea 2:1. In this respect, 2:4 strikes a surprising note, but one that follows logically. With the punishment of the mother, and the identification of the mother as the land made clear, the dependent nature of the children/people to the mother/land cannot be avoided. If the land dries up, the people will be affected.

### Two Judgment Oracles, 2:5-6, 7-9 (MT 2:7-8, 9-11)

Hosea 2:5-9 (MT 2:7-11) twice exhibits the formal elements of a prophetic judgment oracle.[3] [Prophetic Judgment Oracles and Hosea 2:5-9 (MT 2:7-11)] This repetition does not, however, suggest that these verses represent independent units because the first oracle draws upon the reader's awareness of the context, and the second builds upon the outcome of the first. Specifically, Hosea 2:5 (MT 2:7) presumes knowledge of its context conceptually and syntactically by carrying forward the divine speech style and the husband/wife analogy of YHWH and the land. Syntactically, the pronouns ("them" and "her") in 2:5 point back to the children and wife mentioned in 2:4.

Hosea 2:5 (MT 2:7) articulates an accusation against YHWH's wife, and Hosea 2:6 (MT 2:8) announces YHWH's judgment. YHWH's wife has taken other lovers under the mistaken impres-

---

**Prophetic Judgment Oracles and Hosea 2:5-9 (MT 2:7-11)**

Judgment oracles follow a regular pattern, with variations. Three recognizable elements of the genre appear twice in Hos 2:5-6, 7-9 (MT 2:7-8, 9-11): (1) the reason for judgment, often an accusation introduced by "because" (*kî*); (2) a transition marked by "therefore" (*lākēn*); and (3) the announcement of judgment by divine intervention. The second element often includes a prophetic messenger formula, "Thus says the LORD." Since this passage occurs within a lengthy YHWH speech, the messenger formula is not necessary. One can see these elements in the following chart:

| Element | Hosea 2:5-6 (MT 2:7-8) | Hosea 2:7-9 (MT 2:9-11) |
|---|---|---|
| Reason | Because (*kî*) their mother has played the whore; she who conceived them has acted shamefully. Because (*kî*) she said, "I will go after my lovers; they give me my bread and my water, my wool and my flax, my oil and my drink." | . . . Then she shall say, "I will go and return to my first husband, for it was better with me then than now." But she did not know that it was I who gave her the grain, the wine, and the oil, and who lavished upon her silver and gold that they used for Baal. |
| Transition | Therefore (*lākēn*) | Therefore (*lākēn*) |
| Announcement | I will hedge up her way with thorns; and I will build a wall against her, so that she cannot find her paths. | I will take back my grain in its time, and my wine in its season; and I will take away my wool and my flax, which were to cover her nakedness. |

---

sion that they, and not YHWH, have given her life's necessities: bread, water, wool, flax, and drink. The accusation uses polemical language against prostitution to accuse the land/wife of breaking the first commandment (cf. Exod 20:1) by placing other "lovers" before YHWH. The phrasing alludes to the prohibition of following other gods (Deut 6:14; 8:19; 11:28; 13:3; 28:14; Judg 2:12; 2:19; 1 Kgs 11:10; Jer 7:9; 11:10; 13:10; 16:11; 25:6; 35:15), but it substitutes "lovers" for "gods" in keeping with the metaphor of the context. As a result, in 2:6 YHWH prohibits her from seeing her lovers by making it impossible for her to pursue them. YHWH will build a wall of thorns so that she cannot find the paths to her lovers. The imagery of paths also suggests a long-standing practice of betrayal, since she follows "paths" to these lovers.

According to Hosea 2:7 (MT 2:9), YHWH's action will successfully keep his wife away from her lovers. She returns to YHWH not because of a renewed sense of commitment but because she recognizes she was better off with her "first husband." Once she decides to return, YHWH repeats the accusation of 2:5 against her in 2:8 (MT 2:10). The list of elements in 2:8 varies slightly from 2:5, perhaps because someone inserts the language of Joel (1:10; 1:17;

**Fertility Language in Hosea 2:8 and the Book of the Twelve**

Grain, wine, and oil represent a formulaic triad that evokes fertility traditions rooted in Deuteronomy. This combination of elements appears at least nineteen times in Old Testament texts, with five appearing in Deuteronomy (7:13; 11:14; 12:17; 14:23; 18:4) and five in the Book of the Twelve (Hos 2:8; 2:22; Joel 1:10; 2:19; Hag 1:11). This combination provides one piece of a recurring fertility motif highlighted by those responsible for editing the Book of the Twelve. These elements may have already been present in Hos 2:8-9, laying the groundwork for further development in Joel and Haggai by articulating YHWH's control of the fertility of the land.

For additional reading, see James D. Nogalski, "Recurring Themes in the Book of the Twelve: Creating Points of Contact for a Theological Reading," *Int* 61 (2007): 128–30.

**Baal Worship**

Baal was the Canaanite fertility god who played a significant role in the polemic of Old Testament texts against the worship of gods other than YHWH (cf. 1 Kgs 18; 2 Kgs 17:16), especially Judges, Samuel, and Kings. This god was so widely known in ancient Near Eastern cultures that the word *baʿal* came to have three basic meanings in Hebrew: the name of the Canaanite deity, "husband" (Exod 21:3), or a word for "lord" (in the sense of landowner or citizen, e.g., Josh 24:11; or owner, e.g., Exod 22:8 [MT 22:7]). In addition, the word appears in conjunction with local deities often associated with place names (e.g., Baal of Peor in Num 25:3, 5).

According to Canaanite myth, the fertility god Baal was responsible for the life-giving rain. Baal was conceptualized as a virile warrior carrying lightning bolts as his weapons (see the accompanying picture). Hosea uses the word *baʿal* in each of the three basic meanings, and associates the worship of Baal with fertility rites.

Baal with lightening, a stele from the temple of Baal in Ugarit. The god, mounted on a horned altar, marches forward brandishing a mace. Leaves burst forth from his spear, symbolizing the beneficial effects of Baal's storm. Limestone. Louvre, Paris, France. (Credit: Erich Lessing/ Art Resource, NY)

2:19) or other texts in Hosea (2:22 [MT 2:24]; 7:14; 9:1; 14:7 [MT 14:8]). [Fertility Language in Hosea 2:8 and the Book of the Twelve] In addition, YHWH claims that "*they*" used the silver and gold "for Baal." The abrupt change to a third person plural verb stands out stylistically. This change has led scholars to suspect that at least part of 2:8 represents a later insertion.[4] In its current form this verse reflects the accusation of Baal worship, providing explicit detail to the implicit charge of 2:5 (MT 2:7): the land violated the first commandment. The pronouncement of judgment that follows (2:9) mentions the withholding of elements from 2:5 (my wool and my flax) and announces a second punishment. YHWH will remove the food and clothing mentioned in 2:5, 8 that were used to worship Baal.

**Transition from Judgment to Reconciliation, 2:10-15 (MT 2:12-17)**

Hosea 2:10-15 (MT 2:12-17) continues the divine speech, but it begins with a chronological marker that moves the time frame from an undetermined future date to a statement of YHWH's actions for the present. These verses contain two accusations (2:12, 13) and a transitional marker typical of a judgment oracle ("therefore" in 2:14), but they contain two verdicts (2:10-13aa, 14-15) that function differently. The first verdict announces YHWH's punitive actions, while the second promises reconciliation between YHWH and his wife, preparing

**Parallels between Hosea 2:10-15; 2:1-9; and Elsewhere in the Book of the Twelve**

| | | |
|---|---|---|
| 2:10 | Strip her | Hos 2:3 |
| | No rescue | |
| 2:11 | Cause festivals to cease | |
| 2:12 | Lay waste her vines and fig trees | Hos 2:8-9; cf. Joel 1:7 |
| | | (see also Joel 1:12; Mic 4:4; Hag 2:19; Zech 3:10) |
| | Payment from her lovers | Hos 2:8-9; cf. Mic 1:7 |
| | They will become a forest for wild beasts to devour | Mic 3:12 |
| 2:13 | Punish her for the days of the Baals, | Hos 2:8 |
| | when she went after other lovers | Hos 2:5 |
| 2:14 | I am about to entice her to the wilderness | Hos 2:3 |
| 2:15 | where I will give her vineyards | Hos 2:8 |
| | and she will respond as in the days of her youth, | Hos 2:3 (day of her birth) |
| | as when she came out of the land of Egypt | |

the way for the hopeful pronouncements of much of the remainder of the chapter.

The opening Hebrew word of Hosea 2:10 (MT 2:12), "*wĕ'attâ*," shifts the time of YHWH's action to the present: "But now." This word often marks a new unit, but this new section contains verbal and thematic links connecting 2:10-15 with Hosea 2:3-9 (MT 2:5-11). [Parallels between Hosea 2:10-15; 2:1-9; and Elsewhere in the Book of the Twelve] Verse 10 continues immediately with nine more first person singular verbs denoting YHWH as the speaker in 2:10-15 (strip, remove, destroy, lay waste, punish, entice, bring, speak, give). In 2:10, YHWH proclaims he will strip his wife (the land) in order to shame her so that her lovers are no longer interested in her. In 2:10, the husband/wife metaphor figures prominently, but the function of the metaphor becomes clearer in 2:11-12 (MT 2:13-14) because the "stripping" implies not only the loss of the land's fertility (2:13) but also the elimination of the religious festivals (2:12).

The two accusations in 2:12, 13 (MT 2:14, 15) are both marked by *'ăšer* clauses that change the focus to the feminine character to explain how YHWH's wife broke faith. Formally, YHWH justifies his destruction of "her vine and her fig tree" by quoting her claim that these elements were paid to her by her lovers (2:12). Her admission condemns her in two ways. First, using the husband/wife metaphor, she admits to adultery and prostitution. Second, because her "husband" is YHWH, her statement functions theologically as confirmation that she has broken the first commandment by placing other gods before YHWH. As a result, YHWH promises to turn her vine and fig tree into a forest that will become food for wild beasts.

In Hosea 2:13 (MT 2:15), YHWH states that he will "punish her for the days of the Baals." This pronouncement expands upon the festival motifs of 2:11, as can be seen by the way in which the threefold accusation presents her: (1) she burned incense to the Baals; (2) she dressed inappropriately with rings and other ornaments; and (3) she forgot YHWH. These accusations function on the level of the personification by exposing the wife's adulterous behavior. For the third time in four verses, one finds reference to the wife's "lovers," a term chosen for its rhetorical power to convey the image of a "brazen woman" who takes lovers. This chain of accusations culminates with a dramatic, though brief, contrast of her actions designed to please her lovers (burning incense to them and getting dressed up) with the results of these actions with regard to YHWH: ". . . but me, she forgot."

Immediately following YHWH's wounded cry that his wife has forgotten him, Hosea 2:14 begins with "therefore"—the formal marker of transition to the verdict in a judgment oracle. However, this verdict brings a dramatic and surprising change. Rather than pronouncing a harsh judgment befitting the accusations against the wife who has taken lovers, the next four verbal statements in 2:14-15 (MT 2:16-17) proclaim that YHWH will seek to reconcile the relationship that has gone sour. YHWH says he will "entice her into the wilderness," "speak to her heart," "give her vineyards," and "make the Valley of Achor a door of hope." [Achor] YHWH also narrates the response he hopes she will make to these acts: she will respond as she once did. ["Came up from the land of Egypt"] This response assumes there was a time when YHWH's wife was devoted to him, even though that time (the days of her youth) lies in the distant past. Thus, despite everything, YHWH acts to restore the broken relationship of the present in hopes that the future will hold reconciliation.

**Achor**

AΩ Scholars assume the Valley of Achor is located near Jericho (cf. Josh 7:25, 26; 15:7). More important, the statement plays on the Hebrew root *'kr*, meaning "disorder"/"disaster." Thus, the Valley of "Disaster" (Achor) will become a "door of hope."

**"Came up from the land of Egypt"**

AΩ This phrase reflects an idiom for the exodus. It evokes YHWH's deliverance of Israel from slavery as depicted in the story of Moses, but it rarely appears with explicit reference to Moses outside the book of Exodus. Rather, this phrase often emphasizes YHWH's role in the deliverance (cf. Josh 24:17; Judg 2:1; 6:8; etc.).

## Restoring What Is Broken, 2:16-20 (MT 2:18-22)

Hosea 2:16-20 continues to make promises about the future. This section begins with an introductory phrase ("And on that day, it will be that . . .") that often marks a new eschatological unit and builds on the current context. This unit continues until Hosea 2:21 (MT 2:23); it begins with the same introductory phrase, but changes the addressee. The addressee of 2:16-20 begins and ends with direct address to the wife. References to "you" (2fs) in 2:16, 19-20 address YHWH's wife and frame two verses (2:17-18) that do not address her directly. Moreover, the verses with direct references articulate a message of reconciliation between the husband and the wife: "You (2fs) will call me 'my husband,' and you (2fs) will no longer call me 'My Baal.' . . . And I will take you (2fs) for my wife forever; I will take you (2fs) for my wife in righteousness and in justice, in steadfast love, and in mercy. I will take you (2fs) for my wife in faithfulness; and you (2fs) shall know the LORD." The intervening verses shift the focus to removing the names of the Baals from the land, (re)establishing a covenant with creation, and stopping war in the land.

Hosea 2:15 (MT 2:17) concluded the previous unit with the expectation that the wife would "respond" positively to YHWH's gestures of reconciliation. Hosea 2:16 (MT 2:18) relates formally to that response when it begins "on that day." On that day, she will remember to call YHWH her "husband" (lit., "my man"), and she will no longer call him "my Baal" (i.e., "my lord" or "my husband"). In other words, she will decide to forget Baal rather than to forget YHWH (cf. 2:13, 17 [MT 2:15, 19]).

In Hosea 2:17 (MT 2:19), YHWH promises to remove the names of the Baals from her mouth so that these names will no longer be remembered, thus consigning upon them the same fate as YHWH in 2:13. The first half of Hosea 2:18 (MT 2:20) promises to (re)establish a covenant with creation, echoing language reminiscent of creation themes and the Noah covenant. [Covenant with Creation] The latter part of Hosea 2:18 promises an end to war in the land, which echoes the language of the promise to Judah in Hosea 1:7, and it promises security (to "lie down in safety") with a variation on an idiom that appears frequently in Old Testament texts.[5]

In Hosea 2:19-20 (MT 2:21-22), YHWH again speaks of restoring the marital relationship, addressing the land as wife directly with words of promise that sound quite similar to modern wedding vows. YHWH promises to betroth her forever, using two

### Covenant with Creation

Two observations, one syntactical and one interpretive, should be made about the covenant language in Hos 2:18 (MT 2:20). First, the syntax of the phrase "I will cut with them a covenant," is awkward. However, the NRSV erroneously treats the suffix "them" as a scribal error. In fact, it is more likely that the pronoun functions proleptically. In other words, one could translate the phrase: "I will cut with them a covenant, *that is*, with the beasts of the field, the birds of the air, and the creeping things of the ground." Second, the list of animals recalls the creation language of Genesis (cf. Gen 1:26, 28; 2:19), and especially the covenant language following the flood story (cf. 7:14; 9:2, 9-17). Just as Hos 1 includes an allusion to the covenant promises in Genesis (cf. discussion of Hos 1:10), so too does this section.

sets of word pairs that connote attitudes and behaviors.[6] "Justice" implies a proper order, while "righteousness" implies the behavior consistent with this order. Similarly, "steadfast love" implies an attitude of faithful kindness, while "mercy" implies the manifestation of an attitude of steadfast love. Finally, YHWH says he will take her in faithfulness, and she will know YHWH. These last two phrases reverse the depictions of the land as an unfaithful wife who has taken lovers (2:7 [MT 2:9]) and who does not know YHWH as the source of all her good gifts (Hos 2:8 [MT 2:10]).

### Restoring the Land and the Children, 2:21-23 (MT 2:23-25)

These verses begin with an introductory formula ("And it *will be* on *that* day . . .") that sets the action in the future but associates it with the restoration of the previous verses. Hosea 2:21-23 narrates a series of responses to the situation just described that leads to a reversal of the signs of judgment implied by the names of the children introduced in Hosea 1. Hosea 2:21-23 is thus integrally rooted in the immediate and extended literary context, although they comment upon that context more than continue the husband/wife metaphor that dominates Hosea 2.

Hosea 2:21-22 (MT 2:23-25) narrates a chain of responses that culminates in a promise of fertility to Jezreel. [Chain of Responses] The introductory formula alerts the reader that the following events not only relate to the future, but also to the time of reconciliation described in 2:16-20. Once YHWH's wife returns to YHWH and forgets her lovers, YHWH will respond favorably. This response sets off a chain reaction that leads step by step to the fertility of Jezreel: YHWH will answer the heavens, which respond to the land, which in turn triggers the response of the grain, wine, and oil, which finally leads to their response to Jezreel. The reference to Jezreel is more literary than geographic. It marks a shift back to the names of the children mentioned in Hosea 1:2-11. This focus on

---

**Chain of Responses**

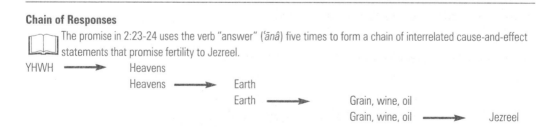

The promise in 2:23-24 uses the verb "answer" (*ānâ*) five times to form a chain of interrelated cause-and-effect statements that promise fertility to Jezreel.

YHWH ⟶ Heavens

Heavens ⟶ Earth

Earth ⟶ Grain, wine, oil

Grain, wine, oil ⟶ Jezreel

the children also marks an inclusio back to the beginning of chapter 2, which addresses the children directly.

Hosea 2:23 (MT 2:25) presents a series of puns on the children's names, each of which removes the judgment that their name implied in Hosea 1. The first pun plays on Jezreel, which means "God sows." In 2:23, YHWH says, "I will sow her."[7] Unlike in Hosea 1:4-5, this sowing is not a pronouncement of judgment. Rather, the second play on words makes clear that YHWH's actions have positive effects. He will pity Lo-Ruhamah (Not-Pitied) and he will say to Lo-Ammi (Not-My-People), "You are my people." Then this people will respond with a one-word affirmation of faith and recognition: "My God" (*ĕlōhāy*). Just as YHWH's wife learned to call him "my husband" (2:16 [MT 2:18]), so also YHWH's people will again learn to call him "my God."

## CONNECTIONS

At its core Hosea 2:1-23 (MT 2:3-25) is about relationships, loyalty, and compassion. This chapter uses a husband/wife metaphor to depict the land as YHWH's wife. As the account unfolds, it evokes powerful images of betrayal in what should be the most intimate of human relationships, that of husband and wife. However, in this relationship, one partner has taken other lovers, causing pain and anger to the other partner.

Before trying to appropriate this passage constructively, one must also recognize the cultural baggage that comes with it, specifically in its presumptions about marriage and adultery, its implicit condoning of the husband's violence, and its assignation of these acts to God. In the ancient Near East, marriage was not the same as marriage in American culture. Women were married through arrangements between families, and the idea of marriage as a partnership of equals was not part of the equation. Women were considered to be under the protection of their fathers until marriage, and once married, they were considered under the control of the husband. In most ancient legal formulations from the ancient Near East that deal with adultery, one sees a decided tendency to protect the honor of the male whose wife has cheated. [Adultery in Ancient Law Codes] Adultery was usually treated as a capital crime, carrying a strong sense of taboo because of the way it dishonored the

### Adultery in Ancient Law Codes

Legal formulations in the ancient Near East rarely demonstrate equal treatment for women, and the societal attitudes toward adultery were extremely harsh. Adultery was considered a capital crime punishable by death. In some cases, the woman was considered the aggressor and the man could escape if he claimed he was seduced (Ur-Nammu §4). In some cases, no specific penalty is even mentioned for the man (Eshnunna §28). Ironically, one legal formulation goes to some lengths to even the punishment for the male and the female, but the intention seems to be to stop retribution against the males. See Middle Assyrian §15, where compassion for the woman must be followed by compassion on the man. Against this cultural context, the biblical codes seem quite similar. Deuteronomy and Leviticus condemn adultery for both males and females, but they share the same assumptions that adultery is a capital crime against the woman's husband. By contrast, the admonition attributed to Jesus in John 8:7 stands out as radically different, when he tells the woman caught in adultery, "Let anyone among you who is without sin be the first to throw a stone at her."

| Source | Law Code |
| --- | --- |
| Ur-Nammu (c. 2040 BCE) | §4: If the wife of a man, by employing her charms, followed after another man and he slept with her, they (i.e., the authorities) shall slay that woman, but that male shall be set free. |
| Eshnunna (c. 2000 BCE) | §28: If (a man) concludes a formal contract with her father and her mother and cohabits with her, she is a housewife. When she is caught with (another) man she shall die, she shall not get away alive. |
| Hammurabi (1700 BCE) | Proven: §129: If the wife of a man has been caught while lying with another man, they shall bind them and throw them into the water. If the husband of the woman wishes to spare his wife, then the king in turn may spare his subject.<br><br>Unproven: §132: If the finger was pointed at the wife of a man because of another man, but she has not been caught while lying with another man, she shall throw herself into the river for the sake of her husband. |
| Middle Assyrian (12th C.) | §13: When a man's wife has left her own house and has visited another man where he is living, if he has lain with her, knowing that she was a man's wife, they shall put the man to death and the woman as well.<br><br>§15: If a man has caught another man with his wife, when they have prosecuted him and convicted him, they shall put both of them to death, with no liability attaching to him. If, upon catching him, he has brought him either into the presence of the king or into the presence of the judges, when they have prosecuted him and convicted him, if the woman's husband puts his wife to death, he shall also put the man to death, but if he cuts off his wife's nose, he shall turn the man into a eunuch and they shall mutilate his whole face. However, if he let his wife go free, they shall let the man go free. |
| Biblical, Deut 22:22 | If a man is found lying with a married woman, then both of them shall die, the man who lay with the woman, and the woman; thus you shall purge the evil from Israel. |
| Lev 20:10 | If a man commits adultery with the wife of his neighbor, both the adulterer and the adulteress shall be put to death. |

husband. These presuppositions about marriage and adultery display a clear preference for the protection of male honor because the woman was deemed more as property than as a person in her own right.

The anthropomorphic depiction of God in Hosea 2 as the dishonored husband reflects many of these ancient cultural assumptions about marriage, and it reflects a male orientation. There is little doubt it was written by males for males in depicting God as the wounded husband who lashes out with words of anger and violence. These acts of violence in our context would constitute spousal abuse, and on this level it is impossible to adopt these images as justifiable ways of speaking about God. God strips and imprisons the wife (2:3, 6, 10). God threatens to kill her and her children (2:3-4). To leave these images of violence unchallenged implicitly condones behavior that is a brutal expression of anger by a powerful spouse misdirected against a weaker partner. The fact that a biblical text uses this imagery for God does not justify the explicit or implicit affirmation of this behavior for contemporary communities of faith. Violence used by one spouse against another should not be tolerated in our congregations and should not be accepted as a legitimate, enduring image of divine behavior.

Nevertheless, especially in communities that traditionally value the Bible as the church's faith book, utterly rejecting the text because of the violence inherent in God's response in this passage is also inadequate. If every violent image in the Bible were merely discarded as a relic of an ancient worldview, then both the Old Testament and the New Testament would be considerably smaller. Responsible interpreters of biblical texts must continue to wrestle with texts of violence in order to present a constructive word of God to the community of faith today. When one asks what that means in the case of Hosea 2, some significant perspectives begin to unfold beyond the violence threatened by one spouse against the other. At least three interpretive avenues arise once one asks how to interpret this problematic text constructively. These paths focus upon the portrayal of God in the ancient context (rather than the modern), the guilt of the spouse (as well as the threatened violence of YHWH), and the multiplicity of perspectives in Hosea 2.

First, if one compares the role of YHWH in Hosea 2 with how the dishonored spouse is expected to behave in the ancient cultural context, the violence that is threatened by YHWH recedes considerably. To be sure, this reduction does not eliminate the problem of divine violence, but neither does it merely reflect the dominant cultural norms of the day. In the ancient world, as already noted, adultery was considered a capital crime punishable by death— usually for both participants. By contrast, Hosea 2 threatens violence, using graphic imagery, but these images give way in the latter part of the chapter to images of God trying to restore the relationship. Although biblical law codes state that a wife caught in adultery should be executed (Deut 22:22; Lev 20:10), other biblical texts suggest this punishment was ultimately deemed too harsh (John 7:53–8:11).[8] Hosea 2:14 depicts God speaking tenderly and promising restoration of the land. Some commentators focus almost exclusively upon how this behavior disturbingly parallels the cyclical pattern of abusive husbands who beat their wives, then express remorse and promise never to do so again, only to begin the cycle all over again because they cannot control their rage. Focusing only upon this element, however disturbing, was certainly not the original intention of the metaphor. For one thing, the "husband" in Hosea 2 does not apologize for his behavior. Rather, he reverses himself by trying to win her back (2:14) and to restore the relationship. To do so, in the logic of the text, requires that she recognize her original commitment. The decision to interpret the expressions of reconciliation as genuine requires that one trust the character of YHWH in this text. Herein lies the difference between what one asks the community of faith to do with this text and what we counsel parishioners who have experienced spousal abuse. Can one trust the God in this text who proclaims a desire for reconciliation? God's conciliatory response differs from the retributive response reflected in the biblical law codes on adultery, but it remains disturbing for many contemporary readers. This text begins with human infidelity and divine anger, but it ends with the desire for divine reconciliation and the hope for human change.

Second, focusing exclusively on the problematic aspects of the anthropomorphism, when applied to God's behavior, bypasses the original challenge entirely. Namely, the extended passage originally focused on spousal infidelity as a metaphor for religious idolatry. Here, unlike modern parallels where the abused spouse suffers innocently from the irrational rage inflicted by a bully, the woman in Hosea 2 (in the logic of the text) can hardly be portrayed as innocent. This partner abandoned her spouse, deliberately sought lovers (2:7), gave them gifts (2:5), and substituted commitment to a spouse for illicit lovers (2:16). In the logic of Hosea 2, the wife has broken faith with her covenant partner. This relationship functions not as a metaphor for human marriage, but as a metaphor for religious infidelity. Challenges to human behavior, not predictions of the future, constitute the chief characteristic of most prophetic literature. While the metaphorical relationship chosen to confront that behavior in Hosea 2 creates real theological dilemmas, one must also take the confrontation seriously because its critique of the wife's behavior symbolizes God's insistence upon fidelity in religious expression. Hosea 2, in this respect, lays the theological foundation for the book as a whole. Human idolatry cannot remain unchallenged in the prophetic worldview.

Third, and related, the message of Hosea 2 reflects a complex web of theological perspectives whose voices must be weighed alongside and against one another. Two of these have already been mentioned: the husband's desire for reconciliation in a context where death was the expected punishment for adultery, and the text's insistence upon the guilt of the woman. Other voices beg to be heard as well. This depiction of a husband and wife is not a newspaper report but an extended metaphor. The husband represents God while the wife plays a multifaceted role. On the most basic level, she represents the land of Israel while her children are its people. On a religious and socio-cultural level, the relationship represents the battle between two religious systems that was taking place in ancient Israel: the worship of a monotheistic deity who demands allegiance or the worship of a fertility god supported by a polytheistic conceptualization of how the world operates. On a theological level, the text emphasizes several key biblical concepts, albeit with troublesome metaphorical images: a God who expects fidelity but extends compassion; a God whose providential care extends to all creation; and human frailty and caprice when it comes to covenant expectations.

# NOTES

1. The NRSV (and others) avoid the problem of the plural objects by substituting the singular, thereby stressing the connection to Hos 1 at the expense of the disjunction in the Hebrew.

2. See Hans Walter Wolff, *Hosea* (trans. Gary Stansell; Hermeneia; Philadelphia: Fortress, 1974) 33; see Gen 31:36.

3. For a more detailed discussion of the prophetic judgment oracle, see Gene M. Tucker, "Prophecy and Prophetic Literature," in *The Hebrew Bible and Its Modern Interpreters* (ed. Douglas A. Knight; Chico CA: Scholars Press, 1985) 325–68, esp. 335–37.

4. For example, Wolff argues that the phrase "they made for Baal" represents a later comment that expands the existing sentence (*Hosea*, 31, 37). Wolff ignores the fact that this scenario presumes an awkward sentence: "And silver I lavished upon her, and gold." Wolff does not explain how silver and gold would have become separated. *BHS* suggests the entire last half of the verse may have been added.

5. The idiomatic expression "to dwell in safety" appears 26 times: Lev 25:18, 19; 26:5; Deut 12:10; 33:12, 28; Isa 47:8; Jer 23:6; 32:37; 33:16; 49:31; Ezek 28:26; 34:25; 34:27; 34:28; 38:8; 38:11; 38:14; 39:6; 39:26; Zech 14:11; Pss 4:9; 16:9; Prov 1:33; 3:29. Note also that the variation "to lie down in safety" appears in Job 11:18 and with a different verb in Isa 14:30. Hos 2:18 probably uses the verb "to lie down" because the 3mp suffix (them) refers back to the animals, and "dwell" would typically imply humans as the subject.

6. See the discussion of *mišpaṭ* and *ṣĕdāgāh* in G. Liedke, "*špṭ* To Judge," in *TLOT* 3:1396. See the discussion of *ḥesed* and *raḥămîn* in H. J. Stoebe, "*ḥesed* Kindness," in *TLOT* 2:453–54. See also Hans Walter Wolff, *Joel and Amos: A Commentary on the Books of the Prophets Joel and Amos* (trans. Waldemar Janzen, S. Dean McBride, Jr., and Charles A. Muenchow; Hermeneia; Philadelphia: Fortress, 1977) 245.

7. NRSV translates "him" to make the gender fit because Jezreel was a boy according to 1:4. However, this decision ignores the role of 2:23 as a comment on Hos 2, where the wife was the primary focus.

8. Even Old Testament texts intimate that treating adultery as a capital offense was not practical. See Elaine Adler Goodfriend, "Adultery," *ABD* 1:83.

# AN ACT OF
# JUDGMENT AND HOPE

## Hosea 3:1-5

## COMMENTARY

The genre of this prose passage is the prophetic symbolic act reported in autobiographical style. [The Prophetic Symbolic Act] This first person style differs from Hosea 1, where the prophet appears in the third person. The prophetic speech also differs from the first YHWH speech of Hosea 2. Hosea 3:1 therefore suggests a different situation than previous chapters. The prose of Hosea 3 also sets this passage apart from the poetry of Hosea 2 and 4.

While YHWH speaks in Hosea 2, the prophet speaks in 3:1-5 as indicated by third person references to YHWH (in 3:1, 5). The word

---

**The Prophetic Symbolic Act**

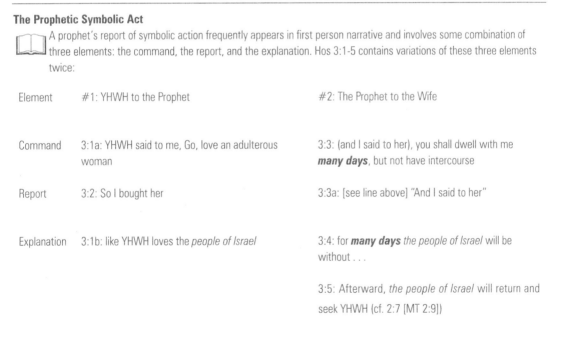

A prophet's report of symbolic action frequently appears in first person narrative and involves some combination of three elements: the command, the report, and the explanation. Hos 3:1-5 contains variations of these three elements twice:

| Element | #1: YHWH to the Prophet | #2: The Prophet to the Wife |
|---|---|---|
| Command | 3:1a: YHWH said to me, Go, love an adulterous woman | 3:3: (and I said to her), you shall dwell with me *many days*, but not have intercourse |
| Report | 3:2: So I bought her | 3:3a: [see line above] "And I said to her" |
| Explanation | 3:1b: like YHWH loves the *people of Israel* | 3:4: for *many days* the *people of Israel* will be without . . . |
| | | 3:5: Afterward, *the people of Israel* will return and seek YHWH (cf. 2:7 [MT 2:9]) |

See Gene M. Tucker, "Prophecy and Prophetic Literature," *The Hebrew Bible and Its Modern Interpreters* (ed. Douglas A. Knight and Gene M. Tucker; Chico CA: Scholars Press, 1985) 342.

### "Again" in Hosea 3:1

AΩ The NRSV associates the word "again" with "say," but it is virtually alone in this respect. Most English translations (KJV, NAS, NJB, NKJV, RSV, NIV), as well as the LXX and the Vulgate, translate "again" with "go." Presumably, the NRSV made this decision based on the disjunctive accent in MT or on the fact that *'ôd* usually comes after the verb when it means "again" (Gen 4:25; 24:20; Judg 13:8; and especially Hos 1:6).

"again" in Hosea 3:1 presents this chapter as related to earlier events, not an independent account, but 3:1-5 is otherwise self-contained. ["Again" in Hosea 3:1] In terms of genre, the chapter recounts a symbolic action report with (1) a formulaic introduction (YHWH said to me . . .); 2) a command from YHWH that includes a rationale with the command to marry an adulteress (3:1); (3) the prophet's response to the command (3:2); and (4) the prophet's command to the wife (3:3) with a two-part explanation (3:4, 5).

The command from YHWH in 3:1 is similar to, but not identical with, the opening command of 1:2. In Hosea 3:1, YHWH commands the prophet to love an adulteress, whereas YHWH tells the prophet to "take a wife of whoredom" in 1:2. Much discussion has focused on the identity of the adulteress, who is probably not Gomer. [The Identity of the Adulteress] Hosea 1 and 3 cite different offenses (harlotry and adultery), but both would have had a similar impact on the reader. Adultery, like other sexual misconduct, is treated as a capital offense (Lev 20:10), and its prohibition appears as one of the Ten Commandments (Exod 20:14; Deut 5:18). YHWH thus commands the prophet to marry a prostitute (1:2) and to love an adulteress (3:1).

### The Identity of the Adulteress

Should the adulterous woman in Hos 3 be equated with "the wife of whoredom" (Gomer) in Hos 1? Interpreters take one of three paths: (1) these chapters offer different accounts of the same event; (2) YHWH gives two different commands to the prophet about the same woman; or (3) these accounts represent two commands to the prophet regarding different women. The first model creates problems. First, the offenses are different. Second, Hos 1 focuses on the birth of three children, while Hos 3 never mentions children; in fact, it indicates that the prophet would refrain from relations with the adulteress (3:3). Finally, the word "again" in 3:1 means that at the point of compilation, these accounts were treated as different encounters. Problems with the second model also make it unlikely. First, the woman is named in ch. 1, but not in ch. 3. Second, one has to construct a narrative scenario explaining how Gomer goes from a former prostitute who bears three children to an adulteress having an affair with a neighbor. Finally, bargaining for a price to pay for the woman (see 3:2) makes no sense if they are already married. The third model creates the least problems. First, "again" in 3:1 makes sense if it is a second woman and a second command. Second, negotiating a price to pay for the woman makes sense if they had no prior relationship with her. Analytically, it is best to treat ch. 3 as a second command concerning a second woman.

The latter half of 3:1 provides the reason for this command, telling the prophet to love an adulteress "just as the LORD loves the people of Israel, though they turn to other gods and love raisin cakes." In other words, YHWH loves the people even though they cheat on him. In "turning to other gods," the people have broken the vow of the first commandment to place no other gods before them (Exod 20:3; Deut 5:7). Moreover, the reference to the people's love of raisin cakes indicates that the people *enjoy* the worship practices associated with the worship of these other gods. [Raisin Cakes]

In Hosea 3:2, the prophet narrates his response to the command of 3:1. The prophet negotiates a price for the unnamed woman. The Hebrew verb used here (*kārâ*) generally indicates bartering. The text does not say whom the prophet paid. However, given that this "purchase" takes place in response to the command of 3:1, it is possible that the reader should assume that the price was given to the (former) husband or perhaps to the woman herself. The amount of this transaction is relatively large, suggesting that the prophet is either purchasing a prostitute like a slave (for a lengthy period) or negotiating for a wife.[1] The NRSV lists the price at fifteen (shekels of) silver, a homer of barley, and *a measure of wine*—a translation based on the LXX text. The MT, on the other hand, has "fifteen (shekels of) silver, a homer of barley, and a *letek of barley*." This difference is not easily explained as a copyist error. The combination of barley and silver is roughly equivalent to 30 shekels, approximately the price of a slave according to Exodus 21:32 and Leviticus 27:4.[2] A "*letek*" is one half of a homer, but ancient measurements are notoriously difficult to equate to modern measurements precisely. [Ancient Measurements] Nevertheless, the amount of grain alone would last for a significant time.

In Hosea 3:3 the prophet tells the woman that she will dwell with him "many days," during which time she will have to remain celibate. She will not sell herself for money, nor will she be able to be with a man intimately. Moreover, the prophet will also not have

---

**Raisin Cakes**

Raisin cakes are mentioned five times in the Old Testament (2 Sam 6:19 = 1 Chr 16:3; Isa 16:7; Hos 3:1; Cant 2:5). Reference to "raisin cakes" in Hos 3:1 implies a polemic against them. This negative connotation derives from the use of raisin cakes as offerings when worshiping other gods. In one account, raisin cakes were clearly given to the people *after* the sacrifice was performed (2 Sam 6:19 = 1 Chr 16:3), even though in that instance the sacrifice had been offered by David to YHWH. Interestingly, four of the five times that the Old Testament mentions raisin cakes, the people consume them in a worship context.

---

**Ancient Measurements**

A general consensus exists regarding the relationship of Hebrew units of measure to one another, but their modern equivalent is difficult because (1) ancient measurements were not standardized from one region to another and (2) the amount involved probably changed over time. Still, the *homer*, *letek*, and *ephah* represented three common measurements of volume for dry goods:

| Term | Ancient Equivalent | Modern Equivalent |
|------|-------------------|-------------------|
| Homer | 10 ephahs, 2 leteks | A homer is listed variously: 11 bushels (Wolff, 61; Sweeney, *The Twelve Prophets*, 39); 5.16 bushels (Mays, *Hosea*, 57), and 6 ½ bushels (Rowell, "Weights and Measures" *MDB*, 958). |
| Letech | 5 ephahs, 0.5 homer | |
| Ephah | 0.1 homer, 0.2 letech | |

Hans Walter Wolff, *Hosea* (trans. Gary Stansell; Hermeneia; Philadelphia: Fortress, 1974).

Marvin A. Sweeney, *The Twelve Prophets* (Berit Olam, vol. 1; Collegeville: Liturgical Press, 2000).

Edd Rowell, "Weights and Measures" *MDB*, 958–59.

sexual relations with her. In short, whether the woman is merely an adulteress or has become a prostitute, the prophet makes it clear that he intends to prohibit her from any type of sexual activity for an indeterminate period. (See [Meanings of "Prostitute"].) This action clearly parallels YHWH removing the wife from her lovers in 2:6 (MT 2:8).

Hosea 3:4 interprets how the prophet's action in 3:3 relates to Israel. The verse lists six items that will be removed from Israel for a lengthy period. These items appear in three groups. The woman going without sex "for many days" in 3:3 symbolizes, according to 3:4, that the "sons of Israel" will be without rulers (no king or prince), without the instruments for offering sacrifice (sacrifice or pillar), and without implements for discerning the future (ephod and teraphim) "for many days." [Pillar, Ephod, and Teraphim] The judgment against the people of Israel pronounced in this verse is directed toward the northern kingdom. It anticipates a period of political and cultic disaster. Hosea 3:4 (see also 3:5) presupposes a polemic against the political and religious practices of the northern kingdom—the kingdom that had disavowed Davidic kingship following the death of Solomon over a century earlier (2 Kgs 12).

Hosea 3:5 takes the prediction of 3:4 a step further by anticipating restoration for the "children of Israel" *after* their punishment is complete. It does so using a play on words that interprets and reverses the judgment. Whereas 3:4 states that the children of Israel would *dwell* (*yēšbû*) without political and religious elements, Hosea 3:5 states that afterward, the Israelites would "*return* (*yāšbû*) and seek YHWH their God and David their king." Thus, Hosea 3:5 interprets the punishment as Israel's exile. The more explicit term "return" implies they had been away (an implication that would not have been required by 3:4 alone). Hosea 3:5 also sharpens the anti-Northern polemic by saying the Israelites will seek YHWH their God (rather than the ephod and teraphim) and David their king (meaning a reunification with Judah and the Davidic kings).

---

**Pillar, Ephod, and Teraphim**

The word translated as "pillar" generally means an uncut memorial stone. Pillars were often placed at sacred places and could be used in funeral rites or with religious rituals. These elements are often condemned as inconsistent with the true worship of YHWH (cf. Hos 10:2; Mic 5:12). The ephod was a cult object, sometimes kept in a shrine (Judg 17:5; 1 Sam 21:10) and sometimes carried (1 Sam 23:6; 2:28; 14:3). Some see it as a priestly garment for carrying items used in divination (see Sweeney, 40). The ephod was used when obtaining a prophetic oracle (1 Sam 23:9; 30:7). It is often paired with teraphim (Judg 17:5; 18:14, 17-18, 20), which perhaps refer to statues of various sizes, which may have functioned as a household deity or been used in ancestral worship. In several texts, one consults teraphim for information about the future (see especially Ezek 21:26). This purpose seems consistent with the several places that mention teraphim in conjunction with the ephod (Judg 17:5; 18:14, 17-20; Hos 3:4; see also Zech 10:2).

Marvin A. Sweeney, *The Twelve Prophets* (Berit Olam, vol. 1; Collegeville: Liturgical Press, 2000).

Hosea 3:5 clearly interprets the punishment announced in 3:4 from a Judean perspective, leading several scholars to assign this verse to a later editor such as the Judean editor of chapter 1, and probably as part of the book's compilation.[3] Hosea 3:5 adds a message of hope to the judgment against the people by means of the prophetic symbolic act and its interpretation.

# CONNECTIONS

This passage involves four entities: YHWH, the prophet, the unnamed woman, and the Israelites (lit., the "sons of Israel"). With whom should the reader identify? One must first understand how the text characterizes each of these entities. YHWH speaks to the prophet because YHWH loves the Israelites (3:1). In the end, YHWH's goodness will draw the Israelites to him in awe and trepidation (3:5). The prophet, on the other hand, obeys YHWH and acts as the mediator of YHWH's message of judgment by pronouncing judgment on the adulteress (3:3) and equating this punishment to what will happen to the Israelites (3:4, 5).

The woman in this chapter functions as a foil that never speaks or responds. She does, however, play an important part as a symbol of the Israelites themselves (3:1, 4, 5). She has committed adultery, and YHWH takes actions through the prophet to prohibit her from having sexual intercourse (3:3). This prohibition serves as the touchstone for equating the woman's fate with that of the Israelites, who in turn will be prohibited from experiencing political and religious life as they have done in the past (3:4). The purpose of this punishment is to admonish Israel to find

**Hosea and Gomer**

In this late medieval manuscript illustration Hosea embraces Gomer, who appears to be irritated by his action.

(Credit: Anonymous. Hosea and Gomer, from the *Bible Historiale*, http://commons.wikimedia.org/wiki/File:Hosea_and_Gomer.jpg)

YHWH, although the prospects for this promise lie in the distant future (3:5). This passage creates many of the same difficulties for contemporary readers as did the metaphorical figure in Hosea 2 (see Connections for Hosea 2). There are no easy solutions. If one eliminates the text because the image is objectionable, one is hard pressed to explain a major metaphor in Hosea. If one tries to make the text meaningful to contemporary communities of faith, one must challenge the violent responses implied in this text, even while trying to understand the text in its ancient context.

Now, one can ask, with whom should the reader identify? On one level, this text equates the adulterous woman with the people. On a secondary level, the text invites the reader to reflect upon the message from a vantage point that includes additional knowledge. Anyone reading this text after 722 BCE would know that the northern kingdom of Israel was indeed destroyed, along with its rulers and religious functionaries. The prediction had come true in that sense, but what about the promise that the Israelites would return and seek the LORD their God and David their king (3:5)? This promise was never fulfilled in any literal sense for the northern kingdom. This historical reflection thus places the reader in a point of tension between despair and hope, between judgment and salvation, between punishment and deliverance.

The reflective reader is privy to knowing YHWH's ultimate intention of restoration, but cannot help asking what happened to the promise. To answer this question, one must recognize several theological affirmations regarding history in Hosea and the Book of the Twelve.

This passage is not the first one in Hosea to vacillate between threat and promise or between judgment and salvation. Each of the first three chapters exhibits this tension. In fact, this tension will return again (especially chs. 11 and 14). These repeated swings between positive and negative messages serve several theological purposes. First, YHWH calls the people to account when they break their part of the covenant. Second, YHWH is not motivated by a perverse desire to destroy. YHWH punishes the people in an attempt to get them to reestablish respect for YHWH's lordship. Third, as will become clearer as Hosea unfolds, the failure of the promised deliverance lies with the people, not YHWH. Every time YHWH provides a chance for repentance and restoration, the people reject it or they give lip service to repentance only to return to their destructive behavior soon thereafter.

This pattern continues beyond the book of Hosea, serving as one of the recurring themes of Old Testament narratives and prophetic writings. The tension between judgment and salvation plays a role in either the structure or the message of every prophetic collection, including the Book of the Twelve. Four of the twelve (Hosea, Joel, Amos, Micah, and Zephaniah) are *structured* to convey this tension with respect to the political and religious continuation of Israel and Judah after 587. Hosea vacillates between judgment and salvation for Israel. Amos overwhelmingly presents a message of judgment on Israel, from which only a remnant will survive. Micah functions in much the same way as Hosea, except Micah focuses on Judah. Zephaniah serves much the same role as Amos, except Judah is the central focus and the promissory elements play a more prominent role for Judah in 3:9-20.

Putting this vacillation into perspective requires engagement and a decision from contemporary communities of faith. [Prediction in Prophetic Texts] The engagement begins with the question of the role of prophetic books as Scripture. If one understands prophetic literature as some kind of magical repository that predicts things from the ancient world that will come true in our time, then contemporary communities of faith will likely be disappointed when reading promises in prophetic texts. The northern kingdom did not return to a Davidic king, at least not in a political sense, so in that sense the promise of Hosea 3:5 will never come true. However, prophetic texts are not some collection of mystical incantations, and literal fulfillments are not the only way that promises can serve a purpose. Prophetic texts offer testimony from ancient communities of faith, testimony that God is at work in the world. Prophetic texts usually call for a decision. Either one chooses, privately and corporately, to live in a way that honors God, or one does not. In a real sense, these decisions parallel the same kinds of decisions we face.

The testimony of Hosea 3 makes statements about political realities. Many, but not all, of those statements came true, not merely for the northern kingdom but also for Judah. It is not difficult to understand how ancient readers saw these warnings and promises extended to them. To the extent that this juxtaposition still helps modern communities of faith to ask questions about the intersection of personal faith and corporate realities, then it serves its

**Prediction in Prophetic Texts**
For a thoughtful analysis of the ways prophetic prediction functions, see J. J. M. Roberts, "A Christian Perspective on Prophetic Prediction," *Int* 33 (1979): 240–53. Roberts illustrates four types of prophetic prediction where fulfillment (1) happens literally; (2) did not and never will come true; (3) has yet to come true; and (4) happens in a way that is less than or more than literal.

purpose as Scripture. How does one face political uncertainty with faith? In prophetic literature several key elements surface repeatedly that help to structure one's response. First, the juxtaposition of judgment and promise presents a continual tension. It is important to recognize this tension and not try to harmonize the two messages. The same prophetic writing contains powerful statements of rejection and of hope. One cannot say that only one of these perspectives represents *the* perspective of the text. Second, this tension forces decisions. Prophetic genres tend to be confrontational speeches that seek to cause a change of behavior by people. The fact that these speeches are recorded after the events implies that those who recorded them wanted later generations to hear these speeches and to reflect upon their meaning. The fact that later readers continued to transmit them implies that they considered the texts to be relevant for their lives. Third, this alternation of political judgment and promise is future oriented, so it forces those who read with the eyes of faith to ask where we are in this picture. Are we heading down the right road as a nation, as a church, as individuals? Did previous generations make the right choices? Will we?

# NOTES

1. Marvin A. Sweeney argues that the amount suggests a permanent transaction (like a marriage) over against a prostitute's fee (*The Twelve Prophets* [Berit Olam, vol. 1; Collegeville: Liturgical Press, 2000] 39). Douglas Stuart calls the money a bride price, but does not explain why the Hebrew term for bride price is not used (*Hosea–Jonah* [WBC 31; Waco: Word, 1987] 66). Others suggest that the prophet is purchasing a prostitute (either as one would purchase a slave or for a lengthy period). Mays and Rudolph suggest that the purchase price could be the purchase of a prostitute for an extended period—essentially buying her as a slave (James L. Mays, *Hosea, A Commentary* [OTL; Philadelphia, Westminster, 1969] 57; Wilhelm Rudolph, *Hosea* [KAT, Bd 13/1; Gütersloh: G.Mohn, 1966] 91–92).

2. Hans Walter Wolff, *Hosea* (trans. Gary Stansell; Hermeneia; Philadelphia: Fortress, 1974) 61.

3. See Mays, *Hosea*, 60. Jörg Jeremias sees 3:5 as a later addition, but he argues it was already in place by the time of Jeremiah (*Der Prophet Hosea übersetzt und erklärt* [Das Alte Testament Deutsch, Neues Göttinger Bibelwerk 24/1; Göttingen: Vandenhoeck & Ruprecht, 1983] 57). Eberhard Bons summarizes the differences between 3:5 and the rest of the chapter, but he is not certain at what point the verse would have been added (*Das Buch Hosea* [Neuer Stuttgarter Kommentar 23/1; Stuttgart: Verlag Katholisches Bibelwerk, 1996] 64–66). Both Jeremias and Bons, however, attribute the verse to the shaping of the book rather than a prophetic speech.

# A LAWSUIT AGAINST THE RELIGIOUS LEADERS AND THE PEOPLE

## Hosea 4:1-19

## COMMENTARY

Hosea 4 begins a lengthy series of judgment sayings that continue unabated until 6:1-3. It contains no hint of the positive message that concluded chapters 1–3. This chapter contains two closely related sections (4:1-6, 7-19) that evoke images of a lawsuit. More pointedly, Hosea 4 conveys a particularly strong invective against the priests and religious leaders who have allowed the people to conduct worship in ways that YHWH abhors. Hosea 4:7-19 returns frequently to the prostitution metaphor from Hosea 2 to explain how dire the situation has become.

### YHWH Brings Charges against the People and their Leaders, 4:1-6

Hosea 4 changes speaker and style from the preceding chapter. Gone are the first person references of the prophet in Hosea 3. Instead, one finds prophetic address both to the people and the priests. Gone too is the message of hope that concluded chapter 3. God appears as the prosecuting attorney in a lawsuit and lays out three specific charges (4:1): Israel lacks faithfulness, covenant loyalty, and knowledge of God. [Lawsuit *rîb*] These charges are then explained (4:2, 6), emphasizing the guilt of the leaders and the effects of these problems on creation.

Hosea 4:1 begins with a call to attention: "Hear the

> **Lawsuit *rîb***
>
> AΩ The use of the covenant lawsuit (*rîb*) in prophetic literature involves some combination of five elements (all of which are present in Hos 4:1-6): (1) a call to open the hearing (4:1a); (2) accusation(s) (4:1b-2, 6a); (3) address by the prosecutor (4:1-6); (4) a reference to the failure of cultic efforts for compensation (4:4); and (5) declaration of guilt and punishment (4:5-6).

### The Command to "Hear the Word" in the Book of the Twelve

The command to "listen" occurs 14 times in the Book of the Twelve, but only in Hosea (4:1; 5:1), Amos (3:1, 13; 4:1; 5:1; 8:4), Micah (1:2; 3:1, 9; 6:1, 2, 9), and Joel (1:2). Thus, the prophetic writings explicitly, or implicitly, set in the eighth century call on the reader/hearer to listen to YHWH's word. All of these texts introduce words of judgment against YHWH's people, and Mic 6:1-2 introduces a lawsuit (rîb) against Judah in much the same way that Hos 4:1 does for Israel.

word of YHWH." The command to "hear" appears in the mouths of judges (e.g., Judg 5:3), kings (e.g., 1 Chr 28:2), emissaries (e.g., 2 Kgs 18:28), and prophets. The command verb appears most commonly, however, to indicate a prophetic message, especially when the object of the verb is "the word (of YHWH)."[1] This command, "Hear the word," plays an intriguing role in the Book of the Twelve. [The Command to "Hear the Word" in the Book of the Twelve]

Hosea 4:1 also cites the reason for calling the people to attention: YHWH brings suit against the inhabitants of the land. The NRSV correctly translates the term for lawsuit, rîb, as "indictment." The latter portion of the verse contains a threefold charge against the inhabitants: there is no faithfulness (or fidelity, 'emet), no loyalty (ḥesed), and no knowledge of God in the land. [The Relational Terms, 'emet and ḥesed] All three of these charges have already been established in Hosea 1–3, especially by the implications of chapter 2.[2]

### The Relational Terms, 'emet and ḥesed

AΩ The term 'emet denotes continuity and a sense of trustworthiness. The continuity may be associated with behavioral attributes of God (Gen 24:7; Exod 34:6) or humans (Exod 18:21; 1 Kgs 3:6; Neh 7:2). As such, it can be translated as trustworthiness, faithfulness, or constancy. It can also refer to the content of statements, made by a person who displays these qualities. Hence, the words of YHWH are true (Ps 19:10) and YHWH speaks truth either directly (Ps 132:11) or through prophets (1 Kgs 17:24). God also can discern those who exhibit 'emet or not (2 Kgs 20:3; Jer 42:5), and God's instruction also conveys 'emet for those who seek it (Pss 25:5; 86:11). God also expects 'emet to be characteristic of God's people, and prophets challenge people when such is not the case (Jer 9:4; Zech 8:16).

The word ḥesed conveys a positive act or behavior that demonstrates continuity in a relationship that comports with what is expected from that relationship. As such, it can be translated as "kindness," "mercy," "loving kindness," or "loyalty," depending upon the context. Most commonly, ḥesed refers to God's behavior (Deut 7:9, 12; Jer 33:11; Joel 2:13) toward the earth (Ps 33:5), God's people (Ps 103:17), or an individual (2 Sam 9:3). It is used as an ideal for humans to seek (Mic 6:8).

Hosea 4:2-3 provides concrete examples of the lack of covenant loyalty. These verses also extrapolate the implications of the absence of ḥesed for the created order. Hosea 4:2 describes the land as suffering from the breaking of those commandments in the Decalogue that deal with human relationships (murder, adultery, robbery, and false witness [cf. Exod 20:13-16]). Hosea 4:2 contains essentially the same elements as these commandments: "swearing, lying, murder, robbery, and adultery break forth." As a result, bloodshed and violence run rampant. It is surely no accident that this larger unit of Hosea 4–11 thus begins with accusations about breaking the last six commandments, while its concluding passage (see discussion of 11:2) essentially accuses Israel of breaking the first two commandments.

Not surprisingly, the land and its inhabitants suffer from the sorry state of affairs cited in 4:2, but 4:3 broadens the implications in a surprising way. The creation language drives home the point that breaking God's commands affects all creation negatively. Citation of "the beasts of the field, the birds of the air, and the fish of the sea" encompasses the created beings of the ground, sky, and sea—all of whom YHWH placed under the dominion of humanity at creation and after the flood (Gen 1:30; 9:2). It implies that the situation has so seriously deteriorated that it threatens God's entire created order.[3] Hosea 4:2-3 draws upon allusions to canonical traditions to emphasize how seriously God takes Israel's abrogation of its covenant obligations.

Hosea 4:4-6 transitions from the charge of the lack of covenant loyalty to a charge based on the lack of knowledge of God (cf. 4:2, 6). This indictment is primarily directed against the priests (and the prophets to a lesser extent) for their failure to present this knowledge to the people. Hosea 4:4 warns the hearers that only God can bring charges in this courtroom drama. Most English translations emend 4:4 slightly to clarify this verse as a strong indictment of the priests in line with 4:5. Hosea 4:5 expresses the totality of the corruption of Israel's religious leaders by using poetic parallelism to indict the priests: "You stumble all day; moreover, the prophet stumbles with you by night." [Poetic Parallelism] This image of the failure of Israel's religious leaders also leads YHWH to announce the land's destruction using the "mother" metaphor of Hosea 2: "And I will destroy your mother." Hosea 4:6 restates the charge, "My people are destroyed for the lack of knowledge."[4] The lack of knowledge results from the priests' failure to impart this knowledge to the people.

Historically, 4:6 presumes a polemic against the religious practices of the northern kingdom. Several passages in Hosea hint at the problem of blending YHWH worship with Baal worship (e.g., Hos 2:10, 18; 13:1).[5] Hosea 4:6 confronts the priests for incorporating Baal elements into their worship and for failing to worship YHWH only. They rejected the knowledge of YHWH, so YHWH rejects them as priests. They

**Poetic Parallelism**

Hebrew poetry, including a large percentage of prophetic sayings, does not rely on rhymes as English poetry often does. Instead, Hebrew poetry generally involves parallelism. Poetic parallelism, or *parallelismus memborum*, involves the use of one or more terms in succeeding lines so that these terms function as syntactical or metaphorical companions. These pairings are especially clear in synonymous and antithetic parallelism. Synonymous parallelism uses different words to express the same meaning, as in Ps 112:1: "Happy is the man who fears YHWH; Who is greatly devoted to his commandments."

Antithetic parallelism uses opposing terms to convey meaning as in Prov 10:1: "A wise child makes a glad father; But a foolish child is a mother's grief."

For a more thorough explanation, see Adele Berlin, "Parallelism," in *ABD* 5:155–62.

**tôrâ**

AΩ The word "Torah" has several meanings depending on the context: law, instruction, legal ruling, or Pentateuch. The word derives from the Hebrew root *yrh* (III), which means to "teach" or "instruct." The noun from this root, *tôrâ* basically means "instruction." Priests performed this "instruction" by teaching and making rulings. Most English translations routinely translate the term as "law," which evokes images of rules and regulations. Several Old Testament texts refer to the Pentateuch as the *tôrâ* of Moses or the *tôrâ* of YHWH, and over time Torah became the term used to designate the first five books of the Bible (Genesis through Deuteronomy). While these books contain the lengthy legal codes of the Old Testament, legal material makes up less than half of the Torah. Since the bulk of the Torah appears as narrative material, the unqualified translation of *tôrâ* as "law" reflects only part of the intention of those texts. This word also connotes "instruction" about YHWH.

forgot God's *instruction*, so God will forget their sons. The word used in 4:6, *tôrâ* is generally translated as "law." [tôrâ] However, the Torah contains far more than legal codes. It is important to understand *tôrâ* in this context as instruction. Since the priesthood passed from one generation to the next through the males of priestly families, this pronouncement of the rejection of the priests' sons effectively announces the end of YHWH's support of the priestly lineage of the northern kingdom.

### Israel's Lack of Faithfulness, 4:7-19

Hosea 4:7-19, the bulk of the chapter, focuses on the ramifications of God's third charge, that God's people lack faithfulness. Each of the four sections making up this unit uses language of prostitution and infidelity to shift the focus from the priests and their sons (4:7-10), to the people (4:11-14), then to the political entities (4:15-16), and finally to the entire Ephraimite region (4:17-19). This imagery contains echoes and allusions to the sexual imagery of Hosea 2.

Hosea 4:7-10 continues the castigation of the priests and their sons for taking advantage of the sins of the people. Hosea 4:7 pronounces judgment replete with contrasts. The verse presumes that the more YHWH provided, the more the priests' children sinned. As a result, YHWH decides to "change their glory into shame." [God Decides to Change their Glory into Shame] The most likely identification for the plural antecedent is the priests and their "sons" mentioned in 4:6. Hosea 4:8 also distinguishes the group from the people. Thus, the plural reference continues the judgment on the priests and their relatives (note 4:9: "like people, like priest"). The charge that "they have devoured the sin of my people" (4:8) also fits this context. Priests were supported in part by eating from the offerings brought by the people. Since the sin of the people included

**God Decides to Change their Glory into Shame**

AΩ The MT reads "I will change" as a continuation of YHWH's speech, but the NRSV follows some ancient interpretive traditions in the Targums (ancient Aramaic translation of the Hebrew Bible) and the Peshitta (Syriac Bible) to read, "They change." This reading was probably changed by the Masoretes, since this verse is one of 18 passages listed in the Tiqqune Sopherim (Emendations of the Scribes), an ancient tradition listing passages changed by the scribes for theological reasons. Later scribes were apparently disturbed by the idea of God associated with shame, especially since the word here (*qâlôn*) can have sexual connotations (Jer 13:26).

bringing offerings to other gods, the accusation in 4:8 implies that the priests partook of these offerings. In other words, they put their own needs above their role as guardians of YHWH's proper sacrifice.

Neither the priests nor the people will escape the consequences of their actions. Hosea 4:9-10 announces judgment on the people and the priests. They will not have enough food to satisfy themselves, and their worship of other gods will not help them increase (lit., "They will prosti-tute themselves, but not increase.") Hosea 4:9 again uses images of infertility and of sexual infidelity in order to accuse people and priests of abandoning their commitment to YHWH. The first line of 4:10 reverses an idiom associated with the fertility of the promised land as expressed in Deuteronomy (6:11; 8:10, 12; 11:15; 14:29; 26:12; 31:20), changing the promise into a curse. This curse serves as part of a fertility motif that unfolds across the Book of the Twelve. ["You shall eat and not be satisfied"]

Hosea 4:11-14 shifts the accent from the priests to the people. Hosea 4:11 implies that the people love the fertility festivals associated with the worship practices of the northern kingdom by condemning the people's love of wine. Hosea 4:12 accuses the people of con-sulting idols. The sarcasm becomes palpable as the prophet mocks those who "consult a piece of wood" or "divining rod" for an oracle. God's prophets rarely missed an opportunity to con-front those substituting superstition and idolatry for reliance upon the living word of God (cf. Isa 44:9-20). This mockery, however, does not mask the serious nature of the accusa-tion against the people. The use of the sexual imagery charges that the root of idolatry lies in the people's infidelity to God: "A spirit of

**"You shall eat and not be satisfied"**

AΩ This phrase and the opposing promise ("You shall eat and be satisfied") play a significant role in a recurring fertility motif. Variations of this phrase appear four times in the Book of the Twelve (Hos 4:10; Joel 2:26; Mic 6:14; Hag 1:6). No other prophetic corpus exhibits this phrase in a form so closely tied to the Deuteronomic language. Hos 4:6 uses the negative form to predict judgment on Israel. Joel 2:26 uses the promise form to anticipate restoration of the land *if* the people repent. Mic 6:14 returns to the negative form as part of a passage that reapplies the message of Amos and Hosea to Jerusalem (cf. the discussion of Mic 6:9-16). Hag 1:6 reads like a fulfillment of the prediction of judgment, since the postexilic community lives in a time described with the negative form of the phrase. This latter description of the land leads to a call for the people to rebuild the temple in order to restore the land's fertility (Hag 1:9-11; cf. Hag 2:19; Zech 8:12).

**Canaanite Goddesses**
Molded figurines of Canaanite goddesses like this one appear in Israel from well before the time of Israel's prophets.

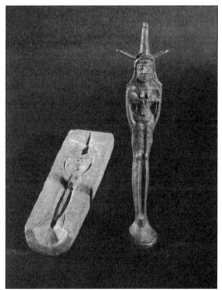

Ancient mould and modern cast of a Canaanite goddess from the "High Place" in Nahariyah. Late Bronze Age, Canaanite. Israel Museum (IDAM), Jerusalem, Israel (Credit: Erich Lessing/ Art Resource, NY)

whoredom has led them astray and they have played the whore." Hosea 4:13 condemns syncretistic practices wherein the people sacrifice to other gods. It mockingly develops the image of people offering sacrifice on any elevated area, where shade from the trees offered a pleasant spot for such activity. Behind this accusation lies the belief that genuine sacrifice should only be made at places that YHWH designated as holy (cf. Deut 12:1-14), not someplace that the people deemed convenient.

The denunciation of illegitimate sacrifice in 4:13a relates to the people's infidelity to YHWH in the previous verse, but it also evokes a parenthetical comment in 4:13b-14. This comment does not treat harlotry as a metaphor for breaking faith with YHWH. Rather, it speaks about the problem of prostitution in a literal sense. A transitional marker, "therefore," abruptly signals the shift from metaphorical to literal prostitution. The prostitution in this section likely reflects cultic rituals and/or the use of prostitution to fulfill religious vows.[6] The author of these comments does not merely denounce the women who prostitute themselves. Hosea 4:14 confronts the men as well, since without their participation prostitution would not occur. The prostitute is no more guilty than the person with whom she has sex.

Hosea 4:15-16 turns the reader's attention to the political entities of Judah and Israel, suggesting in the process that the author judges the situation to be far more problematic for Israel than for Judah. Nevertheless, the author implies that Israel's behavior also threatens to engulf Judah. Hosea 4:15 pleads with Israel not to lead Judah down the wrong path of "harlotry" (i.e., infidelity to YHWH). This charge anticipates important dynamics within the collection of Hosea-Amos-Micah-Zephaniah where Judah's plight continues to deteriorate.[7] Reference to the cultic centers of Gilgal and Beth-aven demonstrates the polemic against the northern cult in Hosea and Amos in particular. [Gilgal and Beth-aven] The word used for incurring guilt (*ʾšm*) generally implies cultic wrongdoing as in Leviticus 4:13, 22, 27.[8] The phrase "YHWH lives" appears in the context of oaths (e.g., Num 14:28;

**Gilgal and Beth-aven**

AΩ  Gilgal was the first cult site established by Joshua according to Josh 4:19-20. The NRSV uses Beth-aven as a transliteration of the Hebrew *betʾawen*. Beth-aven is a polemical slam against the town of Bethel. Bethel means "house of God" in Hebrew (*bêtʾel*), while Beth-aven means "house of disaster." The Hebrew word *ʾawen* has a wide range of connotations, all negative. The word can mean disaster, sin, or falsehood (*HAL*). This same polemic against Bethel and Gilgal also appears in Amos 4:4 and 5:5. Its presence in Hosea, however, seems to take up the attack from Amos. Aaron Schart sees this verse as an addition to Hosea that essentially cross-references Amos's critique of the illegitimate cult of the northern kingdom.

Aaron Schart, *Die Entstehung des Zwölfprophetenbuch: Neubearbeitungen von Amos im Rahmen schriftenübergreifender Redaktionsprozesse* (BZAW 260; Berlin: De Gruyter, 1998) 154.

Judg 8:19; 1 Sam 14:39, 45). Its use in 4:15 with the verb "swear" fits this idiom and admonishes the people not to swear on YHWH's existence.

Verse 16 likens Israel to a stubborn heifer, but shifts quickly to a somewhat ambiguous metaphor for sheep. The context implies a negative statement, so the statement that YHWH will feed them like sheep creates a surprising image for those who think of sheep in docile, pastoral terms. Several translations (NRSV, REV) resolve the problem by treating this metaphorical shift as a rhetorical question, implying that YHWH will not give the lamb food. An alternative resolution recognizes that the word "lamb" over-whelmingly appears in contexts of sacrifice. This conceptualization essentially suggests that YHWH will now fatten the lamb for sacrifice.

Hosea 4:17-19 continues the pronouncements against the cultic abuses in the Ephraimite region. Ephraim is first mentioned in Hosea in 4:17, but it appears in every subsequent chapter.[9] As well, Ephraim is both the name of the major clan of the northern kingdom that comes to signify the entire kingdom and a name for the geographical region of this clan, which includes Bethel and the central hill country.

Hosea 4:17 accuses Ephraim, the heart of the northern kingdom, of idol worship. [Idols and Idolatry] Undoubtedly, religious practi-tioners of the time believed that since their acts of devotion were supported by the priests, then God must be pleased with their behavior. Hosea 4:17, however, confronts that idea with the charge that Ephraim is so irreconcilably involved with idol worship that God has decided to abandon it to its own devices.

Hosea 4:18-19 deals with sex and religion. While 4:18 condemns

**Regions of Ephraim and Judah**

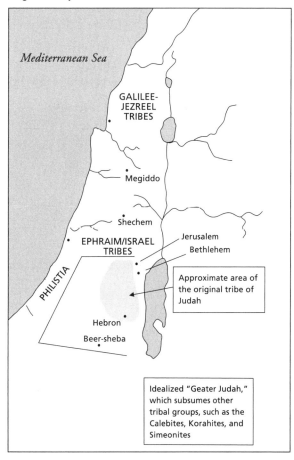

Mediterranean Sea

GALILEE-JEZREEL TRIBES

• Megiddo

• Shechem

EPHRAIM/ISRAEL TRIBES

PHILISTIA

Jerusalem
Bethlehem

Approximate area of the original tribe of Judah

Hebron
•
Beer-sheba
•

Idealized "Geater Judah," which subsumes other tribal groups, such as the Calebites, Korahites, and Simeonites

---

**Idols and Idolatry**

Idols in the ancient Near East have a long history of use in both cultic and private settings. Statues of gods were used in cultic settings from Mesopotamia to Egypt, with the ceremonial feeding of the image playing a significant role. Undoubtedly, these ceremonies helped support cultic personnel by providing food for the deity that was also used for priests. In addition to statues, smaller images are found in abundance. These smaller icons are more prevalent in Syria-Palestine than are the cultic statues. The Hebrew Bible produces a complex picture on the role of idols. On the one hand, the texts of the Old Testament uniformly denounce the worship of any idol. These condemnations appear in texts from the Pentateuch (Exod 20:23; 34:17; Lev 19:4; 26:1; Deut 4:15-19) to the former and Latter Prophets (Josh 24:18-23; Isa 44:12-17; Jer 10:3-5; 11:10-13; Ezek 22:3-4; Hab 2:18-20). Officially, then, worship of idols had no place in Israel, but other texts and archaeological finds suggest that obeying these prohibitions remained a struggle throughout its history.

Stories in Genesis suggest Rebekah carried idols with her from Mesopotamia back to Israel when she returned with Jacob (Gen 31:25-35), and the worship of the calf statue in Exod 32 nearly dooms Israel in the wilderness story. Once in the land, the worship of idols did not disappear as evidenced by texts like Jdg 18:14-26 and 1 Sam 19:11-17. In addition, several texts in Kings refer to reforms whereby idols were removed from the land (1 Kgs 15:12; 16:13) or where kings (1 Kgs 21:6; 2 Kgs 21:11, 21) or the people (2 Kgs 17:12, 15) are accused of worshiping idols. The wide array of figurines that have been found in Israel demonstrate that the use of idols was widespread throughout most of the history of Judah and Israel up to the point of Jerusalem's destruction.

For further reading, see Edward M. Curtis, "Idol, Idolatry," in *ABD*, ed. David Noel Freedman et al. (New York: Doubleday, 1992) 3:376–81 (especially the bibliography at the end). For a survey of the artifacts, see also Othmar Keel and Christoph Uehlinger, *Gods, Goddesses, and Images of God in Ancient Israel* (trans. Thomas H. Trapp; Minneapolis: Fortress, 1998).

---

religious practices that involve the abuse of alcohol and sexual relations with cult prostitutes, 4:19 describes the situation as one in which "a wind has constrained her in her skirts." This phrase can be translated in various ways. The word for "wind" is also the word for "spirit" (cf. Vulgate). The word for "skirts" is frequently translated as "wings," but the sexual innuendo of the previous verse likely draws upon an idiom whose meaning is difficult to reconstruct precisely. At any rate, the point of the verse is not difficult since the association with "altars" at the end of 4:19 also condemns the abhorrent mixture of sexual misconduct and religious rituals. All of 4:17-19 condemns sexual misconduct and drunkenness in religious rituals, not merely illicit deeds performed in private. The accusatory language against the priests earlier in Hosea 4 adds to the impression that the religious establishment of Israel had abandoned the worship of YHWH alone in order to blend the worship of YHWH with the practices of fertility religions. [Fertility Religions]

# CONNECTIONS

This passage lays out the evidence from God's perspective that Israel lacks religious fidelity, kindness, and the knowledge of

YHWH. Its people disavow their long-standing promise to worship YHWH. They commit atrocities against one another, and no one teaches them better because their own leaders have become a major part of the problem. The priests and the prophets are portrayed as having more interest in feeding themselves than in teaching others about YHWH's demands. They accommodate the worship of YHWH to include the worship of other gods. Such accommodation proved popular among the people as the priests participated in worship practices that incorporated fertility rites, wine rituals, and the consultation of idols. In this passage, only a prophet questions these practices or asks what they have to do with the worship of God. Religious expression succumbs to cultural conformity. It becomes impossible to distinguish the worship practices of the northern kingdom from those of its neighbors.

**Fertility Religions**

Largely due to the difficulty of agricultural conditions in the ancient Near East, the fertility of the land represented a continual concern, one that involved life and death. As a result, the concern became a central part of indigenous religious expression. This concern is expressed from the earliest stories of Inanna and Dumuzi whose death and rebirth symbolized the fertility of the land tied to the agricultural cycle. Similar stories circulated later among the Canaanites (with Baal and Anat) and among the Egyptians (with Osiris and Isis). The Canaanite traditions are generally treated polemically in the Hebrew Bible, as Israel gradually replaced the indigenous religion with the worship of YHWH. Recent scholarship focuses upon the polemical nature of the biblical and postbiblical texts that cite these traditions.

See Robert A. Oden, *The Bible without Theology: The Theological Tradition and Alternatives to It* (Cambridge: Harper & Row, 1987).

The issues raised by this passage concerning worship and leadership remain relevant for the church, even though the details have changed. Although modern Christians do not worship wooden idols or engage in fertility rites, ministers and church leaders still face these questions: How far one should go to accommodate worship to the cultural context? How do ministers make worship of God meaningful in a culture that expects to be entertained? Where is the line between real worship that enhances the knowledge of God, and feel-good activities whose main purpose is to put warm bodies in the pew? The words of Hosea 4 challenge today's religious leaders with a record of what can happen when the line is crossed.

Though it takes up far less space in Hosea 4, this passage also challenges the reader to evaluate how one's actions toward others affect all creation. Recent theological treatments of ecology have extrapolated the implications of passages like Hosea 4:2-3 to show how biblical texts often presume interdependence between human action and the divinely created order.[10] This interdependence creates an imperative for humanity to take stock of its role as protector of God's creation. As populations increase and industrialized societies continue polluting the environment, the voice of biblical texts like 4:1-3 needs to be heard. God expects humanity to care about the rest of creation the way that God shows compassion on humanity. [Prophets and the Land]

Finally, how does our own community fare against the three charges God brings against Israel? To be sure, our society as a whole lacks faithfulness to God because it does not claim a covenant relationship to the biblical God. Similarly, one look in the newspaper quickly reveals how easy it is to find reports of horrendous attacks on others. The larger society shows little interest in obtaining knowledge about God. One could make the case that our society is no more compassionate as a whole than was Israel. American society would fare no better than the northern kingdom if we had to defend ourselves against these charges. But what of the church? If we claim to be God's witness in the world, how would we answer the charges as individuals, as congregations, or as denominations? Sadly, in too many instances, we still fail to meet God's expectations of religious devotion, human compassion, and knowledge of

---

### Prophets and the Land

Ellen F. Davis argues that the eighth-century prophets wrote in such a way as to promote a threefold understanding of arable land: (1) it is a gift from God; (2) it is a foundational part of life; and (3) misuse of the land and its workers will lead to destruction of the political system. Davis's reading of Hosea, Amos, Micah, and Isaiah on this point provides an important emphasis on the land and soil that is easy to overlook. Nevertheless, the readings she offers overstate the political basis of prophetic critiques. Davis explores the third point by portraying the prophets as agrarian revolutionaries who anticipate the need to overthrow monarchies because of the change of political structures in eighth-century Judah and Israel. She argues that archaeological discoveries have provided insight into sociological changes where an older economic system (subsistence farming) was replaced by "the development of a centralized system of commodity agriculture controlled by the crown." Further, this change created an economy of "specialized agriculture" whose primary purpose was to feed the administrative structure:

The new system was designed to maximize production of the three most important commodities: grain to feed the cities (the state's administrative and trade centers), and wine and olive oil, the more expensive products, to provide export revenue and to satisfy (directly and indirectly) the taste for luxury now cultivated among the few who were rich.

According to Davis, the prophets direct their poetry toward challenging this system. This reading works with certain passages, but it misses a more foundational element. Specifically, portraying the prophets as primarily driven by political and economic concerns misses the point that the vast majority of the prophetic speeches confronted the people and the religious establishment. These challenges had more to do with creating religious commitment than with economic change. Emphasis upon the grain, wine, and oil become axiomatic expressions of fertility in the Twelve, not merely in the eighth-century prophets, but in much later texts (e.g., Joel 1–2; Hab 3:17; Hag 2:16-19; Zech 8:9-12; Mal 3:11). One could extend the critique of Davis in this sense and suggest that the cult system itself, not the crown, had a vested interest in the economic system, but overemphasizing this economic motive overlooks the complexity of the motivations and does not do justice to the religious motivations and commitments of the prophetic writers.

Ellen Davis, "Running on Poetry: The Agrarian Prophets," in *Scripture, Culture, and Agriculture: An Agrarian Reading of the Bible* (Cambridge: Cambridge University Press, 2008) 121–23.

God. We are too distracted with our own comfort to devote ourselves to God. We remain too concerned about our own welfare to
care deeply about those around us. We yearn for many things, but
knowledge of God typically lies well down the list. This text challenges us to look within and to ask ourselves what we can do to
make a difference.

# NOTES

1. In all, 62 percent (66/107) of the occurrences of this verb form occur in the Latter
Prophets. The command "hear" followed by "word" as the direct object appears 34
times, always in a prophetic writing or in the mouth of a prophet.

2. Note especially Hos 2:19-20 (MT 2:21-22), where YHWH promises to betroth the
personified land in loyalty (*ḥesed*), making her faithful so that she knows YHWH. Hos
4:1 depicts exactly the opposite situation.

3. The use of creation language to display the severity of the threat appears again in
the Book of the Twelve in the anticipation of Jerusalem's destruction in Zeph 1:2-3.

4. See the Connections discussion in Hos 2 concerning the difficulties of this
imagery.

5. See also Jörg Jeremias, "Der Begriff 'Baal' im Hoseabuch und sein
Wirkungsgeschichte," in *Hosea und Amos* (FAT 13; Tübingen: Mohr, 1996) 86–103.

6. For discussion on the ancient practice of women using prostitution for paying
vows to the deity, see Karel van der Toorn, "Female Prostitution in Payment of Vows in
Ancient Israel," *JBL* 108 (1989): 193–205. Van der Toorn makes the case that while
intense religious experience may have inspired women to make vows to pay money,
the fact was that women were economically dependent upon their husbands and often
did not have the means to pay these vows. Consequently, according to van der Toorn,
the desire to pay these vows created socially disruptive situations because it either
meant that husbands had to pay the vows, or if they refused, women were—at least in
some sites—encouraged to have sex for money and use that money to pay their vows.
While this scenario is debatable, there is little doubt that the issue of prostitution as a
means of paying vows was practiced from time to time. Van der Toorn notes that the
condemnation of the practice in texts like Gen 38 and Deut 23:18-19 implies some connection between the *qĕdēšâ* and the *zônâ*. Nevertheless, increasingly, scholars have
noted that claims of cult-prostitution appear overwhelmingly in texts of condemnation,
and scholars now raise questions of how widespread the practice may have been. See
especially Robert A. Oden, "Religious Identity and the Sacred Prostitution Accusation,"
in *The Bible without Theology: The Theological Tradition and Alternatives to It* (San
Francisco: Harper & Row, 1987) 131–53.

7. Note especially Mic 1:5-7, which reflects these same interests but whose contexts become far more critical of Judah and Jerusalem (note especially the
commentary to Mic 3:12).

8. See Marvin A. Sweeney, *The Twelve Prophets* (Berit Olam, vol. 1; Collegeville:
Liturgical Press, 2000) 50.

9. Ephraim appears 37 times in Hosea from this point forward. Outside Hosea, the term appears only four times in the Book of the Twelve, with all of these texts being relatively late (Obad 19; and Zech 9:10, 13; 10:7). The Obadiah text is frequently assumed to be a late addition to the exilic book of Obadiah and the three Zechariah texts come from Deutero-Zechariah, the late Persian period addition to Zechariah.

10. See Terence E. Fretheim, *God and the World in the Old Testament: A Relational Theology of Creation* (Nashville: Abingdon, 2005). See also the discussion in the "Connections" section of Amos 4.

# A GUILTY VERDICT AND COMING DISASTER

## Hosea 5:1-15

## COMMENTARY

Hosea 5:1-15 revolves around two commands (5:1; 5:8) given by YHWH to a group. In Hosea 5:1, YHWH commands the attention of the priests, people, and royal household in order to deliver accusations against the entire people. Hosea 5:1-7 transitions from an emphasis on unfaithful worship in Hosea 4 to announcements of imminent political disasters awaiting Ephraim and Judah in 5:8-15. In so doing, 5:1-7 assumes a trial scene with accusations (5:1-4) and a judge's verdict of judgment (5:5-7). Place names and commentary on eighth-century political events provide 5:1-15 with more specificity than the largely metaphorical thought-world that dominates the images of chapters 1–4.

### YHWH's Accusations and Verdict, 5:1-7

The call to attention in 5:1 signals a trial scene that extends through 5:7, after which 5:8 begins a new series of commands. In Hosea 5:1-3 YHWH speaks in first person, while Hosea 5:4-7 mentions "God" and "YHWH" in third person. Nevertheless, a formal cohesion ties 5:4-7 with 5:1-3. The two sections, linked inextricably by the trial images, present accusations and verdicts against Ephraim (and Judah to a lesser extent).

The subunits of 5:1-7 move from a summons to a verdict that is a type of courtroom drama. [The Lawsuit (*rîb*) in Hosea 5:1-7]

**The Lawsuit (*rîb*) in Hosea 5:1-7**

The elements of the *rîb* in Hos 5:1-7 present themselves somewhat differently than the *rîb* in 4:1-6.

5:1a: Call to attention for judgment
5:1b-3: Recitation of the charges
5:4-7a: Prophetic commentary on the charges
5:7b: The verdict restated

In comparison to the *rîb* of 4:1-6, where YHWH consistently speaks after the opening call, the lawsuit in 5:1-7 changes speakers at a critical juncture. In other words, 5:4-7 speaks about God and YHWH while YHWH speaks about himself in 5:1-3. This change corresponds with the evocation of the language of fornication that appears prominently in Hos 1–3. In this respect, the central section (5:4-7a) functions as prophetic commentary on the charges in light of the opening chapters of the book.

## Places in Hosea 5

Hos 5 mentions several places whose relative positions help one to understand these verses.

YHWH addresses the entire people, as indicated by the three specific groups mentioned in the call to attention in 5:1a: the priests, the house of Israel, and the house of the king. These groups represent the religious leadership, the populace as a whole, and the political leadership—in short the entire population. The reason for the summons is stated succinctly, immediately following the call to attention: "The judgment is for you." From the outset, then, it is clear that the people and their leaders will be found guilty.

Recitation of the charges runs from 5:1b to 5:3. The people and the leaders of Israel are accused of spreading their problems beyond Ephraim to the entire region. In 5:1b, images of a snare and a net presuppose knowledge of hunting practices to imply that Israel's actions led others to behave improperly. The text mentions two villages, Mizpah and Tabor, located toward the southern and northern ends of Israel respectively. According to the text, these villages had engaged in idolatrous practices of Israel that then spread throughout the land. Consequently, God announces punishment on this people.

### Translating Hosea 5:2

AΩ The NRSV and other translations rely on emendations in 5:2a that involve changing the vowels and the consonantal text. Other versions, e.g., NAS and NIV, try to make sense of the text as it appears:

5:2a (NAS): And the revolters have gone deep in depravity. (Translators use an abstraction for *slaughter*.)
5:2a (NIV): The rebels are deep in slaughter.
5:2a (NRSV): and a pit (reading *šḥt* instead of *šḥṭ* dug deep (in) Shittim (reading different vowels).

For a more detailed treatment of the problems of this verse, see Yair Mazor, "Hosea 5:1-3: Between Compositional Rhetoric and Rhetorical Composition," *JSOT* 45 (1989): 115–26.

Translating Hosea 5:2 is difficult, but determining its function is not. [Translating Hosea 5:2] It continues the rationale for judgment that begins in 5:1b. Hosea 5:2 changes from second person plural of 5:1 (you) to third person plural (they/them), but it continues to condemn Israel's depravity in God's eyes.

Hosea 5:3 utilizes parallelism and the language of intimacy to explain the judgment. Ephraim twice appears in parallel with the term Israel, who is not an unknown entity to YHWH. The text presumes that a close relationship with Israel has provided YHWH with ample evidence of how Israel behaves. The relationship has thus been broken by Ephraim/Israel's idolatry, portrayed as prostitution (see the discussion of prostitution in the commentary for Hosea 2). YHWH therefore accuses the northern kingdom of defilement that makes Israel an unfit partner. Specifically, Israel has broken the covenant of fidelity by worshiping other gods. Thus, Hosea 5:3 repeats the charge conveyed earlier in Hosea (2:5 [MT 2:7]; 4:10-18). Here, however, the imagery of prostitution is explicitly used against the northern kingdom in a way that sets up a new topic that will dominate much of Hosea 5-6: the fate of Israel and Judah. The concept "unclean," or "defiled," refers to ritual purity before YHWH. Those who are unclean do not meet the requirements for coming before YHWH to offer sacrifice. The word is particularly prominent in Leviticus, where it refers to lepers, those who have touched corpses, those who have been maimed, and animals, persons, or things that priests should label as unfit to come before YHWH. In Hosea, the root appears again in 9:3-4, where it is also paired with a condemnation of Israel's harlotry (9:1).

Hosea 5:4-7 stands out stylistically from most of the chapter. It does not use first person divine speech. Rather, these verses speak of God (Elohim) and YHWH in the third person. Such a shift is fairly common in Hosea, but it affects the character of these verses so that they function as a prophetic comment on the charges against Israel and Judah, as though the prophet joins the prosecution. Hosea 5:4 declares Israel incapable of repentance. The people's misdeeds prohibit them from returning to YHWH, but the prophetic speaker charges that Israel's infidelity has become ingrained in its very fiber ("The spirit of whoredom is within them . . .") so that "they do not know YHWH." The irony drips from 5:4: YHWH knows Israel (5:3), but Israel does not know YHWH (5:4). The northern kingdom has split its allegiance between various gods for so long that they no longer recognize the true God from the false gods whom they have venerated.

Hosea 5:5-7a restates the charges against Israel, but now includes Judah as well, before culminating in a pronouncement of judgment in 5:7b. The prophet, speaking as a prosecutor, tells the jury that Israel's pride testifies against it. The subsequent poetic lines identify Israel as Ephraim *and* Judah, both the northern and southern kingdoms. Judah's actions, we are now told, parallel those of Ephraim: they seek to placate God with sacrifices (5:6) without changing their behavior, they cheated on YHWH, and they "bear illegitimate children." Hosea 5:5-7a continues to draw upon the marital imagery of the previous verses. The reference to illegitimate children (lit., "foreign children") should not be interpreted literally. Rather, it refers to the false worshipers who had abandoned the worship of YHWH.

Hosea 5:7b pronounces the verdict: punishment will be swift. With the new moon, God's people will be destroyed along with land. The term "fields" in the NRSV does not convey the potency of the word. It often refers to an allotted portion of land (cf. Num 18:20; Deut 18:8; Josh 14:4; 15:13; 18:7; 19:9), and thus potentially implies forfeiting the land promised by YHWH.

### A Cry of Alarm, 5:8-15

Hosea 5:8 begins with the ancient equivalent of a civil defense siren. Blowing the horn (*shôfār*) was done for religious or military purposes. In worship settings, the horn convened religious ceremonies. Militarily, someone blew the *shôfār* to warn the population that an enemy was approaching or to signal troops before or during a battle. In the Book of the Twelve, the horn always appears as warning of an attack against YHWH's people (Hos 5:8; 8:1; Joel 2:1; 2:15; Amos 2:2; 3:6; Zeph 1:16; Zech 9:14). In Hosea 5:8, the warning is repeated by YHWH for two Benjaminite towns (Gibeah, Ramah; see illustration "Places in Hosea 5") and one Ephraimite town (Beth-aven, a derisive term for Bethel; see [Gilgal and Beth-aven]). The region of Benjamin is warned to watch its back. Benjamin was the only tribe other than Judah that remained loyal to the Davidic king when the kingdom split following Solomon's death.

Hosea 5:9 focuses upon the fate of Ephraim as YHWH announces it will become a desolation. In so doing, the fate of Ephraim appears certain while the Benjaminite towns are essentially warned that they are next. Hosea 5:9 refers to a "day of punishment," by which is meant a point of divine intervention, a term that draws on the day of YHWH tradition. [Day of YHWH in Hosea 5] Hosea 5:9 does not detail how the judgment will occur, yet the object of YHWH's wrath is clear: Ephraim. YHWH announces Ephraim's destruction as a warning to all the tribes of Israel. Benjamin and Judah will also be judged (cf. 5:8 and 5:10-15 respectively), but Ephraim is singled out for more severe retribution.

Hosea 5:10 cites the princes of Judah as the source of YHWH's displeasure. Specifically, YHWH compares them to dishonest neighbors who change the boundary markers, a practice condemned in ancient legal codes and the Hebrew Bible (Deut 19:14; 27:17; Prov 22:28; 23:10; Job 24:2). In 5:10, one detects a political situation in which leaders of the southern kingdom are condemned for annexing territory that did not belong to them. For those living in the northern kingdom, this situation corresponds well with the aftermath of the Syro-Ephraimite War. [Syro-Ephramite War] Judah likely took advantage of the situation to expand its territory at Israel's expense. Thus, the charge against Judah in 5:10 is not an afterthought. It reflects YHWH's expectations that nations follow the same rules as individuals. This entire unit vacillates between YHWH's judgments upon the northern and the southern kingdom.

YHWH speaks explicitly of "my wrath" elsewhere only in prophetic texts that refer to severe threats against YHWH's own people (Isa 10:6; Ezek 21:36; 22:21, 31; 38:19; Hos 5:10; 13:11). The wrath of YHWH is known to the psalmists as something terrible that has happened in the past (Pss 78:49; 85:3; 90:9, 11) or something that they hope YHWH will show to their enemies (7:6). It is a powerful concept reserved for times of God's utmost indignation.

## Day of YHWH in Hosea 5

The day of YHWH (or day of the LORD) concept probably derives from the Israelite variation of holy war (*herem*). However, over time this concept also found its way into religious rituals. In Old Testament texts, the concept should not be confused with a final apocalyptic judgment, a view that develops later. At its core, the day of YHWH in the Old Testament refers to a point in the past or the future (imminent or distant) when YHWH will intervene for judgment. This intervention is portrayed differently in various texts: YHWH may act directly; YHWH may use the power of nature; or YHWH may intervene through agents (such as using the army of a nation). The day of YHWH involves judgment for some group perceived as YHWH's enemy. The concept appears most prominently in prophetic texts, especially in Isaiah and the Book of the Twelve. Most of the explicit references using the phrase "day of YHWH" appear in the Book of the Twelve and play a role in shaping the message of this corpus. Other terms may also draw upon this concept, such as the formula "on that day," idiomatic expressions such as "the day of punishment" (Hos 5:9), or even "the day" (Ezek 7:7).

For further reading, see Frank Moore Cross, "The Divine Warrior in Israel's Early Cult," in *Biblical Motifs: Origins and Transformations* (ed. Alexander Altmann; Cambridge: Harvard University Press, 1966) 11–30; A. Joseph Everson, "The Days of Yahweh," *Journal of Biblical Literature* 93 (1974): 329–37; Sigmund Mowinckel, *He that Cometh* (Oxford: B. Blackwell, 1959); James D. Nogalski, "The Day(s) of YHWH in the Book of the Twelve," in *Thematic Threads in the Book of the Twelve* (ed. Paul L. Redditt and Aaron Schart; BZAW 325; Berlin: De Gruyter, 2003) 192–213; Gerhard von Rad, "The Origin of the Concept of the Day of Yahweh," *Journal of Semitic Studies* 4 (1959): 97–108; Rolf Rendtorff, "How to Read the Book of the Twelve as a Theological Unity," in *Reading and Hearing the Book of the Twelve* (ed. James D. Nogalski and Marvin A. Sweeney; Symposium 15; Atlanta: Society of Biblical Literature, 2000) 75–87; and M. Weiss, "The Origin of the 'Day of the Lord'—Reconsidered," *HUCA* 37 (1966): 29–60.

**Syro-Ephramite War**

This war took place between 734 and 732 BCE. As a result of Judah's refusal to join an anti-Assyrian coalition headed by Rezin of Syria and Pekah of Ephraim, these kings attacked Judah. Their goal was to replace Judah's king, Jotham, with a king who would join them in overthrowing Assyria's occupation of the region. Jotham died, and when his young son Ahaz succeeded him, Ahaz contacted Tiglath-Pileser III of Assyria for help. Assyria attacked Syria, causing it to pull its troops out of Judah. Assyria toppled the Syrian king, Rezin, in 732. Pekah of Israel was assassinated around this time and was replaced by Hoshea, whose first act was to pay tribute to Assyria in order to show his loyalty. The royal inscriptions of the Assyrian king imply he conferred his approval on Hoshea as king: "They (Israel) overthrew their king Pekah, and I placed Hoshea as king over them. I received from them 10 talents of gold, 1,000 (?) talents of silver as their [tri]bute and brought them to Assyria" (*ANET*, 284). The exact order of events is disputed, but it is clear that Hoshea received the blessing of the Assyrian king by paying tribute. See also 2 Kgs 15–16.

Hosea 5:11 continues to reflect the situation following the Syro-Ephraimite war, but it changes the focus from Judah to Ephraim. The verse presumes a situation in which Ephraim has been defeated, yet it does not call for pity for Ephraim. Rather, it explains Ephraim's current situation. Hosea 5:11 is difficult to translate, but the sense is clear: Ephraim *willingly* followed its own path rather than YHWH's. In short, Ephraim's rulers did not adequately consider the consequences of their actions in joining Syria to oppose Assyria. In the end, the attempt to stop the Assyrian incursion into the region failed. Syria was destroyed and Ephraim was forced to submit to more stringent economic and political demands from Assyria.

Hosea 5:12-14 offers a series of parallel judgments against Ephraim and Judah. Hosea 5:12 compares YHWH's judgment against these two regions to something that festers and decays. The parallel images of deterioration for Ephraim and Judah continue into 5:13, which uses the image of sickness for Ephraim and of a wound for Judah. This verse offers a study in parallelism that shows how the writer's thought extends over several poetic clauses. [Parallelism in Hosea 5:13] Ephraim may have finally recognized that it was in trouble, but putting its fate in the hands of Assyria only made matters worse. By extension Judah is also warned against making a political alliance with Assyria. Both Ephraim and Judah faced dire consequences from their dealings with Assyria in the aftermath of the Syro-Ephraimite war. Judah became a *de facto* vassal of Assyria, and within a decade Ephraim's new king (Hoshea) led the northern kingdom into another failed rebellion against Assyria. This revolt led to Samaria's

**Parallelism in Hosea 5:13**

The parallelism of 5:13 functions on the level of the names, the problems, and the syntax. The beginning and ending lines of the verse offer parallel judgments for Ephraim and Judah, while the middle line conveys Ephraim's futile attempt to stop the judgment:

When Ephraim saw (3ms) his sickness and Judah (saw) his wound
   then Ephraim went (3ms) to Assyria and sent to the great king
but he is not able to cure you (3mp) or heal your (2mp) wound.

The parallel lines emphasize the futility of the political solutions that Ephraim sought (and Judah by extension), creating problems they should have anticipated.

destruction. From the perspective of Hosea, neither Judah nor Ephraim yet understood the issues, for they sought a political solution to a spiritual problem.

Hosea 5:14-15 changes metaphors but continues the judgment against Judah and Ephraim. Hosea 5:14 compares YHWH to a lion/young lion. These metaphors evoke images of a lion that pounces on its prey—in this case Ephraim and the house of Judah. The lion then violently tears the prey apart. YHWH twice states that he will act in judgment, not for deliverance. Hosea 5:15 changes the imagery again but picks up the phrase "I will go" from 5:14. YHWH plans to depart and stay away until the people return in genuine contrition. At the end of 5:15, YHWH confidently asserts that distress will cause the people to look for him. Several translations, modern and ancient, believe this verse introduces the quote of the people in 6:1-3. YHWH knows that the people will come looking, begging to be taken back, but only when the situation is dire enough that they no longer think they can succeed on their own. Hosea 6 will explore YHWH's turmoil about the fate of this people.

---

### YHWH as a Lion

The portrayal of YHWH as a lion to symbolize God's judgment is a recurring motif in the prophets. This metaphor appears in Hosea (5:14; 11:10; 13:7-8), Amos (3:4, 8, 12), Isaiah (5:29; 31:4; 38:13), and Jeremiah (4:7; 25:38). The lion can also symbolize powerful countries to connote a fierce and awesome power (e.g., Jer 50:17; Nah 2:11-13). Lions were used in architecture as symbols of protective power like the two that guarded the Ishtar temple of Ashurbanipal in the ninth century BCE. Building upon metaphor theory, Brent Strawn offers an exhaustive treatment of the ancient Near Eastern (including Israelite) texts and iconography in an attempt to show how the lion image functioned as a metaphor for deities in that cultural context. In the Hebrew Bible, the metaphor of the lion associated with YHWH overwhelmingly (but not exclusively) plays upon the violent, threatening behavior in the form of the lion's hunting prowess (see Hos 13:7-8), or its frightening roar (see Amos 3:8). This imagery can also be used positively, especially when the lion symbolizes protection of its territory (see Joel 4:16; Amos 1:2).

Brent A. Strawn, *What Is Stronger than a Lion? Leonine Image and Metaphor in the Hebrew Bible and the Ancient Near East* (Orbis Biblicus et Orientalis 212; Fribourg: Academic Press, 2005). See especially his discussion of metaphor theory and theology (pp. 1–16; 58–65).

Walking Lion. From the procession road at Babylon, built under Nebuchadnezzar II (604–562 BCE). Glazed terracotta tiles. Louvre, Paris, France. (Credit: Réunion des Musées Nationaux/Art Resource, NY)

# CONNECTIONS

Hosea 5 reverberates with a message of judgment against the priests, the people, and the politicians. It echoes with the forms of a trial (5:1-7) and a cry of alarm (5:8) as it moves from one warning to another. Judgment is announced for both northern and southern kingdoms.

It is never a good thing to face a trial where the prosecuting attorney and the judge are one and the same. There is little doubt of the verdict. Yet, these verses do not portray a kangaroo court, where the defendant is railroaded for some unproven crime. There is no "reasonable doubt" in these verses. God knows the defendant intimately (5:3), and the people have not only continued in their guilty ways but have also recruited others to join them in their folly (5:1b). In their present state, they are incapable of returning to God, for they are consumed with their own misguided actions of infidelity to God (5:4). They think they will be able to appease God by sacrificing their sheep and cattle (5:6), but God will not be bought or bribed. The biblical God is not one god among competing deities who can be called upon when the worship of other gods fails to bring satisfaction. God expects obedience and commitment.

It is important in this passage to note how God intends to punish the guilty. In their infidelity, they act as if God does not exist, a charge that breaks the first commandment (Exod 20:3; Deut 5:7). Yet, God does not promise to rain down fire and brimstone in retaliation. Rather, God simply withdraws (5:6), leaving these people to their own devices, knowing full well that they are incapable of withstanding the threats they will soon face. [*Deus Absconditus*—The Hidden God]

It is no accident that warning of an impending attack (5:8) follows immediately upon the trial's verdict (5:7).

---

### Deus Absconditus—The Hidden God

Protestant Reformer Martin Luther—among others—emphasized the concept God Hidden (*deus absconditus*) as opposed to God Revealed (*deus revelatus*) as the starting point for discussions of God's justice. Essentially, Luther asserts that without the eyes of faith, God remains hidden.

Temptation and tribulation are part of faith and . . . behind all suffering to which we, our fate, and our world are subject we must recognize the God who through this very suffering is instructing us in steadfastness and calling us to surrender ourselves in prayer to him as our God. In these tribulations, however, God accompanies the Christian along the painful path of disfranchising the "self." It is precisely in this weakness that his strength acquires genuine power, and all attempts at theodicy represent final bastions of human and theological self-assertion along this path. With the parameters of our basic question this means that, just as every theodicy must fail, so also must every attempt at reconciling the *deus absconditus* with the *deus revelatus*. Mediation between the two leaves room for the kind of trust from which faith itself lives. It points to God's promise, in which faith can find its moorings; to prayer, in which he reveals himself as our God; and to the sacrament, as the sign that communion with him is reconciliation and that what we now hope will someday become full reality.

Otto Kaiser, "Deus absconditus and Deus revelatus. Three Difficult Narratives in the Pentateuch," in *"Shall Not the Judge of All the Earth Do What Is Right?" Studies on the Nature of God in Tribute to James L. Crenshaw* (ed. David Penchansky and Paul L. Redditt; Winona Lake: Eisenbrauns, 2000) 77–78.

God's pronouncement of impending devastation is immediately followed by the cry of alarm, which underscores the impression of swift justice facing the people. However, that retribution does not portray YHWH directly attacking the people. The verses speak of YHWH pouring out wrath (5:10b), but the consequences flow from the actions of the leaders of Israel and Judah. Human armies represent the enemies who threaten the people. God's judgment comes when God leaves the people to their own devices, as seen in the final verse of this chapter: "I will return again to my place until they acknowledge their guilt and seek my face."

Two points stand out theologically from Hosea 5. First, actions have consequences. God allows human beings the freedom to make decisions, but humans do not always make them well. Individuals, including religious and political leaders, are capable of doing things that are self-serving, short sighted, and ill conceived rather than making decisions that better the lives of others. Words of confrontation in Hosea 5 remain just as poignant today. Actions set other actions in motion. When we turn our backs on God, or when self-interest controls our decisions, we usually take the low road, the path that requires the least from us. God expects us to serve others in God's name. Corporately, many churches in suburban settings have seen a rise in volunteerism in the last several years, especially among younger members who see themselves as privileged in comparison to the broader culture. Younger members of denominations are calling for more active stands on environmental issues, global warming, and initiatives to deal with poverty. They have begun to challenge the complacency of their parents and grandparents and call for changes in behavior and policies that threaten the world's ability to sustain itself.

Second, God expects human beings to use their freedom to turn to God. The biblical God is not portrayed as a tyrant king who manipulates human beings for his own amusement. God waits for human beings to choose to seek God. God expects righteousness; God expects disciples to work for justice. God does not compromise on these expectations; God waits for us to choose to follow these paths. Too often, the church has been content to reflect its political culture rather than to model a different kind of engagement. In recent years, political engagement in the church has become increasingly pronounced. Battle lines on social issues have been drawn around candidates who espouse the "proper" ideology.

At times, the church has forgotten what belongs to Caesar and what belongs to God. When the church becomes identified with one political party, then it has lost sight of its spiritual mission and substituted a political goal. Often, this has meant adopting political tactics where the end justifies the means. The church should embody love, righteousness, and justice. When church meetings become political gatherings, Hosea 5 reminds us what happens when the people of God confuse political causes with spiritual needs.

# THE WAY TO REPENTANCE AND THE CONSEQUENCES OF FAILURE

## Hosea 6:1-11a

## COMMENTARY

Hosea 6:1-11a relates closely to Hosea 5 by continuing YHWH's message of a coming judgment. It contains three subsections: an invitation to repent (6:1-3), YHWH's struggle over the people's fate (6:4-6), and a description of the violent situation in the land (6:7-11a).

### YHWH's Implicit Call to Repentance, 6:1-3

An invitation to repent (6:1-3) continues YHWH's speech from chapter 5. [Invitation to Repent] Formally, even though the voice of the "speaker" in 6:1-3 changes to the people, it should be interpreted as a continuation of YHWH's speech, as an implicit invitation to the people by telling them what they should say. These verses do not introduce the people as speaker, and nothing has changed regarding Israel's situation once the first person speech of YHWH resumes in 6:4. This lack of change requires one to presume that either YHWH has rejected the repentance of the people as insincere, or that the people have not (yet) spoken these words. (A similar situation exists in Hosea 14:1-9 [MT 14:2-10]). In short, Hosea 6:1-3 shows how the people should return to YHWH, in humility and longing.

**Invitation to Repent**

Hos 6:1-3 presents the first of five calls to repentance in the Book of the Twelve. Hosea ends with an open-ended call for Ephraim to repent that includes a promise (14:1-8 [MT 14:2-9]). Another open-ended call to repentance and promise follows immediately in Joel 1–2, but Joel's call addresses Judah rather than Ephraim. The call to repentance in Zech 1:2-6 plays an important role in the promises of Haggai and Zech 1–8, for it represents the only instance in the Book of the Twelve where a positive outcome is recorded explicitly. The last disputation of Malachi (3:7-12) embeds a call to repentance therein and offers hope that a small group will respond positively (3:16-18).

Hosea 6:1 begins a three-verse speech ostensibly placed in the mouth of the people, but best understood as YHWH quoting what the people *should* say. In this sense, YHWH's speech continues the previous unit. The people acknowledge YHWH's punishment and see it as correction. Thus, YHWH's punishment contrasts with YHWH's salvific intentions: though YHWH has "torn" them like a beast tears its prey (cf. 5:14), YHWH will also heal them if sought by them. In short, though YHWH has punished them, YHWH will also bind up their wounds. These verses speak of genuine contrition and repentance from the people. God wants the people to recognize the true source of the judgment in order that the people will return to God.

### Hosea 6:2 Not a Proof Text for Jesus' Resurrection

Hos 6:2 is often used as a proof text to support the NT fulfillment of Scripture for Jesus' resurrection on the third day. A string of NT texts (e.g., Matt 16:21; Luke 9:22; 24:46; John 5:21; Acts 10:40; 1 Cor 15:4) draw upon the formula of Jesus' being raised "on the third day," but none of these can be clearly tied to the language or context of Hos 6:2. Of this group of texts, only two (Luke 24:45-46; 1 Cor 15:4) explicitly tie the three-day tradition to the fulfillment of Scripture. The words of no less a scholar than C. K. Barrett show the difficulty:

> It is not easy to produce Old Testament documentation for *the third day*. Hosea 6:2 is not very convincing; Jonah 2:1f is used in Matt 12:40, but no other New Testament writer shows a similar interest in Jonah and the whale; 2 Kings 20:5; Lev 23:11 are not more helpful [. . . .] The story of the resurrection of Jesus has no exact parallel or explicit forecast in the Old Testament, but early Christian writers found some passages (e.g. Ps 16:10; Isa 5:7) relevant. It is probably best here too to suppose that the resurrection experience and faith came first; then the conviction that the resurrection must have been foretold; then the documentation.

The difficulties of seeing Hos 6:2 as a foretelling of Jesus' death and resurrection are manifold. First, the Hosea context refers to the revitalization of the people ("He will revive *us*"; "He will raise *us* up."). Thus, it is not a messianic text. Second, the death implicit in these verses is the punishment for the sin of the people, which hardly fits as a parallel to Jesus' death. Third, the revival on the second day in Hos 6:2 has no parallel in any of the NT texts cited. Finally, the purpose of the revival on the third day in Hos 6:2 is so that the people may live before YHWH, which does not easily correspond to the New Testament formulas for Jesus' resurrection.

C. K. Barrett, *The First Epistle to the Corinthians* (HNTC; New York: Harper and Row, 1968) 340.

Hosea 6:2 illustrates that the goal of the people's repentance speech is restoration. They hope that YHWH will revive them after an appropriate time of punishment. This verse calls for YHWH's restoration of the relationship between the people and their God. It has often been misinterpreted by Christians as a proof text for Jesus' resurrection, but such a reading rests on shaky ground because it ignores the context of Hosea entirely. [Hosea 6:2 Not a Proof Text for Jesus' Resurrection] The people speak 6:2 (formally), and it presumes the repentance from 6:1 ("let us return to the Lord," a prayer of repentance), spoken by a guilty people. The speech also presumes their promise that YHWH's restoration will result in their faithful living (". . . so that we might live before him").

The repentance speech concludes in Hosea 6:3 by explaining what it means to live for YHWH, using language that implies a desire to fix what is broken. In Hosea 4, one of the charges levied against the people is that they lack knowledge of God (cf. 4:1, 6). In 6:3a, they should rectify this deficiency. They should pursue the knowledge of YHWH. The latter half of 6:3 affirms YHWH's faithful activity. YHWH's going forth is as certain as the dawn and as gentle as the rain. Hosea 6:3 mentions two types of rain: a general word for rain and latter rain. The latter rains are the rains in the late spring that help the grain mature so it can withstand the summer heat. These rain metaphors presume YHWH's good intentions and YHWH's desire to see the people thrive.

**Gezer Calendar**

(Credit: HolyLandPhotos.org)

The Gezer calendar, pictured here, was found about 18 miles northwest of Jerusalem. This tenth-century BCE calendar lays out the agricultural year as follows, beginning in August: (1) two months of harvest, two months of planting, (2) two months of late planting, (3) a month of hoeing flax, (4) a month of barley harvest, (5) a month of harvest and feasting, (6) two months of (vine) pruning, and (7) a month of summer fruit.

## YHWH Struggles with Judgment, 6:4-6

The second section of Hosea 6 opens with a soliloquy that chronicles a dilemma: YHWH's expectations of loyalty receive trivialities in return; and warnings through the prophets are consistently ignored. The behavior of Ephraim and Judah leaves YHWH little choice but to execute the threats of judgment, creating consternation for a God interested in loving-kindness and fidelity. These verses portray a God who does not rush to act in anger.

Hosea 6:4-6 illustrates that the previous speech by the people should not be understood as a speech actually spoken. Rather, 6:1-3 is a speech that the people should speak, though they show no inclination to turn toward YHWH. Realizing that nothing has changed only heightens the dilemma. YHWH does not wish to punish, but Judah and Ephraim leave YHWH little choice.

Hosea 6:4 portrays the anguished cry of the parent of a wayward child. It poses a rhetorical question to both Ephraim and Judah: "What should I do to you?" God does not really expect a response.

Rather, the question demonstrates YHWH's dilemma in dealing with a recalcitrant child. The latter half of 6:4, however, describes Israel's problem. Israel's loyalty evaporates like the fog and the dew when the sun rises and warms the air. God evaluates Ephraim and Judah as people who are incapable of sustaining love or loyalty.

Hosea 6:5 continues the line of reasoning from 6:4 via the adverb "therefore." Moreover, 6:5a does not express what God will do in the future, but what God has done in the past in an effort to warn them ("hewn them by the prophets" and "slain them with words"). Since they have ignored the warnings, judgment will proceed against the people. [Against the People]

**Against the People**

AΩ The LXX (or the Hebrew source text by the translator) rephrases this verse: "Because of this I have cut down your prophets. I have slain them with the words of my mouth. And my judgment shall go forth like light." Thus, for this reading, false prophets are the object of God's punishment. However, this interpretation fails to see that the judgments of the prophets were intended as warnings to the people in Hos 6:5.

**Prophet vs. Priest**

This and other instances of prophetic confrontations of priests require a context. Generally, these confrontations do not condemn the legitimacy of ritual or the sacrificial system of the cult in its entirety. Rather, the reasons are complex and polyphonic. There is little doubt that prophets and prophecy functioned as part of the Jerusalem cult in both the first and second temple, and in such circumstances prophets are generally calling for a purification and proper performance of sacrifice by both the one bringing the sacrifice and the priest who accepts it (see Mal 1:6-10). At other times, admonitions about sacrifice implicitly challenge priests since they are the ones offering the sacrifice, but the content of the message is more about warning people about assuming one can manipulate God than about condemning sacrifice as such (see Mic 6:6-8). Confrontations of priests in Hosea are more complex than most because some of the sayings may reflect debates from sociological and political settings. Most scholars understand Hosea to have been a prophet from the northern kingdom, where the worship of YHWH took on a different form. The speeches in Hosea often challenge the blending of the worship of YHWH with the inclusion of Baal and other deities. This critique of northern practices gets picked up elsewhere (2 Kgs 17:7-20; cf. Mic 1:5-7). In this respect, these confrontations may well argue for overthrowing the entire cultic system, but in all likelihood, if they had gotten their way, these same prophets would have replaced the sacrificial cults with ones dedicated to YHWH.

For a broader discussion of the social function of prophets, see Thomas W. Overholt, *Channels of Prophecy: The Social Dynamics of Prophetic Activity* (Minneapolis: Fortress Press, 1989).

YHWH's speech culminates in 6:6, a verse that has theological and literary significance. Theologically, Hosea 6:6 presents one of the more explicit statements in the Old Testament regarding the limits of animal sacrifice: "I desire steadfast love and not sacrifice, the knowledge of God rather than burnt offerings" (NRSV). The verse underscores that God is not interested in the externals of religious practices. God looks to the heart of the worshiper. This theological emphasis appears in various forms in prophetic literature, not to condemn the sacrificial cult as such but to remind the people and the leaders that animal sacrifice is not a ritual to appease YHWH's thirst for blood. [Prophet vs. Priest] Sacrifice, when properly given, should be offered out of contrition.

Literarily, the statement that YHWH desires "knowledge of God" alludes back to Hosea 4:1. This phrase is not common, appearing only three times in the Hebrew Bible (Hos 4:1; 6:6; Prov 2:5). Hosea 6:6 recalls 4:1, especially since 4:1 also mentions steadfast love. Although the NRSV translates the two differently, "covenant loyalty" in 4:1 is the same Hebrew word, *hesed*, as steadfast love in 6:6. This concept of *hesed* is a recurring motif in the Book of the Twelve, one that demonstrates a degree of intentionality in places. [*hesed* in the Book of the Twelve] The allusion to 4:1 in 6:6 underscores for the reader the continuity of the situation in Hosea. According to 4:1, *hesed* is one of three elements missing from the land. Hosea 6:6 shows that these elements that God longs to see from the people are still lacking.

## Violence Reigns in the Land, 6:7-11a

The third section of the chapter (6:7-10, 11a) returns the focus to the current situation in which violence rules the land. Hosea 6:7 probably refers to a point at which the city Adam rejected the worship of YHWH. [Adam in Hosea 6:7] Hosea 6:7 does not give specifics about the problems at Adam, but one can assume it has to do with the false worship of YHWH because of the context.

Hosea 6:8 condemns the village of Gilead as a city completely overrun with violence. Normally, Gilead is considered a region. Reference to Gilead as a village may be a poetic device shortening the name of a known village (e.g., Ramoth-gilead or Jabesh-gilead). It is called a village so full of those doing wickedness that it is tracked from the blood of their deeds.

Hosea 6:9, though difficult syntactically, compares priests to a band of raiders waiting to

---

### *hesed* in the Book of the Twelve

AΩ The word *hesed* is translated variously, depending on the context: loving-kindness, covenant loyalty, faithfulness, or goodness. It carries a sense of the willing fulfillment of an obligation. The Book of the Twelve contains nearly one half (13/27) of the prophetic references to this concept (Hos 2:21; 4:1; 6:4, 6; 10:12; 12:7; Joel 2:13; Jonah 2:9; 4:2; Mic 6:8; 7:18, 20; Zech 7:9). These references focus on two different subjects: *hesed* as an attribute of YHWH (Joel 2:13; Jonah 4:2; Mic 7:18, 20) and the people's failure to demonstrate *hesed* as part of their own covenant obligations. Some of these texts, however, appear to depend upon one another. Mic 6:8 shows awareness of Hosea and Amos, and Joel 2:13 and Jonah 4:2 both adapt Exod 34:6-7. See discussion of the word in these various contexts.

### Adam in Hosea 6:7

AΩ Debate exists over whether "Adam" in 6:7 refers to the city, the biblical character, or to humanity as a whole. The city Adam was in the Transjordan, north of the place associated with the Israelite crossing of the Jordan (cf. Josh 3:16). The importance of the city derived from its location near a natural crossing point of the Jabbok river. Those interpreting Adam in Hos 6:7 as the city point out that the mention of Gilead (6:8) and Shechem (6:9) in the immediate context suggest a geographic term is expected here. Conversely, the story of Adam contains no reference to a "covenant," so the allusion of Hos 6:7 is not clear when one attempts to connect it to narrative traditions. Those who believe that Adam refers to the biblical character rely on three arguments. First they argue that the Hebrew preposition "like" (*kě*) affixed to the word "Adam" would need to be "in" (*bě*) if a town were intended (so the editors of *BHS*). They also point out that Hos 12 refers to Jacob, meaning that the Genesis traditions were known to the prophet. Finally, no traditions of the city Adam involve a covenant with YHWH. However, these arguments are weak since numerous places in Isaiah and Jeremiah use the construction "like" (*ke*) + a place name to indicate the people of a town (cf. Isa 1:9; 3:9; 10:9 29:2; Jer 19:12; 23:14; etc.). The LXX reads the term as a reference to humanity (*hōs anthrōpos*), which seems more problematic syntactically than the other two options. Normally, the word "*adam*" takes a singular reference, even when understood collectively, but Hos 6:7 has a plural verb, which makes better sense if "*adam*" were referring to the town's inhabitants.

**Shechem**

Shechem was an Ephraimite town just over 40 miles (65 km) north of Jerusalem. The village plays a major role in the Joshua stories and was probably a significant site in Israel's history prior to the monarchy. Biblical traditions associate Shechem as the place of Joseph's burial and the site of Joshua's covenant renewal (Josh 24). It suffered considerably during the period of the judges at the hands of Gideon's son Abimelech (Judg 9), and despite occasional improvements in its fortunes, it never plays a prominent role again.

ambush unsuspecting travelers. The image of the priests running toward Shechem to plot a crime shows how fully the prophet wished to condemn Israel's priesthood for abandoning their service to YHWH. [Shechem] The activity of the priests in 6:9 involves plotting, an ambush, gang-like activity, and murder of unsuspecting people on the highway. It is difficult to believe that the priests, the religious leaders, could be as wicked as this verse charges. Is this exaggerated rhetoric against the priests of Israel, or does it condemn an actual band of rogue priests? Either way, the description of the priests' actions is intended to shock the reader to the core by describing activity of a criminal gang, not those designated to serve the people for God.

In Hosea 6:10 God continues to speak, condemning Ephraim/Israel for its infidelity. The verse again draws on the metaphor of prostitution to illustrate the offensive nature of Israel's abandoning YHWH (see also 1:2; 2:2-5; 3:3; 4:10-15; 5:3). As well, this verse concludes with a sweeping denunciation of Israel as being "unclean," or defiled. This term is used by priests to designate things or persons who are unfit for cultic rituals. This verse is nearly a refrain of Hosea 5:3; it parallels Ephraim's prostitution and Israel's defilement. [Hosea 5:3 and 6:10] The point is clear from this verse and the entire context: Israel has reached record lows of depravity. The abandonment of YHWH is endemic of the entire region, involving the people and their religious and political leaders. The description of Israel's depravity in Hosea is far from finished; even at this point in the

**Hosea 5:3 and 6:10**

Note the parallels in these verses.

| Hosea 5:3 NRSV | Hosea 6:10 NRSV |
|---|---|
| I know Ephraim, and Israel is not hidden from me; for now, O Ephraim, you have played the whore; Israel is defiled. | In the house of Israel I have seen a horrible thing; Ephraim's whoredom is there, Israel is defiled. |

book, there is little doubt that Israel's activity has left it incapable of meeting its covenant obligations to YHWH.

Hosea 6:11a reads like a gloss, an afterthought announcing punishment for Judah.[1] The preceding verses focus on Israel, but 6:11a warns Judah a harvest awaits them. The imagery in this verse is unusual, since the language of a failed harvest—i.e., a harvest that is withheld or prevented—is more typical of pronouncements of judgment (cf. Isa 18:5; Jer 50:16). However, Jeremiah 51:33 also uses "harvest" to refer to judgment upon a country (Babylon).

# CONNECTIONS

Much of Hosea 6 portrays God like the parents of wayward teens, parents at wit's end, not knowing how to get their children to cease their destructive behavior. Here, God tells the people of Ephraim/Israel what they can do to set things right in 6:1-3, but the rhetoric of 6:4-6 shows that God is not optimistic about the ability of Ephraim to change. God also tries reasoning with them, shocking them with the extent that violence has overtaken the land. Yet if God genuinely doubts Ephraim/Israel will change, why does God go to such lengths trying to get them to do so?

Much has been written about human sinfulness, but we often see this as a problem only from our own point of view. This text forces us to confront how human behavior grieves God. The God who set the world in motion (Gen 1) is also the God who desires to commune in intimate ways with creation (Gen 2). Yet, despite these divine overtures, we continually turn our back on God, often by replacing God with "things" or by taking a "win-at-all-costs" attitude toward our fellow creatures. Imagine the grief of God looking upon wayward priests murdering unsuspecting travelers, when priests should represent God on earth!

Imagine the grief of God looking at our society and our world today. [The Grief of God] God could still find religious leaders more interested in making a profit than in leading others to God. God would still see a world of violence—both physical and figurative—and the church is not immune. Just as the words of Hosea 6 take on the political and religious leaders of an earlier time, they also force us to see how easy it is for our own leaders, religious and political, to abandon the service of God for selfish ambition, whether it be denominational leaders willing to climb their way to the top of the ecclesial structure, or individuals willing to use the simple faith of listeners to line their own pockets. In the lust for power, fame, and wealth, religious and political leaders are still able and willing to use God's name to further their cause. In Hosea, a lone prophetic voice says *no!* In our day, we must be just as vigilant.

> **The Grief of God**
> Ellen Ross offers a well-researched take on how the image of Jesus' suffering depicted in the art of England in the 13th–15th centuries fostered a developed sense of God's mercy and compassion. See Ellen M. Ross, *The Grief of God: Images of the Suffering Jesus in Late Medieval England* (New York: Oxford University Press, 1997).

The leaders of Israel led the people astray, giving people what they thought they wanted: easy answers. The demands of allegiance to God were replaced with ritual practices that would make the people feel good. Sacrifice was accepted without any regard for repentance, because the sacrifice was necessary to keep the priests fed. God looked at the situation and tried to convey a message of love and loyalty: "I desire steadfast love and not sacrifice, the knowledge of God rather than burnt offerings." (6:6). God expresses dismay at the facile way in which Israel abandons its *ḥesed,* its love (NRSV, NIV), goodness (KJV), loyalty (NAS), faithfulness (NET, NKJV), mercy (LXX), and kindness. The dismay will be expressed again in Hosea 11 as God's pain becomes more pronounced. In the Book of the Twelve, rejection of *ḥesed* and justice becomes increasingly obvious because the prophets continue to challenge the behavior of God's people (Mic 6:6-8; Hab 1:2-4).

The awareness of our own shortcomings need not be the end of the story, however. God still shows a remarkable love toward the people of this world. God still invites us to abandon ourselves and turn to live for God in love and service. No individual, church, or denomination is immune to the dangers of replacing God in our lives with things that hold no lasting value. What does it mean today to practice *ḥesed* (loving-kindness) or to know God? The biblical message is remarkably consistent on the expectations God has for human beings. Deuteronomy 6:5 states, "You shall love the LORD your God with all your heart, and with all your soul, and with all your might." When asked to state the greatest commandment, Jesus replied, "You shall love the Lord your God with all your heart, and with all your soul, and with all your mind. This is the great and first commandment. And a second is like it, you shall love your neighbor as yourself" (Matt 22:37-39).

It seems so simple: love God and love your neighbor. Yet most of us have difficulty keeping these two commandments. We need to pause periodically and recommit ourselves to live a life dedicated to serving God. We need to pause to ask ourselves, are we doing all we could do to show God's love to a world in desperate need of compassion and healing?

# NOTE

1. The verse is typically treated as an afterthought, added by an exilic Judean editor who was keen to apply this message to the southern kingdom (see Hans Walter Wolff, *Hosea* [Hermeneia; trans. Gary Stansell; Philadelphia: Fortress, 1974] 123; James L. Mays, *Hosea, A Commentary* [OTL; Philadelphia, Westminster, 1969] 102).

# THE DANGERS OF MIXING FAITH AND POLITICS

## Hosea 6:11b–7:16

## COMMENTARY

This section contains a series of four interconnected units (6:11b–7:4, 5-7, 8-10, 11-16) that explore the religious and political problems facing the northern kingdom. These units are linked by a loose progressive thematic development and catchword connections between the constituent elements. Unlike the previous chapter, which adapted several of the prophetic sayings to Judah, these verses focus exclusively on the fate of the northern kingdom. Thematically, these units move from Ephraim's failure to please the real king (6:11b–7:4) to a picture of political intrigue that threatens Israel's king from within his own household (7:5-7) to a castigation of Ephraim's unwitting contribution to its own destruction by mixing with foreigners (7:8-10). Finally, 7:11-16 culminates with a twofold pronouncement showing how Israel's failed political policies and improper worship practices will lead to destruction.

### Israel Tries to Please the Wrong King, 6:11b–7:4

In Hosea 6:11b–7:4, YHWH speaks in the divine first person. This divine speech begins in 6:11b and describes the wickedness of the people on several levels. Specifically, the speaker in these verses accuses Israel of trying to please the political officials, including the king (7:4), which in turn only serves to anger YHWH. The irony here is stark: in pleasing the ruler who is asking them to worship other gods, the people zealously comply, but in so doing, they ignore the expectations of the king who demands their covenant loyalty. Hosea 6:11b–7:1 uses four synonyms for Israel, moving from largest to smallest: my people, Israel (the kingdom), Ephraim (the tribal name whose region makes up the central portion of Israel, including the capital city), and Samaria (the capital city of the northern kingdom in the eighth century). The sayings contrast YHWH's salvific intent ("when I would restore/heal") with conditions of "iniquity" and "evils," thereby indicating that Israel's behavior prevents YHWH's expression of mercy. The root "heal" (*râf 'â*) involves a play on words with the subject of the next line, Ephraim. It uses three of the same consonants as the root for the Ephraim region, which is used in Hosea as a poetic synonym for the northern kingdom. The wickedness of Israel is further delineated with the comparison of Ephraim/Samaria's behavior to that of thieves and bandits.

Hosea 7:2 forcefully warns that the people's behavior has not escaped YHWH's notice. YHWH states he does not forget what people do, even though the people's behavior suggests they do not think God cares how they behave. The word for "wickedness" (NRSV) is the plural form of "evil" (*râ'â*) that appears in 7:1, 2, 3. As well, the term for "deeds" in the second part of the verse is a word always used in Hosea when referring to wicked behavior (4:9; 5:4; 9:15; 12:3). Israel does not recognize the consequences of its behavior, but YHWH accuses them of performing evil. [The Hebrew root *r*ʿ]

The motivation for the activity condemned in 7:1-2 takes on a political slant in Hosea 7:3, which presumes those performing the wicked deeds desire to impress the political leaders (the king and the princes). This implicit accusation is highly significant for understanding that the previous verses are not to be interpreted merely as ethical problems. The thieves and bandits of 7:1 are somehow operating with political motives: they want to please those in power. Moreover, they are acting with the implicit consent of the rulers, if not at their behest. While it is impossible to reconstruct fully the political corruption to which the prophet is referring, it is clear that Israel's political leaders had been encouraging behaviors that were odious to YHWH.

Hosea 7:4 concludes the unit with a condemnation of the zeal with which evil activity was conducted. YHWH refers to the people as "adulterers." The root appears in Hosea (3:1; 4:2, 13, 14) to refer to the worship of gods other than YHWH. The zeal of

---

**The Hebrew root *r*ʿ**

AΩ The Hebrew root *r*ʿ has a wide semantic range of meaning that includes moral evil (the opposite of good), natural calamities, divine punishment, illegal acts, and unethical behavior. This breadth of meaning is illustrated by the LXX, which uses more than 30 Greek words to translate this one Hebrew root. The dichotomy created by good (*tob*) and evil (*r*ʿ) thus can have legal (justice/injustice), ethical (right/wrong), natural (prosperity/calamity), or providential (reward/punishment) connotations. In Hos 7:1-3 *r*ʿ refers to the ethical and legal misconduct of the people, while elsewhere the same term can refer to the threatened punishment that YHWH chooses to inflict or not (e.g., Jer 18:7-10; Joel 2:13; Jonah 4:2).

those committing adultery (whether metaphorically or literally) is portrayed with a baking metaphor—one of several to play a role utilizing the catchword "oven" (7:4, 6, 7). This metaphor draws upon the imagery of an overheated oven that does not need to be stirred to keep it hot. In the immediate context, the metaphor implies that the "adulterers" are willing partners whose enjoyment of the acts adds to their guilt. Reference to the baker would seem to imply that the prophet envisions an urban context, or perhaps a reference to the king's dwelling in Samaria.

**A Threat to the King from within His Own Household, 7:5-7**

These verses depict danger to Israel's king that comes from within his own house. The king slights the princes, whose anger then puts the king in danger. These verses change in style and subject from 7:1-4, but the two units are linked by a common metaphor (the oven). This type of linkage suggests an editor compiled the chapter by placing a series of short sayings or speech summaries beside one another based on catchwords or theme.

**Ovens**

Flat bread like that mentioned in Hos 7:8 would be placed on the side of the oven to bake after the oven had heated for several hours.

Bread oven from Tel Quasile. Clay (Iron Age). Haaretz Museum, Tel Aviv, Israel. (Credit: Erich Lessing/Art Resource, NY)

Reference to a particular time of celebration (the day of our king) at the beginning of 7:5 might suggest a coronation or an annual celebration of the king's rule, but the details of 7:5-7 remain obscure. Formally, the speaker changes in 7:5. No longer does this passage use divine first person style, but now the prophet identifies with the people when referring to "our king." While the precise celebration may not be known, the speaker describes an incident that has created trouble in the royal household. The king has participated in ridiculing some of the princes who overindulged at his party: ". . . he stretched out his hand with mockers."

Hosea 7:6 continues to unpack the implications of the king's perceived slight toward the officials. The king's mockery causes the drunken officials to resent him, and 7:6 depicts their resentment burning "like an oven." The oven imagery probably accounts for the placement of these verses in this location (see 7:4) even though 7:5-7 presumes a different situation than 7:1-4. Whereas the previous use of the oven referred to the zeal with which the people participated in "adultery," the oven in 7:6 conveys the intensity of anger that rages continually (day and night). Such dissension does not bode well for the king.

In 7:7, reference to "all of them" refers back to the princes from 7:5. The severity of the dissension is reinforced: they are all burning with anger over how the king has mocked them. Never mind that their own actions caused the situation; they blame the king for pointing out their foolishness. The anger of the princes is compared to the heat of an oven, connecting loosely to 7:6. The implications of the dissension in the royal household are significant. The increasing resentment threatens to turn into rebellion. Israel's history provides a backdrop since in the last years of Israel, its kings often fell prey to usurpers. [Kings of the Northern Kingdom] In short, kings did not reign long in the period leading up to the Syro-Ephraimite War.

**Kings of the Northern Kingdom**

It is not known whether this dissension ever resulted in the assassination of the king, but the intent to assassinate the king is certainly implied in 7:7. The tumultuous years leading up to the end of the northern kingdom in the eighth century testify to the volatility of the situation since four kings were assassinated in the northern kingdom from 746–732: Zechariah (746), Shallum (746), Pekahiah (737), and Pekah (732).

## Ephraim Mixes with Foreigners, 7:8-10

Hosea 7:8-10 connects superficially to the immediate context both backward and forward. The baking metaphors of the previous units continue in 7:8, referencing Israel as an unturned cake that is readily associated with the language of the oven (7:4, 6, 7). The links forward are thematic in that the reference to mixing with foreigners has clear parallels to the more politically oriented ideas in 7:11-16, where Israel vacillates between alliances with Egypt and Assyria.

Hosea 7:8 begins a new subject: Ephraim's misconception of its relationship to the peoples of the world. The connection of 7:8-10 to the previous units again draws upon a baking metaphor. In this case, however, it is not the word "oven" that creates the connection, but what one puts in the oven that forms the content of the analogy. The verse characterizes Ephraim as being like an unturned cake. This word "cake" (*ʿugâ*) is not the normal word for bread (*leḥem*), but refers to flat, round loaves that bake relatively quickly and were used on special occasions (Gen 18:6; Exod 12:39; Num 11:8; 1 Kgs 17:13; 1 Kgs 19:6; and Ezek 4:12).

The imagery of an unturned cake means that the cake will burn on one side without cooking all the way through. When placed in an analogy of mixing with other countries, the metaphor suggests a picture whereby Israel becomes overexposed to the nations while not getting the proper energy from God on the other side.

Hosea 7:9 continues the subject of mixing with foreigners that began in 7:8, although the metaphor changes. Foreigners sap the strength of Ephraim. Moreover, Ephraim is implicitly compared to an old man. His hair begins to turn gray without his knowledge. In other words, Ephraim begins to lose vitality.

Israel suffers from pride in its own strength according to 7:10. The phrase "Israel testifies against itself" means that its pride will not let it recognize its need to change. As in English, the Hebrew "pride" can have a positive or negative connotation depending upon whether the pride is well founded. When used positively, pride points to YHWH, as with the royal figure in Micah 5:4. More frequently, however, and especially in the Book of the Twelve, pride is misplaced and becomes a point of accusation. [Pride in the Book of the Twelve] This aspect is clearly implied in Hosea 7:7, which ties pride to Israel's and Judah's unwillingness to turn to YHWH. The people mistakenly believe their own strength is sufficient unto itself. In the context, this accusation means that Israel's pride clouds the people's judgment. They thought they could worship YHWH and encourage foreign practices as well. This prophetic accusation rebuts those assumptions.

## Implications of Substituting Political Expediency for Theological Sense, 7:11-16

Hosea 7:11 begins a new section with a reference to Ephraim, the third time this chapter has begun a unit with such a reference (see 7:1, 8). Hosea 7:11-12 is held together by consistent first person divine speech and third masculine plural references to the people of Ephraim that

**Pride in the Book of the Twelve**

A significant percentage of instances where "pride" appears in the Old Testament (10/47) appear in the Book of the Twelve. They do not, however, develop a consistent motif, since they relate both to accusations against God's people and to foreign nations who have mistreated YHWH's people (Zeph 2:10; Zech 9:6; 10:11). Still, the pride of the northern kingdom appears as a major reason for its destruction in Hosea (5:5; 7:7) and Amos (6:8; 8:7). The positive connotation of "pride in the name of YHWH your God" appears in the promise of an ideal king who will come to lead Judah and Israel (see discussion of Mic 5:4; and compare Nah 2:2 [MT 2:3]).

all draw upon 7:11 for their antecedent. This unit shifts images and subjects as YHWH explores the reasons Ephraim deserves punishment and touches on YHWH's own desire to avoid punishment, but pronounces judgment nonetheless. The unit transitions from threat (7:11-12) to woe oracle (7:13) that articulates reasons and threats while echoing themes from Hosea and beyond (7:14-16).

Hosea 7:11-12 caricatures Ephraim as a dove that YHWH will trap. Unlike modern Western symbols of peace, the dove in 7:11 has a decidedly negative connotation. Taking its cue from the bird's seemingly random movements, the analogy in 7:11 mocks the arbitrary nature of Israel's political alliances. Israel, according to 7:11, has made agreements with both Egypt and Assyria, apparently oblivious to the fact that they are working at cross purposes to their own survival. The content of these agreements is not given, but Egypt had a vested interest in keeping Assyria out of Palestine as Assyria extended its political, military, and economic power. Ephraim makes deals with both, making it highly likely that they will anger at least one of them.

Hosea 7:12 continues the bird analogy as God speaks of casting his net over Ephraim as punishment. Casting the net (*rešet*) refers to a hunting practice for catching birds (as here) or lions (Ezek 19:8). The image in 7:12 implies that the net belongs to YHWH, who will throw the net in order to capture and punish Ephraim as they take off in their flights of political vicissitude.

At the end of 7:12, the "report made to their assembly" requires explanation, since it is often emended and translated in various ways. [Report Made to Their Assembly] Without resorting to emendation, the obscure phrase can be translated as "I will discipline them according to the report about their assembly." One need only assume that this report refers to an assembly's action regarding Egypt and Assyria from the previous verse.[1] It would not be the first time in history that a corporate

### Report Made to Their Assembly

AΩ The reference to "their assembly," because it is so enigmatic, has often been emended to "their wickedness" (e.g., Wolff, *Hosea*, 107) or to "their testimony" (e.g., Sweeney, *The Twelve Prophets*, 81). The latter emendation, admittedly less drastic than Wolff's, refers to the testimony of the treaties made with Egypt and Assyria that makes Israel vulnerable to those entities. While ingenious, it is not convincing text critically, and it is unnecessary. A simpler explanation, one not requiring emendation, presents itself based on the syntax of the phrase and a broad, but documentable, understanding of what constitutes an "assembly." First, Judg 20–21 shows that an assembly can refer to a group gathered for military and political purposes, not just religious observances. Second, the phrasing in Hos 7:12 is unusual in that the word "assembly" is prefixed with a *lamed* preposition (*lě*). Elsewhere, when the word "report" is followed by this preposition (1 Kgs 10:1; Isa 23:5), it refers to the *content* of the report, not the recipients.

Hans Walter Wolff, *Hosea* (Hermeneia; trans. Gary Stansell; Philadelphia: Fortress, 1974).

Marvin A. Sweeney, *The Twelve Prophets* (Berit Olam, vol. 1; Collegeville: Liturgical Press, 2000).

body moved in conflicting directions.

Hosea 7:13-16 heightens the sense of impending disaster. It begins with a woe oracle (7:13), then pronounces destruction with a theological rationale (straying from/rebelling against YHWH), and concludes with a wistful expression of change ("I would redeem them, but they speak lies against me"). These elements are expanded in 7:14-16 with an essentially parallel structure that reinforces both the idea of YHWH's pain and the inevitability of the coming judgment. [Parallel Structure of Hosea 7:13 / 14-16] Thus, Hosea 7:14-16 not only reiterates the same rhetorical elements as 7:13, but it also reminds the reader of previous material in Hosea and anticipates motifs in the developing corpus. [Hosea 7:14-16 and the Developing Corpus]

Hosea 7:14 raises the issue of Israel's sincerity and the problems created by doing one thing and saying another. It describes a people who turn to God, but not genuinely. [Translating Hosea 7:14] "Turning" from YHWH at the end of Hosea 7:14 also evokes themes of improper worship. This verb, *swr*, appears frequently in Kings (1 Kgs 22:43; 2 Kgs 3:3; 10:29; 12:4; etc.) as part of the recurring refrain condemning Israel's kings for not turning from the calf-worship established by Jeroboam at Bethel. In this vein, 7:14 presumes the anti-idolatry polemic of Hosea 2: Israel's festivals (involving agricultural elements) offend YHWH and seduce the people.

In Hosea 7:15, YHWH continues to speak, recalling YHWH's own role of training Israel for battle. The allusion to YHWH's role of preparing them could recall the rationale given

### Parallel Structure of Hosea 7:13 / 14-16

The rhetorical logic of 7:13-16 reinforces the impression of YHWH's struggle over whether to destroy the northern kingdom.

| 7:13 | 7:14-16 |
|---|---|
| Judgment: <br> Woe/destruction | Reasons: <br> (14) superficial cries, desiring grain and wine; revolt against me |
| Reasons: <br> straying from/rebelling against YHWH | Wistful expression that things were different: <br> (15) I trained, instructed, but they plot evil against me |
| Wistful expression that things were different: I would redeem them, but they speak lies against me | Judgment: <br> (16) their princes will die by the sword |

### Hosea 7:14-16 and the Developing Corpus

Hos 7:14-16 summarizes indictments against Israel and hints at YHWH's pain in ways that echo other texts in Hosea and Amos. For example, note the situations depicted in Hos 7:14 and Amos 6:4-6. Both passages presume someone is calling out during a cultic ceremony involving wine and oil while lying on a bed. The fact that this practice is condemned in both texts is no surprise given that it seems to be something associated with Baal worship. The desire to use grain and wine in worship is part of the syncretism that serves as the backdrop for Hos 2 (see 2:8, 13 [MT 2:10, 15]). Moreover, YHWH's desire that Ephraim recognize his debt to YHWH not only conveys sentiments similar to the ideas expressed in Hos 2:14-15 (MT 2:16-17) but also anticipates the dramatic soliloquy concerning YHWH's internal conflict in Hos 11:1-9 (note especially 11:3). In short, Hos 7:13-16 (especially 7:14-16) recalls or anticipates several recurring elements that are of continuing significance in documenting the reasons why YHWH decides, albeit reluctantly, to destroy the northern kingdom in Hosea and Amos.

**Translating Hosea 7:14**

AΩ Translating this verse is difficult, and the text is often emended. Instead of MT's *grr* ("drag away"), the NRSV (following several ancient manuscripts) translates the verb from the root *gdd* as "gash themselves," but this verb also means "gathered themselves," usually referring to troops. The NRSV emendation, *gdd*, can thus be translated as, "They mustered themselves on account of the grain and wine; they turn against me." This accusation against the people accords with Hos 2 where, in conjunction with language of fornication as idolatry, the grain and wine are used for "festival days of the Baals" (see 2:9, 13 [MT 2:11, 15]). As evidence, Jer 5:7 uses *gdd* in the context of Judah's prostitution/idolatry.

**English Translations of Hosea 7:16**

AΩ The text of MT is missing something or has become corrupt. Note how the various translations attempt to deal with this problem.

KJV: They return, [but] not to the most High.
RSV: They turn to Ba'al.
NRSV: They turn to that which does not profit.
NIV: They do not turn to the Most High.
NAS: They turn, but not upward.

Common to all is the clear sense that the action of turning is not appropriate, for the object toward which they turn is not YHWH.

in Judges 3:12, or it could be a more general statement of God's providential care for Israel. Regardless, the accusation is clear: the people show no gratitude. Israel actively turns against YHWH by plotting wickedness (note also "rebel" [7:13], "turn against" [7:14]).

Hosea 7:16 summarizes the contents of the entire chapter thematically and poetically. The first portion is notoriously difficult to translate, as seen by the English translations. [English Translations of Hosea 7:16] Nevertheless, each translation reflects a reason for God's decision to punish Israel. Hosea 7:16 uses military imagery, comparing Ephraim to a bow that is slack. The imagery means that the bow offers no threat because it does not have the power to accomplish anything. Reference to the rage of the rulers' tongues reminds one of the royal intrigue in Hosea 7:5-7. The murmuring of Egypt probably refers to irrational speech, metaphorically referring to speaking nonsense to Egypt (and Assyria?), as in 7:11. Thus, 7:16 recalls the problems that this chapter has treated.

## CONNECTIONS

The content of Hosea 7, with its condemnation of the behavior of the ruling class, its call for purer forms of worship, and its castigation of all things foreign, raises significant issues for relating this issue to our own situation. The context colors the message significantly, both in terms of its geographic and historical focus on the northern kingdom and in the context of the theological aims of the books of Hosea and Amos. This text is not, however, the only text in Scripture that deals with these issues. One must hear these other voices of Scripture before too quickly making direct applications, especially regarding the blending of politics with religion and one's approach to foreigners in a pluralistic, post-9/11 age. [Xenophobia in the Hebrew Bible and Today]

Politics and religion make uneasy companions. The faith of believers is often twisted to political ends by unscrupulous or undiscerning leaders. Conversely, believers often feel their religious beliefs should be codified in political affairs. The desire to please YHWH and the desire to please the king are confused by the people in Hosea 7, and it is hardly different in our own society where people of faith are targeted by politicians as a potential voting block for their agendas—no matter upon which side of the political fence one stands. The prophet's words serve as a warning to distinguish God's expectations from our inclinations, especially in the realm of public policy.

Yet how does one do this? How does one know when it is legitimate to agree with leaders who claim to speak for God and when these leaders should be challenged? The concept of "service" is crucial for understanding the role of king and subject, or of political leaders and ordinary citizens in our context. In Old Testament texts, beginning with Joshua 24:14-24, service to YHWH is the only proper response. Old Testament kings are castigated for failing to serve YHWH (1 Kgs 9:6, 9; 16:31; 22:54; 2 Kgs 10:18ff; 17:12, 16, 33, 35-36, 41; 21:3, 21). This idea is clear enough when speaking of the worship of other gods or idols, but Hosea 7 also presupposes another aspect: a king should act on behalf of the people. One should ask, to whom are the acts of the king directed and who benefits? The king should act in accordance with God's expectations for humans. In other words, the king is to rule with equanimity and accountability: "neither exalting himself above other members of the community, nor turning aside from the commandment" (Deut 17:20). A king is not supposed to get rich at the expense of the people (Deut 17:17). A king should know that serving God involves attending to the

---

**Xenophobia in the Hebrew Bible and Today**

Both the Old Testament and the New Testament contain texts exhibiting negative and positive attitudes toward foreigners. In the OT, xenophobic tendencies can be noted in individual texts (e.g., Ezra 9) and in entire books (e.g., Joshua and Judges). In Ezra 9, Ezra's concern for purity leads him to pray a prayer of confession to God when he learns that men of Judah had taken foreign women (9:1-15). This prayer leads to the imposition of forced divorce for Judean men who had married foreign women (10:9-17). Ezra's attitude reflects much the same attitude one finds in Joshua and Judges, which both display negative attitudes toward non-Israelites, despite the fact that the Joshua narrative depicts Israel as the aggressor nation coming in from outside. Both Joshua and Judges presume that the ideal situation (though it is never achieved) would be the elimination of all the indigenous peoples within the borders of the land promised by YHWH. The fact that this never occurred is seen as a failure on Israel's part (Josh 24:19-28; Judg 1:19-21). The same animosity toward foreigners can be seen in attitudes of the disciples in NT texts (Matt 15:21-26), though it is perhaps less violently expressed.

On the other hand, not every text in the OT demonstrates these xenophobic tendencies. Some OT texts show a clear openness to foreigners and their worship of YHWH. The book of Jonah drives home the point that God's interest in repentance and salvation is not limited to the borders of Israel. Prophetic texts like Isa 56:3-8; Zech 8:20-23; or the parallels in Isa 2:2-4 (= Mic 4:1-3) illustrate that hospitable attitudes were also present in biblical texts. In the end, the church opted for this more open attitude toward non-Jews (Acts 15) in terms of its mission.

### Ideology of Kingship

Deut 17:14-20 lays out the picture of an ideal king, though its rhetorical function also serves as an indictment of kings to come in the grand narrative that tells the stories of the kings of Israel and Judah. The role of the king in the ancient Near East was closely tied to the king's special relationship to the deity and to the expectation that the king headed the military, and was responsible for maintaining order and security in the political realm. In addition to his role as warrior and judge, the king, in most instances, was responsible for maintaining cultic order. In some ancient Near Eastern contexts, the king had a priestly function, though the extent of this function is more difficult to document in Judah. On the one hand, the presence of royal psalms in the Psalter suggests that the king had a significant role in cultic observances, with many suggesting a cultic festival of enthronement could have taken place in Judah like festivals better documented in other contexts. On the other hand, several narratives indicate a tension between priests and kings, especially in delineating the role of the king within the cult. Note especially the rejection of Saul by Samuel for cultic infractions (1 Sam 13:1-13; 15:10-23). Despite this tension, the symbiotic relationship between the king and the cult can be seen in the way that several narratives either praise kings for helping to reform the cult (2 Kgs 10:18-27; 18:4-5; 23:1-25) or critique them for denigrating it (e.g., 1 Kgs 16:32; 2 Kgs 21:2-7). In other words, despite tensions, the state and the cult were closely intertwined during the monarchic period in Judah, and the king was supposed to play a pivotal role in maintaining cultic order and prosperity.

See Hermann Gunkel, *An Introduction to the Psalms: The Genres of the Religious Lyric of Israel* (Mercer Library of Biblical Studies; trans. James D. Nogalski; Macon: Mercer University Press, 1998) 99–120; and Hans-Joachim Kraus, *Psalms 1–59*, (trans. Hilton C. Oswald; Minneapolis: Fortress, 1993) 56–58; Erhard S. Gerstenberger, *Psalms: Part I, with an Introduction to Cultic Poetry* (Forms of the Old Testament Literature 14; Grand Rapids: Eerdmans, 1988) 19.

welfare of all the people, not just the cronies around him (1 Kgs 12:7). [Ideology of Kingship]

These two issues point to dangers faced by those in power at any time, and at any level of society: pride and greed. Modern leaders are often tempted. They expect to benefit financially and socially from their service, even if their reward comes at the expense of setting up responsible systems that benefit all the people. They can place themselves above doing what is right if it benefits themselves or their party. In so doing, they fall prey to the core problems depicted in Hosea 7: they lose sight of those whom they are serving. The kings and princes in Hosea 7 fail to serve God or God's people. They serve other gods and lead the people to do the same (7:3); they enjoy hedonistic pleasures with no regard for the implications beyond their own self-interests (7:5); and the leaders flit from one entity to another in a comedic attempt to protect themselves from all parties (7:11). The end result is a country led by those whose pride will not allow them to ask how they should serve YHWH's people (7:10; see 1 Kgs 12:7). Service should be the visible element of any political leader who dares to claim to act on God's behalf. Moreover, given past abuses, however, people of faith need to develop discernment and a healthy skepticism *any time* politicians claim to speak for God.

How does one deal with this text's condemnation of foreigners and foreign elements in a pluralistic world? Hosea 7 takes one side of an issue that finds more than one voice: how are "foreigners" to be viewed by God's people? Isaiah 56:3-8, on the one hand, and Ezra 9:13-14; 10:2-5, on the other, operate from different assumptions on this issue. Hosea 7:8-10 falls into the more xenophobic category (with Ezra 9–10) for theological reasons. In these texts, foreigners should be avoided because they pose dangers for corrupting the worship of YHWH. By contrast, Isaiah 56 exhibits a more inclusive attitude. Isaiah 56:3-8 and most New Testament texts represent a bolder approach that assumes the relationship between God and God's people knows no geographic boundaries and can withstand the tensions created by the way that religious expression adapts itself to various cultures. This debate continues today, especially in discussions of a post-9/11 world. How do people of different faiths share the same space on this planet? Is it not sadly ironic that the three religious traditions most engaged in hostilities today all claim the God of the Old Testament as their God?

## NOTE

1. See the discussion in Martin A. Sweeney, *The Twelve Prophets* (Berit Olam, vol. 1; Collegeville: Liturgical Press, 2000) 81.

# KINGS AND IDOLS

## Hosea 8:1-14

## COMMENTARY

The extended unit of Hosea 8:1-14 exhibits numerous textual difficulties, contains several thematic overlaps, and is impossible to
organize purely on structural grounds. Nevertheless, the textual difficulties are not so significant that they camouflage the point of the
passage; the thematic repetitions accentuate the core message of the
book; and the rhetorical flow can be followed, even if it is not structured artistically. What is characteristic for this chapter is the number
of times *threatened* punishment alternates with a stated rationale.
[Punitive Action Alternates with Rationale] When this alternation is combined
with thematic and rhetorical considerations, the chapter can be
divided into three interrelated sections: a warning of the broken
covenant and looming threat (8:1-3); the speech that argues that
unauthorized kings led to idol worship and will soon lead to
unwanted kings (8:4-10); and a renewed accusation that improper
sacrifice will lead to a return to slavery and the destruction of the
land (8:11-14).

---

### Punitive Action Alternates with Rationale

In Hos 8 the reasons for judgment on Israel are as varied as the punishments themselves.

| Verse | Reason | Verse | Action |
|---|---|---|---|
| 8:1b | transgressing the covenant | 8:1a | a vulture over the house of YHWH |
| 8:3a | rejecting the good | 8:3b | enemy will pursue |
| 8:4 | unauthorized kings and idols | 8:5a | rejection of calf, anger of YHWH |
| 8:5b-6a | incapable of innocence, crafting idols | 8:6b | calf of Samaria shattered |
| 8:7aa | sow the wind | 8:7ab-8 | reap the whirlwind, crops devastated |
| 8:9-10a | hiring themselves to nations | 8:10b | they will be gathered up and diminish |
| 8:11a | multiplied altars of sin | 8:11b | the altars become altars for sinning |
| 8:12-13a | disrespecting the laws | 8:13b | return to Egypt |
| 8:14a | Israel built palaces/temples Judah increased fortified cities | 8:14b | Fire on its cities will devour its citadels |

### A Cry of Alarm, 8:1-3

Hosea 8:1-3 begins with a cry of alarm spoken formally by YHWH, though YHWH also quotes Israel (8:2) as in 6:1-3. The logic of these verses is clear, even though the text manifests syntactical difficulties: Israel's breaking of the covenant has created a danger (8:1) that causes Israel to petition YHWH for help (8:2), but YHWH turns a deaf ear because Israel's behavior has created the problem. Consequently, the enemy will come (8:3).

Hosea 8:1 abruptly sets forth a call from YHWH to sound the alarm. Both 8:1 and 8:2 use first person references to YHWH ("my covenant," "my law," "to me"), indicating YHWH as the speaker. The alarm is stated quickly (with no verb), adding to the sense of imminent danger: literally, "to your lips, the trumpet!" The word translated "trumpet" is the general word for horn. The *shôfâr* was an animal horn used in a variety of military and cultic contexts. The connotations of blowing the horn depend greatly upon the context. Here, it warns of an impending attack, but the attacker is not identified as a human army until the end of 8:3. Rather, 8:1 identifies the threat as "one like a vulture." Various English versions translate the word *nešer* as either "eagle" or "vulture," but it is best understood as a griffon vulture. In 8:1b, the vulture

**Shôfâr**

An animal horn, usually from a goat, used to signal attack (Neh 4:12; Amos 3:6), to call an army to battle (Judg 3:27), to proclaim victory after a battle (1 Sam 13:3), to proclaim a new king (2 Sam 15:10), and to begin cultic festivals (Lev 25:9; Ps 81:3 [MT 81:4]; Joel 2:15).

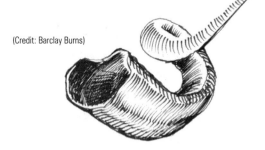

(Credit: Barclay Burns)

**Eagle or Vulture**

The reasons for the different translations have more to do with the connotations of the two birds in English than with the meaning of the Hebrew word *nešer*, which is now widely recognized to be that of the griffon vulture (*gyps fulvus*). Many translators are reluctant to use the word "vulture" because it evokes distasteful images of feasting on carrion. This is particularly true when the word is used to show the protective power of YHWH (Exod 19:4; Deut 32:11). Yet, the *nešer* also connotes speed when attacking, a quality more associated with birds of prey like the eagle in English (e.g., 2 Sam 1:23; Jer 4:13; Hab 1:8).

(Credit: Ingrid Taylor, Griffon vulture at Oakland Zoo, Oakland, California, USA, http://en.wikipedia.org/wiki/File:Gyps_fulvus_-Oakland_Zoo-8a.jpg)

sits above the house of YHWH, so the vulture functions as the threat precipitating the call to alarm. [Temple in Samaria?]

The reason given in 8:1b for the threat is that "they have broken my covenant" and "rebelled against my law." The first phrase, "they transgressed my covenant," has strong connections to Deuteronomic or Deuteronomistic material (Deut 17:2; Josh 7:11; Judg 2:20; 2 Kgs 18:12; Jer 34:18). [Terminology] Amos 2:4 essentially levels the same accusations against Judah. Many scholars treat the

---

## Temple in Samaria?

No scholarly consensus exists regarding which house of YHWH is intended. Does it refer to the Jerusalem temple (as Amos 1:2 refers to YHWH as a lion roaring from Jerusalem), or does it refer to a northern kingdom sanctuary (presumably Bethel) for the worship of YHWH? Some commentators (e.g., W. Rudolph) understand "my house" as symbolic for all Israel, citing Hos 9:15 and various inscriptions that refer to Israel as the "house of Omri."

The ninth-century Mesha inscription, for example, refers to Omri (lines 4-5), his son (line 6), and "his house" (line 7). Others (e.g., M. A. Sweeney) contend that the cultic context of the passage requires some type of temple location. Sweeney even suggests this verse implies that Samaria must have had a temple. Several palace sites have been excavated at Samaria (see the image of the Ahab temple ruins), but according to M. Haran no temple has definitively been located, and no other text implies a temple for YHWH existed in Samaria. 1 Kgs 16:32 does, however, condemn Ahab for building a "house of Baal" in Samaria, a temple that Jehu is later credited with destroying (making its ruins a latrine) in 2 Kgs 10:27. No artifactual evidence for this temple has been located either. Thus, the suggestion that Samaria once had a temple needs further evidence, and one cannot make this claim with certainty, but it would appear plausible. Nevertheless, an actual Israelite temple would make better sense for this threat than a purely metaphorical use of the phrase "house of YHWH.

Haran surveys the biblical evidence for explicit and implicit references to temples, but Samaria is not included in the 13 temple sites he treats.

Wilhelm Rudolph, *Hosea* (KAT, Bd 13/1; Gütersloher: G.Mohn, 1966) 162.

Marvin A. Sweeney, *The Twelve Prophets* (Berit Olam, vol. 1; Collegeville: Liturgical Press, 2000) 85.

Menaham Haran, *Temples and Temple Service in Ancient Israel: An Inquiry into Biblical Cult Phenomena and the Historical Setting of the Priestly School* (Winona Lake: Eisenbrauns, 1985) 26–39.

Mesha Stele: stele of Mesha, king of Moab, recording his victories against the Kingdom of Israel. Basalt, c. 800 BCE. From Dhiban, now in Jordan. (Credit: Neithsabes, http://en.wikipedia.org/wiki/File:Louvre_042010_01.jpg)

(Credit: Todd Bolen/BiblePlaces.com)

Judah oracle in Amos 2:4 as an exilic addition to the oracles against the nations in Amos. The charges against Israel in Hosea 8:1 will be further elucidated in subsequent verses.

In the first part of 8:2, YHWH introduces the cry of Israel, using the same verb as the description of the cry of the Israelites in Egypt (Exod 2:23): "They cry (*z'q*) to me." (Note also how this image returns near the end of the unit in 8:13.) The formulation of 8:2 emphasizes Israel's pain by having God quote Israel crying to God. The logic of 8:2 presumes that Israel recognizes the threat from 8:1 and cries to YHWH, but YHWH ignores the cry according to 8:3. There God summarizes the accusation ("they have rejected good") and pronounces the verdict ("an enemy will pursue him"). In the eighth-century literary setting, this enemy can only be understood as Assyria, who will destroy Samaria (the capital of the northern kingdom) and exile the people in 722. This presumed context—one predicting the downfall of the northern kingdom at the hand of Assyria—becomes even clearer in the next unit.

### Unauthorized Kings, Idol Worship, and Unwanted Kings, 8:4-10

Rhetorical logic and thematic connections to a recurring motif in Kings hold Hosea 8:4-10 together as a compositional unit. It challenges the political existence and religious practices of the northern kingdom. Functionally, 8:4-10 details the reasons for prophetic condemnation. Hosea 8:4-10 begins with a change from the singular pronouns for Israel in 8:3 to the plural pronoun that begins 8:4. Nevertheless, 8:4-10 is not independent of 8:1-3; it shifts from a general warning to a more detailed depiction of the charges against Israel.

Hosea 8:4 introduces the two themes that serve as the focal points for 8:4-10: illegitimate kings and idol worship. The charges in 8:4 differ from those in 8:2a, however. Hosea 8:4 accuses Israel of setting up kings without YHWH's permission and worshiping idols. Two questions arise from the charge of setting up kings YHWH has not authorized. First, what does 8:4 mean when

YHWH refers to their establishing rulers that "I did not know"? In all likelihood, it does not mean YHWH was unaware of what they had done. Rather, it parallels the statement about "kings who were not from me." In other words, it refers to rulers YHWH did not authorize.

Second, what does it mean that they established unauthorized kings? [Interpretive Options for Unauthorized Kings] A decision is not easy, but ties to the Deuteronomistic History in the surrounding context suggest the closest similarities appear in the anti-northern critique in 1–2 Kings, especially when combined with allusions to the anti-idolatry polemic elsewhere in Hosea (for example, see Hos 7:5-7; 2:8 [MT 2:10]; 13:2). The combination of the two themes (rejection of *Israel's* kings and idolatry) not only fits 8:4-10, but the calf reference in 8:5 also evokes images of the "sins of Jeroboam" from Kings. In this respect, Hosea 8:4 connects logically to 8:5 (cf. 1 Kgs 12:32; Hos 7:5-6; 13:2).

> **Interpretive Options for Unauthorized Kings**
>
> At least three options present themselves for consideration. First, it could refer to a rejection of kingship in general, closely akin to 1 Sam 8 (see 1 Sam 8:5-6, 18). Second, it could refer to the establishment of the northern kingdom, whose rejection is especially prominent in the Deuteronomistic History. 1 Kgs 12:26-30 condemns Jeroboam I for establishing rival sanctuaries at Bethel and Dan, and these sanctuaries were recognized by all subsequent kings of the northern kingdom. Third, the condemnation could refer to the events of the eighth century against which the book of Hosea is set, without presupposing the accounts of Kings.

In Hosea 8:5, YHWH addresses Samaria directly ("your calf") *and* speaks about the people in third person plural language. The subject of the verse is YHWH's condemnation of the calf of Samaria (see also 8:6)—a reference to the idol established by Jeroboam I at the sanctuary in Bethel (in the region of Samaria). Erection of the calf becomes the basis for the recurring refrain in 1–2 Kings regarding the sins of Jeroboam.[1] This "sins of Jeroboam" motif culminates in the judgment in 2 Kings 17:21-23, which places singular blame upon this act for the rejection of YHWH, which in turn ultimately causes the downfall of Israel. [Northern Shrines]

Hosea 8:6, like many Old Testament anti-idolatry texts (e.g., Isa 43:12-17), cuts to the heart of the problem with idol worship. If human beings make idols, then worshiping idols as gods is absurd. This verse condemns Israel, meaning specifically the northern kingdom, for idolatry. The phrases "The artisan made it" and "it is not God" continue the theme of idol worship begun in 8:5. This continuation is further evidenced in 8:6b with the pronouncement that the calf of Samaria will be shattered. However, because the calf is as much a political symbol for the northern kingdom as a reli-

### Northern Shrines

While no remains of the shrine have been found at Bethel, the sacred place at Dan has walls from the eighth century BCE that show evidence of earlier walls dating to the tenth century, roughly contemporary with Jeroboam. The structure pictured here shows evidence that it served as the base for another structure (perhaps wooden) that could have supported a shrine with a bull. To the worshipers, this bull represented YHWH, but to the Deuteronomistic Historian, it functioned as an idol and a political symbol of a cult in competition with the temple at Jerusalem.

A cult place behind the gate of the fortification of Tel Dan was probably built by King Jeroboam of Israel in the 10th C. BCE. Dan, Israel. (Credit: Erich Lessing/Art Resource, NY)

gious one, this text quickly makes clear that this threat is not just about the calf itself, but about the destruction of the entire northern kingdom.

In Hosea 8:7-8, YHWH continues to speak, but (re)turns to the subject of the people's guilt rather than the calf of Samaria. The coming judgment is depicted in fearful terms because it will far exceed the crime: "They sowed the wind, but they will harvest the whirlwind." A whirlwind is a sustained, powerful storm. In other words, what the people did will pale in comparison to how God will punish them. This imagery depicts divine judgment in terms that are deliberately intended to illicit fear of YHWH's punishment and to emphasize YHWH's power. The futility of Israel's confrontation with this whirlwind is portrayed poignantly in 8:7b. The vegetation (*ṣmḥ*) will have no grain still on the stalk (*qmh*) because the whirlwind has blown it away. Because there is no head on the grain, there will be no meal from which to make the flour. Finally, the threat is compounded when the last part of the verse says that if *by chance* some stalks did produce grain, the people of Ephraim would not see it because foreigners would be the ones to eat it. The country will soon be swallowed up (8:8) by foreigners who will then swallow up (8:7) whatever grain is present. Israel itself will be exiled "among the nations." This attitude creates difficulty for modern theology, which tends to downplay these direct confrontations as theologically problematic. [Justice of God]

In Hosea 8:9-10 the focus shifts to the political implications of Israel trying to court favor with Assyria. Hosea 8:9 is difficult syntactically, but most commentators recognize the wild ass (*prʾ*) as a pun in referring to Ephraim (*ʾprym*) who has gone off alone trying to hire lovers. The verse thus inverts and applies the harlotry motif

---

**Justice of God**

Consider the statements of James Crenshaw concerning claims of God's justice:

The world has so much randomness that no individual can ever count on reaping the benefits of a noble life. [. . .] This modern shift in understanding removes us from the world of the Bible. [. . .] Nor does historiography that interprets Israel's and Judah's past in the light of this principle do justice to what really happened, as modern scholars have long recognized. The development of history involves numerous imponderables with deep interconnections and any reading of the rise and fall of nations in terms of divine favor or wrath can only be categorized as theology—and bad theology at that.

Random events and human freedom thus challenge an easy connection to the punishment of nations.

Crenshaw acknowledges that this view permeates the historical narratives of biblical texts, creating a difficult sense of dissonance for modern communities of faith. Crenshaw goes on to suggest the dilemma remains mystery, but one should work toward a redeeming goodness:

If understood to be sparked by divine intentionality, such redeeming goodness becomes the finest theodicy of all, as it calls others to participate in the noblest effort under the sun: establishing justice for the victims of oppression, empowered by the mercy of the God of all grace.

James L. Crenshaw, *Defending God: Biblical Responses to the Problem of Evil* (New York: Oxford University Press, 2005) 120, 195.

---

from chapter 2 to the political realm, although it still concerns the relationship between YHWH and Israel. The word "lovers" evokes the harlotry motif of Hosea 2 (2:5, 10, 12 [MT 2:7, 12, 14]). In this scenario, Ephraim bargains for money but does not pay and is thus portrayed as the harlot. References to the harlot's "hire" received by her create a motif that runs from Hosea 2:12 (MT 2:14) to Hosea 9:1 to Micah 1:7. Hosea 8:9-10 uses slightly different wording to show Ephraim "bargaining for lovers" among the nations.

The result of this bargaining, however, is conveyed in the last half of 8:10, where YHWH "will gather them" (Ephraim) for punishment at the hands of a foreign king. Hosea 8:10b creates morphological difficulties, resulting in various suggestions for emending the verb. In addition, the final two words, "king" and "princes," create translation difficulties, as can be seen in various translations. [Different English Versions] The translation is difficult, but the imagery is clear.

**Different English Versions**

These suggestions assume different roots for the verb in 8:10b: "They will writhe" (*hyl*) or "diminish" (*hlh*). The form of the word would seem to derive from "be profaned" (*hll*), which could mean "render invalid" (*HALOT*), though no English translation assumes the root *hll* is correct.

NRSV: They shall soon *writhe* under the burden of *kings and princes*.
NAS: And they will *begin to diminish* because of the burden of the *king of princes*.
NIV: They will begin to *waste away* under the oppression of the *mighty king*.

Ephraim will suffer under the burden of foreign rulers because of its own political actions. Hosea 8:10 alludes to the impending Assyrian occupation when, according to the text, Israel will be subsumed as a result of its abrogation of responsibilities to YHWH. In short, Assyria will control Israel (see 8:3). Israel's kings, unauthorized by YHWH, will lead Israel into a position of subservience to a foreign power.

### Return to Slavery and Destruction of the Land, 8:11-14

Hosea 8:11-14 concludes the unit with a two-part summary of the chapter, rehearsing both the cultic and political reasons why Israel will be punished. Formally, this section contains a speech by YHWH (8:11-12) and a third-party speech about YHWH (8:13-14). The former restates the cultic reasons for YHWH's displeasure: improper sacrifice and ignoring YHWH's instructions (*tôrôt*). The latter announces a cultic problem (improper sacrifice) and punishment (return to Egypt) in 8:13. It also states political signs that God's people have abandoned God (Israel forgot its maker and built palaces; Judah multiplied fortified cities), causing God to destroy the capital cities of the respective kingdoms in 8:14.

In Hosea 8:11, the subject abruptly returns to the issue of improper sacrifice. At issue is the location where sacrifice is performed. This verse picks up on the oblique references to the impropriety of sacrifices as performed in the northern kingdom (see Hos 8:5-6), and condemns Ephraim's sacrifice because it is offered at multiple locations. In so doing, it sends the message that the "sin of Jeroboam" has wrongly kept the northern kingdom from worship at Jerusalem—a perspective consistent with a major motif of the Deuteronomistic History, and one that plays a significant role in Hosea and Amos.[2]

Hosea 8:12 shifts to the theme of Israel's failure to keep its covenant obligations. This verse underscores YHWH's role in the promulgation of the law when YHWH says, "Though *I write* for him the multitude of my instructions . . . ." The only other places that speak of God writing are places describing the giving of the law to Moses (e.g., Exod 24:12, 18; 32:15-16, 32; 34:1; Deut 4:13; 5:22; 9:10; 10:2,4)—though not even all of these describe God actually doing the writing (see Exod 24:4; 34:27-28; Deut 27:8; 31:24; etc.)—and the prophecy of the new covenant in Jer 31:33 that says YHWH will write on the hearts of people. Thus, all of these references (including Hos 8:12) have to do with YHWH writing law/covenant in some form. This background makes the contrast that much more dramatic, when YHWH accuses Israel in Hosea 8:12 of treating his written instructions (*tôrôt*) as foreign things, meaning regulations that they disregard.

Hosea 8:13 first amplifies the accusation of 8:12 and then pronounces a verdict upon Israel for this behavior. The people do not show proper respect when they sacrifice. The most blatant accusation is that when they offer animal sacrifices, they eat the meat intended for the sacrifice—an act that deviates from the stipulations for the sin offering or the guilt offering (see Lev 6:25-30; 7:1-4, 18, 20; Deut 18:1) and the burnt offering (6:9-10). Priests could eat certain portions of some sacrifices, but the ritual participants could not eat these sacrifices. This practice evokes YHWH's ire and becomes part of the judgment against Israel in the Book of the Twelve. [Condemning Sacrifice in the Book of the Twelve] YHWH takes no delight in these sacrifices, and since the purpose of sacrifice was to appease YHWH, this statement renders sacrifice nothing but a ritual of brutality.

The punishment announced in 8:13 also plays off the connotations of YHWH's giving of the law. Since 8:13 refers to the giving of the law(s), the punishment announces Israel's return to the point before they received the law: Israel will return to Egypt. The implications are clear. Israel will not return to commemorate the exodus experience. Since Israel wants to behave as though the covenant stipulations do not apply, YHWH announces they will return to Egypt: the symbolic place of slavery and oppression.

Building on the political implication of the punishment of 8:13, Hosea 8:14 offers a clear signal that the literary horizon of this passage does not merely focus on the immediate context. Since the text has already accused Ephraim of ignoring YHWH's law (8:1, 12) and covenant (8:12), the first line of 8:14 summarizes the current state of the relationship between YHWH and Israel: Israel has forgotten its maker. The accusation is then concretized for *both* Israel and Judah, implying that they think they can rely upon their own strength. Hosea 8:14 charges that Israel has built *hêkâlôt*, a word that can refer to any large building but usually means a royal palace or a temple. Either meaning of *hêkâlôt* fits the context since Hosea 8 deals with improper worship and illegitimate kings. Israel built permanent homes for its illegitimate kings, and it multiplied temples at the expense of worship in the one place YHWH has chosen (Jerusalem). In all likelihood, this perspective reflects the editorial interests of those transmitting Hosea in Judah after the lifetime of the prophet.[3]

### Condemning Sacrifice in the Book of the Twelve

YHWH promises punishment for illicit sacrifice. The condemnation of improper sacrifice is a recurring motif in the Book of the Twelve. The importance of this motif should not be overlooked as it plays a pivotal role in the pronouncement of judgment upon God's people in Hosea, Amos, Micah, and to some extent in Zephaniah (Amos 4:4-5; 5:21-27; Mic 6:6-8; Mal 1:6-14; 3:3b-4,10-12; see also Zeph 1:4). After the restoration of the temple and the repentance of the people (see Zech 1:2-6; the visions of 1:7-6:14; 7:1-7; 8:18-19), YHWH again demonstrates a willingness to forgive. Thus, when Malachi charges a return to improper sacrifice, the cycle of judgment begins anew, essentially returning to where the problems began in the Book of the Twelve.

The second line of 8:14 is surprising in that it accuses *Judah* of building fortified cities. This condemnation stands out because Judah has not appeared in the charges leveled against Ephraim/Israel in Hosea 7–8. Specifically, Judah has not been mentioned since 6:11, nor does Hosea elsewhere criticize Judah for expanding its fortified cities. It seems likely then, that this surprising charge comes from elsewhere. But where? Likely, the charge stems from reflection upon historical tradition and other parts of the Twelve. The Hezekiah narratives associate the end of the eighth century with the Sennacherib invasion of Judah. These narratives relay how *Jerusalem* was miraculously saved, but they also note that the *fortified cities* of Judah were not so fortunate (2 Kgs 18:13 = Isa 36:1; 2 Kgs 19:25 = Isa 37:20). Moreover, another verse in the Book of Four, Zeph 1:16, anticipates judgment on Judah as the day of YHWH that will come against its fortified cities. [Hosea 8:14 and the Book of the Twelve]

**Hosea 8:14 and the Book of the Twelve**

In the Book of the Twelve, Zephaniah is the last writing set before the destruction of Judah. The condemnation of Judah for building these cities also links to a critique of the pride of Judah—a motif that appears in Hos 5:5 and Amos 6:8; 8:7. Amos 6:8 is particularly striking. It connects the pride of Jacob/Zion (see Amos 6:1) with destruction of its citadels (see also Mic 5:4 [MT 5:5]). Moreover, connections to Amos stand out even more clearly when one notes that the concluding portion of Hos 8:14 pronounces judgment on Israel by citing one of the refrains from the oracles against the nations in Amos: "I will send fire upon his cities and it will devour its citadels." (See Amos 1:4 [Syria], 6 [Philistia], 9 [Tyre], 14 [Ammon]; 2:2 [Moab], 4 [Judah]—notably, Israel is not included.) In short, Hos 8:14 reinforces the accusations and punishments within Hos 8 by evoking the broader meta-narrative context— namely, the ongoing story of the fate of Judah and Israel—against which editors of the Book of the Twelve want the words of Hos 8 to be heard.

# CONNECTIONS

Two issues related to this chapter stand out as areas for reflection: the theme of Israel's disobedience and the connections of this chapter to the broader literary transmissions of the Old Testament. Both elements help one understand the function of Hosea in the development of the multivolume corpus. First, the theme of this chapter is not new to Hosea 8. Repeatedly, the problematic relationship between YHWH and Israel is explored in cultic and political terms. While these realms are to some degree separate, the problems are in many ways the same. Israel's kings, like Israel's worshiping community, refuse to see (or are unable to comprehend) their own need of YHWH. Its kings have no meaningful relationship to YHWH (8:4; cf. 7:3, 7). Its people may worship YHWH, but only on their own terms, and these terms are unacceptable to YHWH (8:4-6). Consequently, YHWH threatens Israel in an attempt to force the people to remember their covenant with YHWH (8:1). Throughout their history, according to the logic of the text, the kings of the northern kingdom used religion as a tool to separate the people of Israel from the people of Judah. They succeeded remarkably well at this according to the message of the book of Hosea (8:5-6) and Amos (7:10-17), to the point that Israel's identity as people of *YHWH* is seriously in jeopardy because they no longer serve YHWH in a form that is recognizable as such.

In the grand narrative of Kings, this negative attitude toward monarchs in general appears even before Samuel anoints Saul. The monarchy is portrayed as an ill-advised attempt to substitute human rulers for YHWH (see 1 Sam 8:4-18), which includes YHWH telling Samuel, "Listen to the voice of the people in all that they say to you; for they have not rejected you, but they have rejected me from being king over them" (1 Sam 8:7). This negative attitude becomes even more critical of the northern kingdom when Jeroboam I establishes an altar in two locations, Bethel and Dan, in what is portrayed as a blatant attempt to stop people in Israel from going to Judah to worship in Jerusalem (1 Kgs 12:26-30). Subsequent kings of the north continued these altars, which in the rhetoric of the Judean compiler of Kings meant that they perpetuated the "sins of Jeroboam." Castigation of these kings for accepting these altars creates an ongoing refrain throughout the remaining account of the northern kingdom (1 Kgs 14:16; 15:30; 16:31; 2 Kgs 10:29, 31; 13:2, 11; 14:24; 15:9, 18, 24, 28). The narration of the fall of the northern kingdom includes a long list of reasons for its destruction (2 Kgs 17:7-23), but the final element of this list refers the reader to the fundamental failure of its kings' influence on the people: "The people of Israel continued in all the sins that Jeroboam committed; they did not depart from them" (2 Kgs 17:22).

Unfortunately, parallels to our own time are all too easy to draw. Politicians are quick to state, or at least imply, that God is on *their* side, that no real person of faith could vote for the *other* candidate. Historically, the church has frequently had to relearn the lesson about how dangerous such alliances can be. Church leaders have often demonstrated far too much confidence in their own ability to determine the will of God in the political agendas of the respective parties. Hosea 8 offers a needed warning to distinguish carefully between the call of God and the all-too-human agendas of politicians. Political power is susceptible to corruption, greed, compromise, and convenience. God calls God's people into a covenant relationship in order to learn from God's instruction and to serve those around us. Often this call is at odds with the agendas of political parties. For example, the Black church tied its allegiance to the Democratic Party in the time of the civil rights movement, and that commitment has not infrequently required its pastors to support candidates whose position on social issues differed significantly from their own. Further, with the rise of "Christian" political movements like the Moral Majority of the 1980s and the "Christian Coalition" of the 1990s and early 2000s, many conservative (mostly white) Christians have mobilized over concerns about morality and values, but they were so closely aligned with the agenda of the Republican party that they were often unaware of how the moral rhetoric frequently served as little more than a rallying cry for electing politicians who were focused on other political and economic agendas. At the time of Hosea, the kings of Israel made sure the people could worship as the kings wanted (8:11-13), but allegiance to the king, or a political party, is not the same as worshiping God.

Further, the broader context of the issues addressed in 8:1-14 plays a significant role in understanding the literary and theological function of Hosea in the Book of the Twelve. Reflections on this long view regarding how one speaks of God's role in history belong to the task of theological reflection. The geographic terms used in this chapter (Israel, Samaria, and Ephraim) indicate that the accusations relate to the northern kingdom, not to a generic Israel. Further, these accusations coincide with charges in the Deuteronomistic History (Joshua–Judges, 1 Samuel–2 Kings) that Israel abandoned YHWH for the sake of idols. In Hosea 8, these accusations are preceded by a dire warning of the imminent threat posed by a foreign nation (Assyria) because Israel worshiped idols and followed political policies of their own making. In Hosea, this situation continues to deteriorate: YHWH struggles with the decision to punish Israel (see Hos 11:1-9) and leaves open the possibility that it will repent (14:1-8). Ultimately, however, the northern kingdom rejects YHWH's overtures and warnings (see Amos 4:4-12; 7:10-17). The same concerns will then take center stage for the southern kingdom in Micah. Judah will also receive punishment for its harlotry if it does not change (see 1:5-7). When it does not, Zephaniah pronounces a verdict against Judah and Jerusalem for its idolatry (Zeph 1:4). These two movements—i.e., the rejection of divine warning and the eventual destruction of both Israel and Judah—parallel one another in the Book of the Twelve in ways that are quite consistent with the emphases in the Deuteronomistic History. Israel rejects the warnings of Hosea, and this decision leads to its destruction in Amos. Judah rejects the warning of Micah, and this decision leads to Judah's destruction in Zephaniah. These ideas form the backbone in many respects of significant numbers of prophetic texts.

For modern communities of faith, these ideas create genuine difficulties that should not be ignored, even though they cannot be easily resolved. First, one should not equate ancient Israel or Judah with the modern political entities. Too often, preachers fall into these traps by talking about the United States as a "Christian nation chosen by God," or in some cases confusing the modern state of Israel with the biblical Israel. The former can lead to the assumption that God is on our side, and only our side. Political ideas like Manifest Destiny in the nineteenth century then become infused with religious language and can be used to support policies that are anything but Christian. By equating biblical Israel with the modern state created in 1948, certain Christian groups seek to influence political policy toward Israel because of eschatological convictions about rebuilding the temple in Jerusalem. Neither of these hermeneutical modes reflects the genuine prophetic challenge of these texts. These texts are about commitment to religious fidelity, justice, and mercy. They warn believers about dangers associated with equating political entities with faith communities. They seek a change of behavior on the part of readers; they do not tell faith communities to become political action groups.

## NOTES

1. See 1 Kgs 12:32; 13:33, 34; 14:1, 2, 4-7, 10, 11, 13, 14, 16, 17,19, 20, 30; 15:1, 6, 7, 9, 25, 29, 30, 34; 1 Kgs 16:2, 3, 7, 19; 16:26, 31; 21:22; 22:52; 2 Kgs 3:3; 9:9; 10:29; 10:31; 13:2, 6, 11, 13; 14:16, 2, 24, 27-29; 15:1, 8, 9, 18, 24, 28, 17:21, 22; 23:15.

2. For discussion of this idea, see commentary on Hos 8:4-5.

3. For discussion of how this verse fits in the redactional history of Hosea and Amos together, see Aaron Schart, *Die Entstehung des Zwölfprophetenbuch: Neubearbeitungen von Amos im Rahmen schriftenübergreifender Redaktionsprozesse*

(BZAW 260; Berlin: De Gruyter, 1998) 153–55. Jeremias sees this verse as distinct from the remainder of Hos 8, and argues convincingly that it results from reading Hosea with the themes of Amos in mind. See Jörg Jeremias, "Die Anfänge des Dodekapropheton: Hosea und Amos," in *Hosea und Amos* (FAT 13; Tübingen: Mohr Siebeck, 1995) 39–41.

# A THEMATIC TAPESTRY OF JUDGMENT

## Hosea 9:1-17

## COMMENTARY

Rhetorically, Hosea 9:1-17 provides a pastiche of confrontational sayings with frequently changing stylistic references to Israel. These confrontations convey images that overwhelm the reader with a collage of Israel/Ephraim's corruption, YHWH's righteous anger, and the impending punishment of Israel. The punishment includes threats of military destruction, infanticide, and exile. Thematic overlap plays a significant role in the editorial logic. Clear division of the units is hard to determine, but three groupings emerge because of their internal thematic and lexical ties: 9:1-6, 7-9, 10-17. The first two consistently presume a prophetic speaker. They focus upon improper sacrifice (9:1-6) and corruption (9:7-9). The third thematic section (9:10-17), however, contains a YHWH speech that is twice interrupted by a prophetic response (9:14, 17) and moves three times *from* a botanical metaphor of a healthy/unhealthy tree *to* a punishment related to the death of children.

### Improper Sacrifice Leads to Exile, 9:1-6

Rhetorically, two motifs appear in both 9:1-3 and 9:4-6: the impropriety of Israel's sacrifices and the impending exile to punish Israel's ongoing apostasy. Hosea 9:1-3 draws upon the image of harlotry so prominent in Hosea 1–3 in order to condemn Israel's sacrifices to other gods, while 9:4-6 focuses more on the political dimensions.

Hosea 9:1 begins with a warning to Israel not to rejoice or exult. These verbs are typically associated with cultic celebrations, where festive activities (often associated with the fall harvest) provide a setting in which Israel would normally be called to "rejoice and exult." By reversing this call, 9:1 adds an ominous tone to what the people otherwise would have expected to be a celebration. In Hosea's metaphorical domain, the harlot's pay given on the threshing floor implies that the grain is used to worship other gods.

Hosea 9:2-3 warns of a different scenario. The threshing floor and the wine vat will not feed the people, and there will be no new wine. "Wine press" and "threshing floor" comprise a word pair that occurs elsewhere in the Book of the Twelve. [Wine Vat and Threshing Floor in the Book of the Twelve] The threat is clear that the harvest will not be sufficient to provide for the people, threatening their survival as well as their idolatrous worship. Without grain, with no wine in the vat, and with no new wine, there is little hope that the circumstances will change in the immediate future. At first, this statement merely sounds like the prediction of crop failure, except that 9:3 immediately moves to a pronouncement of *exile*, not famine. Hosea 9:3 anticipates exile for Israel, describing that exile as a single event ("they shall not remain in the land") wherein Israel will return to Egypt and eat unclean food in Assyria. [Exile and Its Theological Function] This event equates the exile to Assyria with the reversal of the exodus. Poetically this imagery depicts punishment on Israel as a return to slavery, but this time as slaves in Assyria.

Albeit from a different perspective than 9:1-3, Hosea 9:4-6 reiterates the problem of offering sacrifice (9:4-5) and the consequences of exile (9:6). Hosea 9:4-5 focuses upon Israel's *inability* to offer sacrifice properly. In this

### Wine Vat and Threshing Floor in the Book of the Twelve

"Wine press" and "threshing floor" comprise a word pair that occurs elsewhere: Num 18:27, 30; Deut 15:14; 16:13; 2 Kgs 6:27. In the Book of the Twelve, the pair also appears in Joel 2:24 and Hag 2:16. The reversal of the threat images in Hos 9:1-2 seems to influence the formulation of restoration promised in Joel 2:23-25. (See the discussion in Joel 2:23. See also the discussion of the harlot's hire in Mic 1:7.) The harvesting of grain involved threshing and winnowing.

In the picture above, one sees an ox threshing corn with a sled-like contraption in modern Egypt. Nile Valley, Egypt. (Credit: Erich Lessing/Art Resource, NY)

In the picture to the right, the man winnows the grain (i.e., throws it into the air to separate the chaff from the grain). Luxor region. Luxor, Thebes, Egypt. (Credit: Erich Lessing/Art Resource, NY)

respect, it presumes a situation different than 9:2-3 (which *anticipated* the unavailability of wine and grain). By contrast, Hosea 9:4-5 does not address a situation in which the elements of sacrifice are lacking. Instead, YHWH refuses to accept them. The people are *commanded not* to pour drink offerings of wine to YHWH, and the sacrifice will not please God. In fact, their sacrifices will be treated by God as funerary bread: unclean and unfit to offer as a sacrifice to the living God. Hosea 9:4 is interpreted in light of 9:3, with the assumption that the people will be in exile, meaning that no food can be properly prepared as a sacrifice by those living in a foreign land. The bread of the exiles will not be good for anything except stopping hunger. It cannot be brought to the temple of YHWH. YHWH's refusal to accept sacrifice means that cultic celebrations will also be ritually impossible, a point driven home by the rhetorical question of Hosea 9:5: "What will you do on the day of appointed festival, and on the day of the festival of the LORD?"

Hosea 9:6 returns to the theme of exile, but this time the place of exile is presumed to be Egypt, not Assyria as in 9:3. The mention of Egypt and its long-time capital Memphis

**Exile and Its Theological Function**

The experience of exile radically reshaped the identity of Judah. While the destruction of Samaria and Jerusalem was devastating, in the aftermath of these events, faith communities developed a stronger sense of who they were and who they should become. The events of 587 (Jerusalem's destruction) were linked with the events of 722 (Samaria's destruction) as God's punishment of Israel and warning to Judah (see discussion of Mic 1:2-7 in this commentary). These discussions were likely fueled by refugees who came to Jerusalem in the aftermath of Samaria's destruction. Jerusalem's destruction was conceptualized as YHWH's punishment for failure to heed this warning. Exile, then, was seen as part of the plan YHWH was developing to reshape Judah and Israel as a faithful people before returning them to the land. These ideas became the primary way in which the exile was theologized. At various points along the way, the collection of prophetic texts indicates a sense that the end of punishment was just around the corner. Some texts reflect the need to rebuild ruined cities (see Amos 9:11-15) and others anticipate an imminent return (e.g., Isa 40–55). Later texts continue to adopt this critique of Israel's and Judah's past as the reason for ongoing punishment "since the time of the kings of Assyria until today" (Neh 9:32) that resulted in oppression, even as they appeal to YHWH to remove this punishment. Hos 9:3 illustrates an important part of this ongoing dialogue whereby the exile of Ephraim (the northern kingdom) is understood as the work of YHWH rather than as the result of Assyrian military expansionism. See also Isa 10:5-11.

See Brad Kelle, *Ancient Israel at War 853–586* (Essential Histories; Oxford: Osprey House, 2007) 66–68, 81–85. Kelle indicates that two groups—the larger group who remained in Judah and the smaller, more influential group exiled to Babylon—were both radically affected. Some of the statements he makes about which books were produced in Babylon and which were produced in Judah (perhaps at Mizpah), are debated, but his description of the general characteristics of these groups generally ring true. For a different understanding of the literary developments, see Rainer Albertz, *A History of Israelite Religion in the Old Testament Period. Volume II: From the Exile to the Maccabees* (trans. John Bowden [Louisville: Westminster John Knox, 1994] 388–90).

implies that these verses address a group that has avoided exile to Assyria and escaped to Egypt. However, the repercussions of their escape offer little solace, since the exiles will die there (Egypt/Memphis will gather/bury them) and the holy items and places they left behind will be overrun with vegetation

**Catchwords in Hosea 9:7-9**

AΩ

9:7 Punishment (root פקד)                    A
  9:7 Prophet                                B
    9:7 Iniquity and Hostility              C
  9:8 Prophet                                B'
    9:8-9 Hostility and Iniquity            C'
9:9 Punish (root פקד)                        A'

(nettles/thorns will possess their silver/tents). Thus, 9:4-6 implies that for those who are removed from their land, cultic worship will disappear.

## The Days of Punishment, 9:7-9

Hosea 9:7-9 is a denunciation of prophetic corruption linked together with a series of repeating verbal connectors. [Catchwords in Hosea 9:7-9] References to the prophet in 9:7 are interpreted variously. Some see this reference as a quote of what Israel is saying about the prophet, meaning that 9:7 portrays Israel as rejecting Hosea.[1] Others see the condemnation of the prophet in 9:7 as the prophet's rejection of Israel's prophets.[2] Elsewhere in Hosea, prophets are seen as both part of the problem (4:5) and as part of God's repeated attempts to warn Israel (6:5; 12:11, 14).

Given other places in Hosea that admonish religious and political leaders and the fact that the immediate context is focusing upon current problems, references to a "prophet" in 9:7-8 more likely presume the corruption of Israel's prophets, not Israel's rejection of Hosea.

Hosea 9:7-9 presents a consistent message: judgment is imminent because Israel refuses to listen. Hosea 9:7 begins by proclaiming that the "days of punishment" and the "days of recompense" have come. Both terms imply that an extended period of judgment is imminent because of the actions of the people. A text-critical debate exists concerning how to understand the transitional phrase connecting the first and second halves of the verse, but there is no reason to emend the text as some translations do. [Text-critical Debate on Hosea 9:7] One should, therefore, read "Israel knows." God quotes Israel in the latter part of the verse, ironically articulating Israel's reasons for rejecting the prophet(s) as the inane babbling of a madman. [Rejecting the Prophet(s) in the Book of the Twelve] The point is clear: Israel has rejected those whose message comes

**Text-critical Debate on Hosea 9:7**

AΩ This verse has a text-critical problem. The NRSV, and others, have "Israel cries" but MT has "Israel knows" (*yēdʿû*). The LXX (*kakōthēsetai*) presumes the verbal root *rʿ* ("to make" / "cause distress"); with the consonantal form of *yērʿû* ("they are evil"), the LXX would require only the graphic confusion of a *resh* and *dalet*. The meaning of "Israel is wicked," however, is about as syntactically awkward as "Israel knows." The NRSV translates "they know" as "they cry," emending to the rarely attested root, *rwʿ*, "to give a thundering cry." In Hebrew, the verb "to know" can also imply knowledge that one expresses. Therefore, one can follow MT "Israel *knows*, 'the prophet is a fool, the man of the Spirit is mad.'"

**Rejecting the Prophet(s) in the Book of the Twelve**

The motif of rejecting the prophet occurs in the Book of the Twelve explicitly and implicitly. The rejection of prophets becomes an explicit point of condemnation in Amos 7:10-17 and Zech 13:2-5. In the former, the people and the religious establishment (in the person of Amaziah) reject God's true prophet. In the latter, YHWH rejects Israel's (false) prophets. Implicitly, the rejection of God's message through the prophets is also part of the fiber of the ongoing "plot" of the Book of the Twelve. Ignoring the warnings from YHWH's prophets leaves God no choice but to bring judgment on the people.

from YHWH, and there are consequences for that rejection.

Hosea 9:8 defends the prophetic role using the metaphor of a sentinel, whose job is to warn Israel of danger. The verse continues the thought from 9:7 by explaining that a prophet should be a sentinel. [Modern Translations of 9:8] The images in 9:8 utilize catchwords from 9:7, and this link sheds interpretive light on the image of the sentinel. [Parallel Catchwords in Hosea 9:7b, 8] The two verses are not only closely interconnected but also contrast the actions of God's prophets with the reactions of God's people, who treat the prophets as madmen. The quote from Israel in 9:7 contrasts with the quote about the prophet in 9:8 where "hostility" is directed toward God's prophet in God's house. Note the word play on Bethel (which means "house of God") and the reference to the hostility in the "house of *his* (Ephraim's) God." The guilt of the people (9:7) parallels the "fowler's snare" (9:8), set to trap Ephraim. In the metaphor of 9:8, hostility against the prophet is the snare that convicts the people, but they are threatening the sentinel rather than paying attention.

Hosea 9:9 compares the actions of the people with the despicable actions of the tribe of Benjamin from the time of the judges. [Gibeah] God will punish Israel, just as God punished Gibeah and the Benjaminites. The concluding line of 9:9 summarizes the punishment of the people of Hosea's generation, tying "their iniquity" back to the iniquity of the people in 9:7.

**Modern Translations of 9:8**

AΩ "Watchman" (NRSV, *sentinel*) is used elsewhere in late pre-exilic and exilic texts to refer to the prophet's task (Isa 52:8; 56:10; Jer 6:17; Ezek 3:17; 33:6-7; see also *piel* forms in Mic 7:7; Hab 2:1; Isa 21:6). The syntax of 9:8, however, is complicated by the question, to which part of the verse does "sentinel" refer? Several suggestions for interpretation or emendation have been offered, as illustrated by modern translations.

MT (no verb)
Ephraim (is *to be?*) a watchman with my God;
A prophet (is) a fowler's snare on all his ways; hostility (is) in the house of his God.

NRSV: The prophet is a sentinel for my God over Ephraim.
NIV: The prophet, along with my God, is a watchman over Ephraim
NAS: Ephraim *was* a watchman with my God, a prophet.
KJV: The watchman of Ephraim was with my God: but the prophet is a snare of a fowler in all his ways, and hatred in the house of his God

**Parallel Catchwords in Hosea 9:7b, 8**

AΩ

9:7b The **prophet** is a fool, the man of the spirit is mad! Because of your great iniquity, your **hostility** is great.

9:8 The **prophet** is a sentinel for my God over Ephraim, yet a fowler's snare is on all his ways, and **hostility** in the house of his God.

**Gibeah**

The verse compares the actions of Ephraim to the "days of Gibeah." The days of Gibeah refer to the story conveyed in Judg 19–21, the story of the brutal rape and murder of the Levite's concubine at the hands of men of Gibeah in the region of Benjamin. The perversity of the gang at Gibeah offers a pointed comparison to those who oppose the mission of the prophet of God. Yet the perversity of the gang at Gibeah was matched by the tribe of Benjamin who refused to punish them, even though the Benjaminites had not participated in the act itself.

### Where Israel Went Wrong, 9:10-17

This thematic unit contains two divine speeches (9:10-13, 15-16) and two prophetic responses to those speeches (9:14, 17). The resulting subunits, 9:10-14, 15-17, may reflect units that were originally independent but were at some point edited together because of their thematic similarity. Three times these verses compare Israel to a tree (9:10, 13, 16) in a manner that castigates the people of the prophet's time. Each time, the punishment of Israel culminates in the death of its children (9:11-12, 14, 16).

Hosea 9:10 compares YHWH's early encounters with Israel to life-sustaining fruit: grapes and figs. First, YHWH claims Israel was once succulent, like grapes in the wilderness. This imagery, perhaps, plays off the well-known metaphor of Israel as a vineyard (see Isa 5), but even if not, the idea is clear. Finding succulent fruit "in the wilderness" would be a welcome sight indeed. In addition, the first fruit of the fig tree (which bears its fruit in August) is another sign of the pleasing nature of Israel to God when he first found/discovered Israel. This pleasure contrasts with Israel's actions in the second part of the verse and (implicitly) with the prophet's audience. Reference to the fathers/ancestors alludes to the generation of the exodus, as noted by the reference to the incident at Baal-peor, which is recounted in Numbers 25. [Baal-peor] Hence the term "wilderness" *and* the incident of "Baal-peor" evoke traditions associated with the wilderness wanderings. However, they also intimate that the issue being condemned in this context is the incorporation of sexual rites into the religious practices of Israel.

**Baal-peor**

Num 25 recounts how the Israelites join in the worship of a local Moabite god, Baal-peor, through the sexual union of worshipers. The extent to which this "worship" angered YHWH can be seen in the large number (24,000) of Israelites the story claims die from the ensuing plague (Num 25:9).

Whereas YHWH punished Israel with a plague in the Baal-peor narrative, YHWH will punish Ephraim in Hosea 9:11-12 with infertility and the loss of its children. The word "glory" here means reputation, or honor, of the northern kingdom that will vanish quickly. The remaining portions of 9:11 tie this loss of glory to a lack of human procreation. Verse 12 adds additional threats. Hosea 9:11implies that no children will be born, while 9:12 assumes that some will be born, but that they too will still suffer the effects of YHWH's punishment. The final statement summarizes the judgment: woe (suffering) will befall them when YHWH departs.

In Hosea 9:13-14, the thematic combination of a tree metaphor and the loss of children appears a second time. In 9:13, YHWH reminisces about the early days of Ephraim. The precise meaning of 9:13a is unclear, although there is little doubt that Ephraim is compared to something planted in a field. [Something Planted in a Field] At any rate, this botanical metaphor is followed by a prophetic response, one in which the prophet addresses Yahweh directly, apparently imploring YHWH to punish Ephraim with miscarriages and a lack of breast milk. Whereas 9:11 promised no conception, the prophet's response calls for Ephraim's children to be stillborn or born to mothers who are unable to feed them. The prophet thus calls for a harsh punishment upon his own people, and sets up a dramatic contrast between the idyllic youth of Ephraim and the terrifying time of punishment come.

Hosea 9:15-17 begins with a divine speech (9:15-16) that is punctuated by a prophetic response (9:17). In Hosea 9:15-16, YHWH rejects the prestigious city of Gilgal (9:15), and for a third time combines the metaphor of Ephraim as a tree (this time one that is not healthy) with punishment of the loss of children (9:16). Given Gilgal's prominence in the northern kingdom as a prestigious worship site from Israel's early traditions (see discussion of Hos 4:15), YHWH's denunciation of Gilgal and its religious practices in Hosea 9:15 appear radically confrontational. The site has become anathema to YHWH because of its religious practices, so much so that YHWH uses the strong word, hate (*šānēʾ*). [YHWH Hates] The idea of YHWH hating is uncomfortable for some, but it is better to acknowledge this discomfort theologically than to tone down the meaning of the word "hate" in Hebrew as many have tried. YHWH's actions demonstrate an aversion to Gilgal by promising to "drive them from my house" and by stating YHWH will no longer love them. In

**Something Planted in a Field**

AΩ The NRSV translates the word *ṣōr* as corrupt and renders it a "young palm," whereas the MT appears to draw a comparison to the city of Tyre, a coastal city, transplanted to a pasture. The difficulty with the imagery has to do with what is planted.

**YHWH Hates**

To "hate" in Hebrew exhibits a strong emotional aversion to someone or something, though not necessarily resulting in wicked action toward that person/thing. It is located in the heart (Lev 19:17) or the being (*nefesh*, 2 Sam 5:8; Ps 11:5). The emotive reaction usually implies emotional aversion to the object of hatred (Gen 29:31, 33: Jacob hates Leah, though still has conjugal relations with her). Hatred, however, is not an excuse for murder or a reason for lessening a charge of murder to manslaughter (Num 35:20). A significant number of texts ascribe hatred of things or people to YHWH, including erection of cultic pillars for worship (Deut 16:22); religious practices of the nations in the land (Deut 12:31); Israel's own hypocritical worship (Isa 1:14; Amos 5:21); false oaths (Zech 8:17); and kingship established at Gilgal (1 Sam 11:14). Like human hatred, YHWH's hate results in withdrawal and aversion (Jer 12:7-8). See also the wisdom list of seven things YHWH hates in Prov 6:16-19: haughtiness, lying, bloodshed, wicked plans, turning to evil, false witness, one who sows contention. In some ways, hate can be a virtue when it is directed toward something to be avoided: evil (Ps 97:10), falsehood (Ps 119:163), arrogance (Prov 8:13).

essence, YHWH repudiates Gilgal in language reminiscent of divorce. The reference to "my house" does not refer to a particular temple here. Rather, the reference to "driving them from my house" should merely be heard in the context of a husband divorcing his wife. Regardless, the combination of the verb "hate" with the statement "I will no longer love" is consistent with divorce language.

Hosea 9:16 describes Ephraim as a withered tree whose root is stricken so that it is no longer able to bear fruit. This metaphor assumes that Ephraim's fruit is its children. The second half of the verse, however, makes this connection explicit when YHWH states his intention to kill any children who are unfortunate enough to be born to Ephraim. This passage expresses God's anger in the strongest terms possible and evokes images of a powerful, angry God whose anger will not easily be assuaged.

In Hosea 9:17, the prophet pronounces what amounts to a malediction by summarizing the reason, the decision, and the consequence of YHWH's action in Hosea 9. The prophet says that the reason God has acted in anger is that people have ceased listening. Hence, YHWH has decided to reject them, and as a consequence they will be forced from the land and will "wander among the nations." Dealing with metaphors of divine hatred and anger, as well as the violence associated with that anger, is an important aspect of understanding prophetic literature.

## CONNECTIONS

Several issues converge around this text and its application, including (1) the threat of exile, (2) failure of the prophets, (3) reference to an idealized past as a rhetorical strategy, (4) the image of an angry God, and (5) observations on application of judgment texts.

(1) Rarely does one pause to consider what it means to be sent into exile. It is difficult in our day to contemplate the fear created by the thought of relocation for those living in ancient Israel. In modern times, families move regularly because of jobs, schooling, or other reasons. Often, when we ask people where they are from, we can detect a pregnant pause while they try to determine where they call "home." The reason for this pause is simply that modern

Western society does not generate a sense of being rooted in a place. In ancient times, however, the kind of relocation threatened in this passage and elsewhere would have evoked considerably more trepidation for two reasons. First, people in the ancient world were more than a little fearful of travel. For most people, vacations simply did not exist, and the world beyond one's village was not a welcoming place. Second, forced relocation did not represent a move toward opportunities. It threatened to upend the entire world as known by the people of that time. So, rather than describing the brutal and horrific battle or the long and tortuous march, the relocation described by the prophet focuses upon what they will lose: their God and their land. They will no longer be able to offer sacrifice, the most visible means of expressing their relationship to God, and the land they call home will revert to an inhospitable region suitable only for growing thorns and thistles. For the prophet, the days of punishment are near, and these images emphasize what is at stake. Life as Israel had known it would cease because of God's revulsion to their behavior.

(2) This text highlights the failure of the prophets of Israel. It depicts the role of the prophet as a watchman over the people, but the prophets of Israel, according to this passage, have failed to recognize the danger at hand or have failed to convince the people anything was wrong. Moreover, the place of worship becomes a place of hostility, and the proclaimers of God's word are treated as fools and madmen. This text warns of a real danger that has faced God's gathered people across the ages: ridiculing those who call them to task when they go astray. Whether the words come from the mouth of a prophet, the actions of Jesus overturning the tables in the temple, Martin Luther's nailing the 95 theses to the door of the church, or Martin Luther King's call to the church for justice, worship communities everywhere and in every age run the risk of losing sight of their purpose. In thesis 27, Martin Luther condemned priests who sold indulgences for money, telling their congregants they would be released from purgatory sooner if they paid more money: "They preach man who say that so soon as the penny jingles into the money-box, the soul flies out [of purgatory]." Martin Luther King, Jr., wrote these words to the church in 1963:

I have heard numerous southern religious leaders admonish their worshipers to comply with a desegregation decision because it is the law, but I have longed to hear white ministers declare: "Follow this decree because integration is morally right and because the Negro is your brother." In the midst of blatant injustices inflicted upon the Negro, I have watched white churchmen stand on the sideline and mouth pious irrelevancies and sanctimonious trivialities. In the midst of a mighty struggle to rid our nation of racial and economic injustice, I have heard many ministers say: "Those are social issues, with which the gospel has no real concern." And I have watched many churches commit themselves to a completely other worldly religion which makes a strange, un-biblical distinction between body and soul, between the sacred and the secular.[3]

The object of worship is God, and the focus of ministry is service in the name of God. When something other than God becomes the focus of worship, or when the focus of ministry is something other than service in the name of God, then God's people need someone to call them back to the right path again. For this reason, God has called prophets to address God's people throughout the ages. Usually these prophets encounter resistance. They may be ostracized or punished, but when they come with a genuine word from God, God's people should pause to hear, to look at their actions individually and collectively, and to acknowledge that they have gone astray.

(3) This passage, along with others in Hosea, evaluates Hosea's generation of Israel with an idealized portrait of the Israel of the past, one that never existed according to the biblical traditions. From the time Israel left Egypt, they began to grumble against God. They set up a golden calf to worship. Israel wandered in the wilderness for forty years because of the people's failure to obey God. Once in the land, they continually turned their backs on God (Judges), and they rejected God as king in favor of human kings (1 Sam 8:4-8).

This rhetorical strategy appears frequently in public discourse today, whether religious, familial, or political. Moralistic speakers are prone to portray earlier times in the life of the family, the nation, or the church as somehow being more in touch with God's expectations. One need only read the editorial pages of denominational newspapers or the resolutions of church conferences from the 1880s, the 1920s, or 1960s to see that the same phenomenon has remained popular through the ages.[4] Perhaps it plays on a deep-seated human desire to live up to the goals and ideals our parents tried to teach us. Yet, if we are honest, our parents' and grandparents' generations struggled with most of the same issues with which we struggle. Only the externals have changed. Parents of an earlier generation complained about the degeneration of youth because they wore bell-bottom jeans and grew hair down to their shoulders. Now parents of this generation look aghast at their children's baggy pants and tattoos. Every generation faces challenges, dangers, and fears. Every generation faces choices about whether and how to live responsibly, live religiously, and live dynamically. Dangerous threats come from many directions, but they always have. These threats can result from our actions, the actions of others, or random events in an imperfect world. In the end, however, how we choose to respond to these events reflects the real character of our faith.

(4) This text portrays the image of an angry God. YHWH charges the people with idolatry and threatens to have them deported. God refuses to accept the offerings of the people because those offerings are tainted. The image of God in this text is a far cry from the syrupy sweet figure depicted in many pulpits across the United States. What does one do theologically with the language of divine hatred and violence? Julia M. O'Brien offers helpful reflections on this troubling topic, but she does not offer easy answers.[5] First, she acknowledges that biblical texts depicting the wrath of God are not limited to the prophetic corpus. Violent metaphors like the Divine Warrior permeate Scripture from the stories of Sodom and Gomorrah in Genesis to the apocalyptic judgment of Revelation. Anyone dealing with biblical texts seriously will encounter claims regarding the wrath of God. Second, a fair reading of the way this language functions in prophetic texts should acknowledge the heuristic value of the frame from which these texts proceed. Namely, texts drawing upon images of divine violence almost universally draw upon this language to portray YHWH as *responding* to some circumstance where unrighteousness or injustice have taken hold. In the logic of the text, it is this problem that rouses anger in YHWH, and YHWH's anger is directed at those perpetuating injustice or breaking covenant promises. In the case of the Divine Warrior, O'Brien points out, YHWH's vengeance is generally directed toward the enemies of Israel and Judah. One should add, however, that similar reactions can be invoked against YHWH's own people, as in Hosea 9, in

response to cultic transgressions. Third, modern responses to these violent images often reflect visceral reactions to either the cause or the effect of this wrath on the part of modern interpreters themselves. Those who justify the portrayal of God in these texts emphasize the injustice that created the response, while those who recoil in horror at these violent images focus largely upon the outcome of YHWH's response (i.e., human suffering). Fourth, O'Brien notes that modern responses to human anger offer a way to reconfigure the problem. Modern discussions of anger fall into at least four categories: (1) anger is a manageable human response; (2) anger is a moral failing to be eradicated; (3) anger can result from righteous indignation and motivate justice; and (4) anger can be used to diagnose our own values. The third and fourth responses play a more prominent role in discussions of divine anger.

O'Brien reminds readers not to discount the human elements of these texts. Psychologists note that anger frequently points to triggers in our own lives, and thus says as much or more about how we evaluate a situation. In the case of prophetic texts that speak of divine anger, God reacts to human betrayal and acts of injustice. Prophets testify of their experience of God, and these testimonies resonate with communities of faith. Nevertheless, the prophets, scribes, and communities of faith that preserved this testimony were all limited to some extent by the time and culture in which they lived. The same is true of us. Our culture, by and large, is not as quick as those in ancient Judah, for example, to assign random weather events to the direct intervention of God, especially since radar systems often allow us to predict both the presence and the path of storms. When the prophet in Hosea 9:14 calls upon YHWH to punish Ephraim with stillbirths and the inability to feed infants, and YHWH promises to do so in 9:16, one must wonder and wrestle with how much more this language says about the prophet's own trigger point than it says about God. From the prophet's perspective, Ephraim's betrayal of YHWH stirs a righteous indignation as powerful as anyone could imagine. That does not mean, however, that God actually did such a thing. Unfortunately, O'Brien does not let us off the hook that easily. She deftly reminds us that our own anger and discomfort with these images also says more about us than it proves about God.

(5) What message can a modern community of faith take from a passage like Hosea 9, with its harsh rhetoric and vitriolic God?

Applying this text does not mean adopting its forms, nor does it require a minister to match the heat of its rhetoric. Applying this text does not mean conveying the image of a God whose righteous character is always on the verge of suffering affront. Rather, applying this text means asking ourselves and our congregations what it means to accept the obligation of being God's people, and reminding ourselves that God is serious about our commitment.

## NOTES

1. For example, see Bruce C. Birch, *Hosea, Joel, and Amos* (Westminster Bible Companion; Louisville, Westminster John Knox, 1997) 86. See NRSV.

2. For example, see Marvin A. Sweeney, *The Twelve Prophets* (Berit Olam, vol. 1; Collegeville: Liturgical Press, 2000) 97. See NAS.

3. Martin Luther King, Jr., "Letter from Birmingham Jail," http://www.mlkonline.net/jail.html.

4. See also the arguments of Christian groups from the 1920s onward regarding the ways that the current generation has deteriorated as a result of movies. One example comes from a character in a short film produced by the film lobby to combat censorship in New York in 1920: "The motion picture is about fifteen years old. Sin is somewhat older than that, yet the censors would have us believe that it was not Satan but Thomas Alva Edison who invented 'The Fall of Man'" (Frank Walsh, *Sin and Censorship: The Catholic Church and the Motion Picture Industry* [New Haven: Yale University Press, 1996] 24).

5. Julia M. O'Brien, *Challenging Prophetic Metaphor: Theology and Ideology in the Prophets* (Louisville: Westminster John Knox, 2008) 101–24. While O'Brien's discussion of violence focuses upon the Divine Warrior motif, her observations extend well beyond the specifics of that motif to prophetic literature in general.

# AGRICULTURAL ADMONITIONS

## Hosea 10:1-15

## COMMENTARY

Hosea 10 divides into two parts delineated by the speakers: the prophet in 10:1-8 and YHWH in 10:9-15. Both sections cohere largely around dominant agricultural metaphors. Hosea 10:1-8 shares two unifying characteristics: the prophetic speaker and the use of agricultural metaphors to describe Israel and its fate. Similarly, Hosea 10:9-15 consistently exhibits a divine speaker and uses agricultural metaphors, though it is far less coherent as a unit because of it changing addressees. This larger composite unit continues the judgment of major sites to illustrate the pervasiveness of the sins of Ephraim. Whereas Hosea 9:15 refers to Gilgal, the first place of encampment in the land, 10:5 and 7 refer to Samaria (the capital), and 10:9 threatens Gibeah, the historic seat of Saul's power (cf. 1 Sam 11:4; 15:34).

### From Fertile Vine to Useless Weeds, 10:1-8

The prophetic speaker in Hosea 10:1-8 explores three images: comparing Israel to a vine that is rotting from within, even while it multiplies altars and pillars (10:1-2); comparing Israel's numerous oaths to weeds growing in the field that will destroy the country (10:3-6); and comparing Israel's coming punishment to thorns and thistles covering the site of the destroyed altar (10:7-8).

*Hosea 10:1-2.* Hosea 10:1 compares Israel to a fruit-producing vine, an analogy that appears elsewhere in the Old Testament, most notably Isaiah 5. [Vine/Vineyard] However, 10:1 deftly uses a double entendre in describing this vine as luxuriant. [Double Entendre] The irony in this comparison is that while the verse describes Israel as a fertile vine, the message of the larger context is that Israel will be laid waste.

## Vine/Vineyard

Victor Matthews demonstrates how the "vine" and "vineyard" play a powerful role in poetic metaphors in Israel and Judah. Matthews indicates that the topography of Israel distinguished it from Egypt in its ability to produce wine (22), and that the full extent of production techniques is more prominent in prophetic texts than is typically recognized (23). He demonstrates how knowledge of these techniques affects the reading of Isaiah 5 in particular. The vine also plays a role as a symbol of the land's fertility (Ps 80:8-11), and tending the vine was a reason to avoid military service (Deut 20:6), demonstrating the importance of the fruit to the economic fate of the country. Poetic texts use the vine as a symbol of peace (Mic 4:4; Zech 3:10; cf. Isa 36:16), and the prophets also use the vine's infertility as a symbol of judgment (Isa 32:10-14; 34:4; Joel 1:11-12).

Victor H. Matthews, "Treading the Winepress: Actual and Metaphorical Viticulture in the Ancient Near East," *Semeia* 86 (1999): 19–32.

## Double Entendre

AΩ The adjective translated "luxuriant" by the NRSV never has this positive connotation anywhere else in the Old Testament. The root *bqq* (which derives from an Arabic word) normally means "to lay waste," but because the context describes a vine that produces fruit, scholars have argued that the word in Hos 10:1 comes from another Arabic word with these same letters that means "plentiful." The two words could simply be an ironic double meaning.

## Altars and Pillars

Altars of the time could be hewn from stone like the one found at Beer-sheva in Judah pictured here from the eighth century. For a pillar, see Hos 3:4.

Reconstruction of an ancient Israelite horned altar (based upon the remnants of the original one) as it was used to sacrifice animals. The original altar was probably dismantled during the time of Hezekiah, the King of Judah, with the centralization of the Israelite cult in the temple of Jerusalem. Tel Be'er Sheva. (Credit: Gugganij, http://en.wikipedia.org/wiki/File:Tel_Be%27er_Sheva_Altar_2007041.JPG)

The latter part of 10:1 describes Israel's booming economic conditions that are about to end.[1] It correlates the increasing fertility of the land with the manifestation of misplaced religious devotion that, in the eyes of YHWH, indicates the people do not understand what they are doing. The building of altars and pillars implies actions taken to increase the number and size of the places of sacrifice. In other words, people are building places to offer sacrifices out of gratitude to the god whom they credit for this agricultural bounty. However, the god whom they credit, and to whom they build altars, is not YHWH.

Hosea 10:2 begins with a statement that flows from the action of 10:1: it denounces Israel's infidelity and pronounces the destruction of its many altars as punishment. In trying to worship multiple gods, Israel has failed to remember the first two commandments (see Exod 20:1-5). Thus, in the first phrase of 10:2, the prophet declares that Israel's heart is false. The word "false" comes from the root "to be smooth" and it can be used in the context of deceptive flattery, as in the phrase "smooth words" (Prov 2:16; 7:5). In these prophetic images, Israel plays the sycophant, saying whatever the context demands.

YHWH's destruction of Ephraim's altars plays an important role in Hosea 10:1-2, 8. [Destruction of Ephraim's Altars] The idea of bearing guilt reflects the widely held theological belief in a causal relationship between an action and its consequences: goodness produces God's beneficence while transgression brings retribution. Hosea 10:1 underscores Israel's disregard of the first two commandments: YHWH does not tolerate the worship of other gods or idols (Exod 20:3-5). The plural "altars" and "pillars" emphasizes the pervasiveness of Israel's sacrifice to false gods. In the immediate context, this punishment results directly from Ephraim's actions in 10:1. Israel has lost sight of the nature of its relationship to YHWH. Here the metaphor of the faithless spouse with which Hosea (see 1:2; 2:2-3, 7; 3:1) began takes concrete form. Israel ignores its covenant obligations with a God who expects fidelity.

*Hosea 10:3-6.* This unit moves from a disputation (10:3) to a quick dismissal of the people's objections (10:4) and finally to a pronouncement of the coming destruction of Bethel's calf (10:5-6). [Disputation] The verses are connected to the preceding verses by a formal transition ("for now") that denotes what follows (10:3-6, 7-8) as the concrete implications of the pronouncement that Israel must bear its guilt (10:2). Hosea 10:3-6 and 10:7-8 overlap thematically, twice combining motifs of the loss of Israel's king (10:3, 7) and the destruction of Bethel's calf (10:5-6, 8). Yet, it is not clear that the two sections belong together originally, since 10:3 presumes the loss of the king has already occurred, while 10:7 anticipates the destruction of the king.

Hosea 10:3 takes the form of a disputation in which the prophet introduces the words of the people in order to refute their position in the verses to follow. The quote from the people provides interesting insight into the prophet's understanding of the people's attitude. The situation presumes the people have heard a threat against the king (or an announcement that the king is dead). Yet, in

**Destruction of Ephraim's Altars**

This motif also plays a significant role in structuring the message of Amos to symbolize God's punishment of the northern kingdom (2:8; 3:14; 9:1). Especially noteworthy in this respect, Amos 9:1 culminates the vision cycle of Amos with a graphic description of the destruction of the altar at Bethel.

**Disputation**

A "disputation" bears some resemblance to a lawsuit (*rîb*) in that charges are addressed. Usually, the subtle differences are best described in the presumption of the setting and in the way the charges are stated. While in prophetic literature a lawsuit usually addresses the people, the charges in the lawsuit more often concern God's actions. Further, the setting of a trial speech usually connects more concretely to a juridical setting. Rhetorically, the disputation also usually connects to other forms. The most extensive use of the disputation in prophetic literature appears in the book of Malachi, where it structures most of that writing.

W. Eugene March, "Prophecy" in *Old Testament Form Criticism*, ed. John H. Hayes (San Antonio: Trinity University Press, 1974) 168.

the mind of the prophet, this news causes them no concern. They believe that they are self-sufficient and that their wealth (see 10:1) makes them invulnerable. More important, if they do not fear YHWH, why would they need a king?

In 10:4, the prophet refutes the prideful statement from 10:3. The translation of the NRSV, however, may be a little misleading, since the Hebrew can be translated in a number of ways. A more contextual translation could proceed as follows: "They speak words of vain curses, cutting off a covenant, and judgment blossoms like poison upon the furrows of the field." Most modern and ancient translations associate "covenant" with the vain curses. The NRSV is unusual in translating the Hebrew word *mispât* with "litigation," implying it refers to a lawsuit, when in the context of this speech it seems more likely that the word should be translated with the more common meaning, "judgment." In 10:4b, the swearing of oaths that mean nothing spreads the seed in the ground already plowed. The fruit of that seed is judgment.

Hosea 10:5 recounts the reactions of the people of Samaria at the news of the destruction of the calf at Bethel. Samaria could connote the capital city of the northern kingdom, or it could simply refer to the kingdom's central region. In either case, it ultimately symbolizes the country as a whole. The reference to Beth-Aven has already appeared as a derogatory term for Bethel (4:15; 5:8). Beth-Aven means "House of Injustice," while Bethel means "House of God." It was the site of one of the golden calves set up by Jeroboam I when Israel seceded from the Davidic empire (1 Kgs 12:25-33). Consequently, the people's mourning implies that the altar at Bethel has been destroyed. This shrine at Bethel was seen as one of Israel's distinguishing characteristics, so the statement that "its glory has departed" would have had roughly the same force as the pronouncement in Ezekiel 10:18 that the glory of YHWH had departed Jerusalem.

The term translated as "idolatrous priests" also casts aspersions upon the religious activity at Bethel. Worship at Bethel and Dan—the two sites of the calf shrines—was never deemed legitimate by those who recognized Jerusalem, the capital established by David, as the place that YHWH had chosen for the legitimate temple. The image of the priests impotently wailing over the destroyed calf stands in stark contrast to the image of 10:3, when the people so brazenly rejected YHWH as unable to offer them anything.

Hosea 10:6 describes the fate of the calf itself. Since the calf was made of gold, it would naturally capture the attention of the invading army of the regional superpower. Seizing local gods was also a common practice in ancient warfare. Thus, although no biblical text relates its fate, it is not hard to imagine that an invading army would have taken the golden calf. This verse describes the fate of that calf in ironic terms: while the calf at Bethel marked the place where offerings were brought to God, here the calf itself becomes an offering to the foreign king. Even the word used in 10:6, *minḥâ*, can refer to a gift, but it often connotes an offering in a religious context (Amos 5:22, 25). Described as Ephraim's glory in the previous verse, the calf is here pejoratively labeled an idol that brings shame to Israel.

**Calf Idols**

The worship of bull calves has a long history in Canaanite and early Israelite history. Old Testament tradition indicates that the worship of calves was an Israelite practice (see Exod 32; 1 Kgs 12:25-33).

Gold-plated bronze calf representing the animal form of the warrior god Resehf, or Baal. The prophets of Israel condemned the idolization of the "golden calf" and the Baal-cult. Byblos, Lebanon. Bronze and gold. Bronze Age. Louvre, Paris, France. (Credit: Erich Lessing/Art Resource, NY)

*Hosea 10:7-8.* These verses, like 10:1-2, 3-6, use a botanical metaphor to depict the consequences of God's judgment on Israel. Hosea 10:7-8 describes the loss of the king and the altar at Bethel. The syntax of Hosea 10:7 is rather awkward, but the sense is clear. Samaria will be silenced because its king was overwhelmed by a much greater power. The word translated as "chip" (NRSV) is interpreted as a twig or branch in some ancient translations, and as a wave in others. In any case, it pales beside the force of the entire ocean.

The denunciation of Israel's worship centers and practices resumes in 10:8, this time referring to them as the high places of Aven (i.e., "shame"). The phrase "high places of Aven" evokes the previous reference to Bethel (10:5), but the use of the plural emphasizes the problematic nature of Israel's worship, since worship on the high places connotes the worship of Baal or some other false deity. The images of thorn and thistle convey the extended period of judgment Israel will experience. The high places become lonely places; unused, they become covered with the vege-

### Hosea 10:8 and the Book of the Twelve

Hos 10:8 anticipates Mic 1:2-7, 3:12, where YHWH appears for judgment and that judgment is expressed in terms that parallel "high places" and "sin" (1:5). The reference to Samaria becoming overgrown with "thorn and thistle" also parallels the images in Mic 3:12, where Jerusalem's fate is similarly described. This motif reflects one of the common recurring elements in the early collection of Hosea, Amos, Micah, and Zephaniah. These four writings show a clear tendency to argue that the destruction of Samaria should have been a warning to Jerusalem and Judah. (See especially the discussions of Mic 1:2-7 and the discussion of "Current State of Redactional Discussions" in the opening chapter of this commentary, "Introduction to the Book of the Twelve." See also James D. Nogalski, "One Book and Twelve Books: The Nature of the Redactional Work and the Implications of Cultic Source Material in the Book of the Twelve," in *Two Sides of a Coin: Juxtaposing Views on Interpreting the Book of the Twelve/the Twelve Prophetic Books* [Analecta Gorgiana 201; Piscataway NJ: Gorgias Press, 2009] 11–50).

tation of the forest, like kudzu on an abandoned automobile. This verse connects to motifs elsewhere in the Book of the Twelve as part of a larger focus on the fate of the northern kingdom used as a warning to Jerusalem. [Hosea 10:8 and the Book of the Twelve] The last part of the verse depicts the shame of this destruction. Metaphorically, the situation will cause the altars to cry out to the mountains and the hills to cover them over.

### Fuming about Farming, 10:9-15

The remaining verses of this chapter presume YHWH as the speaker, marked by first person pronouns in 10:10, 11. However, the pronouns used to refer to Israel fluctuate markedly: second masculine singular in 10:9, 13b-14; second masculine plural in 10:12-13a, 15; third masculine singular in 10:11b; third feminine singular in 10:11a; and third masculine plural in 10:10. This variation provides these verses with a frenetic character, which suggests they reflect a compilation of short sayings. The logic connecting these sayings derives more from the themes of judgment and the agricultural imagery than from a single rhetorical strategy. The smaller, more rhetorically cohesive units convey the following: a statement emphasizing Israel's long-standing problems (10:9), a divine pronouncement of judgment (10:10), an analogy of Ephraim as a stubborn cow (10:11), a call to sow righteousness rather than wickedness (10:12-13), and the pronouncement of the disastrous consequences of a coming military campaign (10:14-15). This amalgamation effectively underscores that Israel's long-standing disregard of YHWH (10:9-11) requires an immediate change in behavior (10:12-13) to avoid the coming judgment (10:14-15).

Hosea 10:9 refers again to the "days of Gibeah" (see 9:9) to convey the long duration of the sinful nature of Israel as well. It also transitions to a pronouncement of judgment against the city by that name (10:9). It is not immediately clear, however, what significance the fate of Gibeah has in this context. Two suggestions have been made: assonance and tradition. First, the reference to the hills (*gĕbā'ôt*) in Hebrew) at the end of 10:8 sounds like Gibeah. Second, the events negatively associated with Gibeah (the rape of the Levite's concubine in Judges 19–21) are perhaps called to mind with this reference. At any rate, 10:9 anticipates that Gibeah too will suffer from a military campaign.

The NRSV offers an idiomatic translation for Hosea 10:10 because of its difficult syntax. [Text-critical Problems in Hosea 10:10] At any rate, like 10:9, Hosea 10:10 pronounces YHWH's punishment upon Ephraim in the form of an anticipated attack from foreign nations. Even though "iniquity" is an emendation, the reference to their double iniquity certainly fits the context that has accented the long-standing nature of Israel's sin (see 9:9, 15; 10:9).

The images in Hosea 10:11 present Ephraim as a female farm animal whose wild spirit makes her difficult to train. The verse implies that YHWH did not hitch her to the plow, but allowed Ephraim space to learn self-control. Now, however, the time for training is over. Instead of threshing wildly, Ephraim must now plow the ground as she was intended to do. The plow implies both responsibility and submission.

The fourth clause of 10:11 applies the metaphor to Judah as well as Ephraim. Even though it relies on the same metaphor, this clause ("Judah must plow") has often been treated as secondary—because Judah has not been the subject of the prophetic speech since 8:14 and because the presence of five couplets creates an uneven pairing of poetic lines. However, the same combination of Ephraim, Judah, and Jacob also occurs in 12:1-2 (MT 12:2-3), where Jacob seems to be selected deliberately as a way of emphasizing both Ephraim and Judah. This emphasis makes sense in light of the recurring warning to Jerusalem and Judah in Hosea, Amos, Micah, and Zephaniah. (See [Hosea 10:8 and the Book of the Twelve].)

Hosea 10:12 interrupts the divine speech with a third person reference to YHWH, but since 10:14 reverts to YHWH addressing "your people," it seems unwise to assume a separate speaker is intended for 10:12-13. Also, 10:12 continues using agricultural metaphors related to planting and harvesting; it only changes the emphasis from the preparatory work to the outcome. The old

### Text-critical Problems in Hosea 10:10

ΑΩ Emendations often occur in three places. First, the verb *bĕavâtî* in the NRSV is translated as "come" (from the root *bô'*) but is a noun that derives from the root *'āvâ* in MT, which means to crave or desire. The second verb is generally emended from a *qal* to a *hif`il* form of the root *yāsar*, which means "to instruct," "correct," or "chastise." Third, the phrase translated as double iniquity changes a *yod* to a *vav* in the Hebrew text in order to make sense of it (MT reads, "their two eyes"). All three of these readings are attested in the ancient versions. The KJV offers a more literal translation of the Hebrew: "[It is] in my desire that I should chastise them; and the people shall be gathered against them, when they shall bind themselves in their two furrows."

adage "you reap what you sow" comes into play. If one plants righteousness (i.e., "right actions" before YHWH), then one will harvest *ḥesed* (fidelity to the covenant obligations). Hosea 10:12 admonishes the people to sow righteousness for themselves.

The second half of 10:12 presents a slightly different picture, since it portrays YHWH casting righteousness. [Casting Righteousness] YHWH throws righteousness, meaning that he is the one who plants the seed. For their part, the people have but to seek YHWH,

**Casting Righteousness**

AΩ Most translations understand the phrase "cast righteousness" as "rain righteousness," based upon the use of an emended form of the verb "to drink, to water" (*rāvâ*) in Hos 6:3. Instead of reading "to throw" (*yārâ*) in the phrase "like the late rain *cast on* the earth" to depict the rain, many assume a variant form of *rāvâ*. However, in 10:12 the metaphors appear to presume preparation of the ground in order that the seed (righteousness) may be cast upon the ground that has been prepared. Thus, there is no reason to emend the verb or presume it comes from *rāvâ*.

though time is of the essence. The transition between these two parts calls upon the people to "break up your fallow ground." Since this activity is part of the preparatory work for planting, the first part of the verse should be seen as a programmatic statement that guides the following lines: break up the dirt clods, seek YHWH, and YHWH will plant the seed (righteousness) in order that the people may harvest *ḥesed*. These extended metaphors illustrate the main point: if one wants to harvest good things, then good things must be planted.

Hosea 10:13 extends the metaphor from the previous verse as a means of confronting Israel's current situation. While the previous verse serves as an admonishment for what Israel ought to do, Hosea 10:13 portrays what they have done by using the same metaphors. Rather than sowing righteousness to reap steadfast love, Israel has plowed wickedness in order to harvest injustice and lies. The last line of 10:13 explicates this metaphor in military and political terms. The NRSV opts for a translation of the word *derek*, which normally means "way" or "path," using a debated sense of the word as "power" (see Jer 3:13; Pss 138:5; 31:3). However, the translation masks an important part of the message. A better translation would be, "because you have trusted in your way (*derek*), in the multitude of your warriors." Essentially, the prophet correlates Israel's behavior with that of a bully. It routinely overwhelms a problem with force. This accusation assumes that such force relies on its own determinations, not on the leadership of God. The idea is similar to that expressed in Psalm 33:16: "A king is not saved by his great army; a warrior is not delivered by his great strength." Superior military strength does not make a cause just if it runs contrary to the ways of God.

### Enigmatic Terms

The precise identities of the place Beth-Arbel and the king Shalman have created debate. Beth-Arbel is the name of a village in Galilee, though some have suggested Arbela in the Trans-Jordan as the intended village. Neither fits the context particularly well, but the former is more likely on morphological grounds. Regarding the identity of king Shalman, we must deal in probabilities because we lack definitive information. Three suggestions have been postulated. The first possibility is Shalmaneser V, king of Assyria (727–722 BCE). The uncertainty of this suggestion lies in the lack of evidence that he attacked Beth-arbel in Galilee or Arbela in the Trans-Jordan, though he did attack Samaria. However, he died during the siege and his successor Sargon II completed the campaign. The second possibility is that Shalman refers to a king of Moab by that name who is roughly contemporary with the time in question. However, no evidence exists of a Moabite attack during this period. The third possibility reaches back roughly a century to Shalmaneser III, king of Assyria (858–824 BCE). He was the first Assyrian king to receive tribute from Israel. Again, there is no direct evidence he attacked Beth-arbel. However, he did attack Israel and Syria on several occasions, and conquered much of southern Syria and northern Israel. Nevertheless, the pointed nature of the judgment oracle would suggest that events in the eighth century are much more pertinent and threatening. Thus, Shalman probably refers to the Assyrian king Shalmaneser V (727–722), who is credited with laying siege to Samaria, the capital of the northern kingdom, though it was his successor, Sargon II, who completed the task after Shalmaneser's death.

---

Hosea 10:14 continues the judgment oracle of 10:13 by announcing the verdict, one delivered with a certain sense of poetic justice. Though the enigmatic terms pose difficulties, the point is clear. [Enigmatic Terms] The situation described in 10:3 notes Israel's penchant for relying on its own military strength. Here, however, the prophet warns in no uncertain terms that Israel has met its match: war will come, and its fortresses will be destroyed.

One of the most horrifying aspects of war, modern or ancient, is the suffering of the innocent, those not involved in the fight who are least able to protect themselves. This verse depicts the ferocity of the Assyrian military power by focusing on its brutal slaying of women and children as a means of putting fear in the heart of the prophet's addressees. [Assyrian Military Cruelty] The idea of brutally slaying an enemy's children in retribution for sins committed by the enemy

### Assyrian Military Cruelty

Warfare has always been a cruel business, and propaganda about warfare has been an important element of political strategy almost as long as warfare has been conducted. Assyrian cruelty in war was well known, in part because the Assyrian kings themselves celebrated their victories with art. The relief here came from the wall of Sennacherib's own palace and commemorates the Assyrian overthrow of the Judean city of Lachish in 701. The scene shows three naked Judeans impaled on poles. Its presence in the palace undoubtedly served as a means of intimidation for those who dealt with the Assyrian king.

Assyrian warriors impaling Jewish prisoners after conquering Jewish fortress of Lachish in 701 BCE. Part of a relief from the palace of Sennacherib, Niniveh, Mesopotamia (Iraq). Assyrian, 8th C. BCE. British Museum, London, Great Britain. (Credit: Erich Lessing/Art Resource, NY)

was common. In Psalm 137:9, the Judean psalmist calls upon YHWH to do the same to the children of Babylon in retaliation for the abuse and taunting suffered by the psalmist during the exile.

To make sure the implications of 10:14 are not lost on its audience, Hosea 10:15 specifies that Israel's destruction at the hands of the Assyrians is coming soon to Bethel and its king. The behavior of Ephraim that has instigated this judgment is characterized by the double use of the word "evil" (lit., the evil of your evil). The same emphasis comes with the verb "to be cut off," where the infinitive absolute precedes the *nifal* perfect of the same verb (lit., "being cut off, he will be cut off"). The prophet conveys the nearness of the destruction by announcing it is coming with the dawn. In military battles, the first light of dawn was often a strategic time to attack.

# CONNECTIONS

This chapter presents a wide array of metaphors for explaining Israel's relationship to YHWH. On one side of the spectrum, 10:1 assumes Israel is a healthy vine, full of good things YHWH has provided, but a vine whose external health belies its rotten core (10:2). As such it reiterates the message of Hosea 2, where Israel did not recognize the source of its good gifts (2:8). On the other end of the spectrum, these verses portray Israel as a people who have rebelled against YHWH from the beginning (10:9, 11). These two ideas function as foundational underpinnings of the Deuteronomistic History. God chose Israel and bestowed favor upon it, but Israel continually turned its back upon its God by breaking its covenant obligations. Thus, these ideas admonish God's people in all generations: a life of faith that does not proceed from gratitude will degenerate into self-absorption. If a believer who has benefited from God's grace behaves as though the benefits are the result of personal initiative, diligence, and drive, then that believer also stands in danger of forgetting God.

Hosea 10:12, 13 focus upon predictable consequences of behavior. These verses illustrate the old adage, "You reap what you sow," in both positive and negative terms. Hosea 10:12 calls upon Israel to "sow righteousness" in order to reap "steadfast love." Sadly, Hosea 10:13 conveys the reality of Israel's situation in opposing terms. They have plowed wickedness and reaped injustice. They have harvested the fruit of lies.

Today, it is all too easy for Christians to overlook passages of prophetic judgment. We treat them as warnings from a bygone era that no longer apply to us. We want to let ourselves off the hook, often reminding one another that Jesus came with a new covenant, one of grace in which we are not judged by our works. But a covenant is an agreement with obligations for both parties. The new "covenant" also implies covenant obligations, both personal and corporate, for God's people. Hence, when we ignore the needs of those around us, or when we think our good fortune results from things we have done, we fall into the same trap as Israel in the eighth century. We think our special status as God's people entitles us to special considerations, but actions have consequences. We reap what we sow. These verses challenge the church as God's people to look to God, to live honestly, and to show kindness.

These religious and ethical admonitions remain interconnected for communities of faith. In the religious realm today, church congregations tend to reflect American culture in ways similar to the ways religious practices of ancient Israel were affected by their culture. American congregations tend to see religious expression in more individualistic terms. We can become so transfixed on the question of how to worship that we forget why we worship. In the case of Israel in Hosea, pillars and altars symbolized religious expression, but the prophets condemned those expressions because they pointed to deities other than the true God. All too often, American religious expression tends to take similar routes that confuse the worship of the true God. As churches grow, physical expressions of that growth become a significant means by which we mark that experience. We think we need bigger and bigger boxes where people can experience God in greater and greater comfort. Soon, the tail can wag the dog and larger facilities take up more of the resources to operate, creating disincentives for ministry. Which honors God more, a 9,000-seat sanctuary in the suburbs of a large metropolitan area, or a soup kitchen serving the city's poorer neighborhoods that is funded by the church? The answer likely depends upon where one sits for most of us. Hosea 10 makes us uncomfortable because the prophet looks past the things that make us comfortable to remind us that bigger is not always better, that more is not always greater, and that health is not always judged by the externals. If we build sanctuaries to God to keep us feeling good about our own situation, sooner or later those sanctuaries become symbols of isolation rather than engagement of the world in the name of God.

# NOTE

1. Much of the eighth century saw economic prosperity under the reign of Jeroboam II (782–742 BCE), though Hosea's early material reflects a time of transition as political unrest and religious deterioration (in the perspective of Hosea and Amos) begin to settle in. See discussion in Marvin A. Sweeney, *The Twelve Prophets* (Berit Olam; Collegeville: Liturgical Press, 2000) 3–5, 192–94.

# A COMPASSIONATE FATHER AND A REBELLIOUS SON

Hosea 11:1-11

## COMMENTARY

This unit alternates between YHWH's statements about Israel and YHWH's reminiscing as a father over a wayward son. This act of remembering is at once loving and rueful, because the child has abandoned his father. This unit has three movements, although the third one is complex. The first movement, Hosea 11:1-4, presents YHWH's reflections on the early life of a rebellious son, Ephraim. Then in 11:5-7, YHWH articulates the need to punish this people for their disrespect. In the last movement, Hosea 11:8-11 conveys YHWH's decision to remove the punishment, although much of 11:10 takes a different tone, likely reflecting a later commentary influenced by Joel and Amos. Further, not only does Hosea 11:8-11 conclude this threefold unit, but by reiterating God's salvific intentions for God's people, it also effectively concludes Hosea 4–11.

### When Ephraim Was a Child, 11:1-4

Hosea 11:1-4 focuses on the tender acts of Father God in attempting to raise his beloved son to adulthood. Meanwhile, despite YHWH's nurturing, the son proceeds to disregard his father like a rebellious teenager whose resistance to parental authority becomes more important than the relationship to the parent.

Hosea 11:1 opens in a way that depicts two sets of symbols: the father-son relationship between YHWH and Israel/Ephraim, and an Israel-Egypt dichotomy that alludes to the exodus story as the formative event of Israel's history. Throughout this chapter, both sets of symbols continue to play a role in exploring God's love on the one hand and the actions of the political entity Israel on the other. Hosea 11:1 begins an extended soliloquy where YHWH expresses—as

### God as Father

The image of God as father is treated in more detail in Hos 11 than anywhere else in the Old Testament. Although abundant in the teachings of Jesus and elsewhere in the New Testament, the concept of God as father in the Old Testament typically has to be extracted from names or metaphors. For example, the epithet "Abiel" in 1 Sam 9:1 literally means "My father is El/God." Indirectly, the notion of God as father can also be derived from metaphors like those found for God in Hosea. Hosea metaphorically refers to God's people as the children of his wife, thereby alluding to God's fatherhood. In Hos 2, in particular, this wife is the land personified, and elsewhere in the prophetic corpus, Lady Zion is treated (metaphorically) as the wife of YHWH (e.g., Isa 50:1) whose children are her inhabitants (Isa 49:25). Mal 1:6 and 2:9 also infer God as father of the people. Jesus expands upon this idea when he depicts God as the loving father in the parable of the prodigal son, and especially when he refers to God using the endearing term "Abba" (Mark 14:36)—an image that was not lost on Paul (Rom 8:15, 16, 21; 4:6; 9:8; Phil 2:15) or other early Christians since the number of references to God's children increases dramatically in the New Testament (e.g., John 1:12; 11:52; 1 John 3:1, 10; 5:2).

nowhere else in the Old Testament—the pathos of a father's love over a wayward child. The chapter presumes a father who desperately loves his child (11:4, 8) in spite of the fact that the child continually turns his back on the father (11:3, 7). These conflicting images create internal turmoil (11:8-9) that is all the more poignant because the father is YHWH.

This chapter is remarkable for several reasons. First, the portrayal of God as "father" is unusual in the Old Testament. [God as Father] Second, the powerful image of a loving, gentle parent offers a striking contrast to the images of the mighty, angry, wrathful God presented in Hosea 4–10. Hosea 11:1 states God's love for Israel, the "young boy." This statement emphasizes that God's love is a long-standing love. The metaphor of Israel as a young boy allows the reader to distinguish between Israel of the distant past and the Israel whom God has been confronting in chapters 4–10. How far in the distant past becomes clear in the second half of 11:1 when God says, "I called my son out of Egypt"—a clear reference to the exodus story.

Hosea 11:2 shifts gears by alluding to what has happened to the relationship since Israel has grown and changed.[1] The first half of the verse draws upon the image of a parent calling a child over and over again; all the while, the child refuses to

### God Rebukes Israel

God rebukes Israel for burning incense to idols (11:2). Altars excavated at Arad, a city in southern Judah that had an important sanctuary before Hezekiah's late-eighth-century reforms.

(Credit: Jim Pitts)

acknowledge the voice of the parent. However, the child does not merely ignore the parent, but in this case moves ever farther away. Shifting gears yet again, the second half of the verse returns to the corporate symbol of Israel, the country and its people. It provides a concrete illustration of how Israel has turned its back on YHWH (see 11:1). Specifically, Israel has continually offered sacrifices to the Baals (see Hos 2:13, 17) and burned incense to idols rather than YHWH. These acts imply that Israel has rejected YHWH's lordship in a specific way. The first two things God commanded Israel at Sinai were (1) that they were to have no other gods before YHWH and (2) that they were not to make idols. Yet in 11:2, YHWH accuses Israel of placing Baal before YHWH and making idols to worship other gods (see the discussion of Baal worship in Hos 2:7, 13). Thus, it is clear that Israel has broken the first two commandments, the foundational statements outlining YHWH's command for allegiance from his people. Moreover, this allusion to the Decalogue associates 11:2 topically with the beginning of the extended section on judgment from Hosea 4–11. In Hosea 4:2, the prophet accuses Israel of breaking four of the last six commandments—that is, those related to human conduct toward other humans. Since 11:2 accuses Israel of breaking the first two commandments, these combined allusions imply that Israel has completely ignored the commandments given at Sinai.

Hosea 11:3-4 returns to the father metaphor, using the more specific term "Ephraim." YHWH endearingly recounts his tender actions toward young Ephraim: teaching a child to walk, holding a child in an embrace, and nursing a sick child back to health (11:3). Hosea 11:4 continues to describe YHWH's tender acts as YHWH's gentle leading of Israel and YHWH's loving nurture. The first half of the verse ("With human cords I will draw them, with bonds of love" [NRSV]) depicts the tension of a parent raising a child, a parent who leads by example and whose restrictions represent the limits of one who is wiser than the child. [Cords in Hosea 11:4]

The second half of 11:4, admittedly difficult to translate, compares YHWH to those lovingly raising an infant to kiss it on the cheek according to the NRSV. While a beautiful image, this translation departs from the wording in the MT in rather significant ways, but text-critical problems with this verse are numerous. [Text-critical Problems in Hosea 11:4b] Despite the problems, the NRSV is here preferred because of its contextual consistency. The NRSV con-

## Cords in Hosea 11:4

AΩ Three possible meanings can be found for the noun formed from the three Hebrew consonants (*ḥbl*) that make up this word: "cords" (NRSV and most English translations), "destruction" (LXX, see also Mic 5:2), and "birth pangs" (Sweeney, 114). The first two nouns from this root have identical vowels but come from different etymological backgrounds. Sweeney argues the term "cords of human kindness" (NRSV) should be "human labor pains" (reading *ḥēbel* instead of *ḥebel*). His suggestion is then, "I pulled them out with human labor pains, bonds of love" (implying God as mother). This word also appears in Hos 13:13 where it means "birth pangs." While none of the three is without difficulty, the verb "to pull, or drag" (*mšk*) in MT makes the most sense with "cord," meaning the NRSV's "led with cords" makes better sense than "pulled with birth pangs." The kind of cord is also disputed. MT has "cords of man" where "man" (*ʾādām*) is taken as a synonym for "humane" (hence, human kindness in NRSV that parallels "bands of love" in the next phrase). *HALOT* suggest that *ʾādām* could derive from an Arabic root meaning skin or leather. *HALOT* also suggests that the Hebrew word translated as "love" (*ʾahăbâh*) could derive from another Arabic word and could thus also mean "leather." These suggestions go far afield, though, from the positive tenor of the passage.

Marvin Sweeney, *The Twelve Prophets* (Berit Olam, vol. 1; Collegeville: Liturgical Press, 2000).

## Text-critical Problems in Hosea 11:4b

AΩ The MT reads as follows: "but then I will be like those raising a yoke upon their cheek that will stretch out to him; I will feed" (see NAS). The comparison in the Hebrew refers to the removal of the work implements (a yoke) from a farm animal's jaw or cheek in order to feed it. The NRSV reads the word "yoke" (*ʿōl*) as "infant" or "suckling" (*ʿûl/ʿul*) rather than "yoke," assuming a defective spelling. The consonantal text would be the same in both cases (*ʿl*). Both options pose difficulties. On the one hand, the idea of raising a yoke would more naturally fit with the idea of putting the yoke on the animal and then removing it. On the other hand, it is not clear why one would raise an infant to one's cheek in order to feed it. The LXX translates, "When men were destroyed, I drew them with the bands of my love: and I will be to them as a man smiting his own cheek; and I will watch him closely, I will prevail with him." Apparently, the Septuagint sees the consonants used in "cord" as the word *ḥbl* (3), "to deal corruptly" (see the noun form in Mic 2:8 and Job 21:17). The last portion of this verse in the Septuagint does not coordinate readily with the Hebrew, but probably represents an attempt to derive the verb from *ykl* (to "prevail") rather than *ʾkl* (to "cause to eat" in the *hifʿil*). In the end, the emendation followed by NRSV, and others, creates the fewest conceptual difficulties. The comparison of the tender act, raising infants to one's check (or jaws), seems a more apt picture than feeding a farm animal in this context.

strues the image of a gentle father that continues the logic of 11:3.

## Punishment for Ephraim's Rebellion, 11:5-7

Hosea 11:5 combines references to Egypt and Assyria as a means of connecting the period of slavery in Egypt with impending exile to Assyria. While other possibilities exist for translation, the NRSV translates this imagery similarly to Hosea 9:3 so that Hosea 11:5 threatens Israel/Ephraim with a return to Egypt, meaning a return to the slavery from which YHWH originally delivered Israel. [Other Possibilities for Translation of Hosea 11:5]

However, the next line makes clear that 11:5 does not mean a literal return to Egypt, for YHWH equates the return to Egypt with subjugation to the king of Assyria. Hence, YHWH intends to exile Israel/Ephraim to Assyria, where the people will live under the oppression of the Assyrians in the same way that they once lived under the oppression of the pharaoh. The reason given for this punishment is Israel's stubborn refusal to return to YHWH. The concept of the covenant holds the two parts of this verse together. When Israel came out of Egypt (Exod 24) and conquered the land (Josh 24), the Israelites willingly agreed to abide by the obligations YHWH set before them. Since they have now abandoned that covenant, YHWH decides to send them back where he found them, back to slavery, oppression, and bondage. These symbols send a powerful message: "because you turned your back on me, I will turn my back on you."

Hosea 11:6 explicates the consequences of Israel's rejection with the pronouncement of a military conquest. The verb used in the image of the sword raging (*ḥûl*) in the cities of Israel implies a military battle or a series of battles. Typically, this verb implies frenetic activity and is used, for example, to refer to the activity of whirlwinds (Jer 23:19; 36:23). As well, the word translated by the NRSV as "oracle-priests" is an unusual word, appearing elsewhere in exilic texts (Isa 44:25 and Jer 50:36). The precise meaning, however, is unknown, and other options exist, but it probably refers to priests using divination to predict the future. [Other Options for Hosea 11:6] Regardless, this verse cites their activity as the rationale for the impending military invasion.

Hosea 11:7 condemns the people for worshiping another deity. The image of the people turning from YHWH in this context implies deliberate choices (lit., "they hang on to their apostasy"). Moreover, the second half of 11:7 charges that though the people "call him *ʾel-ʿal* (translated

---

**Other Possibilities for Translation of Hosea 11:5**

AΩ The MT has a particle of negation that the NRSV treats emphatically. Other translations keep the negation and treat the second line as an adversative "but" to contrast with the upcoming Assyrian subordination. For example, the NAS reads, "They will *not* return to the land of Egypt; but Assyria—he will be their king, because they refused to return (to me)." In either case, the point seems to be that the impending exile to Assyria will be at least as fearful as Israel's time in captivity in Egypt.

---

**Other Options for Hosea 11:6**

AΩ The Hebrew word *bad* can derive from five different etymological backgrounds, making interpretation of the word quite different, depending upon how one understands the metaphors, as evidenced by the various translations of the word.

NRSV: The sword rages in their cities, it consumes their oracle-priests, and devours because of their schemes.
NAS: And the sword will whirl against their cities, And will demolish their gate bars And consume *them* because of their counsels.
KJV: And the sword shall abide on his cities, and shall consume his branches, and devour *them*, because of their own counsels.
NIV: Swords will flash in their cities, will destroy the bars of their gates and put an end to their plans.

Further, Sweeney (115)—with NAS and NIV—interprets this word as a metaphor for city gates, apparently taking the more common Hebrew word *bad* (meaning 2 in BDB), "pole," as referring to the poles holding the city gates closed, instead of the infrequent *bad* (meaning 5), "oracle priest." While "pole" could make sense, it would require treating "city" (*ʿir*) as masculine instead of feminine, and it hardly flows smoothly with "schemes" in the next line. Wolff (*Hosea*, 192) translates with *bad* (meaning 4), "idle talk" / "braggarts." Rudolph (*Hosea*, 211) emends to "his sufficiency" (*bĕdayô*).

Marvin Sweeney, *The Twelve Prophets* (Berit Olam, vol. 1; Collegeville: Liturgical Press, 2000).
Hans Walter Wolff, *Hosea* (Hermeneia; trans. Gary Stansell; Philadelphia: Fortress, 1974).
Wilhelm Rudolph, *Hosea* (KAT, Bd 13/1; Gütersloh: G.Mohn, 1966).

**God Most High**

AΩ It is difficult to translate *'el-'al*. 7, as can be seen by the divergence in the translations. Most take *'el* as the preposition "to" rather than the construct form of "God." The NRSV has "to the most high they call, but he does not raise them up at all." The NAS has "though they call them to *the One* on high, none at all exalts *Him*." NIV translates, "Even if they call to the Most High, he will by no means exalt them." However, the MT makes good sense if one translates *'el* as God and includes "together" with the first part of the verse: "And together they call him God Most High (*'el-'al*); he will not exalt them."

the God Most High), "he will not raise them up." [God Most High] The background of the term refers to the most high deity in the Canaanite pantheon, either Baal or El. The point of the verse is that the people are turning to impotent Canaanite deities instead of YHWH. YHWH speaks about the people turning to this god who is unable to answer their plea. The verb "raise up" or "exalt" has a double entendre, since it can also mean "to raise/rear" children (Isa 1:2; 23:4). It thus functions well as a contrasting image in this chapter where YHWH has already shown himself to be the one who raised Ephraim (see 11:3).

### YHWH's Compassion toward Ephraim, 11:8-11

The remaining verses of this chapter once again change the tenor of the message. Readers are now invited to hear how YHWH struggles, despite Israel's apostasy, with the idea of giving up on them. In fact, YHWH's compassion and salvific inclinations take over in most of this unit. Despite the egregious violations with which YHWH has charged Israel in the previous verses, YHWH's love and compassion make it difficult for YHWH to consider abandoning this wayward child. The pathos expressed by YHWH in these verses portrays the inner turmoil of a God who does not desire to resort to punishment. [The Pathos of God]

**The Pathos of God**

📖 Abraham Heschel treats the tension between God's judgment and mercy as a result of the pathos of God. Heschel notes, however, that "These words [. . .] were neither a final judgment nor an actual prediction. Their true intention was to impart the intensity of divine anger. And yet, that anger did not express all that God felt about the people. Intense is his anger, but profound is his compassion." Heschel already seems to imply what later scholars such as Crenshaw and others explore in more explicit treatments—that God can no longer be responsibly described in terms that involve God in violence of the type described in Hosea or elsewhere in biblical texts. The danger for abuse of this language is simply too great. In this sense, Hos 11:1-9 stands out dramatically as counter-testimony to the more dominant message in Hosea and elsewhere in the prophetic corpus.

Abraham J. Heschel, *The Prophets: An Introduction* (Harper Torchbooks; New York: Harper and Row, 1955) 46.

In 11:8, the places Admah and Zeboiim are cities destroyed along with Sodom and Gomorrah (Deut 29:23 [MT 29:22]; Gen 14:2, 8; 19:24-28; 10:19; 13:10-12). Hosea 11:8 thus reiterates the special nature of the relationship between Israel and YHWH. Unlike God's dealings with the cities like Gomorrah, it grieves and pains the God of Abraham to think of destroying Israel. God is here portrayed anthropomorphically, as a father who grieves at the idea of punishing Ephraim: his heart aches and his compassion comes to the fore. ["My Heart Recoils"]

As a result of the inner turmoil, Hosea 11:9 relates YHWH's decision to withhold wrath against Ephraim. Instead, YHWH chooses to take the high road, stating that it is his divinity (contrasted with humanity) that causes YHWH to refrain from punishment: "I am God and no mortal." Ironically, this statement comes immediately after what is perhaps the most humanlike portrayal of divine emotional suffering in all of Scripture. The irony in 11:9 is that while YHWH expresses the effects of his compassion and grace, he becomes more distant in doing so. YHWH refuses to enter the city (for judgment) because he is not human, and YHWH remains in the midst of Ephraim, but as the Holy One, not the tender father. [YHWH Refuses to Enter the City]

Hosea 11:10 marks a parenthetical shift in style. This verse deviates from the "divine I" style of the remainder of Hosea 11 by referring to YHWH in the third person, indicating the prophet/narrator as speaker. Hosea 11:10 portrays Israel's reaction as children who will follow the sound of a roaring lion. This imagery presumes that God's roaring will be sufficient to create fear in those who hear it. By the lion's sending the warning, the children know they must appear before him. Though they tremble in fear at the voice of the lion, they will come.

Two things are unclear about this verse. First, why is the lion roaring? Is it roaring because it has found food and is ready to feed its young? This is the image upon which Amos 3:4 draws: "Does a lion roar in the forest when it has no prey? Does a young lion cry out from its den if it has caught nothing?" The verb "tremble," however, would seem to argue against that image because the element of fear underlies this action. In that sense, 11:10 seems to be talking about God's judgment. Second, why do the children of

**"My Heart Recoils"**

AΩ The NRSV translation of YHWH's response reflects an English idiom for a Hebrew verb that may in actuality express an even stronger idea. The Hebrew verbal root behind "recoil" is *hpk*, which means "to overturn." More literally, the Hebrew phrase means "my heart is overturned upon myself." It represents one of numerous places where God talks about changing God's mind in the Old Testament. (See discussion of the use of Exod 34:6-7 in Joel 2:13; Amos 7:1-3, 4-6; Mic 7:18-19; and Nah 1:4, where this idea comes back into play.)

**YHWH Refuses to Enter the City**

AΩ The NRSV translates the last line of 11:9 as "I will not come in wrath." The Hebrew of the MT reads "and I will not enter the city." The NRSV alters the spelling of the Hebrew by dropping a letter and translating this word as a noun from the root *b'r*, meaning "to burn." While the image of burning anger is certainly not unknown to Hebrew, the more common root to express this idea was already used at the beginning of this verse. Because of the changes required, both vocalic and consonantal, this emendation seems unlikely. Instead, YHWH's pronouncement that he will not enter the city should be seen as a proclamation that he will not attack the city. The verb used here, *bô'*, and the preposition *bĕ* can be an idiomatic expression that means "to go against" or "attack" (Josh 2:18; Judg 11:18; Dan 11:40). A military attack on cities has already been mentioned in 11:6. The city in this case would probably be Bethel.

this lion return from the west? General consensus among commentators suggests the west implies the farthest reaches of civilization, thus making it a broad promise of the people's return. Given the abrupt change of style, and the unusual adoption of the lion metaphor, it is helpful to note that Hosea 11:10 has a wider literary horizon than the immediate context, one that takes account of Hosea, Joel, and Amos in Book of the Twelve. [Hosea 11:10 in the Book of the Twelve]

Hosea 11:11 continues the images from the previous verses, though it simultaneously changes the metaphor by which they operate. This verse connects both to 11:9 and 11:10, but distinctly. The plural verb "tremble" is the same verb used in 11:10, and it presumes the subject (i.e., children/sons) from that verse. However, the metaphor of children, used to depict Israel, changes to birds in order to contrast more fully the image of the people trembling before the mighty lion. The image of the people trembling emphasizes the power of the lion, though several commentators have argued that 11:11 originally connected to 11:9 and likely used the verb "to tremble" to portray the speed with which the birds returned, not birds trembling in fear.

This final verse of Hosea 11 (according to the MT's versification) is often seen as a counterpart to 7:11. The first word used for bird (*ṣipôr*) is a generic term, but the image of the dove (*yônâ*) has already appeared in Hosea 7:11, where its characteristics connote foolishness. In 11:11, however, the "birds" speed back to the land from Assyria and Egypt, receiving a promise of resettlement from the mouth of YHWH. In other words, this verse assumes that judgment will take place, but that YHWH will bring his people home afterward.

## Hosea 11:10 in the Book of the Twelve

Erich Zenger suggests Hos 11:10 was added in order to anticipate the lion imagery of Joel and Amos. According to him, the motif of a roaring lion plays a salvific role in Hosea (5:14; 11:10), calls the people to repentance in Joel (2:11), and roars judgment in Amos (3:6; see also Amos 1:2 and Joel 3:16 =MT 4:16). Thus, Hos 11:10 connects the perspectives of Hosea, Joel, and Amos, where passages warning God's people with a trumpet blast (Hos 5:8; Joel 2:1; Amos 3:6) culminate in a lion metaphor for YHWH (Hos 5:14; Joel 2:11; Amos 3:4). Zenger also notes that Hos 11:10 anticipates both the image of the lion as (potential) savior for God's people (as in Joel) *and* the image of the lion roaring judgment, though not annihilation (as in Amos).

See Erich Zenger, "'Wie ein Löwe brüllt er . . .' (Hos 11:10): Zur Funktion poetischer Metaphorik im Zwölfprophetenbuch," in Erich Zenger, ed., *"Wort JHWHS, das geschah . . .": Studien zum Zwölfprophetenbuch* (Herders Biblische Studien 35; Freiberg: Herder, 2002) 33–45.

## CONNECTIONS

The images in Hosea 11:1-8 depict YHWH as a tender, loving father in a way unlike any other biblical text. The passage's form comes close to that of a soliloquy, providing the reader the ability to hear YHWH's internal struggle over whether to punish his wayward child. The images of tenderness depicting YHWH's paternal nature do not reflect the machismo of the warrior God that comes to mind when most people consider the God of the Old Testament. Rather, Hosea 11 expresses the relationship between God and Ephraim/Israel through the eyes of a parent who longs for a time when parenting was simpler, and who wishes his/her recalcitrant teenager would willingly choose to obey. The father calls to the child, but the child goes in the other direction (11:2). The parent teaches the child to walk, and carries him when he cannot, but the child does not acknowledge the parent's actions (11:3). The parent playfully kisses the child (11:4). The parent's compassion creates second thoughts about the punishment of the child (11:8).

These images of a conflicted father intertwine with accusations against his wayward son and culminate in two separate statements of God's intention. First, God will withhold wrath, choosing to take the high road because "I am God and not man" (11:9). Second, and more ambiguously, God will bring the exiles home from the lands to which they have been sent (11:10b-11). This second image shows God's restorative intentions, but a return presumes that the children have been expelled from the land. In the end, the message of compassion and the presumption of judgment stand over against one another, furthering the impression of a parent struggling mightily over the question of how to deal with a child who will not listen.

For many, the idea of God vacillating runs counter to their preconceived notions of God's sovereignty. The biblical God, however, is not a mechanistic deity whose actions and decisions are set forever in stone. Rather, the biblical God tempers wrath with patience and compassion (Exod 34:6-7). In Hosea 11, the soliloquy characterizes God as agonizing over whether to give up on a wayward child. God has invested much in a son who continually turns his back on the parent who raised him, taught him to walk, fed him, and nurtured him to maturity. Yet God cannot help loving this child, even though the child prefers other gods (11:1-2). Moreover, although God trained and healed this child, the child accepts no limits (11:3-4). Thus, while God's character defaults to compassion (11:8b) and refuses to give in to human urges of retaliation (11:9), God abhors the behavior of this child. In the end, the vacillation of YHWH shows God's compassion at war with God's holiness.

This dialectic between God and God's people remains even to this day. God's children still find many ways to turn their backs on God, yet God still wants their acknowledgment, desires that they recognize God's compassion, and hopes they will extend that compassion to others in God's name. Yet while we are quick to call upon God's compassion for ourselves and for those like us, we are just as quick to want God's punishment for those who cause us pain. As well, we know we should offer sustenance in Jesus' name (Matt 25:40), but we usually turn our backs on those in need. When we compare ourselves to the loving parent who has reared us, how do our lives stack up? Are we rebellious children, or are we willing to obey? Are we oblivious to what God has done for us and how our actions grieve God? Are we willing to deny our sense of anger and justice so we can seek to show compassion instead?

# NOTE

1. The NRSV correctly follows the LXX here, which presumes the Hebrew form *kĕqârî*. The MT, by contrast, has the plural verb *qâr'û* (they called), but there is no suitable antecedent for this plural. The form behind the LXX involves two changes to the consonantal text, but these are preferable to trying to make sense of the MT (see NAS, KJV). See Hans Walter Wolff, *Hosea* (Hermeneia; trans. Gary Stansell; Philadelphia: Fortress, 1974) 190–91.

# JACOB AND MOSES AS LESSONS FOR THE PRESENT

## Hosea 11:12–12:14

## COMMENTARY

This chapter structures its accusations against Israel's treachery in the present by drawing upon characters of the past. "Ephraim" refers to the present generation and is accused of political stupidity (12:1 [MT 12:2]), ethical violations (12:6-7 [MT 12:7-8]), and improper religious practices (12:11 [MT 12:12]). In between these accusations, the stories of Jacob (12:2-4, 12-13 [MT 12: 3-5, 14-15]) and the exodus (12:9-10, 13 [MT 12:10-11, 14]) serve as reminders that sin brings consequences, even in a relationship characterized by providence and compassion.

The syntactical divisions in this chapter create at least six short sections (11:12-12:1; 12:2-6, 7-8, 9-11, 12-13, 14). The brevity, complexity, and relative syntactical independence of these units create ambiguities that are reflected in textual and interpretive difficulties. That said, the thematic unity of Hosea 12 derives more from repetition than from a clear rhetorical structure. Recurring ideas include treachery (11:12; 12:7), iniquity (12:8, 11) and recompense (12:2, 14). However, the rhetorical flow of this chapter is accomplished through the interplay of accusation, illustration, doxology, paronomasia (word play), allusion, and summation.

### The Deceit of Ephraim, 11:12–12:1 (MT 12:1-2)

The core of 11:12–12:1 charges Ephraim, the northern kingdom, with lies and deceit, but these charges in turn create two points of contrast with their context. First, in contrast to the previous chapter depicting YHWH's compassion, this small unit (and the entire chapter) focuses upon the sin of Ephraim. Second, this unit contrasts the actions of Ephraim with those of Judah.

### The Meaning of Hosea 11:12b

AΩ The last half of 11:12 changes speaker and topic: instead of the divine speech, it refers to God in third person; instead of Ephraim, it deals with Judah. The entire phrase has a parenthetical character. Both sentences in 11:12b are ambiguous as can be seen by glancing at several English translations.

RSV: but Judah is still known by God, and is faithful to the Holy One.
NRSV: but Judah still walks with God, and is faithful to the Holy One.
KJV: but Judah yet ruleth with God, and is faithful with the saints.
NIV: And Judah is unruly against God, even against the faithful Holy One.
NAS: Judah is also unruly against God, even against the Holy One who is faithful.

In the first sentence, the word translated as "walks" (NRSV) means "to wander." Translations of this word interpret Judah positively (RSV, NRSV, KJV) or negatively (NIV, NAS). The second sentence creates more difficulty, with three points of variation. First, KJV, RSV, and NRSV translate Judah as the subject of "is faithful," while the NIV and NAS assume YHWH is the subject. Second, the translations maintain the same attitude toward Judah in 11:12b as 11:12a. Finally, though the MT clearly has a plural noun, "holy ones" (KJV: saints), most translations treat it as a singular reference to God (Holy One). The MT does make sense, however, if "holy ones" refers to the people of Judah who heeded the prophet's message. The subject of the verb "is faithful" then has to be God, not Judah. This statement is positively directed toward Judah, and there is no compelling reason to change the last word of the MT, hence: "but Judah still roams with God, and he (God) is faithful with his holy ones."

### Vassals Carrying Gifts

Israel followed the pattern of many smaller near-eastern nations in entering into vassalage to the rising Assyrian empire.

Tributaries (i.e., vassals) carrying gifts and dues to King Shalmaneser III. Basalt bas-relief. Black stele of Shalmaneser III of Assyria. 9th C. BCE. British Museum, London, Great Britain. (Credit: Erich Lessing/Art Resource, NY)

Hosea 11:12 (MT 12:1) changes tone abruptly from Hosea 1:1-11 by bluntly accusing Ephraim and the house of Israel of deceit and lies against God. Accusations that God's people lie have already been levied in 7:3 and 10:13, but in 11:12, these accusations set the theme for the entire chapter. The second half of the verse (often considered an editorial addition) focuses on Judah, although the meaning of Hosea 11:12b has long been debated. [The Meaning of Hosea 11:12b] It should be translated, "but Judah still roams with God, and he (God) is faithful with his holy ones." Even though 11:12b stands out from the context and functions parenthetically, the positive treatment of Judah appears elsewhere in Hosea (1:7, 11; 4:5).

Hosea 12:1 (MT 12:2) expands the accusation against Ephraim (11:12a) into the political realm. Its image of Ephraim herding the wind and pursuing the east wind connotes the absurdity of Ephraim's political behavior. The latter half of 12:1 explains in concrete terms what is meant by these images: trying to appease Assyria and Egypt simultaneously. The vested interests of these two powers were frequently at odds, so signing a treaty with Assyria (political appeasement) while providing merchandise in the form of olive oil to Egypt (economic commerce with political implications) was bound to create political problems.

## Indictment against Judah and Jacob, 12:2-6 (MT 12:3-7)

Hosea 12:2-6 comprises a complex rhetorical unit where 12:2-4 announces an indictment and a call for recompense against Judah/Jacob (12:2), which is subsequently illustrated with allusions to the Jacob story (see below). These allusions show that Jacob's propensity for treachery was ultimately overcome by YHWH's care (12:3-4). A doxology (12:5) then interrupts the flow before 12:6 returns to admonish the current generation.

With its indictment against God's people, 12:2 (MT 12:3) begins Hosea 12–14 quite similarly to 4–11. Like 4:1, Hosea 12:2 begins with a formal indictment using the Hebrew term *rîb*: 4:1 addresses the land, and 12:2 indicts both Judah and Jacob. Hosea 12:2 differs from 11:1-11 by including Judah in the accusation, setting up the same rapid change of fate for Judah (see 11:12b) as occurred with Ephraim from 11:1-11 to 11:12-12:1 (MT 12:1-2).

"Jacob" is an unusual word in Hosea, appearing elsewhere only in 10:11 and 12:12 (MT 12:13), with the latter referring to the ancestor Jacob specifically. Elsewhere, when not referring to the ancestor, "Jacob" can be used in prophetic texts as a synonym for Judah (Obad 10-11), as another name for the northern kingdom (Amos 7:2, 4; Mic 1:5), or as a metaphor for the entire kingdom (Hos 10:11). Given that in both 12:2 and 10:11 the immediate context mentions first Ephraim and Judah and *then* Jacob, "Jacob" in 12:2 likely intends the entire kingdom. In other words, this *rîb* (indictment) is not limited to Judah but is directed against both kingdoms.

Hosea 12:3-4 (MT 12:4-5) moves directly from the reference to "Jacob" as the land in 12:2 to Jacob the ancestor, who from birth deceitfully sought advantages for himself at the expense of others until his striving with God at the Jabbok River (Gen 32:22-32) profoundly changed him. To accomplish this, 12:3-4 alludes to several parts of the Jacob story simultaneously. [Hosea 12:3-4 and the Jacob Story] Much

### Hosea 12:3-4 and the Jacob Story

Explanations for how Hos 12:3-4 relates to the Jabbok story typically take one of three paths (McKenzie, 314–15). First, some treat Hos 12:4-5 as a midrash on Gen 32:23-33 wherein details have been added. Second, some have argued that Hos 12:4-5 relays a different version of Jacob at the Jabbok. Third, the source for the Jacob references in Hos 12:4 is not just Gen 32:23-33, but includes the encounter with Esau in Gen 33. The third way helps to account for both the concept of mercy and the image of Jacob weeping. The encounter of Jacob and Esau in 33:4-10 begins with the two men weeping (33:4) and culminates in Esau's acceptance of Jacob's gifts because Jacob "has found favor" from Esau (33:10-11). The problem with this view (as articulated by McKenzie) is that it does not flow naturally from the text because only one of the nine singular references in 12:3-4 must be understood as Esau. Interpreting the reference to "his" favor as Esau's favor would have to skip the masculine nouns "angel" and "God" in order to go back to the previous verse and assume Esau as the antecedent. However, it is plausible that the denouement of Jacob's return, his acceptance by Esau, affected the formulation of Hos 12:4 (MT 12:5) since the role of the Jabbok story is closely related to Jacob's impending encounter with Esau. Thus, the midrashic elements of Hos 12:4, as is often the case with midrash, draw from the larger context.

Steven L. McKenzie, "The Jacob Tradition in the Hosea 12:4-5," *VT* 36 (1986).

has been written about how references to Jacob here differ from the Jacob tradition in Genesis. However, when one understands how the allusions combine various parts of the Jacob tradition for a particular purpose, the differences in detail are relatively minor.

The first half of 12:3 (MT 12:4) alludes to the tradition in Genesis 25:24-26, the etiology explaining Jacob's name (*ya'ăqōb*) and character. Jacob and Esau were twins, and though Esau was born first, Jacob came out holding his heel. The verbal root "to supplant" (*'āqab*) actually means "to grab by the heel" or "to trip." However, the negative connotations of this name do not become clear until the speech in Genesis 27:36, where Esau says of Jacob, "Is he not rightly named Jacob, for he has *supplanted* me these two times." Hosea 12:3 (MT 12:4) uses the same verb (*'āqab*), recalling the birth account, then quickly moves to the Jacob/Esau conflict.

The second half of 12:3 refers to the episode of Jacob at the Jabbok River (Gen 32:22-32), wherein Jacob's name is changed to "Israel." Again, the allusion is made via the verb used in the Genesis story: *he strove* (*śārâ*) with God (see Gen 32:29). Both allusions draw upon the Jacob cycle story to show that from the beginning Jacob/Israel had a contentious character.

This use of the Jacob story continues into 12:4, but it is here that the comparison begins to deviate from the plot found in Genesis. The allusions of 12:4 go from the Jabbok story ("he strove . . . and prevailed") in Genesis 32 to the story of Jacob's dream at Bethel in Genesis 28:11-19. [Bethel in Hosea 12] The first part of 12:4 relates to the story of Jacob at the Jabbok, but differences exist with the story as presented in Genesis (specifically the striving with God [12:3], an angel [12:4], or a man [32:24-25]). The second part of Hosea 12:4 alludes to the dream account in Genesis 28:11-19, where Jacob saw angels ascending and descending on a ladder. However, in the Genesis story line, Jacob's dream at Bethel took place as Jacob was leaving Canaan some twenty years earlier. It is neither possible nor necessary to harmonize this variation because the plot is not the point in this allusion. Rather, both episodes refer to numinous experiences where Jacob finds protection from God (see Gen 28:20-22; 32:29-30).

In addition to the confusing jump between the stories, Hosea 12:4 incorporates motifs from the extended story in Genesis. Neither recounts Jacob's weeping, for example. Along with the language of seeking favor, this weeping motif comes from Genesis 33

**Bethel in Hosea 12**

The reference to Bethel in 12:4 as founded by Jacob lacks the polemical moniker Beth-Aven for Bethel (see 4:15; 5:8; 7:4; 10:5, 8) found elsewhere in Hosea.

(see [Hosea 12:3-4 and the Jacob Story]). At any rate, Hosea 12:3 and 12:4 draw two distinct lines of characterization for Jacob by alluding to *different* narrative episodes to make their points. Hosea 12:3 draws on Genesis 25 (assuming the connotations of 27:36) and Genesis 32 in order to highlight Jacob's penchant for seeking an advantage for himself. On the other hand, Hosea 12:4 draws upon Genesis 32 (assuming the reconciliation of 33:10-11) and Genesis 28 to highlight God's patient providence in dealing with Jacob.

Hosea 12:5 (MT 12:6) shifts to a doxological style. It could be a later comment, as is often suggested, because it interrupts the flow of 12:4 to 12:6 (MT 12:5 to 12:7). Whether or not this verse is a later addition, this doxology has an explanatory character, identifying the one who spoke to Jacob at the end of 12:4.

Hosea 12:6 (MT 12:7) turns the reader's attention to the moral of the Jacob story for the current generation. Hosea 12:6 calls Israel to repentance, a significant catchword for the theology of Hosea and the Book of the Twelve. [Hosea 12:6, 7 and the Book of the Twelve] Repentance is indicative of the behavior YHWH seeks from the people, namely, repentance (*šub*) that results in loyalty (*ḥesed*), in justice (*mišpaṭ*), and in the expectation (*qâvâ*) that God will act. Repentance (*šub*), used twenty-three times in Hosea, has the basic meaning "to turn around." Hosea 12:6 calls the entire nation (see Judah and Jacob in 12:2) to act. Just as Jacob went to a foreign land and returned a changed man after his encounters with YHWH, so too the people should turn to God and live like their faith made a difference in their lives.

> **Hosea 12:6, 7 and the Book of the Twelve**
>
> These catchwords establish thematic connections to the books of Amos, Micah, and (to a lesser extent) Zephaniah because of the frequency with which they appear: *ḥesed* (Hos 2:19 [MT 2:21]; 4:1; 6:4, 6; 10:12; Mic 6:8; 7:18, 20) and justice (Hos 2:19 [MT 2:21]; 5:1, 11; 6:5; 10:4; 12:7; Amos 5:7, 15, 24; 6:12; Mic 3:1, 8, 9; 6:8; 7:9; see also Zeph 2:3; 3:5, 8, 15). In particular, Mic 6:8 has this same tripartite concept: *ḥesed*, justice, and walking with God. In addition, Hos 12:6 conceivably serves as the anchor text for the beginning of Mic 6:8, which says, "He *has told you*, O man, what is good . . . ." No text in Micah prior to 6:8 mentions *ḥesed*, so assuming 6:8 has a particular text in mind, Hos 12:6 is by far the most likely text. (See the discussion in [*ḥesed* in the Book of the Twelve].)
>
> Further, in Hos 12:7, accusations concerning improprieties using scales with false measures reflect a recurring motif in Hos 12:7, Amos 8:5, and Mic 6:11. Hosea and Amos use the same phrase ("false scales") while Micah refers to wicked scales, but these texts accuse Israel and Judah of ethical violations.

## Historical Lessons Arranged by Catchwords and Alliteration, 12:7-8, 9-11, 12-13, 14

These verses constitute short sayings whose function is to reinforce the message of this chapter, even though they are not integrally related to one another syntactically.

*Hosea 12:7-8 (MT 12:8-9).* These two verses almost read like independent proverbs, but the Hebrew syntax more clearly connects the two than is apparent in most English translations. Most English versions mask the harsh rhetoric of the original language at the beginning of 12:7. The word "trader" in Hebrew is the word "Canaanite" (*kĕna'ănî*). Apparently, equating Canaanites and traders derives from the stereotypical assignation of a profession to an ethnic group.[1] The rhetorical barb of Hosea 12:7 becomes even more poignant when it is paired with 12:8.

Hosea 12:8 begins with a *vav* conjunction, "*and* Ephraim said," linking Ephraim's speech in 12:8 to the description of the dishonest Canaanite in 12:7. Hosea 12:8 quotes Ephraim, who claims its wealth has been obtained honestly. Ephraim's speech, taken at face value, is a proclamation of innocence, but when linked to 12:7, the quote becomes a satirical accusation in line with the theme of the chapter: the treachery and deceit of Ephraim.

*Hosea 12:9-11 (MT 12:10-12).* The style of 12:9-11 changes, setting these verses apart from 12:1-8, but the logic of their placement seems clear. Following several accusations against the nation in 12:1-8, 12:9-11 pronounces YHWH's punishment. YHWH speaks in the first person in 12:9, first drawing upon the exodus as a symbol of the covenant relationship and then reversing that symbol into a pronouncement of punishment. "The days of the appointed festival" means, simply, the time of the wilderness wandering. Israel will be returned to the wilderness, living in tents outside the land. The wilderness imagery in 12:9 functions primarily as a judgment motif, not a sign of salvation or God's mighty acts.

YHWH continues to speak in 12:10, claiming credit for sending prophets from the exodus to the present. YHWH affirms the use of numerous prophets, and the recognition of multiple visions underscores the numerous times YHWH sent messengers to the kingdom. It does not imply a dichotomy of false visions versus real visions. YHWH proclaims that the message of the prophets will be a message of destruction. [Destruction]

Divine judgment continues in 12:11 (MT 12:12), focusing on two places of historic significance: Gilead and Gilgal. The playful style of 12:11 belies its serious message, since the phrasing is replete with word plays. Gilgal is accused of iniquity. In 12:11, Gilead refers to the region east of the Jordan River across from

**Destruction**

AΩ According the NRSV, the prophets bring a message of destruction, but other translations derive this word from a different root.

NAS: and through the prophets I gave parables.
NRSV: and through the prophets I will bring destruction.
NIV: and told parables through them.

The NRSV derives the word from the root *dāmâ* (3), while the NAS and NIV derive the root from *dāmâ* (1).

Jericho and northward (see also 6:8). Significantly, this region contains the Jabbok River. The word translated as iniquity by the NRSV is a word rife with paronomasia, making a single word translation inadequate. [Word Play on Iniquity] This word play forces the reader to consider Gilgal as the place of power, wealth, disaster, and guilt.

Gilgal was a city of importance, especially for the book of Joshua where it serves as one of the two major staging points for the conquest (see Josh 4:19-20; 9:6; 10:6-7, 9, 15, 43; 14:6; 15:7). The city has already (Hos 4:15; 9:15) been the subject of polemical attacks critiquing cult traditions of the northern kingdom. The charge here is no different. The word used in 12:11 for "bulls" (*šěvārîm*) is not the more common word (*par*), but fits the artistic phrasing of 12:11. [Alliteration in Hosea 12:11]

*Hosea 12:12-13 (MT 12:13-14).* Hosea 12:12 alludes to the story of Jacob, who fled the wrath of Esau by returning to his mother's home country. This allusion refers to the flight recorded in Genesis 28 and the story of Jacob's marriage to Leah and Rachel in Genesis 29. However, Genesis 29 calls the home of Laban "Haran," while Hosea calls the place "Aram," which usually refers to Syria. Explanations for this difference usually suggest that Hosea knows a different version of the Jacob story, or that Aram was at some point thought to extend to Mesopotamia, so that Haran (which is in the upper Northwest Mesopotamia) could have once been considered part of Aram. Whether this concept ever reflected political reality is an open question, but the association of Aram with Abraham/Jacob can be made on several fronts, not the least of which is the introduction to the episode of Esau's Canaanite wife in Genesis 28:5, which names Laban's father, "Bethuel the *Aramean.*" Hosea 12:12 also seems to know the larger Jacob/Israel story since (1) it uses both Jacob and

**Word Play on Iniquity**

AΩ The word translated as "iniquity" has multiple meanings; its use as a homophone is also suggestive and (together with "Gilead") helps explain the unit's placement. The consonantal text (*'vn*) has been pointed in the MT as *'āven*, but those consonants also spell *'ôn*. The word *'āven* has a wide range of meanings, all negative: disaster, injustice, sin, deception, and nothingness. The word *'ôn* has more positive connotations around various forms of "power," including wealth. Both *'ôn* and *'āven* are near homophones to another Hebrew word, *'avôn*—the common word for "iniquity." Both *'ôn* and *'avôn* appear in Hos 12:8 (MT 12:9), while 12:11 has *'āven*, meaning that all three words appear in close proximity. The word play on iniquity gives way to a series of alliterative combinations in the remainder of the verse.

**Alliteration in Hosea 12:11**

AΩ Artistic phrasing typifies 12:11: "In *Gilead* there is iniquity, they shall surely come to nothing (*šāv'*). In Gilgal they sacrifice (*zibbēḥû*) bulls (*šěvārîm*), so their altars (*mizbēḥotām*) shall be like stone heaps (*kěgallîm*) on the furrows of the field."

| Gilead | A1 | | |
| *šāv'* (nothing) | B | B' | *šěvārîm* (bulls) |
| Gilgal | A | C' | *mizbēḥotām* (their altars) |
| *zibbēḥû* (they sacrifice) | C | A2 | *kěgallîm* (heaps) |

Note that the A elements repeat the first (A1) and second syllable (A2) of Gilgal (A). Also, the repeated elements on the right hand side of the chart all add a *mem* to the end of the word.

Israel as the name for the ancestor; and (2) it subtly incorporates the entire twenty-year period of Jacob's sojourn, since the phrasing ("he served for a wife"/"guarded *sheep*") includes the time Jacob worked for both marriages to Leah and Rachel as well as the subsequent time he worked with Laban's sheep. [Jacob's Sojourn]

Hosea 12:13 (MT 12:14) alludes to Moses, highlighting his role as prophet. Hosea 12:13 is formulated to draw attention to 12:12. Recent study suggests 12:12 and 13 reflect two different traditions for Israel's origin, one genealogical and the other prophetic.[2] As well, connections between the two verses share rhetorical markers: the dual use of "by a wife" (12:12) and "by a prophet" (12:13), combined with forms of the verb "to guard" (*šāmar*) in both verses. Hosea 12:13 subtly challenges the claim that one belongs to "Israel" by birth. Rather, it implies that paying attention to God's word as mediated by the prophets determines who belongs to Israel and who does not.

*Hosea 12:14 (MT 12:15).* Hosea 12:14 summarizes the accusation and punishment of the unit by accusing Ephraim of provoking YHWH's punishment. Elsewhere this provocation can involve pagan worship (e.g., Deut 4:25; 9:18; 32:16), and Ephraim's crimes probably assume the idolatry already described in Hosea 12 as well as 4–10.

The NRSV ("insults" rather than reproach) tones down the language of 12:14b. A more literal translation reads, "And his bloodshed is given over to him, and his Lord will return his reproach upon him." The reproach motif recurs periodically in the Twelve. [Reproach in the Book of the Twelve]

---

**Jacob's Sojourn**

AΩ Hos 12:12 refers to Jacob's wives, and the stories surrounding them, by means of the catchwords "work" (*ābad*) and "guard" (*šāmar*). This rather unusual phrasing picks up the verbs from two sections of Jacob's dealings with Laban in Genesis. The word "work" (*ābad*) is the verb used in 29:15, 20, 28, 30 when Jacob negotiates with Laban for Rachel and Leah. However, the verb "guard" (*šāmar*) is used when Jacob negotiates to keep Laban's sheep in Gen 30:31, starting a six-year period during which time Jacob received all of the sheep that were not solid black or white. Thus, as with the previous references to the Jacob story, 12:12 also uses catchwords from the larger narrative to make its point.

---

**Reproach in the Book of the Twelve**

The disgrace, or reproach, of God's people is a recurring motif in Hosea—Zephaniah. A string of texts announces Israel's reproach (Hos 12:14; Mic 6:16; Zeph 2:8) and offers to take it back (Joel 2:17, 19; 3:18).

---

## CONNECTIONS

Hosea 12 not only continues to develop a picture of a caring, compassionate God who is willing to forgive, but also portrays a God who has expectations regarding how people should live. This God is no stranger to Israel because Israel's own testimony tells the story of the many times it has disappointed that God. In Hosea 12, the story of Jacob lingers in the background as a reminder of what God has done: God protected Jacob as he fled the country after swindling his brother, and God protected Jacob when he returned after a twenty-year sojourn, during which time he was cheated by his own father-in-law. Yet, Jacob became wealthy even though some of his wealth resulted from some rather clever scheming on his part. Israel kept this story alive, telling and retelling it, presenting Jacob, warts and all, as a person who finally came to rely upon God's care, and as a person who learned to change his priorities for life as a result.

Hosea 12 creatively alludes to Jacob's story from the past in order to remind those in the present of their own need to turn to God. This chapter presents a collage of images in which the past meets present in order to reiterate a spiritual truth about the human condition: left to its own devices, humanity—including God's people—will act in their own selfish interests. The biblical God, however, calls us beyond ourselves to a dynamic, living relationship with the God who has a track record of being present to those who turn, or return, to God.

Hosea 12 also uses another of Israel's cherished traditions to challenge its assumptions that it is somehow immune from danger. Deftly drawing on the exodus, the story of God's liberation of Israel from bondage in Egypt, Hosea 12 reminds its original audience that their liberation obligated them to obedience to the God who liberated them. Indeed, the God who brought them out of the wilderness can send them back. God's deliverance does not guarantee them immunity from future trials, especially those brought about by their own recalcitrance. Consequently, the Moses of significance in Hosea 12 is Moses the prophet and lawgiver. Birthrights do not carry much weight in Hosea. God warns God's people through prophets because God's relationship with God's people is ongoing, ever developing, and ever relevant. This dynamic God challenges us today as well. Few will doubt that God was on the side of justice in the civil rights movement or in the overthrow of apartheid, but we do not ask where injustice lies in our own communities today, or what is our role in the perpetuation of injustice. Or, consider the caricature of "Ephraim" in 12:7-8, assuming that God blessed his economic endeavors because he stayed inside the limits of the law while amassing wealth, though he had benefited from a system that was rigged in his favor. God asks for commitments that seek love and justice, not power and wealth (12:6).

Yet, Hosea 12 does not present its message in a neat package that promises great spiritual and material rewards to its readers. Hosea 12 bombards us with accusations, challenging God's people to change from duplicity to integrity. It begins with direct assaults against a people who say one thing and do another, who hope to benefit from illicit behavior and yet think that God will not notice (11:12). It accuses God's people of chasing illusions without owning up to their own responsibility (12:1). It accuses God's people of trying to walk a dangerous line between military powers of the day without turning to God (12:1). It accuses God's people of business dealings whose sole purpose is increasing the bottom line, even if it means cheating the customer (12:7). Finally, Hosea 12 accuses God's people of worshiping other gods (12:12).

Moreover, the accusations of Hosea 12 do not come as idle threats. The chapter frames its message with clear reminders that actions have consequences (12:2, 14). Thus, the nation has created its own crisis—politically, economically, ethically, and spiritually.

**Experiencing the God of Justice**

A recent work by Tony Campolo and Mary Albert Darling explores the connections between justice and mysticism. See Anthony Campolo and Mary Albert Darling, *The God of Intimacy and Action: Reconnecting Ancient Spiritual Practices, Evangelism, and Justice* (San Francisco: Jossey-Bass, 2007).

So what can God's people do? Does this chapter offer nothing but a warning of divine rejection and doom? No. This prophet, like other prophets, calls for a change. In fact, this call to change appears in the middle of the chapter. Sandwiched between the warnings and the accusations, Hosea 12:6 presents a clear, pithy call to repent and live as though one's faith makes a difference: "But as for you, return to your God; hold fast to love and justice; and wait continually for your God." [Experiencing the God of Justice]

This call emphasizes three major theological movements: (1) repentance that leads to (2) the life of commitment that (3) lives expectantly for the future. First, the prophet addresses a people who think they can deceive God. They behave as though lies and deceit have no consequences. To them, and to us, God's message to God's people calls for a radical change of direction, one as great as Jacob's change or Israel's liberation. Second, this call to change, or repent, is based upon a simple set of expectations from God. God expects *ḥesed*, *mišpaṭ*, and hope. The Hebrew concept of *ḥesed* is a loaded word. It implies a range of attitudes and actions within a covenantal relationship. *Ḥesed* means kindness and mercy: we must show the same benevolence to others that God has shown to us. *Ḥesed* means keeping faith with promises made: when we tell God we will do something, we must do our best to follow through. *Ḥesed* means remembering who we are: we belong to God.

The Hebrew concept of *mišpaṭ* means justice, but not a one-sided view of justice as retribution. The idea of *mišpaṭ* means to do what is right and proper in small things and in large. It means not only making sure we behave properly but also making sure the right thing is done for society. The concept of *mišpaṭ* applies the same obligations to the poor and the wealthy, to the weak and the powerful; it means holding leaders accountable to behave with integrity; it means not letting the wealthy buy their way out of legal troubles; it means not letting the powerful make laws that benefit only themselves. The concept of *mišpaṭ* means not letting the widows and the orphans go hungry because it is not convenient to feed them; it means not ignoring the poor of society because the poor will be with us always; it means making sure our economic, judicial, and educational systems are fair and just. Why? Because it is part of God's expectation of God's people that we do what is right.

# NOTES

1. Similar associations happen with this word in Zeph 1:11; Zech 14:21; Prov 31:24; and Isa 23:8. Wolff notes that "Canaanites" is a derogatory reference to Ephraim, a land "filled with a Canaanite spirit of harlotry and commerce" (Hans Walter Wolff, *Hosea* [Hermeneia; trans. Gary Stansell; Philadelphia: Fortress, 1974] 214). For Jeremias, the equation of Canaanite with trader is a later concept, though he sees 12:8 as an early speech (Jörg Jeremias, *Der Prophet Hosea. übersetzt und erklärt* [Das Alte Testament Deutsch 24/1; Göttingen: Vandenhoeck & Ruprecht, 1983] 155).

2. See Konrad Schmid, *Genesis and the Moses Story: Israel's Dual Origins in the Hebrew Bible* (trans. James D. Nogalski; Siphrut 3; Winona Lake: Eisenbrauns, 2010) 74–75. Another recent redactional study of Hosea argues that the compositional form of Hos 12 reflects an exilic setting not far removed from the time of the Deuteronomistic History (Roman Vielhauer, *Das Werden des Buches Hosea: Eine redaktions-geschichtliche Untersuchung* [Beihefte zur Zeitschrift für die alttestamentliche Wissenschaft 349; Berlin: De Gruyter, 2007] 178–79).

# RECAPPING THE MESSAGE

## Hosea 13:1-16 (MT 13:1–14:1)

## COMMENTARY

Two characteristics stand out regarding Hosea 13: its trifold chronological movement and the intertextual features of its formulations. The trifold chronological movement combines past and current activity with future punishment. [Trifold Chronological Movement] The first movement (13:1-3) reflects upon the death of Ephraim's glorious past, its continuing rejection of God, and its imminent punishment. In the second movement (13:4-10), reference to Israel's history and its rejection of YHWH gives way to warning of a swift, surprising, and ferocious attack followed by a rhetorical question reminding Israel it currently has no king. The third movement (13:11-16 [MT 13:11–14:1]) reflects upon the history of Israel's failed political leadership and then characterizes Ephraim as a clueless child about whom God must make a decision that could determine the fate of the northern kingdom. At several points, Hosea 13 reflects a later, more reflective perspective than the bulk of Hosea 4–11, suggesting this chapter functions as a redactional compilation, especially because of its use of other texts.

The intertextual features of Hosea 13 include (1) themes, citations, and motifs found in Hosea and parts of the Book of the Twelve (Joel, Amos, Micah); (2) traditions about the exodus and entering the land; and (3) Deuteronomistic texts (1 Sam 8). [Intertextual Features of Hosea 13] These features create a kind of theological collage at

---

**Trifold Chronological Movement**

**Past**–13:1: Ephraim's past greatness died when Ephraim worshiped Baal.
**Present**–13:2: *Now* they continue to sin through false worship.
**Future**–13:3: *Thus*, they will soon disappear.

**Past**–13:4-6: I was their savior who brought them out of Egypt, but they abandoned me.
**Future**–13:7-9: I will attack them swiftly and ferociously.
**Present**–13:10: Destruction is coming, so where now is your king?

**Past**–13:11: I gave you kings and judges against my better judgment.
**Present**–13:12-14: Since Ephraim's sin and iniquity are clear, shall I redeem them? No.
**Future**–13:15-16: YHWH will send an east wind to dry up the land, and Samaria will fall by the sword.

| **Intertextual Features of Hosea 13** | |
| --- | --- |
| **Hosea** | **Quotations, Parallel Themes, and Motifs** |
| 13:1 | 12:14; 4:15; 5:15; 10:2 |
| 13:2 | 8:4; Amos 6:4; Mic 6:6 |
| 13:3 | 6:4 |
| 13:4 | 2:15; 7:11, 16; 8:13; 9:3, 6; 11:1, 5; 12:9, 13 |
| 13:5 | exodus and entering the land |
| 13:6 | 2:13 [MT 2:15]; 4:6; 8:14 |
| 13:7 | 5:15; 11:10 |
| 13:8 | Amos 5:18-19 |
| 13:9 | |
| 13:10 | 3:4, 5; 5:1, 13; 7:3, 5, 7; 10:3, 6, 7, 15 |
| 13:11 | 1 Samuel 8 |
| 13:12 | 4:8; 8:13; 9:9 |
| 13:13 | 7:11; 11:1; 14:9 (MT 14:10) |
| 13:14 | 11:8-9 |
| 13:15 | Joel 1:17, 19, 20; 2:3, 22; 4:18, 19 |
| 13:16 | 13:1; 10:14; Amos 7:9, 11 |

this important juncture in Hosea—the penultimate chapter that recaps significant elements of the book's message before the final call to repentance in Hosea 14. Consequently, the character of Hosea 13 is similar to Amos 8, which also is a theological recapitulation in the penultimate chapter before the book's final pronouncement(s).

## The Death of Ephraim's Glorious Past, 13:1-3

Hosea 13:1-3 exhibits no formal indicators that definitively mark the speaker. Rather, it falls between a unit where a prophet speaks (12:12-14) and another where God speaks (13:4-10). The opening verse continues the theme of 12:14. The form of 13:1-3 reflects the outline of a judgment oracle: the problem of past actions (13:1) continues into the present (13:2), inevitably leading to the pronouncement of impending punishment (13:3). [Prophetic Judgment Oracle]

Hosea 13:1 laments the death of the once glorious political entity Ephraim. Ephraim is the name of the central region of the northern kingdom, the region where Bethel and Samaria (see 13:16) were located. The tribe that had commanded respect as a political power has now died because of its guilt. Its guilt came about through the worship of Baal. Moreover, this accusation coincides with the charges leveled elsewhere in Hosea (2:8, 13, 16, 17; 7:16; 9:10; 11:2) and against the northern kingdom in 1–2 Kings, charges often seen as Deuteronomistic. Hosea 13:1 conveys a hint of polemical sarcasm in the statement about Baal.

**Prophetic Judgment Oracle**

The prophetic judgment oracle consists of four basic parts: (1) an introduction (usually in the form of a commission or an appeal to attention); (2) an indication of the situation (often in the form of an accusation); (3) a prediction or pronouncement of verdict (often introduced by the phrase, "therefore, thus says YHWH"); and (4) a concluding element (often providing motivation or confirming the outcome).

See W. Eugene March, "Prophecy" in *Old Testament Form Criticism* (ed. John H. Hayes; San Antonio: Trinity University Press, 1974) 159–60.

The statement declares Ephraim dies as a result of Baal, but the Baal story ends with Baal coming back to life in order to take care of the earth. No such restoration awaits Ephraim. [The Baal Myth]

Hosea 13:2 continues the accusation against Ephraim, but specifically characterizes the current time ("and now") as sinful. The "cast image" generally appears (as here) in the context of idols for worshiping pagan deities (Deut 27:15; Judg 17:3-4; 18:14; Nah 1:14). This image refers to a figure made from pouring molten metal into molds. Thematically, this accusation parallels the charge in Hosea 8:4 (which also contains anti-king polemic similar to that found in 13:10-11). The word translated "artisans" literally means "metal workers" and comes from the root meaning "engrave." The noun of this root also appears in Hosea 8:6, another text condemning the worship of idols. Hosea 13:2 alludes to another cultic practice, but it is not readily apparent in the NRSV. The phrase "sacrifice to these" (NRSV) changes the MT, which has "those sacrificing men." Thus, the NRSV downplays the gruesome accusation of human sacrifice, but human sacrifice was known in the ancient world (including Israel, see Mic 6:7). [Human Sacrifice] Also, while the word "calves" used in the NRSV technically refers to young bulls, it often refers to metal replicas used in worship, especially in Samaria. These calf figures were condemned in Hosea 8:5-6, and similar condemnations also occur in Amos 6:4 and Micah 6:6.

The change from the death of Ephraim (13:1) to Ephraim's continued sinning (13:2) seems illogical at first. The gap from "then" to "now" created by the movement from 13:1 to 13:2 cannot be explained literally, so most commentators explain the tension conceptually and politically. Conceptually, one finds the idea in

### The Baal Myth

For a recent critical English translation of the Baal myth, see William W. Hallo et al., eds., *Canonical Compositions from the Biblical World*, vol. 1 of *The Context of Scripture* (Leiden: Brill, 2003) 243–73, as well as the brief introduction preceding the translation by Dennis Pardee (p. 241–42) documenting the difficulties of piecing the text together from the extant pieces. This Ugaritic text from the second millennium tells the story of Baal defeating Yam (Sea) in a battle for kingship. Baal builds his own palace on the high places, but he is eventually defeated by Mot (god of the underworld). Baal's sister and perhaps lover, Anat, the goddess of war, defeats Mot so that Baal is returned to his throne. While Baal is in the underworld, the world suffers, and when he is returned, fertility of the land resumes.

### Human Sacrifice

Acts of human sacrifice are universally condemned in the Hebrew Bible, but this condemnation also presumes that the practice was being conducted by persons of despicable repute. In some form, child sacrifice appears in 24 texts: Gen 22:2; Lev 18:26; 20:2-3; Deut 12:31; Josh 6:26; Jdg 11:30-31; 1 Kgs 16:34; 2 Kgs 3:27; 16:3; 17:17; 21:6; 23:10; 2 Chr 33:6; Isa 57:5; Mic 6:7; Jer 7:31; 19:5; 32:35; Ezek 16:20-21, 36; 20:26; 23:37; Ps 106:37-38. At times, this practice is euphemized as "passing through fire," where the practice is either used to praise cultic reforms of kings who stopped it (Josiah in 2 Kgs 23:37) or to condemn kings who practiced it (Manasseh in 2 Kgs 21:6). The practice generally appears in polemical contexts, as part of condemnations, so its prevalence is a matter of some debate. For example, Joshua forbids the rebuilding of Jericho lest the builder lose his firstborn and youngest sons (Josh 6:26), but in the time of Ahab (Israel's most despised king in the book of Kings), Hiel the Bethelite chooses to "honor" this endeavor by sacrificing his oldest and youngest son as a sign of his (wayward) devotion.

**Calf Shrines**

Metal calf shrines have been found in the Levant and were apparently used in the late bronze and iron ages as religious icons.

Two bulls, from the Jordan Valley. Bronze (Late Bronze or Early Iron Age). Reuben & Edith Hecht Collection, Haifa University, Haifa, Israel. (Credit: Erich Lessing/Art Resource, NY)

**Changes from 733 to 722**

After the Syro-Ephraimite war (733), Hoshea was put on the throne by the Assyrians, against whom he soon began to plot. Later, Hoshea began to rebel against the Assyrians before he was taken prisoner by the Assyrians (724), and the destruction of Samaria followed after a three-year siege (722). Several commentators see the events between 724 and 722 as the background for Hos 13:2 and 13:10.

Hebrew texts, especially in Psalms, that someone in mortal distress can be addressed as though they are already dead (e.g., Ps 30:3, where the speaker speaks of being "restored to life from among those gone down to the Pit.").

This dead-but-not-yet-dead scenario also fits as a metaphor describing political changes in Israel. [Changes from 733 to 722] In this scenario, Ephraim refers to the rump state ruled by Hoshea after 733 BCE, when two-thirds of the country fell under Assyrian authority. The prophet has fled Ephraim because he sees what others do not: namely, that by rebelling against the Assyrians, Hoshea has put Ephraim on a path to inevitable destruction because Ephraim cannot possibly overpower the Assyrians. The setting for this unit presumes a time after Israel's monarchy failed (724 BCE, see 13:10) and before Samaria's complete destruction (722 BCE, 13:16). Given the various chronological indicators in Hosea 13, this chapter may be a later construct reiterating the book's message prior to the final call to repent (see Hosea 14).

Hosea 13:3 introduces the punishment using "therefore," a typical marker in a judgment oracle. Thus, 13:3a echoes Hosea 6:4, comparing Ephraim to the morning fog or dew that quickly evaporates. However, in 6:4 the phrase is part of an accusation where God charges that their *loyalty* disappeared like the dew and the mist, while in 13:3 the similes reflect Ephraim's punishment: *they* will disappear quite quickly. Thus, the images earlier used for the accusation are now used to announce the imminent punishment. To this comparison, the second half of the verse adds two more images of elements that are easily blown by the wind: chaff and smoke.

## Rejection of YHWH Leads to Disaster, 13:4-10

This second movement in Hosea 13—covering past (13:4-6), future (13:7-9), and present (13:10)—links more integrally with the movement that follows (13:11-16). The link between these two movements is formed through the shared perspective of the divine speaker and the use of rhetorical questions when addressing the present time. Hosea 13:4 begins with an allusion to the exodus event and the exclusive nature of Israel's relationship with God. Allusion to the exodus occurs elsewhere in Hosea (2:15; 11:1; 12:9, 13), and 13:4b paraphrases the first commandment ("I am the Lord your God [. . .] you shall have no other gods before me" [Exod 20:2-3]). [Exodus Allusions in Hosea]

Hosea 13:5 continues YHWH's speech, referring to YHWH's relationship with Israel that began "in the wilderness." It alludes to the wilderness period and YHWH's provision for Israel during Israel's sojourn in Egypt. The NRSV, apparently influenced by the LXX ("I tended you"), translates the first verb "fed," but the MT has "I knew you" in the wilderness. This latter concept is attested in Deuteronomy (2:7; 8:2; 9:24), and need not be changed in Hosea 13:5.

While 13:5 refers to the wilderness period, commentators differ on whether 13:6 refers to the wilderness or the entry into the land. Hosea 13:6 implies that YHWH provided for Ephraim, but the Ephraimites took YHWH for granted. Some think 13:6 refers to the wilderness, though it makes no specific reference to manna or to the grumbling of the Israelites. Others argue that this verse extends the metaphor to a period in which Israel entered the land. For this view, one must assume the image of YHWH as shepherd who has brought the sheep into the pasture. The extended parallelism of 13:6 presumes a process: feeding leads to satisfaction, satisfaction then leads to pride, and finally pride leads to abandoning YHWH.

Whether 13:6 limits itself to the wilderness period, however, is not a major issue. Rhetorically, YHWH is challenging the current generation. When 13:6 says, "they forgot me," this accusation runs counter to commands that specifically expected the people "to remember" what YHWH had done in Egypt and the wilderness (e.g., Deut 5:15; 7:18; 8:2; 9:7; 15:15). This phrase also reiterates a

### Exodus Allusions in Hosea

References to the exodus tradition appear in various forms in Hosea. One finds phrases used to refer to YHWH's salvific acts of the past in idyllic terms, and which serve as a hopeful pattern for the future (2:15; 11:1). The exodus also serves as warning for judgment in the sense of a repeat of the wilderness wandering (12:9). Moses' prophetic leadership is also credited for protecting Ephraim (12:13). Hos 13:2 alludes to Baal worship by drawing a parallel to the golden calf incident (Exod 32) in order to reiterate that YHWH, not Baal, is the one who brought Israel out of Egypt (Hos 13:4-5).

charge found elsewhere in Hosea (2:13 [MT 2:15]; 4:6; 8:14) that Israel has forgotten YHWH—a charge that represents an important testimony for Israel's identity.

YHWH's future actions are described in 13:7 using metaphors that draw upon images found in Hosea and Amos. Moreover, Hosea 13:7 presents the consequences of Israel turning its back on YHWH. It threatens Ephraim with a surprise attack from which there is no escape. The logic connecting 13:6 to 13:7 is significant: *because* the people have forgotten, YHWH will dramatically remind them. This reminder takes the form of lion imagery that plays a role elsewhere in Hosea (5:15; 11:10) and is one of the motifs connecting Hosea, Joel, and Amos (see the discussion of Hos 11:10).

Hosea 13:8 continues to portray YHWH as a wild animal, in this case a she-bear whose cubs have been taken. With 13:7, the ferocity of these images emphasizes the speed and anger of the attacker, underscoring YHWH's ability to attack at will and the vulnerability of the nation. Adding to this violent image is the phrase "covering of their heart," which literally means "heart container" and refers to the chest cavity. This image of a ferocious she-bear ripping open the one she thinks responsible for taking her cubs is a deliberately shocking metaphor designed to startle the people who take YHWH for granted (see 13:6). Several commentators note similarities between 13:7-8 and Amos 5:18-19, where the move to escape a lion leads to the attack of a bear.

Hosea 13:9 asserts the implications of YHWH's surprising and devastating actions. The verb "destroy" in 13:9 can refer to the work of a lion (Jer 4:7). Influenced by the LXX, the NRSV emends the text to make YHWH the destroyer, but the MT suggests the fault lies with Israel because they turned against YHWH. [Emending 13:10] The NAS offers the closest translation of the MT by expressing the same idea one finds in Jeremiah 2:17. At any rate, Hosea 13:9 drives home the point of the animal metaphors, even as it transitions to a discussion of the futility of resistance. If one is frightened by the image of a lion or bear attacking, then how much more daunting should it be that YHWH, not an animal, threatens to attack. There is no

**Emending 13:10**

AΩ English translations of 13:10 illustrate its complexity:

NRSV: I will destroy you, O Israel; who can help you?
RSV: I will destroy you, O Israel; who can help you?
KJV: O Israel, thou hast destroyed thyself; but in me is thine help.
NIV: You are destroyed, O Israel, because you are against me, against your helper.
NAS: It is your destruction, O Israel, that you are against Me, against your help.

escape; there is no point in fighting back; and there is no help on the way.

Finally, Hosea 13:10 takes up the issue more pointedly by asking two rhetorical questions whose answers are patently obvious. The first deals with the impotence of Israel's king, implying both that the king cannot save Israel from YHWH *and* that the king is no longer in the picture. "Where now" emphasizes the absence of the king. It alludes to the imprisonment of Hoshea by the Assyrians as described in 2 Kings 17:4. Hosea 13:10a plays on the name of the last king of Israel, Hoshea, whose name means "he (YHWH) will save," while 13:10 asks, "Where is your king that *he may save you?*" Hosea 13:10b mocks the power of Israel's king by alluding to 1 Samuel 8, where the elders ask Samuel to give them a king since his sons were not fit to lead.

## Ephraim's Failure as a Political Entity and as a Child, 13:11-16 (MT 13:11–14:1)

The third movement from past to present to future continues with YHWH's reference to his *past decision* (13:11) that causes him to reflect upon his *current decision* (13:12-14), before the pronouncement of YHWH's *future actions* (13:15-16 [MT 13:15–14:1]) against Samaria. Hosea 13:11 sets up a dichotomy between the accommodation of YHWH in giving Israel kingship ("in my anger") and the removal of the king ("in my wrath"). As with Hosea 13:10, the backdrop of giving a king is also 1 Samuel 8, where YHWH tells Samuel to anoint a king for the people, even though this meant Israel was rejecting YHWH as king (1 Sam 8:7). First Samuel 8 largely exhibits a negative view toward kingship in general because human kingship removed YHWH from YHWH's rightful place. Hosea 13:11 also presupposes the end of Israel's kingship, although 724 (the imprisonment of Hoshea) or 722 (the destruction of Samaria) would be the earliest point for dating this passage because of its reflective qualities. This reference to kingship that began and ended with YHWH's anger hermeneutically moves the reader to the present, where YHWH evaluates Ephraim's current state in 13:12-13. [Kingship and the Prophets]

Hosea 13:12 presents a short saying that utilizes assonance and parallel expressions. The two subjects (iniquity and sin) of this verse display a synonymous parallel, while the two verbs begin with

## Kingship and the Prophets

The role of kingship in the prophets has a long and complex history. W. Zimmerli notes that the relationship of Yahwism to the monarchy has always had its tensions, as indicated by the bifurcated narrative in 1 Samuel 8–12, which tells of the prophetic role in anointing Saul and David but also conveys Samuel's ambivalence toward kingship in general. The continuing rule of a Davidic monarch for 400 years adds to the impression of validity of promises of eternal rule. These expectations become the starting point for messianic expectations.

B. Lang suggests four types of hopes associated with royal figures in Jerusalem: (1) a messianic monarchy, which articulates the king's close association with the deity; (2) a conservative royalist restoration party of the exilic period with specific but unrealistic aims of national independence with a Davidic monarch; (3) non-messianic religion centered in the temple that rejects both the idea of an independent state and a Davidic descendant; (4) an apocalyptic movement that thinks in terms of a universal kingdom ruled by two messiahs (one religious and one military) that requires divine intervention. The first type describes official Davidic orientation of Jerusalem prior to 586 BCE, while the fourth type arises in the second century BCE. The second and third groups competed with one another, from the exilic period onward, with the third group representing the more powerful group for much of that period.

R. Albertz sees not two, but several groups vying for control from the exilic period onward, and also suggests these groups do not speak with one voice concerning kingship. Ezekiel and Jeremiah were quite critical of the monarchs, but the Deuteronomists were by and large convinced they were a necessary part of a future kingdom. A prophetic group influenced by the Deuteronomists, which Albertz labels JerD, was more cautious about the monarchy, making their existence contingent upon the need of the monarchy to care for the weak. A time of renewal would only come at the instigation of YHWH, not the reestablishment of the monarchy. In time, the Deuteronomists concluded that true restoration could come about only through complete allegiance to YWH, and the restoration of the state cult. A third group that plays a role is the group dominated by pious laypersons who commit to complete devotion of YHWH as well.

P. L. Redditt demonstrates how these attitudes play out in the development of the Twelve. He notes a decidedly negative attitude toward kingship present in the early portions of the Book of Four (Hosea, Amos, Micah, Zaphaniah) while Haggai and Zechariah 1–8 are much more open and present Zerubbabel as the "first step toward the restitution of the monarchy." By contrast, Redditt sees a redactional, "pro-Davidic recension" experienced by the Book of Four. Ultimately, Zechariah 9–14 reassess the role of the Davidides and makes clear that the house of David would need to repent before it could be used fully of God.

Walther Zimmerli, *Old Testament Theology in Outline* (trans. David E. Green; Edinburgh: T & T Clark, 1978) 92–93.

Bernhard Lang, *Monotheism and the Prophetic Minority: An Essay in Biblical History and Sociology* (SWBA 1; Sheffield: Almond Press, 1983) 132–36.

Rainer Albertz, *From the Exile to the Maccabees* (vol. 2 of *A History of Israelite Religion in the Old Testament Period*; trans. John Bowden; OTL; Louisville: Westminster John Knox, 1994) 382–94.

Paul L. Redditt, "The King in Haggai–Zechariah 1–8 and the Book of the Twelve," in *Tradition and Transition: Haggai and Zechariah 1–8 in the Trajectory of Hebrew Theology* (Library of Hebrew Bible/OTS 475; New York: T & T Clark, 2008) 56–82.

the same Hebrew letter and together present a kind of process: binding and storing away. The word pair "iniquity and sin" appears elsewhere in Hosea (4:8; 8:13; 9:9), and once again, the core concern of this saying draws upon motifs that play a significant role in the book's message, namely the "iniquity" (4:8; 5:5; 7:1; 8:13; 9:7, 9; 10:10; 12:9; 13:12; 14:2, 3) and "sin" (4:8; 8:13; 9:9; 10:8; 13:12) of Ephraim/Israel. Yet, the point is not merely to repeat key words. This short saying characterizes the repetitive nature of Ephraim's rejection of YHWH. God's patience, by implication, has reached its limit.

Hosea 13:13 draws upon other recurring motifs in Hosea to characterize Ephraim. Hosea 13:13 presents a sardonic picture of Ephraim as a child with no sense. In this picture, Ephraim neither knows what to do, nor when to do it. Hosea 13:13 draws upon the image of childbirth to make the point: even an infant knows when to be born, but Ephraim does not respond "at the proper time" to the message of the prophet. In this image, if the child refuses to be born, it can only mean death for the child and the mother.

This image of the young child has counterparts elsewhere in Hosea, notably Hosea 11. The perspective of 13:13 ties together the motif of the young child (see 11:1) and the foolish meandering of Ephraim (7:11) in a type of summary pronouncement on its fate.

A series of four rhetorical questions addressing Death and Sheol structure 13:14, and a fifth line answers those questions. The questions are not existential so much as they call on Death and Sheol to do their job. [Sheol] Hosea 13:14 functions as the antithesis to the emotion-laden YHWH speech of 11:8-9. YHWH speaks to YHWH, thus mimicking the style of the divine soliloquy about what to do with Ephraim in 11:1-9. However, 13:14 shows none of the pathos over Ephraim's fate found in Hosea 11. In 11:8-9, YHWH's compassion took precedence, while here judgment takes over. [1 Corinthians 15:55 Cites Hosea 13:14] The final line makes a definitive pronouncement: unlike in 11:8-9, YHWH will not intervene to deliver Ephraim.

Finally, Ephraim's future is laid out in 13:15-16. Stylistically, these verses change from first person divine speech (13:15) to third person prophetic speech (13:16). In 13:15, YHWH uses metaphors to pronounce the coming destruction of the Assyrians, while in 13:16 the prophet explicates those metaphors with a theological rationale.

The first phrase is difficult to translate, but most of 13:15 pronounces judgment on Israel in the form of a drought caused by an east wind

**Sheol**

ΑΩ "Sheol" is the Hebrew word for the abode of the dead. However, it is not identical with the New Testament concept of Hades. The New Testament concept of Hades reflects a period prior the development of the idea of an eternal afterlife, which came about during the Hellenistic period (332–63 BCE). Sheol was the place to which all those who died went. Moreover, unlike its New Testament counterpart, Sheol was not a place of torment. It was simply the place of the dead from which no one returned. Other texts personify Sheol as in Hos 13:14 (Prov 1:12; Isa 5:14; Hab 2:5), and a significant number of words are used as synonyms elsewhere. These include "ditch" (Ps 16:10), "pit" (Ps 28:1), "death" (Ps 6:5 [MT 6:6]), and "perdition" (Abaddon, Ps 88:11).

**1 Corinthians 15:55 Cites Hosea 13:14**

Hos 13:14 functions differently in Hosea than when Paul cites it in 1 Cor 15:55. In Hosea, the verse assumes that YHWH controls the plagues and that he can use them as he chooses. Paul treats these questions in isolation from the Hosea context as existential laments of the power of death. However, Paul combines these questions with the idea of YHWH defeating death that appears in Isa 25:8, and he puts this affirmation into the context of a life in Christ. In one sense, both assume God has ultimate control over death, but the Hosea passage assumes that this control is used as a weapon against Ephraim while Paul sees Christ's resurrection as the reversal of this sentence.

### The First Phrase of Hosea 13:15

AΩ One phrase has textual variations. The NRSV translates the accusative of the first phrase "flourish *among the rushes*." The MT says, "for he will flourish *between brothers*." The NRSV assumes a different text, but one that cannot be justified text critically. It reads *'āḥû* instead of MT's *'aḥîm*. Such a reading would involve changing two consonants (a *yod* and *mem* for a single *shureq*) for no apparent reason.

### Hosea 13:15 in the Book of the Twelve

Hos 13:15 contains several images that come back into play in the Book of the Twelve as part of a recurring fertility motif. This verse may have played a role in Joel's formation or placement, since Joel 1–2 follows Hosea in the MT order of the Twelve and combines the images of locust plagues, military invasion, and drought to describe the situation with which that book begins. Links between Hos 13:15 and Joel abound: the wilderness (Joel 1:19, 20; 2:3, 22; 4:19), spring (4:18), and storehouse (1:17). Subsequently, the Book of the Twelve contains a promise to restore the agricultural fertility from seed in the storage pit once temple construction begins (Hag 2:19) and a call to bring the tithe into the storehouse (Mal 3:10) after the temple has been restored. See discussions of these texts.

### Phrases from Hosea and Amos

AΩ The phrase "they shall fall by the sword" is reminiscent of Amos 7:9, 11 (see also 4:10), the prediction of the death of the house of Jeroboam. The phrase "their little ones will be dashed in pieces" recalls Hos 10:14, which speaks of Ephraim/Judah/Jacob (10:11) whose mothers are dashed in pieces with their children. The phrase "their pregnant women ripped open" is virtually identical to the phrasing of the Ammonite oracle in the Amos 1:13, not coincidentally for its treatment of Gilead (see Hos 12:11). See also 2 Kgs 15:16.

coming from the wilderness. [The First Phrase of Hosea 13:15] The drought will dry up the water supply of the land, causing stockpiled grain in the storehouse to disappear. Many commentators interpret the east wind as a metaphor for Assyria. They note how well the metaphor fits in the time after the capture of King Hoshea and Assyria had taken over the region. Hosea 13:15 may also have played a role in the formation of the Book of the Twelve. [Hosea 13:15 in the Book of the Twelve]

Hosea 13:16 combines phrases from Hosea and Amos in a final statement about the guilt and punishment of the northern kingdom, specifically addressing the capital Samaria. [Phrases from Hosea and Amos] The verb "to bear guilt" began this chapter equating Ephraim's sin with the worship of Baal. Its recurrence here undoubtedly connects back to 13:1. In short, the punishment in 13:16 describes the aftermath of military destruction and degradation at the hands of a foreign army, thus interpreting the east wind of 13:15 more concretely as a military power than the metaphorical language of 13:15 alone.

## CONNECTIONS

Hosea 13 appears to be a theological collage summarizing the message of the book by drawing upon particular phrases from Hosea and other traditions. Hosea 13 offers this summary before the final call to repentance that dominates Hosea 14. This is no accident. Amos 8 does the same thing for Amos before the book's fifth and final vision. Hosea 13 also exhibits a perspective considerably later than most passages elsewhere in Hosea, for it presumes the king of Ephraim has already disappeared (13:10). This later perspective, combined with allusions to Israel's historical traditions, gives this chapter a reflective quality. Hosea 13 recapitulates the message of Hosea in order to provide further evidence of the depth of Israel's problems before once again moving to a call to repentance (14:1-9 [MT 14:2-10]).

Three times the reader learns that past sins continue into the present and that these sins will lead to punishment. [Remembering the Past] The sins about which the chapter speaks are the sins about which the book has already spoken: the worship of Baal and idols (13:1-2), forgetting YHWH (13:6), and sinful and foolish behavior (13:12-13). The imminent punishment (13:3, 7-8, 15, 16) connects images from Hosea, Amos, and Joel. These connections probably did not happen simultaneously, but the final form of Hosea in the Book of the Twelve receives continuity from them, however one explains them. In addition, links to this prophetic message extend beyond the Book of the Twelve to the Pentateuch and the story of the monarchy. Hosea 13 refers to the exodus, the wilderness wanderings, and the conquest of the land (13:4-6). These stories concern Israel's deliverance and its entry into the land. Hosea 13 also alludes to problems with the judges and the kings, with particular emphasis upon the important text of 1 Samuel 8.

By placing Hosea 13 alongside the references to the exodus and the Jacob story in Hosea 12, one finds clear allusions to the Pentateuch and the Former Prophets.[1] These references to Israel's story underscore YHWH's patience and grace. Hosea 13 depicts Ephraim as having forgotten YHWH repeatedly, but Ephraim's existence testifies to YHWH's patience. Three times this chapter shows the long-standing nature of the problem, and three times YHWH warns of impending punishment on Ephraim and Samaria, a punishment described in 2 Kings 17. In short, the canonical allusions in Hosea 12–13 emphasize the lengths to which YHWH had gone to preserve a relationship with Ephraim. Now, however, the time had come to recognize that Ephraim would

## Remembering the Past

The philosopher George Santayana is the source of the maxim: "Those who cannot remember the past are condemned to repeat it." The broader context of that quote, while dated in its formulation, nevertheless raises important issues. Where are we headed as a society, as individuals, and as a community of believers?

Progress, far from consisting in change, depends on retentiveness. When change is absolute there remains no being to improve and no direction is set for possible improvement: and when experience is not retained, as among savages, infancy is perpetual. Those who cannot remember the past are condemned to repeat it.

Hosea 13 attempts to frame the future for its readers by citation of Israel's past. Such use of the past differs from merely citing the past of some type of ideal from which the current generation has deviated.

George Santayana, *Reason in Common Sense* (vol. 1 of *The Life of Reason: Or The Phases of Human Progress*; New York: Charles Scribner's Sons, 1905; repr., New York: Dover, 1980) 284.

never learn to rely upon YHWH without radical changes. Still, the prophet's message comes in the form of a warning in Hosea 13; it is a warning of impending doom as just punishment, and yet a warning that is still not the end of the story. Hosea 14 will, once again, extend a call to Israel to repent.

Many believers do not like to dwell on the judgment of God. They prefer the tender father in Hosea 11 to the God whose compassion is hidden in Hosea 13. Yet, other believers act as though God's tenderness is a sign of weakness. They prefer to portray God as a deity ready to strike at a moment's notice to correct God's wayward children. The Bible (both Old and New Testaments), however, portrays God as loving and judging, as merciful and wrathful. The abrupt changes in the portrayal of God in Hosea 11–14 dramatically reiterate both judgment and grace. The grace of God is no less real because it is followed by judgment in Hosea. God's judgment is no less daunting because God prefers love and respect. No one is beyond the reach of God, but they must recognize the problem and return to God. However, the decision on when, how, and to whom God responds is not ours to make. God's justice and God's grace begin and end with God (obliquely, one finds this stated in Joel 2:14; it is more explicit in Jer 18:7-10).

# NOTE

1. See Roman Vielhauer, *Das Werden des Buches Hosea: Eine redaktions-geschichtliche Untersuchung* (Beihefte zur Zeitschrift für die alttestamentliche Wissenschaft 349; Berlin: De Gruyter, 2007) 180–81.

# AN OPEN INVITATION

## Hosea 14:1-9 (MT 14:2-10)

## COMMENTARY

Hosea 14 divides into three sections (14:1-3, 4-8, 9 [MT 14:2-4, 5-9, 10]), the first two of which relate integrally to one another while the third reflects upon the entire book. Hosea 14:1-8 is universally treated as a call to repentance, though the relationship of its two parts elicits debate. Hosea 14:1-3 contains the call proper, addressed to the people by the prophetic voice, and 14:4-8 contains the divine response. Since 14:8 addresses rhetorical questions to the present generation, and since these questions presume idolatry as an ongoing problem, 14:1-8 serves as an open-ended call to repentance. Finally, Hosea 14:9 (MT 14:10) functions as the motto for the book, and it is associated often, but not universally, with wisdom tradents.

### An Open-ended Call to Repentance, 14:1-8 (MT 14:2-9)

Hosea 14:1-8 (MT 14:2-9) divides into two parts based on the speaker: the prophet's call to repentance (14:1-3) and the divine response (14:4-8). Each of these parts also has two sections. The prophet's call to repentance begins with the call proper (14:1-2a) and then conveys the specific prayer that the prophet wants the people to pray (14:2b-3). The divine response begins with a promise of God's compassionate deliverance (14:4-7) before turning to a rhetorical question and response challenging the current generation (14:8).

*Hosea 14:1-3* (MT 14:2-4). The prophet begins this call to repentance with an imperative verb "return," which is the theological expression used to call someone to reverse direction. In contrast to the previous chapter, 14:2-9 specifies Israel, not Ephraim, as the addressee. This change in moniker causes some to see "Israel"—who is mentioned in 14:1, 5 (MT 14:2, 6)—here as an epithet for both the northern and southern kingdoms. However, since the previous verse announces the imminent demise of Samaria, the capital of Israel, one should assume this call to repentance is directed toward the northern kingdom. Also, 14:8 offers a promise to Ephraim, and it is an integral part of the call to repentance. The reason for the need to repent is Israel's iniquity, a concept associated with the guilt of various groups throughout Hosea (4:8; 5:5; 7:1; 8:13; 9:7, 9; 10:10; 12:9; 13:12; 14:3). Specifically, the idea of "stumbling in iniquity" already appeared in 5:5, and as with chapters 12 and 13, the larger thematic unit exhibits a recognizable inclusio at the beginning and end of the unit (14:1, 9), using the verb "to stumble."

Hosea 14:2 (MT 14:3) continues the call to repent by explaining what the people should say when they return to YHWH. The people should ask YHWH to remove their guilt, the reason given in 14:1 (MT 14:2) for the need to repent. As a result, the people shall bring their genuine spoken promises to YHWH instead of meaningless sacrifices. [Spoken Promises] Thus, this prayer reiterates the devaluation of animal sacrifice as in Hosea 6:6 (see also Mic 6:6-8). Instead, the image created by this prayer is that of a pious worshiper who offers a vow/sacrifice, but the offering is neither a pledge nor an animal; rather, it is a changed life, a confession to YHWH, and a petition for YHWH to remove the guilt of former actions.

Hosea 14:3 (MT 14:4) expands the prayer to include recurring motifs from the book: Israel will not find deliverance in political entities or in the worship of idols. Rather, Israel hopes to find mercy like that which YHWH shows to orphans. Implicitly, then, 14:3aa indicates that Israel had failed to recognize that YHWH, not Assyria, is the true force behind political and military power. "Horses" are military instruments in 14:3. The point of the line, then, is that Israel will disavow Assyria as a source of deliverance (see 5:13; 7:11; 8:9; 12:1). Next, 14:3ab picks up the anti-idolatry polemic that plays a prominent role in the book (4:12-13, 17; 8:5-6; 11:1; 13:2). Finally, 14:3b picks up the motif of Ephraim as a child, yet this time portraying Israel as an orphan, since Hosea 11 portrays their father (i.e., YHWH) as having acquiesced to their

**Spoken Promises**

AΩ This portion of Hos 14:2 (MT 14:3) reads, "And we will repay bulls (by) our lips." Some translations, like the NRSV, follow the LXX and translate "fruit" (*perî*) rather than "bulls" (*pārîm*), but this translation only attempts to smooth difficult syntax without explaining how the MT originated. Instead, it is better to understand "bulls" as the sacrificial animals used as a guilt offering (Lev 4:3) or a peace offering (Exod 24:5; Num 7:88). This liturgical reference makes sense in the immediate and extended context since Israel's false worship has been a major source of concern in Hosea. It goes without saying that the spoken sacrifice must be genuine this time, since 6:4-6 rejected the promise of 6:1-3 as inauthentic.

disavowal of his parental status by withholding his compassion (13:14). In 14:3, the orphan will find compassion, using the verbal root from the name of Hosea's daughter, *Lo-Ruhamah*. Thus, the prophetic call to repent suggests a prayer for the people that recognizes their guilt—guilt that has been laid out throughout the book of Hosea.

*Hosea 14:4-8* (MT 14:5-9). YHWH responds to the prayer in 14:4-8 first with a salvific promise (14:4-7) and then with a rhetorical admonition (14:8). This proleptic response resolves God's dilemma—whether to judge Israel or not—that has played a major role in Hosea's structure, especially in Hosea 11/12–13. The response underscores God's love, compassion, and willingness to forgive, but it requires a commitment to change from Israel.

The speaker changes to YHWH in Hosea 14:4. The formulation contains a play on words in Hebrew between the words Ephraim and "I will heal" (*'erpâ*). God promises healing, love, and the cessation of anger. This promise depends contextually upon the condition that the prayer suggested by the prophet in 14:1-3 has been spoken by the people. Herein lies a significant debate among commentators. Should the reader assume that the people have spoken the words in 14:1-3, or is the invitation still open? The answer to this question does not come definitively until the end of the unit (14:8), where the admonition presumes that Israel is still steeped in idolatry. The effect of this delayed admonition underscores God's willingness, even at this late point, to take Israel/Ephraim back. Moreover, this theological affirmation lays the groundwork for a series of allusions later in the Book of the Twelve to Exodus 34:6-7.[1]

In contrast to the way it is used previously in Hosea (see 6:4; 13:6), Hosea 14:5 uses the dew simile positively. The comparison in 14:5 draws upon the hydrating qualities of dew, not the speed with which it evaporates as in the previous references. Hosea 14:5 offers two images of healthy plants. Together these images underscore the fertility YHWH promises to Israel: the lily blossoms upward, with the flower symbolizing its fertility, while the roots of the cedars of Lebanon shoot downward and supply the trees their strength. The word "forests" in the NRSV does not appear in the MT "His roots will be like the Lebanon." It is deduced from the context. Lebanon was known for its cedars in the ancient world. Cedars were prized for fine lumber because of their longevity and aromatic character. Lebanon is also used in metaphors in 14:6, 7, though 14:7 refers to the wine of Lebanon, not the cedars.

Hosea 14:6 (MT 14:7) continues the promise to Israel using metaphors of fertile plants, specifically an olive tree and a cedar. The olive tree, especially when full of fruit, connotes a tree with a thick canopy of intertwining branches and twisted trunks. The word "beauty" may conjure different images than the tree conveys for most westerners, but the olive tree often grows where other trees do not. Its fruit is the source of food and oil (for cooking and for lamps). "Lebanon" again implies the cedars of that region and their aroma.

The NRSV attests to the rather strange turn taken by the syntax and the images in 14:7. The Hebrew text of 14:7 reads differently than the NRSV. [The Problematic Hebrew Text of Hosea 14:7] A more literal translation of the MT is presumed here: "My inhabitants will return in his shade; they will revive grain and they will blossom like the vine; his renown will be like the wine of Lebanon." The NRSV deviates unnecessarily from this text. References to Ephraim have used third masculine singular pronouns, but 14:7a suddenly changes to plural pronouns that refer to the inhabitants, while the singular references continue to refer to Israel. "Shade," or "shadow," can be used metaphorically to refer to protection, whether that protection is from God (Pss 17:8; 36:8), a king (Lam 4:20), a citizen (Gen 19:8), or a nation (Isa 30:2). Here, one must decide whose protection the inhabitants will enjoy. Syntactically, the protection refers to Israel, but this depends upon YHWH's promise to restore Israel.

The rhetorical question that opens 14:8 continues with YHWH as speaker, but moves from the realm of promise to the sphere of Israel's current condition. Specifically, this verse makes clear that the promise of 14:4-7 has not already been granted, but remains subject to the response of the people. Thus, the rhetorical question reminds Ephraim to abandon its worship of idols and turn to YHWH.

**Olive Tree**

(Credit: Mewasul. Olive trees in Gethsemane, Jerusalem, http://commons.wikimedia.org/wiki/File:Getsemane1.JPG)

Adjacent to the Church of All Nations is an ancient olive garden. Olive trees do not have rings and so their age cannot be precisely determined, but scholars estimate their age to anywhere between one and two thousand years old. It is unlikely that these trees were here in the time of Christ because of the report that the Romans cut down all the trees in the area in their siege of Jerusalem in 70 CE.

**The Problematic Hebrew Text of Hosea 14:7**

AΩ The NRSV differs from the seemingly nonsensical MT ("The 'inhabitants of' shall return in his shade"). The MT has a construct form ("inhabitants of") not followed by a noun in the absolute state. At least five possible emendations have been suggested. First, the NRSV takes *yōšbê* ("inhabitants of") as a copyist error since the first three letters of the first two words of 14:7 are identical. The NRSV takes the first verb to mean "they shall do again" (rather than "they shall return") and emends *yōšbê* into a plural verb *yōšbû* ("they shall dwell"). Second, the *yod* (ʻ) on the end of "inhabitant" could be a copyist error that should have been a *vav*, which would have then been translated "his inhabitant." Third, the existing consonants could be repointed, resulting in "my inhabitants" (*yōšbay*) instead of "inhabitants of" (*yōšbê*). Fourth, a pronominal suffix may have fallen away, which means the original reading could have been "his inhabitants." Fifth and finally, a *mem* could have fallen away, the restoration of which would then read "inhabitants." The most likely of the possibilities would be option three since it is the emendation that involves no changes to the consonantal text. The consequence of this reading is rather significant,

since it means the speaker continues to be YHWH, but the third person suffix on "shadow" must refer to Israel/Ephraim. In other words, the restored text involving no consonant changes would be translated "my inhabitants will return in his shade." "My inhabitants" would mean God's inhabitants, while "his shade" would refer to the protection offered by Israel (see below).

The NRSV translates the second phrase "they shall flourish as a garden," but the word in the MT is "grain" (*dāgān*), not "garden" (*gan*). The verb in the MT (*ḥāyāh*) generally means "to live" or "exist," but it can also mean "to return to life" or "revive"; in this case grain is the object of "to grow again." Thus, "They shall again grow grain." The final phrase of 14:7 in the NRSV reads as though it is identical to the last phrase in 14:6, but it is not. The MT of 14:7 contains the word "his renown" rather than "his fragrance." So as reconstructed here, the verse could be translated as follows: "My inhabitants will return in his shade; they will revive grain and they will blossom like the vine; his renown will be like the wine of Lebanon."

## Wisdom Motto for the Book, 14:9 (MT 14:10)

This final verse, it is widely recognized, functions as the motto for Hosea and displays characteristics of the wisdom tradition. [Wisdom Tradition] YHWH is no longer the speaker, but is referenced in the third person. The verse is addressed to the wise reader, who is asked to apply "these things" to the reader's own life. It assumes the reader knows that the words of the book point one to the ways of YHWH, and that those who understand this connection will follow (or "walk in") these ways. By contrast, those who rebel against the words will stumble and fall. This open-ended admonition to the reader ties in well with the open-ended character of the call to repentance for Israel (14:1-8). However, 14:9 probably reflects a later editor's desire to keep the message of Hosea current, since the destruction of Ephraim/Israel had long since passed. In this sense, the verse fits with other passages that take this later reflective attitude. In other words, for this editor the enduring message of the book extends beyond the northern kingdom. Every generation of believers is expected to walk in the paths of YHWH.

---

**Wisdom Tradition**

Characteristics that 14:9 shares with wisdom literature include the form of the question (see Eccl 8:1; Ps 7:43) and vocabulary that is typical of wisdom works (discerning, wisdom, and the contrast of the upright with the rebellious). The expressions suggest that the motto combines these wisdom motifs with key phrases from Hosea. Ephraim has already been named as an unwise son (Hos 13:13) who has stumbled (14:1), but here the reader is essentially invited to choose whether or not to follow Ephraim or follow the paths of YHWH. For a history of the association of Hos 14:10 with wisdom tradition, see Kåre Berge, "Weisheitliche Hosea-Interpretation? Zur Frage nach Kohärenz und literarischem Horizont von Hosea 14,6-10," in *Wer darf hinaufsteigen zum Berg JHWH's: Beiträge zu Prophetie und Poesie des Alten Testaments* (ed. Hubert Irsigler et al., Arbeiten zu Text und Sprache im Alten Testament 72; St. Ottilien: EOS, 2002) 3–5.

---

# CONNECTIONS

Hosea ends with an open-ended call to repentance (14:1-8) and an invitation to reflect upon the words of the book (14:9). Hosea 14:1 ties the need for repentance to the guilt of the people, and the prayer suggested in 14:2-3 ties into motifs already delineated in Hosea. Specifically, it contains a profession of true religious devotion (14:2), a disavowal of reliance upon political and military powers (14:3), a rejection of idolatry (14:3), and an affirmation of divine mercy for the child who has been abandoned by its parents (14:3). These statements address guilt that has been discussed previously in Hosea. Moreover, the divine promise (14:4-7) depicts a merciful God who is ready to forgive if and when the people truly repent, and it does so using subtle but clear affirmations of YHWH's supremacy over other deities. This promise, then, reiterates the portrayals of God that the book has already charted. However, the call to repentance and the promise of deliverance should by no means be taken as a fairytale ending. The promise depends upon the response of the people to whom it is addressed, both then and now.

Hosea 14 *offers* salvation one more time, but the response of eighth-century Israel is never recounted because the book, in its final form, wants to be heard on two levels: historically and theologically. The book of Hosea presents the prophetic message delivered primarily to the people of a particular historical time, the northern kingdom of the eighth century. Moreover, as the northern kingdom did not disappear by some accident of history, neither does Hosea portray some arbitrary deity who woke up angry and decided to lash out. Rather, a recurring alternation between words of judgment and words of promise constitutes a major structural component of the entire book. This vacillation does three things with respect to Israel of the eighth century. First, it documents God's salvific desires, even while holding Israel accountable to its abandonment of its own covenant obligations. Second, it conveys the repeated instances in which God's patience and compassion prevented God from destroying God's own rebellious people. Third, by concluding with an open-ended call to repentance, the book of Hosea leaves a clear impression that Israel could still change its fate, though time is running short.

This prophetic reflection upon the history of Judah and Israel continues to play a major role throughout the Book of the Twelve. What does this historical background mean for persons of faith today? Or, put more pointedly, why should an ancient prophet's interpretation of Israel's history have relevance for the community of faith today?

Theologically, Hosea 14 ends a book that has been compiled and edited in order to convey the dynamic nature of the word of God. God's message to Israel should not be shelved as a relic of the past; it opens a window for the people of God to listen and learn from the mistakes of the past. In numerous places within the book, the prophet's message to the northern kingdom was expanded and applied to the southern kingdom. Here, at the end of Hosea, this dynamic process of application, meditation, and discernment addresses the *readers* of every generation. The upright, those who want to please God, will contemplate the implications of God's expectations for God's people. They will ask, how does our community fare in light of Hosea? Have we learned that God's way is not the way of "might makes right"? Political and military powers will not save us. Have we learned that God's way involves our whole being, not just the things we do or the words we say while we are in church? God is not impressed with our words of devotion if our actions do not show fidelity, compassion, and consistency. When we fail, are we strong enough to admit it? Can we return to the God who desires commitment rather than self-obsessed behavior? The invitation is open, but the jury is still out for the community.

What is clear, however, is the portrait of God. The end of Hosea presents a God who is willing to forgive those who have done wrong if and when they express a genuine change of heart. God desires to show mercy, and God has a history of compassion and patience. In this text, the prophet provides the words, and God promises compassion will result from a willingness to change. The final verse of Hosea reaffirms that the choice belongs to those who reflect upon the book. The paths of God are straight, and the righteous walk those paths while the rebellious stumble over them.

# NOTE

1. These allusions are documented by Raymond C. Van Leeuwen, "Scribal Wisdom and Theodicy in the Book of the Twelve," in *In Search of Wisdom: Essays in Memory of John G. Gammie* (ed. Leo G. Perdue, Bernard Scott, and William Wiseman; Louisville: Westminster/John Knox Press, 1993) 31–49; and Ruth Scoralick, *Gottes Güte und Gottes Zorn: Die Gottesprädikationen in Exodus 34:6f und ihre intextuellen Beziehungen zum Zwölfprophetenbuch* (HBS 33; Freiburg: Herder, 2002). See discussions in this commentary of Joel 2:13; 3:19; Jonah 4:2; Mic 7:18-19; Nah 1:2-3.

# SELECT BIBLIOGRAPHY
# FOR HOSEA

Andersen, Francis I., and David Noel Freedman. *Hosea*. Anchor Bible 24. Garden City: Doubleday, 1980.

Birch, Bruce C. *Hosea, Joel, and Amos*. Westminster Bible Companion. Louisville: Westminster John Knox, 1997.

Emmerson, Grace I. *Hosea: An Israelite Prophet in Judean Perspective*. Journal for the Study of the Old Testament: Supplement Series 28. Sheffield: JSOT Press, 1984.

Guenther, Allen R. *Hosea, Amos*. Believers Church Bible Commentary. Scottdale PA: Herald Press, 1998.

Holt, Else Kragelund. *Prophesying the Past: the Use of Israel's History in the Book of Hosea*. Journal for the Study of the Old Testament: Supplement Series 194. Sheffield: Sheffield Academic Press, 1995.

Jeremias, Jörg. "The Interrelationship between Amos and Hosea." In *Forming Prophetic Literature*, edited by James W. Watts and Paul R. House, 171–86. Sheffield: Sheffield Academic Press, 1996.

King, Philip J. *Amos, Hosea, Micah: An Archaeological Commentary*. Philadelphia: Westminster Press, 1988.

Limburg, James L. *Hosea–Micah*. Interpretation. Atlanta: John Knox, 1988.

Mays, James L. *Hosea*. Old Testament Library. London: SCM, 1969.

Stuart, Douglas K. *Hosea–Jonah*. Word Biblical Commentary 31. Waco: Word Books, 1987.

Wolff, Hans Walter. *Hosea*. Translated by Gary Stansell. Hermeneia. Philadelphia: Fortress Press, 1974.

Yee, Gale A. *Composition and Tradition in the Book of Hosea: A Redaction Critical Investigation*. Society of Biblical Literature Dissertation Series 102. Atlanta: Scholars Press, 1987.

# JOEL

# INTRODUCTION TO THE
# BOOK OF JOEL

## Dating the Prophet and the Book

Dating Joel with any precision creates notorious difficulties for both modern and ancient interpreters. [Joel in Jewish Tradition] In the past, suggestions have ranged from the tenth to the second centuries BCE.

In the last thirty years, however, scholars have reached a broad consensus that Joel is a postexilic writing. Attempts to narrow the parameters further have focused upon two possibilities: toward the end of the sixth century or near the beginning of the fourth century. Extensive reviews of the arguments have been published in recent commentaries by James L. Crenshaw and John Barton, so that work need not be repeated here.[1] A summary of the pertinent textual evidence will suffice to demonstrate the issues.

Evidence for dating Joel essentially stems from five lines of reasoning: the lack of a king, the presence of a functioning temple, the citation of other texts, the reference to Jerusalem's physical structures, and the depiction of political constellations. [Dating Joel] These observations provide sufficient grounds for a Persian period date, yet they lack the incontrovertible specificity for narrowing that consensus further.

### Joel in Jewish Tradition

Debate surrounding the prophet Joel did not suddenly arise with the onset of critical scholarship. Jewish tradition places the prophet in four different periods, and debates regarding whether the locust plagues are literal or symbolic are already reflected in rabbinic literature. This variety likely results from the character of the book, which exhibits little interest in the realia of its day. The prophet Joel in rabbinic literature has been associated with (1) the son of Samuel (eleventh century); (2) a prophet in the reign of Jehoram of Israel (849–842); (3) a prophet during the reign of Manasseh of Judah (687–642); (4) a postexilic prophet; and (5) an otherwise unknown prophet shortly after the time of Hosea in the eighth century.

The time of Jehoram is extensively treated in rabbinic literature, although this date has not withstood critical scrutiny. The attraction of Jehoram draws primarily from two associations: the king's dealings with another prophet (Obadiah) that corresponds to the name of another undated prophetic writing in the Twelve, and a tradition of the seven-year famine associated with the reign of Jehoram. According to these traditions, the seven-year famine was halted as a result of the preaching of Joel. Legendary elements of this tradition include descriptions of the repentance of the people who did not even have enough grain to sow for seed, so that at the prophet's urging the people found seed hidden in anthills and mouse holes. This seed, once planted, took only eleven days to grow so that it could be harvested. This tradition assumes that the call to repentance in Joel 1–2 was successful, an assumption that rests upon ambiguous textual evidence. The time following Hosea is presupposed by the admonitions of Jerome, who states that each undated prophecy should be dated to the time of the previous dated prophet.

## Dating Joel

First, the book never mentions a king, or any member of a royal family, despite the fact that Joel 1 calls virtually every other level of society to the temple to fast and lament. It is inconceivable that a prophet determined to gather the entire community would omit the king if a ruling monarch actually sat on the throne.

Second, Joel presumes the functioning presence of the temple in Jerusalem (1:14, 16; 2:1, 17; 4: 17, 18). This simple observation eliminates the period of the exile (587–520 BCE) after the temple had been destroyed but not yet rebuilt. Third, the person who compiled Joel worked extensively with other texts, even texts that presuppose Jerusalem's destruction—including the explicit citation of Obadiah (see the discussion below of Joel as scribal prophecy).

Fourth, the description of YHWH's cosmic army (2:1-11) refers to this army's scaling the wall of Jerusalem (2:7, 9). Those who opt for the earlier date downplay this observation, seeing the reference to the wall as illustrative of any city, not specifically Jerusalem. They argue that portions of the wall remained intact so that one could speak of a wall, even though it afforded no protection militarily. Those who opt for the later date emphasize the significance of the wall, since the wall was not rebuilt until 445 BCE during the governorship of Nehemiah. They claim that 2:1-11 can have no other city in mind than Jerusalem. The opening verse of this passage, Joel 2:1, specifies Zion as the place under threat, and the Jerusalem setting is self-evident elsewhere in the book from the references to the temple and the priests.

Finally, the political constellation depicted in Joel 3:4-8 (MT 4:4-8) corresponds best to the period near the beginning of the fourth century, though explanations have also been proposed for the end of the sixth century. H. W. Wolff has put forward the most extensive arguments for the political alignments toward the beginning of the fourth century. Citing Pseudo-Phylax (a travel itinerary from the fourth century) as evidence, Wolff notes that the combination of Tyre, Sidon, and "all the regions of Philistia" corresponds politically to this time when the coastal region functioned more or less cohesively. In this scenario, the rebellion of the Phoenicians against the Persians, quashed

in 353 BCE, would serve as the latest date of this passage. Reference to the Greeks (3:6) could certainly signal their rise as an economic power in the fourth century, which would culminate in the conquest of Alexander in the latter third of the century. Critique of this dating focuses primarily on the reference to the Sabeans in 3:8 (MT 4:8) and evidence for commerce with Greece from the sixth century onward. Critics point out that the Sabeans lost control of the trade routes to the south and east of Judah by the end of the fifth century. Assuming the citation of the Sabeans requires that they were a viable regional power, these critics opt for a date toward the end of the sixth century, when the Sabeans had more clout in the region. These scholars tend to treat the Phoenicians, Philistines, and Greeks as generic references that could fit anywhere along the time line. Thus, the most concrete political references seemingly point in opposite directions, depending upon how one weighs the evidence.

This commentary will assume the later date, despite the objections, for the following reason. The roles of the Greeks and the Sabeans are not equal in the rhetoric of the passage. In 3:6, the Greeks receive Judean slaves from the coastal regions of Phoenicia and Philistia (presumably acting in concert). Joel 3:6 presumes the thriving economic power of the Greeks. The selling of slaves from the coastal regions to the Sabeans, however, has more to do with poetics of the punishment fitting the crime than with economic viability of the Sabeans. As well, it is only a potential event, a threat, and one that as far as we know never materialized. In short, the Sabeans (who still existed as a political entity) function poetically as a foil for poetic justice. The coastal regions sold the Judeans to a country northwest of Palestine and separated from the land by a large body of water (Greece). As recompense, YHWH promises that Judah would do the opposite. They would sell the coastal population as slaves to the southeast across a large, dry desert. The Sabeans were located in what is today Yemen, south of Saudi Arabia. The judgment is not concerned so much with economic reality or viability as with creating a picture of poetic justice.

Hans Walter Wolff, *Hosea* (Hermeneia; trans. Gary Stansell; Philadelphia: Fortress, 1974).

When one evaluates all the evidence concerning the date of Joel, one finds reasons for both confidence and caution. The evidence for a postexilic dating offers a high degree of confidence in the wake of numerous evaluations. A more specific date is less clear, but for the reasons delineated in [Dating Joel], this commentary assumes a date near the beginning of the fourth century.

## Literary Form, Structure, and Unity of Joel

The issues surrounding the form, structure, and unity of Joel are no less complex than those of its date. On the one hand, great strides have been made in recognizing and understanding the unifying elements of the book. On the other hand, the disparate elements within the larger units defy easy solutions to the origins of Joel. As a result of these two conflicting realities, scholars have postulated or presumed several different models to explain the final form of the book.

Joel divides into two parts, each of which exhibits a particular rhetorical function: the communal call to repentance in 1:1–2:17 and the series of contingent promises in 2:18–3:21 (MT 2:18–4:21). This unifying rhetorical flow can be easily summarized. The ominous threat facing Judah constitutes YHWH's punishment for which the people must repent (1:1-20), but it pales in comparison to the punishment God is about to send against Zion (2:1-11). Only by throwing themselves upon YHWH's mercy can Judah (implied by the reference to land in 1:2, 14; 2:1) hope that YHWH will relent (2:12-17) before the day of YHWH comes. If the people genuinely repent, YHWH will remove the punishment (2:18-27), leading subsequently to the outpouring of God's Spirit on all believers who survive the coming day of YHWH in Jerusalem (2:28-32 [MT 3:1-5]). At that time, God will punish the nations who took advantage of Judah and will restore the land's abundance to a degree it had never known before (3:1-21 [4:1-21]).

Despite the clear flow, tensions complicate the fluidity. These tensions revolve around the character of the day of YHWH, the nature of the threats facing Joel's audience, and the lack of accusations. The impending day of YHWH constitutes a unifying motif, but one that changes dramatically as the book unfolds. In the beginning of the book, the day of YHWH functions as a threat to Judah (taking 1:2 as a reference to Judah) and Jerusalem, while in the second half of the book the day of YHWH functions as part of a promise to Judah and Jerusalem because it is directed against foreign nations.

The threats facing Judah at the beginning of the book defy a single, all-encompassing explanation. Instead, the picture developed by the various descriptions creates a mosaic of dangers not easily reconciled with one another. This picture contains a *series* of locust plagues (1:4; see 2:25), an attack from a foreign nation (1:6-7) and YHWH's army (2:1-11), drought (1:11-12), and fire (1:19). While this variety has long been recognized, attempts to harmonize the divergent elements into a single setting often become difficult to conceptualize, especially when scholars try to explain how this situation changes to a message of promise.

One neglected problem raised by the study of Joel concerns the utter lack of accusation to provide a rationale for the punishment the land experiences at the beginning of the book. This problem not only creates the sense that the reader is joining a conversation "in progress" but also creates significant theological dilemmas, making Joel unique among the prophets. No other prophetic book pronounces judgment against God's people without explaining the reasons for this punishment. In the latter part of the book, the reasons God would punish the nations are provided (3:4-8, 9-17), but no reasons for the utter devastation of the land appear in Joel.

Any attempt to explain *both* the unifying flow and the divergent elements of Joel must assume a model by which to interpret the relationship of the parts of Joel to one another. In the past, scholars have presumed one of four models: an oral setting, a work reflecting a liturgy, an organized collection of speeches, or a corpus that expands in two to five stages to reach its final form. Recently, variations of a fifth model have arisen. These newer approaches treat the book as a theological reflection whose compilation treats Joel as (1) a scribal prophet exploring the concept of the day of YHWH (S. Bergler), (2) a prophetic exploration of theodicy (Crenshaw and Barton), or (3) a book compiled for its location in the Book of the Twelve (Nogalski).[2]

This fifth model will be explored more fully below, but it takes seriously both the unity and the diversity of Joel as a composition utilizing preexisting elements designed from the outset to fit between Hosea and Amos. As such, the Book of the Twelve receives a theological focus on Judah and Jerusalem near the beginning of the corpus that is simply not present to the same degree until Micah, if Joel were not here. Hosea and Amos speak largely to and about the northern kingdom, Israel, though each has been edited with periodic references to Judah. By contrast, Joel focuses its message upon Judah and Jerusalem.

Hosea ends with an extended call to repentance to the northern kingdom, a call whose response is never narrated. Joel begins by doing the same for Jerusalem and Judah. Joel takes up the images of Hosea 2 and its threat to the land while calling Judah and Jerusalem to repent. Amos begins with a series of oracles against the nations and culminates in the confrontation of Israel (2:6-16) that introduces a message of judgment against the northern kingdom, which does not change until the eschatological promise at the end of Amos (9:11-15). Joel ends with its own message to the nations who have extended the punishment Judah will face in the Book of the Twelve. The end of Joel punctuates its message to the nations with quotes from the beginning and end of Amos. More will be said about this model of Joel as theological reflection as it becomes clear how intricately the message of Joel functions within the broader recurring motifs of the Book of the Twelve.

## The Message of Joel

The message of Joel revolves around several interlocking theological and tradition-laden combinations of motifs. This combination includes repentance, guilt, and punishment; Joel's presuppositions about God; the cultic orientation; the day of YHWH; and YHWH's sovereignty, compassion, and justice.

*Repentance, guilt, and punishment.* From the outset, Joel presents an urgent, communal call to repentance. A heretofore unimaginable threat permeates the current reality in Joel's depiction of the land. In Joel, the manifold disasters facing the country elicit calls to lament, mourn, and repent in the face of the calamitous situation. The calls are addressed to groups (elders, inhabitants, drunkards, farmers, vinedressers, priests, ministers) and assume that these groups share responsibility for causing God to punish this people. While this assumption is sometimes challenged (Crenshaw), Joel never explains or otherwise conveys what Judah has done to warrant this punishment. Recent explorations of the interplay between the writings of the Book of the Twelve raise the question of whether the reader of the Twelve should extend the accusations leveled in Hosea to the groups mentioned in Joel.

One significant avenue for conveying guilt in Hosea rested with the failure of the priests to instruct the people in the knowledge of

YHWH (4:1-6; 6:6). In Joel, the call to repentance led by the priests (2:17) leads to a series of promises. The culmination of the first of these promises not only reverses the situation described in Joel 1 (with the refertilization of the land and the removal of the attacking army) but also leads to a new relationship of the people with YHWH, a relationship that now presumes the people's *knowledge* that YHWH is in the land (2:27).

A second venue for connecting Joel and Hosea comes with the open-ended call to repentance that concludes Hosea. This call to repentance concludes with a *contingent* promise. When the beginning of Joel asks, "Has this happened?" (1:2), the syntactical awkwardness in that context dissipates considerably if one reads Joel as a continuation of Hosea. The missing antecedent to "this" suddenly has a clear referent, namely the promise of Hosea 14:4-8. Additionally, the expected answer to this question of Joel 1:2 ("No") makes sense if the reader assumes Joel continues Hosea. The people have not repented, and thus the promises have not been fulfilled. In fact, the description of the situation in Joel 1 reflects the mirror image of the promise of Hosea 14, a promise of fertility that belies the reality of devastation in Joel 1. This juxtaposition of promise and reality moves the reader forward on the one hand to a time of punishment, and on the other hand helps to explain the urgency of the prophet.

Third, the paradigm of the relationship between YHWH and the land metaphorically depicted in Hosea 2 coincides remarkably well with what happens in Joel if one assumes that the people have turned their backs on YHWH. In Hosea 2, YHWH addresses the land personified as YHWH's wife. YHWH removes the gifts he has heretofore provided (Hos 2:8-9 [MT 2:10-11]; Joel 1) because they had been given to "Baal" (Hos 2:8, 13, 16-17) "in the days of her youth" (Hos 2:15). YHWH longs for the day when she will call YHWH "my husband" (*'îšî*) instead of "my Baal" (*ba'lî*). Joel 1:8 addresses the personified land as well, evoking the images of Hosea 2 to command the land to "lament like the *bĕtulâ* (virgin) on account of the *baal* (husband) of her youth" because of the agricultural elements God has taken away, precisely those YHWH threatened to remove in Hosea 2 (the grain, the wine, and the oil in Joel 1:10; see Hos 2:8).

*God.* The portrayal of God that results from an isolated reading of Joel, apart from the larger context of the Book of the Twelve, creates theological difficulties. The devastation of the land, according to the prophet, requires a response from the people, but that response and, more important, its presuppositions do not present a satisfying scenario. The rhetoric of Joel 1 not only conveys a sense of urgency at the situation but also implies that the current situation either (1) constitutes punishment from God or (2) has come about without God's knowledge. In the second instance, Joel becomes a kind of prophetic counterpart to Job to raise the problem of theodicy. Calamity comes as part of life, though the readers are never told why. When disaster comes, the only response with any possibility of success (and it is not guaranteed—see 2:12-14) is to go to God with the hope of arousing God's compassion. Such is largely the portrayal of Joel presented by Crenshaw. This picture, however, creates several problems. Chiefly, it presumes a passivity on God's part not typical of the prophetic outlook, and it does not adequately account for God's response toward the nations in the second half of the book. To a certain extent, the resultant picture of God in this model presumes God must punish someone, so if Judah is to be rewarded, then the nations must be punished.

A portrayal of Joel as theodicy does, however, take seriously the problem created by the widespread assumptions that the current situation must be viewed as punishment from YHWH. Yet, treating the calamities of Joel 1–2 as punishment, when read in isolation, creates significant theological problems because Joel never explains the grounds for this punishment. Joel never accuses Judah or Jerusalem of any wrongdoing. This omission makes Joel unique among the prophetic writings. While both Testaments portray God as capable of acting in wrath, reasons for God doing so are generally provided. Typical responses to this problem among commentators (ancient and modern) do little to resolve it. First, the biggest majority simply ignore the missing accusation. Second, some suggest that Joel reflects an oral setting where the reasons for punishment required no explanation, for Joel's audience knew what they had done. This suggestion fails to account for the literary character of Joel. Joel's incorporation of allusions, citations, and quotations requires considerable artistry and reflection. Recent studies classify this prophet as a "scribal prophet" or "scripture interpreter" for this reason.[3] This style does not give the impression of an ad hoc speech. Third, several commentators argue that Joel reflects the outline of a liturgy that can be applied to any number of situations. All these responses to the problem require something beyond the confines of the final form of the book. Joel offers no explanation for the devastation of the land that begins the book, and yet most commentators think Joel presumes that these events constitute punishment.

*Cultic orientation.* In Joel, the fact that the devastation threatens temple operations magnifies the threat, yet that temple as the source of genuine religious community, along with its priestly leaders, also holds the key to changing the situation. The temple features prominently in the major sections of the book (1:13, 14, 16; 2:12-17; 3:18), even though the address to the priests conveys anger toward them. The rhetorical edge toward the priests derives primarily from the urgency of the situation. Joel's summons addresses a wide array of groups within the community, and it includes descriptions of the devastation of the land pertinent to those groups: the elders (1:2, 14), drunkards (1:5), priests (1:14), farmers (1:10), and vintners (1:10). However, when the time comes to prescribe action and not just describe the problem, Joel calls on the priests to take the lead (1:13-14; 2:15-17). Joel's interest in the cult percolates through these calls because they reveal a concern that the devastation hurts the people's ability to offer sacrifice (1:9, 13, 16; 2:14). The answer, no matter what caused the calamities that beset the land, must be sought in community, at the temple, in genuine repentance. Poetically, the temple sustains the entire land, at least in Joel's anticipation of the way things will someday work (3:18 [MT 4:18]).

*Day of YHWH.* The day of YHWH forms the literary, theological, and poetic backdrop throughout Joel, but the purpose and imagery of YHWH's day changes dramatically as the book unfolds. In prophetic literature, the day of YHWH functions as a day of divine intervention, usually for judgment, against YHWH's people or against the nations. In Joel, both YHWH's people and the nations are threatened with this intervention. Moreover, this concept in Joel functions as a kind of anthology in that Joel's terminology for the day illustrates the prophet's familiarity with other parts of the Book of the Twelve.

The day of YHWH sayings in Joel are not unique formulations. Rather, Joel's references to the day of YHWH all manifest significant parallel formulations in other prophetic writings. Joel 1:15

emphasizes the nearness of the day, as do 2:1 and 3:14. The first two portray the day of YHWH as a threat to Jerusalem, while 3:14 anticipates the day of YHWH as judgment for the nations. This formulation, "the day of YHWH is near," appears later in the Book of the Twelve when Zephaniah 1:7 and 14 use this phrase to describe another day of impending threat against Jerusalem. Joel 2:2 does not use the phrase "day of YHWH," but describes this day as day of darkness using synonyms that not only function within Joel (see 2:31 [MT 3:4]; 3:15) but also foreshadow motifs associated with the day of YHWH in other texts in the Book of the Twelve (Zeph 1:15; see also Amos 5:18-20). Joel 2:11 echoes Malachi 4:5 (MT 3:23) and 3:2. Joel 2:31 (MT 3:4) also uses the language of "great and terrible day of YHWH" that concludes the Book of the Twelve (Mal 4:5 [MT 3:23]). It introduces the day of YHWH in the second half of Joel as a day of judgment against the nations. Joel 3:14 (MT 4:14) stresses the nearness of the day of YHWH against the nations, using language from Obadiah 15.

What purpose does this interlocking language play? It aids the paradigmatic quality of Joel by putting down markers in advance to alert the reader to how the day of YHWH "plays out" as one reads the Book of the Twelve. Linguistically and literarily, Joel prefigures YHWH's judgment against Jerusalem in Zephaniah, though Joel was compiled later than Zephaniah. The same is true for the day of YHWH directed against various nations within the Book of the Twelve: hence, the interplay with Obadiah, Nahum, Habakkuk, Zechariah 12-14, and Malachi. The day of YHWH functions as a major motif in Joel, and Joel's day of YHWH sayings also anticipate the recurrence of the day of YHWH in the Book of the Twelve.

*YHWH's Sovereignty, Compassion, and Justice.* Another significant issue in Joel revolves around the book's pivotal use of Exodus 34:6-7. Joel 2:13 cites Exodus 34:6 as the reason one should turn to God in a desperate situation. Exodus 34:6 offers a self-characterization of YHWH to explain the decision not to destroy the people who have just broken the covenant for the first time: "YHWH, YHWH, is a God merciful and gracious, slow to anger, and abounding in steadfast love and faithfulness." Joel quotes this part of YHWH's self-disclosure as the reason for returning to YHWH before the coming day of punishment. YHWH has continually shown compassion to those who have thrown themselves upon the divine mercy.

This quote is no magic formula to manipulate YHWH. YHWH decides when to manifest this compassion. After 34:6, Exodus 34:7 describes the flip side of YHWH's character, YHWH's justice. Just as YHWH is a God whose loving-kindness endures for a thousand generations, YHWH also holds the guilty accountable: "yet by no means clearing the guilty, but visiting the iniquity of the parents upon the children and their children's children, to the third and fourth generation." This affirmation does two things. It accentuates God's compassion over God's wrath (one thousand generations of compassion versus four generations of judgment), and it creates a tension consistent with the biblical portrait of God as both the one who judges and the one who redeems. This tension remains throughout the biblical narrative and the prophetic writings, and it is only resolved by God's sovereignty. God, and only God, chooses who receives compassion and who will be judged. These issues play out in Joel. Facing devastation that will soon bring the day of YHWH, Joel announces that one's only hope lies in turning to YHWH for deliverance, because the very character of YHWH exudes compassion. However, Joel presumes that the people need to change. Hence, Joel calls for repentance, led by the priests at the temple. Yet Joel also knows this "return to YHWH" by no means guarantees that YHWH will instead choose to show compassion: "*Who knows whether* he will not turn and relent, and leave a blessing behind him . . ." (2:14). However, 2:18 clarifies God's response in this instance by offering a series of promises that God will restore the fertility of the land, remove the foreign army, and punish *the nations* who have taken advantage of God's people. Compassion, sovereignty, and justice all play a role in this transition, and all are connected as ruminations on Exodus 34:6-7.

While YHWH's compassion evokes the language of Exodus 34:6 in Joel 2:12-13, the extension of YHWH's justice to the nations in Joel 3 raises the issues addressed in Exodus 34:7, explaining why Joel 4:21 closes the book with language from Exodus 34:7: YHWH will by no means clear the guilty. Thus, Joel cites both Exodus 34:6 and 34:7 at key points in the book. Further, Exodus 34:6-7 plays a significant role elsewhere in the Twelve, specifically in the transition from Micah to Nahum, and in Jonah 4. Micah 7:18-19 draws upon Exodus 34:6 to affirm YHWH's compassion on YHWH's people, while allusions to Exodus 34:7 in Nahum 1:3 reiterate YHWH's judgment on the guilty in order to introduce the punishment of Assyria. Jonah 4:2 presents the thematic counterpoint. Namely, if God's justice and wrath extend to the nations, then does it also not hold true that God's compassion should extend to the nations as well? This contemplation takes place in Jonah 4:2 via the citation of Exodus 34:6. The formulations of Joel concerning the compassion and justice of YHWH thus point beyond Joel and move from the Torah's presentation of YHWH into other writings in the Book of the Twelve.

## Joel and the Book of the Twelve

In Joel one encounters the recurring theological motifs of the Book of the Twelve. These recurring elements all run through Joel, making it the literary anchor of the larger corpus. In addition to the day of YHWH and theodicy discussed above, recurring elements include the fertility of the land, Joel's paradigm of history, and how these issues portray sin and repentance.

*The Fertility of the Land.* Joel develops imagery from Hosea with respect to the fertility of the land and to the need for the community to repent. Hosea 2 already anticipated the removal of fertility from the land (and her children) as punishment for pursuing other gods. The land will be laid waste, and the joy of cultic celebration brought to an abrupt end (Hos 2:11-12 [MT 2:13-14]), which is precisely the situation with which Joel begins. In Joel, food and fertility have been cut off so that joy and gladness have disappeared (Joel 1:12, 16). The elements God anticipates removing in Hosea 2 have been taken away in Joel 1. Only a change of behavior will cause God to restore the situation to what it had been (Hos 2:23-24 [MT 2:25-26]; see Joel 2:19). This threat to the fertility of the land using images one finds in Joel appears later in the Book of the Twelve: Amos 4:6-11 (a passage that has clear connections to Joel 2:12-14); Habakkuk 3:17 (anticipating the destruction of Jerusalem); and Haggai 1:10-11. Fulfilling these promises begins with the laying of the foundation of the temple (Hag 2:19) after the people have repented (Zech 1:2-6; this passage predates the appearance of Haggai's last message [Hag 2:10, 20; Zech 1:1] and is most likely associated with the joining of Haggai and Zechariah). This explicit repentance begins the process of restoring the land's fertility (see discussion of Zech 8:9-12). This fertility is threatened again according to Malachi by the response of the people who revert to familiar patterns of ignoring YHWH's expectations. Malachi 3:6-12 confronts the people for not bringing YHWH his due. Contrary to Joel, where the storehouses are empty because of the devastation to the land (1:17), the storehouses in Malachi are empty because the people *choose* not to bring the tithes and offerings. YHWH promises that if the people will act faithfully, the fertility of the land will increase exponentially as the windows of heaven open (Mal 3:10).

The agents of devastation in Joel include a series of locust plagues, droughts, and enemy attacks. This same combination appears in the Amos 4:6-11 expressing YHWH's frustration that these punishments have *not* resulted in repentance from the people. Further, the combination of Nahum and Habakkuk portrays the transition from Assyrian hegemony to Babylonian control by comparing these two entities to the attack of one locust swarm by another (Nah 3:15-16) and by a description of Babylon as a "horde of faces" that move forward militarily in a description (Hab 1:7-11) "reminiscent" of YHWH's army in Joel 2:1-11. In the end, God will remove the devourer, meaning locusts, from the land if the people respond faithfully (Mal 3:11).

*Paradigm of History and the Fate of the Country.* The book of Joel comprises one of only two writings in the Twelve (Obadiah is the other) that do not relate clearly to the unfolding chronological structure created by the six dated superscriptions (Hosea, Amos, Micah, Zephaniah, Haggai, and Zechariah) or by the four books whose content requires a certain placement within the developing chronological flow (Jonah, Nahum, Habakkuk, and Malachi).

As noted above, connections between Joel and its literary context suggest that Joel was aware of this chronological flow, but that Joel's theological agenda transcends this chronology in favor of an eschatological portrait. In the Twelve, Joel functions on at least two levels: to actualize Hosea's message for a Judean context and to present a paradigm for the whole.

First, in its canonical context, Joel juxtaposes God's salvific promises with confrontations of the current reality. Following Hosea's promise of God's restoration of Israel *should* they repent, Joel begins with a question: "Has this happened?" Both the question, which expects a negative answer, and the subsequent depictions of the "current" devastation demonstrate that Joel's "community" has not responded to the call for repentance from Hosea 14. At the other end of Joel, Joel's promise of future judgment on the nations (3:1-21), contingent upon the people's decision to repent (2:12-17), leads to the oracles against the nations in Amos (1:2–2:16) that constitute specific allegations against those nations but that culminate in accusations against Judah (2:4-5) and Israel (2:6-16). Those accusations leave a clear impression to the reader of the Book of the Twelve that Joel's audience, like Hosea's before him, did not respond positively to the call to repent in Joel 1:2–2:17. If that impression was not enough, Amos 4:6-11 specifies no fewer than five failures of God's people to repent following calamities sent by YHWH. Thus, Joel contrasts the current reality with the future promise for God's people.

Second, Joel's paradigm for repentance and restoration serves as the literary cornerstone for understanding that what happens later in the Book of the Twelve reflects God's fidelity to the promises God made at the beginning of the book. Allusions to Joel appear unexpectedly, serving as scribal bookmarks reminding the reader of the Twelve to notice connections they might otherwise miss. Nation-locusts that devastate the land only to be followed by more locusts form the metaphorical domain of Nahum 3:15-16. YHWH's commitment to hold the guilty accountable connects Nahum 1:2-3 and Joel through clear allusions to Exodus 34:6-7. Punishment will come to Judah and Jerusalem on the day of YHWH (Zeph 1:2-18), though God does not forget the promise to "restore the fortunes" "at that time" (Zeph 3:20; see Joel 3:1). A change in the fertility of the land and punishment of the nations begins almost immediately after the people repent (Zech 1:2-6; see Hag 2:19; Zech 1:12-14). This restoration also functions as a test for God's people before ushering in more complete judgment of the nations (see Zech 8:9-12). The situation in Malachi, however, makes clear that the community as a whole has again failed the test, though God is still willing to remove "the devourer" so that the land may prosper (Mal 3:6-7, 8-12).

## NOTES

1. John Barton, *Joel and Obadiah: A Commentary* (OTL; Louisville: Westminster John Knox, 2001); James L. Crenshaw, *Joel* (AB 24C; New York: Doubleday, 1995).

2. Siegfried Bergler, *Joel als Schriftinterpret* (Beiträge zur Erforschung des Alten Testaments und des antiken Judentums 16; Frankfurt: Peter Lang, 1988); Crenshaw,

*Joel*, 39–46; Barton, *Joel and Obadiah*, 34–36; James D. Nogalski, "Joel as 'Literary Anchor' in the Book of the Twelve," in *Reading and Hearing the Book of the Twelve* (Symposium 15; Atlanta: Society of Biblical Literature, 2000) 91–109.

    3. Bergler, *Joel als Schriftinterpret*, 21–32; Nogalski, "Joel as Literary Anchor," 94–109.

# OUTLINE OF JOEL

I. Joel 1:1: Superscription of the Book

II. Joel 1:2-14: A Summons to Communal Repentance

III. Joel 1:15-20: A Warning and a Prayer

IV. Joel 2:1-11: YHWH's Attacking Army

V. Joel 2:12-17: A Renewed Call to Repentance

VI. Joel 2:18-27: First Promise—Restoration of the Land

VII. Joel 2:28-32: Second Promise—A Different Day of YHWH

VIII. Joel 3:1-21: Third Promise—Two Sides of the Day of YHWH

    A. Joel 3:1-3 (MT 4:1-3): Thematic Introduction

    B. Joel 3:4-8 (MT 4:4-8): Slave Traders Become Slaves

    C. Joel 3:9-17 (MT 4:9-17): Judgment in the Valley

    D. Joel 3:18-21 (MT 4:18-21): Fertility beyond Measure

# A CALL TO REPENT BEFORE THE IMPENDING DAY OF YHWH

## Joel 1:1-20

## COMMENTARY

The prophet speaks beginning with 1:2, and the prophetic voice continues until 2:17 when YHWH takes over as the dominant speaker for the remainder of the book. The long prophetic address (1:2–2:17) can be read as a single speech, though scholars debate the extent to which preexisting material has been collected and adapted for its present location. As a single (albeit composite) rhetorical unit, Joel 1:2–2:17 functions in its current location as an extended call to repentance to the people of Jerusalem and Judah, a call that unfolds in three broad movements. The first major section of Joel, 1:2-20, urgently addresses a series of groups in order to describe several grave threats facing the land (1:2-14) and to call the people to gather for repentance in the face of imminent danger—danger that is none other than the day of YHWH (1:15-20). The second section, 2:1-11, sounds an alarm and describes the cosmic army YHWH will lead against the prophet's people on the day of YHWH. The third section, 2:12-17, offers an even more urgent call to repentance before the coming day of YHWH.

Joel 1:1-20 divides into three sections: 1:1, 2-14, and 15-20. Joel 1:1 functions as the superscription to the book. The middle unit contains five smaller rhetorical subunits (1:2-4, 5-7, 8-10, 11-12, 13-14), each with its own addressee, but each calling for some type of lament before YHWH. The prophetic voice consistently speaks in 1:2-20, though the addressees change repeatedly in 1:2-14 as the prophet turns to different groups and calls them to notice the devastation before them. In the latter part of the chapter (1:15-20), the prophet equates the destruction to the coming day of YHWH and then prays on behalf of the people to YHWH.

## Superscription to the Book, 1:1

Joel 1:1 functions as the superscription to the entire book. Its form is that of a word-event formula similar to but not identical with the form of the superscription that begins Hosea 1:1. [Word-Event Formula] What distinguishes Joel 1:1 from Hosea 1:1 is that Joel contains no reference to a king during whose reign Joel prophesied. This lack of a historical marker has resulted in a wide range of suggestions for the date of the prophet in both ancient and modern times, as even a cursory glance at the portraits of Joel in rabbinic literature will show. (For Joel in Jewish tradition, see the introduction to Joel.) This commentary is based on a date near the beginning of the fourth century BCE (see the introduction).

One may readily classify the phrase "word of YHWH" as a prophetic expression. It appears 231 times in the Old Testament, with the vast majority found in the Latter Prophets (146) or in the Former Prophets (60) related to prophetic activity. It appears only six times in the Torah, and there in the context of prophetic activity (e.g., Gen 15:1, 4; Exod 9:20, 21; Num 15:31; Deut 5:5). In the section of Hebrew canon known as "the Writings," it appears in one psalm with respect to creation (Ps 33:4, 6), once in Ezra (1:1), once in Daniel (in a reference to the word of YHWH in Jeremiah), and fifteen times in Chronicles, all related to prophetic activity.

The name "Joel" means "YHWH is God." "Son of Pethuel" functions as both a clarifying and an enigmatic marker, distinguishing "Joel" from the other persons named Joel in the Old Testament and yet offering no help to the modern reader in identifying the setting of the book. [Joel, Son of Bethuel] The book uses such typical language that the book can be, and has been, plausibly set in a wide variety of periods. In the end, the word-event formula and the theophoric name of the prophet in this superscription validate the message of the book as being God's word through an otherwise unknown prophet.

**Word-Event Formula**

AΩ The phrase, "the word of YHWH came to x," where x is the name of the prophet or a pronoun referring to the prophet, introduces prophetic books and speeches. This formula draws upon God's authority by claiming to speak a "word" from God, staking an important claim for the community about the message.

**Joel, Son of Bethuel**

The name "Joel" appears 19 times, mostly in postexilic books. Of these, 17 occur in Ezra, Nehemiah, and 1–2 Chronicles. Ezra and Nehemiah cite persons named Joel within the postexilic community, while the Chronicler mentions people named Joel only in genealogical material. None of these persons can be plausibly linked to the prophet, since the prophet's father, Pethuel, is otherwise unknown outside Joel 1:1. The LXX names Joel's father Bathouel, a similar sounding name that occurs more frequently (Gen 22:22, 23; 24:15, 24, 47, 50; 25:20; 28:2, 5; 29:1; 1 Chr 4:30), though none of these people named Bathouel has a son named Joel.

## A Summons to Communal Repentance, 1:2-14

In Joel 1:2-14, the naming of specific groups (1:2, 5, 9, 11, 13, 14) creates a visual image within which the prophet addresses groups of people from various walks of life. [Groups in Joel 1:2-4] In the process, this shifting focus divides the larger unit into six smaller rhetorical units (1:2-4, 5-7, 8-10, 11-12, 13, 14) where the prophetic speaker illustrates how the impending threat will affect each group. Once the groups are addressed, the final rhetorical unit (1:15-20) describes the effects of the impending threat as the day of YHWH (1:15-18) before invoking the language of prayer for the devastated land (1:19-20).

*Joel 1:2-4.* Because it begins "hear this," Joel 1:2-4 is usually described as a teacher's call to attention that has roots in the wisdom tradition. However, of the eight times in the MT where the phrase "hear this" appears (Isa 47:8; 48:1, 16; Hos 5:1; Joel 1:2; Amos 8:4; Ps 49:2; Job 34:16), only the last two actually appear in wisdom contexts. The other six occur in prophetic texts. Moreover, apart from Joel 1:2, only Psalm 49:2 begins a unit without taking up the preceding context. This raises the question, What is the antecedent of the feminine singular pronoun "this"? Is it a proleptic antecedent as is normally presumed, meaning "this" refers to something that has yet to be named? Or does "this" refer to something that has already been mentioned? We will return to this question after looking at 1:2b.

> ### Groups in Joel 1:2-4
> The order and identity of the groups mentioned in Joel 1 are not as random as they might appear at first glance. Three combinations of groups in pairs occur twice. The first pairing encompasses the entire population and its leaders. The second grouping includes those who have abused cultic elements (specifically the wine) along with those who have grown these elements (farmers/vine dressers). The third group includes those responsible for leading cultic celebrations (priests/ministers of YHWH).
>
> | Verse | Groups |
> |-------|--------|
> | 2 | A Elders/Inhabitants |
> | 5 | B Drunkards/Wine Drinkers |
> | 9 | C Priests/Ministers |
> | 11 | B' Farmers/Vine Dressers |
> | 13 | C' Priests/Ministers |
> | 14 | A' Elders/Inhabitants |

The second half of 1:2 asks a rhetorical question whose answer is presumed to be obvious: Has *this* (a feminine singular demonstrative pronoun) happened in your days or in the days of your fathers? Once again, a pronoun appears that has no clear antecedent. This type of rhetorical question presumes the answer is "no," implying that the prophet refers to something rare that has not come to pass in previous generations. What the prophet does not say, however, is to what "this" refers. Two possibilities present themselves depending upon the literary horizon of the reader. If one reads Joel in isolation, "this" is a pronoun that can be interpreted as a proleptic reference to the devastation described in 1:4-20.

If, however, one chooses to read Joel in the context of the Twelve, the antecedent can be interpreted as the extended call to repentance and its attendant promise from Hosea 14:1-8, or even the entire book of Hosea. Regarding the latter, R. Scoralick has convincingly shown that the call to repent that begins in 1:2 bears a striking resemblance to Hosea 4:1 and 5:1, the beginning of the accusations against Israel that dominate Hosea 4–10.[1] She demonstrates that Hosea 4:3 links the summation of the crimes (Hos 4:1-2) to the breaking of the Ten Commandments with the resulting devastation of the land to follow (4:3). It is the language of Hosea 4:3 upon which Joel 1 expands. In so doing, Joel assumes that the crimes delineated in Hosea 4–14 have been committed in the land and have caused devastation. In short, the book of Joel does not need to describe the crimes of the people because those crimes have already been documented in Hosea. Moreover, the open-ended call to repentance of Hosea 14:1-3 has not resulted in the fulfillment of YHWH's promise (Hos 14:4-8) when the reader encounters the scene described in Joel 1:2-20. Only gradually does the reader learn that "the land" in Joel has shifted to a focus on Judah.

Joel 1:3 gives a command that points the reader in the opposite direction of 1:2. Rather than searching the past, a command is given to recount "it" to future generations, making sure that the message is conveyed for four generations. The antecedent of the feminine singular pronoun "it" still has not been stated, but that will change with 1:4. Joel 1:3 relates syntactically and conceptually to 1:2, meaning that the inhabitants are to "listen" (1:2) and "recount" (1:3) what they hear. Significantly, then, this dual command refers to the message the prophet wants to convey, not to an event.

Joel 1:4 describes a process whereby four locusts successively devour what the others left behind. Two points should be noted. First, the sequential nature of this destruction does not describe one invasion by four types of locusts. Rather, each locust devours what the previous locusts left behind. Second, the number of locusts corresponds to the number of generations who are to be told of "it" in 1:3. As Joel unfolds, the symbolic nature of these locusts clarifies so that it becomes increasingly pos-

**Locusts**

Throughout history, locusts have sometimes brought devastation to crops.

(Credit: G. Eric and Edith Matson Photograph Collection at the Library of Congress, http://commons.wikimedia.org/wiki/File:Locust_from_the_plague_in_Palestine,_1915.jpg)

sible to identify the locusts as foreign powers who invade the land at YHWH's initiation. Early rabbinic tradition often associated the locusts with four kingdoms. [Four Kingdoms] These four locusts are mentioned again in 2:25 where they symbolize YHWH's promise of restoration that is contingent upon the repentance of the people.

*Joel 1:5-7.* In the next subunit, the prophet begins a series of calls to specific groups, usually naming them in pairs, as here when addressing the "drunkards" and "wine-drinkers." The two groups receive three imperatives: wake up, weep, and wail. The verbs demand action from those incapable of comprehending what has happened. Those asleep in a drunken stupor are called to wake up and show remorse (weep and wail). The devastation to the land from the sequential locust plagues (1:4) demands an active response. The terms "drunkards" and "wine-drinkers" are pejorative and communicate

### Four Kingdoms

In rabbinic tradition, as part of the punishment for Abraham treating Lot like an heir, God decides that Abraham's descendants will be trodden by the four kingdoms as the earth is trodden. These four kingdoms were sometimes symbolically associated with Joel's four locusts (Ginzberg, 6:314). The identity of the four kingdoms changed over time. Some traditions saw the four kingdoms as Assyria/Babylon, Media/Persia, Macedonia/Greece, and Rome. Later traditions omitted Assyria and added Edom and Ishmael, which symbolized Rome and Arabia respectively (see Ginzberg, 1:229, 5:223, and 6:314). Christian interpreters were no different in this respect. Several pre-critical interpreters relate the locusts to kings of Assyria, including Theodore of Mopsuestia (fifth century) and Isho'dad of Merv (ninth century). For these and other symbolic readings, see Alberto Ferreiro, ed., *The Twelve Prophets* (Ancient Christian Commentary on Scripture, OT 14; Downers Grove: Intervarsity Press, 2003) 60–61. The case can be made that this multivalent reading is present in Joel from the outset of its work. This symbolic interpretation would be buttressed by references to attacking nations as locusts in the Book of the Twelve (e.g., Nah 3:15; Hab 1:9; Mal 3:11; see also Amos 4:9). In the Book of the Twelve, the four locusts would not include Rome but would include Assyria, Babylon, Persia, and Greece or Egypt.

Louis Ginzberg, *The Legends of the Jews*, 7 vols. (Philadelphia: The Jewish Publication Society of America, 1947).

a sense of disdain. However, Joel elicits a cultic context so that these rebukes are not calls for abstinence. Joel 1:5b provides the rationale for calling them to attention. The consequences of the devastation anticipated in 1:4 have implications: the crops are ruined, and life as they know it has changed. The cultic celebrations they took for granted are no longer possible because the crops are no longer available.

Joel 1:6 explains why the wine and sweet wine have been cut off, but the rationale differs from the reason connecting 1:4-5. Specifically, according to 1:6-7, an attacking nation of great size and power has created the agricultural problems. The description compares this nation to a ferocious lion attacking YHWH's land. This single lion-nation has destroyed the land (1:6), or more specifically has devastated the vines and stripped the fig trees of their bark and leaves (1:7). This image is odd—a carnivorous lion attacks the vegetation of the land. Herein lies the clue to connecting 1:4, 5, 6. Most scholars treat the nation as a metaphor for the attacking locust hoard, a move that resolves some but not all of the conceptual problems. This equation of the locust hoard-nation-lion makes sense to the extent that it can explain the reference to the power and number of the attacker and the fact that the lion attacks the plants in 1:7. It overlooks the fact, however, that 1:4 described a *series* of locust plagues, not a single plague. Joel 1:6-7 utilizes nation imagery because the locust is itself symbolic of the devastation that the land will experience from numerous attackers. Increasingly, Joel introduces threats other than locusts.

Joel 1:7 continues to describe the devastation caused by the lion-nation of 1:6, and the attacker is singular, not plural. The same is true for the vine and the fig tree (contrary to the NRSV transla-tion): "*It* (the nation) has laid waste my *vine*, and splintered my *fig tree*; *it* has stripped off *its* bark and thrown *it* down; *its* branches have turned white." Identifying the singular pronouns is significant rhetorically and has implications for interpreting 1:6-7 in relation to 1:4. *If* the locust were the original antecedent, it would be only one of four locust plagues. Instead, this "nation" who acts like both lion and locust affects God's produce (my vine, my fig tree).

*Joel 1:8-10.* Joel 1:8 begins a new rhetorical subunit by issuing a command to a new addressee. Joel 1:8-10 sets itself apart from 1:5-7 (addressed to the drunkards) and 1:11-12 (addressed to the farmers). The addressee in 1:8 is an unnamed feminine entity, as seen in the feminine singular command to lament. By taking other prophetic texts into account, two possible identities for the addressee present themselves: Lady Zion or the land. Since Lady Zion does not appear in the remainder of Joel, and since the com-pilation of Joel provides evidence of having been influenced by Hosea, where the personified land plays a major role in Hosea 2, the personified land becomes the stronger candidate for this femi-nine singular entity.

The picture created by 1:8 and its conceptual links to Hosea requires attention. The command to lament evokes images of sadness and trouble, while the reference to sackcloth can imply mourning or repentance. However, the command to lament given to the personified land evokes a simile that intensifies the feelings expected with this lamentation. The land should lament like a virgin wailing over the "husband of her youth," an image that implies the loss of said husband. However, this comparison creates several difficulties not often addressed adequately by commentators: how a virgin has a husband; the fate of said husband; and the chronological distance implied by the phrase "husband of her youth." Before addressing these difficulties directly, it helps to note that several ideas relate this verse to the extended metaphor of Hosea 2. There, the land is personified as YHWH's unfaithful wife whom he punishes by removing the gifts of grain, wine, and oil given by YHWH that she wrongly used as gifts for the Baals (2:8 [MT 2:10]). See the illustration "Baal Worship" in Hosea 2:7. In Hosea 2:16 (MT 2:18), YHWH anticipates a time when she will call YHWH "my husband" (*ʾîšî*) rather than "my Baal" (*baʿĕlî*). The word "*baal*" can refer either to the Canaanite deity or a "husband" (Gen 20:3; Exod 21:3). In a double entendre, Joel 1:8 uses the word *baʿal* as "husband." In Hosea 2:15 (MT 2:17), YHWH hopes that by punishing the wife/land, she will again respond to him as "in the days of her youth." For a woman, "youth" normally meant the time *before* she was married or betrothed, when she still lived in her father's house (Lev 22:13; Num 30:16 [MT 30:17]). It is also the same word used in Joel 1:8. Even more oddly, in Joel 1:8 the phrase "husband of her youth" implies this lamentation looks back on a time in the past. It is like saying, "her husband of long ago." The image of a *virgin* with a *husband* in the *distant past* is a strange picture indeed. So what does Joel 1:8 mean? Given the increasing recognition of Joel as a book of scribal prophecy (see discussion of "Literary Form, Structure, and Unity" in the introduction of Joel), 1:8 makes more sense as a metaleptic allusion to the constellation in Hosea 2. [Metaleptic] First, without changing the consonantal text (since the definite article *h* would assimilate), the word "like a virgin" can be translated as "like *the* virgin." Second, "the virgin" would readily be understood as an abbreviated form of the title "virgin Israel" (e.g., Jer 18:13; 31:4, 21; Amos 5:2), and as such makes more sense in the constellation of Hosea 2 than it does as an aphoristic image. In Joel 1:8, the personified land is told to lament like the virgin (Israel) for the *baal* (lord/husband) of her youth, which, following Hosea 2, assumes YHWH as the husband who provided for her.

Joel 1:9-10 provides the reason for the land's lamentation: without grain or grape, no offering can be made to YHWH, and

**Metaleptic**

Metalepsis is a type of allusion that points the attentive reader to another text, but that then assumes knowledge of the entire passage to which it alludes. See Richard Hays, *Echoes of Scripture in the Letters of Paul* (New Haven: Yale University Press, 1989) 14–21.

the priests, YHWH's ministers, cannot perform their sacrificial duties for the people. The verbs used about the land imply violence. The land has been ransacked and can no longer provide produce for sustenance and worship. This language could be appropriate for destruction caused by either a locust plague or a foreign army, but 1:9 assumes the aftermath of that destruction. Because the field has been devastated, the products it provides are not available. The implicit logic of 1:9-10 segues to the next subunit. The land is called to mourn because the offerings have been cut off from the temple, which causes the priests to mourn (1:9). The arable land and its crops are devastated (1:10), which in turn leads to a call to those who harvest the produce to mourn (1:11).

*Joel 1:11-12.* This new rhetorical subunit proceeds from the logic of 1:10. The previous subunit, 1:8-10, concluded with a reference to the devastation of the fields and their produce, specifically grain and wine. Now, 1:11 directs the call to mourn and wail at the farmers who produce the grain (wheat and barley) and the vine dressers who harvest the vine. Further, the devastation extends to other products in 1:12 (the fig, pomegranate, and apple trees). The result of the devastation then extends in 1:12b to the people as a whole, for whom joy is now gone. The cultic orientation of these verses implies the devastation does not derive primarily from the loss of food, but from the loss of joy because the people cannot bring their offerings.

*Joel 1:13-14.* Attention turns to the priests with 1:13-14, where they are specifically called to mourn and wail, even though 1:9 has already described the mourning of the priests. The verbs at the beginning of 1:13 portray lamentation, implying they demonstrate sorrow and regret. The first verb, translated by the NRSV as "put on sackcloth," literally means prepare oneself, but it often appears in the context of mourning. Preparation for mourning included changing into the clothes used in funeral rituals, specifically sackcloth. Here, as elsewhere in Joel, no reason is given as to why the land is suffering, but the text assumes the devastation of the land represents punishment from God because of the people's behavior. Commentators have searched in vain within Joel for a specific clue indicating what the people have done to merit God's punishment. However, only the effects of the punishment are stated in Joel. As will be noted (2:12-14), because Joel's extended call to repentance culminates in language reminiscent of Amos and Hosea, these two books provide plenty of reasons for divine punishment. Hence, it is no accident that Joel 1 formulates its call to attention with allusions to Hosea 2 and 4–5, where the evidence for the political, ethical, and cultic violations has been laid forth in detail.

## A Warning and a Prayer, 1:15-20

Formally, Joel 1:15-20 functions as an intercessory prayer with an introduction (1:15), a reiteration of the situation for the congregation (1:16-18), and the intercession proper (1:19-20). Contextually, these verses indicate an important shift. Whereas previously the prophet sent out a call to a wide range of groups asking them to gather and to mourn the devastation of the land (1:2-14), now the prophet joins them. Interpreting the situation as evidence that the day of YHWH is at hand (1:15), the prophet not only recounts the situation (1:16-18) but also joins his voice with those who suffer. This transition is evidenced by the first person plural pronouns in 1:16, where the prophet says the food is cut off before "our eyes" causing joy to disappear from the temple of "our God." The image described in 1:17-18 reinforces this bleakness: seed has been planted, but the lack of water means nothing will come of the planting; storehouses and granaries hold no fruit or grain; and the fields contain no vegetation upon which animals may feed. Then, in images reminiscent of the first two visions of Amos (see Amos 7:1-3, 4-6), the prophet cries to YHWH because fire has destroyed the land so that even the animal kingdom has nowhere to turn for water (1:19-20). [The First Two Visions of Amos] Events have gone from bad to worse in that it is no longer merely a drought but fire that threatens the land.

For the first time in the Book of the Twelve, Joel 1:15 uses the term "day of YHWH." ["Day of YHWH" in Joel 1] It has become widely acknowledged that the day of YHWH is a major recurring motif in the Twelve, and Joel plays a major role in that constellation. No other corpus in the Old Testament refers specifically to the day of YHWH as frequently. In the Book of the Twelve, one finds thirteen of the seventeen

### The First Two Visions of Amos

Comparison to the visions of Amos is not accidental, since those two visions recount the prophet's intercession in the face of a powerful locust attack (Amos 7:1-3; cf. Joel 1:4) and a fire of cosmic proportions (Amos 7:4-6; cf. Joel 1:19-20).

### "Day of YHWH" in Joel 1

In the Old Testament, the day of YHWH, or the day of the LORD, refers to a particular point in time, past or future, that the prophets portray as a day of divine intervention. Overwhelmingly, YHWH intervenes for the purpose of judgment, though the recipient of that judgment can be a foreign nation or YHWH's own people.

examples of this phrase: Joel 1:15; 2:1, 11; 2:31 (= MT 3:4); 4:14; Amos 5:18, 20; Obadiah 15; Zephaniah 1:7, 14 (twice); Zechariah 14:1; Malachi 4:5. Elsewhere, the phrase "day of YHWH" appears in the Old Testament only in Isaiah 13:6, 9 and Ezekiel 13:5; 30:3. This distribution, of course, tells only part of the story, since other phrases can also elicit similar ideas: for example, the day of distress (Obad 12), the day of disaster (Obad 13), the day of his coming (Mal 3:2), the day of clouds and thick darkness (Joel 2:2; Zeph 1:15), and many others.

## CONNECTIONS

Rhetorically, Joel 1 creates a vivid picture of the devastation threatening an entire community. The prophet gathers the community and challenges specific groups to recognize the severity of the problems. With each new description of the devastation, problems increase because a new threat enters the picture until 1:15-20 increases the threat exponentially by equating it with the day of YHWH. God is portrayed as the source of the disaster, and the prophet intercedes to YHWH on behalf of the people. Yet, as dire as the situation appears, it will get worse when a cosmic army commissioned by YHWH goes up against Jerusalem (2:1-11). It is helpful to think of its message both for modern persons of faith and its role in the Twelve.

First, responsible theologians today are slower to attribute natural disasters to the direct intervention of God than were their counterparts in the ancient world. The modern study of weather patterns makes droughts much more predictable than they once were. Hurricanes can be tracked, and their paths predicted, days before they make landfall. And yet, for all our knowledge, we still cannot control the powerful forces of nature. Attempts to control the devastation often result in little more than mandating evacuations, transporting supplies from regions not affected, and managing the cleanup. Political games ensue in the aftermath of major devastations, with politicians taking credit when recovery efforts go well and pointing fingers when they do not.

In the end, we live in an uneasy tension of knowing more and knowing less than those of Joel's world. We know more about anticipating natural calamities and getting aid to the regions in need, but we often know less about bringing God into the picture. We rightly reject the picture of an arbitrary God choosing to punish one street with flooding while sparing another. We do not ask, until it is too late, how our commitment to God could have alleviated the effects. In Joel's world, everyone suffered from the devastation. In our world, the degree of devastation and its consequences often depend upon systemic factors and political decisions. The tsunami of 2004 was made worse by prior decisions of some governments not to invest in early warning systems. The flooding after Hurricane Katrina in 2005 resulted from economic decisions not to build the levies to withstand a category 5 hurricane. The earthquake in Haiti in 2010 exposed what happens when no construction standards are in place to protect a population. After the disasters, people wished those decisions had been different. What if someone had asked, what would God have us do? Would it have made a difference to the politicians making the decisions if the most affected areas included their own homes rather than the homes of the poorest of society? Joel's plaintive cry to look at the devastation reminds us that the human cost of natural disasters should be part of the equation.

Just as important, God is no stranger to suffering. God can and should be sought for solace, comfort, and courage in the aftermath of natural calamity. Joel assumes that the people's behavior caused God to send the calamities described in Joel 1 without specifying what the people did. Persons of faith today should take a different approach. The image of the God who suffers with the world offers important corrective in both the Hebrew Bible and the New Testament. The pathos of Hosea 11 already drove home God's painful dilemma when dealing with a recalcitrant Israel. This image of the suffering of God, however, is not limited to Hosea 11. [The Suffering of God in the Old Testament]

The mystery of the power of calamity can unite the people of God who serve a Messiah willing to suffer on their behalf. Doctrine matters little in the face of hunger. Stands on political issues seem petty in the face of social upheaval. Jesus would be with the victims, no questions asked. Jesus stilled the storm; he did not cause it. Jesus confronted religious leaders

**The Suffering of God in the Old Testament**

A. Heschel wrote eloquently of the role of divine sorrow as a major component for Isaiah. Heschel reasons from the text that YHWH's anger develops from YHWH's sorrow from having been deserted by the people. T. Fretheim takes these ideas further when he writes of YHWH suffering "because," "with," and "for" humanity. For Fretheim, God's decision not to deal with humanity on strictly legal terms obligates God to suffering in the form of Israel's rejection.

Abraham J. Heschel, *The Prophets: An Introduction* (Harper Torchbooks 421; New York: Harper and Row, 1962) 79–83. Terence Fretheim, *The Suffering of God* (OBT 14; Philadelphia: Fortress, 1984) 107–48.

who had all the answers, who had their God packaged in a neat little box. He broke Sabbath customs to heal a man (Matt 12:10-13). He did not shy away from confronting moral issues, nor did he blame those who suffered when a tower collapsed in Siloam (Luke 13:1-5). Instead, he admonished followers to work from compassion and serve those in need as though they were serving him (Matt 25:41-45).

Second, from a descriptive perspective, Joel 1:2-20 provides a pivotal hermeneutical component of the theological affirmations of the Book of the Twelve. While this text conveys a cause-and-effect theology that can be abused, it also does five things that underscore the accountability before God's ethical and theological expectations. First, this passage extends the message of Hosea, which is important for the Book of the Twelve for at least two reasons: it presumes the charges leveled against God's people in Hosea are still valid, and it underscores both the call to repentance and the failure of God's people to respond to this at the end of Hosea (14:1-8). Second, Joel 1 lays the groundwork for the continuing effect of God's word upon God's people. God has offered a chance to repent, but the people have chosen to ignore it, thus creating consequences for God's people. Third, as will become clearer beginning with 2:1, the cultic setting of Joel 1 begins to shift the focus more explicitly to Jerusalem and Judah, whereas Hosea largely focuses upon the northern kingdom. This southern focus has implications for readers old and new. Were it not for the inclusion of Joel—a writing whose Jerusalem orientation becomes increasingly clear as the book unfolds—it might have been possible to read Hosea and Amos (the first and third writings in the Book of the Twelve) as messages designed for someone else (that is, the northern kingdom of Israel). This expansion of the message invites all readers who think they are part of God's people to hear Joel's words with the words of Hosea. Fourth, even though God's judgment threatens God's people, Joel 1 shows that the relationship continues. The prophet brings a message from God to challenge the people to turn back to God. Finally, while Joel 1 is oriented toward the suffering of the here and now, chapters 2–3 will also lay out a paradigm of history that foreshadows what will happen to Israel and Judah as the Book of the Twelve unfolds. In a real sense, Joel anticipates, at least symbolically, Israel's story through time. God sends a series of locust-nations, and they devour the land until it cannot sustain life as they knew it. Only God's consistent deliverance of a remnant creates the possibility for a return of the people, the reconstruction of the temple, and the renewal of the fertility of the land.

# NOTE

1. Ruth Scoralick, *Gottes Guete und Gottes Zorn: Die Gottespraedikationen in Exodus 34:6f und ihre intextuellen Beziehungen zum Zwoelfprophetenbuch* (HBS 33; Freiburg: Herder, 2002) 164.

# A THREAT, A CALL TO REPENT, AND TWO PROMISES

## Joel 2:1-32

## COMMENTARY

Joel 2 (MT 2:1–3:5) continues the themes from Joel 1 but raises the stakes considerably following the introduction of the day of YHWH in 1:15. The chapter unfolds in four interrelated sections: an impending threat (2:1-11), a call to repent (2:12-17), and two promises (2:18-27; 2:28-32). Joel 2:1-11 describes the cosmic army that YHWH will lead to battle against Jerusalem on the impending day of YHWH. This attack is not a normal invasion, since the attacking army will be utterly unique (2:2) and will be led by none other than YHWH himself (2:11). Joel 2:12-17 follows with a call to repent, delivered to the people of Jerusalem. With 2:18, the style of speech shifts to divine first person as YHWH responds to the call to repent with a promise. Joel 2:18-27 renews God's promise of restoration to the people, should they choose to repent, by reversing the situation of Joel 1. The fertility of the land will be restored and the invading army removed, preparing the land and the people for a life of service to YHWH. Joel 2:28-32 (MT 3:1-5) extends the promise into a more distant future where all of God's people shall speak for YHWH and serve as catalysts for the entire world to recognize YHWH as God.

### YHWH's Attacking Army, 2:1-11

The structure of 2:1-11 consists of a thematic frame (2:1-2a, 11b) surrounding three descriptions of YHWH's army, each paired with a response to that army by a different entity (land, people, and cosmos). [Structure of Joel 2:1-11] The thematic frame announces the impending day of YHWH. Both parts of the frame accentuate the fearsome nature of the army and the nearness of the day of YHWH, and both parts use language about the day of YHWH found else-

The structure of Joel 2:1-11 emphatically depicts a fearsome enemy and the response of the land, people, and cosmos. The army belongs to and will attack on the day of YHWH, as underscored by allusions to the other Day of YHWH texts in the Book of the Twelve (see [Day of YHWH Quotes]):

2:1-2a Be Afraid. The day of YHWH is here (ends with allusion to Zeph 1:7)
   2:2b Description of YHWH's Army
     2:3 Response of the Land
     2:4-5 Description of YHWH's Army
     2:6 Response of the People
     2:7-9 Description of YHWH's Army
     2:10 Response of the Cosmos
     2:11a YHWH Is at the Head of His Vast Army
2:11b Be Afraid. The Day of YHWH is here (ends with allusion to Mal 3:2; 4:5)

where in the Book of the Twelve. [Day of YHWH quotes] The imminent arrival of the day of YHWH (2:1b) connects thematically with 1:15b, but the formulation of 2:2a is even more similar to Zephaniah 1:7 (though the motif appears in other texts as well in the Book of the Twelve). Further, Joel 2:11b echoes day of YHWH language in Malachi 3:2 and 4:5 (MT 3:23). These parallels anchor the day of YHWH in Joel to the broader corpus.

Joel 2:1 announces a call to alarm. The phrase "blow the trumpet" in 2:1, 15 begins two calls to attention, but for different reasons. In 2:1 the trumpet signals an impending attack on the day of YHWH, while in 2:15 the horn calls the people together for cultic reasons. The fearsome description of the day of YHWH continues in Joel 2:2 with references to the "day of darkness and gloom, a day of clouds and thick darkness." This description evokes theophanic language often associated with the escape from Egypt, presence at Sinai, and the wilderness wandering. Simultaneously, it elicits fear of the presence of YHWH.
[Theophanic Language]

Joel 2:2b-11a unfolds in four movements (2:2b-3, 4-6, 7-10, 11a), each containing a description of the army interwoven with depictions of responses from three different entities. The land

**Day of YHWH Quotes**

The thematic frame of Joel 2:1-11 draws upon other day of YHWH texts in the Book of the Twelve.

Joel 2:1-2: Blow the trumpet in Zion; sound the alarm on my holy mountain! Let all the inhabitants of the land tremble, for the day of the LORD is coming, it is near,

Joel 1:15; 2:1; 4:14; Obad 15; Zeph 1:7, 14: (for) the day of the LORD is near

a day of darkness and gloom, a day of clouds and thick darkness! Like blackness there is spread upon the mountains a great and powerful people; their like has never been from of old, nor will be again after them through the years of all generations.

Zeph 1:15: A day of wrath is that day, a day of distress and anguish, a day of ruin and devastation, a day of darkness and gloom, a day of clouds and thick darkness,

Mal 4:5: Lo, I will send you the prophet Elijah before the great and terrible day of the LORD comes.

Joel 2:11b: Truly the day of the LORD is great; terrible indeed—who can endure it?

Mal 3:2: But who can endure the day of his (YHWH) coming, and who can stand when he appears?

(2:3), people (2:6), and cosmos (2:10) respond to YHWH's army with similar-sounding words, drawing attention to similar reactions. In Joel 2:2b-3, one finds the first description of YHWH's massive cosmic army followed by a statement about the effect of this army upon the land. The army is described as unique in that its likes have never been seen before, nor will they be seen again. The description emphasizes the sheer size and destructive power of the army. Moreover, the effect of the army upon the land contrasts the idyllic time before the army's arrival—when the land was like the garden of Eden—with the state of utter devastation after the army's arrival—when the land will be "a desolate wilderness." [The Garden of Eden]

The second description of the army appears in 2:4-5. This description focuses upon military similes to depict the danger (e.g., they have the appearance of horses, like charging war horses, like chariots). The people's response illustrates the impossibility of resistance in 2:6. Merely the sight of the army panics the people, and they respond in utter terror. They writhe and become flushed. The idiom, "their faces become pale," recurs in Nahum 2:10 (MT 2:11), where the Babylonian destruction of Nineveh is portrayed. Habakkuk extends this description of Babylon as an army sent by YHWH (1:5-12), whose horses and horsemen convey a sense of inevitable destruction (1:8; cf. Joel 2:4-5). Joel 2:1-11, like Habakkuk, presumes this impending day of YHWH's attack will strike Jerusalem. The association of this imagery with Babylon in the Book of the Twelve suggests one should hear the reference to the day of YHWH as a warning about the "coming" destruction of Jerusalem that will play out in the Book of the Twelve, a suggestion supported by the echoes of Zephaniah 1:15 in Joel 2:2.

The third description of YHWH's army (2:7-9) depicts the horde-like, unwavering movement of the army in ways that, like 2:4-5, remind the reader of the Twelve of the Babylonian juggernaut described in Habakkuk 1:6-11, where the soldiers move forward like a (locust) horde, or a group marching *en masse* (Hab 1:9), as they laugh at the defenses of other nations (1:10). Joel 2:7 (1) depicts the army scaling the wall of Jerusalem (see 2:1), the

---

**Theophanic Language**

ΑΩ A theophany is a narrative or poetic text that tells of God appearing on earth, as indicated by etymology of the word that comes from the Greek words for God (*theos*) and "appearance" (*phaneros*). See Exod 13:21, 22; 14:9, 20, 24; 16:10; 19:9, 16; 24:16, 18; 33:9-10; 40:34-38; Num 9:17; etc. These theophanic images, paradoxically, do two things simultaneously: they provide comfort of YHWH's presence, but they also create fear of the power and glory of the Almighty. Prophetic theophanies are poetic texts that almost always presage an appearance of God for judgment, either against foreign nations (e.g., Nah 1:2-8; Isa 63:1-6) or against YHWH's own people (Mic 1:2-4). Joel's use of theophanic language draws more explicitly on motifs associated with exodus traditions.

See Siegfried Bergler, *Joel als Schriftinterpret* (Beiträge zur Erforschung des Alten Testaments und des Antiken Judentums 16; Frankfurt: Peter Lang, 1988) 247–94.

## The Garden of Eden

The reference to the "garden of Eden" in 2:3 functions *intertextually* on two levels. First, it presumes knowledge of the paradise story from Genesis to the extent that the "garden of Eden" serves as a metaphor for undisturbed fertility of the land. It is not addressing the issue of human sinfulness, but merely comparing the land to a symbol of health and fertility. Second, beyond the use of Eden as symbol, Joel 2:4 portrays the functional opposite of two other prophetic texts (Ezek 36:35; Isa 51:3).

**Joel 2:3:** Fire devours in front of them, and behind them a flame burns. Before them the land is like the garden of Eden, but after them a desolate wilderness, and nothing escapes them.

**Ezek 36:35:** And they will say, "This land that was desolate has become like the garden of Eden; and the waste and desolate and ruined towns are now inhabited and fortified."

**Isa 51:3:** For the LORD will comfort Zion; he will comfort all her waste places, and will make her wilderness like Eden, her desert like the garden of the LORD; joy and gladness will be found in her, thanksgiving and the voice of song.

Of these two, Ezek 36:35 uses remarkably similar language so that Joel 2:3 may be a direct allusion to Ezek 36:35. The contrast of the message is that Ezek 36:35 and Isa 51:3 move from images of destruction to the promise of Eden, while Joel 2:3 looks back on the past as a time of Eden while the future will be one of desolation. Joel 3:10 functions similarly in that a promise appearing elsewhere in the prophetic canon (Isa 2:4; Mic 4:3) is reversed from a promise of peace for the nations to a call to arms for the nations.

The treatment of Eden as an allusion to the fertility/infertility of the land, while evocative, is not as theologically laden as later artistic renderings. Consider the work of Lucas Cranach (1472–1553) below from around 1530, where Eden serves as the idyllic backdrop for various scenes from Gen 2–3 that were more focused upon documenting the consequences of the fall from grace that took place in Eden. In this painting, the confrontation with God stands in the foreground while other scenes from the Genesis narrative are depicted in miniature all around the frame, including (from left to right) the angel's expulsion of the couple, the couple's hiding, the creation of woman from man, the serpent tempting the couple with an apple, and the creation of man. Eden, of course, has symbolized theological discussion on everything from original sin to the question of the immortality of the human soul. On the latter, see particularly, James Barr, *The Garden of Eden and the Hope of Immortality* (Minneapolis: Fortress, 1992). "Eden" also played a significant role in temple ideology as "a mythopoetic realization of heaven on earth."

Lawrence Stager, "Jerusalem as Eden," *BAR* 26/3 (May/June 2000): 38.

Lucas Cranach, the Elder (1472–1553). *Paradise*. 1530. Oil on limewood. Kunsthistorisches Museum, Vienna, Austria. (Credit: Erich Lessing/Art Resource, NY)

primary means of a city's defense, and (2) notes that the wall shows no visible signs of slowing the forward movement of the army itself. The "soldiers" do not break ranks but move forward unabated. These two images of 2:7 are repeated in reverse order in 2:8-9, providing an A-B-B'-A' chiastic structure to this strophe. [The Chiastic Structure of Joel 2:7-9] Joel 2:8 describes the invincibility of the forward push of the army that does not deviate from its path, while Joel 2:9 describes the army's scaling of the wall, the houses, and the windows of the city. The army scales the city's defenses and enters the homes with no effective resistance to stop them.

Joel 2:10 portrays a third response to YHWH's army in this passage, this time expanding the fearful reaction of the earth, the heavens, the sun, the moon, and the stars. In other words, this response affects the entire cosmos. All creation fears the actions of this army. The earth and the heavens tremble, while the cosmic luminaries lose their light. The reactions of the cosmic entities evoke images of earthquakes and theophanies, images designed to convey monumental threats.

Joel 2:11 rounds off the unit with a final descriptive element (2:11a), placing YHWH at the head of this massive army, and a second citation—this time from Malachi's description of the day of YHWH (Joel 2:11b, cf. Mal 3:2; 4:5). Thus, the citations that begin and end 2:1-11 evoke texts in the Book of the Twelve related specifically to the impending day of YHWH, from the last writing prior to Jerusalem's destruction (Zephaniah) and from the final writing (Malachi).

### Horses of War

Joel describes the locusts as horses of war. His imagery reappears in John's Apocalypse in the description of the locusts that come upon the earth after the fifth angel blows the trumpet (Rev 9:7-10).

Fifth trumpet: men stung by locusts (Rev 9:7-12). *Commentary on the Apocalypse*, by Beatus of Liebana. Spain (Leon), c. 950. The Pierpont Morgan Library, New York, NY. (Credit: The Pierpont Morgan Library/Art Resource, NY)

### The Chiastic Structure of Joel 2:7-9

A [7a]Like warriors they charge, like soldiers they scale the wall.

  B [7b]Each keeps to its own course, they do not swerve from their paths.

  B' [8]They do not jostle one another, each keeps to its own track; they burst through the weapons and are not halted.

A' [9]They leap upon the city, they run upon the walls; they climb up into the houses, they enter through the windows like a thief.

## A Renewed Call to Repentance, 2:12-17

As a rhetorical unit, Joel 2:12-17 does three things: it calls the people to repent in hopes of changing YHWH's mind (2:12-14); it connects the call to the threats of Joel 1–2 (2:15); and it calls upon the priests to intercede for Jerusalem (2:16-17). Thus, the presupposition of the unit becomes clear: showing repentance to YHWH may convince YHWH to change Jerusalem's fate.

Joel 2:12 marks a major turning point in the book. Whereas 2:1-11 describes the army's attack on the impending day of YHWH, 2:12 addresses the people, calling them to repent before the day of YHWH comes. In Joel 2:12, YHWH commands the people to repent ("return to me"), describing repentance in both internal and external terms. Internally, the repentance requires "all your heart," while externally it involves fasting, weeping, and mourning. Joel 2:13 continues the call to repent, though YHWH now appears in the third person. It also references internal and external acts of repentance, but emphasizes the internal in that the call to "rend your hearts" is given preference over the external "tearing of garments." The second half of 2:13 reiterates the call to return/repent that began 2:12. In other words, the chiastic structure of 2:12-13 has YHWH imploring the people (a) to return with (b) sincere acts of repentance, followed by the prophet calling for (b) sincere acts of repentance and (a) a call to return to YHWH, your God.

Joel 2:14 culminates 2:12-17 by asking a rhetorical question: who knows whether YHWH will change his mind? [Does God Change God's Mind?] The point of the repentance in 2:12-13 is to attempt to change YHWH's mind. The rhetorical question in 2:14 assumes this change is possible, but that only YHWH knows whether YHWH will relent.

By utilizing self-quotes from 2:1 and 1:14, Joel 2:15 draws together the two major portions of the book so far: gathering the people (1:2-20) and warning of the impending day of YHWH (2:1-14). [Self-quotations from Joel 2:1 and 1:14] Joel 2:16 extends 2:15's call to gather by specifying the elderly, the children, the groom, and

### Does God Change God's Mind?

Modern theological assertions about God's sovereignty often go too far with the intractability of God out of concern that God not appear weak. However, the Old Testament remains content to portray God as capable of changing God's mind about something God has done or is about to do. Old Testament texts use the verb *nḥm* with its idea of "to be sorry" in seven key texts: Gen 6:6; Exod 32:14; 2 Sam 24:16; Jer 26:13; Jer 26:19; Amos 7:3; Amos 7:6. God's action can even be described using the verb *šûb*, meaning to turn or repent (Deut 13:17; Josh 7:26). This change of course is not a mechanical response to words of distress. God did not always respond by relenting or changing a decision, even when called upon (Deut 1:45; Jer 23:20). The assumption of a reciprocal change can also be portrayed where YHWH will change course (*šûb*) if and only if the people change first (Zech 1:3; Mal 3:7).

the bride. This combination covers the entire extended family, emphasizing what is at stake—the continuing existence of the people itself. Finally, Joel 2:17 explains the purpose of this gathering. The people are gathered to witness the priest's intercession to YHWH to spare YHWH's people. The reason for this intercession is YHWH's own reputation, much like the rationale used by Moses when interceding to YHWH in the wilderness after the people worshiped the golden calf (Exod 32:11-12).

**Self-quotations from Joel 2:1 and 1:14**

Joel 2:15 begins with the same command to blow the trumpet that began 2:1, but the purpose for the command differs. Whereas 2:1 commanded the trumpet be blown as a warning of the impending attack, 2:15 introduces a call to gather the community for public prayer, specifically intercession to YHWH to spare the people. The second half of 2:15 quotes 1:14 ("sanctify a fast, call a solemn assembly"), a verse that concluded the initial call to the community before transitioning to the scene of the day of YHWH.

## First Promise—Restoration of the Land, 2:18-27

Joel 2:18-27 offers a promise in three rhetorical sections: an affirmation of YHWH's response (2:18-20); a call for rejoicing from creation (2:21-23); and a statement of consequences (2:24-27). The first section (2:18-20) affirms that YHWH will act on behalf of the land and people (2:18). [Joel 2:18, Past or Future?] After YHWH decides to show zeal (2:18), YHWH will provide the land with symbols of fertility, specifically grain, wine, and oil (2:19). This recurring triad represents the produce of a healthy land (cf. Deut 28:51; 33:28). [Fertility of the Land in the Book of the Twelve] More important, for Joel, this promise of fertility reverses the state of the plants in Joel 1 (see 1:10; see also 1:5, 17).

---

**Joel 2:18, Past or Future?**

Joel 2:18 poses a major interpretive problem for the book, as evidenced by the disagreements in English translations. At issue is whether this verse should be read as a continuation of the call to repentance, or whether it presumes the people had repented. The debate affects whether the verb, *to become jealous*, is translated as narrated past (RSV, NRSV, ESV) or describes YHWH's action in the future (NIV, KJV, NASB, NLT). Syntactically, both are possible, so to a large extent, the translation depends upon how one understands the larger context, or even the function of the book. If one assumes an oral setting for Joel, then Joel's structure likely reflects a cultic event wherein the people have repented following the command to do so in 2:12-13. In this case, the narrator marks the turning point with YHWH's decision "to become jealous" for the land and the people who have already repented. However, translating this verb as past tense creates a chronological island, since the preceding verses presuppose the need for repentance and intercession, and the subsequent verses refer to actions that YHWH will do in the future. Further, the broader context of Joel argues strongly for literary associations. Joel 1–2 imitates the open-ended call to repentance that concluded the book of Hosea, the text where the people's response was also not narrated. The compiler of Joel makes extensive use of allusion and citation in these chapters, including self-quotation (2:25) and allusion to Hosea (2:24). The paradigmatic quality of Joel for the Book of the Twelve also plays an anticipatory role in this respect. The one place in the Book of the Twelve where YHWH's people do explicitly repent (Zech 1:6) is followed by the first vision of Zechariah, where YHWH's first words fulfill Joel 2:18: "I am very jealous for Jerusalem and for Zion" (Zech 1:15). Thus, Joel 2:18 portrays a future reality contingent on Israel's repentance.

---

**Fertility of the Land in the Book of the Twelve**

Variations of this motif recur in key locations in the Twelve as allusions to the promised fertility of the land (Hos 2:8, 22 [MT 2:10, 24]; 14:7; Joel 1:10; Hag 1:11; 2:19; Zech 8:9-12; Mal 3:10-11). The motif reminds the reader that the land's suffering results from God's punishment of the people. Hos 2, by personifying the land as YHWH's wife, portrays this infertility in terms of YHWH's removal of his gifts in order to show his wife that other gods have not provided them (Hos 2:8-9). Joel advances the metaphor on two fronts: (1) Joel 1–2 depicts the current suffering of the land while Hosea 2 portrays the loss of these elements as a situation in the future; and (2) Hosea deals primarily (though not exclusively) with Israel while Joel deals primarily with Jerusalem. By contrast, Haggai and Zechariah utilize this motif as part of a promise *being realized* after the temple reconstruction had begun. Finally, Malachi turns again in the direction of contingency: *if* the people will bring the tithes correctly, *then* YHWH will restore fertility and remove the devourer (locust). These images parallel those of Joel 2:19-20. This address to the present generation with an open-ended call to repent/change helps one see the function of Joel and Malachi in the Book of the Twelve: the former prefigures the basic flow of the story of Israel and Judah presumed in the Twelve, while the latter confronts the "current" generation (and readers) with the danger to which, despite everything that has occurred (as portrayed in the Book of the Twelve), God's people have returned—the same dangerous abuses with which the first prophets (Hosea, Joel) had to deal.

---

The promise of fertility in 2:19 is underscored by a related act in 2:20. YHWH will also remove the invading army from the land, a statement that reverses the threat of the locust/enemy attack so prominent in 1:2–2:11.

Joel 2:21-23 directs a series of imperatives to the land (*'ādâmâh*, 2:21), the animals (2:22), and the people of Zion (2:23): take courage and rejoice. Like the previous section, these commands reverse the imagery of Joel 1–2, which addresses the lamentations of the people, the land, and the animals. While the commands of 2:21-23 utilize antonyms, the subjects address the same entities affected in 1:2–2:18—the people of Zion, the land personified (1:8), and the animals (1:18)—to reverse YHWH's punishment. Each verse provides reasons for rejoicing: YHWH will act (2:21), fertility will return to the land (2:22), and rains will begin again (2:23). Punishment was directed against the people, and all creation had suffered. Fittingly, the promise offered in 2:21-23 affects not just the people, but all creation as well.

Joel 2:24-27 provides an extended rationale to the calls for joy and courage by presenting the consequences of YHWH's change of heart. Agricultural bounty will return (2:24); restitution of what the *series* of locusts removed will occur (2:25); people will have food to eat (2:26); they will praise YHWH (2:26), realize YHWH's presence in the land (2:27), and no longer be ashamed (2:26, 27). These consequences relate specifically to the preceding sections in two ways. They not only extend the rationale for the commands of 2:21-23 but also describe the consequences of YHWH's zeal for the land and the people in 2:18-20. [Interrelated Motifs of Joel 2:18-27] The three parts of this extended unit—YHWH's promise (2:18-20), the call for creation to rejoice (2:21-23), and the description of the consequences (2:24-27)—form a sophisticated network of images.

However, this promise is limited in two ways. First, the promise and its consequences depend upon the people's response to the call to repent in 2:12-17, a response that is never narrated. Second, the promise of 2:18-27 does not end the book. Two additional, extended promises (2:28-32; 3:1-21) will enter the picture in order to extend the implications of the people's potential repentance and to redefine the nature of the day of YHWH respectively.

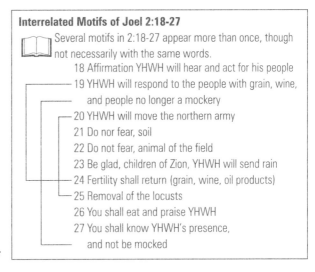

**Interrelated Motifs of Joel 2:18-27**

Several motifs in 2:18-27 appear more than once, though not necessarily with the same words.

- 18 Affirmation YHWH will hear and act for his people
- 19 YHWH will respond to the people with grain, wine, and people no longer a mockery
- 20 YHWH will move the northern army
- 21 Do nor fear, soil
- 22 Do not fear, animal of the field
- 23 Be glad, children of Zion, YHWH will send rain
- 24 Fertility shall return (grain, wine, oil products)
- 25 Removal of the locusts
- 26 You shall eat and praise YHWH
- 27 You shall know YHWH's presence, and not be mocked

## Second Promise—A Different Day of YHWH, 2:28-32

In its current form and location, Joel 2:28-32 portrays a second promise to the people should they choose to repent, but it differs from the first promise (2:18-27) in three ways. The differences are so stark that these verses have often been perceived as a later addition, either alone or with 3:1-21. First, 2:28-32 describes the events as subsequent to those described in 2:18-27, as noted by the introductory formula ("and it will happen afterward"). Second, the promise is not related to the fertility imagery of Joel 1–2. Rather, 2:28-29 focuses upon the prophetic function of the *entire* Jerusalem population. Third, this prophetic function announces a new day of YHWH (2:30-32), but this new threat is directed against the nations. Only those on Mount Zion will be spared. The two subunits of this second promise (2:28-29, 30-32) serve a single function: to point toward a more distant day of YHWH for which the people will be prepared, if and when they repent. Further, while the focus shifts from that of Joel 1–2, it anticipates certain thematic movements that will play a role elsewhere in the Book of the Twelve. [Joel 2:28-32 and the Book of the Twelve]

Joel 2:28 (MT 3:1) begins the second promise whose description runs from 2:28-2:32. The chronological transition at the beginning of the verse places this promise subsequent to the restoration of the fertility and

**Joel 2:28-32 and the Book of the Twelve**

Joel 2:28-32 transitions from a promise that focuses upon the re-fertilization of the land to a promise of a purified Jerusalem, where the entire population functions like prophets (2:28-29) and where "those who call on the name of YHWH" find refuge on the coming day of judgment against all the earth (2:30-32). While at this point unexpected in Joel, the theme of judgment against the nations on the coming day of YHWH serves as the central theme for the final chapter of Joel. In addition, this eschatological framing of judgment against the nations prepares the reader of the Twelve for the move from Joel to Amos. Further, the rationale cited in Joel 2:32 cites Obad 15 and uses its imagery.

The vision of Joel 2:28-29 is not so unusual when one understands the implications of other texts. For example, Gen 1 goes to considerable lengths to make the point that woman and man are created in the image of God. The narrative history of Israel and Judah makes room for women as prophets (Miriam in Exodus–Numbers; Deborah in Judg 4–5 [she is also a judge]; Huldah in 2 Kgs 22; and several unnamed female prophets). The situation changes in the postexilic period when the temple is reconstructed around a male priesthood. However, even in the time of Nehemiah female prophets can still be found. Noadiah, the prophetess, is named in Neh 6:14 as one of the enemies of Nehemiah because she worked against him, not because she was a prophet. Jesus battled prejudice against women by including women among his disciples. Not surprisingly, Joel 2:28-29 serves as a proof text for the writer of Acts to illustrate the power of the arrival of the Spirit at Pentecost (Acts 2:17-21), a power that descended upon all who were present that day. Female prophets in the Hebrew Bible and in ancient Israel in general have been the subject of significant study of late, which suggests they were more prevalent than many modern commentators have assumed. Though she may overstate some of the evidence, see Wilda C. Gafney, *Daughters of Miriam: Women Prophets in Ancient Israel* (Minneapolis: Fortress, 2008).

The imagery in 2:31 of the darkening of the cosmic luminaries as a precursor to the day of YHWH already appeared in 2:10, and it will return in 3:15 (MT 4:15). However, those being judged in Joel 2:31 and 3:15 differ from those in 2:10. The first reference in 2:10 depicts the cosmic response to the impending attack on YHWH's people, while the nations are the object of judgment on the day of YHWH in 2:31 and 3:15 (MT 3:3; 4:15). This imagery of the darkening of the cosmic luminaries as a precursor to the day of YHWH also appears in Amos 8:9 as a precursor to the destruction of the northern kingdom.

the removal of the enemy nation described in 2:18-27. This second stage is notable for two reasons. First, it describes a new relationship between YHWH and YHWH's people—one unlike any in Israel's history in which all people function as *prophets*. Both prophesying and dreaming dreams connote the act of communicating for and with YHWH. Second, this passage emphasizes that *all* of God's people will be called to function in this new manner. Given the patriarchal structures of the time, this promise to include women, children, and slaves, as well as men and elders, in the work of YHWH is unparalleled in Old Testament texts. [Women as Religious Leaders in the Old Testament]

The focus shifts in 2:30-32 to the cosmic dimensions of the day of YHWH. At first glance, these verses stand out for their negative implications, given that the verses on either side contain promises. However, careful attention to the larger context illuminates the verses as presuming the dark side of the day of YHWH for the nations, not for YHWH's people. In this respect, 2:28-32 fits better into the logical context of Joel's structural flow than is typically recognized. To be sure, the verses do not pronounce judgment on the nations so much as they presume it, but this presumption helps to explain the promise of deliverance on Mount Zion for whoever calls on the name of YHWH (2:32). In short, these verses presume a day of YHWH will come against the entire world, while those who worship YHWH in Jerusalem will be delivered. [Cosmic Upheaval and the Day of YHWH] This presumption of judgment upon the nations builds upon the promise to remove the northern army (2:20) and the effects of the "locusts" (2:25). Finally, this presumption also anticipates a major theme of the final chapter of Joel—the day of judgment will come on the nations while deliverance will come to Zion.

## CONNECTIONS

Theological reflection on Joel 2 concerns more than application for the modern community of faith. One should reflect upon the nature of the chapter as a paradigm of the history of Judah and the theology of prayer.

*Joel 1–2 as a Paradigm in the Book of the Twelve.* Readers who knew Israel's story well would have heard more in the description of YHWH's army in 2:1-11 than just a threat from an angry God. The combination of these images, with motifs elsewhere associated with the Babylonians and with the destruction of Jerusalem, suggests the compiler presumed a paradigmatic quality for Joel that extends beyond the book. The series of "locusts" who attack Judah and Jerusalem plays out in the Book of the Twelve, where Assyria and Babylon devour successive portions of the country (see discussion of Nah 3:15-16; Hab 1:9) and where "locusts" continue to plague the land even after the people rebuilt the temple (Mal 3:10-12). In addition, the promised return to fertility after an extended period of infertility, if God responds favorably to the people's repentance, also plays out in a series of texts in the Twelve (see [Fertility of the Land in the Book of the Twelve]). These two motifs—devouring locusts and promised fertility—are linked to the fate of Israel and Judah in the Book of the Twelve. The locust motif consistently refers to external threats that appear suddenly and in large numbers. Sometimes these "locusts" are literal (see Amos 4:9), but in other passages they clearly function as metaphors of foreign military power (Nah 3:15-16; Hab 1:9; Mal 3:10). Related, the calls to repentance that conclude Hosea (for Israel) and begin Joel (for Judah and Jerusalem) both extend a contingent promise to God's people if the people repent. However, despite these promises, neither book stipulates how the people actually respond. The recurring motifs of "locusts" (nations), the continuing allusions to the infertility of the land, the contingent nature of the promise, and this lack of narrated response certainly pose the question: How is one to interpret the people's response to this call to repent in the Book of the Twelve?

Traditionally, when Hosea and Joel are interpreted in isolation from one another, and in isolation from the other writings in the Twelve, interpreters tend to assume the people respond positively. However, the positive response assumed by so many for Hosea and Joel appears less likely when one looks at the Twelve in its entirety for at least three reasons: the repetition of the call to repent from Hosea to Joel, the subsequent citations of the people's failure to repent (most notably in Amos 4:6-11), and the one specific passage, Zechariah 1:2-6, that does recount the people's repentance. The fact that Hosea ends with an open-ended call to repent, and then Joel follows immediately with another, longer, and more urgent call strongly suggests that the need for God's people to repent intensifies. To be sure, Joel changes the focus from Israel to Judah, but this shift underscores the extent of the problem. Joel contains no new accusations because the accusations from Hosea are still in effect. In Amos 4:6-11, YHWH lays out a series of actions intended to bring God's people back, but which fail to have the desired effect. These actions read like a litany of the threats in Joel 1–2: famine (4:6), drought (4:7-8), blight and mildew that destroy the produce of the land (4:9), and plagues on the magnitude of those from the exodus story (4:10). Finally, Zechariah 1:2-6 represents the one place in the Book of the Twelve that does portray, in the form of a narrative report, the repentance of the people. This report refers back to the previous rejection of YHWH's calls to repent by the ancestors of the generation that returns from exile. Just as important, the report of Zechariah 1:2-6 introduces a series of night visions, the first of which recounts YHWH's response to the situation in terms remarkably reminiscent of the promise language of Joel. In other words, when the people actually do repent (Zech 1:6), YHWH begins to make good on his promise.

These thematic links invite the reader to step back and look at Joel in light of the entire history of Judah and Israel from the eighth century forward. The long view of history, as though seen from God's perspective, plays a pivotal role for understanding the nature of the Book of the Twelve as a compendium of God's prophetic message to Judah and Israel interpreting events from the eighth century through the Persian period. This unfolding compendium documents a theological understanding of history for the ancient community of faith that witnesses to God's enduring compassion, even as it challenges the community of faith to return to its God before the coming day of YHWH. In the larger scheme of the Twelve, that day of YHWH takes at least two different forms. First, through Zephaniah, the reader of the Twelve intuits the impending destruction of Jerusalem looming ahead. Second, following a successful return and a reconstruction of the temple (Haggai and Zechariah 1–6), the message of Zechariah 7–14 and Malachi increasingly turn the reader's attention to unfinished business in the aftermath of the temple's reconstruction.

*A Theology of Prayer.* The theology of prayer present in Joel 2:12-14, 16-17 invokes a dynamic sense of God's involvement with the world and God's people. The theology behind the prayer involves at least four important affirmations about the way God relates to God's people. First, the call to pray presumes God can and *may* change God's mind once the decision to punish has been made. God is not some immutable, immovable, implacable force devoid of feeling for the people with whom he has tangled for so long. This conviction regarding God's willingness to respond to the cry of a people in need derives from teachings within Israel's own sacred texts from the outset. When Israel cried out under the oppression it suffered in Egypt, God responded. Then when Israel turned its back upon God and worshiped the golden calf, God changed God's mind about annihilating his people in response to the intercession of Moses (Exod 32:14). Second, the theology of prayer in Joel 2:14 presumes that the choice to change the decision belongs to God. Any hope for a pardon requires a change of heart from the people (2:12-13), but the prophet is not espousing some mechanistic ritual whereby the people repent and God is required to forgive them. Rather, 2:14 reminds people of the uncertainty of God's response. Third, the hope that God would change God's mind rests upon one of the chief attributes of God, namely God's compassion. Drawing again from lessons learned from the story of the golden calf, Joel 2:13 cites Exodus 34:6: "Return to YHWH, your God, for he is gracious and merciful, slow to anger, and abounding in steadfast love, and he relents from punishing." Thus, compassion and mercy constitute an essential part of God's character. Fourth, the theology of the prayer acknowledges that the fate of God's people reflects upon God. If God annihilates God's people, it makes God look weak before the nations: "Spare your people, YHWH, and do not make your heritage of mockery, a byword among the nations. Why should it be said among the peoples, 'Where is their God?'" (Joel 2:17) To be sure, when their lives hang in the balance, the people's petition to God that God remember God's *reputation* can seem self-serving. Nevertheless, this line of reasoning also appears on the lips of Moses in the story of the golden calf (Exod 32:12). If God desires to use God's people as a sign to the nations, the task will certainly become significantly more complex if God punishes his people more severely than those who do not worship God. Whether one perceives this argument as genuine or manipulative depends upon how one perceives the motives of those who pray. In either case, however, it arises from a sense of desperation, and in the end it underscores an important, too often forgotten aspect of God's election of God's people. Namely, God's people are not chosen so that they may receive special privileges. Rather, they are chosen so that they might represent God to those who have not encountered God. [For Further Reading]

**For Further Reading**

Regarding further resources for a theology of prayer that focus on the Hebrew Bible, see especially Samuel E. Balentine, *Prayer in the Hebrew Bible: The Drama of Divine-human Dialogue* (OBT; Minneapolis: Fortress, 1993) 260–71; and Patrick D. Miller, *They Cried to the Lord: The Form and Theology of Biblical Prayer* (Minneapolis: Fortress, 1994) esp. 46–48, 307–13; and Walter Brueggemann, *Worship in Ancient Israel: An Essential Guide* (Abingdon Essential Guides; Nashville: Abingdon, 2005) esp. 49–52.

# TWO SIDES OF
# THE DAY OF YHWH

## Joel 3:1-21

## COMMENTARY

Joel 3 contains four subunits artfully combined into a coherent whole. Two independent units (3:4-8, 9-17*) have been adapted for this context along with an introduction to the chapter (3:1-3) and a conclusion to the book (3:18-21). As a composite whole, Joel 3 deals with eschatological judgment on the day of YHWH during which the nations will be judged for what they have done to Judah, while Jerusalem will be spared. The outer sections (3:1-3, 18-21) appear to be composed for the context in order to introduce the chapter and close Joel within the Book of the Twelve. [Structure of Joel 3]

> **Structure of Joel 3**
>
> 📖 The thematic introduction (3:1-3) presents three specific themes that reappear in reverse order in the subsequent subunits. Joel 3:1-3, 18-21 were composed to incorporate 3:4-8 and the portions of 3:9-17 that already existed into Joel.
>
> A Restoration of Judah and Jerusalem (3:1)
>   B Judgment in the valley of Jehoshaphat (3:2)
>     C Punishment for selling of God's people into slavery (3:3)
>     C' Punishment for selling of God's people into slavery (3:4-8)
>   B' Judgment in the valley of Jehoshaphat (3:9-17)
> A' Restoration of Judah and Jerusalem (3:18-21)

### Thematic Introduction, 3:1-3 (MT 4:1-3)

Joel 3:1-3 introduces the themes of the remainder of the chapter. Joel 3:1 begins with an unusual eschatological formula: "in those days and at that time." ["In those days and at that time"] This dual formula connects the two actions of Joel 3—the restoration of the fortunes of Judah and Jerusalem (3:1), and the judgment against the nations in the symbolic valley of Jehoshaphat (3:2)—to the same time as the formula in 2:28. The phrase "restore the fortunes" implies restoration in the aftermath of the Babylonian captivity, and it serves as a type of refrain in the Book of the Twelve (Hos 6:11; Joel 3:1; Amos 9:14; Zeph 2:7; 3:20). ["Valley of Jehoshaphat"] Further, 3:2 is also linked to the

---

**"In those days and at that time"**

AΩ The dual reference points are unusual. The phrase "at that time" typically appears in narrative literature, where it universally refers to something in the past. Only in the prophetic corpus does the phrase refer to a time in the future. Ezekiel never uses this phrase; it appears eight times in Jeremiah but only three times in Isaiah; it appears six times in the Book of the Twelve (three of which are in Zeph 3:19-20); and it appears three times in one verse in Daniel (12:1). The combined phrase "in those days and at that time" appears elsewhere only in Jeremiah (33:15; 50:4, 20). Besides Joel 3:1, only Zeph 3:20 combines the phrase

"at that time" with the idiom of restoring fortunes. Given the secondary nature of Zeph 3:20 (long recognized as such in scholarly discussions) and its function as a transition to Haggai (see commentary to Zeph 3), a link between Joel 3:1 and Zeph 3:20 can be assumed, though the question of intentionality is more difficult. In the Book of the Twelve, Zeph 3:20 anticipates the restoration of Judah while pointing to Hag 1, where that restoration has taken place. Literarily, then, Joel 3:1 anticipates this "distant" promise as a turning point for the corpus.

---

**"Valley of Jehoshaphat"**

📖 In Joel 3:2 and 3:12, YHWH announces that judgment will take place in the "valley of Jehoshaphat" against those nations who have scattered God's people Israel. The location of this valley should not be sought on a map. Rather, this toponym is symbolic (Jehoshaphat means "YHWH will judge"), which is why it can also be given another name (i.e., "the valley of decision") in 3:14.

preceding promise, meaning that the judgment of the nations in 3:2 is part of the restoration of the fortunes of Judah and Jerusalem in 3:1. Finally, the reason for this judgment is the scattering of God's people and the dividing of God's land.

Joel 3:3 further explicates the meaning of "scattering" my people in 3:2 by accusing these nations of slave trading. It depicts the motive of the slave trade as sexual and drunken revelry: trading boys for prostitution and selling women for wine to drink. One should note, however, that the situation presumed is not the actual destruction of Jerusalem but the opportunistic acts of nations who have taken advantage of Judah's plight in the aftermath of that destruction. Such a scenario is further extrapolated by the depiction in 3:4-8, which lists the nations who did not participate in the Babylonian invasion but who have been selling Judeans to the Greeks.

**Logic of Joel 3:4-8**

📖 The core logic of the punishment of the coastal regions is clear. Because the Phoenicians and Philistines (the sea peoples) sold Judah's inhabitants into slavery across the sea to the Greeks, they will be punished by having the returning population of Judah sell them into slavery across the desert to the Sabeans.

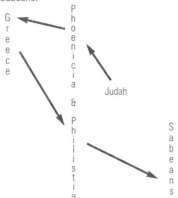

### Slave Traders Become Slaves, 3:4-8 (MT 4:4-8)

Joel 3:4-8 has its own logical structure as well as transitional markers at its beginning ("Moreover") and end ("... for YHWH has spoken"). [Logic of Joel 3:4-8] Because this unit interrupts the two references to the valley of Jehoshaphat (3:2, 12), it has often been argued that 3:4-8 represents a later insertion.

However, the thematic structure of the chapter suggests otherwise. While 3:4-8 appears to be a preexisting unit, the more important question relates to its function in Joel 3. In this respect, Joel 3:4-8 offers something not present anywhere else in the book, namely, specific charges against nations whom God has decided to punish. In short, God will punish the coastlands for their aggressive acts against the land and people of YHWH.

Joel 3:4-8 unfolds in two rhetorical movements: 3:4-6 lays out the charges against Tyre and Sidon (the Phoenicians) and "all the regions of Philistia," while 3:7-8 pronounces YHWH's verdict against these people. The crimes, as delineated in 3:4-6, include looting YHWH's land of its treasures (3:5) and selling YHWH's people into slavery (3:6). The speech reflects a polemical accusation from YHWH who interprets these aggressive acts as crimes against YHWH himself. YHWH has been aggrieved, and YHWH will execute retribution against the guilty parties.

The mention of Tyre and Sidon (Phoenician cities) would imply some distance of time from the Babylonian destruction, since Tyre was also attacked by Nebuchadnezzar (Ezek 26:7-14; 29:17-20) around the time Jerusalem was destroyed (587 BCE). They would not have been in a position to infiltrate Judah on slave runs while Babylon held control of the region. By contrast, Tyre and Sidon had more autonomy under the Persians, but by the middle of the fourth century were in open rebellion against Persian authority, creating a scenario in which one could imagine raids into Judah (a region with stronger ties to Persia) to capture slaves. The rebellion of the Phoenician cities was put down by 343 BCE.

In the second rhetorical movement, 3:7-8 conveys a sense of poetic justice by recounting YHWH's verdict. Those who sold Judah into slavery will, in turn, be sold into slavery by Judah. Those who stole YHWH's silver and gold will become the currency for reimbursing YHWH's people. The sea peoples who sold the Judeans into slavery *across the ocean* to the Greeks (3:6) will themselves be transported as slaves *across the desert* to the Sabeans (3:8). The image is brutal, but the speech is designed to convey the idea that the punishment fits the crime.

## Judgment in the Valley, 3:9-17 (MT 4:9-17)

Joel 3:9-17 changes style and content in a manner that suggests it begins a new speech, and the intertextual citations within it suggest it has been edited to fit the current context in the Book of the Twelve. This new unit begins in 3:9 with the plural imperative "Proclaim this among the nations." As a whole, this unit introduces a call to judgment in the Valley of Jehoshaphat (3:12, see also 3:14)

**Judgment against the Nations**

(Credit: Illustration by Viktor Koen)

In this picture, God prepares to strike the United States while at least one angel cannot bear to watch. Many people imagine the God of the Old Testament as an angry, out of control deity whose wrath frequently gets the better of him. Unfortunately, people generally pay little attention to the contexts of Old Testament judgment scenes. These scenes often, as in Joel 3, presume that the warrior God acts on behalf of God's people who have been attacked.

that anticipates judgment against all the surrounding nations (3:11) on the day of YHWH (3:14). The unit continues through 3:17, after which a new introductory formula in 3:18 begins the final unit of Joel.

The rhetorical logic of 3:9-17 is not difficult to follow, but it is complicated by a change of speakers and by allusions and quotes from other prophetic texts. The rhetorical flow contains (1) a call to battle (3:9-11a), (2) the prophet's prayer that YHWH send his warriors against the nations (3:11b), (3) YHWH's proclamation as judge that the time for judgment is at hand (3:12-13), (4) a series of descriptions of the day of YHWH (3:14-16), and finally (5) two purpose statements: to show YHWH's power (3:17a) and to remove strangers from Judah and Jerusalem (3:17b).

Two options exist for describing the integrity of this unit: (1) it is either a unified composition or (2) it is a preexisting unit expanded for the context of Joel in the Book of the Twelve. Characteristic of this unit is the incorporation of numerous allusions to other prophetic texts. First, Joel 3:10 reverses the call to peace found in Isaiah 2:4 (= Mic 4:2). Then Joel 3:14b repeats the phrase, "Near is the day of YHWH," from Joel 1:15 (see also 2:1)—a recurring phrase within the Book of the Twelve (Obad 15; Zeph 1:7, 14). Next, Joel 3:15 reiterates the phrase, "The sun and the moon are darkened," a phrase taken from Joel 2:10 (see also 3:4) but one that also evokes images elsewhere in the Book of the Twelve (Hab 3:11; see also Amos 5:18, which depicts the day of YHWH as a day of darkness). Finally, Joel 3:16 cites the beginning of Amos 1:2. These allusions, coupled with the fact that the final unit of Joel (3:18-21) begins by citing the concluding verses of Amos, particularly 9:14, shows the nature of this passage as scribal prophecy. These citations of other prophetic texts are not random, but draw upon images of the day of YHWH as punishment for foreign nations and/or the destruction of Jerusalem.

Joel 3:10 draws upon Isaiah 2:4 (= Mic 4:3), but makes two significant changes. First, it reverses the imagery from peace to war. Second, it changes the narrative description of a future ideal in Isaiah 2:4 into a direct address that issues a call for battle. These changes create a scenario for the Joel context whereby the nations are called to account by YHWH, as warrior and judge. Within Joel, this judgment upon these nations will rectify the abuses the nations have perpetrated upon Israel as described elsewhere in Joel (1:6-7; 2:20; and the series of "locusts" symbolizing military invasions in 1:4 and 2:25). Joel 3:10b functions satirically as a call to battle, juxtaposing the pride of the nations against the power of YHWH. The weakling, implying the nations, will mistakenly presume himself to be a mighty warrior, a presumption that is not only wrong but that will end in disaster for those who try to defeat YHWH.

Joel 3:11 switches addressees in the middle of the verse. It begins with a plural verb that continues the command of 3:10. By contrast, Joel 3:11b changes to singular, which can only be understood as a brief prayer from the prophet to YHWH, calling upon YHWH to intervene by sending his heavenly warriors to fight the nations. The taunt of 3:10b is strengthened: the weakling who thinks himself to be a warrior will now face the warriors of YHWH, the heavenly host.

Joel 3:12-13 provides YHWH's response to the prophet's prayer: calling the heavenly tribunal to order. YHWH, as judge, convenes the court in the valley of Jehoshaphat to judge the nations. This verse alludes to the symbolic name mentioned in 3:2. The defendants in this trial are "all the surrounding nations," a phrase that suggests not only the neighbors to the west of Judah (Philistia and Phoenicia) mentioned in 3:4-8, but the countries north and east as well (Syria, Edom, Ammon, and Moab). This phrase signals that 3:9-17 functions as an expansion of 3:4-8 on the one hand, and on the other hand as an eschatological transition to a broader context, the oracles against the nations that begin Amos. [Joel 3:9-17 and Amos]

Joel 3:13 reiterates the nearness of the time for judgment using agricultural metaphors for harvesting. The sickle was used to cut grain at harvest time, while the overflowing wine press depicts the

**Joel 3:9-17 and Amos**

Is it accidental that Amos, the next writing in the Book of the Twelve, presents an extended, carefully crafted call to judgment of the surrounding nations (Amos 1:3–2:5; see also [Encircling Israel])? To be sure, the oracles against the nations that begin Amos do not have the eschatological setting of the judgment scene in Joel 3:9-17, and rhetorically, those countries function as foils to get to the main focus of YHWH's wrath in Amos—Israel. Nevertheless, no other collection of oracles in the Book of the Twelve so closely fits the phrase "all the surrounding nations." Most telling of all in this respect, however, are the citations of Amos in Joel 3:16, 18. Those citations derive from the beginning and end of Amos (1:2 and 9:14 respectively) and imply more than a casual connection between Joel and Amos. The end of Joel anticipates Amos to a significant degree, just as the beginning of Joel contains allusions to the beginning and end of Hosea.

abundant grape harvest as ready to trample. These harvest images, however, connote the imminent judgment of the nations, not the fertility of the land (see 3:18).

Joel 3:14-16 describes the coming day of YHWH by relating it to other texts. The scene emphasizes the extensive number of persons involved and utilizes another symbolic name for the valley in which the judgment will take place, the valley of threshing. It plays on the judgment scene of the broader context (YHWH holding court in the valley of Jehoshaphat). By changing the name of the place to "valley of threshing," Joel 3:14 underscores the point of 3:13-14, namely that the judgment is at hand. One should note that the word "decision" used in most English translations actually comes from the word *ḥārûṣ*, which means "threshing sledge" (Isa 28:27; Amos 1:3), which in the current context could imply the threshing of grain after the harvest. The word *ḥārûṣ* is never translated as "decision" anywhere else. Consequently, one should consider the possibility that Joel 3:14 anticipates the first of the oracles against the nations in Amos 1:3, where Damascus is condemned for "threshing" (*ḥārûṣ*) Gilead with iron sledges. As with Joel 3:4-8, poetic justice comes into play: those who have threshed other nations will themselves be threshed on the imminent day of YHWH.[1]

Joel 3:15 emphasizes the dramatic nature of the day of YHWH by citing an earlier text about the darkening of the celestial luminaries (2:10, see also 2:31). This citation effectively transfers the threat of YHWH's army ready to attack Judah to an image underscoring the impending threat against the nations about to be judged in the valley of Jehoshaphat/threshing.

Joel 3:16a is identical with the beginning of Amos 1:2, but 3:16b has been adapted for the Joel context. [Joel 3:16 and Amos 1:2] The adaptation of this quote draws upon the themes of the surrounding context: judgment on (1) the nations, represented by the shaking of the heavens and earth (3:9-17), and (2) Jerusalem as a place of protection for God's people because of YHWH's presence (3:18-21). Both elements represent key affirmations of Zion theology, though the omission of any reference to the Davidic king reflects the postexilic situation, when hope for a Davidic king's return to power was not paramount. [Zion Tradition]

Joel 3:17 lays out the theological and political objectives of these acts of judgments on this particular day of YHWH. Specifically, the judgment has two aims: (1) to prove to the people that YHWH dwells in Zion and (2) to remove foreigners from Jerusalem as a sign of YHWH's power.

## Fertility beyond Measure, 3:18-21 (MT 4:18-21)

Joel 3:18-21 creates a picture of fertility for the land that is utopian in its scope. This final unit begins with another "on that day" formula, which is then followed by the promise of a restored land. This promise revolves around the dual axes of the unparalleled fecundity of Judah on the one hand and the promise of divine justice on the other, the latter being the punishment of those nations who had added to Judah's suffering. In principle and in details this promise reverses the situation with which Joel began. Joel 3:18 depicts the fertility of the land with a series of three poetic images of abundance. First, sweet wine (ʿâsîs; see 1:5) and milk flow like rivers from the hills. Second, the creek beds of Judah, many dry much of the year, will flow regularly, providing a continuing source of water (cf. 1:20). Third, a fountain in the temple will become a continuing source of water for the creek bed at Shittim. The symbolism of this final image should not be missed. Shittim is the name of the place on the far side of the Jordan River where the Israelites camped before entering the land (Josh 2:1; 3:1). The topography of Palestine is such that no one would confuse this image as a natural phenomenon. Rather, this poetic image portrays the life-giving water at Jerusalem's temple as the headwater for the place where Israel's entry into the land began.

### Joel 3:16 and Amos 1:2

Joel 3:16: The LORD roars from Zion, and utters his voice from Jerusalem, and the heavens and the earth shake. But the LORD is a refuge for his people, a stronghold for the people of Israel.
Amos 1:2: And he said: The LORD roars from Zion, and utters his voice from Jerusalem; the pastures of the shepherds wither, and the top of Carmel dries up.

Both verses present YHWH's judgment in the imagery of a lion, which is very much at home in the book of Amos (see 3:4, 8, 12). Amos 1:2, as scholars have often noted, functions as the motto of the book, summarizing Amos's message about YHWH's judgment against the northern kingdom of Israel. Thus, even though Amos 1:2 plays a redactional role in its own book, it was probably already in its place by the time of the composition of Joel.

### Zion Tradition

The Zion tradition had a long history, serving as the theological underpinnings of royal ideology in the monarchic period, and as the source of hope for restoration in the exilic and postexilic periods. With YHWH as the king of supreme ruler, one finds three poles of Zion theology include (1) YHWH's choice of Jerusalem as the place for his name to dwell; (2) YHWH's protection of the city and the nation from its enemies; and (3) YHWH's selection of a Davidic king to serve as YHWH's representative in Jerusalem. One sees these three elements in numerous psalms (e.g., Pss 2, 22, 47, 48), though later psalms downplay the Davidic connection in favor of accentuating the role of YHWH as king (see Pss 92, 94, 110; cf. Zech 1:12-21). It is important to note that the king plays no role in Joel's promise. In fact, the utopic depiction of 2:28-32 displays a decided democratization when seen through the lens of Zion theology. At the same time, YHWH's name dwells in Zion (2:32), and while YHWH's enemies will be destroyed (2:30), those calling on YHWH's name in Zion will be delivered.

**Egypt and Edom**

Given Israel's long history with both of these entities, some have suggested Egypt and Edom are mentioned because they evoke memories of the exodus: leaving Egypt the land of slavery and passing through Edom on the way to Shittim in Moab. Others have suggested dates at the other end of the chronological spectrum, where Egypt represents the Ptolemies and Edom stands for any unnamed enemy. More likely, one should take one's clue from the formulation of Joel 3:19, where these countries are condemned for incursions into Judah in the aftermath of Jerusalem's destruction. For many years, it seems, Judah lost territory to its neighbors because it had no effective defense. During the 200 years after 587, Edom, in particular, began encroaching upon Judean territory. It is less clear, but plausible, that Egypt also made forays into Palestine.

Joel 3:19 pronounces judgment upon Egypt and Edom. The sudden appearance of these two countries has provoked numerous theories. [Egypt and Edom] This punishment, for the second time in Joel, alludes to Exodus 34:6-7 to underscore that the punishment will come because of YHWH's own character. [Joel 3:19-21, Exodus 34:6-7, and the Book of the Twelve] Joel 3:20-21 contrasts the desolation of Egypt and Edom with the restoration of Judah. Judah and Jerusalem will be inhabited into perpetuity, but Egypt and Edom will suffer vengeance from YHWH for the bloodshed of YHWH's people. Also, 3:21 returns to the theme with which the chapter began, the restoration of Judah and Jerusalem (see discussion of the chiastic structure of Joel 3).

**Joel 3:19-21, Exodus 34:6-7, and the Book of the Twelve**

Joel 3:21 draws subtly, but unmistakably, upon Exod 34:7 in a manner that is noteworthy on several fronts.

**Exodus**

34:6 The LORD passed before him, and proclaimed, "The LORD, the LORD, a *God merciful and gracious, slow to anger, and abounding in steadfast love* and faithfulness, 34:7 keeping steadfast love for the thousandth (generation), *forgiving iniquity and transgression* and sin, yet *by no means clearing the guilty*, but visiting the iniquity of the parents upon the children and the children's children, to the third and the fourth (generation)."

**Joel**

2:13 rend your hearts and not your clothing. Return to the LORD, your *God*, for he is *gracious and merciful, slow to anger, and abounding in steadfast love, and relents from punishing*.
4:19 punish those who shed "innocent blood"
4:20 Jerusalem inhabited for "generations"
4:21 I will avenge their blood, and I will *not leave the guilty unpunished*, for YHWH dwells in Zion.

The promise to avenge Judah's blood in Joel twice uses the verb *nqh*, the same verb used twice in Exod 34:7. Both passages see the implications as multigenerational. Perhaps one might not see the allusion to Exod 34:7 if Joel 2:13 had not already incorporated a more explicit allusion to Exod 34:6 into the call to repentance.

The use of Exod 34:6-7 takes on more prominence in the Book of the Twelve since it appears in three other locations. Mic 7:18-20 draws upon Exod 34:6 to offer promise to YHWH's people at the end of Micah, while Nah 1:3 draws upon Exod 34:7 to affirm YHWH's punishment of YHWH's enemies. As with Joel 2:13 and 3:19-21, the two parts of the Exodus presentation of YHWH (compassion and wrath) serve to evoke promises that YHWH's compassion and justice are still operative at the end of Micah and the beginning of Nahum. By contrast, the book of Jonah (most likely added later to the Twelve), combines Exod 34:6-7 to challenge the idea that the promise of compassion does not apply to the nations as well. In Jonah 4:2, Jonah cites Exod 34:6 (YHWH's compassion) but applies it to the Assyrians, not Judah or Israel. At the end of the day, this intertextual dialogue in the Book of the Twelve thus affirms that YHWH's justice and compassion operate both for Israel and the nations.

The restoration anticipated in this final unit (3:18-21) contains utopian promises of the land's fertility (3:18) and the continual habitation of Judah and Jerusalem into perpetuity (3:20). The unit also promises that the guilty will be punished, meaning those who exploited Judah's situation during its time of punishment (3:19, 21). These three promises (fertility, habitation, and punishment of enemies) not only round off the themes of the final chapter, but they also reverse the situation with which Joel began: the land that had been devastated in ways never seen before (1:2) will now abound with wine, milk, and water (3:18); the land desolated by enemy attack (1:6) will see those enemies punished by YHWH (3:19, 21); and the land that could not support inhabitants because of numerous threats will be inhabited forever (3:20). The sweet wine that had been cut off (1:5) will flow from the mountains (3:18), and the creek beds that had dried up (1:20) will now flow with water continually (3:18).

# CONNECTIONS

The promise of Joel 3 portrays retribution against the nations and restoration of the fertility of the land as acts of direct, divine intervention on the day of YHWH. Joel 3 has no need for humans to participate in holy war—God will judge the surrounding nations. [Holy War] God will provide an abundance of products necessary for the sustenance of life. On one level, these images are hyperbole; no one really expects wine and milk to flow from the hills. On another level, however, one can wonder how someone from the ancient world would view life in our society. In a world where every field producing fruit or grain had to be tended by hand, where the slow, tedious work of planting and harvesting was complicated immensely by the hot climate and the rocky soil, one can only

**Holy War**

Old Testament scholars often distinguish what they refer to as "holy war" from the way the term is often used in popular culture, or from later forms of religious war such as jihad or the Crusades. These descriptions attempt to make a distinction between human wars fought for reasons of religious conviction and the holy war traditions in the Old Testament where YHWH does battle, with or without human aid. R. D. Nelson describes holy war as a theological construct:

> Holy war was never a uniform or normative sequence of practices but a constellation of religiously oriented military procedures and customs that varied according to time and circumstance. Nor was holy war something distinctive or unique to Israel's culture and religion. Holy war was not only, or even primarily, a set of actual military practices, but more foundationally a theological construct intended to relate belief in the LORD as cosmic warrior to Israel's narrative traditions, national identity, and insecure position in the world.

In short, the idea of God as Warrior par excellence represents a mode of expression, culturally conditioned, not a reason for battle. Eschatological texts like Joel 3 depict YHWH as the primary actor in the battle scene (see also Zech 14), but other texts can imply that humans will join YHWH in a battle (see Obad 18-20).

Richard D. Nelson, "Holy War," *NIDB*, 2:854.

suspect an ancient writer might well be amazed at things we take for granted. Trucks and trains roll across our hills bringing food to the shelves of grocery stores, food for which we have never lifted a finger. Packages line entire aisles of our supermarkets with cereal boxes containing processed grain for which we never toiled. In our time, what would a utopian promise look like? We have become so accustomed to getting what we think we want, when we want it, that a promise like Joel 3:18 hardly moves us. However, the events of the last several years have made our country stop in its tracks. Whether one speaks of terrorist attacks, like those of 9/11 in New York, Washington, and Pennsylvania, or whether one speaks of natural disasters the likes of Hurricane Katrina, when devastation strikes, we realize how truly dependent we are upon God's enduring mercy, upon one another, and upon the sustaining structures of society developed through the use of technology and the search for wisdom. Gifts from God should not be taken lightly, whether they flow from the hills or sit on store shelves. Promises given by God can be fulfilled in surprising ways.

What about God and the foreign nations? History resounds with examples of wars fought under the conviction that "God is on our side." Repeatedly, tyrants, clergy, and committed believers have gone to war the world over, utterly and completely convinced that they fought on behalf of their deity. Worse yet, political leaders through the centuries have wrapped themselves and their rhetoric in religious symbols and phrases designed to convince the public that God needed their help to make the world a safer place. Frequently, the truth comes out only in retrospect, when the hidden agendas of those in power become known. Historically, believers have responded variously to this type of manipulation, from feeling betrayed and angry to lashing out in denial at those who uncovered the truth.

Some commentators call the prophet Joel "nationalistic" because his portrait of a peaceful future imagines the destruction of other nations and the utopian bliss of his own. While Joel 3 creates uneasiness for modern readers who do not share Joel's social setting, one should not dismiss this chapter without first contemplating the implications of what Joel does not do. Joel does not spur Judah to action as human distributor of divine wrath. Joel does not rally the troops to march under the banner of a crusading military campaign. Joel does not act in a vacuum.

In Joel 3, God acts as judge (3:12) to punish the nations who have wreaked havoc upon Jerusalem and Judah. Joel seeks vindication from God; he does not call the people to battle. Moreover, the battle is a defensive battle to remove foreign powers from the land, not a battle of aggression. Joel petitions God to use God's armies (3:11) so as to reinstate the order the surrounding nations have violated. Joel does not put faith in human armies and weapons, but in God's capacity to restore order and administer justice in the face of violence and injustice. Finally, the literary context of Joel should not be forgotten. The promises of Joel 3 do not constitute nationalistic absolutes demanding that God protect God's chosen. Rather, the prophet delivers these promises only after he has confronted God's people with their own need for repentance in chapters 1–2. The prophet speaks, in this sense, on behalf of victimized Judah, who has suffered the aggression of military attack compounded by the devastation of natural disasters (Joel 1–2). Consequently, Joel 3 functions as a plaintive cry of hope that Judah's fate can and will improve, if only Judah will reorient its own communal response (see 2:14). Those who receive the promises of Joel 3 are those whose current reality (Joel 1–2) has left them helpless to resist.

On its own, Joel leaves loose ends literarily and theologically. One who reads Joel in isolation never learns what God's people have done wrong, how God's people respond to the prophet's call to repentance, or whether these utopian promises of life in the distant future ever materialize. Yet the reader of Joel need not read it as an isolated book. More than any other writing in the Book of the Twelve, Joel can be read meaningfully within the context of the Book of the Twelve as both an invitation to every generation and a foreshadowing of the history of God's people in Judah (see the introduction to Joel and recurring themes in the Book of the Twelve).

# NOTE

1. See Aaron Schart, "The First Section of the Book of the Twelve Prophets: Hosea–Joel–Amos," *Int* 61 (2007): 145–46.

# SELECT BIBLIOGRAPHY
# FOR JOEL

Allen, Leslie C. *The Books of Joel, Obadiah, Jonah, and Micah.* New International Commentary. Grand Rapids: Eerdmans, 1976.

Barton, John. *Joel and Obadiah: A Commentary.* Old Testament Library. Louisville: Westminster John Knox, 2001.

Bergler, Siegfried. *Joel als Schriftinterpret.* Beiträge zur Erforschung des Alten Testaments und des antiken Judentums 16. Frankfurt: Peter Lang, 1988.

Birch, Bruce C. *Hosea, Joel, and Amos.* Westminster Bible Companion. Louisville: Westminster John Knox, 1997.

Crenshaw, James L. "Who Knows What YHWH Will Do? The Character of God in the Book of Joel." In *Fortunate the Eyes That See*, edited by Astrid B. Beck et al., 185–96. Grand Rapids: Eerdmans, 1995.

———. *Joel.* The Anchor Bible 24C. New York: Doubleday, 1995.

Deist, Ferdinand E. "Parallels and Reinterpretation in the Book of Joel: A Theology of the Yom Yahweh." In *Text and Context*, edited by W. Claassen, 63–79. Sheffield: JSOT Press, 1988.

Dozeman, Thomas B. "Inner-Biblical Interpretation of Yahweh's Gracious and Compassionate Character." *Journal of Biblical Literature* 108 (1989): 207–23.

Nogalski, James D. "Joel as 'Literary Anchor' for the Book of the Twelve." In *Reading and Hearing the Book of the Twelve*, edited by James D. Nogalski and Marvin A. Sweeney, 91–109. Atlanta: Society of Biblical Literature, 2000.

Ogden, Graham S., and Richard Deutsch. *A Promise of Hope—A Call to Obedience: A Commentary on the Books of Joel and Malachi.* International Theological Commentary. Grand Rapids: Eerdmans, 1987.

Prinsloo, Willem S. "The Unity of the Book of Joel." *Zeitschrift für die Alttestamentliche Wissenschaft* 104 (1992): 66–81.

Redditt, Paul L. "The Book of Joel and Peripheral Prophecy." *Catholic Biblical Quarterly* 48 (1986): 225–40.

Stuart, Douglas K. *Hosea–Jonah.* Word Biblical Commentary 31. Waco: Word Books, 1987.

Sweeney, Marvin A. "The Place and Function of Joel in the Book of the Twelve." In *Thematic Threads in the Book of the Twelve*, edited by Paul L. Redditt and Aaron Schart, 133–54. Beihefte zur Zeitschrift für die alttestamentliche Wissenschaft 325. Berlin: Degruyter, 2003.

Wolff, Hans Walter. *Joel and Amos.* Hermeneia. Translated by Waldemar Janzen, S. Dean McBride, Jr., and Charles A. Muenchow. Philadelphia: Fortress, 1977.

# AMOS

# INTRODUCTION TO THE BOOK OF AMOS

## Dating the Prophet and the Book

The prophet Amos is one of four eighth-century prophets—Amos, Hosea, Isaiah, and Micah—who have books named after them within the prophetic corpus. A few pieces of tradition provide details about his life, but those details are only suggestive in the biblical text, though ancient Jewish tradition contains quite a bit of elaborative material. [Amos in Jewish Tradition] Amos 1:1 refers to Tekoa as the prophet's hometown, a village within ten miles of Jerusalem. To understand the rhetoric and the reception of Amos, one should recognize that this background makes the prophet an outsider to those to whom he preached. Although he came from the southern kingdom, the vast majority of the prophetic material addresses the people and leaders of the northern kingdom.

Amos 1:1 also places the ministry of the prophet during the reign of Jeroboam II (782–742 BCE), king of Israel, and Uzziah (786–746 BCE), king of Judah. The inserted narrative of 7:10-17 also presumes the prophet works during the reign of Jeroboam. Given the political stability and economic prosperity (at least for the ruling class) of Jeroboam's lengthy reign, most scholarship has concurred that the prophet Amos likely appeared between 760–750 BCE. Since the early portions of both of these kings' reigns involved military activity that helped stabilize and expand their kingdoms' borders, it stands to reason that the relative economic prosperity, which several of the oracles in Amos presuppose, reflects a time after this stabilization has occurred. Moreover, after the deaths of these two long-reigning kings, both Israel and Judah soon experienced significant turmoil that greatly affected the standard of living. Hence, the decade from 760–750 BCE has much to offer as the time of the prophet. While this date may be fairly reliable, one has no way of knowing how old the prophet Amos was when he began prophesying in the northern kingdom, or how long his prophetic mission lasted. Still, from the relatively consistent portrait of an affluent society within Amos, one receives the impression that Amos's ministry did not last long. The

---

**Amos in Jewish Tradition**

Texts in early Jewish literature tend to cluster around three issues: the date of Amos, the aftermath of his encounter with Amaziah (recorded in Amos 7:10-17), and the violent death of Amos. Regarding the date, while modern scholarship frequently cites Amos as the oldest of the "writing prophets," rabbinic sources more typically list him after Hosea's prophetic ministry and yet before Isaiah's. The reasoning behind this date for Amos appears to have been influenced by canonical arrangement, since the book of Hosea always precedes that of Amos in the arrangements of the Book of the Twelve and since the rabbis generally interpreted Hos 1:2's "when God first spoke to Hosea" to mean "God spoke first to Hosea."

The rationale for dating Amos before Isaiah is also textually driven, yet it derives from two different lines of reasoning. First, since Amos 1:2 dates the prophet "two years before the earthquake," and since Isaiah 6 appears to incorporate earthquake imagery into the prophet's call narrative, it is not surprising that the rabbis connected the "earthquakes" in these two texts. Hence, following this logic, Amos preached two years prior to the call of Isaiah. Of course modern scholarship, being less textually creative in its search for connections between texts, has pointed out that the language of Isaiah 6 has more to do with a theophany than with a literal earthquake. The second reason for the traditional Jewish dating of Amos is that several rabbinic texts (and at least one manuscript of the pseudepigraphic work, "The Ascension of Isaiah") treat Isaiah as the son of Amos. Apparently, the ancient rabbis mistakenly read Isaiah's name in Isa 1:1 as Isaiah ben *Amos* rather than Isaiah ben *Amoz*, which of course sound similar but use different letters in Hebrew. The pseudepigraphic reference in Ascension of Isaiah 1:1, however, goes well beyond Isa 1:1 by referring to "Isaiah son of Amoz the prophet." The final form of the Ascension of Isaiah was edited in Christian circles, but in all likelihood, the tradition of Isaiah's lineage reflects some of the Jewish interpretive traditions that were circulating at the beginning of the second century CE.

One of the most interesting lines of rabbinic tradition, in part because it differs so radically from modern interpretations, concerns the aftermath of the prophet's confrontation with Amaziah recounted in Amos 7:10-17. Most modern commentators, including this one, presume that Amaziah succeeded in silencing Amos, thereby symbolizing Israel's rejection of the prophet's message. By contrast, rabbinic midrash uses the story of Amaziah's confrontation to resolve another problem. In rabbinic tradition, Jeroboam II refuses to act against Amos, either because he thought Amos incapable of treason or because he realized the prophet was only speaking what God had told him to speak. As a result of Jeroboam's forbearance, God rewarded Jeroboam with a prosperous reign. This reward solves the problem created by the Deuteronomistic History, which does not explain why God allowed Jeroboam II to rule for forty years—a time during which the northern kingdom prospered economically and expanded its territory (2 Kgs 14:23-29). These midrashic stories resolve the issue by asserting that Jeroboam was rewarded for his treatment of Amos.

Concerning the prophet's death, rabbinic tradition typically understands Amos to have died at the hands of King Uzziah of Judah (a contemporary of Jereboam II) rather than in the northern kingdom of Israel. Thus, in the Jewish tradition, Amos appears as an equal-opportunity offender: after returning from Israel, the prophet angers the Judean king, who then promptly hits Amos in the forehead with a red-hot poker. Variations of this story have Amos dying after being hit in the head with a stick by the son of Amaziah, the priest at Bethel.

See Darrel D. Hannah, "Isaiah, Ascension of," in *New Interpreter's Dictionary of the Bible* (Nashville: Abingdon, 2008) 3:74–75.

---

rhetoric is intense, garnering the notice of the officials in Israel who subsequently sought to deport Amos back to Judah (7:10-17).

In all likelihood, Amos was the first of the four eighth-century prophets to appear on the scene, though for theological reasons the book that bears his name appears third (MT order) in the Book of the Twelve (see below, "Amos and the Book of the Twelve"). The message of Amos consistently denounces the kingdom of Israel for blatantly disregarding its ethical responsibilities (2:6-7; 3:10; 4:1), allowing religious aberrations (2:8; 3:14; 4:4-5; 5:21-23), and disavowing righteousness and justice (5:7, 14-15, 24)—and this behavior is in spite of the kingdom's relative prosperity. By contrast, the book of Hosea consistently presents its message by juxtaposing words of judgment with words of promise, providing a sense of uncertainty regarding the fate of Israel. Thus, while Amos precedes Hosea historically, the message of Hosea (with its uncertain outcome) makes a better starting point for the Book of the Twelve than Amos (with its certainty regarding Israel's destruction).

The book of Amos underwent a lengthy process of collection, arrangement, and expansion before it reached its final form in the postexilic period. Several passages reflect concerns of the eighth century, but exilic and postexilic perspectives can be detected in the book as well. The issues surrounding these editorial processes will be discussed in more detail in the following section.

## Literary Form, Structure, and Unity of Amos

The book of Amos typically divides into four sections (1–2; 3–6; 7:1–9:6; and 9:7-15) based upon the genre and stylistic similarities of the material within each of those sections. More debated is the question of how and when those sections were combined into a single corpus.

Amos 1–2, in its final form, unfolds primarily as a series of eight highly stylized oracles against the nations. The first six pronounce judgment upon surrounding foreign nations (Syria, Philistia, Phoenicia, Edom, Ammon, and Moab), followed by oracles against Judah and Israel. These oracles begin with the same formulaic introduction ("For three transgressions of 'x' and for four I will not take it back"), and their arrangement deliberately encircles Israel before the focus turns to the northern kingdom as the cumulative entity. In other words, the oracles against the nations and Judah serve as prelude to the word of judgment against Israel.

Scholars have long suggested that three of these oracles (those against Tyre, Edom, and Judah) were added after the time of the prophet Amos, probably in the exilic period, in part because these three oracles differ from the other five stylistically, and because their wording better suits the exilic situation. Despite some objections in recent years, the likelihood of editorial accretions to the collection appears well founded.

In addition, both the superscription to the book (1:1) and the book's motto (1:2) owe their existence to the editorial processes that shaped the book, not to the (oral) speeches of the prophet. Because of the complexity of the superscription's syntax, scholars often suggest that 1:1 itself reflects editorial work at more than one level, with at least one portion being tied to the editorial activity of an early multivolume corpus that included Hosea, Amos, Micah, and Zephaniah (though even this process occurred in stages—see "Introduction to the Book of the Twelve"). Amos 1:2, which poetically summarizes the message of the book, likely originated with the process of compiling the first three collections of Amos (1–2; 3–6; 7:1–9:6) into a single entity.

Because of the nature of the material, it seems likely that the second section of Amos (3–6) experienced its own transmission process over a considerable period before being combined with the oracles against the nations cycle (Amos 1–2) and the vision cycle (7:1–9:6). Amos 3–6 exhibits different dominant unifying characteristics than chapters 1–2. The material in 3–6 can best be described as sayings, largely due to the relative brevity of most of the units within these chapters. Few of these units span more than a few verses, and this section lacks the cohesive hermeneutical movement that is present in both the oracles against the nations and the visions. Nevertheless, signs of an editorial hand can be detected, especially in the similarities of headings in the chapters (3:1; 4:1; 5:1; and to a lesser extent 6:1), in the placement of the material (using thematic arrangements and catchwords), and in a few places where an original oracle against the northern kingdom has been expanded to include a Judean perspective (5:5; 6:1). The core of this material reflects the gist of the messages delivered by Amos, or at least the messages that focus upon God's word of judgment to the northern kingdom in the eighth century BCE.

Amos 7:1–9:6, like the first major section of Amos, displays a rhetorical movement deriving largely from the combination of similarly styled units, in this case a series of five vision reports (7:1-3, 4-6, 7-9; 8:1-3; 9:1-4). The stylistic similarities of these five vision reports follow a 2-2-1 pattern that invites close comparison. (To see how the first two vision reports are structured more closely to one another, see [The Structure of the Visions of Amos (NRSV)].) These vision reports are interrupted before the fourth and fifth vision reports. The first interruption is accomplished by the insertion of a prophetic narrative (7:10-17) germane to the rhetorical movement of this section and to the book as a whole. The narrative recounts the rejection of Amos by Amaziah, the chief priest at Bethel. The second interruption constitutes a mosaic of sayings (8:4-14), which evokes the formulations and themes of the book as a whole. The rhetorical movement focuses upon the inevitability of judgment for the northern kingdom, a theme expressed throughout the book, but one particularly pronounced in both the fourth and fifth vision reports (the former proclaims the end has come; the latter recounts the destruction of the northern kingdom temple).

Amos 9:7-15 divides into two thematic units that deal with the surviving remnant (9:7-10) and a future restoration for a reunified Davidic kingdom (9:11-15). Both units stand largely outside the main themes of the book, and both units reflect multiple perspectives. In 9:7-10, a statement rejecting the unique nature of Israel's status before God anticipates its total destruction (9:7-8a), but elicits a response depicting the devastation as the removal of sinners so that a purified group might remain (9:8b-10). In 9:11-15, hope for restoration and rebuilding in the aftermath of destruction (9:11, 14-15) frames statements regarding an aggressive campaign to retake the lands of the former Davidic kingdom (9:12) and a utopian refertilization of the land (9:13). The expansive statements of 9:12, 13 relate to the books on either side of Amos in the Book of the Twelve (MT order). Amos 9:12 essentially summarizes a major theme of Obadiah (Judah will repossess Edom and the surrounding nations), while Amos 9:13 reflects the same hyperbolic hope for refertilization one finds in Joel 3:18 (MT 4:18).

## The Message of Amos

Clearly, the book of Amos presents a portrait of an angry God for whom judgment has become the operative paradigm. However, in order to understand that portrait, one must first understand its presuppositions. Specifically, it tacitly assumes that God expects justice and righteousness to form the basis of human behavior in the world—an expectation Amos accuses Israel of violating. Periodically, Amos explicitly communicates these expectations via commands or accusations. However, most of the material in Amos *presumes* these accusations and focuses instead upon the imminence of judgment.

Justice and righteousness are YHWH's expectations for the people. Israel's failure to meet these expectations creates a crisis that Amos is called to address at YHWH's behest (7:15). The widespread inhumane treatment of others, especially by those with the means and the power to help those less fortunate, makes a mockery of YHWH's expectations. Insensitivity toward those in need is rampant and extends into the religious realm, where Israel's religious expression also deviates widely from YHWH's expectations. These two issues, how one behaves toward others and toward God, constitute the bulk of Amos's accusatory language.

Inhumane treatment and disregard of others figure prominently in the accusations made by the prophet. These accusations include failing to see suffering and ignoring the needs of the poor, either because of a misguided sense of entitlement or because of self-absorbed behavior by people who are too intent on satisfying their own desires to notice the needs of others around them (2:7; 6:4-6). In addition, these accusations imply that those who have the means and power to do so are obligated to help those who are less fortunate. Finally, Amos's accusations emphasize that ethical behavior is a starting point for all humanity, not merely an expectation for God's people. [Universal Ethics] This universal ethic is evident in Amos's opening chapters, which accuse the surrounding nations of forgetting what it means to behave humanely even toward one's enemies (1:3–2:3).

Amos uses harsh language to confront the audience, challenging their bravery (2:14-16), insulting them by calling them cows (4:1), and speaking to them as though they are dead (5:1-2). Amos presents the inevitability of judgment (3:2; 5:18-20), but implicitly embeds instructions for restoring the relationship by seeking YHWH (5:4-7). And yet, in the course of the book, when the severity of the judgment is revealed to the prophet (7:1, 4), it is Amos who intercedes twice on Israel's behalf, causing YHWH to change YHWH's mind regarding this destruction (7:3, 6).

---

**Universal Ethics**

B. Birch articulates the concept of universal ethics often assumed in prophetic condemnation of the nations:

Interestingly the prophets often addressed messages of judgment and calls to accountability for the nations. Since the nations knew nothing of the specific channels through which God had made known the divine character and will this suggests that the prophets understood some notion of moral vision as inherent being human and a part of God's creation. Some actions are ethically abhorrent to all nations and persons and the demands of behavior and character which eschews such practices is understood by the prophets to be universal.

Bruce C. Birch, "Ethics in the OT," *New Interpreter's Dictionary of the Bible* (Nashville: Abingdon, 2007) 2:347.

Two things become clear when one asks the question, what does God expect from Israel in Amos? First, God expects a spiritual searching, a return to YHWH unencumbered by forms of worship and behavior considered anathema by God. "Seek me and live; but do not seek Bethel, and do not enter into Gilgal or cross over into Beer-sheba; [. . .] Seek the Lord and live" (5:4, 6). Second, God expects behavior that demonstrates one has found the path toward YHWH. In other words, God expects justice and righteousness to be the pillars that orient behavior for the faithful (5:7, 10-12, 14-15, 24; 6:12). "Hate evil and love good, and establish justice in the gate" (5:15).

In the religious realm, the failure to return and to change leads to Israel's inability to find YHWH. The ethical and religious practices of the people have inured them to any message of religious fidelity to YHWH. The worship of idols is assumed as part of the polemic against Bethel in Amos. Bethel was the southern religious center of the northern kingdom, one of two sites where Jeroboam I established shrines for worship that included the figure of a bull (1 Kgs 12:25-33). (See illustration "Northern Shrines.") Presumably, the bull was conceptualized as the animal that YHWH would ride, though YHWH was not portrayed on the bull. Nevertheless, those in the southern kingdom who expected orthopraxy felt strongly that these shrines violated the first two commandments. It is unclear whether, from the perspective of the northern kingdom, this bull itself became the subject of worship over time, but the polemic from southern kingdom writers certainly portrayed it that way. Further, Amos occasionally alludes to syncretistic practices (2:7; 5:26?) in such a way that the portrayal of Israel's religious expression resembles those condemned in more detail by the prophet Hosea (e.g., 4:16-19; 8:6, 11). In short, the peculiarity of Israel's cult demonstrates closer affinities to Canaanite practices than Jerusalemite adherents would tolerate.

Amos also accuses Israel of a superficial understanding of sacrifice (4:4-5; 5:21-24), one where sacrifice provides an excuse for gathering and celebrating but does not affect the behavior of those involved toward those around them.

I hate, I despise your festivals, and I take no delight in your solemn assemblies. Even though you offer me your burnt offerings and grain offerings, I will not accept them; and the offerings of well-being of your fatted animals I will not look upon. Take away from me the noise of your songs; I will not listen to the melody of your harps. But let justice roll down like waters, and righteousness like an ever flowing stream. (5:21-24)

Here, Amos presents the rationale for God's impending judgment in the form of accusations against YHWH's own people, but the majority of the book is cast in rhetorical forms that should be understood as warnings more than accusations. Using diverse genres and rhetorical devices, the book of Amos emphasizes that judgment is coming. Beginning with the oracles against the nations, and then focusing upon Israel itself, the book presumes YHWH's patience has reached its limit. The reasons are provided, but only periodically. The message of impending judgment is far more pervasive. This message (1) presumes a history of human provocation (both for the nations and Israel); (2) assumes a purpose for the judgment; and (3) portrays this judgment through various images.

(1) The history of provocations meriting God's judgment is articulated explicitly at several points, beginning with the oracles against the nations (Amos 1:3–2:16). These oracles all begin with the same numeric formula: For three transgressions and for four . . . I will not take it back. The recurrence of this formula does several things. First, it makes clear that the judgment announced by the prophet comes only after a series of incidents that could have incited the wrath of YHWH. Thus, the prophet does not portray the wrath of YHWH as some arbitrary, capricious act of a deity who is out of control. Rather, YHWH has already exercised restraint. Second, this formula indicates that God's patience has limits. Finally, since it introduces oracles against other nations besides Israel, the refrain implies that Israel is not alone. While the rhetorical culmination of this passage focuses on Israel, it does so only after documenting the crimes of its neighbors, including Judah. Thus, from the beginning of the book, the reader learns that God's patience has ended for Israel and its neighbors because of repeated missteps.

Besides the refrain in Amos 1–2, Amos 4:6-12 recounts a series of unsuccessful attempts by YHWH to change Israel's behavior. YHWH recalls attempts to change the people using famine, blight, mildew, and pestilence, but Israel fails to heed the message ("yet, you did not return to me"). As a result, readers not only gain the impression that YHWH's judgment is inevitable but also attain insight into the purpose of this judgment.

(2) In several texts, the purpose of judgment implies a chance to change the behavior (and perhaps to avoid punishment). To be sure, texts in Amos do not emphasize this option, which, rhetorically, adds to the impression of urgency. Nevertheless, Amos periodically provides a hint in this direction using calls to seek YHWH or to seek goodness (5:6-7, 14-15), intercessions made by the prophet (7:1-3, 4-6), and reports of failures to return to YHWH (4:6-12).

(3) From the beginning of the book, though, neither YHWH nor the prophet anticipates the response will be different this time. For this reason, the prophet depicts the coming judgment in the strongest possible terms, but the images used to convey this judgment are diverse. They include military invasion by foreign powers (6:8, 11), exile into foreign lands (5:27; 6:7), and cosmic upheaval on the day of YHWH (3:14-15; 5:18-20). Occasional references imply that a few may survive the judgment (3:12; 5:3; 6:9-10; 9:8b-10), but their lot will be far from pleasant. These allusions to a remnant are not formulated as a reason for hope, with the exception of 9:8b-10, but imply the remnant will serve as witness to the horrific nature of the judgment. When the judgment comes, the prophet warns, Israel will be powerless to resist. No amount of pride over previous battles will help Israel at that time, and their military fortifications will prove to be of little value (6:8, 13). In summary, the rhetoric of the book of Amos conveys a powerful sense of urgency and fear before the wrath of YHWH. Only the last five verses of the book (9:11-15) pause to reflect upon what life might look like beyond this judgment.

## Amos and the Book of the Twelve

The editors of the Book of the Twelve incorporated Amos into its current position for chronological, theological, and geographical reasons. Chronologically, Amos appears during the eighth century under the reign of Jeroboam II, and for this reason it fits closely with Hosea and Micah. Amos as a book, however, is preceded by Hosea in both the MT and LXX ordering of the Book of the Twelve. Later rabbis explained this predilection for Hosea being the first writing in the Book of the Twelve as a result of a peculiar reading of Hosea 1:2 ("when the Lord *first* spoke through Hosea"). However, if one grants a more sophisticated editorial process, a more plausible theological rationale emerges: the vacillation between judgment and promise in Hosea (see "Literary Form, Structure, and Unity of Hosea" in the introduction to Hosea), combined with an open call to repentance at the end of Hosea (14:1-8 [MT 14:2-9]), leaves the reader with the impression that the question of the fate of the northern kingdom is still undecided. By contrast, the overwhelming tone of judgment in Amos, combined with the final two vision reports that predict the end has come, leaves no uncertainty. Rather, the theological message of Amos concerns judgment from beginning to end. Only the last few verses offer any real promises (9:11-15). In all likelihood, however, these verses not only come from a later editorial hand but also presuppose that judgment will come before restoration. Thus, theologically, Hosea's message would seem superfluous were it to come after Amos in the Book of the Twelve. In addition, this same dynamic regarding the fate of the southern kingdom occurs in both Micah and Zephaniah. Micah alternates its message of judgment with one of hope, while the eschatological message of hope appears in Zephaniah only at the end of the book (3:11-20) in passages largely deemed to reflect later redactional interests. (See the introduction to the Book of the Twelve for more information on the history and function of this book of four writings that have likely been edited in conjunction with one another before joining a larger corpus.) Lastly, Amos is not only chronologically and theologically situated but also has the same geographical focus as Hosea, namely that of the northern kingdom. Thus, whereas Micah and Zephaniah focus geographically on the southern kingdom of Judah, Hosea and Amos address their oracles primarily to the northern kingdom.

Two issues in Amos intersect with recurring theological motifs in the Twelve regarding the kingdom's fate. These issues concern judgment and promise, with judgment directed against the northern kingdom and designed as a warning to Judah and Jerusalem. By contrast, the words of promise and restoration are filtered through the lens of a restored Davidic kingdom.

The bulk of Amos concerns the impending destruction of the northern kingdom of Israel. Yet, a few passages extend this message to Israel's neighbor to the south. Most of them likely reflect redactional activity sometime after Samaria's destruction. [Samaria] One such passage includes the oracle against Judah (2:4-5) that mirrors the style of the other oracles against the nations in 1:3–2:3. In addition, the inclusion of the southern town of Beer-sheba in 5:5 and 8:14 implicitly warns Judah that it could suffer the same fate as Israel. The opening to the dirge in 6:1 addresses the arrogant in Jerusalem and Zion. Also, readers would have likely transferred some confrontations to Judah by assuming a new location in which the message was pronounced. For example, Amos 5:21-23 challenges the superficiality with which sacrifices were brought in Israel, but a Judean hearing these verses might readily think of Jerusalem temple practices, given the general terms (festivals, solemn assemblies, burnt offerings, etc.). In short, the message emphasizes that the northern kingdom will not last, and it subtly warns Judah that it faces the same danger. These warnings will be expanded explicitly in Micah and Zephaniah, especially in the transitional passage in Micah 1:2-9.

**Map of Places in Amos**

Beer-sheba represents one of the southernmost towns in Judah while Dan represents the northern extremity of Israel. Jerusalem and Samaria are the capital cities of the two kingdoms. Bethel is south of Samaria on the way to Jerusalem.

Amos expresses hope for a renewed Davidic kingdom, and while this hope appears elsewhere in the Twelve, Amos is reticent regarding its leadership. For example, Hosea 1:11 articulates this hope in terms of one king, as does Micah 5:2. By contrast, the reference in Amos 9:11 to the "fallen booth of David" focuses on the restoration of the kingdom (see 9:14) rather than on kingship per se. Haggai also anticipates a Davidic ruler, Zerubbabel, but it carefully avoids explicit reference to that ruler as king (see Hag 2:23). The ambiguous terminology of Amos 9:11 does not necessarily require a Davidic king, since other texts in the Twelve advocate a return to

**Samaria**

Samaria was destroyed in 722 BCE by the Assyrians, but its destruction was used in 2 Kgs 17 as a warning to Jerusalem. For more detailed discussion, see the treatment of Mic 1:5.

the kingship of YHWH (e.g., Zeph 3:15; Zech 14:9, 16, 17; Mal 1:14). Still, given the number of other thematic and linguistic connections between Hosea, Amos, and Micah in particular, one should probably presume that a Davidic king was assumed with the pronouncement of Amos 9:11.[1]

Amos 4:6-12 echoes several motifs that the reader of the Twelve has encountered in Hosea and Joel. These motifs center on YHWH's use of calamities in an attempt to get YHWH's people to return to their God; e.g., famine, drought, blight, mildew, and locust plagues (cf., Amos 4:6-12; Hos 2:8-9; Joel 1–2). In keeping with the message of Amos, however, these motifs function differently in Amos than in Hosea and Joel. In Hosea and Joel, these motifs were part of a call to the people to change, while in Amos YHWH's attempts to motivate Israel to change via natural disasters are reported as failures leading to pronouncements of punishment.

The hope for fertility also links Amos to other writings in the Twelve. As articulated in 9:13-14, this hope essentially reverses the judgments made earlier in Amos that affect the land (e.g., 4:6-11; 7:1-3, 4-6). Yet 9:13 and 14 present two substantially different paradigms. The first displays a utopian scenario, where the only problem is harvesting all the produce prior to the time of replanting and where wine flows from the mountains and hills like water. To be sure, these images are poetic and probably not intended literally; nevertheless, the images depict a carefree setting where life's sustaining needs are met unequivocally. By contrast, the second image in 9:14 appears far less ambitious. In this scenario, it is enough to replant and rebuild with the hope of being present to participate in the harvest. The hope for restoration of the supra-abundant and normal fertility of the agricultural processes (9:13, 14 respectively) likely entered the text at different points. Amos 9:14-15 may well have followed 9:11 as a unified promise of restoration for the Davidic kingdom that was expanded with 9:12, 13 in order to connect Amos with Obadiah (9:12) and Joel (9:13). This development is evidenced in the fact that both 9:12 and 9:13 significantly expand the scope of the surrounding promises (9:11, 14).

Amos also plays a role in Haggai's message regarding the fertility of the land. Haggai 2:17 draws upon Amos 4:9 in order to call attention to the effects of rebuilding the temple. Haggai 2:19 also alludes to Joel for similar reasons: to place a marker in Haggai that the call to repentance has been answered (see the discussion in Zech 1:2-6), ending the long period of YHWH's judgment. Thus, Haggai's citation of Amos reverses the judgment against Judah following the return from exile, a perspective not dissimilar to the Judean appropriation of the words of Amos noted in the discussion of the transmission history of Amos above.

## NOTE

1. Paul L. Redditt, "The King in Haggai-Zechariah 1-8 and The Book of The Twelve," in *Tradition in Transition Haggai and Zechariah 1-8 in the Trajectory of Hebrew Theology* (New York: T & T Clark International, 2008) 56–82.

## OUTLINE OF AMOS

I. Amos 1:1–2:16: The Lion Roars
  A. Amos 1:1: Layered Superscription
  B. Amos 1:2: The Book's Motto
  C. Amos 1:3–2:16: Oracles against the Nations and Israel
II. Amos 3:1–6:14: Sayings from the Prophet and Disciples
  A. Amos 3:1-15: Signs, Sin, and Identity
  B. Amos 4:1-13: Missing the Signs and Paying the Consequences
  C. Amos 5:1-27: Lamenting the Lack of Justice and Righteousness
  D. Amos 6:1-14: Ignoring the Ruin of Joseph
III. Amos 7:1–9:6: Visions of Impending Destruction
  A. Amos 7:1-3: First Vision—Locust Plague
  B. Amos 7:4-6: Second Vision—Cosmic Fire
  C. Amos 7:7-9: Third Vision—A Dangerous Ball of Tin
  D. Amos 7:10-17: Confrontation between Amos and Amaziah
  E. Amos 8:1-3: The Fourth Vision—The End Has Come
  F. Amos 8:4-14: Recalling the Prophet's Message
  G. Amos 9:1-4: The Final Vision—Watching the Destruction
  H. Amos 9:5-6: The Final Doxology
IV. Amos 9:7-15: A Remnant and Hope
  A. Amos 9:7-10: (Only) A Remnant Will Survive
  B. Amos 9:11-15: Political Restoration and Fertility

# THE LION ROARS

## Amos 1:1–2:16

## COMMENTARY

The first two chapters of Amos contain the superscription (1:1), the motto of the book (1:2), and a series of judgment oracles against six surrounding countries, Judah, and Israel (1:3–2:16). The stylized nature of these oracles, each with obvious introductory refrains, makes the parameters of the individual units clearly recognizable. Yet, it just as clearly suggests that attention needs to be paid to the rhetorical aims of the oracles as a group.

### Layered Superscription, 1:1

The superscription shows evidence of growth over time. Initially, the earliest elements probably included the attribution to Amos and the reference to the earthquake that had happened two years earlier. It is possible that this early superscription originally introduced the collection of Amos 3–6, since their content best fits the description, "the words of Amos." Chapters 3–6 have often been classified as prophetic sayings, given the relatively short length of the units. The remaining elements in the superscription can be tied to the growth of the corpus. The reference to the shepherds of Tekoa presumes knowledge of the prophetic narrative in 7:10-17, inserted into the cycle of visions for rhetorical purposes. The mention of kings Uzziah of Judah and Jeroboam II of Israel, on the other hand, likely reflects the redactional linking of Amos to Hosea, Micah, and Zephaniah. (See discussion in Hos 1:1.)

The phrase "the words of Amos" is unusual since "word" in prophetic superscriptions typically refers to the word of YHWH, not the word of the prophet. Only Jeremiah begins similarly. Little is known about the person Amos, apart from what is provided here and in 7:10-17. These two passages claim that he was a herdsman and a dresser of sycamore trees (7:14). Together, these tidbits suggest a person of some means, since he would need land and cattle to do these jobs. Beyond that, little about the prophet is claimed in the book, though one finds additional speculation on Amos within rabbinic sources. (See [Amos in Jewish Tradition].)

Information concerning the earthquake is sparse, but reference to it suggests it once introduced an early collection of the prophet's sayings, when knowledge of "the earthquake" was still known. In this respect, it connotes a monumental event that shapes a generation, not unlike the way references to Pearl Harbor, the Kennedy assassination, the *Challenger* disaster, or 9/11 function in our culture as references to pivotal events.

The two kings mentioned in Amos 1:1 not only help set the context for hearing the book of Amos but also provide insights into the agenda of those who compiled the words of Amos. No serious challenge has been leveled against the historicity of the tradition that Amos preached during the reign of these two kings who were roughly contemporary with one another. Both Uzziah (786–746 BCE) and Jeroboam II (786–746 BCE) had lengthy reigns covering most of the first half of the eighth century, though during the last ten years of Uzziah's reign his son was co-regent because of Uzziah's illness. The precise time Amos appeared is not stated, but because the economic status of Israel appears fairly robust, it is generally assumed that Amos preached in the last decade of Jeroboam's reign (786–746 BCE). [Economic Status of Israel] The mention of one king from the north and one from the south corresponds to the pattern one finds among the tradents of the Deuteronomistic Historian, as seen in the book of Kings, where stories about the kings of Judah alternate with those of Israel's kings. The book of Amos addresses Israel and

**Economic Status of Israel**

The political and economic situation presupposed in Amos differs markedly from that of Hosea. Amos reflects the stability and the economic prosperity of the reign of Jeroboam II in the northern kingdom, which is one of the mains issues in Amos. On the other hand, Hosea alludes to a situation characterized by political intrigue and royal instability that best reflects the time after the death of Jeroboam II. This means, in all likelihood, that Amos preached 15–20 years prior to the time of Hosea. Yet, in all the various orders of the Book of the Twelve, Hosea precedes Amos. Two explanations for the preference of Hosea as the first writing in the Twelve can be seen, though they are not mutually exclusive. First, much has been made of the phraseology of Hos 1:2, which begins, "when YHWH *first* spoke . . . ." Of course, Hos 1:2 probably refers merely to the time when Hosea began receiving prophetic messages, but one can easily see how later readers could have understood this chronological datum to pertain to the prophets in general. Second, and more likely, a theological rationale may account for the placement of Hosea before Amos. The structure of Hosea invites assessment and engagement for the reader, since it continually alternates messages of judgment with words of promise and since it ends with an open-ended call to repentance. By contrast, the message of Amos contains virtually no hint of promise, as though the decision for judgment against Israel has already been reached, at least until the last two units of the book (9:7-10, 11-15). Following the narrative logic of the Book of Four, Micah significantly begins with the assumption of the destruction of Samaria (Mic 1:2-7), thus picking up on the message of Amos and Hosea. In Micah, however, the same decision presented to Israel in Hosea (and evidently rejected in Amos) is now presented to Jerusalem and Judah, and their decision will determine whether they will suffer the same fate as Samaria.

Judah, not just Judah (as one finds in Chronicles).

## The Book's Motto, 1:2

Amos 1:2 functions as the motto for the book in the form of a theophany portrayal. [Theophany] The brief poem depicts the book's message in which Amos, who comes from the outskirts of Jerusalem, delivers God's words of judgment against Israel. Amos 1:2 uses the metaphor of a lion roaring from its den (see also 3:4, 8) when describing YHWH uttering his voice from Jerusalem. The verse also presents a cause-and-effect scenario: YHWH utters his voice from Jerusalem (i.e., pronounces judgment), and the northern kingdom withers from the "pastures of the shepherds" to "the top of Carmel" (i.e., a high, prominent peak in Israel). This promontory forms a poetic counterpart to Jerusalem because of its height and its religious significance. Carmel was the site of the famous battle between Elijah and the prophets of Baal (1 Kgs 18:19-40). Obliquely, this mountain represents the religious syncretism of the northern kingdom, an issue that will surface again in the book of Amos and one that is explored even more fully in Hosea.

### Theophany

AΩ The word "theophany" stems etymologically from the Greek words for God (*theos*) and appearance (*phaneros*) and means just that, an "appearance of God." In Old Testament contexts, a theophany can refer to any account, visual or audible, whereby God appears to a person or persons. Hence, the term is often used in narrative context to refer to encounters as diverse as the Eden stories (Gen 2–3), Noah's encounter with God before the flood (Gen 6), Moses' encounter with the burning bush (Exod 3), or God in the terrifying cloud at Sinai (Exod 19). These appearances may also reflect dreams or visions in which YHWH appears at key places or pivotal moments, as in Jacob's dream of God at Bethel (Gen 28:10-22) or his wrestling match with God at Peniel (Gen 32:22-32). These appearances generally demonstrate favor upon a person, a people, or a place.

Conversely, especially in prophetic literature, theophanies frequently can take a different shape. One encounters theophanies, or more specifically theophanic portrayals, as poetic portrayals of God's arrival for judgment. In these texts, YHWH's appearance creates cosmic reaction and fear from the enemies. In these cases, one sees a two-part pattern in which (1) YHWH goes forth (as though for battle) and (2) nature reacts dramatically to YHWH's movement. Portrayals of YHWH's appearance as warrior that follow this pattern occur in texts that scholars typically date early (e.g., Judg 5:4-5) and in texts that post-date Old Testament texts (e.g., Sir 43:16-17). In such instances, key components of the theophanic portrayal result when one questions from whence YHWH comes (e.g., Zion, heaven, or Sinai) and toward whom the wrath is directed. For further reading, the most extensive treatments of theophanies are found in the writings of Jörg Jeremias. His English article offers an excellent summation of his monograph.

Jörg Jeremias, "Theophany in the OT," *Interpreter's Dictionary of the Bible* (New York: Abingdon, 1972) 5:898–98; and *Theophanie: Die Geschichte einer Alttestamentlichen Gattung* (Wissenschaftliche Monographien zum Alten und Neuen Testament 10; Neukirchen-Vluyn: Neukirchener Verlag, 1965).

## Oracles against the Nations and Israel, 1:3–2:16

Amos 1:3–2:16 constitutes, in its final form, a series of eight carefully fashioned oracles whose patterned presentation requires analysis individually and as a group. The recurring pattern will be treated first before we turn a brief analysis of the individual oracles.

*The Pattern of the Oracles.* [Pattern of the Oracles] Five recurring elements form a rhetorical pattern: (1) introductory refrain; (2) reason

**Pattern of the Oracles**

| | 1:3-5 | 1:6-8 | 1:9-10 | 1:11-12 |
|---|---|---|---|---|
| **Region/City** | Syria | Philistia | Tyre | Edom |
| **Refrain** | Thus says the LORD: For three transgressions of Damascus, and for four, I will not revoke the punishment; | Thus says the LORD: For three transgressions of Gaza, and for four, I will not revoke the punishment; | Thus says the LORD: For three transgressions of Tyre, and for four, I will not revoke the punishment; | Thus says the LORD: For three transgressions of Edom, and for four, I will not revoke the punishment; |
| **Reason for Punishment** | because they have threshed Gilead with threshing sledges of iron. | because they carried into exile entire communities, to hand them over to Edom. | because they delivered entire communities over to Edom, and did not remember the covenant of kinship. | because he pursued his brother with the sword and cast off all pity; he maintained his anger perpetually, and kept his wrath forever. |
| **Description of Punishment** | So I will send a fire on the house of Hazael, and it shall devour the strongholds of Ben-hadad. I will break the gate bars of Damas-cus, and cut off the inhabitants from the Valley of Aven, and the one who holds the scepter from Beth-eden; | So I will send a fire on the wall of Gaza, fire that shall devour its strongholds. I will cut off the inhabi-tants from Ashdod, and the one who holds the scepter from Ashkelon; I will turn my hand against Ekron, | So I will send a fire on the wall of Tyre, fire that shall devour its strongholds. | So I will send a fire on Teman, and it shall devour the strongholds of Bozrah. |
| **Result of Punishment** | and the people of Aram shall go into exile to Kir, | and the remnant of the Philistines shall perish, | X | X |
| **Concluding Formula** | says the LORD. | says the Lord GOD. | X | X |

| 1:13-15 | 2:1-3 | 2:4-5 | 2:6-16 |
|---|---|---|---|
| Ammon | Moab | Judah | Israel |
| Thus says the LORD: For three transgressions of the Ammonites, and for four, I will not revoke the punishment; | Thus says the LORD: For three transgressions of Moab, and for four, I will not revoke the punishment; | Thus says the LORD: For three transgressions of Judah, and for four, I will not revoke the punishment; | Thus says the LORD: For three transgressions of Israel, and for four, I will not revoke the punishment; |
| because they have ripped open pregnant women in Gilead in order to enlarge their territory. | because he burned to lime the bones of the king of Edom. | because they have rejected the law of the LORD, and have not kept his statutes, but they have been led astray by the same lies after which their ancestors walked. | because they sell the righteous for silver, and the needy for a pair of sandals— (7) they who trample the head of the poor into the dust of the earth, and push the afflicted out of the way; father and son go in to the same girl, so that my holy name is profaned; (8) they lay themselves down beside every altar on garments taken in pledge; and in the house of their God they drink wine bought with fines they imposed. |
| So I will kindle a fire against the wall of Rabbah, fire that shall devour its strongholds, with shouting on the day of battle, with a storm on the day of the whirlwind; | So I will send a fire on Moab, and it shall devour the strongholds of Kerioth, . . . . I will cut off the ruler from its midst, and will kill all its officials with him, | So I will send a fire on Judah, and it shall devour the strongholds of Jerusalem. | (9-12) A HISTORICAL SUMMARY<br><br>(13) So, I will press you down in your place, just as a cart presses down when it is full of sheaves. |
| then their king shall go into exile, he and his officials together, | and Moab shall die amid uproar, amid shouting and the sound of the trumpet; | X | Flight shall perish from the swift, and the strong shall not retain their strength, nor shall the mighty save their lives; (15) those who handle the bow shall not stand, and those who are swift of foot shall not save themselves, nor shall those who ride horses save their lives; (16) and those who are stout of heart among the mighty shall flee away naked in that day, |
| says the LORD. | says the LORD. | X | says the LORD. |

for the punishment; (3) description of the punishment; (4) results of the punishment; and (5) the concluding formula. The final oracle (2:6-16) departs from this linguistic pattern. Of the remaining seven oracles, four contain all the elements in roughly the same order, while the oracles against Tyre, Edom, and Judah lack the final two. In addition to these stylistic variations, linguistic and historical considerations also suggest that the three deviating oracles were added to the collection during the exilic period.[1] The recurring elements provide continuity to the whole, and yet because of the refrain, the concluding formula, and the variations in the crimes, each of the oracles also functions independently. Before turning to the individual units, then, it will help to look at issues raised with the refrain and the rhetorical goal of the series.

The refrain introduces each new oracle with the same formula: "for three transgressions of X and for four, I will not turn *it* back." The "X" stands for the various cities or countries named in the indictment. The first three are addressed to cities (Damascus, Gaza, Tyre) that represent regional seats of power and symbolize a country. The other five concern countries (Edom, Ammon, Moab, Judah, and Israel). Three questions about the refrain have puzzled scholars to various degrees: how to understand the numerical phrase, the best connotation of the verb "return," and the antecedent for the pronoun "it." First, two options exist for the numerical phrase "for three and for four." Either it can be seen as a poetic device, as numbers can be used in introductory clauses to introduce a specific number of items in a list (see Prov 30:15-17, 18-19, 21-23, 24-28, 29-31), or it can be understood abstractly to indicate "a significant number and then some." The latter option seems more likely in Amos, since none of the oracles list three or four specific crimes. [Other Suggestions for "Three and Four"]

Second, translating the *hif'il* verb *šûb* has generated several suggestions: (1) "to turn back"; (2) "to return"; (3) "turn away"; or (4) "to take back." Most commentators and translations interpret the verb to mean "take it back," with the assumption that God has released God's word of punishment and has no intention of reversing it.

Third, scholars have offered various explanations for the missing antecedent for the masculine singular pronoun "it." Several commentators suggest that the antecedent is the "voice" of YHWH that roars in 1:2, but this option ignores the syntactical independence of

## Other Suggestions for "Three and Four"

The argument by F. Andersen and D. N. Freedman that the seven nations leading up to Israel constitute the "three and then four"—meaning that YHWH prefigures the oracular sequence in its entirety in each refrain—is not convincing for stylistic, rhetorical, and theological reasons. Stylistically, their arguments only work if one counts one crime committed for each nation, yet the multiplicity of formulations in three of the oracles' rationales describes more than one crime. Second, their arguments that these seven oracles themselves divided into one group of three and another group of four reflect extremely subtle distinctions that would elude listeners. Rhetorically, two observations stand out. The first builds upon the stylistic objections by noting how difficult the multiple crimes of the Tyre, Edom, and Judah oracles would make following such a speaker's outline. Second, one can hardly deny that Israel functions rhetorically as the ultimate goal of this collection, but according to Andersen and Freedman, this oracle does not follow the pattern. Theologically, the resulting portrait of God from Andersen and Freedman's line of argument creates a troubling picture: YHWH would have to be a petulant deity who has "had it up to here" with the lot of these nations. As a result, because all of these nations have received divine forbearance on at least one occasion, YHWH now intends to punish all of them. In short, Andersen and Freedman's arguments portray God's wrath as punishing everyone within a geographical region on account of the sins of just a few.

Francis I. Andersen and David Noel Freedman, *Amos* (AB 24A; New York: Doubleday, 1989) 231–33.

---

1:2 from that which follows.[2] Most commentators have understood "it" as anticipatory of that which follows, where this proleptic "it" essentially means "punishment." Several English translations exhibit this cataphoric interpretation by inserting the word "punishment" for clarity (NRSV, NKJV, NAS; NIV inserts "my wrath" instead). Schart even suggests the end of Hosea was intended.[3] While this argument may not have found many supporters to this point because it builds upon redactional hypotheses concerning the larger corpus, one can nevertheless learn from Schart's reasoning that the end of a book does not stop the word of YHWH. Learning to pull back and see the entirety of the prophetic message (especially in the Book of the Twelve) against the continuing story of Israel and Judah is an important aspect of interpreting prophetic literature.

The rhetorical goal of this collection of oracles culminates in the final oracle that pronounces judgment upon Israel itself. Moreover, the arrangement of these oracles is no accident. Rather, the prophet verbally encircles Israel as he programmatically makes his way around the region—moving from northeast to southwest and then northwest to southeast—before turning to Judah and Israel. [Encircling Israel] This

## Encircling Israel

The seven countries named prior to the oracle against Israel were not selected at random. Rather, it is evident that these countries were listed because they geographically encircle the northern kingdom of Israel: (1) Syria to the northeast; (2) Philistia to the southwest; (3) Phoenicia to the northwest; a group of three kingdoms to the east and southeast, specifically (4) Edom, (5) Ammon, (6) Moab; and finally, (7) Judah, Israel's sister kingdom to the south.

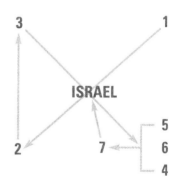

sequence was calculated to provide maximum shock value to the readers/hearers. Since Amos came from Tekoa, a village just ten miles south of Jerusalem, one can imagine this southern prophet would have elicited suspicion had he merely begun by pronouncing judgment upon Israel. By beginning with "foreigners," the passage taps into xenophobic attitudes. People then, as now, are more apt to critique the sins of others than to examine their own actions. Thus, Amos paves the way for the rebuke of Israel by subtly pulling the people along, gaining trust with each passing condemnation of someone else before lowering the boom on Israel. Recognizing this rhetorical goal does not mean, however, that the charges leveled against these nations should be deemed inconsequential. These oracles against the nations display a number of important theological presuppositions. It is important to look at the individual units and the crimes that Amos delineates.

*Amos 1:3-5: Syria.* Amos 1:3-5 pronounces punishment upon Syria, referring to the country by the name of its capital city (Damascus), the name of the people (Aram), and its royal house (Hazael, Hadad). The reason for the pronouncement of punishment has to do with war atrocities for which the king, the city, and the people are all held culpable. Specifically, Amos accuses the Syrians of torturing the people of Gilead, treating them like a grain to be broken under the weight of a metal sledge. The delineation of punishment pronounces judgment upon the king, the city, and the people. This first pronouncement of punishment is the most extensive in the cycle, because it introduces phrases used to pronounce punishment later in the cycle (e.g., sending fire upon the nation/city and devouring the citadels).

Theologically, this pronouncement makes several significant presumptions. First, it presumes YHWH has power over nations outside Israel. Second, it presumes YHWH holds foreign nations accountable for their behavior when they transgress accepted military norms. Abusing the people of other countries by torture and humiliation stands as an affront to God's expectations for humanity. Third, it presumes YHWH holds entire nations accountable for the actions of a few. Thus, this text does not just ask who was in charge of the military unit who conducted the torture. Rather, it pronounces an end to the entire kingdom under whose aegis the torturers acted. In short, the punishment anticipates the exile of the entire people of Aram (1:5).

Three place names are used in the description of Aram's punishment: (1) the Valley of Aven, which means the valley of sin; (2) Beth-Eden, which probably refers to a region near the Euphrates River then controlled by Syria; (3) and Kir, perceived as a region in Mesopotamia from which the people of Syria had escaped (see Amos 9:7). This punishment, given the statements in Amos 9:7, is like telling the people of Israel that they will return to Egypt.

*Amos 1:6-8: Philistia.* The second refrain in 1:6 names Gaza as the addressee, but it quickly becomes apparent that the entire Philistine region is the subject of the oracle in 1:6-8. Gaza was one of five Philistine cities whose rulers worked in consort with one another (see "Map of Places in Amos"). Four of those five are mentioned specifically in the punishment of this oracle: Gaza, Ashdod, Ashkelon, and Ekron. Only Gath is not specified in these verses.

Following the introductory refrain, 1:6 provides the reason for punishment—one that is simultaneously specific and ambiguous. The oracle accuses Gaza of slave trade with Edom that is excessive. They "deported an entire population" to another country (Edom). It was not unusual in the ancient Near East to take slaves after a battle, but 1:6 castigates Gaza for going too far. They did not use the slaves themselves, but sold an entire people to Edom. This charge suggests a policy rather than a singular incident, but a specific historical context is difficult to ascertain.

The punishment expands the accusation—including not just Gaza, but Ashdod, Ashkelon, and Ekron as well. Further, it addresses the same sociological constellation as 1:3-5 (city, people, and king). Amos 1:7-8, however, specifies different geographical recipients for each punishment in order to cover the entire Philistine region. So the punishment specifies the city of Gaza, the inhabitants of Ashdod, and the king of Ashkelon. Amos 1:8 then adds the unleashing God's power against Ekron before pronouncing punishment upon the entire "remnant of the Philistines," thereby confirming that this oracle affects the entire region, not just one part.

*Amos 1:9-10: Tyre.* The oracle against Tyre represents the first of three oracles in 1:3–2:5 often considered as exilic expansions for stylistic and historical reasons. Stylistically, this oracle deviates from the pattern. It lacks both a result clause and a concluding formula (see [Pattern of the Oracles]). While 1:9-10 contains two reasons for punishment, the first merely repeats the accusation from 1:6. The second refers to an unknown covenant, but one that perhaps refers to an agreement that resulted from a meeting in 593 during Zedekiah's reign (Jer 27:1-8). After Jerusalem's destruction, oracles against Tyre became more prominent than they were in the eighth century.

*Amos 1:11-12: Edom.* The oracle against Edom (1:11-12) constitutes the second oracle that deviates from the basic pattern and that is often treated as a later addition to the series. The stylistic reasons are the same as with 1:9-10: it lacks a result clause and a concluding formula. The Edom oracle is particularly relevant to an exilic historical context, since there is no evidence of hostilities between Edom and Israel or Judah during the time of Amos. By contrast, reference to Edom "pursuing his brother with the sword" coincides with exilic traditions that Edom aided Babylon following Jerusalem's destruction (Obad 11-14; see the introduction to Obadiah). Amos 1:11 adds two additional charges, namely that Edom stifled its compassion and did not control its anger. The pain behind this oracle lies not only in the charge of military engagement but also in the fact that the aggression took place against "his brother." Some have attempted to soften this charge by understanding brother generically, as any ally. However, in the Hebrew Bible too many references connecting Edom to the descendants of Esau, the brother of Jacob, make this formulation unlikely (e.g., Obad 10, 12; Mal 1:2). While "brother" could imply a military ally, if this were intended in 1:11, one would expect some other formulation to avoid confusion. Most likely, reference to the brother of Edom/Esau would have been understood as Israel/Jacob. (For an introduction to the role of Edom in the Old Testament, see [Edom in Biblical Tradition].)

*Amos 1:13-15: Ammon.* The subject of the fifth oracle is Ammon, a small kingdom beyond the Jordan River, east of Israel, and north of Moab and Edom. Like the preceding oracles, the accusation against Ammon concerns war crimes, but in this case ones committed against civilians in Gilead. An Israelite region beyond the Jordan, Gilead became the target for conquest in the eighth century. Gilead is the region victimized by the Syrians in Amos 1:3. In this oracle, however, Amos accuses Ammon of slaughtering the pregnant women of Gilead, an egregious military act designed to terrify and brutalize one's enemy. Once again, YHWH holds foreign nations accountable for war crimes violating basic human rights. The punishment pronounced is destruction of the city of Rabbah and its royal family via a military defeat and exile respectively.

*Amos 2:1-3: Moab.* The accusation levied against Moab reflects abuses committed in the aftermath of war, specifically the defamation of the body of the defeated king of Edom. The exact setting of these charges cannot be verified, but the fact that Amos accuses Moab of burning the bones of the Edomite king would imply that this king was already dead.

The punishment is directed against the city of Kerioth and its political leaders (judge and princes). Kerioth was a prominent Moabite city, though its exact location is debated. Evidence from the Moabite Stone suggests that the city had a temple dedicated to the god Chemosh, and that it contained royal or administrative officers in association with this temple. The result clause in this oracle—"Moab will die amid tumult with war cries and the sound of a trumpet"— implies that the fate of Kerioth will be the fate of all of Moab. The synecdoche of Kerioth for all of Moab explains why the result clause of this oracle appears in the middle of the description of the punishment rather than immediately preceding the concluding formula as in 1:5, 8, 15.

*Amos 2:4-5: Judah.* The oracle in 2:4-5 against Judah is the third oracle often considered a later addition to the original cycle for two reasons: first because it contains the same stylistic variations as the oracles against Tyre (1:9-10) and Edom (1:11-12), and second because its accusation differs so dramatically from other oracles. Unlike the previous oracles, the accusation against Judah contains no hint of military or humanitarian abuse. Neither does it exhibit explicit concern for social justice like the oracle against

**Slavery**

Stone panel from the Central Palace of Tiglath-pileser III (745–727 BCE). The king is shown in his chariot, while in another scene above Assyrian soldiers drive out prisoners and flocks from a fortified city. Nimrud (ancient Kalhu), northern Iraq. Neo-Assyrian, about 730–727 BCE. British Museum, London, Great Britain. (Credit: © The Trustees of The British Museum/Art Resource, NY)

Israel. Rather, Judah's crime is expressed solely in religious terms. They have failed to keep the law of YHWH, and they have fallen prey to the same "lies" as their ancestors. In all likelihood, the second charge relates to the first. The idea of a lie "after which one walks" refers to a lifestyle that does not take seriously YHWH's covenant relationship with the people. That this accusation would be leveled against Judah presupposes the charges that Judah has taken up the worship of other gods and abandoned its covenantal obligation to YHWH (cf. Isa 28:15, where the rulers of Jerusalem are accused of making a "covenant with death" and taking refuge in their lies and falsehoods).

The closest parallels to Amos's charge against Judah appear in Isaiah 5:24 and Hosea 4:6. In the former, Jerusalem and Judah (picking up on the vine metaphor) will dry up because they have rejected the law of YHWH Sebaoth. In the latter, God rejects the people because they rejected knowledge and forgets them because they forgot the law of YHWH. The phrase "law of YHWH" is less common than one might think, appearing only nineteen times in the Hebrew Bible.[4] For example, in 2 Kings 10:31, Jehu is castigated for not "walking after the law of YHWH"; whereas in Psalm 119:1, those who "walk in the law of YHWH" are blessed. One can see from these references that the phrase "law of YHWH" refers to a lifestyle oriented toward YHWH's instruction, not a slavish legalism as is typically understood by many Christian congregations. This oracle accuses Judah of abandoning YHWH's instruction, which certainly included specific statutes; yet it is the rejection of the desire to please YHWH that is at issue here, not the listing of specific shortcomings.

*Amos 2:6-16: Israel.* That the oracle against Israel, the northern kingdom, functioned as the ultimate rhetorical target can be seen from two observations. First, it comes as the last element in the series, a position that often serves as the series' rhetorical climax. Second, the charges leveled against Israel are longer and less formulaic than those in the other oracles.

The reasons for punishing Israel revolve primarily around issues related to social justice rather than military crimes. (See illustration "Temple in Samaria?".) The powerful and the wealthy abuse the weak and the poor. Amos 2:6 charges Israel with trafficking its own people into slavery, selling the righteous for silver and the destitute for shoes. These two terms ("the righteous" and "the destitute") are used as parallel expressions, but they do not point to the same group. Rather, the parallelism includes both. Amos 2:7 charges that the wealthy/wicked benefited economically by taking advantage of groups who could not defend themselves. In 2:7a, apathy toward society's unfortunate begins the accusation, while 2:7b transitions to the charge of cultic prostitution (see [Meanings of "Prostitute"]). Amos 2:8 charges Israel with profaning the sacred by lounging upon garments taken as collateral for religious vows and by partying in the temple at Bethel, imbibing in wine paid for by temple taxation. [Cultic "Parties"]

All of this aberrant behavior occurs despite YHWH's past benefaction. Amos 2:9-11 reminds Israel of how God had once destroyed the Amorites and delivered the Israelites from Egypt. According to at least some texts in the Pentateuch (Gen 15:16; Deut 1:7), the Amorites were the primary people group living in the land at the time of Israel's conquest. The book of Amos depicts the Amorites as a once powerful force that was utterly devastated. In Amos, God emancipated the Israelites from slavery in Egypt and then used them to displace the Amorites. [Amorites] This subtle reminder of YHWH's power chips away at Israel's sense of uniqueness. YHWH reminds Israel that God has replaced powerful nations in the past, implying God can do so in the future. YHWH subtly reminds Israel that while they had once suffered oppression as slaves, their leaders have since become the oppressors. In short, Israel's status as God's chosen people is not a license to mistreat others. God's election of Israel was for service, especially to those who are powerless to act for themselves. God set apart some in Israel for service. Amos 2:11-12 mentions two specific groups who were set apart: the Nazirites who had taken vows of abstinence and the prophets who speak on YHWH's behalf. Amos, however, condemns Israel for thwarting their work by making

## Cultic "Parties"

AΩ This reference in Amos 2:8 appears to refer sarcastically to a cultic gathering, *marzēaḥ*, that was common in the ancient Near East. Similar words appear in Ugaritic, Aramaic, and Phoenician. These parties are referenced explicitly and derisively in Amos 6:7 (see also Jer 16:5). Their background likely comes originally through the El cult, and while different manifestations of a *marzēaḥ* reflect local culture and theologies, the core concept appears to be a communion with a deity at a great hall (not always a temple) accomplished through a sacral meal.

For a treatment of the development of the concept, and its wide distribution across time and locations, see Heinz-Josef Fabry, "*marzēaḥ*," in *Theological Dictionary of the Old Testament* (Grand Rapids: Eerdmans, 1998) 9:10–15. See also the important study by Barstad that surveys the texts referring to the *marzēaḥ*: Hans M. Barstad, *The Religious Polemics of Amos: Studies in the Preaching of Am 2, 7b-8; 4:1-13; 5:1-27; 6:4-7; 8:14* (VTSup 34; Leiden: E.J. Brill, 1984) 33–36, 127–42; and Peter J. King, "The *marzēaḥ* that Amos Denounces," in *BAR* 14/4 (1988): 1–12.

## Amorites

The Amorites appear in portions of the story about the conquest of Canaan. Their origins remain obscure, perhaps reflecting ancient oral traditions of a people called the *Amurru* in ancient Akkadian documents from as early as the third millennium BCE. In the Pentateuch, the Amorites are first mentioned among the nations in Gen 10, but their main role is as one of the nations who occupy the land prior to the conquest (see Exod 3:8, 17; 23:23; 33:2; 34:11; Num 13:29; Deut 7:1; Josh 3:10; and Gen 15:19-21). Amos 2:9-10, by contrast, mentions only the Amorites. For further reading on the complicated and difficult task of reconstructing the history (or even delineating the existence) of the Amorites, see J. Andrew Dearman, "Amorites," *New Interpreter's Dictionary of the Bible*, 1:132.

the Nazirites drink wine and making the prophets cease their prophesying.

Amos 2:13-16 functions as the pronouncement of punishment in the oracle against Israel, using agricultural and military images to convey the imminent destruction "on that day" (2:16) when God will act. Amos 2:13 draws upon a metaphor of a cart overloaded with grain to depict the power God's judgment will exert upon Israel. Such a cart would have strained under the weight of its load, so that the creaking would alert everyone to the difficulty. Similarly, YHWH announces his intention to press down upon Israel so that they will find themselves feeling like that cart, over-burdened, unable to move, and in danger of breaking apart. This metaphorical picture of judgment is then followed by pronouncements of chaos in the time of battle. Warriors who had once exhibited the skill necessary to survive in battle will suddenly find that skill has abandoned them. The fleet of foot will not be able to run; the strong will become weak; the brave will become frightened; and the archers will be unable to stand and shoot. The cumulative effect of these images portrays a battle scene in which Israel's army is utterly decimated. Even though the phrase "day of YHWH" is not used explicitly in this description, the concept probably derives from the images here since God threatens to act (2:13) directly on the day of battle. Certainly Amos 5:18-20 shows the book's keen awareness that the coming day of YHWH should not be an idea of comfort for Israel. Rather, "on that day" (2:16) Israel will be routed militarily by an army God will send, and the outcome is hardly in doubt.

# CONNECTIONS

Theologically, the oracles against the nations are important as a group for at least four reasons. [Oracles Against the Nations] First, they presuppose YHWH's universal control over human powers. God's interest in how nations behave does not stop at the borders of the holy land. Second, they presuppose moral principles by which even nations who do not recognize YHWH as God must abide. The nations are held accountable for their actions, even in times of war, because some things are beyond the pale of what it means to be human. Third, claiming to be the people of God invites additional scrutiny. The charges leveled against Judah (rejection of the law) appear tame in comparison to those of the other nations, but YHWH treats Judah's rejection on the same level as the war crimes of Syria, Ammon, or Philistia. Judah's punishment is just as severe as that of any other nation. According to 2:4-5, Judah receives no "pass" because of its special relationship with YHWH. Fourth, the refrain in all the oracles ("for three transgressions and for four") presumes an ongoing series of crimes as judged by YHWH, even if only one is specified in the oracle that follows. YHWH's judgment then is measured, not impulsive. It represents, in these oracles, a response that comes only after numerous instances of rebellion.

These oracles typically make modern Christians nervous. For some, the idea of God judging nations creates theological problems because of their understanding of Jesus' teachings on violence (e.g., Matt 5:39; Luke 6:29). For others, these oracles conjure up images of a vengeful God that makes them uncomfortable with the Old Testament. Still others shy away from the idea of God judging nations because of the abuses of theocratic rulers throughout history who have used religious language to claim a divine mission to propagate their own agenda and usually to fill their own coffers. Yet images of God's judgment cannot be excised from the Bible, either the Old Testament or the New Testament. Jesus and Paul both speak of God's wrath (Luke 21:23; Rom 1:18; 2:5).

These texts cannot be easily swept aside. Neither, however, should these texts serve as one's only source for understanding God. In fact, when taken as a group, these oracles offer several important rejoinders against those who are all too eager to see God punish others. First, none of these texts justify human aggression in the name of God. The prophet does not say he will lead an army to

**Oracles Against the Nations**

Oracles against foreign nations in the prophetic writings raise a host of theological, literary, and historical dilemmas. For further reading, see the following sources:

John Barton, *Amos's Oracles Against the Nations: A Study of Amos 1.3–2.5* (Cambridge: Cambridge University Press, 1980).

Duane L. Christensen, *Transformations of the War Oracle in Old Testament Prophecy: Studies in the Oracles Against the Nations* (Missoula: Scholars Press, 1975).

Dereck Daschke and Andrew Kille, *A Cry Instead of Justice: The Bible and Cultures of Violence in Psychological Perspective* (New York: T & T Clark, 2010).

John B. Geyer, "Mythology and Culture in the Oracles Against the Nations," *VT* 36 (1986): 129–45.

Donald E. Gowan, *Significance of the Oracles Against the Nations* (Chicago: University of Chicago Press, 1964).

John Haralson Hayes, "Usage of Oracles Against Foreign Nations in Ancient Israel," *JBL* 87 (1968): 81–92.

Harold R. Mosley, "The Oracles Against the Nations," *TTE* 52 (1995): 37–45.

Graham S. Ogden, "Prophetic Oracles Against Foreign Nations and Psalms of Communal Lament: The Relationship of Psalm 137 to Jeremiah 49:7-22 and Obadiah," *JSOT* 24 (1982): 89–97.

exact God's vengeance, nor does he see the execution of judgment as the role of the state. Rather, the oracles of Amos speak only of God holding the nations accountable. Second, the arrangement of these oracles serves as a reminder that 1:3–2:16 is more interested in the sins of Judah and Israel than in the sins of other nations. These oracles culminate in judgment against God's own people. This collection is not intended to bolster xenophobic, nationalistic claims that "foreigners" are to blame for the mess in this world. God holds all people accountable for their own actions. Third, most of the crimes indicted reflect God's objection to the way people treat one another. God cares how our societies provide for the poor, the righteous, and the downtrodden. One need only contemplate the oracle against Israel to understand that God is not interested in claims of supremacy, but in actions of advocacy.

Concerning the judgment against Israel, Amos 2:6-16 accuses Israel of inverting true religious expression by making the sacred profane (2:7-8, 11-12) and making the profane sacred (2:7b). These accusations portray a people who have lost sight of what it means to worship, to ascribe worth to one's God. These charges coincide rather closely with the emphasis in Hosea that castigates Israel for the impropriety of its worship (e.g., Hos 4:4-6, 12-13; 7:14-15; 8:4-5).

In addition, 2:6-16 involves one of the constituent elements of the message of Amos, specifically a sense of social justice that pervades this writing. God expresses solidarity with the poor and oppressed by challenging the behavior of the wealthy and the powerful. The affluent are not judged for their status but for their behavior. Much like our world today, the world of Amos was a world of haves and have-nots. Amos charges Israel with the complete apathy and antipathy that people show for those less fortunate than themselves. Specifically, the picture created in 2:6-16 is of two groups of people: one group suffers economically and spiritually, while the other exploits the needs of the oppressed or remains completely oblivious to the needs around them. In the first group, those who suffer economic hardship are forced to sell themselves and their loved ones for money (2:6), and the text paints a picture of so many of those suffering that they block the pathway of those trying to enter the temple (2:7). In the other group, some of the affluent simply ignore the plight of the poor, while others treat the economically downtrodden with violence (2:6-7). The picture created by 2:7b-8 depicts this wealthy group as eager to be rid of the poor and suffering because they are in a hurry to get to the party at the temple. The quick transition from violence against the poor to prostitution and drunkenness in the temple lends itself to this picture. Further, not only does this group appear not only to be obsessed with the perpetration of injustice but their very presence in the temple profanes the name of God.

Amos paints a haunting picture. It would be easy merely to point fingers at those oblivious reprobates of another time and another place, but the word of God has a habit of not letting us off the hook so easily. How much more pleasant it would be, from our safe vantage point, if we could merely identify with Amos? But when we let Amos speak to us, and we hear this message in our community of faith, with whom are we supposed to identify? Do we really see ourselves as those who are suffering outside the gate, unable to enter the temple, or do we get an uneasy feeling that, even though we are more subtle in how we go about it, as individuals and as a group we too often turn a blind eye to the suffering and economic hardships of those in our community? To be sure, we rarely physically push people aside, but we do avoid them. We know the neighborhoods they live in, but we stay away. Like the priest and the Levite in the parable of the good Samaritan (Luke 10:29-37), it is easier to keep walking, to cross over to the other side of the street, and not to invest time and energy trying to improve the lives of the poor in our own communities. We know this haunting feeling, but it is easier to push it to the side than to face the challenge Amos and Jesus put before us and our congregations (Amos 2:7; Matt 19:16-22). But as long as we read the Bible, that haunting feeling will not go away, for it lies at the core of genuine ministry—namely, that showing compassion to the poor and oppressed in society is a means of expressing genuine faith and gratitude for all that God has done for us.

## NOTES

1. Linguistically, the three deviating oracles all shorten the infinitive clause and lengthen the verbal clause. The three later oracles lengthen the reason for punishment while shortening the announcement of punishment, and all three lack reference to specific acts while condemning motives and "subjective attitudes" (Hans Walter Wolff, *Joel and Amos* [trans. Waldemar Janzen et al.; Hermeneia; Philadelphia: Fortress, 1977]

139–40). Historically, Tyre and Edom as targets make more sense after Jerusalem's destruction, while antagonism of this magnitude is harder to document for the eighth century. See Rainer Albertz, *From the Exile to the Maccabees*, vol. 2 of *A History of Israelite Religion in the Old Testament Period* (trans. John Bowden; OTL; Louisville: Westminster John Knox, 1994) 372–73.

2. Francis I. Andersen and David Noel Freedman, *Amos* (AB 24A; New York: Doubleday, 1989) 234.

3. Aaron Schart, *Die Entstehung des Zwölfprophetenbuchs: Neubearbeitungen von Amos im Rahmen schriftenuebergreifender Redaktionsprozesse* (Beihefte zur Zeitschrift für die alttestamentliche Wissenschaft 260; Berlin: de Gruyter, 1998) 145–47.

4. Exod 13:9; 2 Kgs 10:31; 1 Chr 16:40; 22:12; 2 Chr 12:1; 17:9; 31:3f.; 34:14; 35:26; Ezra 7:10; Neh 9:3; Pss 1:2; 19:8; 119:1; Isa 5:24; 30:9; Jer 8:8; Amos 2:4.

# SIGNS, SIN, AND IDENTITY

## Amos 3:1-15

## COMMENTARY

Amos 3–6 constitutes the second major section of the book. Two characteristics of this section stand out: the introductions at the beginning of each chapter (3:1; 4:1; 5:1; 6:1) and the relatively brief character of the units within these chapters. Amos 3, unlike 1–2 or 7:1–9:6, does not cohere rhetorically via an easily recognizable structure or transitional refrains. Instead, these fifteen verses divide into five moderately short units (3:1-2, 3-8, 9-11, 12, 13-15). Most of these units could stand independently, but the consistent message of judgment against God's people for the abuse of worship and neglect of the poor continues the drumbeat begun in Amos 1–2. First, Amos 3:1-2 calls the people of Israel to attention, reminding them of God's saving acts when they came from Egypt. Surprisingly, they now function as reasons for punishment. Amos 3:3-8 engages the hearer to recognize what God is doing in compelling the prophet to speak. The judgment oracle in Amos 3:9-11 then calls the nations to watch as YHWH condemns Israel for its violence and thievery. Sardonically, Amos 3:12 suggests the survival of a remnant, but it offers little hope in doing so. Finally, Amos 3:13-15 challenges Bethel's religious establishment and ruling class to understand that their power is no match for YHWH.

*Amos 3:1-2.* Amos 3 begins with a call to attention that is virtually identical to the calls in 4:1 and 5:1. [Hear this Word . . .] Amos 3:1 does two things: it announces judgment against the sons of Israel (this word YHWH has spoken against you), and it recalls God's ongoing relationship that began with the exodus from Egypt. The juxtaposition of these two elements (judgment and election) reverberates with implications for God's people.

Amos 3:2 pronounces a word of judgment against the "people of Israel" (see 3:1), but these two verses lack a rationale that is typically

**Hear this Word . . .**

In Amos 3–6, each chapter begins with a call to attention delivered to a named group followed by short prophetic oracles, sayings, and exhortations:

3:1  Hear this word but the Lord has spoken against you, O people (*běnê*) of Israel, against the whole family that I brought up out of the land of Egypt:

4:1  Hear this word, you cows of the Bashan who are on Mount Samaria, who oppress the poor, who crush the needy, who say to their husbands, "Bring something to drink!"

5:1  Hear this word I take up over you in lamentation, O house of Israel:

6:1  Alas for those who are at ease in Zion, and for those who feel secure on Mount Samaria, the notables of the first of the nations, to whom the house of Israel resorts!

The first three of these introductions begin identically ("Hear this word . . ."). Successive, subtle, and perhaps deliberate changes become evident as one evaluates the addressees of these introductions. The first two change genders, addressing first the "sons" (*běnê*) of Israel and then the women of Bashan/Samaria, ignominiously denigrated with a bovine metaphor as cows with husbands. In 5:1, a more inclusive term, house of Israel, is used, but the situation has become even more dire with the reference to a dirge. The introduction changes with 6:1, both in terms of its form and its addressees, the latter having been expanded to include the southern kingdom of Judah. The addressee of 6:1 includes the inhabitants of Mount Samaria (i.e., Israel), but also "those at ease in Zion." This incorporation of Zion hints at an important shift in the larger corpus of the Twelve. When Amos transitions to Micah, a shift explicitly takes place in that the judgment against Israel is then taken as a warning to Jerusalem and Judah (Mic 1:2-7; 3:12).

provided in judgment oracles (cf. Amos 1–2). (See [Prophetic Judgment Oracle].) Thus, Amos 3:1-2 is incomplete formally and rhetorically. The logic of 3:2 by itself is strange indeed: "I have known only you, therefore you are the one I will punish." As is, this verse makes more sense as a transition from the oracles against the nations, within which Israel is the last, than it does as an introduction to what follows. Whether this linking function refers back to 2:6-16, forward to 3:3-15, or to both simultaneously, the presumption is clear. God's people are not free to behave as they please simply because they have benefited from God's deliverance in the past. If anything, the opposite is true: knowledge of God's past deliverance carries with it certain obligations and does not guarantee that God will deliver again.

*Amos 3:3-8.* Amos 3:3-8 forms the next rhetorical unit, although 3:8 appears to be a transitional verse connecting 3:3-7 with the more formally recognizable judgment oracle in 3:9-11. Amos 3:3-6 coheres through a series of seven rhetorical questions, the culmination of which is the theological affirmation about God and God's messengers in 3:7. These seven rhetorical questions all draw upon images involving a cause-and-effect relationship. Each question is formulated to imply a clear answer, and that answer is "no." This string of questions seeks to force the reader/hearer to recognize the warning signs of an impending threat. In fact, the concluding affirmation in 3:7 puts Israel on notice that, indeed, God has revealed something of significance to "his servants the prophets."

The first rhetorical question begins innocuously enough, evoking a shared journey that begins with a rendezvous, agreed upon in advance. The next four rhetorical questions, however, become more ominous since each draws a picture from the animal world that would be familiar to hunters, and each question also threatens the death of something. The last two questions deal with threats against humans (3:6). Then, after the concluding affirmation of 3:7, Amos 3:8 testifies to the prophet's own sense of mission by adding two additional rhetorical questions, both of which also presume a cause-and-effect relationship. These rhetorical questions combine images from the larger context and 3:1-7.

Several things occur simultaneously when 3:8 asks the question, "The lion has roared; who will not fear?" First, the immediate answer to the question is implied: anyone who is close enough to hear a lion roar, and who has any sense, certainly knows to be afraid. Second, the image of the lion roaring in 3:8 also forms an inclusio with 3:4 to accentuate the nearness of judgment. Third, Amos 1:2 (the book's motto) introduced YHWH with the image of a lion whose roar symbolizes judgment. This same metaphor comes back into play in 3:8b, but now the roar of the lion (Adonai YHWH) is perceived by the speaker as a command to prophesy. As a result, 3:1-8 functions as a kind of commission testimony to explain why the prophet feels compelled to pronounce judgment: God, the lion, has made it impossible to resist prophesying.

*Amos 3:9-11.* Amos 3:9-11 possesses all the elements typical of a judgment oracle, albeit with a twist. As expected, one finds the call to attention (3:9), the accusation (3:10), and the punishment (3:11). The object of the judgment (that is, the one who receives the punishment) is the inhabitants of Mount Samaria (that is, Israel). Yet one only learns who is being judged after the call to attention is delivered to the Philistines and Egyptians (3:9). Once again, as with Amos 1–2, judgment against Israel comes surprisingly. Moreover, this connection to the oracles in Amos 1–2 is not coincidental, since the message is proclaimed to the "strongholds" of Ashdod and Egypt, the very word that appeared in the punishment pronouncements of several of the oracles against the nations (1:4, 7, 10, 12, 14; 2:2, 5). Thus, what appears initially to be a pronouncement against the Philistines and Egyptians quickly turns into judgment against Israel once these foreign nations are summoned to observe YHWH's wrath on Israel. In short, the foreign nations become witnesses of God's judgment rather than the objects of it.

The accusation (3:10) brought by God against Israel is broad and ethical in its orientation. Amos charges that they do not know how to behave properly, but instead demonstrate a propensity for violence and theft. Thus, as with 2:6-16, YHWH accuses Israel of acting improperly toward persons and property. Thus, Amos does not debate theological dogma but challenges how Israel's people behave toward one another.

The punishment brought against Israel in 3:11 anticipates the arrival of a foreign enemy who will lay siege to the land, wear down its defenses, and loot its strongholds. Historically, Israel does not fall for another twenty to thirty years after the time of the prophet Amos, and yet this poetic picture corresponds rather closely to what actually happened when the Assyrians did lay siege to Samaria before finally destroying it around 722 BCE.

*Amos 3:12.* Amos 3:12 stands out formally and conceptually. The messenger formula ("Thus says YHWH") signifies a new oracle whose images offer a macabre sense of hope. The comparison in 3:12 hints that rescue may be part of God's intension, but this rescue provides little confidence to those who pause to hear what it is genuinely saying. The rescue that awaits Samaria is likened to a shepherd who "rescues" a piece of a sheep's carcass from the mouth of a lion. That which is rescued (two legs or part of an ear) will hardly recover. The parallel image of Samaria (3:12b) does not compare this "rescued" remnant to a portion of the people. Rather, the second half of the verse compares the remnant of Samaria to pieces of furniture pulled from the rubble. Thus, only body parts and debris will remain after God's judgment.

*Amos 3:13-15.* Amos 3:13-15 focuses the punishment more specifically upon Bethel (3:14), the site where Jeroboam I established a competing shrine with Jerusalem. This competing sanctuary, along with the one in Dan in the northern part of the kingdom, was anathema to the Deuteronomistic Historian who compiled the book of Kings. For that act, not only was Jeroboam condemned but also every northern king after him because they allowed those sanctuaries to continue to exist. For the Deuteronomistic Historian, this act became known as the "sins of Jeroboam" that caused every northern king thereafter to be castigated (1 Kgs 14:16; 15:30; 16:31; 2 Kgs 3:3; 10:29, 31, 13:2, 11; 14:24; 15:9, 18, 24, 28). Reference to the horns of the altar in 3:14 presumes knowledge of the shape of ancient sacrificial altars. (See the illustration "Altars and Pillars.") Destruction of the horns implies destruction of the entire altar.

Amos 3:13 begins with a summons, "Hear and testify against the house of Jacob." Here, the house of Jacob means the northern kingdom, since the follow-up in 3:14 specifies Bethel. Amos 3:14 also draws upon the concept of the day of YHWH, though it does not use the phrase. Rather, by using the refrain language of the oracles in Amos 1–2, Amos 3:14 specifically reminds the reader of the oracle against Israel and the portrait of the Day of the Lord in it.

Amos 3:15 mentions four types of houses (winter, summer, ivory, and great houses). Rhetorically, these four types of houses paint a picture of wealth and power, but they also convey a serious ironic word play. Since the previous verse had announced the destruction of the "house of God" (the English meaning of the word *Bethel* in Hebrew), the prophet now turns his attention to the destruction of human houses. The "ivory" house is typically a house built by kings (1 Kgs 22:39; Ps 45:9), but the list mentions numerous *houses* (plural) of the wealthy, not merely the king. The list includes houses for summer and winter (the dry and the wet seasons respectively), and it alludes to the splendor of houses inlaid

**Ivory Sphinx**
This picture from the Israel Museum in Jerusalem shows an ivory sphinx that was found in the palace of Israelite kings in Samaria from the ninth or eighth century BCE.

Winged sphinx in a lotus thicket. Ivory (open work) from Megiddo, Israel. Phoenician. Israel Museum (IDAM), Jerusalem, Israel. (Credit: Erich Lessing/Art Resource, NY)

with ivory as well as their number (many houses). In short, God threatens to tear down the houses of the powerful, a not-so-subtle way of telling them that their wealth will not save them. (See [Economic Status of Israel] and the illustration "Ivory Sphinx.")

## CONNECTIONS

The sayings in this chapter remind readers of three things: (1) the importance of proclaiming that actions have consequences, (2) the nature of the community of faith, and (3) the character of those on whose behalf God acts. The series of seven rhetorical questions in 3:3-8 bombards the reader with metaphorical images, forcing the reader to ponder the warning through the lens of cause and effect. For those willing to look and listen, signs of danger can be seen and heard. The lion's roar warns others to stay away or suffer the consequences. A hunter's success in using traps requires careful preparation, but those who know what to look for can avoid the bait—thereby avoiding the trap. As well, the sentinel's alarm means danger is within sight.

Three implications—one personal, one communal, and one theological—permeate these verses. *Personally*, the prophet has heard YHWH's call as clearly as a lion's roar. Having seen the problem, the prophet cannot remain silent (3:8) no matter how daunting the task.

In these verses, the *community* is threatened if they do not heed the sound of the trumpet or the voice of the prophet. When alarms sound, we must assess whether they represent real danger. In our own day, we are assailed daily with warnings: newspapers hype terrorist plots, even when details are sketchy; twenty-four-hour news programs warn us of coming pandemics; overzealous weathercasters scream about the potential dangers posed by this year's new round of hurricanes and tornadoes; and when calamity does strike, religious shamans hawk their message that the catastrophe shows God's wrath will not be assuaged. The message comes through time after time: be afraid, be very afraid. And yet, day in and day out, we go about our business, increasingly numb to the dangers that may or may not await us as the day unfolds. Why is that? Because these warnings are not the kind about which Amos speaks. We intuit the severity of these warnings from the blatant self-interest of those promoting them. But Amos speaks of warnings about which he cannot be silent because he has heard the warning from God. He is not selling airtime or asking for donations; he is confronting the elite of Israel who do not understand the danger they pose to themselves and others, and he does so at considerable personal risk.

In Amos, one sees how this risk becomes real when the prophet is expelled from Israel (7:10-17) for speaking out against the king. Modern prophets hardly fare better. Martin Luther King, Jr., was often called a modern prophet. His interest in connecting issues of social justice to Christian ideals helped to change a culture, but it also created resistance that ultimately cost him his life. In American church culture, one often finds that attitudes toward social justice can create divisions within congregations or separate one congregation from another. Recently, however, young Christians have begun to ask why their churches have failed to take seriously the needs of the poor.

The community to whom Amos speaks is not just any community. It is a *theological* community of faith, a community who can recount God's gracious acts of the past as a sign of God's blessing. Yet, this community is dominated by persons of power who believe that God's redemption inoculates them from the consequences of their own behavior. They think they already possess God's redemption because they have been chosen to receive it. But they have lost sight of what that redemption means. God redeemed them for a purpose: namely, to become God's people redeemed from bondage and to testify to the greatness of God before the nations (e.g., Num 22:3; Deut 2:25; Josh 2:9; 4:24; 9:24). Now, however, the nations will see God undo the exodus (3:9) because the elite of this nation have used their power for their own benefit, as already seen in 2:6-16. God is not blind to their hording of wealth and the intimidation of the powerless; God sees their actions, and God will not condone them. In short, God's beneficence is not something that is ever owed, but it's something that can be forfeited by violence and greed. When humans use power to oppress, God stands not with them but with their victims.

# MISSING THE SIGNS AND PAYING THE CONSEQUENCES

## Amos 4:1-13

## COMMENTARY

Amos 4:1 begins the second subsection of Amos 3–6 with the phrase, "Hear this word," the second of three times time this phrase appears, followed by the address of a particular group (see 3:1; 5:1). The chapter contains four units (4:1-3, 4-5, 6-12, 13) that function coherently on their own, but whose sequence emphasizes YHWH's decision to punish the northern kingdom. These four units function as a judgment oracle (4:1-3), an ironic call to worship (4:4-5), a divine rehearsal of Israel's failure to repent and its consequences (4:6-12), and the first of three Creator doxologies in Amos (4:13).

*Amos 4:1-3.* Amos 4:1-3 exhibits the general structure of a judgment oracle:[1] a call to attention ("Hear this word . . ."), a description of the current situation, and the sentencing of imminent judgment. The first element addresses the metaphorical "cows of Bashan," while the second condemns them for their willful neglect of the poor and their selfish preoccupation with their own comfort (4:1). The sentencing phase follows a transitional formula ("the time is surely coming upon you, when . . .") and proclaims imminent judgment in the form of a military defeat and a brutal exile (4:2-3). Finally, a concluding formula marks the end of the unit: utterance of YHWH. Aside from the general structure, one should also note that there is some variation in the gender and number of 4:2, although feminine plural verbs remain dominant throughout 4:1-3.

In 4:1, the prophet addresses the "cows of Bashan," a derogatory metaphor used either (1) to castigate and denigrate the wealthy women of the region for whom Amos apparently holds particular disdain or (2) to refer derogatorily to the warriors of Bashan as women. [Cows of Bashan] The latter tends to take preference in more recent commentaries.

## Cows of Bashan

AΩ Several commentators (e.g., Andersen/Freedman, Rudolph) astutely suggest the term "cows" should be understood ironically and/or sarcastically as a derogatory reference to warriors, who can be compared to bulls to emphasize their strength and virility (Ps 22:12 [MT 22:13]; Jer 50:27). By calling them "cows" rather than bulls, the prophet uses a feminine term designed to shame and mock them.

Wilhelm Rudolph, *Joel—Amos—Obadja—Jona* (Kommentar zum Alten Testament 13/2; Gütersloh: Gütersloher Verlagshaus, 1971) 167.

Francis I. Andersen and David Noel Freedman, *Amos* (AB 24A; New York: Doubleday, 1989) 421, 446–47.

Bashan is a region in Israel known for its fertility. It lies east of the Jordan, north of the region of Gilead, and south of Mount Hermon. A flat plain for the most part, Bashan was renowned for its ability to support cattle (Ps 22:12) and oak trees (Isa 2:13). Because of its fertility, Bashan was a desirable territory. Because it bordered Syria, control of the region was often contested. By the last third of the eighth century BCE, Israel had lost control of it. [Amos's City on a Hill]

The metaphor of cows—whether for women or soldiers—creates a powerful but strange image when one considers the prophet's indictments. Amos levels three charges at these "cows": they oppress the poor, crush the needy, and command their husbands/lords to bring them more to drink. The first two charges typify the message of Amos, who has long been the prophet most noted for issues related to social justice—specifically, expecting the wealthy to help the weak, poor, and marginalized. Understanding the third charge depends upon the identity of the "cows." Most of the

## Amos's City on a Hill

The hill of Samaria was in the tribal territory of Manasseh, but apparently was not significantly inhabited until the time of King Omri (Ahab's father). For the next 160 years, the city was the capital of the northern kingdom, apparently reaching a size of 150 acres (as large as Jerusalem in Hezekiah's time). Samaria is well situated with steep slopes on all sides. This geographical reality is reflected in the history, as Samaria withstood sieges by the Arameans (2 Kgs 6), Assyrians for 3 years (2 Kgs 17), and Hasmoneans for one year.

English versions translate "their lords" (*ʾădōnêhem*) as "husbands," but neither of the typical words used for husband (*ʾîš* or *baʿal*) appear in 4:1. Those interpreting "cows of Bashan" as the women of Israel believe that Amos found the idea of wealthy *women* taking advantage of their wealth—that is, living a life of leisure, partying, and issuing orders—at the expense of the poor and needy to be particularly offensive. If the cows, however, refer to warriors, then "their lords" would refer to the political leaders or to idols, conveying an image where the soldiers are using their power for personal gain and pleasure. In either case, the picture created by this verse is rather

(Credit: Todd Bolen/BiblePlaces.com)

strange. The metaphor paints a picture of a relationship that is the reverse of what it should be. "Cows" do not order "their lords" around, and they should certainly not be taking advantage of the poor and needy.

The image takes another bizarre twist in 4:2, where Amos pronounces the judgment that these "cows" will be carried off on meat hooks and fish hooks. The military nature of the punishment (defeat and exile) seems to raise the likelihood that the "cows" metaphor derides the pride of Israel's warriors rather than the wives of wealthy men.

The phrase "the time is surely coming" is essentially synonymous with "the day of YHWH," a time when God chooses to intervene, usually for judgment. The fact that YHWH has sworn by his holiness signifies the import of this threat. God has taken it seriously enough to swear an oath, and that oath portends disaster for Israel.

*Amos 4:4-5.* Amos 4:4 begins a new unit marked by two masculine plural imperatives, "come" and "transgress," that open an "ironic" call to worship. The end of the unit is marked with a concluding formula as in 4:3. In this new unit the prophet deftly issues a call to worship but ironically inverts that call into an accusation of insincere worship. The call beckons the people to come to two of the more important cultic cities in Israelite tradition, Bethel and Gilgal. Bethel, as already noted, was the site of the northern kingdom's major altar, where the priests could offer sacrifice. Gilgal, also an important place of religious significance, represents one of the major staging points of the conquest in the book of Joshua. Gilgal was the first place the people of Israel camped after crossing the Jordan, and one of the sites where Joshua erected a monument of twelve stones taken from the Jordan (Josh 4:1-9, 19-20). That Gilgal retained its importance as a historical shrine and an ongoing worship center can be inferred from this context.

*Amos 4:6-12.* A new unit begins with 4:6 and runs through 4:12. The unit, placed in the mouth of YHWH, unfolds with a series of statements documenting how YHWH has previously attempted to get Israel's attention by sending various calamities against it, although none of these disasters can be associated with specific events from the time of Amos. [History and Amos 4:6-11] A refrain follows each calamity's description in which YHWH expresses incredulity at Israel's failure to perceive the message, not once but five times (4:6, 8, 9, 10, 11): "yet you did not return to me.

## History and Amos 4:6-11

Scholars have had no luck re-creating the precise events to which Amos 4:6-11 alludes. Hans Walter Wolff sees these verses as a later addition from the time of Josiah, a composition inspired by Josiah's moves against Bethel. He also argues that the writer articulated them replete with echoes to Lev 26 and 1 Kgs 8. Rudolph sees no reason to deny them to the time of Amos, and he believes the culmination in 4:11 refers to the same earthquake mentioned in 1:1. Mays thinks the generic nature of the events derives from regional experience: "By their nature nothing can be said about them as historical occurrences except that they all represent the type of misfortune which happened from time to time in Syria-Palestine." He continues, "The raw material for Amos' narrative certainly lay at hand in the experience of a people for whom life was often nasty, brutish, and short. One need not assume that these misfortunes were either contiguous or contemporary." Andersen/Freedman pinpoint the events to the midpoint of the career of Amos. Jeremias rejects the notion that they were intended to refer to specific historical events, but thinks they refer generically to the people's experience up to and beyond the destruction of Jerusalem, which he thinks is the actual apex of the passage. From this brief review, one can see that the nature of the calamities and the presumptions of the reader lead to significant variations when interpreting this text.

Hans Walter Wolff, *Joel and Amos* (Hermeneia; trans. Waldemar Janzen, S. Dean McBride, Jr., and Charles A. Muenchow; Philadelphia: Fortress, 1977) 212–14, 217–18.

Wilhelm Rudolph, *Joel—Amos—Obadja—Jona* (Kommentar zum Alten Testament 13/2; Gütersloh: Gütersloher Verlagshaus, 1971) 173–74, 180.

James L. Mays, *Amos* (OTL; London: SCM, 1969) 78–79.

Francis I. Andersen and David Noel Freedman, *Amos* (AB 24A; New York: Doubleday, 1989) 421, 446–47.

Jörg Jeremias, *Der Prophet Amos* (Das Alte Testament Deutsch 24/2; Göttingen: Vandenhoeck & Ruprecht, 1995) 50–54.

Utterance of YHWH." Thus, Amos 4:6-12 states in no uncertain terms that the northern kingdom, Israel, has failed to repent, to change its behavior with respect to YHWH. This failure not only has implications for the tenor of the book's message but also constitutes a significant text for understanding the development of the repentance motif in the Book of the Twelve. [Repentance in Amos 4:6-12 and the Book of the Twelve] In Amos 4:6-12, YHWH's actions have become increasingly severe and culminate with a final, dire warning that YHWH's patience has run out. Death is at hand.

In 4:6, YHWH claims to have sent famine. Far from a dentist's dream, clean teeth in the ancient world would have been unthinkable as long as there was food. Rather, as one can see from the parallel in the second half of the verse, this image indicates famine. Amos 4:7-8 speaks of drought caused by the lack of rain. This longest of the five subunits paints an unpleasant picture. In the hot, summer climate the lack of rain would have had terrible consequences on the population, let alone the crops. At most, city water systems at that time would have included a few cisterns but not running water. Intermittent bursts of rainfall would quickly dissipate in the dry ground. Rumors of rain in a neighboring village could send entire populations to those villages in search of water, but water from a single rainfall would not last long. Amos 4:9 describes a series of calamities that had destroyed the land's ability to produce, creating dire consequences. In the past, YHWH struck with blight (caused by too little water) and mildew (caused by too much water), so that vegetation and vines ceased growing. Locusts destroyed the trees needed to produce the staples of the regional diet, figs and olives. The loss of olive trees hurts doubly because

Amos 4:6-12 plays an important role in the Book of the Twelve regarding the recurring motif of repentance. This motif plays a major role in Hosea and functions as the pivot point in the book of Joel (2:12-17). Hosea ends (14:1-3), and Joel begins (1:2–2:17), with calls to repentance followed immediately by divine promises in the event that the people respond positively (Hos 14:5-8; Joel 2:18-27, 28-32; 3:1-21). Yet two issues must be borne in mind in the larger context of the Book of the Twelve. First, the addressees of these two calls to repentance are not the same. Hosea addresses the northern kingdom, while Joel addresses Judah. Second, the promises that follow these calls to repent must be seen literarily and theologically as contingent upon the people's response; yet neither Hosea nor Joel records the response of Israel or Judah. Canonically, Amos 4:6-12 leaves no doubt from YHWH's perspective that the northern kingdom of Israel has *failed* to return (*šûb*). In fact, the book of Amos leaves the clear impression that Israel has squandered its last chance to avoid punishment. Even the "salvific" promises at the end of the book (9:7-10, 11-15) offer hope, but only *after* judgment has been meted out. Later in the Twelve, the question of how Judah will respond to YHWH's prophetic message becomes the focal point of Mic 1–3 (see discussion of Mic 1:2-7). Judah also squanders its opportunity so that by Zeph 1 one finds many of the same dynamics present in YHWH's decision to punish Israel in Amos, but they are applied to Judah. Only in Zech 1:2-6 is the reader of the Book of the Twelve specifically informed that the people actually repent. Thus, it is hardly coincidental that in Hag 2 and in the first night vision of Zechariah (Zech 1:7-20) one finds language reminiscent of Joel that suggests that YHWH begins to fulfill the promises made in Joel 2:18–3:21.

they also provide oil used for everything from candles to cooking. In short, for those reading the Book of the Twelve, Amos 4:9 echoes the language of Joel 1–2.

In 4:10 the litany becomes canonical, alluding to the plagues YHWH used against the Egyptians to force Pharaoh to release Israel to Moses (Exod 7–12). However, in a manner fairly typical of the book of Amos, YHWH's past actions of salvation are now turned against God's people. YHWH is portrayed as having sent plagues against Israel like those he sent against Egypt. In addition, Israel's army is envisioned as the army of Pharaoh, utterly decimated by the warrior YHWH. YHWH struck Israel's soldiers and carried away its horses, so that the smell of the bodies in the camp became overwhelming. In 4:10, Israel replaces Egypt and Pharaoh as the group who foolishly stands in YHWH's way.

The canonical allusions continue in 4:11, working their way backwards with a reference to the destruction of Sodom and Gomorrah in Genesis 19. As with these fated cities of old, 4:11 implies that YHWH, Israel's own God, has randomly destroyed some of Israel's towns, presumably with the same cataclysmic force of raining down fire and brimstone. [Random Acts] Within the terrifying analogy of 4:11, those who survived barely escaped: they "were like a brand snatched from the fire."

After spending several lines reminding listeners of past calamities, YHWH reveals what will happen next. Given the calamities in

## Random Acts

The idea expressed in Amos 4:11 creates a theological conundrum, but one that is hardly new. Amos 4:6-11 implies that God has randomly selected portions of the kingdom to punish with rain (4:7) and then with cosmic destruction (4:11) in order to "cajole" others in the kingdom to return. Because they do not get the "hint," Amos 4:12 announces a more severe form of destruction on the entire kingdom. This image, taken in isolation, presents a distorted view of God. The rhetorical point of 4:6-11 uses language of various calamities to admonish Israel for disregarding the prophetic warnings and for abandoning faithfulness to YHWH, but the image of God arbitrarily and actively selecting groups to punish in order to deliver others should be challenged on broader biblical and theological grounds. The flip side of this argument also plays out in recent theological discussions about Divine passivity. Can we talk about random suffering without implying God is apathetic to suffering? Can we talk about God intervening without indicting God as a co-conspirator who allows evil and suffering to exist?

For further reading, see Joel S. Burnett, *Where Is God? Divine Absence in the Hebrew Bible* (Minneapolis: Fortress, 2010); and Daniel Castelo, *The Apathetic God: Exploring the Contemporary Relevance of Divine Impassibility* (Paternoster Theological Monographs; Milton Keynes UK: Paternoster, 2009). Recent theological treatments focus upon the mystery of suffering, the complex role of the cross for Christian communities of faith, and the role of covenant. These discussions do not resolve the dilemmas, but they do help to throw it into sharp contrast.

4:6-11, one should not underestimate the rhetorical power of the first word of 4:12—that is, "therefore" (*lākēn*). This word typically signals the verdict in judgment oracles. What becomes clear with the beginning of 4:12, however, is that the disasters of 4:6-11—with descriptions of YHWH's past punishments and a refrain condemning Israel's failure to return to YHWH—have all been but a prelude to the pronouncement that YHWH is now about to make. Unlike the descriptions of past judgments, 4:12 contains no reference to an expected return (*šûb*) to YHWH. Rather, the omission of this detail from the pronouncement of judgment in 4:12 is both ominous and ironic: because all this did not cause you to return to YHWH, now "Prepare to meet your God, Israel." Needless to say, this phrase, "to meet God," does not connote a pleasant encounter. It means the end is near.

*Amos 4:13.* Amos 4:13 constitutes the first of three so-called "doxologies" in Amos. These three doxologies (4:13; 5:8-9; 9:5-6) stand out for their hymnic style, their recurring language, their focus on creation, and the disjunctures they create in their contexts. [Three Doxologies in Amos] It seems wise to approach these hymnic pieces from two directions: first, what they have in common, and then how they relate to their current contexts. To begin with, these doxologies share two general themes—(1) that YHWH created the world and (2) that YHWH has the power to destroy it—that intersect one another by repeating phrases, especially some form of the phrase "YHWH is his name." Regarding this phrase, neither its form nor its placement is identical in all three passages. Nevertheless, despite this variety, the common focus on identifying YHWH by name cannot be ignored. Concerning the theme of creation, Amos 4:13 speaks of God's primordial creativity in the world (forming the mountains and creating the wind) and the ongoing creative processes in nature (changing daylight to darkness). Amos

**Three Doxologies in Amos**

Many of the commentaries in the twentieth century, relying on source-critical work, argue that these three doxologies constitute fragments of a single hymn, portions of which were split into three parts and placed in their current locations. Attempts to reconstruct the original hymn based on various criteria have not produced any consensus, and such attempts have largely been abandoned. The stylistic peculiarity of these pieces has created a significant consensus that they represent additions to Amos during the exilic or early postexilic periods.

| 4:13 | 5:8-9 | 9:5-6 |
|---|---|---|
| For lo, the one who forms the mountains, creates the wind, reveals his thoughts to mortals, *makes the morning darkness*, and treads on the heights of the earth—the LORD, the God of hosts, is his name! | The one who made the Pleiades and Orion, and *turns deep darkness into the morning*, and darkens the day into night, *who calls for the waters of the sea, and pours them out on the surface of the earth*, the LORD is his name, who makes destruction flash out against the strong, so that destruction comes upon the fortress. | The Lord, GOD of hosts, he who touches the earth and it melts, and all who live in it mourn, and all of it rises like the Nile, and sinks again, like the Nile of Egypt; who builds his upper chambers in the heavens, and founds his vault upon the earth; *who calls for the waters of the sea, and pours them out upon the surface of the earth*—the LORD is his name. |

Attempts to describe these doxologies, however, as the conclusion of significant versions of the book of Amos have also failed to generate unanimity because only the first and third of these doxologies currently appear at clear breaking points in the collection. Thus, their investigation has led in conflicting directions. On the one hand, there is little doubt that these three passages are interrelated. On the other hand, they stand out so dramatically from the contexts that it is not readily apparent why all three of these appear where they do.

For additional reading, see James L. Crenshaw, *Hymnic Affirmation of Divine Justice: The Doxologies of Amos and Related Texts in the Old Testament* (Missoula: Scholars Press, 1975); Jörg Jeremias, *Der Prophet Amos* (Das Alte Testament Deutsch 24/2; Göttingen: Vandenhoeck & Ruprecht, 1995) 56–58.

5:8-9, on the other hand, speaks of YHWH's creative activity in the heavens (creating the constellations of Pleiades and Orion) and expands reference to the creative processes in nature (darkness to light, light to darkness). Finally, Amos 9:5-6 also draws upon the cosmic creation of the heavens (creation of the chambers and vault of YHWH). In short, a pattern of recapitulation emerges regarding this theme: an element in the first doxology is repeated in the second; the second doxology introduces another element, which is then recalled in the third doxology.

When one looks at the imagery related to the second theme, one finds an increasing threat. Amos 4:13 hints at YHWH's destructive power using theophanic images ("the one who treads on the heights of the earth"), which elsewhere typically evoke YHWH's arrival for judgment (e.g., Mic 1:3). Amos 5:8-9 brings judgment more explicitly into view with language of the primordial chaos battle (calling forth the waters of the sea) and the flood story (pouring out waters on the face of the earth). This second doxology then portrays YHWH's judgment against the people and their fortresses. Thus, this portrait shows that the flood imagery is not intended literally as another all-encompassing flood—which God had promised never to do (Gen 9:11)—but as a symbol of YHWH's destructive power. Similar use of creation and flood motifs are also directed against Judah in Zephaniah 1:2-3. Finally, Amos 9:5-6 expands God's universal judgment to include the melting of the earth and a devastating earthquake, again evoking the same watery chaos language of 5:8-9. Thus, as with the previous theme, a pattern begins to emerge, but this time it is a pattern of movement rather than of recapitulation. Indeed, the creation imagery moves from the earth to the stars to the heavens. Moreover, the destruction imagery increases exponentially. The net result is that YHWH's power is more clearly avowed and increasingly destructive, especially as it is turned toward the judgment of the northern kingdom.

Having dealt with what the doxologies have in common, one can now explore how they function in their contexts. The key, in each case, is to recognize the focus upon YHWH himself. The first doxology follows the command, "prepare to meet your God." It seems appropriate that this command be followed by an extended description of who YHWH is (4:13). It is important that this description contains a unique element not recurrent in other doxologies, namely YHWH's revelation of his thoughts to humanity. This idea echoes—albeit obliquely since the wording is not identical—the idea that culminated the opening unit of the previous chapter (Amos 3:7): YHWH has revealed his secrets to the prophets so that they would, in turn, reveal that message to others. The second doxology, 5:8-9, also follows an imperative regarding YHWH: "Seek YHWH and live [. . .] You who turn justice into wormwood" (5:6-7). This imperative essentially calls the people to make a decision to find YHWH for the second time (see 5:4); however, the accusations that follow in 5:10-12 make it clear literarily that Israel will not change. The doxology provides a pause between these two elements, effectively conveying the escalating danger from YHWH's judgments to the hearers/readers. The third doxology, 9:5-6, follows YHWH's definitive statement, "I will fix my eyes on them for harm and not for good" (9:4). Next, the destruction language of 9:5-6 contains theophanic imagery in which God's appearance causes the earth to melt and shake, and the inhabitants to mourn. This doxology coincides with the imagery of the destruction of Samaria in 9:1 with the shaking/shattering of the sanctuary thresholds, a judgment that results in the death of the people of the northern kingdom. In short, each doxology has some thematic connection to its literary setting. While these connections are not so close as to require these hymns to have been written for their location, they are clear enough to suggest someone has placed these hymnic pieces purposefully. The first (4:13) connects the God of creation with an emphasis upon God's revelation; the second (5:8-9) creates a transitional pause to reflect upon the cosmic power of YHWH after a call to seek YHWH; and the third (9:5-6) warns of destruction by correlating the shaking of the northern kingdom with the shaking of the cosmos.

## CONNECTIONS

The God portrayed in Amos 4 is unpalatable for many today who believe in a sanitized, neutralized, and ultimately trivialized deity who offers comfort without upsetting the status quo. Amos 4:6-11 poses a theological dilemma for modern believers by presupposing a cause-and-effect theology that runs the danger of portraying God as a judge who becomes violent when he does not get his way. Some tension will always be present as readers try to wrestle with the vengeance of God because the Old and New Testaments both portray God as one willing and able to execute judgment and as one capable of using many means to bring about change. In the end, two things appear striking about Amos 4:6-11: God's use of creation for the purpose of judgment, and (once again) God's decision to exercise this judgment against God's own people.

The danger of seeing Amos 4:6-11 in isolation lies at two extremes: universality and irrelevance. First and foremost, this passage is not universally applicable. God does not sit in heaven casting lightning bolts toward unsuspecting humans in fits of divine anger, even though the Bible not infrequently portrays God in these terms. In an age when satellites can track weather patterns across the nation and when radar can pinpoint the movement of thunderstorms and tornadoes down to a few blocks, one must come to terms with the ways in which the ancients viewed natural calamities as signs of a deity's displeasure. In the intervening 2,700 years since the time of Amos, humanity has learned a great deal more about the causes and patterns of weather-related disasters. The very predictability of such devastation and the concomitant ability to issue warnings in the face of such disasters tell us incontrovertibly that storms, tornadoes, floods, hurricanes, earthquakes, drought, and the like are a part of natural phenomena built into the way creation functions. In the aftermath of Hurricane Katrina (in 2005), religious opportunists proclaimed the decimation of the Gulf Coast as God's wrath visited upon New Orleans for its wickedness. Such charges, by and large, rang hollow because of the large-scale devastation extending across much of the Gulf Coast, not just New Orleans, and because of the relatively small amount of damage experienced by the French Quarter, arguably the epicenter of the kind of behavior those preachers railed against. People are not easily sold on the idea that God would choose to devastate a 500-mile wide swath of coast in order to punish people for activities on a single street. For many, the idea that God arbitrarily chooses targets for his wrath, without care for collateral damage, represents a kind of "bogeyman" theology that has no place in the modern world. Such theology, at best, may serve to curb the immoral behavior of a few out of fear. However, it does little to convey the love of God or to motivate people to serve others in the name of God. Such a God soon becomes irrelevant.

Still, Amos 4:6-11 creates a sense of theological discomfort because it claims God has acted directly, using natural disasters, to punish a wayward people. Admittedly, this unease is not easily dismissed, yet two issues help mitigate some of the problems. First, like the drama of the plague narratives in Exodus 7–12, Amos 4:6-11 attests to the failure of natural calamities to bring about human repentance on a large scale. In the ancient world where natural disasters such as drought, floods, and famine occurred all too frequently, and in the modern world where the conditions for such phenomena can be tracked and predicted to some degree, it is impossible for most people to tell which calamity results from the hand of God and which to attribute to the random, uncontrollable power of nature. Surely God has noticed how ineffective such means have become, if repentance is the goal. Second, as the recent work by T. Fretheim has shown, the symbiotic relationships among God, humanity, and creation provide a healthy perspective from which to counterbalance cause-and-effect theology. When speaking of Amos 4:6-13, Fretheim reiterates the interrelatedness of creation, sin, order, judgment, and salvation:

> The moral order is fundamentally a matter of creation, built into the very infrastructure of God's cosmic design. That sins will have adverse consequences is fundamentally a matter of the way in which the world works; ill effects are intrinsically related to the deed. And so, it is a natural theological move for the prophet to follow the strong indictment and oracles of judgments (experienced and anticipated) with a word about creation.[2]

Fretheim reminds the reader that Amos also depicts salvation and restoration in terms of creation language (9:11-15). He tries to explain the tension by describing the language as metaphor:

> Amos's recurrent use of references to the natural order and the linking he draws to human words and deeds cannot be reduced to poetic imagery [. . .] The word *metaphor* is appropriate here, providing one does not deny continuity between language and reality, recognizing the yes as well as the no in all metaphoric language. The natural order is *actually* affected by human behaviors; social order and cosmic order are in fact deeply interrelated.[3]

Fretheim essentially embraces the tension of cause-and-effect theology without feeling compelled to explain every calamity as God's direct intervention, yet recognizing an indissoluble link between human action and consequences for the natural order. In short, to the extent that God becomes involved, God does so because of God's relationship with creation and humanity.

> God has a future in store for the entire created order, not just human beings. For the sake of that future—a new heaven and a new earth—God's salvific activity catches up every creature. The need for such a comprehensive divine activity is, most fundamentally, to be laid at the door of human decisions and actions. While human faithfulness could lead to blessing for the natural order [. . .] human sin has had a deeply negative effect upon all creatures, as is clear from the beginning of the Bible (Gen 3:17-19; 9:2-3) [. . .] The close interrelatedness is characteristic of the entire Old Testament, [. . .] sometimes explicitly associated with judgment (Isaiah 24–27; Jer 4:23-28; Amos 4:6-11), sometimes not (Hos 4:1-3). Judgment on

Israel and the nations may be specifically designed as a divine action on behalf of the land (e.g., Lev 26:32-43). While there is no indication that every "disruption" in the natural world is the effect of human sin (including earthquakes, famines, and wild animals [. . .]) human sin has resulted in the degradation of the environment. Given this link between moral order and cosmic order, human redemption must be accomplished in order for this destructive cycle to be stopped.[4]

In the case of Hurricane Katrina and its aftermath, one need not see God as the direct source of the hurricane in order to understand the extent to which human actions, or inaction, exacerbated suffering. [Human Suffering and Divine Presence] Had someone decided decades ago to build stronger levies, flooding in and around New Orleans would have been greatly reduced. Had governmental agencies had better plans in place for evacuation, the number of deaths would have been fewer. Had wetlands around the city not been diverted to make way for human habitation, natural buffers would have lessened the force of the water that made it inland. Choices have consequences; moral values affect the natural world; we must recognize the interrelatedness of nature, humanity, and God; these are the lessons of cause-and-effect theology regarding nature.

## NOTES

1. See [Prophetic Judgment Oracle].

2. Terence E. Fretheim, *God and the World in the Old Testament: A Relational Theology of Creation* (Nashville: Abingdon, 2005) 169.

3. Ibid., 171.

4. Ibid., 194.

## Human Suffering and Divine Presence

Seen from the perspective of one who survived Hurricane Katrina, the anxiety, sadness, and mourning over what happened are often juxtaposed with joy, gratitude, and relief that they have survived. God is present for the one in the midst of calamity. One survivor's story illustrates the conflicted feelings. She took her twelve-year-old son with her, but her husband stayed behind because he worked for the school board:

> I would not have left if I had not had a 12 year old. I left, *praying for the best*, and went to Alabama. On Monday morning, my husband called me from St.Bernard and told me that the *worst seemed to be over*, and it did not look too bad. I told him we would be home on Tuesday. About 10 min. later, after he hung up, he said the water came pouring into the parish. *Thank God* I did not know this at the time!

She did not make it to Alabama, but got stranded in Mississippi at a hotel that had no electricity. Consequently, she had no food and no power for her cell phone. She was all but out of gas, but no one had had any gas to sell for nearly four days:

> On Thursday, someone told me that they were going to start selling gas at Walmart, so I drove there *praying I had enough gas to get there*.

While waiting for the gas station to open the next morning, she borrowed a cell phone, and her daughter arranged for a cousin to drive to her with gas. She was finally able to complete her trek to family:

> I have never been *so glad* to see someone!! He filled my van up, and we followed him to Jackson. It was around 3 in the morning by this time. I fell asleep as soon as we got there. I had only been sleeping about 2 hours when my husband called and said to come pick him up in Lake Charles. I got up, showered and drove straight there. I was so *happy to see him* and know that he was okay.
> It was then, that I learned that our house was completely under water, and the entire parish was under water. *I was devastated.* After staying in Jackson for a week, my aunt in Young Harris, GA., invited us to come

> stay with her *in an empty trailer* on her property. It was *beautiful* up there, and just what we needed to be in the mountains and get out thoughts and decisions made about the future. We finally got to go visit our home in October, and once again, the *devastation* floored me. Everything we owned was gone. I sat on the backporch and *cried, and was angry* at the same time. We went back to GA, and stayed there until February, until my husband got called back to work at the school. We bought a home in Poplarville, MS., because we wanted to be *as far away from the wreckage* as possible. It has not been easy starting over, and we miss our families and friends who lived who lived in St. Bernard. Most, like us, did not return, and it is difficult to have 35 years of your life taken away. I lost my job, my home, my friends, my family, and most of all, a way of life that I had always known. Many people say, just get on with your life . . . . That would be good, but how do you do that when everything you have ever known is gone in just a day? I will always feel an *emptiness* inside for the life we had before. But, *I thank God* for all He has done for us, and is still doing for us.

The difference between the perspective of this story and the perspective of Amos 4:6-11 reflects more than a cultural shift. This story is told from the perspective of the victim of a random act while Amos 4:6-11 takes on a metahistorical perspective, trying to provide meaning to past troubles in order to change the attitudes of the present listener. To do so, it ignores questions about the victims of the previous acts that appear random, in order to provide a certain kind of meaning to those whom the prophet addresses. The problem with Amos 4:6-11, theologically speaking, comes when one shifts the focus to those whom the prophet is claiming God has terminated in order to change the nation. By contrast, this story is told from the lens of someone who experienced calamity beyond measure, as though encompassing the calamities of Amos 4:6-11 and Job together. From her vantage point, the words of Amos 4:6-11 would depict a rather brutish and heavy-handed deity.

For the complete story recounted by Lucy Juneau, along with the stories of other survivors, see Lucy Juneau, "Untitled," Hurricane Digital Memory Bank, Object #42702, 1 June 2010, http://www.hurricanearchive.org/object/42702.

# LAMENTING THE LACK OF JUSTICE AND RIGHTEOUSNESS

## Amos 5:1-27

## COMMENTARY

The sayings in Amos 5 are just that, a series of eleven more or less independent units (5:1-2, 3, 4-7, 8-9, 10-12, 13, 14-15, 16-17, 18-20, 21-24, 25-27) whose sequential compilation hammers home a message of judgment against the northern kingdom because of its improper worship and lack of social justice. The resulting mosaic does not detail the fate of the people in consistent terms, but the effect of the whole underscores the prophet's sense of the danger Israel faces. A few preliminary examples are in order here. To begin with, some of the sayings presume that the destruction is already underway (5:1-2, 13, 14-15), while other sayings presume that the destruction is imminent (5:3, 4-7, 10-12, 16-17, 18-20, 21-24, 25-27). Several of these units, on the one hand, hint that a small remnant will remain, although the emphasis clearly lies on the destruction of the kingdom (5:3, 13, 14-15). The remaining units, on the other hand, do not mention a remnant. Finally, one of the units (5:3) presumes that destruction will result from a large military battle, while others focus on exile as punishment (5:4-7, 27). Still others leave the means of the destruction ambiguous (5:10-12, 16-17, 18-20).

*Amos 5:1-2.* This unit begins the third subsection of Amos 3–6 with the same call to attention that began the first two subsections (3:1; 4:1: "Hear this word . . ."). The ominous perspective of this unit, however, is provided by the genre it mimics (a dirge). [Dirges] Using personification, Amos 5:1-2 signals a decided shift to the reader, for it presumes Maiden Israel [Maiden Israel] has been destroyed: "fallen, no more to rise." In all likelihood, this unit comes from the tradents who compiled this collection of sayings, for (especially after 4:12) it plays an important role by suggesting that Israel will not

## Dirges

AΩ A dirge is a song or chant that accompanies a funeral procession. The Hebrew word *bĕtûlat* used in Amos 5:1 can be translated as "lamentation" (NRS, KJV), "dirge" (NAS, Tanach), or "funeral song" (NET). Jer 9:20 and Ezek 32:16 imply that such funeral songs were the craft of professional mourners, women who were paid to accompany the funeral march. Women were not, however, the only ones who are recounted as singing a dirge since prophetic texts also command the people (Ezek 19:1), the prophet (Ezek 27:2), or leaders (26:17) to do so, and one text even assigns the task to YHWH (Jer 9:9 [MT, but see LXX, which changes the first person, common gender, singular (1cs) report "I will take up a dirge" to a command to the people "take up a dirge"]). Dirges were composed for kings or military leaders as well (e.g., 1 Sam 31:13; 2 Sam 1:12; 3:31-34). In some instances, figurative aspects may be elicited by rhythmic connotations, as a 2-3 meter could mimic the slow rhythmic march of the funeral procession. In Amos 5:1, the significance of the reported dirge implies that "Virgin Israel" (5:2) is already dead in the eyes of the prophet.

For further reading, see Hermann Gunkel, *An Introduction to the Psalms* (trans. James D. Nogalski; Mercer Library of Biblical Studies; Macon GA: Mercer University Press, 1998) 100; Sigmund Mowinckel, *The Psalms in Israel's Worship* (trans. D.R. Ap-Thomas; The Biblical Resource Series; Grand Rapids: Eerdmans, 2004) 27–28; and G. Fleischer, "*qînâ*," in *Theological Dictionary of the Old Testament* (Grand Rapids: Eerdmans, 2004) 13:17–23.

## Maiden Israel

AΩ NRSV translates *bĕtûlat* Israel in Amos 5:2 as "Maiden Israel" even though it represents the same title elsewhere translated more literally as "Virgin Daughter." One finds in the prophets several instances where geographic regions (primarily cities) are personified with the title "Virgin Daughter X" (*bĕtûlat bat*): Isa 23:12 (Sidon); 37:22 ("Zion" = Jerusalem); 47:1 (Babylon); Jer 14:17 ("my people" = Jerusalem); 46:11 (Egypt). Three places in Jeremiah use the same phrase as Amos, "Virgin Israel" (Jer 18:13; 31:4; 31:21), to refer to the country as a whole, though all three are translated as "Virgin Israel." See also the discussion of Joel 1:8 and Hos 2 where the land is personified as a woman. The honorific title in Amos 5:2 personifies the region with a phrase connoting beauty and youth, making her death all the more poignant.

avoid punishment, despite the pleas that Israel seek YHWH in order to live (5:4, 6, 14). This call to attention—with its lamentation over the fallen "house of Israel" or "Maiden Israel"—colors everything that follows.

*Amos 5:3.* This new unit begins with its own introductory messenger formula ("Thus says YHWH . . ."), although the enclitic particle (*kî*, translated "for" or "because") formally ties it to the preceding unit. Initially, this particle sets up the verse as an explanation for why "Maiden Israel" has fallen in 5:2. If 90 percent of the military force is decimated, then that army is defeated. The logic of this reading, however, soon collapses. The next unit (5:4-7) begins precisely like 5:3, but 5:4 extends an invitation for the people to seek YHWH in order to live, whereas 5:3 indicates that YHWH's decision to execute judgment has already been made. In short, the enclitic particle cannot be understood as indicative of a causal relationship, either between 5:1-2 and 5:3, or 5:3 and 5:4-7. Rather, each of these units appears to be an independent saying. The focus of 5:3 is on the future destruction, not the remnant left behind, and its message is formulated as a threat, not as hope that some will survive.

*Amos 5:4-7.* Amos 5:4 begins with the same introductory messenger formula as 5:3. Extending through v. 7, this unit divides in two parts: the first comes from the mouth of YHWH (5:4-5), but the second speaks of

YHWH in the third person (5:6-7). Otherwise, both parts are remarkably parallel, offering a similar message in the form of an imperative admonition (seek me/YHWH and live) followed by a threat against Bethel and others.

Amos 5:4-5 unfolds as a contrast between choosing the proper or improper object of worship and death. As the proper object of worship, YHWH provides the source and hope for life, while Bethel and Gilgal (improper objects of worship) offer only hopelessness and death, for Gilgal will be exiled and Bethel destroyed. Three place names appear in the threat in 5:5. The combination of Bethel and Gilgal has already appeared in Amos 4:4-5, representing the premier religious centers of the northern kingdom. By contrast, Beer-sheba is a city that is in southern Judah, not Israel (see also 8:14). Further, while the people are commanded not to cross over to Beer-sheba, no explicit threat against Beer-sheba follows. As one of the southern kingdom's religious centers, Beer-sheba serves as a focal point in the ancestral traditions of Abraham, Isaac, and Jacob. [Beer-sheba] Thus, rather than pronouncing punishment on Beer-sheba, Amos warns the northern kingdom with a series of imperatives against bringing syncretistic practices to the southern kingdom.

> **Beer-sheba**
>
> Beer-sheba was a town that traditionally represented the southernmost boundary of Judah (about 45 miles southwest of Jerusalem), though some see these references as an idealized border. In biblical texts, Beer-sheba has two stories of its founding, one with Abraham (Gen 21:22-34) and one with Isaac (Gen 26:23-33), both of which play off the meaning of the name. Beer-sheba either means "well of oath" or "well of seven." Both the number seven and the oath play a key role in the etiological narrative of the well in the Abraham version, while the oath takes primary importance in the Isaac version.

This warning, intrusive as it is, reflects one of the editorial concerns in the development of the books of Hosea, Amos, Micah, and Zephaniah, where the progressive deterioration of God's people begins in the northern kingdom and then moves to the southern kingdom. The focus of this motif transitions to the south in Micah 1:2-9; 3:12. As in the Deuteronomistic History (e.g., 2 Kgs 17), the destruction of the northern kingdom should be taken as a warning by the southern kingdom and Jerusalem that they too could suffer the same fate and that they must do something to avoid it; namely, they must seek YHWH and worship YHWH as their God, not worship idols or blend the worship of Baal with the worship of YHWH.

Following the command to seek YHWH, the parallel statement in Amos 5:6-7 expands the threat in 5:4-5 by including Bethel *and* "the House of Joseph." This phrase essentially implies the entire northern kingdom, drawing from the immediate context and from the Joseph tradition in which Joseph was given the double portion of the tribal lands via his two sons Manasseh and Ephraim (see Gen 48:8-21; Deut 33:17; Josh 16:6; 17:17; Isa 9:21). Their allotment makes up the central corridor on the eastern and western side of Jordan, and Bethel is situated in the tribal land of Ephraim.

The threat in this subunit also evokes images from the larger context of Amos. In retrospect, the threat of fire as the means of destruction echoes the threats within the oracles against the nations (1:4, 7, 10, 12, 14; 2:2, 4), where Israel is the only nation that is not threatened with fire. Subsequent to this independent saying, the prophet again envisions a destructive fire in the second of Amos's five visions (Amos 7:4-6; see also discussion of 5:27).

Amos 5:7 provides the accusation for this unit (5:4-7): those to whom the prophet speaks have subverted justice and righteousness. [Justice and Righteousness] This verse presents the first of three times in Amos (see also 5:24; 6:12) where justice and righteousness are used as parallel terms. In one sense, these two terms are close to one another, at times being virtually synonymous. If, however, these two terms can be distinguished from one another, the combined pair emphasizes deeds to honor YHWH (righteousness) and deeds designed to do the right thing toward one's fellow human being (justice).

*Amos 5:8-9.* Amos 5:8-9 provides an emphatic pause to the admonitions of 5:4-7. As the second of three Creator doxologies in Amos (see the discussion of 4:13), the inclusion of this doxology stresses the name of YHWH, articulates YHWH's power over cre-

---

**Justice and Righteousness**

According to Wolff, in Amos, *justice*

means that order which establishes and preserves peace under the law; this order is realized in practice through the legal decisions made in the gate, where matters of local jurisdiction were settled. "Righteousness" designates behavior which is in keeping with this order, e.g., the willingness of one who himself is legally "in the right" to stand up in defense of another who [. . .] has been unjustly accused (cf. 2:6 and 5:12).

*Righteousness* also has to do with how one honors relationships, relationships that can be social, juridical, or covenantal.

The concept deserves some negative definitions. In the OT it is not behavior in accordance with an ethical, legal, psychological, religious, or spiritual norm. It is not conduct which is dictated by either human or divine nature, no matter how undefiled. It is not an action appropriate to the attainment of a specific goal. It is not an impartial ministry to one's fellow men. It is not equivalent to giving every man his just due. Rather, righteousness is in the OT the fulfillment of the demands of a relationship, whether that relationship be with men or with God. Each man is set within a multitude of relationships: king with people, judge with complainants, priests with worshipers, common man with family, tribesman with community, community with resident alien and poor, all with God. And each of these relationships brings with it specific demands, the fulfillment of which constitutes righteousness. The demands may differ from relationship to relationship; righteousness in one situation may be unrighteousness in another. Further, there is no norm of righteousness outside the relationship itself. When God or man fulfils the conditions imposed upon him by a relationship, he is, in OT terms, righteous.

Hans Walter Wolff, *Joel and Amos* (trans. Waldemar Janzen et al.; Hermeneia; Philadelphia: Fortress, 1977) 245.

Elizabeth R. Achtemeier, "Righteousness in the OT," *IDB* (New York: Abingdon, 1962) 4: 80.

ation, and escalates the threat against Israel in comparison to the previous doxology. The rationale for locating this particular doxology, or hymnic fragment (see discussion of 4:13), is not immediately clear, but even though it does not end a major unit like 4:13 or 9:6-7, Amos 5:8-9 does play a role in emphasizing YHWH's power over creation and the impending threat against Israel.

*Amos 5:10-12.* Amos 5:10-12 begins and ends with accusations directed against the wealthy and powerful about improper activity in the gate. In the center of this unit, 5:11 pronounces YHWH's verdict against the wealthy and the landowners. Amos 5:10 brings the first accusation in the form of two parallel lines directed against an unspecified group. Two possibilities could account for this lack of identity. First, if 5:10-12 continues 5:4-7—interrupted by the insertion of the second Creator doxology—then the identity of the group would be the same as 5:4-7: specifically, those causing injustice and unrighteousness cited in 5:7. Second, since these short units in Amos do not always identify the group to whom they are addressed, it is possible that the intended group is already specified in the repeated introductions to the blocks of material in 3:1; 4:1; and 5:1. [Economic Situation in the Eighth Century]

The accusation in 5:10 speaks of this group's animosity toward the one who is "in the gate," who is acting with principles of righteousness and justice. The activities this hated individual performs are formulated in broad terms that could be used to describe prophets, elders, judges, or witnesses in a trial. These actions suit the context of the city gate in the ancient Near East, where a number of public proceedings took place, including trials, contract disputes, and other matters of local justice (Deut 21:19; 25:7; Ruth 4:11). These formulations emphasize that the place of public justice has become the home of rampant corruption. Amos 5:11a continues the accusations, but instead of dealing with attitudes (hating, abhorring), it deals with specific actions (trampling on the poor, demanding payments of grain). The first charge probably reflects figurative language for actions that deni-

### Economic Situation in the Eighth Century

Much has been made of the economic changes experienced by Israel and Judah in the eighth century. The early and middle portions of the century saw long, stable kingships under Uzziah of Judah (786–746) and Jeroboam II of Israel (786–746). The economic boon was particularly strong in Israel, but as is often the case, not everyone benefited equally. Disparity between the classes became exaggerated during this time, though some think Israel became stronger economically and militarily than Judah. For example, Andersen and Freedman consider Uzziah and Jeroboam II to be equals who coordinated an expansionist military strategy in the decade between 765–755 BCE before the rise of Tiglath-Pileser II and the Assyrian Empire. By contrast, Marvin Sweeney sees Jeroboam and Israel as the more powerful partner who took advantage of Judean landowners like Amos.

Francis Andersen and David Noel Freedman, *Amos* (AB 24A; New York: Doubleday, 1989) 18–23.

Marvin A. Sweeney, *The Twelve Prophets* (Berit Olam, vol. 1; Collegeville: Liturgical Press, 2000) 192–95.

grate, ignore, or worsen the plight of the poor, while the second charge condemns the wealthy who are benefiting from taxing the poor.

The punishment of the oracle announced in 5:11b essentially reverses the Deuteronomic blessing (e.g., Deut 8:12) in a manner reminiscent of the curses of Deuteronomy 28:30, 39. Within the Book of the Twelve, this same curse reappears in Zephaniah 1:13, where it is applied to Judah in much the same way Amos applies it to Judah. This motif is one of several connecting Amos and Zephaniah, illustrating their parallel functions within the larger corpus, namely to pronounce judgment unequivocally upon Israel (Amos) and Judah (Zephaniah) in the Book of the Twelve.

*Amos 5:13.* On several fronts, Amos 5:13 complicates any description of the units in this chapter as a single, cohesive composition. First, although the verse relates itself to the preceding unit by means of the word "therefore" (*lākēn*), the function of this conjunction does not, however, introduce a verdict as one would expect. Instead of a verdict against those who abuse the poor in the gate (5:10-12), Amos 5:13 is taken as a warning or a continuation of the problem. Depending upon how one interprets the verb, as a jussive or as a simple imperfect, one could translate the verse as an exhortation ("The prudent should keep silent . . . for it is an evil time") or as a continuation of the problem (the prudent remain silent). To maintain silence contrasts markedly with the role of the prophet presented in Amos. Elsewhere, Amos confronts injustice and unrighteousness directly, and Amos 2:12 condemns those who seek to silence the prophets. Finally, the place where one finds the closest parallels to the idea of the prudence of silence is within Proverbs (e.g., 11:12; 13:3; 17:27), providing a greater affinity to wisdom literature than prophetic texts.

The better way of interpreting this verse in context treats "therefore" as introducing the implications of the accusation of 5:10-12: because the wealthy and powerful hate those who speak the truth, the wise remain silent out of a desire for self-preservation. "Therefore" connects Amos 5:13 to the problem of 5:10-12. It does not advocate silence in the face of injustice. Rather, it indicates that the caution of the prudent ones when facing overwhelming evil only allows the wicked more space. This simple imperfect would mean that remaining silent only compounds the situation.

*Amos 5:14-15.* This unit presents a series of interrelated imperatives and suggests that a remnant of the northern kingdom will endure if they behave as YHWH desires. In 5:14, the command to "seek good and not evil" is tied to two purpose clauses: (1) "so that you will live" and (2) "so that YHWH . . . will be with you." In 5:15, three commands (hate evil; love good; establish justice in the gate) extend the imperatives of 5:14 in hopes of persuading YHWH to show mercy. Given the situation of injustice "in the gate" described in 5:10-12, these four commands represent nothing short of a complete reversal of the situation that currently exists.

The phrase "remnant of Joseph" presupposes the devastation of Israel as a reality, and it contrasts with assumptions of the phrase "house of Joseph" in 5:6. Various explanations for dating this unit have been offered: the 740s after Assyria begins to be a threat, during the Syro-Ephraimite war (734–733), and the period after Israel's destruction in 722. Likely, in this unit a later hand reflects upon events in the aftermath of Assyrian incursion. In any case, Israel has experienced some type of devastation. Moreover, the fate of this remnant remains contingent upon YHWH, who will only react positively *perhaps*, if the situation of injustice and unrighteousness is reversed. [Amos 5:14-15 and the Book of the Twelve]

*Amos 5:16-17.* Immediately after mentioning the remnant in 5:15 who *might* survive if they change the situation, the description of mourning and lamentation in 5:16-17 abruptly ends any fleeting thoughts that the judgment might somehow be averted. Instead, God's judgment is portrayed as passing through the midst of Israel, overwhelming a wide social and geo-

> **Amos 5:14-15 and the Book of the Twelve**
>
> Though the linguistic similarities are not identical, one can hardly miss the similarity between the calls to repentance of Amos 5:14-15 and Joel 2:12-17. Effectively, these two passages provide similar responses, one for the northern kingdom and one for the southern kingdom. One cannot claim literary dependence, but it is significant that a prophetic figure confronts both Jerusalem/Judah and the House of Israel with a call to change so that "perhaps" YHWH might relent. Theologically, these calls to repent emphasize YHWH's repeated attempts to bring the people back (see also Amos 4:6-11).

graphical spectrum from the streets of the city to the rural fields. Socially, the lamentation will include the farmers (*ʾikkār* probably refers to those who work the fields, not the owners) and professional mourners. Geographically, the description of the city is equally all encompassing, including the open squares, where people could gather publicly, and the streets, more like narrow alleys than boulevards. As well, this unit extends the divine wrath from the city all the way to the vineyards, from whence the farmer presumably came. Finally, the phrasing of this unit emphasizes the totality of God's judgment via the triple use of the word "in every" (*bĕkāl*).

## Woe Oracle

AΩ A woe oracle, like a dirge (see Amos 5:1) connotes images and moods typically associated with funerals. The structure of the woe oracle typically contains four elements: (1) the interjection *hôy* (translated as "woe" or "alas"; 5:18); (2) a participle indicating the subject of the woe ("you who desire the day of YHWH"); (3) an explanatory sentence (in Amos 5:18b, this takes the form of a rhetorical question and a warning: "Why do you want the day of YHWH? It is darkness and not light."); and (4) an announcement of judgment, though this frequently comes after several oracles (and is not formally present in 5:18-20, but is implied by the description of the day of YHWH as a day of darkness in 5:18b, 20). Elsewhere, woe oracles can appear in groups (see Hab 2:5-20; Isa 5:8-24,) or as individual pronouncements (Mic 2:1-4). For additional examples and summaries of the debates about the original life-setting (*Sitz im Leben*) of the forms, see Eugene March, "Prophecy," in *Old Testament Form Criticism* (ed. John H. Hayes; San Antonio: Trinity University Press, 1974) 164–65.

*Amos 5:18-20.* As a woe oracle, Amos 5:18-20 begins with the telltale interjection *hôy* ("alas," "woe"). [Woe Oracle] The oracle corrects false assumptions concerning the day of YHWH, directing its message to those who believed God's judgment was saved for someone else. The unit presumes that people have heard the phrase "day of YHWH" and expect God will intervene on their behalf. Amos 5:18-20 challenges this belief. Rather, when the day of YHWH comes, divine wrath will be directed toward them. [Amos 5:18-20 and the Book of the Twelve] Thus, Amos 5:19 presents three images designed to frighten the reader with the inevitability of God's wrath. A man flees from a lion only to encounter a bear; in the safety of his home, he rests a hand upon a wall only to be bitten by a snake. Given the context of the day of YHWH, the point of these images is clear: if YHWH decides to intervene, then there will be no escape.

It does not take a lot of imagination to visualize those to whom 5:18-20 is addressed. It is clearly aimed at those who assume God's election precludes them from facing the consequences of failing to abide by God's behavioral expectations. This motif reemerges in Amos 9:7-8, where YHWH determines to destroy the house of Jacob, but not totally. Although Amos never uses the word "covenant" in association with God's behavioral expectations for Israel, this unit cuts to the core those who see the covenant promise as an all-encompassing protective umbrella. Indeed, YHWH demands that his people take seriously their response to the covenant.

## Amos 5:18-20 and the Book of the Twelve

The language used for the day of YHWH in 5:18-20 (a day of darkness, not light) frames the images of inevitability in 5:19. This phrase, "day of darkness," here used in association with the day of YHWH, appears elsewhere in the OT only in the Book of the Twelve in Joel 2:2 (see also 2:31 [MT 3:4]) and Zeph 1:15. This recurring phrase, chronologically appearing first in Amos, reflects a scenario in the Book of the Twelve wherein language for the day of YHWH in one writing often reflects the phraseology found elsewhere in the Book of the Twelve, adding to the impression that the day of YHWH becomes a major motif for understanding the larger corpus.

*Amos 5:21-24.* Arguably the most famous text in Amos, this passage elevates justice and righteousness above religiosity. The text is a ringing denunciation of all things religious, but not because religious expression itself is meaningless.

Rather, the rhetoric of these verses only presupposes religion to be meaningless when it does not result in justice and righteousness.

The passage divides into three parallel sets of negative statements (5:21-23) that express YHWH's rejection of festivals, sacrifices, and music. These statements culminate in a positive expression of YHWH's desire for justice and righteousness (5:24). The first set of parallel lines (5:21) uses three expressive verbs (hate, despise, take no delight) followed by two objects (festivals, solemn assemblies). The second set of parallel lines (5:22) focuses upon three types of sacrifice (burnt offerings, grain offerings, offerings of well-being) that YHWH rejects. In the third set of parallel lines (5:23), YHWH commands that songs cease and refuses to hear the instrumental music. These parallel formulations have a cumulative effect as, rhetorically, YHWH distances himself from all these religious expressions. By referring to these expressions as "yours," YHWH insists that they belong to the people. In essence, YHWH spurns the entire cult here by rejecting the reasons for gathering, the expressions of piety, and the sounds of worship. Worship performed when justice and righteousness are ignored rings hollow.

The word translated as "solemn assemblies" in Amos 5:21 generally refers to a ritual ceremony. Elsewhere, it means recurring holiday celebrations such as the festival of booths (Lev 23:36; Num 29:35; Neh 8:18), temple dedications (e.g., 2 Chr 7:9), or ad hoc ceremonies (Joel 1:14; 2:15). *Festivals* (Heb. *ḥag*) "is never applied to family festivals, the nomadic festival of sheepshearing, or the sabbath and new moon which derive from the lunar calendar (Ezek 45:17)." Rather, the word refers to "a community festival of the Israelites, determined by the solar year, even when the festival is considered illegitimate (Exod 32:5; 1 Kgs 12:32)."[1] Noticeably lacking from the named festivals and solemn assemblies is the mention of Sabbath.

The types of sacrifice in 5:22 include burnt offerings, grain offerings, and offerings of well-being. Burnt offerings, also known as whole offerings, consume the entire animal (usually a bull) as an act of atonement. Grain offerings (Heb. *minḥâh*) appear in prophetic texts only when paralleled with other types of offerings, and only when the prophets are taking on the misunderstandings of the sacrificial system.[2] Outside prophetic texts, the word can refer to most any sacrifice and can mean tribute, offering, or gift. It is not limited to the offering of grain. The offering of well-being appears only here in the singular in the Old Testament. It refers to sacrifices of three subtypes: the thanksgiving, the vow, and the freewill offering.[3]

Why does YHWH reject these elements from Israel? The rejection has little to do with the elements themselves. Rather, Amos 5:24 implies that YHWH rejects the worship elements because they do not result in righteousness and justice—those relational terms signifying the combination of religious belief with the actions by which one demonstrates that belief. Genuine worship affects one's behavior toward others. Any other type of worship deludes the practitioner.

*Amos 5:25-27.* This passage builds off the subject of the abuse of sacrifices in 5:22, beginning with a rhetorical question: "Did you bring to me sacrifices and offerings in the forty years in the wilderness, . . . Israel?" The question creates linguistic and canonical tension. Linguistically, the question implies a negative response, meaning the prophet's audience would assume the people did not sacrifice during the wilderness period. Canonically, however, the Pentateuchal narrative indicates sacrifice was offered in the wilderness (Exod 24; 32 [though not to YHWH]; Lev 9; etc.). How does one resolve this issue? One can only assume that a version of the wilderness story existed at the time that did not recount sacrifices in the wilderness. The logic of 5:25-27 presupposes a negative response since allegiance to other gods becomes a reason for exile (5:26-27). In addition, one other Old Testament text implies a tradition that people did not sacrifice in the wilderness (Jer 7:21-23). In short, Amos 5:25-27 essentially portrays YHWH as avowing, I brought you out of the wilderness even though you did not sacrifice, but now I will send you back because you are sacrificing improperly.

In 5:26, Sakkuth and Kaiwan create problems for understanding. The word *sikkût* in MT probably refers to an Assyrian God, and Kaiwan refers to the planet Saturn, perhaps represented by a star. [Standards] Thus, though the syntax of this verse is notoriously difficult, these images represent allegiance to the Assyrian king. Yet, the ambiguity of the images makes it difficult to know whether 5:26 is (1) a prediction leading to the punishment to come in 5:27 (NRSV); (2) a continuation of the question begun in 5:25[4]; or (3) part of an accusation of past behavior, contrasting with 5:25 (NAS, NIV, NLT). While it may be impossible to tell with certainty, the

**Standards**

Symbolic standards were used in the ancient Near East from Egypt to Mesopotamia for everything diplomatic, from missions to military engagements, as can be seen in the military scene depicted on the Egyptian chest here, where footmen behind the king's chariot carry the standards, or from a Schist panel from Mari, where the standard bearer leads the victory celebration.

Otto Eissfeldt, "Lade und Stierbild," *ZAW* 58 (1940/41): 209.

Painted wooden chest of Tutankhamun showing the king in a battle against Asiatics. Egypt, 18th dynasty. Egyptian Museum, Cairo, Egypt. (Credit: Scala/Art Resource, NY)

A soldier approaches a Mari dignitary who carried the standard of Mari. Detail of a victory parade, from the Ishtar temple, Mari, Syria, 2400 BCE. Schist panel inlaid with mother-of-pearl plaques. Louvre, Paris, France. (Credit: Erich Lessing/Art Resource, NY)

end result of 5:26 is to separate YHWH from YHWH's people who have turned, or *will* turn, to other deities and other kings for protection. Carrying standards into battle designates allegiance, and these images do not belong to YHWH.

The final pronouncement in the chapter (5:27) anticipates punishment for Israel, describing it as an "exile beyond Damascus"— a phrase that neither requires nor eliminates Assyria as the perpetrator of this exile. Subsequently, Amaziah the priest condemns Amos for this prediction (7:11, 17). This pronouncement of exile suggests an interesting phenomenon. In the opening section of Amos 1–2, the punishments pronounced in the first seven oracles tended to repeat themselves. One finds predictions of fire (1:4, 7, 10, 12, 14; 2:2, 5), destruction of strongholds (1:4, 7, 10, 12, 14; 2:2, 5), and exile (1:5, 6, 15) listed among the punishments. However, these recurring elements do not appear in the oracle against Israel (2:6-16), so it is noteworthy that two of these elements, fire (5:6) and exile (5:5, 27), appear as judgments against Israel in Amos 5, the central chapter of the book. Both of these elements also appear as threats in the vision cycle of Amos 7. Fire is the threat of the second vision (7:4), and the prediction of exile is the subject of contention for Amaziah in the narrative following the third vision (see 7:11, 17). When one notes that the destruction of the strongholds of Israel appears as the subject of an oracle in 6:8, then one finds that the punishments missing from the Israel oracle (2:6-16) appear in the concluding chapters of the center panel of Amos, chapters 5–6.

## CONNECTIONS

Amos 5:18-20 speaks clearly about the prospects of accountability. Too often, those who scream the loudest for God's judgment assume they will be spared because they know the mind of God. Like Amos, Jesus too combated this mindset on several fronts. Jesus warned against thinking that the sins of others are viewed by God as worse than the sins we commit (Matt 7:1-5), and he also warned against hypocrisy, evidenced by those who worry more about impressing other people than impressing God (Matt 6:2-6). He warned religious leaders (the Pharisees) against thinking they had all the answers when spouting theological dogma. God cares at least as much about proper relationships as correct theology (Matt 5:38-42, 43-48).

The inevitability of judgment in Amos seems harsh when taken in isolation, but two elements serve as reminders that this chapter is not the entire story. First, by using the phrase "the remnant of Joseph" (5:15), this chapter hints that the judgment may not imply complete oblivion. Second, the fact that the call to repentance is reminiscent of but not dependent upon Joel reminds the reader of other calls to repent within the Book of the Twelve, which forces the reader to infer that God's people have rejected previous warnings (Hos 6:1-3; 14: 1-8; Joel 1:2-2:18; Amos 4:6-11). Whatever the outcome, God's people cannot say they were not warned.

What is the purpose of worship? The legal sections of the Torah are rife with commands about worship, including extensive sections about the proper way to conduct the very sacrifices that YHWH rejects in 5:21-24. Does Amos 5:21-24 throw out the entire sacrificial system? Does it rebuke the sacrifice of the northern kingdom because it is not performed in Jerusalem? The text itself offers no hint that the latter is the case, and the formulations in 5:21-23 show clearly that the rejection is not merely about the sacrifices. Rather, this denunciation includes the music (5:23) and the meetings themselves (5:21), meaning that YHWH is rejecting the worship of Israel in its entirety. The text does not provide the reason for this rejection until the contrast of 5:24. The reason YHWH rejects the entirety of Israel's worship is that it has no effect on their lives. Their gatherings, their sacrifices, and their music have no effect upon God because they have no effect upon their own behavior. Amos repeatedly condemns those who use religious gatherings for their own benefit (2:8; 4:4-5) and who take no notice of the suffering around them because of their own relative prosperity (2:6-7; 4:1; 5:10-12).

Righteousness and justice are relational terms about the proper way to regulate society, jurisprudence, and religious expression. It would be a mistake, and a misunderstanding of the prophetic spirit, to think that the words of Amos should be relegated to a religion and a culture that have long since passed from the scene. These words presuppose an understanding of the very nature of God and God's relationship to those who profess to follow God. Religious expression old and new is not commanded because God needs it. Rather, God requires religious expression, or worship, of humans in order to testify to the reality of the deity who transcends our petty desires, who lays claim on our lives and behavior. Our gatherings, songs, chants, and offerings have no physical effect upon God. God does not weigh the relative benefits of an organ over an electric guitar; God does not prefer contemporary praise music over traditional hymnody; God does not care whether we ascribe to specific creeds and faith statements. God cares about how our religious faith and practices affect the way we relate to those around us. Do we stand up to those with power and wealth when they abuse the system so that the rich get richer while the poor continue to suffer? Do we look at those around us and ask ourselves who is suffering? Do we encourage one another? Do our worship services remind us that God expects righteousness and justice from us? Amos 5:21-24 does not merely highlight somebody else's problems. Indeed, it challenges us to look at our own faith and ask tough questions. This passage is the Old Testament equivalent of Matthew 25:31-46, the haunting challenge of Jesus: "then they also will answer, 'Lord, when was it that we saw you hungry or thirsty or a stranger or naked or sick or in prison, and did not take care of you?' Then he will answer them, 'Truly I tell you, just as you did not do it to one of the least of these, you did not do it to me'" (Matt 25:44-45).

Passages like Amos 5:21-24 represent in many ways the canonical underpinnings of Jesus' teachings. It is difficult to worship when animosity (Matt 5:21-22, 23-24) or arrogance (Matt 7:3) controls one's life. It is difficult to claim Jesus is Lord if one refuses to see those in pain and physical need (Matt 25:31-46), or if one acts only out of self-interest (Matt 7:12).

## NOTES

1. B. Kedar-Kopfstein, "חַג chagh; חגג ḥgg," *TDOT* (ed. G. Johannes Botterweck and Helmer Ringgren; Grand Rapids: Eerdmans, 1974) 4:206.

2. H. J. Fabry, "מִנְחָה minḥâ," *TDOT* 8:415.

3. Gary Anderson, "Sacrifice and Sacrificial Offering," in David Noel Friedman, ed., *ABD* (New York: Doubleday, 1992) 5:878.

4. Hans Walter Wolff, *Joel and Amos* (trans. Waldemar Janzen et al.; Hermeneia; Philadelphia: Fortress, 1977) 259–60.

# IGNORING THE
# RUIN OF JOSEPH

## Amos 6:1-14

## COMMENTARY

Amos 6:1-14, the final large block of the sayings section (Amos 3–6), begins differently than the first three chapters, each of which began with "Hear this word" (3:1; 4:1; 5:1). Amos 6 begins with a woe oracle against the complacent ones in Judah *and* Israel. The chapter divides into five units: the first is a relatively long woe oracle that culminates in a pronouncement of punishment (6:1-7); next follow four smaller units (6:8, 9-10, 11, 12-14) whose relationship to one another results more from their rhetorical arrangement than from an integrated logic.

*Amos 6:1-7.* Amos 6:1 begins with a woe oracle (see [Woe Oracle]) addressing God's people in a way that specifically incorporates Israel *and* Judah by castigating the idle rich in the capital cities of Samaria and Jerusalem (= Zion). The depiction of these groups' activities continues through 6:6, after which the conjunction "therefore" introduces the pronouncement of punishment in 6:7. In Amos 6:1, the prophet polemically confronts those "at ease" and those "who feel secure." In addition, the latter half of the verse suggests that they rely upon these persons as "the notables of the first of the nations, to whom the house of Israel resorts." This group must refer to the elite of the kingdom, presumably in the north and south.

Amos 6:2 uses four imperatives and two rhetorical questions to goad Israel's upper class. The imperatives mention three different places at opposite ends of the kingdom: Calneh, Hamath, and Gath. Calneh was a provincial capital in northern Syria captured by the Assyrians in 738 BCE. The city of Hamath was also in Syria, but the phrase "the entrance of Hamath" also denotes the northernmost region of the ideal boundaries of the kingdom of Israel (Num 34:8; Ezek 47:15). Gath, on the other hand, was one of the major cities of

Philistia at the southwestern end of the kingdom. All three of these cities were conquered by the Assyrians between 738–734 BCE. Because these dates appear late for the prophet Amos, scholars have suggested this passage comes from a disciple of Amos. At any rate, the speaker does not expect his audience to go physically to these cities, but rhetorically asks them to compare their kingdom to others. The text presumes that anyone who looked objectively could not possibly consider Israel to be in better shape than these other regions, despite its status as the people of YHWH. One finds similar prophetic challenges elsewhere in Amos, where the prophetic message reminds the audience that God owes them nothing simply because they belong to the people of Israel (5:11, 18-20; 9:6-7).

It is not clear what 6:3 means in its current context, but the broader literary context—both within Amos and the prophetic canon—has intertextual associations that are hard to ignore. Amos 6:3 refers to scattering or making distant the "day of evil" while bringing near a reign of violence. Modern readers can readily associate the day of evil with the day of YHWH described in 5:18-20. In the context of Amos, knowing what happens in the last third of the eighth century, one should associate the "reign of violence" with Assyrian hegemony.

In rapid succession, Amos 6:4-6 challenges two groups whose behavior the prophet finds particularly repulsive. The imagery used in this text essentially accuses the idle rich (6:4) and musicians (6:5). Both sets of images share at least one common denominator: whiling away time while society languishes. This trait is clear enough in the first group. The image of those sprawling on couches and lying on beds inlaid with ivory while devouring fine meat (lamb and veal) displays a polemical edge toward those who have the means to afford these luxury items, but who use their time to stuff their faces. (See [Economic Situation in the Eighth Century] concerning the changing economic situation of Israel and Judah in the eighth century.) They do not merely lie down; they also sprawl upon exquisite furniture in a drunken, sated stupor.

The polemical rant against the musicians, however, raises several questions: Why does the composition of music irritate the prophet? Why is the improvisation on musical instruments "like David" not to be considered a compliment? Is the reference to music about the cultic performance of Psalms, or is this anti-music attitude about people who spend their time playing music rather than working?

The spirit of this confrontation portrays these revelers as persons who think of themselves more highly than they ought to do. Partying among the elite also plays a significant role in Hosea 7:3-7, which denounces officials who party and abuse their positions as a factor in the collapse of the northern kingdom. Two things seem clear. First, the actions of these music makers created an affront to the sensibilities of the prophet because they lacked dignity and purpose. More forcefully stated, the rhetorical barb here is quite strong. Whether they describe the abuse of a cultic situation or merely a Saturday night bash is almost beside the point. Second, the extravagance symptomatically reflects the arrogant disregard of resources, station, and dignity that one would normally not expect leaders to display. (See the discussion of *marzēaḥ* in [Cultic "Parties"].)

**Ivory**

Amos denounces those "lying on ivory beds" to confront those who spend their wealth on frivolous items that merely help them waste their time.

Lotus buds and blossoms. Ornamental relief on a carved ivory plaque, from Samaria, Israel. Israel Museum (IDAM), Jerusalem, Israel. (Credit: Erich Lessing/Art Resource, NY)

The images in 6:6 continue to denounce unbridled drinking and indulgent extravagance. In short, these images portray excess and arrogance. The revelers drink wine in such excess that they need mixing bowls rather than goblets. These bowls were used to mix wine and spices, but they were not intended as drinking utensils for individuals. One the other hand, the pouring of fine oils upon the head was done for aroma and for the cooling sensation it provided to the skin. One anointed honored guests at festivals and other special occasions (Ps 23:5; Luke 7:37-38). Yet in the portrayal of Amos 6:6, these revelers arrogantly anoint themselves.

The last line of 6:6 provides the reason for the agitation. These persons are partying while the nation is falling apart: "they are not grieved over the ruin of Joseph!" The metaphorical use of Joseph here refers to the northern kingdom since Joseph is the progenitor of Ephraim and Manasseh, whose tribal regions comprise the bulk of the central section of the kingdom.

This series of indictments culminates with an announcement of punishment in 6:7. Those with the means and the power to change the situation will be the ones sent into exile. They should be the ones who foresee the implications for society. Instead, they live in luxury at the expense of those who do not have the means or the power to protect themselves (note the same dynamic for Judah's elite in Mic 2:1-4; 3:1-4). Amos charges these elite groups with neglecting their duty by being completely oblivious to the dangers around them, and with being more concerned about their parties than the fate of their nation.

*Amos 6:8.* Amos 6:8 stands apart formally in that it contains a rather cumbersome introductory formula, twice presenting YHWH as the speaker. This composite introductory formula is then followed by four lines of divine speech. The first two lines announce, in parallel, YHWH's revulsion at "Jacob's" pride and power. The last two lines pronounce YHWH's impending destruction of "the city" and everything in it.

Amos 6:8 functions as the source of an allusion made in Amos 8:7, one that refers back to YHWH swearing on account of the pride of Jacob. Yet to whom does "Jacob" refer? In any given prophetic text, Jacob can refer either to the northern kingdom (Mic 1:5), to Judah (Isa 2:3,5; Jer 5:20; Obad 10, 17-18), or to both when referring to the ideal kingdom (Isa 9:8; 10:20-21; 41:8; Ezek 20:5). The same is not true in Amos, where several texts clearly use "Jacob" as an epithet for the northern kingdom (3:13; 7:2, 5). There is no reason to suggest otherwise in Amos 6:8, even though 6:7 uses "Joseph" to mean the northern kingdom. However, since Amos 5:6 and 15 also use Joseph to represent the northern kingdom, one can only assume the two terms, Jacob and Joseph, are synonymous in the book of Amos, barring clear indications to the contrary.

*Amos 6:9-10.* Perhaps the most enigmatic passage in the entire book, 6:9-10 presents shocking images of utter annihilation combined with reports of a conversation whose responses are impossible to understand fully. The first portion of 6:9 describes the complete annihilation of a family living in a house. Confusion begins when a relative is dispatched to burn the bodies. It would appear that burning the bodies would thus be part of the burial procedure, but such a procedure is not documented elsewhere in the Old Testament, except for vengeance (1 Sam 31:12) or punishment in extremely despicable cases (Lev 20:14; Josh 7:25). Burning the bones of the king of Edom was denounced as an abomination committed by the Moabites in Amos 2:1. In short, cremation seems to imply shame, but that does not seem to be the point in Amos 6:10, which presumes cremation to be necessary because of the scope of the devastation.

Next, this relative carries on a conversation with someone in the house whose identity is not clear since, according to 6:9, everyone in the house has perished. Yet, somehow one must account for two people in this scene. The relative asks a question of someone in the house: "Is there anyone else with you?" The response confirms there are no survivors with a simple one-word answer, "no one" (*'āpes*, a particle of nonexistence). Yet, the relative's final statement rebukes the one who responded, but the reason makes little sense: "Shut up, for we shall not mention the name of YHWH." Most commentaries contend that this final response reflects, in some way, the speaker's fear that mentioning the name of YHWH in the context of those who have died in such a violent manner might further provoke God's wrath. [Mentioning the Name of God] Why this speaker expresses this fear is not recounted, but the text assumes that danger is real.

*Amos 6:11.* Amos 6:11 formally links to the preceding conversation via a connecting formula ("for behold"), though the saying that follows is not intrinsically related. Nevertheless, this connecting formula demonstrates how the compiler saw the connection between 6:9-10 and 6:11. In short, the compiler understood the image of 6:10—specifically, the relative's fear of YHWH's name being uttered—to indicate that God's word of judgment will have consequences for all of society, from the "great house" to the "small house" (6:11). Moreover, the imagery of destruction in 6:11 not only coincides more with that of an earthquake (shatters into bits and pieces) but is also consistent with the destructive imagery of the fifth vision in 9:1-4.

*Amos 6:12-14.* Amos 6:12 is a classic example of a text-critical problem wrought by the dividing of words in an unpointed text. Since the Hebrew text was originally unpointed (meaning the vowels were not included), mistakes could arise when copying manuscripts if two words were combined into one by omitting a space. The NRSV translates an emended text because the MT does not make sense. [Text-critical Problem in Amos 6:12] No one plows the sea with oxen. In the end, the rhetorical questions in the first half of 6;12 illustrate the absurdity, from YHWH's perspective, of the

### Mentioning the Name of God

J. K. Rowling uses a similar motif in her Harry Potter novels, where the vast majority of characters refer to the evil Lord Voldemort as "He-Who-Must-Not-Be-Named," afraid that saying his name out loud would land the speaker under his influence. At first, only the hero, Harry Potter, refuses to be cowed into submission. In the Old Testament, saying the name "YHWH" is generally not frowned upon, but texts like Amos 6:9-10 and 2 Sam 6:3 do emphasize the power of YHWH's name as a potentially dangerous harbinger of wrath. Many of the Qumran manuscripts from the first century BCE write the name YHWH in an archaic script indicating it had a sacred status among those scribes. Later, the Masoretes treated YHWH as too holy to pronounce, so the vowel pointing for Adonai (Lord) was adapted to the consonants YHWH, and readers of Hebrew Scripture even today pronounce the Tetragrammaton as *'adonai* or *Ha-shem* (the Name). Not pronouncing the name YHWH can be a sign of respect, but it should not be endowed with magical powers.

**Text-Critical Problem in Amos 6:12**

The NRSV translates the relevant phrases,
"Do horses run on rocks?
          Does one plow the sea with oxen?"
By contrast, a literal rendering of the MT translates,
"Do horses run on rocks?
          Or does one plow with oxen?"
Since the first question implies the answer "no,"
one expects the second question to have the same
answer. However, oxen are used to plow, so one
finds a rhetorical disconnection within the MT.
However, when one notes that the word for "oxen"
(*bāqār*) never appears anywhere else with the
plural absolute form (*bāqārîm*) because it is a col-
lective noun, then a solution to this conundrum
begins to emerge. If the plural ending (*îm*) was
originally separated from the word "oxen," the two
letters (*yôd, mêm*) could have been the word
"sea,"—thus providing the translation in the NRSV
and simultaneously providing the expected "no"
response. (Thus, NRSV reads *bqr ym* rather than
*brrym* in the MT.)

people's actions. Namely, the country has taken two things that YHWH holds dear (justice and righteousness) and turned them into things that are lethal and useless ("poison" and "wormwood," respectively).

The mention of the towns in 6:13, Lo-Debar and Karnaim, provide substantive and figurative connotations. They probably reflect places taken by Jeroboam II when expanding Israelite territory to its ideal borders. Lo-Debar was an Ammonite town, and Karnaim was a city in Syria. These regions would have been consistent with the expansion of Jeroboam. However, these city names also work as wordplays in the larger rhetorical unit of 6:12-14. Lo-Debar means "no-thing." The implications are obvious: Israel is celebrating because they have taken nothing. Karnaim means "two horns." Marvin Sweeney has noted how this name conjures images of the act of grabbing the horns of the altar out of desperation—taking refuge from one's enemies (see 1 Kgs 2:28).[1] Such an act of desperation, needless to say, would not help the person if the king determined to execute him anyway, as is the case in the story of Joab and Solomon (1 Kgs 2:28-34). Such is also the case in Amos 6:12-14. Celebrating over the "two horns" will not protect Israel if YHWH determines judgment is at hand, as YHWH indeed announces in 6:14.

Amos 6:14 contrasts the deluded strength of Israel with YHWH's strength and warns of an imminent, ominous future. Amos 6:14 brings theological, geographical, and canonical issues into play. Theologically, YHWH decides to judge Israel by sending a nation against them. The implications are clear: YHWH's patience has run out. In addition, the portrayal of God's power in 6:14 shows God as one who can change the fate of one nation by manipulating another. Geographically, this judgment is directed against the "house of Israel," a term that means both Judah and Israel in 6:14 because the place names Lebo-Hamath and the Wadi Arabah refer to places at the far northern and southern ends of the ideal kingdom borders. In the eighth century, the Assyrians destroyed the political entity of Israel and placed such severe economic hardships upon Judah that it nearly failed as a state. Canonically, the reader should assume Assyria is the nation YHWH intends to send. Identifying this nation as Assyria not only makes sense within Amos, but also within the Twelve. The formulation of this judgment in 6:14 reappears almost identically in Habakkuk 1:6, except there God promises to raise up the Babylonians against Judah using almost identical terms. [Amos 6:14 in the Book of the Twelve]

**Amos 6:14 in the Book of the Twelve**

This verse parallels the formulation in Hab 1:6. Functionally, this parallel creates a conceptual link connecting God's use of a *foreign* nation to punish Israel (with the Assyrians in Amos 6:14) and Judah (with the Babylonians in Hab 1:6). In all likelihood, the formulation in Habakkuk draws from Amos at this point.

# CONNECTIONS

Amos 6:4-7 offers powerful condemnations, and it would be easy to construct a straw man to make ourselves feel superior. Such, however, would not have been the intention of Amos. In modern congregations, one would be hard-pressed to find those who would support wealthy, self-centered, indolent, drunken, party-loving leaders who think life holds nothing greater than indulging one's every whim. [*What Would Jesus Buy?*] It would be easy to take up the polemic of Amos to caricature some perceived enemy. However, to do so would be to miss the principle behind the rhetoric. One of the major responsibilities of a deepening spirituality lies in self-reflection about our own lifestyles. Two fundamental problems lie behind the charges of Amos 6: arrogance and apathy. When one's life revolves around one's self, sin results. When we are so arrogant we think our needs must be met entirely before we can help somebody else, sin grows. When congregations use all their resources to meet their own perceived needs, sin kills ministry. If nobody cares about the poor, then congregations may argue about the color of the carpet. If nobody cares that public policy is creating the "ruin of Joseph," then it is okay to turn our backs on the elderly, the underinsured, the immigrants, and any number of disenfranchised groups. Apathy and arrogance can affect individuals and congregations, but the words of Amos challenge us all; they make us uncomfortable and cause us to wonder whether we have done enough to change the world.

**What Would Jesus Buy?**

In 2007, the "documentary" titled *What Would Jesus Buy?* took a comedic look at the way commercialism and the American culture create "need" and "markets" where none really exist. Part "mockumentary" and part social commentary, it pokes fun at the dark side of American consumerism. The exaggerated desire to buy the newest gadget or the trendiest toys for children can create a society that rivals the portrayal of Israel in the polemic of Amos. The social critique of Amos offers a sobering call to look at the ways one's actions within one's own society create problems on a bigger scale. As this film shows, the church is not immune. When the desires of churches and their members get wrapped up in the same kinds of impulses, genuine calls for "righteousness" and "justice" can go unheard (Amos 6:4-6).

How does one read the signs of the times? Amos 6:11-13 raises this issue poignantly. In the days of Jeroboam II, one could make the case that life in Israel was pretty good. The king was expanding the territory with the aim of restoring territory that had been lost over time. The economy was booming, at least for part of the country. But trouble loomed in the not-too-distant future. The prophet saw it, though few others cared to listen. They partied and celebrated Pyrrhic victories because they had captured No-Thing (Lo-Debar). Like the image of Nero fiddling while Rome burned, most people could not see that the world around them was changing and that their own behavior was destroying their society. Changes were taking place outside the land while Amos's antagonists became increasingly self-absorbed. In order to fuel their appetites, those with whom Amos contended lined their pockets at the expense of the poor and the weak.

One wonders what Amos would say in our context. Are we trying to make the world a better place, or do we delude ourselves into thinking the world owes us? Do we turn a blind eye to suffering as long as it does not affect us? If so, Amos is coming. Will we have the courage to see and hear the needs of others even if we believe their fate is not our problem?

As the story of the fate of Israel and Judah embedded in Amos unfolds, Amos 6:14 adds an ominous warning for Israel, one that will be echoed later for Judah. God will not remain idle but will "raise up a nation" that will oppress the entire nation. Within Amos, it will become clear that even this danger could still be averted if Israel changed. The five visions of Amos (7:1–9:4) will deliver this message. When Israel does not change, God will act to keep Judah from falling into the same trap. Hints of this message have surfaced in Amos, but they will become explicit in Micah 1–3. An image of God continues to emerge and finds its clearest expression in Exodus 34:6-7: God desires to show *ḥesed*, but God will not leave the guilty unpunished.

# NOTE

1. Marvin Sweeney, *The Twelve Prophets* (Berit Olam, vol. 1; Collegeville: Liturgical Press, 2000) 248.

# VISIONS OF IMPENDING DESTRUCTION

## Amos 7:1–9:6

## COMMENTARY

Amos 7:1–9:6 contains a series of five vision reports (7:1-3, 4-6, 7-9; 8:1-3; 9:1-4). [Prophetic Vision Reports] The first four vision reports share structural features that invite comparison of the individual reports. The final vision report stands apart from the first four, but it also serves an important function for the series and for the book. In addition, comparison of these vision reports shows movement at several levels as the reports unfold. The first three vision reports appear in rapid succession with no interruption. However, prior to the fourth and fifth vision reports, two passages (7:10-17; 8:4-14) are inserted into the series that give dramatic pause before the final two vision reports. Both of these intervening passages play a role in understanding the book as a whole.

The first four vision reports share a structure involving three components: (1) a report of what YHWH shows the prophet, (2) a conversation between YHWH and the prophet, and (3) a pronouncement from YHWH regarding the vision's significance. [The Structure of the Visions of Amos (NRSV)] The first two vision reports contain additional information about the object of the vision. Interpreting these visions must take account of at least two contexts: the visions by themselves and within the larger context of Amos. The visions (without 7:10-17 and 8:4-14) unfold in a 2-2-1 pattern, meaning that visions one and two

**Prophetic Vision Reports**

Vision reports are relatively common in prophetic literature, but especially in Ezekiel, Zechariah 1–6, and these five in Amos 7–9. The three-part structure of the vision report is fairly simple: (1) an introduction containing a form of the verb "to see"; (2) a description of the event or item seen; and (3) a concluding explanation. Three types of vision reports have also been identified: the "presence vision," the "event vision," and the "wordplay vision." The five visions of Amos fall into the latter two categories as visions 1, 2, and 5 describe events the prophet sees, while visions 3 and 4 constitute wordplay visions.

For information on structure see Eugene March, "Prophecy," in *Old Testament Form Criticism* (ed. John H. Hayes; San Antonio: Trinity University Press, 1974) 170.

For information on types see Friedrich Horst, "Die Visionsschilderungen der alttestamentlichen Propheten," *Evangelische Theologie* 20 (1960): 193–205.

## The Structure of the Visions of Amos (NRSV)

| Element | 7:1-3 | 7:4-6 | 7:7-9 | 8:1-3 | 9:1-4 |
|---|---|---|---|---|---|
| (1) Introduction | This is what the Lord God showed me: | This is what the Lord God showed me: | This is what he showed me: | This is what the Lord God showed me | I saw the Lord standing beside the altar, and he said: |
| Description of Object Seen | he was forming locusts at the time the latter growth began to sprout (it was the latter growth after the king's mowings). | the Lord God was calling for a shower of fire, | the Lord was standing beside a wall built with a plumb line, with a plumb line in his hand. | a basket of summer fruit. | *YHWH's Monologue*: Strike the capitals until the thresholds shake, and shatter them on the heads of all the people; and those who are left I will kill with the sword; not one of them shall flee away, not one of them shall escape. Though they dig into Sheol, from there shall my hand take them; though they climb up to heaven, from there I will bring them down. Though they hide themselves on the top of Carmel, from there I will search out and take them; and though they hide from my sight at the bottom of the sea, there I will command the sea-serpent, and it shall bite them. And though they go into captivity in front of their enemies, there I will command the sword, and it shall kill them; and I will fix my eyes on them for harm and not for good. |
| Additional Observations about the Object | When they had finished eating the grass of the land, | and it devoured the great deep and was eating up the land. | | | |
| (2) Conversation | I said, "O Lord God, forgive, I beg you! How can Jacob stand? He is so small!" | Then I said, "O Lord God, cease, I beg you! How can Jacob stand? He is so small!" | And the Lord said to me, "Amos, what do you see?" And I said, "A plumb line." | He said, "Amos, what do you see?" And I said, "A basket of summer fruit." | |
| (3) YHWH's Decision and Explanation | The Lord relented concerning this; "It shall not be," said the Lord. | The Lord relented concerning this; "This also shall not be," said the Lord God. | Then the Lord said, "See, I am setting a plumb line in the midst of my people Israel; I will never again pass them by; the high places of Isaac shall be made desolate, and the sanctuaries of Israel shall be laid waste, and I will rise against the house of Jeroboam with the sword." | Then the Lord said to me, "The end has come upon my people Israel; I will never again pass them by. The songs of the temple shall become wailings in that day," says the Lord God; "the dead bodies shall be many, cast out in every place. Be silent!" | |

relate closely to one another, as do three and four, before the final vision deviates. This 2-2-1 pattern, however, becomes less significant when one notes how the visions function within Amos, because 7:10-17 and 8:4-14 pull attention away from the visions themselves in order to convey something important for the book.

## First and Second Visions, 7:1-3, 4-6

The first two vision reports begin identically. Both narrate an ominous sight from the prophet. The first (7:1-3) reports that the prophet sees a locust plague coming upon the land. Since the crop is about to sprout, it requires little imagination to perceive the devastating consequences. If the grain is destroyed by locusts, hunger and death will result. The seed, saved from the previous harvest, is already planted. The ancient world had no modern garden store where farmers could go for additional seed, and the brutal heat of the summer would make it difficult, if not impossible, for new growth to survive even if it could be replanted.

The second report (7:4-6) describes an even more threatening scenario of cosmic proportions. The prophet sees YHWH calling forth a "shower of fire" that devours "the great deep" and "the land." The great deep conveys various connotations. It is closely associated with creation texts and can convey oblique references to the Babylonian creation myth of the great chaos battle between Marduk and Tiamat. [Tiamat and Marduk] However, more apropos to the current context, the great deep (*tĕhôm*) represents the gathering of waters that have been corralled by YHWH and now serve to water the land (see Deut 8:7; Ezek 31:4; Job 38:16; Pss 104:6; 33:7; Prov 8:24). In other words, when the second

### Tiamat and Marduk

The ancient Babylonian story, Enuma Elish, tells how the god Marduk came to power by defeating the forces of chaos led by the goddess Tiamat. Several motifs from the plot carried over into other Semitic creation stories. In the climactic battle scene, Marduk defeats Tiamat, frightening her allies who were themselves soon defeated:

Then joined issue Tiamat and Marduk, wisest of gods.
They strove in single combat, locked in battle.
The Lord spread out his net to enfold her,
The Evil Wind, which followed behind, he let loose in her face.
When Tiamat opened her mouth to consume him,
He drove in the Evil Wind that she close not her lips.
As the fierce winds charged her belly,
Her body was distended and her mouth was wide open.
He released the arrow, it tore her belly,
It cut through her insides, splitting the heart.
Having thus subdued her, he extinguished her life.
He cast down her carcass to stand upon it.
After he had slain Tiamat, the leader,
Her band was shattered, her troupe broken up;
And the gods, her helpers who marched at her side,
Trembling with terror, turned their backs about,
In order to save and preserve their lives.
Tightly encircled, they could not escape.
He made them captives and he smashed their weapons.
Thrown into the net, they found themselves ensnared;
Placed in cells, they were filled with wailing;
Bearing his wrath, they were held imprisoned.

After killing her, Marduk uses the slain Tiamat's body to create the earth and the heavens.

Text from "The Creation Epic," trans. E. A. Speiser, *ANET*, 67.

vision reports that the shower of fire devours the great deep, it means the springs and wells that provide water for the land, cattle, and people will now dry up.

The "land" (NRSV; NIV) in 7:4 reflects a word translated as "portion," but it can refer to farm land (2 Kgs 9:10, 36-37; Hos 5:7) and makes sense as such in this context (see NAS). The syntax and sequence of the vision implies movement: the fire devours the great deep and begins moving into the land, immediately threatening Israel's crops and its people.

In the first two vision reports, immediately after the prophet describes what he sees, he offers an intercessory prayer, first asking God to forgive (7:2) and then asking God to cease (7:5) because Jacob cannot endure. In both cases, the prayer succeeds in convincing YHWH to change YHWH's mind. In both instances, the prayer succeeds, and God refrains from executing judgment. One should understand how these vision reports function in Amos. Specifically, one must remember Amos 3:7: "Surely the Lord God does nothing without revealing his secret to his servants the prophets." Within the vision reports, YHWH reveals YHWH's *intention* to the prophet. The events seen by the prophet, in this case, have not occurred. In the case of the first two visions (7:1-3, 4-6), YHWH decides not to follow through after Amos intercedes for "Jacob, who is so small," and YHWH changes YHWH's mind. [YHWH Repenting]

## The Third Vision, 7:7-9

The third and fourth visions (7:7-9; 8:1-3) form the second pair in the 2-2-1 pattern, but in their canonical context they are interrupted by a prophetic narrative (7:10-17). Visions 3 and 4 resemble each other more closely than do either the first pair (7:1-3, 4-6) or the final vision report (9:1-4). See [The Structure of the Visions of Amos (NRSV)]. This structural similarity also coincides with their surprisingly ominous subject matter: a lump of tin and summer fruit. The danger in the first two visions is clear because

---

**YHWH Repenting**

📖 The idea of YHWH repenting, relenting, or changing YHWH's mind surprises many Christians who have grown up hearing language of predestination and God's immutability. Yet, the Hebrew Bible repeatedly reports that God repented concerning something God had done or was about to do. This happens at least 21 times in the Old Testament: Gen 6:6; Exod 32:12, 14; Judg 2:18; 1 Sam 15:11, 35; 2 Sam 24:16; Jer 18:8, 10; 26:3, 13, 19; 42:10; Joel 2:13, 14; Amos 7:3, 6; Jonah 3:9, 10; 4:2; 1 Chr 21:15. Several things can motivate YHWH's change of heart, including human intercession, divine compassion, and human repentance. This variety also occurs in phrases using the verb turn (*šûb*) as in Zech 1:3; Mal 3:7; Pss 6:4; 90:13. This portrayal means that the future is open for the biblical God. Over and over, whether in terms of human behavior or human pleading, God responds to the responses human beings make. To be sure, this idea of "repentance" differs from human repentance from sin. YHWH's changing YHWH's mind generally flows from YHWH's mercy overcoming YHWH's wrath. YHWH's repentance is not based on sin but on compassion.

the objects themselves (locusts, fire) are immediately recognizable as threats. The first two reports accelerate this threat by describing the action being performed by the object of the vision. The locusts and the fire were devouring the land. By contrast, the objects seen in the third (plumb line, lump of tin) and fourth (summer fruit) vision reports initially seem quite tame, but the puns they provide become the vehicles for deceptively deadly judgment.

The meaning of the puns unfolds during a conversation between YHWH and the prophet. Where the conversation in the first two vision reports begins with the prophet's speech about the destruction he sees, YHWH begins the conversation in the third and fourth vision reports with identical questions: "Amos, what do you see?" In both cases, Amos confirms that he has seen what YHWH revealed to him. In 7:7, the prophet reports that YHWH showed him a lump of tin (NRSV, NIV: plumb line), and he answers YHWH's question in 7:8 with the same information. Similarly, in 8:1 the prophet reports that he sees a basket of summer fruit and answers YHWH's question accordingly in 8:2. The surprising, deadly nature of these objects is quickly revealed to the prophet through the explanation of *the significance* of what he had seen (7:8b-9; 8:2b-3).

The distinguishing characteristics of the third vision report (7:7-9) focus upon the charges against the people. Amos 7:8 conveys judgment through an oblique wordplay. Some ambiguity exists because the word for the object (ʾānāk) appears only here, but scholars agree that ʾānāk refers to a lump of tin. Most English versions translate the word as "plumb line." Since YHWH stands beside a wall (7:7) and places the tin in the midst of Israel (7:9), they assume YHWH must be measuring Israel's suitability, similar to the way a carpenter would use a plumb line to make sure a wall is straight. However, this interpretation creates significant difficulties because tin is not a suitable material from which to make a plumb line. It is too light. Even in the ancient world, lead would have been the material of choice. A second line of interpretation takes its cue from the fact that the fourth vision uses the wordplay that is clearly recognizable (see below). In this case, it is significant that the word used for tin (ʾānāk) sounds similar to the Hebrew word for mourning (ʾānāhâh). Thus, YHWH is not measuring the people; rather, YHWH is placing mourning in their midst— meaning death is near. In either interpretation, the rhetorical effect is the same: something that looked harmless becomes a message of destruction from YHWH.

### Confrontation between Amos and Amaziah, 7:10-17

As with the vision cycle, one should interpret Amos 7:10-17 both as a relatively independent episode and as a unit whose placement serves a literary and theological purpose. By recounting Amaziah's banishment of Amos, 7:10-17 is a prophetic narrative, one of a very few in the Book of the Twelve (see Hos 1), and one whose significance is best understood in relation to other narrative accounts of the dealings between prophets and kings. [Prophets and Kings] In short, in prophetic narratives in the Latter Prophets, the basic tenor of the relationship between prophets and kings reflects a far more confrontational attitude than the counterparts of prophets addressing kings at Mari. [Prophets and Kings at Mari]

The structure unfolds with the narrator's account of Amaziah's actions (7:10-13), followed by a clearly structured judgment oracle against Amaziah (7:14-17). The narrator introduces him as the chief priest in Bethel (7:10) who writes Jeroboam (in Samaria), informing him that Amos is preaching treason. He quotes Amos by paraphrasing 7:9. Then, in a telling exchange, and without waiting to hear back from the king, Amaziah claims the king's authority and forbids Amos from prophesying at Bethel, demanding that Amos go back to Judah. The sarcasm drips from the last line of 7:13, as the chief priest does not claim that Bethel belongs to God, but that it is a "sanctuary of the king and the temple of the kingdom." Amaziah accuses Amos of preaching for money when he says, "Seer, go, flee away to the land of Judah, earn your bread there and prophesy there" (7:12). Amaziah not only questions the motives of Amos and sends him packing but also in the process shows that his true allegiance lies with the king rather than YHWH.

---

**Prophets and Kings**

Other stories of confrontations between prophets and kings reveal the rather consistent way YHWH's prophets confront kings (Exod 7–12; 1 Sam 13; 15; 2 Sam 12; 1 Kgs 18:17-46; 21:1-29; 22:1-38; 2 Kgs 3:13-20; 20:1-11, 12-19). This quality stands out markedly when one contrasts the prophetic behavior of Judah's prophets toward kings and others in power with the prophetic behavior at Mari, for example, where both requests and forms of speech show a more symbiotic relationship between prophets and kings. In Mari texts, prophets, male and female, worked at temples and spoke for the deity of that temple. Female prophets generally worked at temples for goddesses and males worked at the temples of gods. They frequently requested favors from the king in return for messages of future success, or they claimed responsibility for success on behalf of the god for whom they spoke.

See Daniel E. Fleming, "Prophets and Temple Personnel in the Mari Archives," in *The Priests in the Prophets: The Portrayal of Priests, Prophets, and Other Religious Specialists in the Latter Prophets* (ed. Lester Grabbe and Alice Bellis; Library of Hebrew Bible/OTS 408; New York: T & T Clark, 2004) 44–64.

For a brief analysis of the story form relative to prophetic speech, see also Mark Roncace, *Jeremiah, Zedekiah, and the Fall of Jerusalem* (Library of Hebrew Bible/OTS 423; New York: T & T Clark, 2005) 23–24.

---

**Prophets and Kings at Mari**

Prophets and prophecy were complex phenomena in the region of Mari. One relative constant, however, appears in the close association of prophetic activity and temple support. The temples were located across the land, and the texts attest to a complex structure of temple personnel where only prophets communicated the divine will from temples. Sometimes these pronouncements dealt with big issues such as the deity's conferral of favor upon the current king, but many of the reports have to do with more immediate events or needs. To illustrate the former, consider the statement of Abiya, a prophet in Alleppo, when speaking for the deity Addu: "Thus says Addu: 'I gave all the land to Yahdun-Lim and because of my weapons, he had no rival. He abandoned me, however, and so I gave to Samsi-Addu, the land that I had given to him."

As with most such prophetic pronouncements, this statement was delivered through an intermediary (this one named Nur-Sin) who was normally a local government official. What is clear from the letter is that the prophet Abiya conveys the deity Addu's support of Zimri-Lim, even while claiming that Addu was responsible for giving power to Yahdun-Lim (father of Zimri-Lim) and for taking away that power. In this text, Addu (through Abiya) asks only that Zimri-Lim act with justice in his role as judge. In another instance, an official consults a prophet on Zimri-Lim's behalf, but the oracle is concerned specifically with the safety of the king at a particular time. The text is broken, but the context provides the gist of the response to a localized event: "The very next day, I assembled the *nabû* (prophets) of the tent-dwellers. I had an omen taken for the safety of my lord, saying 'If my lord stays seven days on the outside when he performs [his] ritual bathing.'" At this point, the account breaks off, so the response is not reported, but clearly the official had a specific event in mind.

For an overview, see Daniel E. Fleming, "Prophets and Temple Personnel in the Mari Archives," *in the Priests in the Prophets: The Portrayal of Priests, Prophets, and Other Religious Specialists in the Latter Prophets* (ed. Lester L. Grabbe and Alice Ogden Bellis; JSOTSup 408; London: T & T Clark, 2004) 46, 50–53, 56. For a survey of topics and patterns in prophecies, and their implications, see Simon B. Parker, "Official Attitudes toward Prophecy at Mari and in Israel," *VT* 43 (1993): 50–68. For an assessment of the expansive presence of prophets at Mari and the royal controls used by the king that includes a collection of significant texts in translation, see William L. Moran, "New Evidence from Mari on the History of Prophecy," *Bib* 56 (1969): 15–56.

Text cited from Fleming, "Prophets and Temple Personnel," 52.

---

In 7:14-17, Amos defends his honor as one genuinely called of God (7:14-15), and then pronounces a judgment oracle against Amaziah (7:16-17). Amos begins by denying that he is a professional prophet who has come to Israel to make money. Amos claims not to be a prophet or the son of a prophet (usually interpreted as a prophet's disciple; see 2 Kgs 2:3, 5, 15; 4:1, 38; 6:1; 9:1). Moreover, Amos claims YHWH called him when he was gainfully employed as a shepherd and a tender of sycamore trees, meaning he did not need to come to Israel to make money. The case has often been made that Amos must have been a man of some means to have owned both cattle and orchards. [Prophet, Shepherd, Tender of Trees] Typical of judgment oracles, Amos recapitulates the current setting, though from a perspective quite different from that of Amaziah. Next, Amos pronounces YHWH's verdict, introducing it with a speech as bombastic as the one Amaziah leveled at him: "You say, 'do not prophesy against Israel, and do not preach against the house of Isaac.'" Afterward Amos predicts Amaziah's wife will be forced into prostitution, his children killed in battle, and his land parceled out to strangers, while Amaziah will die in a foreign land when Israel is exiled. Such specific threats are unusual from a prophet, and one could certainly draw a parallel to the confrontation between Jeremiah and Hananiah in Jeremiah 28:12-16. At any rate, the narrative breaks off abruptly so that the fourth vision report (8:1-3) then concludes the judgment oracle.

Intertextuality plays a role in this narrative since Amaziah's accusations charge Amos with predicting the death of the king and the exile of the people. Both charges are essentially accurate. Amos 7:9 pronounced God would act against the "house of Jeroboam with the sword." While some try to obfuscate this charge by claiming it related to only to the king's descendants, such fine distinctions would probably mean little to a sitting king. In addition, the prediction of exile accurately reflects some of the sayings (5:5, 27; 6:7). The veracity of Amaziah's charges is not at issue within the narrative, for Amos has done exactly what the priest charges him of doing. Rather, at issue is the question of authority. Amaziah recognizes the king as the ultimate authority, while Amos speaks from his sense of obligation to God.

The narrative in 7:10-17, taken by itself, makes a subtle point with a strong dose of irony. No sooner does Amaziah forbid Amos from prophesying than Amos prophesies against Amaziah himself. Amaziah tells Amos that the land cannot bear his prophecies about exile, and Amos tells Amaziah, "You are going with them." Amos refuses to let Amaziah have the last word.

However, the rhetorical effect of the narrative looks different when interpreted with the visions. The narrative ends abruptly with the pronouncement of judgment against Amaziah in the judgment oracle, but the judgment oracle lacks a concluding element. Usually, judgment oracles end with a formulaic statement or with some indication of how the situation plays out, but 7:10-17 does not. As soon as Amos pronounces the verdict against Amaziah, the fourth vision begins. Moreover, this fourth vision stresses that the end is near (8:2). By inserting the narrative between the third and fourth visions, the author creates a new dynamic. Instead of emphasizing the irony of a prophet forbidden to prophesy who prophesies, the hammer drops on Israel in the fourth vision. Amaziah, the chief priest at Bethel, Israel's religious center, rejects Amos, and the placement of 7:10-17 represents Israel's rejection of the message of Amos in the broader context. This official rejection appropriately precedes the pronouncement of the end because it illustrates for the reader that Israel left God no choice when it rejected the message of his prophet.

### The Fourth Vision—The End Has Come, 8:1-3

The structural similarities between the third and fourth vision reports were introduced at the beginning of the discussion of the third report (7:7-9). Here, the discussion will concentrate upon the distinguishing characteristics of the fourth vision report (8:1-3) and its role in Amos.

The play on words in 8:1-3 is more recognizable than the pun in 7:7-9. In 8:1-3, the object that the prophet sees is not only recognizable but is desirable; he sees a basket of *summer fruit*, and tells YHWH so when asked. Summer fruit represents a general term for any number of fruits that ripen in the summer including figs, pomegranates, grapes, and melons. This vision would be particularly appealing, both to the imagination and the senses. Pleasant notions evaporate, however, with the explanation of the vision. It uses a pun on the word for summer fruit (*qāyiṣ*) when YHWH suddenly announces that the end (*qēṣ*) is near. YHWH then describes the end of Israel in graphic detail that flows from YHWH's decision not to withhold punishment any longer. The songs of worship will become funeral songs, and corpses will pile up everywhere. As if to emphasize the finality of this decision, 8:3 ends with a single word that leaves no room for the prophet to intercede: YHWH simply and forcefully concludes, "hush."

The conversation by which YHWH explains the puns in the third and fourth reports contrasts with the first pair of vision reports because it replaces the prayer of intercession from the prophet. In other words, once the pattern is established that the prophet intercedes when he realizes the threat against Israel, his failure to intercede in visions 3 and 4 cannot be overlooked. Thus, one forms a different impression if one reads the visions in isolation than if one reads them in their current canonical context, where 7:10-17 is inserted between the third and fourth visions and the theological summation of Amos appears in 8:4-14 between the fourth and fifth visions. Amos 7:10-17 emphasizes Israel's rejection of YHWH's prophet. We now turn to 8:4-14, which creates a literary summation before the final vision (9:1-4).

### Recalling the Prophet's Message, 8:4-14

Beginning with the command, "Hear this," Amos 8:4-14 returns to a style of sayings reminiscent of Amos 3–6. Significantly, Amos 8:4-14 presents nothing new. The themes of these sayings have already surfaced, and many of the phrases used in this passage echo those found earlier in the book. [Recurring Language in Amos 8] Four

---

### Recurring Language in Amos 8

AΩ Amos 8 presents something of a montage, combining and rearranging images, phrases, and themes that the reader has already encountered in the book. Functionally, coming between the fourth and fifth vision reports, 8:4-14 provides a theological summary of the message of Amos to Israel.

| Amos 8 | | Elsewhere in Amos | |
|---|---|---|---|
| 8:3: | dead bodies; Hush! | 6:9-10: | dead bodies; Hush! |
| 8:4: | Hear This! | 3:1; 4:1; 5:1: | Hear this! |
| 8:4: | Trample (*š'ap*) on the needy (*'ebyôn*) | 2:7: | Trampling (*š'ap*) on the head of the poor |
| 8:5: | (abuse of sacred days) | 5:21-23: | (YHWH despises the festivals) |
| 8:6: | buying the needy (*'ebyôn*) for a pair of sandals and taking grain (*bar*) from the needy for profit | 2:6: | Selling the needy (*'ebyôn*) for sandals |
| | | 5:11: | taxing the poor for grain (*bar*) |
| 8:7: | Swearing by the pride of Jacob | 6:8: | YHWH swearing, hating the pride of Jacob |
| 8:8: | land trembles and inhabitants mourn | 9:5: | the earth melts and its inhabitants mourn |
| 8:9: | on that day I will make a day of light into darkness | 5:18-20: | The day of YHWH will become a day of darkness and not light |
| 8:10: | I will turn your feasts into mourning Your songs become laments | 5:21: | I despise your festivals |
| | | 5:16: | farmers mourn and funeral singers will lament |
| 8:11: | famine on the land; (not a) thirst for water, | 4:6: | lack of bread in the cities |
| 8:12: | but wandering (*nû'a*) the land to seek (*bāqaš*) the word of YHWH | 4:8: | wandering (*nû'a*) for water |
| | | 5:4-6: | Seek (*dāraš*) YHWH and live |
| 8:13: | young maidens (*bĕtûlâh*) and men will faint from thirst | 5:1: | Maiden (*bĕtûlâh*) Israel has fallen, no more to rise |
| 8:14: | (idolaters) will fall and not rise | | |

rhetorical shifts characterize the subunits of this passage, 8:4-7, 8-10, 11-12, 13-14.

*Amos 8:4-7.* The theological summation of 8:4-14 begins the same way as the first three chapters of the sayings: "Hear this!" (3:1; 4:1; 5:1). This formula not only echoes the beginnings of those chapters, but the content that follows also takes up the themes and formulations from elsewhere in the book, albeit often combined in different ways.

Amos 8:4 addresses those castigated in Amos 2 and 5: the insensitive wealthy, whose lack of concern for how they make their money evokes denunciation from the prophet in 8:7. In between, 8:5-6 extends the accusations, portraying this group's anxious longing for the religious observances to end so that they might resume their commerce—commerce built on dishonest and unethical practices. Here, the prophet mockingly quotes not only their desire to resume selling but also their confession that they use dishonest scales to cheat their customers. The prophet accuses these merchants of using weights that are heavier than they claim to be, meaning they are charging more for less than they claim. However, Amos 8:4-6 also reiterates that their actions have not gone unnoticed, and, ominously, 8:7 declares that YHWH will hold them accountable for what they have done. YHWH will not forget their deeds.

*Amos 8:8-10.* Amos 8:8 begins with a rhetorical question that explores the implications of the preceding statement. Implications of this question are obvious: anyone who understands this declaration in 8:7 should be scared. The rhetorical question also implies the reason that the land should tremble: creation itself will become involved as the earth will heave violently, rising and falling like the River Nile. This language evokes images of an earthquake or a theophany. (For a discussion of portrayals of a theophany in prophetic literature, see [Theophany].) In Amos, the blending of earthquake and theophany images happens as a sign of divine judgment, both at the beginning (1:1-2) and near the end of

**Weights and Scales**

Stone weights from roughly the time of Amos show a relatively complex system of fractions of shekels (from 1/2 to 2 shekels). In the set pictured here, a shekel weighted about 11 grams, but these weights varied from location to location, and they changed over time.

Stone weights. Iron age, 930–580 BCE. Reuben & Edith Hecht Collection, Haifa University, Haifa, Israel. (Credit: Erich Lessing/Art Resource, NY)

the book (9:1). In fact, 8:8 anticipates motifs occurring in the final creation doxology in 9:5, and contains the only allusion that points forward to another text in Amos within 8:4-14, a passage that serves as a summation of the book's message prior to the final vision of the destruction of the temple and the kingdom.

Amos 8:8-10 describes the effect of this upheaval upon the land (8:8), the cosmos (8:9), and the people (8:10), all guided by the formula "on that day" (8:9). The land will show the kind of upheaval associated with earthquakes, while the cosmos will alter radically with the sun going dark in the middle of the day. The people will gather to mourn rather than celebrate. They will put on the garb of mourning and repentance, perhaps in order to seek YHWH (see 8:12), but by then the die will be cast. These verses describe the effects of the coming day of YHWH on Israel, even though they do not use the specific phrase. To solidify the association of this destruction with the day of YHWH, the concluding phrase of the verse describes the end of this destruction as being "like a bitter day," like a day of mourning for an only son who has died. The focus of this unit falls upon the human misery of those who are suffering in the aftermath of the destruction.

*Amos 8:11-12.* A new introductory formula begins, "behold the days are coming." This phrase signals a new unit but not necessarily a new time frame. The reader must determine whether these verses parallel the action described in the preceding units or whether they presage what follows. The verses predict a famine, but a lack of sustenance in this case does not mean a lack of food or water. The famine about which 8:11-12 speaks is the unavailability of the word of YHWH, which implies a lack of prophetic speech (see discussion in Joel 1:1). Thus, the unit likely refers to a removal of YHWH's prophets from the land. This charge is more poignant following the rejection of Amos depicted in 7:10-17. While the unit does not specify how the time frame relates to the preceding verses, the fact that it refers to the time as "days that are coming" rather than the singular "on that day" *suggests* the verses are intended to be read in close proximity to one another. A time of devastation (8:8-10) will lead to a period when YHWH's word is absent (8:11-12), that will in turn lead to a time of death for idolaters in the land (8:13-14). [Seeking the Word]

*Amos 8:13-14.* The last unit of the chapter begins with another introductory formula, "on that day." These verses offer little hope for the population. This implied fate of 8:12 affects even those in society who would otherwise be the elite of the next generation, as even the young women and men will faint from thirst. Those who put their trust in other gods shall fall and not get up (8:13).

Amos 8:14 references three places and three acts whose combination shows how pervasive the prophet deemed the problem: (1) those swearing by Ashimah of Samaria; (2) those saying, "as your God lives, O Dan"; and (3) those saying "as the way of Beer-sheba lives." These three lines each specify an

> **Seeking the Word**
>
> Given that the "word of YHWH" implies prophetic activity, the imagery in 8:11-12 implies that the coming time will see a cessation of prophetic activity from YHWH. Hence, the people will no longer hear prophets speaking on YHWH's behalf, even though they seek it. The irony of this judgment becomes clear when one hears this statement in light of the actions of Amaziah who forbade YHWH's prophet Amos from speaking (Amos 7:10-17).

act of idolatry or apostasy, and the places represent the central kingdom (Samaria), the northern end of the country (Dan), and the far southern region of Judah (Beer-sheba). Two options for explaining the charges in the first line are reflected in differences among English translations. "Those who swear by Ashimah of Samaria" (NRSV) in the first line connotes apostasy, describing an act of allegiance to a goddess, while the "guilt of Samaria" (NAS, NIV) implies a broader array of iniquity. Thus, Amos 8:14 could refer to a goddess Ashimah worshiped in Samaria at the time, but about whom we know nothing. Evidence for a goddess whose name is spelled similarly appears in 2 Kings 17:30. In addition to the different spelling, the goddess in 2 Kings 17:30 is worshiped by the people of Syria, not Samaria. The second, more likely interpretation treats *’ašmat Samaria* as a feminine construct noun that means guilt/shame (NAS, NIV). This phrase, "guilt of Samaria," could also represent a wordplay on Asherah in much the same way that Bethel (House of God) is named Beth-Aven (meaning House of Disaster) in Hosea 4:15 (see also Amos 4:4 and 5:5). Likely, the echo of Hosea 4:15 is not coincidental, given that Hosea 4:15 accuses Beth-aven of swearing "as YHWH lives," precisely the charge leveled in the second line of 8:14 against against those in Dan who say, "as your God lives." The third line transfers the charge of idolatry to the southern town of Beer-sheba. At any rate, the point is clear. Collectively, all three lines of 8:14 portray the entire region of Israel as abandoning allegiance to YHWH and replacing it with allegiance to other gods, a clear violation of the first two commandments (Exod 20:1-6; Deut 5:6-10).

### The Final Vision, 9:1-4

The fifth and final vision deviates significantly, but purposefully, from the first four reports. The structure is so different that the fifth vision is widely treated as a later addition to the corpus. More important than the question of authorship, however, is the *function* of this final vision in its current context. The key to this function appears in the very deviation of the structural elements. In the fifth vision, the prophet is an ancillary character, a passive observer who merely reports the devastation of Israel's temple and the annihilation of its people. Using language of earthquakes and theophanies, the vision describes the crumbling of the capitals in the thresholds of the temple and the futile attempts of people trying to escape the wrath of YHWH. Although the text does not specifically mention Bethel or Samaria, the context demands relating this vision to the destruction of the northern kingdom.

### The Final Doxology, 9:5-6

The final doxology in 9:5-6 shares phrases and themes with its counterparts in 4:13 and 5:8-9. (See the discussion in 4:13, where the methods of connection and the thematic movement are explained.) The three doxologies accentuate two themes: (1) YHWH created the world, and (2) YHWH has the power to destroy it. These themes culminate in 9:5-6 where, following the description of the final vision (9:1-4), these verses reaffirm YHWH's power over creation.

In addition to the connections to the other doxologies, Amos 9:5 also contains the images of the land melting, the people mourning, and the land undulating up and down like the River Nile. All three of these images appear in the pivotal verse of 8:8—the center of the theological summary between the fourth and fifth visions. Thus, even more than the first two doxologies, Amos 9:5-6 connects closely to its larger context. Many have argued that this doxology served as the conclusion of the book prior to the exilic and postexilic additions of 9:7-10 and 9:11-15. Whatever its point of entry into the text, there can be little doubt that 9:5-6 functions as a final emphatic chord, underscoring God's judgment upon Israel in Amos.

Unlike the book of Hosea, which alternates a message of judgment and promise for the people of Israel, the book of Amos has from the beginning focused exclusively on God's impending judgment, the reasons for God's judgment, and God's attempts to change the people. Up to this point, only a few texts in Amos have referred in passing to those surviving the destruction and aftermath of God's judgment, as the message of the book has placed little emphasis upon this remnant. That will now change in the two remaining units (9:7-10, 11-15); even so, it is clear in these passages of hope that nothing will be as it once was.

## CONNECTIONS

The changing role of the prophet in this vision sequence sheds light on the portrayal of God, underscores the accusations against God's people, and offers challenges for our own situation. According to these visions, God twice changes God's mind (7:3, 6). Some people find it threatening to think that God would change God's mind. However, in the Old Testament, the image of God changing God's mind is a function of God's sovereignty. Exodus 34:6-7 provides the basis for several texts in the Book of the Twelve that explore the ramifications of a God willing to forgive but who still expects obedience. Canonically speaking, Exodus 34:6-7 plays a pivotal role in understanding the attributes of God. God has just brought Israel to the base of Sinai (Exod 19), where God has delivered the Book of the Covenant (Exod 20–23) to which the people have agreed to submit themselves (Exod 24). Next, while God commands Moses how to build the tabernacle (Exod 25–31), the people turn to Aaron to lead them into apostasy by worshiping the golden calf (Exod 32–33). As a result, God determines for the first time to destroy Israel for disobedience (Exod 32:10), but Moses intercedes on Israel's behalf and YHWH changes YHWH's mind (Exod 32:11-14).

Additional texts in the Book of the Twelve explore God's motives for this behavior from several perspectives (Joel 2:12-17; 3:21; Jonah 4:2; Mic 7:18-20; Nah 1:3). These texts illustrate the significance of worshiping a long-suffering, faithful, and merciful God, but one who articulates a desire to hold the guilty accountable. None of these attributes reflects mechanical processes, for God, and only God, decides whether to exercise grace or punish the guilty. Human statements on the nature of God's justice do not limit

God; God chooses when and how to act. Human repentance does not force God into forgiveness; God chooses when and whom to forgive. Human repentance *may* cause God to reconsider, but God chooses when and whether that will happen. Even after God has made the decision to punish, God may choose to reverse course. (See [YHWH Repenting].)

Most instances where the Bible speaks of God changing God's mind involve human repentance or intercession. Theologically, this means we serve a dynamic God for whom the future is open. We do not serve a God who has preordained what will happen, but a God willing to wait for humans to change even though that waiting causes pain. We serve a God who is faithful and compassionate, even though that compassion sometimes extends human suffering. And, on the other hand, we also serve a God who will not be mocked, a God of justice for the oppressed and the oppressor, a God of redemption and wrath, a God who delivers the poor and punishes the powerful. God changes God's mind *because* God responds to the responses human beings make, and the future unfolds accordingly.

The prophet's successful intercession in the first two visions contrasts with the people's failure to heed the prophet's message, resulting in further charges and predictions of Israel's destruction in 7:7–9:6. Then the third and fourth vision reports (7:7-9; 8:1-3) frame the narrative of Amaziah's rejection of the prophet (7:10-17). The location of the narrative occurs at precisely the point in the vision reports where one finds the prophet interceding on Israel's behalf in the first two vision reports. Put another way, the prophet's successful intercession does not occur a third time because the narrative of Amaziah's rejection of Amos takes the place of the prophet's intercession. The placement of the narrative thus removes from the scene the one person who had twice proven successful in intervening on Israel's behalf. Moreover, rejecting the messenger is representative of Israel's rejection of Amos's message. As a result, YHWH determines the time has come to bring an end to the kingdom. In short, this rejection has both religious and ethical causes in the book of Amos, and both aspects appear prominently in the rehearsal of the charges in 8:4-14. Specifically, the ethical charges include oppression of the poor and cheating in the marketplace (8:4-6), while the religious causes include idolatry (8:13-14).
[Prayer and Its Literary Contexts]

In modern communities of faith, one must ponder an important question about these visions: "What of Amos's charges today?" Do the accusations of this prophet carry any weight in a modern, pluralistic world for people of faith? Some might say the prophet Amos preaches a message that is too nationalistic to be valid. Others might say the message of Amos confronts a political system that does not correlate to our own. Still others might say that talk of God judging nations is no longer adequate as a theological paradigm. What relevance do these prophetic words have, since they confronted a kingdom that disappeared from the scene over 2,700 years ago? What significance do the words of an ancient Jewish prophet have for modern believers? The answer lies not in a prediction about the end of the world or in a proclamation of some grand "I told you so."

Even at the beginning of the twenty-first century the message of Amos provides a starting point for personal and national self-reflection. The situations that motivated Amos to speak against the kingdom, its rulers, and its elite have not been solved. As long as wealthy nations take advantage of poor nations, and the wealthy within nations continue to oppress the poor, the words of Amos need to be heard. As long as problems continue to be addressed by violence that one group, rich or poor, perpetrates upon another, the words of Amos need to be heard. As long as our treasured religious practices are more important than establishing just and equitable systems by which to live and relate to others, the words of Amos need to be heard. Justice and righteousness lie at the heart of the message of Amos, and people of faith must continue to struggle with how to implement justice and righteousness in our day.

Amos confronts greed and oppression, especially when it is done in the name of God Almighty. Amos confronts religious pomposity that places ceremony above righteous acts. Amos confronts political superiority that considers itself unassailable. Amos does all of this in the conviction that God has established an order for this world that transcends the buildings where we worship, that supersedes the

---

**Prayer and Its Literary Contexts**

The literary function of prayer is not always noted. Frequently, prayers in biblical narratives reinforce the larger narrative context and play a role in connecting the discourse. Similarly, the prayers of intercession in Amos's first two visions follow such a close linguistic pattern twice that the reader expects a third prayer in Amos 7:9, only to be told instead about the banishment of Amos (7:10-17), a narrative that connects to the third vision report by pronouncements of Jeroboam's death by the sword in YHWH's pronouncement (7:9) and Amaziah's rebuke of Amos (7:11).

Note the intricate relationship of the prayer for divine intervention in the Hezekiah narrative to its narrative context (2 Kgs 19:15-19), and the role of prayer as discourse in the Deuteronomistic History and Chronicles as illustrated by Samuel E. Balentine, *Prayer in the Hebrew Bible* (Overtures to Biblical Theology; Minneapolis: Fortress, 1993) 91–100.

petty interests of kings and kingdoms, and that demands from all believers that we find ways to harmonize our lives with the order God would see established. When this does not happen, political entities threaten to fall apart, and the world itself totters and shakes. So let justice roll down like waters, and righteousness like an ever-flowing stream; let the wealthy sell their sandals for the poor and pull the afflicted out of the dust; let the Sabbath be a day of rest and a day for contemplating words of peace; let us pray that the day of YHWH will be a day of enlightenment and not darkness; and let us find the word of YHWH in our day to be words of peace and not fear, words of justice and not oppression, words of righteousness but not self-righteousness.

# A REMNANT AND HOPE

## Amos 9:7-15

## COMMENTARY

The move from judgment to hope typical of several prophetic writings occurs in Amos 9:7-15 in at least two units (9:7-10; 9:11-15). It is doubtful, however, that either represents a text from the time of Amos. Rather, the complete change of tenor from judgment to promise has largely been determined to be the product of exilic or postexilic editing. Not only does the theme change but the texts, especially 9:11-15, also represent a Judean perspective and an eschatological orientation far more consistent with exilic and postexilic literature.

*Amos 9:7-10: (Only) A Remnant Will Survive.* Amos 9:7-10 represents a thematic unit, but its message appears to present two sides of a debate concerning the fate of the kingdom. Amos 9:7-8a forms a divine speech that rejects any notion of Israel being unique among the nations (9:7) and confirms YHWH's intention to remove "the sinful kingdom . . . from the face of the earth" (9:8a). By contrast, the second half of this unit (9:8b-10) places limits upon the destruction, suggesting that a remnant will remain because only the guilty would be destroyed.

Amos 9:7 takes aim at Israel's most prized tradition, its sense of election.[1] Similar challenges to a sense of entitlement appeared in Amos 3–5. Consequently, it undercuts any claim that Israel could expect special treatment from YHWH. Specifically, it affirms YHWH's role in delivering Israel out of Egypt but treats this salvific act as evidence of the nature of God, not a sign of special status for Israel. God also claims to have delivered the Philistines and the Syrians as well. In other words, God's work is not confined to the borders of Israel, and God works salvifically on behalf of nations near and far. Caphtor and Kir represent the hostile, adjacent countries of Philistia and Syria respectively. On the other hand, reference to the

Ethiopians (the Cushites) evokes a sense of an exotic, faraway people—a people who would seem as far removed from Israel culturally and historically as they are geographically. Thus, Amos 9:7 affirms that God acts on behalf of all these foreigners, regardless of culture and proximity, just as he does for Israel—no more, no less. Amos 9:7 challenges those in Israel who believe that being God's chosen keeps them safe from external threats. Yet God has structured the world so that actions have consequences, and when human beings work at cross purposes to God's intentions, God will allow, or cause, those consequences to come to fruition.

Amos 9:8 provides a classic example of communicating truth through paradox, since 9:8a and 9:8b present conflicting claims. The first half of the verse claims God will utterly destroy "the sinful kingdom" from the face of the earth, while the second half equivocates about the extent of destruction. The claim of 9:8a that YHWH will destroy the sinful kingdom is undercut in the next line: "I will *not* utterly destroy the house of Jacob." Explanations of this discrepancy have generally sought either a linguistic or diachronic solution. Some try to create linguistic nuances between the formulations used in the two halves. Even though the same verb appears in 9:8a and 9:8b, some argue that the verbal expression in 9:8b is more emphatic, distinguishing the phrase "destroy" from "utterly destroy." This line of reasoning creates problems since the (arguably) weaker form of 9:8a ("I will destroy") is followed immediately by the expression "from the face of the earth," which leaves the clear impression of utter destruction. A second linguistic approach attempts to distinguish between the identity of "the sinful kingdom" in 9:8a and the "house of Jacob" in 9:8b. For example, Andersen and Freedman argue that "house of Jacob" refers to the entire kingdom (Judah and Israel), a problematic assertion since elsewhere in Amos Jacob clearly stands for the northern kingdom (3:13; 7:2, 5; 6:8; 8:7).[2]

A diachronic explanation typically suggests that the harsh, fatalistic statement in 9:7-8a elicited comment from a later hand after the destruction of the country, when it became clear that a remnant had survived in the northern kingdom. However one explains the conflicting claims of 9:8, it is clear that 9:9-10 build upon the ideas expressed in 9:8b: some would survive.

Amos 9:9-10 interprets Israel's destruction as the work of God, but work that is in some way limited to the destruction of the sinful among the kingdom. Amos 9:9 formally connects to 9:8b via the conjunction "for," linking a description of a remnant in 9:9-10 with those who survived the destruction of 9:8. The unit describes God's judgment with the metaphor of a sieve wherein the house of Israel is shaken "among the nations" while pebbles remain in the sieve. The connotations of this metaphor portray two groups: a smaller group that survives but is scattered among the nations, and the larger pebbles that remain in the sieve, which will be destroyed. Amos 9:10 identifies the latter group as "the sinners of my people." In this metaphor, then, the entire "house of Israel" experiences judgment, but not everyone dies. This group of sinners is further character- ized as those who believe they are safe from calamity. In the context of the book of Amos, identifying these two groups is not easy. Does this remnant refer to fugitives from Israel after the destruction of Samaria who made their way to Jerusalem? Or does it refer to Judah who sur- vived the onslaught of the Assyrian military machine in the latter third of the eighth century BCE? Both interpretations are possible.

*Amos 9:11-15: Political Restoration and Fertility.* The promise (9:11-15) contains two parts (9:11-12, 13-15), as indicated by the introductory formulas in 9:11 and 9:13. [Diachronic Notes on Amos 9:11-15] Amos 9:11-12 offers a promise of restoration of the Davidic kingdom (9:11) and an attendant purpose statement (9:12). The promise in 9:11 unfolds in a series of four parallel lines complicated by an enig- matic phrase (fallen booth of David) to which three different pronominal suffixes refer back. The variation in suffixes does not, as is often presumed, result from a corrupt text. A comparison of the ancient versions indicates they all struggle with how to translate the variation in suffixes.[3] Rather, the parallelism of these lines sug- gests a deliberate, artistically constructed poetic image promising the rebuilding and restoration of the Davidic kingdom of old. [Parallelism of Amos 9:11] The larger context indicates that the metaphor of the fallen booth of David connotes the Davidic kingdom as a whole, though it presumes Jerusalem's destruction in 587 along with other cities. The situation presumed by 9:11-15 reflects the destruction of cities (9:14) in need of rebuilding and repopulation,

**Diachronic Notes on Amos 9:11-15**

The material in Amos 9:11-15, as widely recognized among scholars, does not belong to the time of the prophet Amos in the eighth century. Additionally, Amos 9:11-15 is not the composition of a single author. Amos 9:11-15 contains material from at least two different hands. The first portion comes from the early exilic period (9:11, 14-15) because it brings a message of hope for rebuilding Jerusalem (9:11) and the devastated cities of the kingdom (9:14-15). This earlier portion is aware of Amos 9:7-10, which also presupposes the breakup of the kingdom. The remaining verses (9:12-13) expand upon this material with more elaborate eschatological aims and contain a thematic summary of Obadiah (9:12) and a quote of Joel 3:16 (9:13b).

The summary of the development of Amos 9:11-15 draws upon more extensive analysis in James D. Nogalski, *Literary Precursors to the Book of the Twelve* (BZAW 217; Berlin: De Gruyter, 1993) 110–22.

---

**Parallelism of Amos 9:11**

The presence of four clauses using three nearly synonymous verbs signals the parallelism, while the alternating suffixes treat the phrase "fallen booth of David" collectively (third feminine plural), then refer to David (3ms) and booth (3fs) specifically.

| I will raise up | I will repair | I will raise up | |
|---|---|---|---|
| the fallen booth (3fs) | ← | ← | I will rebuild it (3fs) |
| of David (3ms) | ← | his ruins (3ms) | |
| | ← their (3fp) breaches | | |

---

and it promises the retaking of land formerly part of the ideal Davidic boundaries, including Edom and other nations (9:12).

Thematically, 9:12, which emphasizes the possession of "the remnant of Edom" along with "all the nations who are called by my name," is interesting on several fronts. First, the promise of repossessing foreign territories when cities lie in ruins (9:14) reflects a more aggressive stance toward those foreign territories than would be expected in the early exilic period, when survival and rebuilding were the pressing issues. Second, the phrase "remnant of Edom" presumes that some type of destruction had already taken place, or at least was already underway. Neither the time of Amos nor the early exilic period can account for the idea of a remnant with respect to Edom; though by the end of the sixth century, the nomadic tribes, specifically the Nabateans, had begun to push the Edomites out of their territory and into what had been southern Judah. [Nabateans and Edomites] This loss of land to desert tribes continued for the better part of a century, and it appears to be reflected in the opening passage of Malachi (1:2-4). Third, the twin themes of the destruction of Edom and the reconstitution of the Davidic kingdom represent the two major themes of the book of Obadiah, which follows imme-

**Nabateans and Edomites**

The Nabateans were a group of Arab tribes whose incursion into lands formerly held by Edom began in the Persian period. Over time, the Nabateans forced Edomites west and north until by the time of Jesus "Idumea" was directly south of Judea, whereas in the time of the prophet Amos, "Edom" was well south and east of the Jordan from Judah. The Nabateans became increasingly powerful as they ultimately controlled the southern trade routes from the Persian Gulf to Egypt to the west or north to the Syrian Desert, from at least the fourth century BCE. An exact sequence of events in the fifth century is difficult to construct due to the sparse nature of sources and the uncertainty of the relationship between the Nabateans and the Nebaioth. The Nabatean city of Petra (in modern Jordan) represents one of the marvels of ancient architecture, with its massive building facades carved into the rock face, like the treasury pictured here whose carved front stands 130 feet high.

See John R. Bartlett, *Edom and the Edomites* (JSOTSup 77; Sheffield: JSOT Press, 1989) 163–74.

Facade of Al Khazneh (Treasury), Petra, Jordan. (Credit: Bernard Gagnon, http://en.wikipedia.org/wiki/File:Al_Khazneh.jpg)

diately after Amos. [Amos 9:11-15 and the Book of the Twelve] Fourth, Amos 9:12 plays a significant role in Christian history and mission, though not one that is consistent with its Amos context. [Amos 9:12 in MT, LXX, and NT]

Amos 9:13-15 continues the eschatological promise from 9:11-12, though parts of it reflect grander expectations and an awareness of the larger context. Amos 9:13 begins almost identically to Amos 8:11: "Behold the days are coming says *Adonai* YHWH." Coupled with the phrase "on that day" that appears in Amos 8:9, the parallel introductory formulas in 8:9, 11 suggest that 9:11-15 mirrors the structural elements of the preceding chapter. The promise of 9:13, set in a vague point in the

## Amos 9:11-15 and the Book of the Twelve

See the discussion in Joel of the doublet between Joel 3:18a (MT 4:18a) and Amos 9:13b. This verse forms part of the connection with the end of Joel, where Joel 3:16, 18 (MT 4:16, 18) contains citations of Amos 1:2 and 9:14. The end of Joel cites the beginning and end of Amos. When one also recognizes that Amos 9:12 connects linguistically and thematically to the book of Obadiah, it certainly raises the likelihood that the wording and placement of these three sequential writings in the Book of the Twelve (Masoretic order) cannot be explained as coincidence. More will be said about these commonalities in the treatment of the structure of Obadiah.

---

## Amos 9:12 in MT, LXX, and NT

AΩ Acts 15:16-18 cites Amos 9:11-12 in support of Paul's mission to the Gentiles, a hermeneutical move made possible by the changes made by the LXX translator of the Hebrew text. Understanding the changes from MT to LXX allows one to see as well the changes made by Luke's portrayal of James's speech. The critical changes in these three versions take place in two lines:

| Amos 9:11-12 MT | Amos 9:11-12 LXX | Acts 15:16-18 |
|---|---|---|
| [11]On that day I will raise up the fallen booth of David . . . | [11]On that day I will raise up the fallen booth of David . . . | [16]After this I will return, and I will rebuild the fallen booth of David . . . |
| [12]so that they may possess (ירש) the remnant of Edom (אדום) and all the nations who are called by my name, says YHWH who does this. | [12]so that the remnant *of men* (אדם) and all the nations upon whom my name is called may seek (me) (דרש) | [17]so that the remnant of men may seek *the Lord*, even all the Gentiles who bear my name, says the Lord would does these things [18]*known from long ago.* |
| The statement in Amos (MT) is a promise of hope for the restoration of the ideal boundaries of the Davidic kingdom through conquest (that is, possession). | LXX reflects three substantive changes to MT:<br>(1) The nation Edom (אדום) is changed to humanity (אדם) by dropping one letter from the Hebrew consonantal text.<br>(2) "Remnant of men" and "all the nations" become the subject, rather than the direct object, by dropping the direct object marker (את) from MT.<br>(3) The verb "possess" (ירש) changes to "seek" (דרש) by changing the first letter of the root. | Acts follows the LXX, but also makes three changes:<br>(1) Acts changes "On that day I will raise" to "After this, I will return," presumably for christological reasons.<br>(2) Acts inserts "the Lord" as the direct object of "seek," thereby correcting the awkward syntax of LXX (which lacked a direct object) and simultaneously emphasizing "even all the Gentiles" for contextual reasons.<br>(3) Acts adds an editorial comment, "known from long ago." |

What makes these variations so interesting is that the fluidity of translation, especially when combined with the theological and christological lenses of the New Testament writers, radically changes the original meaning of the Hebrew text from a message of conquest to a model of openness to foreigners. The LXX's deliberate change for a new context (the Greek-speaking Jewish Diaspora) opens the door for James to offer the crucial support of Paul's mission to the Gentiles that changed the course of Christian history.

future ("and behold the days are coming"), offers hope for refertilization of the land, the likes of which the land had never known. The hyperbolic images of the promise evoke a picture of agricultural abundance in poetic pairings.[4] Because the harvest is so plentiful, the one who plows will find that the fields are still being harvested when it is time to replant them, and workers will still be treading the harvested grapes when they will be needed to sow the seed. Indeed, the mountains themselves, where grape vines were often planted, "shall drip with sweet wine." The word translated "sweet wine" (*ʿâsîs*) is not one of the common words used for wine, but it probably refers to newly threshed or freshly fermented wine.

Amos 9:14 speaks of restoration in the aftermath of military destruction and exile. Like 9:11, Amos 9:14 refers to rebuilding and repopulating the cities that have been destroyed. This promise makes sense in the aftermath of the destruction of Judah, especially in light of the promise that the population will once again plant vineyards and gardens and will be able to benefit from those labors. In addition, Amos 9:15 emphasizes that YHWH will plant the people on the land so that they will never be removed again. Both promises (replanting and refertilization) coincide with the general scenario anticipated in 9:11, but they are superfluous when read in conjunction with the promise of 9:13. What need does one have to replant if the land is already producing an abundance of grain and wine? Oddly, then, Amos 9:11 and 14-15 stress the need to rebuild, replant, and restore while 9:12 and 13 go well beyond these simple hopes. The fact that vv. 12 and 13 also connect to Obadiah and Joel suggests the possibility that the promise elements in 9:11-15 come from at least two different hands.

## CONNECTIONS

The story of Israel in Genesis to Kings is not the complete story of God. Even when one includes the remaining narrative, prophetic, and poetic books of the Old Testament, one does not get the entire picture. The Old Testament presents Israel's testimony of how God acted in the lives of its people, shaped its history, and communicated its understanding of who God is. As a result, these biblical books testify to the powerful presence of God in Israel's past. What one must not forget is that this testimony is filtered through the lens of Israel's experience. Only occasionally, as in Amos 9:7, do the writers pause to reflect on the broader range of YHWH's activity in the world. Like the people whom this text originally addressed, testimony of religious experience cuts two ways. On the one hand, it offers a powerful and moving witness that God is actively at work in the lives of believers and in communities of faith. Without this concrete testimony, God would remain an abstract deity far removed from daily life.

On the other hand, a focus solely upon the experience of God by one person, one congregation, one denomination, or one nation attempts to place limits on God's activity. We tend to judge others by what we have experienced without trusting that God is bigger than our own experience. We need to remember both sides of this testimony. We need to recount the ways we have experienced God, but we also need to hear others recount their experience. Otherwise, when we only talk of God in small circles, we will be tempted to believe that God must act toward others in the same way God has acted in our own experience. Why is it, for example, that so many Christian congregations in the United States feel compelled to fly the American flag in God's sanctuary, while many Christian congregations in Europe refuse to fly the flag of any nation within the walls of the sanctuary? For many in the United States, flying the flag represents a kind of prayer for God's protection of the nation. For others, though, it represents an affirmation that God has chosen this country from all the countries in the world for special blessing. In Europe, especially among Baptists and other Free Church traditions, the lessons of history are still too fresh regarding what happens when the church *submits* to the aims of the state without asking what God expects. Crusaders of the Middle Ages left Europe to take the Holy Land for Christianity by force, with the blessing of the church. Anabaptists and other Free Church reformers were drowned at the behest of the state in Europe, and the official church watched. Jews were burned and gassed under Hitler's regime, and the church rarely said a word. The power and fate of a nation should not be equated with the grace of God. Amos 9:7 reminded Israel that God is God over Philistia and Syria, countries that did not have Israel's interests at heart; we would do well to remember that lesson.

Hope is a powerful theological motif because it provides something the human condition requires. Viktor Frankl, renowned therapist of the twentieth century, was imprisoned in several different concentration camps during World War II only because he was Jewish.[5] He observes that those who survived the arduous life of the concentration camp were those who found reason to live. For some it was the hope of seeing family again; for others it was a desire to return to their life work; for others it was the meaning they found from the suffering itself that gave them the strength to continue. Such desire is hard to fathom in an age of instant gratification, in a society where our needs and desires can be met with little effort. Yet, when things are taken away, as they were for Frankl, how does one cope with radical change on a societal level?

Amos 9:11-15 knows the message of Amos but does not speak to the same audience. The passage speaks to those for whom the "booth of David" had fallen (9:11). This phrase functions as a metaphor for a kingdom that had ceased to exist with the destruction of Jerusalem in 587. It speaks to those who knew their cities had been destroyed and to those whose labor no longer resulted in enjoying the produce of their land (9:14). Yet, these verses do not say "I told you so," nor do they present a homily saying, "Amos was right." Rather, they address a people humbled by circumstance, searching for a reason to put the pieces back together. They convey the message, "the story is not over." These verses assume a relationship with a faithful God and offer hope that the future will be better, that God will not abandon the promises of the past. In fact, the writer assumes—hopes—that only God can restore what God has taken. In the ruins of the fallen booth of David, only God could restore a kingdom. In the devastation and rubble that follow war, only God could rebuild the cities. In the aftermath of forced deportations, only God could replant the people. The words of this author cannot change the suffering; they can only offer hope that the suffering is not the end of the story, not the end of the relationship, and not the end of the people.

In the aftermath of communal devastation, one must seek hope for the future. In the aftermath of Katrina, blame does not get homes rebuilt in the Gulf Coast. After the Gulf oil disaster, anger at companies and governmental agencies can only go so far. Plans for moving forward must take its place. A message of hope does not mean ignoring the current devastation; it means clearing out the rubble, evaluating what went wrong with safety regulations, and maybe holding people accountable, but it also means rebuilding, reimagining what can be, and articulating goals for the future so that people can live in security, or, in the words of Amos 9:15, "so that they shall never again be plucked up out of the land that I have given them says, the LORD."

## NOTES

1. See also the discussion of Joel S. Kaminsky's exploration of election in the "Connections" for Mal 1:2-5 in James D. Nogalski, *The Book of the Twelve: Micah–Malachi* (Smyth & Helwys Bible Commentary Series).

2. For example, see Francis I. Andersen and David Noel Freedman, *Amos* (AB 24A; New York: Doubleday, 1989) 870.

3. James D. Nogalski, "The Problematic Suffixes of Amos 9:11," *VT* 43 (1993): 411–18.

4. In addition to the hyperbole, Andersen and Freedman (*Amos*, 891) insightfully call attention to the cyclical nature of this fertility promise since the four agricultural activities mentioned in 9:13 (plowing, sowing, reaping, and treading grapes) occur across the four seasons respectively (fall, winter, spring, and summer in order).

5. Viktor E. Frankl, *Man's Search for Meaning: An Introduction to Logotherapy* (trans. Ilse Lasch; New York: Washington Square Press, 1963).

# SELECT BIBLIOGRAPHY
## FOR AMOS

Andersen, Francis I., and David Noel Freedman. *Amos: A New Translation with Introduction and Commentary*. Anchor Bible 24A. New York: Doubleday, 1989.

Asen, Bernhard A. "No, Yes and Perhaps in Amos and the Yahwist." *Vetus Testamentum* 43 (1993): 433–41.

Auld, A. Graeme. *Amos*. Old Testament Guides. Sheffield: JSOT, 1986.

Barré, Michael L. "The Meaning of *l' 'sybnw* in Amos 1:3–2:6." *Journal of Biblical Literature* 105 (1986): 611–31.

Birch, Bruce C. *Hosea, Joel, and Amos*. Westminster Bible Companion. Louisville: Westminster John Knox, 1997.

Carroll R., Mark Daniel. *Amos—The Prophet and His Oracles: Research on the Book of Amos*. Louisville: Westminster John Knox, 2002.

Coggins, R. J. *Joel and Amos*. New Century Bible Commentary. Sheffield: Sheffield Academic Press, 2000.

Coote, Robert B. *Amos among the Prophets: Composition and Theology*. Philadelphia: Fortress, 1981.

Hayes, John Haralson. *Amos: The Eighth-Century Prophet: His Times and His Preaching*. Nashville: Abingdon Press, 1988.

Jeremias, Jörg. "The Interrelationship Between Amos and Hosea." In *Forming Prophetic Literature*, edited by James W. Watts and Paul House, 171–86. Sheffield: Sheffield Academic Press, 1996.

———. *The Book of Amos: A Commentary*. Old Testament Library. Louisville: Westminster John Knox, 1988.

Martin-Achard, Robert, and S. P. Re'emi. *God's People in Crisis: A Commentary on the Book of Amos*. International Theological Commentary. Edinburgh: Handsel Press, 1984.

Nogalski, James D. "The Problematic Suffixes of Amos ix 11." *Vetus Testamentum* 43 (1993): 411–18.

Paul, Shalom M., and Frank Moore Cross. *Amos: A Commentary on the Book of Amos*. Hermeneia. Minneapolis: Fortress, 1991.

Soggin, J. Alberto. *The Prophet Amos: A Translation and Commentary*. London: SCM, 1987.

Stuart, Douglas K. *Hosea–Jonah*. Word Biblical Commentary 31. Waco: Word Books, 1987.

Sweeney, Marvin A. *The Twelve Prophets*. Berit Olam. 2 volumes. Collegeville MN: Liturgical Press, 2000.

Watts, John D. W. *Vision and Prophecy in Amos*. Macon GA: Mercer University Press, 1997.

Wolff, Hans Walter. *Joel and Amos: A Commentary on the Books of the Prophets Joel and Amos*. Translated by Waldemar Janzen, S. Dean McBride, Jr., and Charles A. Muenchow. Hermeneia. Philadelphia: Fortress, 1977.

# OBADIAH

# INTRODUCTION TO THE BOOK OF OBADIAH

### Dating the Prophet and the Book

The prophet behind the sayings of Obadiah remains unknown. The Jerusalemite setting is not disputed given the centrality of the Zion tradition in Obadiah 16-21, as well as the concern for Edom's role in the destruction of Jerusalem in vv. 11-14. Attempts to identify a prophet with specific persons named Obadiah mentioned elsewhere in the Bible have not met with critical concurrence. A few commentators have questioned whether the name is an eponym, though most tend to treat the prophet as an actual person who is not known apart from the book.[1]

With respect to dating the book, the issues are no less complex. Three lines of evidence suggest a date of compilation for Obadiah that precludes anything before the sixth century. First, Obadiah 10-14 presumes knowledge of Edom's role in the aftermath of Jerusalem's destruction. Second, the parallels with Jeremiah 49 and Obadiah 1-5 likewise point to a time in the early sixth century as the earliest point for the compilation (see the discussion of the literary form, structure, and unity below). While the direction of dependence is debated, an analysis of the text in its context in the Book of the Twelve suggests that the Obadiah parallels derive from the Jeremiah context and not the other way around. Third, Obadiah 16-21 makes promises of restoration that presume the end of the sixth century as the earliest time of origin. However, given that vv. 16-21 are appended to an existing collection, one has to contend with the uncertain date of the combination of the two units as well as the dates of composition. Within Obadiah 16-21, vv. 19-20 comment upon vv. 17-18 and reflect a setting after Jerusalem's resettlement that was no longer an issue, which one can assume presupposes a time after Nehemiah (c. 450). To the extent these verses adapt an existing block as part of the combination of Obadiah 1-14+15b with 15a+16-18, 21, one can assume this adaptation takes place no earlier than the mid-fifth century.

Thus, the date of Obadiah depends on whether one speaks of the book in its final form or of the prophet presumed responsible for the early portions. Most critical scholars tacitly or overtly consider Obadiah to be the otherwise unknown prophet who wrote the bulk of the book (Obad 1-14+15b), adapted from an earlier source (Jer 49:14-16, 9), but it is doubtful that the book in its entirety comes from a single hand.

### Literary Form, Structure, and Unity of Obadiah

Obadiah is often treated like an oracle against any nation, but such assumptions are too facile toward Edom. Edom was considered a brother nation because of traditions regarding the common ancestry of the twin sons, Jacob and Esau, born to Isaac and Rebekah. [Edom in Biblical Tradition] These conflicting traditions suggest that hostility toward Edom jumped dramatically after the exile because Edom's actions (somehow working in concert with the Babylonians) were perceived as betrayal by Judah. [Obadiah in Jewish Tradition] This betrayal stung worse because it was Edom, whom Judah considered an ally. For this reason, one finds Edom receiving condemnation in the Book of the Twelve in a manner that is structurally and thematically parallel to the destruction of Israel in Amos 9. From a Judean perspective, Edom's fate had to be equal to that of Israel.

The final form of Obadiah is a complex mixture of component pieces thematically arranged around two foci—the condemnation of Edom and an impending day of YHWH that will institute justice on the surrounding nations and will restore Judah. The first part of this short booklet (Obad 1-14) focuses upon the former, while the bulk of the latter portion of the book (vv. 16-21) reflects on the Day of YHWH. Obadiah 15 transitions between the two sections. Despite the thematic coherence, critical scholarship generally recognizes that neither of these two blocks of material can be readily explained as the composition of a single author working from scratch. The sections 1-14, 15b and 15a, 16-21 suggest that more than one hand has shaped these verses. For such a short book, Obadiah's compositional features appear amazingly complex. The opening unit has a close parallel to Jeremiah 49:14-16, 9, but the differences are as important as the similarities. The diversity of situations, stylistic patterns, and theological perspectives presumed in the building blocks of this book belie the simplicity of its message.

## Edom in Biblical Tradition

Edom had a long history with Judah and Israel, as indicated by the Jacob/Esau narratives in Gen 12–35, which presume Esau as the progenitor of the Edomites (e.g., Gen 36:1) and which portray Jacob and Esau as the twin brothers born to Isaac and Rebekah (Gen 25:19-23). These stories portray a familial relationship between Jacob and Esau, but one that was also contentious. These ambivalent attitudes are also displayed in a series of Old Testament texts that vacillate between respect and disdain for the Edomites. For example, in Deut 2:4-6, Moses forbids Israel from taking any territory from Edom because they are descendants of Esau, and 23:7-8 admonishes Israelites to respect Edomites because of the kinship ties. Conversely, texts in Samuel and Kings record that Saul (1 Sam 14:47), David (2 Sam 8:13; 1 Kgs 11:15-16), and Solomon (1 Kgs 11:14) all fought battles with Edom, with the result that David brutally killed "every male in Edom" (1 Kgs 11:15). Of course, this last claim reflects hyperbole, but Israel considered Edom part of the full territory controlled by the Davidic kingdom (e.g., Ps 60:6-9). In 2 Kgs 3, an unnamed King of Edom joined forces with the kings of Israel and Judah against Mesha of Moab in the ninth century BCE. Ancient traditions also list Edomite territory as the place from which YHWH comes in several theophanies (Deut 33:2; Judg 5:4; Hab 3:3), but a late text in Isaiah turns that tradition in the opposite direction as YHWH comes from Edom with bloody garments after a battle (Isa 63:1-6). This defeat of Edom is associated with a "day of vengeance" (63:4), but one already anticipated literarily in Isa 34, a bridge text connecting earlier portions of the Isaiah corpus with one another. Mal 1:2-5 also indicates Edom has been threatened, probably by the Nabateans though they are not named (see illustration "Nabateans and Edomites"). See discussion of Mal 1:2-5 in James D. Nogalski, *The Book of the Twelve: Micah–Malachi* (Smyth & Helwys Bible Commentary Series) to see how that text takes up Obadiah, in much the same way as Isa 63 takes up Isa 34 (see O. H. Steck).

The biggest change in attitude toward Edom came in the aftermath of Jerusalem's destruction (in 587 BCE) by the Babylonians, in which Edom seems to have participated in some way. Several texts suggest as much (e.g., Obad 11-14; Lam 4:21-22; Jer 49:7-22; Ezek 25:12-14). Bartlett is illustrative of those who try to play down Edom's role in the aftermath of Jerusalem's destruction by reading these texts as ambiguous reflections of stock formulations. Such readings, however, fail to take account of how the venom became so much more closely associated with Edom than with other countries. Later, both Mal 1:2-5 and Isa 63:1-6 point to events in the middle or late Persian period that were interpreted as YHWH's judgment on Edom. Yet, by the first century, Idumea lay directly south of Judea. This change of position implies that while the Edomites were driven from their homeland (presumably by the Nabateans and other factors), they were ultimately able to secure land in territory that once belonged to Judah. Specifics of this process are not available, but the effects are clear. For a more extensive survey of Edom in the Latter Prophets, see P. R. Raabe's survey. Raabe clearly demonstrates the importance of Edom as a state, not merely a cipher for all nations. He does not, however, explore the role of Edom in Jerusalem's destruction in any detail there, as either a literary trope or as a historical event.

At any rate, J. R. Bartlett admits the difficulty of determining precise events. Surveying scholars regarding various scenarios of devastation from the beginning of the sixth century to as late as the fourth, Bartlett concludes from the archaeological evidence that, "there seems little doubt that sometime in the sixth century BCE, the kingdom suffered a disaster" … "most probably inflicted by Nabonidus, king of Babylon" in 552 (p. 161). This defeat, however, was not annihilation, but Bartlett considers it probable that the Edomite king was replaced at this point with a Babylonian governor, which then led to the end of Edom as an independent state.

Odil Hannes Steck, *Bereitete Heimkehr. Jesaja 35 als redaktionelle Brücke zwischen dem Ersten und dem Zweiten Jesaja* (Stuttgarter Bibelstudien 121; Stuttgart: Katholisches Bibelwerk, 1985).

Paul R. Raabe, *Obadiah* (AB 24D; New York: Doubleday, 1996) 33–47.

John R. Bartlett, *Edom and the Edomites* (JSOTSup 77; Sheffield: JSOT Press, 1989) 151–57.

*Parallels between Obadiah 2-5 and Jeremiah 49:14-16, 9.* Obadiah 2-5 shares too much of its structure, wording, and imagery with Jeremiah 49:14-16, 9 for the similarities to be considered a coincidence. [Obadiah 1-5 and Jeremiah 49:14-16, 9] Of late, several

## Obadiah in Jewish Tradition

Modern scholarship assigns authorship of the book to an otherwise anonymous prophet from the Babylonian or Persian Period, but ancient rabbinic references presume that the book is named for the Obadiah associated with king Ahab of Israel (873–851 BCE). Rabbinic traditions about Obadiah provide a colorful portrait of a prophet known for courage, rewarded for piety, and provided with a message against Edom. The Obadiah assumed by most of these traditions is mentioned in 1 Kgs 18:3-7, 16 as one "who revered YHWH greatly," an affirmation of his role in saving 100 prophets from Jezebel's persecution (1 Kgs 18:4). Details of this persecution are sparse, but later tradition assumes Obadiah suffered for protecting the prophets. They claim Joram (son of Ahab) charged Obadiah exorbitant interest when Obadiah had to borrow money to help feed the prophets. Some of these traditions also interpret the prophets for whom Obadiah provided as prophets who did not bow down to Baal as Jezebel had commanded (Ginzberg, 4:240; 6:355-356, note 20). In 1 Kgs 18:5, Ahab also appoints Obadiah to help him find water in the third year of a drought, whereupon Obadiah encounters Elijah, a prophet whom he greatly respects (18:7). Obadiah apparently helps to arrange a meeting between Ahab and Elijah (18:16).

Traditions surrounding Obadiah's piety develop from the statement about his reverence of YHWH (1 Kgs 18:4). In rabbinic tradition, Obadiah's piety places him in charge of the first of the seven divisions of paradise (Ginzberg, 1:21; 5:31, note 91). The rabbis note Obadiah is in select company because the text refers to him as one who feared YHWH greatly, since this statement is used elsewhere only of Abraham, Joseph, and Job (Ginzberg2:124; 5:361). Also, Obadiah's piety plays a role in ancient tradition to identify the unnamed widow of 1 Kgs 17:9-24 as Obadiah's wife. These stories tie her plight to the king's attempt to force Obadiah's children to pay Obadiah's debt. For this reason, she petitioned her dead husband, and he told her from heaven that Elisha would come to her aid.

Speculation about Obadiah's genealogy also receives attention. One finds traditions equating the prophet of 2 Kgs 18 with the author of Obadiah. Because the book rebukes Edom, several legends assume Obadiah was himself Edomite. Several mention Eliphaz, the Temanite, as Obadiah's ancestor. Teman was a city in Edom, and Eliphaz was one of Job's friends whom God rebuked. In rabbinic tradition, this rebuke involves further punishment. One of the descendants of Eliphaz, Obadiah, would be commissioned to pronounce punishment upon Edom. This motif attempts to explain Obadiah's harsh rhetoric against Edom as a part of divine punishment initiated by the actions of one of its progenitors (Ginzberg, 1:422; 5:322, note 319).

Other traditions portray Obadiah as a reluctant prophet on this issue, prophesying only after he is convinced to do so by the heavenly council (Ginzberg, 6:344; see [Heavenly Council]). Edomite heritage also explains why the rabbinic tradition also claims Obadiah was a proselyte, who converted to Judaism (Ginzberg,1:21).

In the end, even though the book of Obadiah can no longer be traced to a ninth-century prophet, these traditions about the ninth-century prophet Obadiah provide insight into the mindset of those who dealt with these texts in the formative periods of Judaism. This early date for a prophet Obadiah *may* have provided supporting rationale for Obadiah's position in the Book of the Twelve, but if so, only tangentially. The ninth century prophet Obadiah lived well before Hosea or Amos, and that fact would not have escaped those who arranged the writings in the Book of the Twelve. On the other hand, these traditions point to a basic presupposition about the writers of biblical books. Even a book as vitriolic as Obadiah was presumed to have had holy and honorable reasons behind it. These traditions portray the book as the word of YHWH, a word so important it was delivered through one of four persons known for their reverence of YHWH, a word so important it was not delivered by one believed to be a Judean (lest he be accused of petty jealousy), but by a fellow Edomite, whose piety YHWH recognized.

Louis Ginzberg, *The Legends of the Jews*, 7 vols. (Philadelphia: The Jewish Publication Society of America, 1947).

commentators suggest that both texts adapt a common source no longer available. Many of the arguments rest upon close analysis of the Hebrew text, so detailed presentation of these arguments cannot be treated in this commentary. However, I argue elsewhere that the Jeremiah context appears closer to the original wording.[2]

**Obadiah 1-5 and Jeremiah 49:14-16, 9**

| Obad 1-5 | Jer 49:14-16, 9 |
|---|---|
| [1]The vision of Obadiah. | |
| Thus says the Lord GOD concerning Edom: | |
| We have heard a report from the LORD, and a messenger has been sent among the nations: | [14]I have heard tidings from the LORD, and a messenger has been sent among the nations: |
| "Rise up! Let us rise against it for battle!" | "Gather yourselves together and come against her, and rise up for battle!" |
| [2]I will surely make you least among the nations; you shall be utterly despised. | [15]For I will make you least among the nations, despised by humankind. |
| | [16]The terror you inspire |
| [3]Your proud heart has deceived you, you that live in the clefts of the rock, whose dwelling is in the heights. You say in your heart, "Who will bring me down to the ground?" | and the pride of your heart have deceived you, you who live in the clefts of the rock, who hold the height of the hill. |
| [4]Though you soar aloft like the eagle, though your nest is set among the stars, | Although you make your nest as high as the eagle's, |
| from there I will bring you down, says the LORD. | from there I will bring you down, says the LORD. |
| [5]If *thieves* came to you, if plunderers by night—how you have been destroyed!—would they not steal only what they wanted? If *grape-gatherers* came to you, would they not leave gleanings? | [9]If *grape-gatherers* came to you, would they not leave gleanings? If *thieves* came by night, even they would pillage only what they wanted. |

Further, I suggest that the number of structural and thematic parallels between Amos 9 and Obadiah suggests that the compiler of Obadiah cast an eye toward Amos 9 while putting the pieces of Obadiah together. Space and technical argumentation do not allow detailed replication of the arguments here, but for the sake of this commentary, it is not absolutely necessary that one accept the influence of Amos 9 upon the *composition* of Obadiah in order for the similarities to function meaningfully. Given the ancient tradition of the Book of the Twelve, these common features raise the suspicion that, at the very least, they played a significant role in the *placement* of Obadiah beside Amos in the MT. As such, these common features certainly invite readers of the Twelve to relate Amos 9 and Obadiah to one another. A brief introduction to these common features will function to extend an invitation to read Obadiah alongside Amos 9.

*Structural and Thematic Parallels with Amos 9.* The similarity of structural markers, repeating vocabulary, and shared themes draw one's attention to similarities between the final chapter of Amos and the entire book of Obadiah. [Parallels between Amos 9 and Obadiah] The cumulative effects of these parallels are difficult to ignore.

First, Amos 9 begins the fifth and final vision in the writing, describing the destruction of Bethel and with it the entire northern kingdom. Obadiah has a superscription classifying it also as a "vision" (Obad 1), though of Edom. Second, the theme of the inability to escape from YHWH is present in both Amos 9 and Obadiah, and it contains an unusual verbal parallel. The phrase "from there I will bring them/you down" appears in only three places in the Hebrew Bible: Amos 9:2; Obadiah 4; and the parallel text from Jeremiah 49:16. In all likelihood, this phrase already existed in the Jeremiah context and served as the motivation for bringing the prophetic condemnations of Edom into this context in the Book of the Twelve.[3] Third, Amos 9:2-4 contains five clauses that all have the phrase "if . . . from there," while the parallel text in

---

**Parallels between Amos 9 and Obadiah**

| Structural and Thematic Parallels | | Amos 9 | Obadiah |
|---|---|---|---|
| Vision | | 9:1 | 1 |
| Five "if/though" (*'im*) clauses | | 9:2-4 | 4-5 |
| No escape from YHWH : "from there I will bring them/you down" | | 9:2 | 4 |
| Destruction & remnant motifs (using agricultural imagery) | | 9:7-10 | 5 |
| Thematic shifts/text markers with: | "Is it not" (*hălô'*) | 9:7 | 8 |
| | "on that day" (*bayyôm hahû'*) | 9:11 | 8 |
| | "utterance (*nĕ'ūm*) of YHWH" | 9:7,8,13 | 8 |
| Introduction with eschatological "day" | | 9:11 | 15 |
| Allusion to destruction of Jerusalem | | 9:11 | 16 |
| Restoration of Davidic kingdom | | 9:11 | 19f. |
| "Possession" of Edom and other nations | | 9:12 | 17f.,19f. |
| Eschatological/agricultural abundance | | 9:13 | — |
| Restoration of captivity/exiles | | 9:14 | 19f. |
| Restoration/reclamation of cities | | 9:14 | 20 |
| Concluding promise for the restoration of the land/kingdom | | 9:15 | 21 |

Obadiah 4-5 has five "if" clauses (only two of which appear in the parallel text in Jeremiah). This combination of "if . . . from there I will bring you down" along with a total of five "if" clauses, whether intentional or not, certainly causes the reader of Obadiah to hear the echo of the final vision of Amos.

In addition to the close verbal parallel in Obadiah 2-4 with Jeremiah 49:14-16, Obadiah 5 picks up a previous saying from Jeremiah 49:9, but reverses the order of its two parts. No satisfactory explanation has been offered regarding either change. Why was it necessary to go back to Jeremiah 49:9, and why does the parallel reverse 49:9b and 49:9a? A simple explanation presents itself if one assumes that the compiler of Obadiah is following the rhetorical/thematic flow of Amos 9. Amos 9:7-10 uses agricultural metaphors both to describe the coming destruction and to introduce the theme of a surviving remnant. Both motifs appear prominently in Jeremiah 49:9, but in the opposite order than they appear in Amos 9:7-10. By inverting the order of Jeremiah 49:9a,b, Obadiah 5 brings its message of judgment and remnant into line with Amos, using agricultural metaphors to introduce the topics of destruction and a remnant. Of course, the message differs for the respective entities: in Amos 9:7-10, destruction will come but a remnant of Israel will survive, but Obadiah 5 implies that the coming destruction will leave no remnant for Edom.

Obadiah 8 begins uniquely with three sequential phrases that create an awkward introduction: "is it not," "on that day," and "utterance of YHWH." They are followed by the conjunction "and" (*vav*), which in turn introduces the subsequent subordinate clause. While odd as a single phrase, it can hardly be coincidental that the three transitional phrases introduce thematic shifts in Amos 9 in precisely the same order as they appear in Obadiah 8: "is it not" (9:7), "on that day" (9:11), and "utterance of YHWH" followed by a *vav* (9:13).

Moreover, the thematic and verbal parallels between Amos 9:11-15 and Obadiah 15-21 are equally striking (see [Parallels between Amos 9 and Obadiah]). To be sure, the subjects are different, with Amos 9:11-15 focusing on the restoration of Judah, Jerusalem, and the Davidic kingdom, while Obadiah 15-21 focuses on the day of YHWH and repopulating the land outside Jerusalem (see especially the commentary on Obad 19-20). Nevertheless, the general themes mirror one another closely.

The cumulative effect of these parallels suggests a close affinity between Amos 9 and Obadiah. The parallels in the first portion of Obadiah reflect formal similarities by using similar text markers and linguistic formulations. By contrast, the parallels with Amos 9:11-15 tend to be thematic and formal. One can, however, offer an explanation for this difference. In places where one finds structural and linguistic similarities, they serve a larger rhetorical purpose. Namely, they document a message of incontrovertible judgment against Israel (Amos 9) and Edom (Obad 1-14). In so doing, the fate of the two nations is joined. Both political entities will be destroyed. However, the thematic parallels in the latter portions of these two texts shift from words of judgment against Israel and Edom to promises of restoration for Judah. Here, the messages of the two passages are largely the same, though they reflect different historical settings and points of view. The message of restoration in Amos 9 focuses upon the rebuilding and replanting of YHWH's kingdom, while the restoration of Obadiah 15-21 reflects a more militarily aggressive set of expectations for restoring the borders for Judah and for the security of Zion. The positioning of Obadiah after Amos 9 thus confirms the promise of restoration for Judah but draws a parallel to prophetic judgment announced against the two "brother" kingdoms of Judah. On the one hand, Jacob/Israel will be destroyed for its failure to heed the warnings of YHWH, while on the other hand, Esau/Edom is condemned for its pride and warned that its actions will also lead to God's judgment should they not change. In other words, judgment is pronounced upon the northern kingdom and upon Edom, though remnants of Judah and Jerusalem will survive.

*The Composition of Obadiah.* How do all of these things come together in this short book? Various explanations have been offered, including multiple redactional layers, a single author writing with alternating styles, and the merging of several originally independent units. Peter Weimar analyzes the literary and historical tensions reflected in Obadiah and argues that seven redactional layers are needed to account for these divergent tendencies.[4] While he demonstrates a keen analytical eye, few scholars have been convinced that a twenty-one-verse book would require seven redactional layers to reach its final form. Ehud Ben Zvi argues that Obadiah constitutes a composition of Persian period authors whose varying stylistic tendencies and ambiguities function as part of the identifiable characteristics of this book.[5]

Josef Wehrle focuses on four "communication levels" in Obadiah.[6] However, he sees additional hands behind these communication levels creating, selecting, and modifying material. His view of redaction reflects a more fluid model that concerns the innovations in a text demonstrated by deviation and change over against both its reworked traditions and its genre predecessors. In this, selection and combination play a significant role over against the received traditions and forms. Frequently, however, a precise separation of traditional from redactional material is no longer possible.[7] Wehrle focuses "upon the question of the decisive factors for the coherence of a text, but also the question of the driving perspectives and purposes that lie at the base of a composition."[8]

In this respect, perhaps one should simply recognize Obadiah as a mosaic of anti-Edom sayings in two parts. Obadiah is frequently treated as a collection of anti-Edom sayings, though commentators disagree about the extent to which the two main sections (1-14, 16-21) reflect a single compositional hand. While it cannot be subdivided as a rhetorical unit, the parallel in Jeremiah shows clearly that Obadiah 1-5 has been adapted from preexisting material. Obadiah 6-7 follows smoothly enough on 1-5, but the aphoristic character of 6-7 could just as easily mean they comprise independent units. Obadiah 8-9, 10-14 + 15b likewise play a role in the larger rhetorical context, and flow more smoothly than 6-7, but they could also come from a different hand. In fact, the formulation of the unique introduction in Obadiah 8 could be influenced by its location in the Book of the Twelve. In short, these sayings serve a rhetorical function, but nothing in these four subsections demands that they come from a single hand or a single setting. In fact, Obadiah 1-14 clearly comes from a preexisting context given the use of Jeremiah 49:14-16, 9 in Obadiah 1-5. The same is true for Obadiah 15a + 16-21, wherein vv. 19-20 have frequently been attributed to a "later redactional hand" because they seem to presuppose a different scenario than vv. 11-14.

The first part of Obadiah in particular appears to have been modified with an eye toward Amos 9 (see Amos 9:11-15 and [Diachronic Notes on Amos 9:11-15]). Similarly, the theme of vv. 16-21 fits well with their location (following Amos 9) and other texts in the Book of the Twelve (notably, Joel 3:1-21). For these and other reasons, it seems unwise to postulate a lengthy redactional history for Obadiah. Rather, the more cautious approach would be to treat the literary and historical tensions as the result of the divergent building blocks in the compilation of this short writing for its location in the Book of the Twelve. Like Joel, the final form of Obadiah results from piecing together several smaller units with an eye toward adapting the material to its broader literary context.

## The Message of Obadiah

The message of Obadiah centers on three interrelated aspects of the fate of Edom. First, betrayal *by* Edom will be punished by the betrayal *of* Edom. Obadiah 7 depicts Edom's downfall as the result of betrayal from those whom it considered to be allies. Obadiah 10-14 portrays Edom's betrayal of Judah in Judah's time of need. These two pronouncements combine in a simple cause-and-effect relationship in Obadiah 15b: "As you have done, it shall be done to you; your deeds shall return on your own head."

Second, Edom will forfeit its reputation as a place known for its wisdom (Obad 8) because its actions were motivated by pride and deceit (Obad 3). The judgment that Edom will experience comes from YHWH, and as such, no resistance or counter arguments from Edom's side will change the outcome (Obad 3-4). Its power is no match for the power of YHWH.

Third, divine retribution will come on the impending day of YHWH. Retribution is not limited to Edom. Judah has already experienced YHWH's wrath (Obad 16), and that wrath will soon be turned upon the surrounding nations. However, as a result of the day of YHWH, Judah will be restored and the promises of a kingdom dedicated to YHWH will remain in effect (Obad 21).

Behind these three points about Edom, the portrayal of the deity in Obadiah raises troubling images. Obadiah depicts YHWH as a God whose vengeance must be appeased, first as presumed by the punishment of Judah and Zion and then by the punishment of the surrounding nations. Obadiah's God is certainly a God to be feared, but this portrayal of God hardly resembles the warm, fuzzy portrayal of God one hears in most American pulpits on any given Sunday. However, several points need to be remembered regarding the original setting of Obadiah. The message of Obadiah was not directed toward a community of believers who lived in a wealthy society and worshiped in relative comfort. The message of Obadiah was directed toward a community of believers whose world, both physically and theologically, had been radically overturned.

Jerusalem, its temple, and its king had been destroyed; and the God upon whom they all relied for protection had not prevented the devastation.

In the aftermath of this changed world, Obadiah's harsh words offer hope for restoration on several levels simultaneously. First, the suffering of Judah had a purpose: to restore holiness to the kingdom (vv. 17, 21). Second, the moral compass of the cosmos had not changed. Evil would be punished, and betrayal had consequences because YHWH is a God of justice. Third, this portrayal of a God who has the power to overturn the status quo would have been "good news" to a poor, downtrodden community that had suffered at the hands of more powerful nations. A God with the power to set things right provides a potent theological symbol to those in need. Yet such a God presents a frightening challenge to those who think they are in control.

## Obadiah and the Book of the Twelve

Three motivating factors appear in the parallels of the Book of the Twelve that would help account for the compilation of Obadiah. First, Obadiah deals with the perceived betrayal of Judah by Edom in the aftermath of 587. Even though Edom is addressed briefly in other texts in the Book of the Twelve (Joel 3:19 [MT 4:19]; Amos 1:11-12), those responsible for the Book of the Twelve apparently concluded that Edom required its own book. Second, the theological conviction that YHWH will punish nations other than Judah rests upon a strong belief in divine justice. Edom's betrayal must be punished. Third, interpreting Edom's changing circumstances in the Persian period as a sign that divine justice against the surrounding nations would soon occur helps account for the assignation of this activity to an imminent day of YHWH (see the discussion of Mal 1:2-4).

As noted above, subtle yet noticeable alterations to the source texts of Obadiah suggest a significant interest in drawing parallels between the fate of Edom and the fate of Israel. These alterations help account for Obadiah's position after Amos 9. In addition, Malachi's allusion (see Mal 1:2-4) to Obadiah offers another important linchpin for understanding the function of Obadiah in the Book of the Twelve. Malachi presumes that Edom suffers defeat as a sign that God's love for Israel did not stop with Jerusalem's destruction.

What would motivate the compilation of a group of anti-Edom sayings into its own separate corpus? Answers to this question have occupied Obadiah scholarship for a long time. Several scholars have suggested that Edom was simply a symbol for any nation. However, references to Edom exhibit specific data and traditions in terms of Edom's cities (Obad 9), reference to Edom's ancestor Esau (Obad 6, 8, 9), and Edom's involvement in Jerusalem's destruction (Obad 10-14; see also Ps 137:7; Lam 4:22). This specificity suggests that "Edom" actually means the country in Obadiah. Usually, scholars explain the book as a response to Edom's betrayal of Judah in the aftermath of 587 BCE. This tradition grew so that in the third century, 1 Esdras 4:45 even blames Edom for burning the temple in 587. However, this attitude alone cannot adequately explain the peculiar form of the commands in Obadiah 10-14. If *Schadenfreude* (rejoicing over the troubles of another) were the sole motivation, then one can that imagine other, less ambiguous avenues would have been available by which the prophet could have essentially said, *you have gotten what you deserved.*

Here, expanding one's literary horizon beyond Obadiah itself to include the Book of the Twelve helps one to see other theological issues at work, specifically in the structural parallels between Amos 9 and Obadiah and in the interplay between Obadiah and Malachi 1:2-5. (The parallels between Amos 9 and Obadiah are detailed above.)

While Obadiah anticipates Edom's punishment, Malachi 1:2-5 presents Edom's punishment as underway (see [Edom in Biblical Tradition]). In Malachi 1:2-5, the prophet's disputation uses Edom's devastation as proof to Israel of God's love. The Malachi passage alludes to Obadiah in the process of conveying this message, thereby confirming that Obadiah's message of judgment has begun to come to pass.

Similarly, the structural parallels between Obadiah and Amos 9 do more than create an artistic linchpin between two writings. The structural parallels draw attention to the common fate of the two neighboring countries, conceptualized by Judah as its closest kin. Judah and Israel are portrayed in the historical narratives as one people, separated by rebellion but joined by blood. Likewise, from the narratives of Genesis onward, Edom is not a foreign nation like other nations. Biblical accounts portray the people of Edom as descendants of Esau, the twin brother of Jacob (who is later named

Israel). To be sure, in biblical narratives this relationship between Judah/Israel and Edom was often strained, but until the events of 587, the relationship was not broken. That changed in the aftermath of Jerusalem's destruction, when Edom participated with the Babylonians in the sacking of Jerusalem. Obadiah's placement presumes this betrayal to be on the same level, theologically, as the northern kingdom's abandonment of YHWH and YHWH's chosen king so prominent in the Deuteronomistic History and elsewhere in the Old Testament texts (see Mic 1:2-9; 2 Kgs 17). Both Israel and Edom had kinship ties to Judah that go beyond geographic boundaries according to biblical tradition. What better place in the Book of the Twelve to anticipate the destruction of Edom than immediately after the place that most graphically anticipates the destruction of Israel in the Book of the Twelve? "You *should not* gloat over your *brother* on the day of his misfortune" (Obad 12). Obadiah plays the role of confirming God's justice by holding Edom just as accountable as Israel and Judah: "As you have done, so it will be done to you" (Obad 15). In the Book of the Twelve, this statement does not function as an idle threat against a brother's betrayal.

# NOTES

1. See John D. W. Watts, *The Books of Joel, Obadiah, Jonah, Nahum, Habakkuk, and Zephaniah* (Cambridge: Cambridge University Press, 1975) 53; Otto Kaiser, *Introduction to the Old Testament: A Presentation of Its Results and Problems* (trans. John Sturdy; Oxford: Blackwell, 1975) 260. See also Ehud Ben Zvi, *A Historical-Critical Study of the Book of Obadiah* (Beihefte zur Zeitschrift für die alttestamentliche 242; Berlin: de Gruyter, 1996) 14–15. However, Ben Zvi argues that the name was intended to refer to Obadiah, officer in the court of Ahab, an approach that finds much in common with rabbinic tradition (see [Obadiah in Jewish Tradition] ). Concerning arguments that the prophet Obadiah was an otherwise unknown prophet, see Hans Walter Wolff, *Obadiah and Jonah: A Commentary* (trans. Margaret Kohl; Minneapolis: Augsburg, 1986) 44.

2. James D. Nogalski, *Redactional Processes in the Book of the Twelve* (Beihefte zur Zeitschrift für die alttestamentliche 218; Berlin: de Gruyter, 1993) 71–74.

3. See Nogalski, *Redactional Processes*, 61–74.

4. Peter Weimar, "Obadja. Eine redaktionskritische Analyse," *BN* 27 (1985): 35–99.

5. Ehud Ben Zvi, *A Historical-Critical Study of the Book of Obadiah* (Beihefte zur Zeitschrift für die alttestamentliche 242; Berlin: de Gruyter, 1996).

6. Josef Wehrle, *Prophetie und Textanalyse der Komposition Obadja 1-21. Interpretiert auf der Basis textlinguistischer und semiotischer Konzeptionen* (Arbeiten zu Text und Sprache im Alten Testament 28; St. Ottilien: EOS, 1987).

7. Ibid., 347 (my translation).

8. Ibid., 348 (my translation).

## OUTLINE OF OBADIAH

I. Obadiah 1-14: Announcing the Destruction of Edom

  A. Obadiah 1-5: "From there I will Pull You Down"

  B. Obadiah 6-7: Esau Has Been Deceived

  C. Obadiah 8-14: The Coming "Day" of Destruction

II. Obadiah 15b,a + 16-21: Punishing the Nations, Restoring Judah

# JUDGMENT AGAINST EDOM

## Obadiah 1-21

## COMMENTARY

At least two independent units have been woven together to comprise the twenty-one-verse book known as Obadiah. The first, Obadiah 1-14 + 15b, addresses Edom directly using second masculine singular pronouns and verbs, condemning Edom for its pride (v. 3) and its role in the sacking of Jerusalem (vv. 10-14). The second unit, Obadiah 15a, 16-21, has a broader scope (the fate of the nations on the day of YHWH) in which Edom constitutes one of several subjects. Each of these units includes subdivisions where the focus of the passage shifts as the unit unfolds.

The compilers of Obadiah brought together preexisting units, though it appears unlikely that they originally derived from the same prophet. Rather, this mosaic contains anti-Edom sayings that are linked thematically and that proceed from the conviction that YHWH will not allow Edom's betrayal to go unpunished. In this respect, and only in this respect, one can say that Edom serves a paradigmatic function. The anti-Edom sayings in vv. 1-5, 6-7, 8-14 begin by pronouncing Edom's fate (destruction) before providing the reasons for its punishment (its treatment of Jacob).

Obadiah's first major unit (vv. 1-14+15b) unfolds in three sections (1-5, 6-7, 8-14+15b). This first unit (1-14, 15b) contains a superscription ("the vision of Obadiah") followed by a messenger formula

**Bozrah**

The ancient Edomite capital, Bozrah, was located on the site of the modern city of Buseirah.
(Credit: Todd Bolen/BiblePlaces.com)

("thus says the Lord God . . ."). This passage also exhibits two transition points (6, 8) signaled by formulaic elements that can introduce new units ("how" and "on that day"), although in Obadiah they introduce subunits of the larger passage. The resulting tripartite subdivision (1-5, 6-7, 8-14 +15b) pronounces judgment against Edom, taunts Edom for its political alliances, and explicates the rationale for God's action. (See [Edom in Biblical Tradition].)

## Announcing the Destruction of Edom, 1-14+15b

*"From There I Will Pull You Down," 1-5.* The superscription of Obadiah, "The vision of Obadiah," separates itself syntactically from the remainder of the unit and functions as a title for the book. [Obadiah 1 and the Book of the Twelve] "Vision" appears as a superscription elsewhere in the prophetic corpus (Isa 1:1; Nah 1:1b), but more commonly it refers to the constitutive actions of a prophet.

Nowhere is this clearer than in Ezekiel 7:26, where the functions associated with prophets, priests, and elders are listed as the visions, instruction (*torâ*), and counsel respectively. Prophetic visions can happen during the night or be received in some type of revelatory act that has a more ritualized form, since "vision" appears in parallel both in the context of dreams (Isa 29:7) and divination (Jer 14:14; Mic 3:6). A vision can be misleading (Jer 14:14; 23:16; Ezek 13:16), but it can also refer to distant or delayed events (Ezek 12:24, 27; Hab 2:2-3). Misleading visions can result from words of peace spoken by false prophets in the face of disaster that YHWH has intended (Jer 14:14; 23:16; Ezek 12:24; 13:16), or the confusion may even stem from YHWH himself (Hos 12:10 [MT 12:11]).

The name "Obadiah" means servant of YHWH. Several Old Testament personages bear this name, though none of these have been convincingly linked to the prophet for whom this book is named. (Compare the discussion in [Obadiah in Jewish Tradition].) Ancient

### Obadiah 1 and the Book of the Twelve

The "vision of Obadiah" offers a significant point of contact with the end of Amos. Whether or not this superscription was deliberately added with Amos 9 in view, the beginning of Obadiah as a "vision" beckons the reader of the Book of the Twelve to compare this new vision with the cycle of five vision reports in Amos (7:1-3, 4-6, 7-9; 8:1-4; 9:1-4). Such is all the more the case given the other points of contact between Obadiah and Amos 9. In this respect, while the final vision of Amos anticipates the imminent destruction of Israel, the northern kingdom, Obadiah's vision anticipates the destruction of another kingdom with close familial ties to Judah—namely Edom.

Additionally, the messenger formula appears 13 times in Amos 1–5 (1:3, 6, 9, 11, 13; 2:1, 4, 6; 3:11, 12; 5:3, 4, 16) plus twice in narrative inserted into the vision cycle (7:11, 17). Note also the use of *"Thus*, he showed me" to begin the first four visions. In the Book of the Twelve only Zechariah uses the messenger formula more frequently (20 times). Neither Hosea nor Joel uses this introductory formula. Given that the messenger formula in Obad 1 is not part of the parallel with Jer 49:14-16, it is possible (but admittedly not provable) that this formula echoes Amos intentionally. In fact, only three other occurrences of the messenger formula in the Book of the Twelve refer to the deity specifically as *"Adonai YHWH,"* and all three occur in Amos (3:11; 5:3, 16).

scholars (and periodically modern ones as well) have sought to create a biographical profile, but this endeavor has not succeeded because of the paucity of material in Obadiah and the real possibility that the two major units of the book do not even come from the same person. Most recent scholarship tends to treat the name either as a pseudonym or the name of an otherwise anonymous, exilic prophet (see the introduction to Obadiah).

The remainder of v. 1 begins with an introduction to the subunit of Obadiah 1-7, consisting of the combination of a messenger formula ("Thus says Adonai YHWH") followed by the subject of the vision ("concerning Edom"). Typically, the messenger formula introduces a message delivered from YHWH to a prophet, who then conveys it to the audience. In the case of Obadiah 1, a report of indirect speech follows the messenger formula: "We have heard a report from YHWH, and a messenger has been sent among the nations." It is not immediately clear whether "we" assumes the people of Judah, a group of prophets, or some type of heavenly council, the leader of which is now conveying this message to the prophet. [Heavenly Council] It is clear, however, that the origin of the message to attack comes from YHWH. The content of the report addressed to the nations is a call to battle against Edom: "Rise up! Let us rise against her for battle!"

**Heavenly Council**

The idea of a heavenly council has a long history in the ancient Near East, including Israel. In polytheistic systems, the idea originated as an assembly of the deities, like the *ilū* in Mesopotamia, where the senior deities conferred. Sometimes these groups included fifty deities, while other times they included only seven. In Israelite tradition, this idea was transformed over time to fit a monotheistic system, although it is largely recognized that several texts contain echoes of earlier times when the existence of more than one deity may not have been denied as forcefully as it was later in Israel's history. In most biblical texts, YHWH functions as the only deity, although YHWH gives commands and receives reports from angelic figures: "men" on horseback in Zech 1–2; *cherubim* and *seraphim* in Isa 6; and the "sons of God" in Job 1–2 (cf. Pss 29:1; 89:7). There are, however, several texts in the Hebrew Bible where the concept of the assembly may still be dealing with an idea of a divine assembly, with YHWH as the chief deity among others. The most noteworthy example comes in Ps 82:1, where God (*Elohim*) convenes the divine assembly but then pronounces judgment upon other gods, announcing that these gods will die like humans (82:6-7). It has often been asserted that the plural language used by God in Gen 1 also draws upon the idea of the divine assembly in some form (cf. Gen 1:26). It is in this context that some commentators have attempted to explain the plural language in Obad 1: "*We have heard a report from YHWH.*"

The feminine pronoun (often translated "it") must refer back to Edom, but a feminine reference to Edom appears nowhere else in the Hebrew Bible. Normally, Edom is masculine. An explanation for this variation, however, appears when analyzing the parallel text in Jeremiah 49:14 (see introduction to Obadiah), where the antecedent to the pronoun in that speech refers to the city Bozrah (49:13). Cities, in contrast to countries, take feminine verbs and pronouns. This represents but one indication that the parallel text in Jeremiah 49:14-16, 9 reflects an earlier form of the parallel to Obadiah 1-5.[1]

Obadiah 2-5 represents a judgment oracle that begins with the consequences (v. 2), then moves to the rationale (3), before taunting Edom with the inevitability of judgment (4-5). Beginning with Obadiah 2, YHWH becomes the formal speaker who addresses Edom directly using second masculine singular forms, a style that continues unabated through the remainder of the unit (1-14+15b). Obadiah 2 conveys the consequences of the battle. Edom's status among the nations will diminish, and it will become an object of derision. The rhetoric of Obadiah 2 manifests hostility toward Edom, though the reason will not be clear until Obadiah 11-14, where its role in attacking Jerusalem becomes clear as the motivating factor.

Obadiah 3-4 provides the first glimpse into the reason for judgment. Edom's self-deception regarding its own importance and security serve as focal points of Obadiah 3-4. Edom relied for safety upon its isolated location and rocky terrain, but they provided no protection. As a literary device, YHWH quotes Edom itself to convey this pride: "Who will bring me down to the ground?" Pointedly, YHWH answers the question in Obadiah 4 in a way that challenges Edom's self-perception. YHWH's response mocks Edom's self-importance by essentially saying, "Your pride is misplaced; your power is no match for YHWH." The motif of a nation's pride evokes more than conceit. When this motif appears elsewhere in prophetic literature, it tends to refer to countries that have attacked God's people. For example, see the anti-Assyria polemic in the boast of the king of Assyria (Isa 10:5-11) followed by YHWH's response (10:12-19), and the portrayal of Babylon in Jeremiah 50:29-30.

Obadiah 5 conveys Edom's total annihilation by asking a rhetorical question whose unstated response implies devastating consequences. The question uses two images, thieves and plunderers, to make one point: a threat from human enemies pales compared to the threat of what will happen once YHWH decides to punish them. Metaphorically, if Edom were robbed or looted, something would be left. By contrast, destruction from YHWH will leave nothing.

*Esau Has Been Deceived, 6-7.* These verses extend the imagery from Obadiah 5 but manifest a different chronological perspective toward Edom's fate. Obadiah 6 changes the epithet for Edom to

Esau. [Esau] Paradoxically, Edom and Israel/Judah shared a relationship that was perceived as different from the relationships that Israel/Judah had with other nations bordering the country. Yet, Edom and Israel/Judah did not always treat one another in a brotherly fashion. (See [Edom in Biblical Tradition].)

Obadiah 6 presupposes Esau/Edom has suffered significant devastation. The formulations in Obadiah 6, with two verbs in perfect tense, presume this devastation has already happened. Such a presumption is one of the reasons Obadiah has long been treated as a sixth-century prophet, since this kind of devastation can best be explained as a result of the invasions that began in the sixth century by the Nabateans, an Arabic tribe from the desert. In addition, the Babylonian king Nabonidus (556–539 BCE) claims to have mounted a military campaign against Edom in 552. In the eyes of Judah, such destruction undoubtedly seemed fitting punishment given Edom's role in helping the Babylonians loot the temple of Jerusalem in 587 (Obad 11-14; Ps 137:7). [Edom in Psalm 137:7]

Obadiah 7 portrays Edom's situation as the result of betrayal. [Political Betrayal] In short, Obadiah 7 assumes a situation where an ally has turned against Edom, with the result that Edom has been forced to flee to the border of its own land. As with Obadiah 6, this poetic image coincides with Edom's gradual loss of traditional territory that begins in the sixth century.

*The Coming "Day" of Destruction, 8-14.* A new unit begins with the introductory formula in Obadiah 8 ("On that day, says

### Esau

Esau was the older twin brother of Jacob in Genesis. Esau's descendants are depicted as the Edomites, while the descendants of Jacob become the twelve tribes of Israel. In the story, enmity existed between these two brothers from the time of their birth until Jacob fled to Mesopotamia before Esau killed him. Jacob and Esau ultimately reconcile (Gen 33:1-17), though some tension remained. This tension reflects much of the history of Edom and Israel (see [Edom in Biblical Tradition]).

---

### Edom in Psalm 137:7

Ps 137 laments the destruction of Jerusalem from the perspective of an exile who is homesick, who is tired of being taunted by his Babylonian captors, and who thinks that the Zion tradition of worship is gone forever:

By the rivers of Babylon—there we sat down and there we wept when we remembered Zion. On the willows there we hung up our harps. For there our captors asked us for songs, and our tormentors asked us for mirth, saying "Sing us one of the songs of Zion!" (Ps 137:1-3).

From this context, it is clear that when Ps 137:7 offers an imprecatory prayer, i.e., a curse, the psalmist blames the Edomites for participating in Jerusalem's destruction in some way:

Remember, O LORD, against the Edomites
The day of Jerusalem's fall,
How they said, "Tear it down! Tear it down!
Down to its foundations!"

When compared with other texts, it is not always clear that Edom participated directly, and the Babylonians get an even stronger imprecation in 137:9, but it is hard to imagine that the Edomites would have been singled out if they were not involved in some way. See discussion of Obad 11-14.

---

**Political Betrayal**

📖 Obad 7 contains four parallel lines, with the first three conveying an image of an ally who has turned against its compatriot.

> The men of your covenant have sent you to the border.
> The men of your peace have deceived you, overpowered you.
> They placed your bread beneath you as a trap.
> There is no understanding in him.

This translation of the third line differs from the NRSV, because the NRSV (and other English translations) has emended "your bread" to a plural participle, "those eating your bread," on the assumption that the third line requires a plural entity to parallel the first two lines. However, this emendation creates linguistic, syntactical, and conceptual problems that are avoided when one understands that "your bread" is a metaphor for a political alliance that parallels covenant and peace. The plural verb in the third line assumes the antecedent has already been stated.

See discussion of these issues in James D. Nogalski, "Obad 7: Textual Corruption or Politically Charged Metaphor?," *ZAW* 110 (1998): 67–71.

---

YHWH"). In contrast to Obadiah 6-7, v. 8 portrays the destruction of Edom as something that will occur in the distant future. This verse draws upon traditional portraits of Edom as the home of wisdom. [Wisdom in Edom] YHWH promises to destroy the sages.

**Wisdom in Edom**

📖 It has long been noted that Edom is a place associated with "wisdom" in various ways. See Jer 49:7; Bar 3:22-23; see also Job 2:11, where Eliphaz came from Teman. Reasons for these associations are not clear. Some see the wisdom connection as the result primarily of literary associations alone (P. R. Raabe), or as the consequence of Edomite wisdom literature (R. H. Pfeiffer), technological (E. A. Knauf and C. J. Lenzen), or political skills (W. Rudolph) for which they became famous.

Paul R. Raabe, *Obadiah* (AB 24D; New York: Doubleday, 1996) 164.

Robert H. Pfeiffer, "Edomitic Wisdom," *Zeitschrift für die Alttestamentliche Wissenschaft* 44 (1926): 13–25.

Ernst Axel Knauf and Cherie Joyce Lenzen, "Edomite Copper Industry," in *Studies in the History and Archaeology of Jordan III* (Amman: Department of Antiquities, 1982) 83–88.

Wilhelm Rudolph, *Joel—Amos—Obadja—Jona* (Kommentar zum Alten Testament 13/2; Gütersloh: Gütersloher, 1971) 308.

Obadiah 9 continues the threat from YHWH but focuses on the destruction of Edom's warriors and its population.

With Obadiah 10, the focus shifts to the reason for YHWH's vendetta. Obadiah 10-14 lays out a series of charges against Edom based largely on Edom's role in helping the Babylonians destroy Jerusalem in 587. The phrasing of these verses adds to the chronological confusion of Obadiah, as evidenced by various English translations. [Translations of Obadiah 10-14]

Obadiah 10 accuses Edom of the slaughter of Jacob. While Obadiah 6 and 8-9 refer to Edom by the name of its progenitor, Esau, Obadiah 10 uses the ancestral name for Israel, Jacob. Thus, it accentuates the familial relationship. Accusing Esau of killing *Jacob* heightens the sense of familial betrayal when contrasted with the Genesis account where Esau and Jacob reconcile.

Two lines of thought concerning Edom's role in Jerusalem's destruction tie Obadiah 11-14 together. First, the allusion to Jerusalem's destruction uses a series of phrases presuming the events represent a day of YHWH, which the NRSV lists as follows: the day you stood aside (11), the day strangers carried off his wealth

**Translations of Obadiah 10-14**

AΩ The NRSV, for example, translates the commands as past perfects ("you should not have . . .") while the NIV translates them as warnings against action in the future ("you shall not . . ."). Do these verses represent the words of a prophet interpreting Edom's recent defeat as punishment from God *because* Edom aided Babylon when Jerusalem was destroyed? Or do they represent a prophetic warning to Edom to stay away, to refrain from allying itself with Babylon against Jerusalem? Syntactically, both are possible. The choice depends on the context one assumes as one reads Obadiah. In terms of the original setting, the former appears more likely to modern scholars, who tend to read Obad 10-14 as the rationale for punishment. Hence, the NRSV's translation of the verbs condemns Edom for past actions ("you should not have . . ."). However, modern scholars did not compile Obadiah. Rather, Obad 1-5 adapts an existing text that also appears in Jer 49:14-16, 9, and in that literary context, these verses confront the Edomites in the present (though the message is really intended for the Judean audience reading or hearing the words). However, Obad 8 and 15 begin new units with a future orientation. Obad 8 begins "on that day" and Obad 15 begins "For the day of the LORD is near." One must therefore distinguish the original setting of the Obadiah units from their current literary function. While Obadiah clearly reflects the aftermath of Jerusalem's destruction, as well as events from later in the sixth century, the future orientation of the larger context (especially regarding the introductions in Obad 8 and 15) suggests that the voice of Obadiah is intended to be heard as someone speaking prior to these events.

(11), the day of his misfortune (12), day of distress (12, 14), day of their calamity (13), day of his disaster (13). Second, verses 11-14 portray an increasingly active role for Edom in the destruction. Obadiah 11 castigates Edom for the aid it provided Babylon. Taken by itself, this verse presupposes Edom's passivity added to the pain Jerusalem experienced. This verse implies Edom should have come to the aid of its brother Judah. The fact that it did not means, for Judah, that Edom was just as guilty as if it joined the attack. However, verses 12-14 increasingly depict an active role for Edom. In Obadiah 11 Edom appears passive, but Obadiah 12 depicts its enjoyment of Judah's destruction: Edom gloats and boasts over it. Verse 13 goes a step further, accusing Edom of entering the city gate and the temple "on the day of their calamity," and Edom plundering those areas. Finally, Obadiah 14 continues to describe Edom acting against Judah, this time by capturing refugees and turning them over to Babylon. The role of Edom in these verses, then, increases in severity. At the end, one can hardly imagine a more onerous role for an enemy. To be sure, Edom did not initiate the attack, but merely joins the Babylonians. However, the long tradition of alliance and blood kinship would make the actions of Edom in many ways more despicable than those of Babylon, which never claimed to be an ally, a friend, or a brother. The vitriol so prominent from the beginning to the end of Obadiah has its roots in betrayal.

### Punishing the Nations, Restoring Judah, 15b,a + 16-21

The somewhat euphemistic presumption of Jerusalem's destruction as a day of YHWH in Obadiah 11-14 gives way to a new discussion in Obadiah 15-21 concerning broader implications for a day of YHWH against the nations. Stylistically, the bulk of Obadiah 15-21 changes from singular address to plural because it refers to the nations rather than to Edom alone. The exception to this change appears in Obadiah 15b, which maintains the singular reference. For some time, scholars have argued that this singular style in Obadiah 15b in all likelihood originally constituted the end of 11-14. Thus the singular "you" in Obadiah 15b offers a fitting conclusion to the charges against Edom in vv. 11-14, even if they are expressed as a warning. The logic of 11-14 charges Edom not to do several things (though knowing full well that they would), and it only stands to reason that these charges would conclude with a kind of verdict, precisely the kind that one finds in 15b: "As you (2ms) have done, it will be done to you (2ms); your (2ms) deeds shall return upon your (2ms) own head." This 2ms threat would have been directed specifically to Edom.

In contrast to Obadiah 15b, 15a changes to a pronouncement that the day of YHWH is near against *all* nations. Beginning with Obadiah 16 these nations are addressed directly and collectively using masculine plural forms. Thus, 15a anticipates the thematic shift that continues in Obadiah 16, while 15b concludes the castigation and threat to Edom that served as the focal point in Obadiah 1-14. By dovetailing the introduction to 16-21 with the conclusion of 1-14, the compiler has effected a transition whereby Edom's fate illustrates what awaits the nations in general on the day of YHWH. In Obadiah 15-21, one finds the portrayal of the day of YHWH, at its core, as a day of restoration for Jerusalem and of justice in the form of punishment for the nations.

Obadiah 16 flows thematically quite well on the heels of 15b, even though the two were not originally composed for one another. The threat of 15b that Edom (using second masculine singular address) will get what it deserves gives way to the same essential retribution against the nations in 16 (using third masculine plural language). In addition to speaking about the nations, Obadiah 16 also addresses a group directly (using second masculine plural language): "for as you have drunk (2mp) on my holy mountain, all the nations around you shall drink (3mp)."

The identity of the group who is addressed directly in Obadiah 16 deserves comment. Two possible interpretations find their way into the discussion. A smaller number of scholars suggest the addressee should be assumed to be Edom, in spite of the change from singular to plural address, because no formal change of addressee has otherwise been mentioned.[2] On the whole, however, the majority of scholars treat the addressee as the people of Jerusalem.[3] This explanation has several advantages: it fits the immediate context, better situates itself tradition-historically, provides a better explanation why this group is on YHWH's holy mountain, and makes better sense within the Book of the Twelve.

[Tradition History] The context of Obadiah 16-21 changes the tenor from the castigation of Edom to the restoration of Jerusalem that involves the punishment of the surrounding nations on the day of YHWH. Tradition-historically, this concept fits well with the idea of the "cup of reeling" one finds in the prophetic corpus (Isa 51:17-23; Jer 25:15-29; 48:26-27; 49:12; 51:7-8, 39; Ezek 23:31-35), Lamentations (4:21), and Psalms (60:3; 75:8). The basic plot line of this tradition remains relatively consistent. Zion is punished with YHWH's cup, causing her to stumble and stagger. When this punishment ends, YHWH then attends to the nations who have tormented her in her time of trouble. At times, prophets use this tradition to confront Jerusalem (Ezek 23:31-35), while at other times the tradition comforts Zion by announcing the end of her time of punishment. YHWH then turns to another nation. The other nation can vary from text to text, including Moab (Jer 48:26-27), Edom (Jer 49:12; Lam 4:21), or Babylon (Jer 51:7-8, 39). In one case, the order is reversed and another country's drinking of the cup leads to Jerusalem's turn for punishment (Ezek 23:31-35).

**Tradition History**

Tradition history seeks to determine the developmental range of meanings of a given word, phrase, or text complex to provide a profile of the author's intellectual milieu. Tradition history presupposes that the meaning of linguistic expressions in a given context rely ultimately upon the thought world of the author. For further reading, see Odil Hannes Steck, *Old Testament Exegesis: A Guide to the Methodology* (2d ed.; trans. James D. Nogalski; Atlanta: Society of Biblical Literature, 1998) 17–20, 121–42.

In many respects Obadiah 17 reflects the central message of Obadiah 16-21: a remnant of Judah (the house of Jacob) will be restored upon Zion and retribution will occur for the damage done to Jerusalem. Obadiah 17 conveys poetic justice when those who have been possessed will possess those guilty of injuring YHWH's people. This attitude toward the nations largely coincides with the attitude of justice toward the nations that one finds within Joel 3,

## Obadiah 17 and the Book of the Twelve

Obad 17 connects to other passages in the Book of the Twelve in at least three ways. First, Amos 9:12 thematically anticipates Obad 17, since "possession" language depicts a remnant that will rise up and restore the Davidic kingdom. Second, Joel 2:32 (MT 3:5) quotes Obad 17 explicitly when it refers to the remnant who will survive the day of YHWH: "for in Mount Zion and in Jerusalem there shall be those who escape as the Lord has said." Third, the association of Judah with the punishment of Jacob also occurs in Mic 1:2-7, a passage that would have begun the next writing in the Book of the Twelve before Jonah entered the corpus, although Jacob means the northern kingdom there (see discussion of Mic 1:5 and the section "Current State of Redactional Discussions" in the introduction to the Book of the Twelve at the beginning of this commentary).

most prominently Joel 3:4-8 (MT 4:4-8). [Obadiah 17 and the Book of the Twelve]

One finds the themes of Obadiah 17 reiterated in the final verse of the book, Obadiah 21. Both emphasize the centrality of Zion, the restoration of Zion's status through the punishment of other nations, and the holiness of Zion and the kingdom. Obadiah 21 also presupposes an extension of these motifs in ways that suggest it takes account of Obadiah 18, 19-20.

Obadiah 18 extends the thought of Obadiah 17 by providing a metaphor for the power of the remnant that will survive on Zion, which both verses label "the house of Jacob." Obadiah 18 calls the house of Jacob "fire," a metaphor of an unstoppable destructive force. This fire has a purpose—to destroy Edom. Obadiah 18 resorts to ancestral epithets, referring to the house of Jacob and Esau. This terminology does three things. First, it emphasizes the familial relationship assumed in the tradition, a relationship portrayed as strained from the beginning. Within the Jacob story, competition leads to betrayal, and nearly to death before time and distance allow the brothers to reach a rather tentative truce (Gen 25:22-23; 27:1–28:8; 33:1-17). Unlike the Genesis account, in Obadiah Esau betrays Jacob, implying a need for justice. Second, in Obadiah these terms also serve a political function. The house of Jacob and the house of Esau refer to the countries of Judah and Edom. Third, the terms Jacob and Esau connect Obadiah 16-21 with 1-9 and 10-14. Obadiah 6, 8, and 9 refer to Esau, while 10-14 evokes the familial relationship by charging Edom with taking advantage of its "brother" (10, 12) and "Jacob" (10). Obadiah only twice specifies Edom (1, 8) while mentioning Esau seven times (6, 8, 9, 18 [twice], 19, 21).

Obadiah 18 seems to conclude a unit with a formulaic but emphatic attribution of the message to YHWH: "for YHWH has spoken." However, Obadiah 19 begins anew by delineating the extent of the repossession more concretely than did the metaphor of fire in the Obadiah 18.

**Repossessing the Land**

The chart shows the relative movements of two waves of occupation whose purpose serves primarily to strengthen occupation of the land surrounding Jerusalem. In essence, the population realignment indicated by these statements in Obad 19-20 anticipates movements in two stages: (1) from the central portions of Judah outward (darker arrows), and (2) reinforcements from outlying districts to fill gaps (lighter arrows). The first wave (Obad 19) describes movements from Judah outward by statements that inhabitants from Negeb will push Edom back while those from the Shephelah will move into Philistine and Ephraimite (and Samarian) territory. At the same time, inhabitants of Benjamin (the other traditional tribal region that made up Judah during the divided monarchy) will move northeast to retake Gilead (a region lost to the Assyrian invasions of the eighth century). The second wave (Obad 20) anticipates Israelite exiles possessing Phoenician territory and Jerusalemite exiles (currently located in Sardis) filling in the land of the Negeb (which had been vacated by those moving out toward Edom). These movements essentially describe a process of postexilic resettlement that seeks to recreate the Davidic kingdom borders. The end result of this plan is extension of Judah in every direction. There is no evidence to suggest that this movement ever took place either militarily or peacefully.

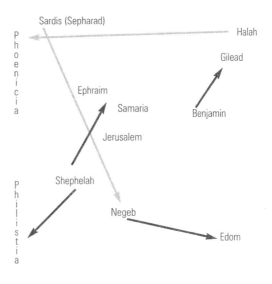

The places mentioned in Obadiah 19-20 presume a conceptual logic that concretizes the more programmatic statements of Obadiah 18. The movement implied by these statements unfolds in two stages to reconstitute the old boundaries of the Davidic kingdom: from the inside out (19) and from the outside in (20). [Repossessing the Land] Obadiah 19 states that the Negeb (a designation for the southern region of Judah) will possess the mountain of Esau, implying eastward movement from Judah, while the Shephelah (the foothills between the Philistine plain and the hills of Judah) will do the same to the Philistines, conquering land to the west and south. This same group from the Shephelah will head north to retake the land of Ephraim/Samaria, while Benjamin moves northeast to reclaim the land of Gilead. Thus, Obadiah 19 describes a conquest from within Judah that expands the boundaries to retake land associated with the Davidic kingdom. The second phase (Obad 20) involves resettling exiles in a way that completes the expansion of Judah to the northwest and south. Reference to the "exiles of Jerusalem" in "Sepharad" completes the picture of the second phase, even though the location of Sepharad is debated. [Sepharad] These exiles return to the land south of Jerusalem that had been vacated by the group that had expanded

**Sepharad**

Most see reference to Sepharad as the Aramaic spelling of Sardis, the capital of Lydia in Asia Minor. An ancient inscription has been found spelling Sardis with the same consonants as Obad 20, and a monument from the fifth century BCE attests to a Jewish presence in Sardis that could be roughly contemporary with the time of the compilation of Obadiah.

into Edomite territory. Simultaneously, exiles of Israel will take Phoenicia to the north and west of Ephraimite territory.

At any rate, the general effect is clear. Judah will be expanded as a nation. Obadiah 18 presupposes that Edom has begun infiltrating land previously occupied by Judah. Obadiah 18-19 makes sense if Jerusalem has already been resettled, since the exiles are not brought back there. In all likelihood, this passage presupposes a Persian period context when some hope of expanding Judah existed. How far into the Persian period is a matter of debate. Several scholars see 19-20 as a fifth-century addition, though these scholars generally date the person Obadiah close to the time of Jerusalem's destruction.[4] Others date these verses to the fourth century.

Obadiah 21 concludes the book with a summary statement. The statement has two parts, the first highlighting the centrality of Zion over Esau and the second emphasizing that the kingdom belongs to YHWH. Since these two parts appear similar to ideas expressed in Obadiah 17-18, it has been suggested that Obadiah 21 originally followed Obadiah 18 before the insertion of Obadiah 19-20.[5] Such may be the case, but one should not ignore the connections between Obadiah 21 and Obadiah 19-20. Obadiah 21a fits better with the more limited scope of Obadiah 17-18, which deals with Edom's punishment. However, Obadiah 19-20 expands the concept of restoration well beyond Edom, and this expansion fits Obadiah 21b: "The kingdom shall belong to YHWH." Obadiah 19-20 reflects a model of restoration along the lines of Amos 9:11-12: so that "the fallen booth of David . . . may possess the remnant of Edom *and all the nations who are called by my name,* says YHWH who does this." In this respect, Obadiah 21 functions aptly as both the conclusion to Obadiah 17-18 (punishment of Edom) and 19-20 (restoration of YHWH's [Davidic] kingdom).

As noted previously, Obadiah 21 builds upon motifs expressed in Obadiah 17, but extends them to incorporate the "action" of Obadiah 18 (and perhaps 19-20). Obadiah 17 emphasizes Zion's centrality, but the focal point references those who escape, while Obadiah 21 emphasizes the power of those who *have* returned. Obadiah 17 also emphasizes the holiness of the Zion, while Obadiah 21 expands this motif to include a promise that the *kingdom* shall belong to YHWH. Thus, Obadiah 17 presumes Zion's holiness, while Obadiah 21 touts the kingdom's relation to YHWH. In between, Obadiah 19-20, which describe the re-conquest of the kingdom by those in the land and exiles who have returned, makes this move from Zion to kingdom understandable. Additionally, the combination of Obadiah 17 and 21 helps account for the expansion of the third motif shared by the two verses: namely, the punishment of offending nations. Here, though, Obadiah 17 states that the remnant will "possess those who dispossess them," while Obadiah 21 refocuses the attention specifically upon Esau, representing the first of the surrounding nations to be punished, a focus suited to summarizing the message of the book.

## CONNECTIONS

Obadiah reflects prophetic pronouncements that concern betrayal, national pride, and divine retribution. Few things in life hurt more than the pain inflicted by a friend or family member. Because the relationship involves a bond of trust, those closest to us know more about us and know what we hold dear. As a result, betrayal rarely seems trivial, and the desire to strike back out of pain and frustration can be difficult to restrain. One sees this sense of betrayal in biblical texts as well as in life itself. The story of Jacob and Esau in Genesis tell the story of a son's betrayal by his mother and twin brother. Jacob stole his father's blessing through treachery and deceit, and his mother helped him do it (Gen 27:1-40). [Family Betrayal] Yet Genesis does not tell the story from the perspective of the aggrieved party, Esau. Instead, the narrator's light shines upon the transformation of Jacob when he himself is betrayed by his father-in-law (Gen 28–31).

In Obadiah, one finds a new chapter in the story of this dysfunctional family. To be sure, Jacob and Esau are not the subject, but

---

**Family Betrayal**

The betrayal of family members, especially in the societies where clan identity plays a pivotal role, represents a pain that is excruciating to experience. In the Jacob and Esau story, this betrayal is compounded by the fact that the parents take sides and compound the problem. The pathos of Esau is palpable when he learns he has been deceived by both his brother and his mother:

Now Esau hated Jacob because of the blessing with which his father had blessed him, and Esau said to himself, "The days of mourning for my father are approaching; then I will kill my brother Jacob." But the words of her elder son Esau were told to Rebekah; so she sent and called her younger son Jacob and said to him, "Your brother Esau is consoling himself by planning to kill you. Now therefore, my son, obey my voice; flee at once to my brother Laban in Haran, and stay with him a while, until your brother's fury turns away—until your brother's anger against you turns away, and he forgets what you have done to him; then I will send, and bring you back from there. Why should I lose both of you in one day?" (Gen 27:41-45)

Obadiah is not a narrative about two brothers, but the familial betrayal is nevertheless evident (see Obad 7, 10, 12). Of course, the perspective of Obadiah changes in that it is Esau who is the subject of Jacob's anger.

### Imprecatory Psalms

The role of curse literature in the cult is associated with blessing for the community as well as the individual. D. McBride offers a clear statement on this connection:

> The official Yahwistic cultus, eventually centered at the Jerusalem Temple and idealized in the tabernacle traditions of the Pentateuch, sought to assure the constancy of these and other blessings of the Lord (e.g., Exod 20:24; 39:32-43; Lev 9:22-24; Num 6:22-27; Ps 128). Also understood to be of critical importance for the well being of the worshiping community and its individual members were cultic means to identify, preempt, and either execrate or expiate anything that threatened adversity. Such means included imprecatory oaths that invoked divine assistance in distinguishing between innocent and guilty parties (e.g., Num 5:11-31; Deut 29:18-21 [Heb. 29:17-20 ]; 1 Kgs 8:31-32); other forms of cursing were deployed against the plots and assaults of both personal and national enemies (e.g., Pss 54–56; 79; 83; 109; 129 ; compare Luke 6:27-31). In brief, cultic institutions functioned to maximize the actualization of blessings and to minimize, thwart, or redirect the injurious effects of cursings.

The collection of numerous sayings regarding foreign nations likely flows from this cultic background.

S. Dean McBride, "Blessings and Cursings," *NIDB*, 1:474.

their story is echoed in the fate of the nations representing their descendants. This time, however, Jacob is the one betrayed by the brother, and unlike the Genesis story, which devotes virtually no space to the perspective of the party who had been wronged, Obadiah delivers its message from the perspective of the one betrayed. In this respect, Obadiah functions similarly to the imprecatory psalms (e.g., 69:22-26). [Imprecatory Psalms] The desire to make those who hurt us suffer as we have suffered is a powerful human emotion, but the desire to retaliate, or to have God retaliate, runs counter to the teachings of Jesus, as well as other biblical texts (Matt 5:7, 9, 38-48; Mic 6:6-8; Lev 24:22; 1 Sam 19:4-6; 24:1-10). However, Obadiah takes this idea further. Obadiah treats Edom's betrayal of Jacob as the betrayal of God, and it portrays God as the one who will administer justice. Whereas the imprecatory psalms turn the calls for vengeance over to God but never recount God's response, Obadiah portrays YHWH as the one who will punish Edom. To understand this image of divine retribution, it is also important to remember that Obadiah's Esau is *not* a person but a country whose arrogance has caused it to act in direct opposition to God.

In Obadiah, the root of Edom's problem rests in its own self-deception and arrogance (Obad 3). Like a bully's henchman, Edom does not attack because Edom had been wronged. Edom joined Babylon in attacking Judah to curry Babylon's favor because it deemed Babylon more powerful and chose to gloat over the destruction of its brother (v. 13). Rejoicing over the misfortune of others, and especially one's relative, evokes the prophet's calls for justice (15b).

National aggression is a terrifying, violent repudiation of human and divine law. Rarely in the history of humanity has the brute force of one nation had the lasting impact the attacking nation desires, yet nations continue to attack other nations to further their own agendas. Edom appears to have become a willing partner in Babylon's attack on Judah. We do not know precise details regarding how this happened, but in Obadiah we catch a glimpse of how Judah perceived this act as the betrayal of a brother. Obadiah offers not one word of condemnation for Babylon, whom we know initiated the attack on Jerusalem, though Obadiah warns Edom that its newfound allies will turn on them as well (vv. 7, 15b).

What of today? In an age when military industrial powers confront terrorism, have things changed? Is military violence necessary to preserve security and way of life? Frequently, politicians say military responses are necessary, but the community of faith needs to remind the world that military action comes with a price. The church should call the world to peace in order to honor Jesus' teachings that violence toward one's neighbor perpetuates retaliation. National violence begets death and human suffering on a grand scale. Resentment lingers for generations.

When confronted in Gethsemane, Jesus did not call out the troops. When confronted with an occupying military presence, Jesus commanded his disciples to return kindness for evil (Matt 5:38-42). Nowhere does Jesus issue a call to arms, yet from the Crusades to the present, the church has frequently aligned itself with national interests instead of God's interests. When the church becomes the tool of the state rather than the voice of God in this world, the mission of the church suffers. Obadiah approaches national conflict differently. These prophetic sayings portray God announcing justice: "I will surely make you least among the nations" (v. 2); "I will destroy the wise out of Edom and understanding out of Mount Esau" (v. 8); "as you have done, it shall be done to you" (v. 15). The divine retribution present in both the Old and New Testament texts troubles many. It is hard to reconcile commands to love and forgive one's neighbor with portrayals of God as avenger. Yet one must recognize that retribution is part of a worldview that demands justice from God. Lest evil triumph, there must be an arbiter to whom we turn in the face of injustice, violence, and aggression. Sometimes the Bible speaks of God's use of humans to accomplish justice, but human agents can lust for power and attribute victory to themselves (see discussion of Hab 1:5-12 in

James D. Nogalski, *The Book of the Twelve: Micah–Malachi* [Smyth & Helwys Bible Commentary Series]). Obadiah expects justice as punishment for Edom. However, this punishment comes not at the hand of the country that has been wronged. Rather, punishment comes from God, and it comes because of Edom's own deeds require a response from God.

In addition to divine retribution, Obadiah's sense of justice demands restoration, though once again Obadiah tends to portray restoration in terms of land retaken (vv. 18-21). Judah has lost its land, its king, and its temple. Judah saw the land as God's gift, promised to Abraham, delivered after the exodus, and promised again to David the king. For justice to be complete, in the view of Obadiah, the restoration and purification of Jerusalem is not enough. Judah must reclaim the land it had once possessed, but it must do so recognizing that this kingdom belongs to YHWH. What does one make of the fact that this promise is never fulfilled in Obadiah's time, and as yet not in ours? These promises become the substance of hope: hope for restoration and justice, hope for purification and returning to God. In a time when there are wars and rumors of wars, prophetic eschatology reminds us that hope for a changed world can only be found in God.

# NOTES

1. Contra Ehud Ben Zvi, *A Historical-Critical Study of the Book of Obadiah* (BZAW 242; Berlin: de Gruyter, 1996) 36–37.

2. See Marvin A. Sweeney, *The Twelve Prophets* (Berit Olam, vol. 1; Collegeville: Liturgical Press, 2000) 294.

3. So Hans Walter Wolff, *Obadiah and Jonah: A Commentary* (trans. Margaret Kohl; A Continental Commentary; Minneapolis: Augsburg, 1977) 63; John Barton, *Joel and Obadiah: A Commentary* (OTL; Louisville: Westminster John Knox, 2001) 151–52.

4. For example, see Wolff, *Obadiah and Jonah*, 19.

5. For example, see Jörg Jeremias, *Die Propheten Joel, Obadja, Jonah, Micha* (Das Alte Testament Deutsch 24/3; Göttingen: Vandenhoeck & Ruprecht, 2007) 71, 73–74.

# SELECT BIBLIOGRAPHY
# FOR OBADIAH

Barton, John. *Joel and Obadiah: A Commentary*. Old Testament Library. Louisville: Westminster John Knox, 2001.

Ben Zvi, Ehud. *A Historical-Critical Study of the Book of Obadiah*. Beihefte zur Zeitschrift für die alttestamentliche Wissenschaft 242. Berlin: Walter de Gruyter, 1996.

Emerton, John A. "Looking on One's Enemies." *Vetus Testamentum* 51 (2001): 186–96.

Kodell, Jerome. *Lamentations, Haggai, Zechariah, Malachi, Obadiah, Joel, Second Zechariah, Baruch*. Old Testament Message 14. Wilmington, Michael Glazier, 1982.

Mason, Rex. *Micah, Nahum, Obadiah*. Old Testament Guides. Sheffield: JSOT Press, 1991.

Nogalski, James D. "Obadiah 7: Textual Corruption or Politically Charged Metaphor?" *Zeitschrift für die Alttestamentliche Wissenschaft* 110 (1998): 67–71.

Ogden, Graham S. "Prophetic Oracles against Foreign Nations and Psalms of Communal Lament: The Relationship of Psalm 137 to Jeremiah 49:7-22 and Obadiah." *Journal for the Study of the Old Testament* 24 (1982): 89–97.

Raabe, Paul R. *Obadiah: A New Translation with Introduction and Commentary*. Anchor Bible 24D. New York: Doubleday, 1996.

Renkema, Johan. "Data Relevant to the Dating of the Prophecy of Obadiah." In *Past, Present, Future*, ed. Johannes Cornelis de Moor and H. F. Van Rooy, 251–61. Leiden: E. J. Brill, 2000.

———. "The Literary Structure of Obadiah." In *Delimitation Criticism*, ed. Marjo C. A. Korpel and Josef M. Oesch, 230–76. Assen: Van Gorcum, 2000.

Robinson, Robert B. "Levels of Naturalization in Obadiah." *Journal for the Study of the Old Testament* 40 (1988): 83–97.

Snyman, S. D. "Cohesion in the Book of Obadiah." *Zeitschrift für die Alttestamentliche Wissenschaft* 101 (1989): 59–71.

Snyman, S. D., and Bloem Fontein. "Yom (YHWH) in the Book of Obadiah." In *Goldene Äpfel in Silbernen Schalen*, ed. Klaus-Dietrich Schunck and Matthias Augustin, 81–91. Frankfurt am Main: Peter Lang, 1992.

Stuart, Douglas K. *Hosea–Jonah*. Word Biblical Commentary 31. Waco: Word Books, 1987.

Wehrle, Josef. *Prophetie und Textanalyse der Komposition Obadja 1-21. Interpretiert auf der Basis textlinguistischer und semiotischer Konzeptionen*. Arbeiten zu Text und Sprache im Alten Testament 28. St. Ottilien: EOS, 1987.

Weimar, Peter. "Obadja. Eine redaktionskritische Analyse." *Biblische Notizen* 27 (1985): 35–99.

Wolff, Hans Walter. *Obadiah and Jonah. A Commentary*. Translated by Margaret Kohl. Continental Commentary. Minneapolis: Augsburg, 1977.

# JONAH

# INTRODUCTION TO THE BOOK OF JONAH

Modern scholars assume that Jonah is an anonymous short story of theological fiction. By contrast, large numbers of lay readers operate from the assumption that the events in this short story actually occurred. These views naturally affect one's interpretation of the text [Jonah in Jewish Tradition] The truth of the book, however, goes far deeper than historical questions. The portrayal of God in Jonah represents the central focus of the book. Nevertheless, some orientation to the critical issues surrounding the book will aid one's interpretation.

## Dating the Prophet and the Book

Only two prophets for whom biblical books are named are also mentioned by name in 1–2 Kings: Isaiah (2 Kgs 18–20) and Jonah, the son of Amittai. According to a brief note in 2 Kings 14:25, Jonah was a prophet during the reign of Jeroboam II (786–746 BCE), king of Israel. In that context, Jonah is the prophet whom YHWH uses to predict Jeroboam's success in restoring the boundaries of Israel to the extent that they had been during the reign of Solomon. As such, the mention of Jonah would raise conflicting images for later readers. On the one hand, in 2 Kings 14:25 Jonah operated at YHWH's command. On the other hand, the effect of Jonah's message expanded Israel under a king (Jeroboam II) who is otherwise evaluated negatively, like the other kings of the northern kingdom (see 2 Kgs 14:24). For this reason, it is doubtful that the keepers of tradition in Judah would have viewed Jonah favorably. Perhaps this legacy made "Jonah" the perfect foil for the postexilic author of the book.

Critical scholarship has virtually abandoned the task of dating the book of Jonah with any real precision. There is widespread acknowledgment that the book as we have it stems from the postexilic period, but scholars are split over whether it comes from the early, middle, or late Persian period, or even from the Greek period. Reasons for dating the book so late center on linguistic features, Jonah's use of other biblical material, and the history of ideas. Undoubtedly, Jonah's

## Jonah in Jewish Tradition

Not surprisingly, the legendary material surrounding Jonah in rabbinic sources is more extensive than that of most of the other prophets in the Book of the Twelve. Traditions grew about this prophet concerning his background, his time on the ship, his time in the fish, and the aftermath of his preaching to the Ninevites. Rabbinic tradition claims Jonah was a disciple of Elisha and anointed Jehu king of Israel. One of the reasons Jonah was concerned about YHWH's proclivity toward forgiveness was that Jonah was already known as a false prophet because he predicted the fall of Jerusalem. However, after its people repented, YHWH relented about destroying Jerusalem. This change, however, reflected negatively on Jonah's veracity, and Israelites began to see Jonah as a false prophet. Jonah's concern about YHWH showing compassion in 4:2 was thus interpreted to have less to do with Jonah's dislike of foreigners than with protecting his reputation as a reliable prophet.

The people on board the ship, according to rabbinic legend, came from the 70 nations of the world. The people on the ship did not want to kill Jonah so they tested the effect by dunking Jonah three times. The first time they dunked him into the water up to his knees, and the sea calmed until they took him out. Then they placed him into the sea up to his neck (cf. 2:5 [MT 2:6]) and again the sea got calm. Finally, they were convinced that they had to throw him in if they wanted to survive. Subsequently, the conversion of the pagan sailors is recounted even more dramatically by the rabbis than by the book of Jonah.

Several traditions, both competing and harmonizing, can be detected in rabbinic material about Jonah's time in the fish. One tradition arises from the use of two different words for fish in the narrative, twice masculine (1:17 and 2:10) and once feminine (2:1). The harmonizing traditions thus put Jonah in a masculine fish first.

This fish was appointed from the beginning of time to be ready for Jonah. However, this fish was also destined to be destroyed by Leviathan once Jonah was inside. Jonah, however, convinced Leviathan not to eat the fish. Out of gratitude the male fish gives Jonah the ride of his life, showing him the great undersea marvels of the world. As a result, Jonah is having such a great time that God sends a female fish that is pregnant with 365,000 baby fish to take Jonah. At that point, Jonah's discomfort forces him to pray for deliverance. The heat from the belly of the fish dissolves his garments, makes his hair fall out, and causes sores to develop on his body. These ailments add to his discomfort when waiting in the sun outside Nineveh.

In rabbinic tradition, Jonah learns a valuable lesson from YHWH's speech to him after YHWH destroys the plant. Jonah shows contrition. He prostrates himself and implores YHWH: "O God, guide the world according to your goodness." Thus, while the book of Jonah ends with an open-ended question, rabbinic tradition tends to portray Jonah as having been enlightened by the experience with the plant and the worm. Jonah's punishment in the fish had been so severe that Jonah was spared death and taken to paradise while he was yet living. Nineveh's deliverance lasted as long as their repentance. At the end of the 40 days, they returned to their sinful ways and Jonah's prophecy overtook them. This last portion ties specifically into Nahum (see Beatte Ego, "The Repentance of Nineveh in the Story of Jonah and Nahum's Prophecy of the City's Destruction: Aggadic Solutions for an Exegetical Problem in the Book of the Twelve," in Aaron Schart and Paul Redditt, eds., *Thematic Threads in the Book of the Twelve* [Beihefte zur Zeitschrift für die alttestamentliche Wissenschaft 325; Berlin De Gruyter, 2003] 155–64).

For additional reading, see Louis Ginzberg, *The Legends of the Jews*, 7 vols. (Philadelphia: The Jewish Publication Society of America, 1947) 4:246–53 and 6:343–52.

composition was complete by the time of Sirach (c. 200 BCE) since Sirach 49:10 refers to the Twelve. Jonah appears as the fifth book in the Twelve in the MT sequence and the sixth in the LXX tradition (see "The Order of the Book of the Twelve" in the introduction to this commentary). Jonah likely represents the latest complete book added to the Book of the Twelve, though some suggest Jonah developed in stages or entered the Twelve with another book.[1] Some have suggested that Jonah entered the Twelve with (at least portions of) Zechariah 9–14.[2] Others see it entering with Malachi.[3]

## Literary Form, Structure, and Unity

The book of Jonah stands alone among the Latter Prophets in that it does not offer a collection of prophetic sayings. Rather, it is a narrative about a prophet's dealings with YHWH. Thus, it is similar to prophetic narratives that comprise short portions of other prophetic books (e.g., Amos 7:10-17), but the Jonah narrative is more elaborately constructed. Recent discussions of Jonah have classified it as a novella, a satire, or a midrash. [The Genre of Jonah] No matter what specific designation one assigns to it, the booklet has characteristics of all three of these types of literature. Jonah tells a short story that conveys a plot line, though it has significant points of disjuncture. Jonah is also satirical since the prophet serves as the foil, not the hero of the book. Jonah also makes several theological points dramatically and powerfully. It portrays a God who is not only interested in the well-being of all creation but who is in complete control, who can act unilaterally, and who can reverse course when deemed appropriate.

> **The Genre of Jonah**
>
> A *novella* is a short novel. Those who see Jonah as a *satire* see the focus of the message as poking fun at the narrow-minded theological perspective Jonah represents. A *midrash* is a genre unique to Judaism. It is a story told to explain a theological point that is generally related to a biblical text. In the case of Jonah, it has often been suggested that Jonah is a midrash on Jer 18:7-10, a text that articulates YHWH's freedom to act in judgment or salvation toward any nation.

Recent holistic treatments of Jonah focus upon the book's episodic action as its structural key. For instance, the final form of Jonah divides into four scenes: Jonah on the sea (1:1-16), Jonah in the sea (1:17–2:10), Jonah in Nineveh (3:1-10), and Jonah outside Nineveh (4:1-11). With each scene, Jonah changes location. The shift allows each section to focus upon interaction with others—with the (foreign) sailors, with God, with the people of Nineveh, and with God again—as a means of exploring the Jonah's view of God and its implications for his ministry.

Despite the recent focus on the final form of prophetic books, Jonah has received its share of attention from source critics and redaction critics who have questioned whether the form as we have it constitutes the earliest form of the book. Several scholars suggest that the style of chapters 3–4 is so different from 1–2 that they must have been transmitted separately.[4] These ideas represent a minority opinion because the narrative logic requires something to

### The Prophet Jonah

Michelangelo's Sistine Chapel portrayal of Jonah captures the anguish of the reluctant prophet.

Michelangelo Buonarroti (1475–1564). The Sistine Chapel; ceiling frescos after restoration. *The Prophet Jonah*. Located on the altar wall as a symbol of the resurrection of Christ. Sistine Chapel, Vatican Palace, Vatican State. (Credit: Erich Lessing/Art Resource, NY)

precede 3:1, and the literary structure of chapter 1 makes the arguments for a multi-staged growth of this chapter rather strained. More frequently, and more convincingly, one finds the argument that the poetic material of the book (2:2-9 [MT 2:3-10]) represents a redactional addition to the book in order to portray the prophet more positively.[5] While these arguments carry considerable weight in this commentary, it should be noted that the insertion of this psalm was not made without careful contemplation and that it functions meaningfully in its current context.

### Jonah in the Book of the Twelve

Jonah's unique features are not limited to its genre or narrative style. Its transmission and its theological perspective also set Jonah apart from the remainder of the Book of the Twelve. Jonah is the only writing with a different placement in all three of extant orders of the Book of the Twelve. It appears fifth in the MT order. In the LXX order, however, it appears in the sixth position between Joel and Nahum. In both instances, it logically precedes Nahum, a book that predicts and presupposes the destruction of Nineveh. Thus, even though Jonah's composition is widely dated to the postexilic period, its position falls into the preexilic writings (Hosea–Zephaniah). The third sequence of the Book of the Twelve is attested in only one manuscript in the Qumran caves, 4QXII[a]. [4QXII[a]] This manuscript fragment from the second century BCE contains a portion of Malachi followed by Jonah, which indicates that Jonah would have been the last book on the scroll for this manuscript. The reasons for this variation are unknown, and while the potential implications are not insignificant, they are largely limited to speculation about the order in which the writings entered the Twelve.

More significant than the order of transmission is the theological perspective of Jonah, which differs from the remaining writings in the Twelve. Jonah lacks several significant motifs that appear in other writings of the Book of the Twelve. It exhibits no eschatological focus, no specific or formulaic references to the Day of YHWH, no promises about the fertility of the land, and no message of political judgment on Judah or Israel. Jonah does contain a message of impending judgment on a hated nation (Assyria), but the book turns on the unparalleled acts of repentance of that nation, resulting in YHWH's decision not to punish Nineveh. While one periodically finds texts in the Book of the Twelve that allow for the salvation/deliverance of certain foreign peoples (e.g., Zech 8:22-23; 14:16; Mal 1:11), only Jonah implicitly castigates those in Israel, who (like Jonah) resent God showing compassion on the nations.

Yet, for all its uniqueness, Jonah is not disconnected from the Book of the Twelve and other Old Testament texts. Jonah's reason for fleeing YHWH, according to 4:2, cites Joel 2:18 (which in turn cites Exod 34:6). Moreover, Micah 7:18-19 has long been associated with Jonah in Jewish synagogue worship. Jonah's placement also raises questions for the reader of the Twelve about God's concern for Assyria when compared to the book of Nahum. While Jonah speaks of Nineveh's repentance and deliverance, Nahum condemns Nineveh and portrays its destruction. These connections

**4QXII[a]**

AΩ The nomenclature of this fragment follows the standard patterns of naming manuscripts and fragments from the caves around Qumran. "4Q" means it was found in cave 4 at Qumran. "XII" is the Roman numeral for twelve used as the abbreviation for the Book of the Twelve. The superscripted "a" means it was the first such manuscript of the Book of the Twelve found in cave 4. In this case, this was the first named fragment from cave 4 of a total of seven (4QXII[a-g]). It is one of the oldest manuscripts found among the Qumran caves, stemming from approximately 150 BCE. See the discussion of the text's characteristics in Russell Fuller, "The Text of the Twelve Minor Prophets," in *CurBS* 7 (1999): 81–95. While Fuller indicates that the text and order of the manuscript evidence exhibits diversity, this diversity is not nearly as broad as in Jeremiah, Ezekiel, and several other books.

demonstrate Jonah has a complex purpose. On the one hand, it is steeped in the traditions of Israel's prophets. On the other hand, it is critical of the narrow nationalistic use of the traditions from which it draws. Jonah functions in the Book of the Twelve as a reminder not to attempt to force God into a box. God's grace and compassion are a scandal to the prophet Jonah when offered to foreigners. The book holds Jonah's bigotry up to the light of day so that its readers see how ludicrous that bigotry appears against God's desire to reconcile with all. The prophet attempts to limit God's compassion to those like himself, but the book of Jonah knows better. The foreigners in the book are model characters who are willing to be enlightened (the sailors) and who are quick to repent (the Ninevites). It is Jonah who is portrayed as obstinate, arrogant, unwilling to change, and self-centered. More important, Jonah serves as a paradigmatic character after whom Israel should not pattern itself. Jonah's futile attempt to limit God's compassion is all the more ludicrous in light of Jonah's own experience of God's grace in the form of miraculous delivery from certain death.

### The Message of Jonah

Because of Jonah's narrative form, the main points of the book are not stated explicitly. Rather, the reader is invited to contemplate the meaning, a task aided by noting the implicit factors related to the portrayal of God and God's relationship to humanity. The book of Jonah underscores several theological points relating to God's power and freedom, God's compassion, God's response to human actions, and human recognition of God's purpose.

In Jonah, God displays control over all creation, while displaying a penchant to allow humans the same freedom of action even when limiting their actions. God's power over creation is displayed in several ways. First, God calls and then compels Jonah to perform his bidding to deliver a word of judgment to Nineveh. Second, God utilizes living and nonliving objects from the created order to persuade Jonah of a certain course of action or to confront Jonah's attitudes: God controls the wind for specific purposes (1:4; 4:8); God appoints a fish (1:17) to receive Jonah and deposit him back onto dry land; God appoints a plant (4:6) and a worm (4:7) to make a point to Jonah. In Jonah, God is not limited by the way the created world normally functions because God is utterly in control of the world God created. The effect of this control over nature underscores God's power, but it also highlights God's freedom. God, for some unstated reason, wants Jonah to go to Nineveh, and God is free to use any means to make sure Jonah gets there.

Even though God established the order of creation, God can choose to bypass that order. This presumption of divine freedom is not limited to the book of Jonah, but resounds throughout Scripture. God chose to respond to Israel's distress when they were in Egypt. God chose to accept Abel's offering, which infuriated Cain. God's freedom finds clear expression in Jeremiah 18:7-10, within which God claims the right to change the balance of political power as God sees fit:

> At one moment I may declare concerning a nation or a kingdom, that I will pluck up and break down and destroy it, but if that nation, concerning which I have spoken, turns from its evil, I will change my mind about the disaster that I intended to bring on it. And at another moment I may declare concerning a nation or a kingdom that I will build and plant it, but if it does evil in my sight, not listening to my voice, then I will change my mind about the good that I had intended to do to it.

In every instance, it is not humanity, but God, who controls what happens and when.

A second theological point undergirding the narrative is that God's actions toward humanity are motivated by compassion, not a desire for retribution. This compassion is not a sanguine "anything goes." Even when God speaks words of judgment, God is prepared (but not obligated) to withhold punishment in response to human change of heart. Jonah 4 emphasizes this point by noting that Jonah fled because he knew God was too compassionate toward people (4:2). YHWH, however, defends YHWH's own compassion by asking Jonah a rhetorical question that challenges the prophet to consider his own response to the plant that withered. If Jonah could show pity on a plant, why would God not have compassion on the living things of Nineveh?

A third significant point about God appears when one recognizes that Jonah does not portray God mechanistically. God consistently responds to the responses that human beings make. God does not merely set things in motion like a watchmaker who winds a clock. The God of Jonah, indeed the God of the Bible, interacts with humanity. God does not predestine the responses people make, and God responds to humans in any number of ways. God commands Jonah to go to Nineveh, but Jonah refuses, so God's sends a wind capable of destroying the ship on which Jonah has sought to flee. The foreign sailors throw Jonah into the sea at God's request (1:14-15), and then God calms the storm. The people of Nineveh repent, unsure whether it will change their fate (3:9), and then God decides not to punish them. Jonah becomes angry with God (4:1), and God sets out to teach him a lesson. The biblical God is one who actively and dynamically participates in the ebb and flow of life.

A fourth area for theological reflection is the way that God relates to humanity. God's actions are inscrutable, and God's reasons often lie beyond human comprehension (cf. Job 38:4–40:2). Yet the biblical portrait of God depicts two paradoxical paradigms that help explain much of what God does when relating to human beings: God's expectations for proper conduct and God's compassion toward humanity. These paradigms play a large role in Jonah. God's expects human beings to behave honorably. Amos condemns foreign nations not because they fail to worship YHWH but because they mistreat other human beings (Amos 1:2–2:3). In Jonah, God sends the prophet to proclaim judgment on Nineveh because of its wickedness—not its worship of foreign gods (Jonah 1:2).

God also exhibits compassion, pity, and forgiveness when dealing with flawed human beings. The sailors, ignorant of YHWH, come to recognize God's power when God calms the storm. God takes compassion on Nineveh when it repents, despite its history of wickedness that had provoked God in the first place. God delivers Jonah from the depths of the sea when Jonah prays not because God had to do so but because God has compassion on disobedient prophets who turn to him just as he did to the ignorant sailors and the wicked Ninevites. The God portrayed in Jonah is not a vindictive God but a God of compassion who desires his followers to show the same compassion on others as they have received. Though never made explicit, the thrust of God's expectation for Jonah relates closely to Jesus' articulation of the Golden Rule in Luke 6:31: "Do to others as you would have them do to you." Jonah did not wish to learn that lesson. Instead, Jonah's actions are designed to stop God from showing compassion on Nineveh, but Jonah is the only one who gets hurt in the process. It is Jonah who nearly drowns and who then gets burned in the sun as he sulks in anger. In the meantime, the pagan sailors become God-fearers and the Ninevites are saved from extermination. How ironic that Jonah's desire to limit God's salvific activity to certain people turns out to allow Jonah to serve as an instrument by which others come closer to God.

## NOTES

1. See James D. Nogalski, *Redactional Processes in the Book of the Twelve* (Beihefte zur Zeitschrift für die alttestamentliche Wissenschaft 218; Berlin–New York: de Gruyter, 1993) 255–73. One Qumran manuscript (4QXII^a) places Jonah after Malachi, which causes Jones to wonder whether its inclusion in the Twelve was quite late (Barry Jones, *The Formation of the Book of the Twelve* (SBLDS 149; Atlanta: Scholars Press, 1995) 213–18. See also Russell Fuller, "The Minor Prophets Manuscripts from Qumran, Cave IV" in *The Prophets* (ed. Eugene Ulrich; vol. 10 of *Qumran Cave 4*; DJD 15; Oxford: Clarendon Press, 1997) 221–318. For a recent example of Jonah's gradual accretion within the Twelve, see Jakob Wöhrle, *Der Abschluss des Zwölfprophetenbuches: Buchübergreifende Redaktkionsprozesse in den späten Sammlungen* (Beihefte zur Zeitschrift für die alttestamentliche Wissenschaft 389; Berlin: de Gruyter, 2008) 365–99.

2. Nogalski, *Redactional Processes in the Book of the Twelve*, 272–73, 278–79.

3. Aaron Schart, *Die Entstehung des Zwölfprophetenbuchs: Neubearbeitungen von Amos im Rahmen schriftenuebergreifender Redaktionsprozesse* (Beihefte zur Zeitschrift für die alttestamentliche Wissenschaft 260; Berlin: Walter de Gruyter, 1998) 289–303, 315.

4. See discussion in Hans Walter Wolff, *Obadiah and Jonah: A Commentary* (trans. Margaret Kohl; A Continental Commentary; Minneapolis: Augsburg, 1977) 78–80. For a proponent of Jonah as a narrative that developed over time, see Peter Weimar, "Jon 4,5. Beobachtungen zur Entstehung der Jonaerzählung," *BN* 18 (1982): 86–109.

5. See [Literary Tension between Jonah 2:2-9 and the Narrative] for discussion and bibliography concerning the issues involved.

## OUTLINE OF JONAH

I. Jonah 1:1-16: Jonah's Commission and Flight
   A. Jonah 1:1-3: Jonah's Prophetic Commission and Pathetic Flight
   B. Jonah 1:4-16: YHWH's Storm and the Sailors' Fear
II. Jonah 1:17–2:10: Jonah in the Fish

A. Jonah 1:17–2:1: Narrative Frame

B. Jonah 2:2-9: A Song of Thanksgiving

C. Jonah 2:10: Narrative Frame

III. Jonah 3:1-10: A Reluctant Prophet Speaks to a Receptive People

A. Jonah 3:1-3: God Reissues the Command to Jonah

B. Jonah 3:4: Jonah Delivers a Brief Message to the Ninevites to Satisfy YHWH

C. Jonah 3:5: The People of Nineveh Respond

D. Jonah 3:6-9: The King Responds

E. Jonah 3:10: God Shows Mercy to Nineveh

IV. Jonah 4:1-11: Jonah's Protestations and God's Response

A. Jonah 4:1-4: Jonah's Petulant Prayer and God's Response

B. Jonah 4:5-8: Jonah's Passive Aggressive Challenge

C. Jonah 4:9-11: God's Final Lesson

# JONAH'S COMMISSION
# AND FLIGHT

## Jonah 1:1-16

## COMMENTARY

Jonah 1:1-16 takes Jonah from the restful security of his own country on a chaotic flight across the sea that lands him in the ocean depths. The story unfolds in stages as the narrator artistically and dramatically shifts the spotlight back and forth between Jonah and the sailors, as can be seen from the basic structure of the plot. [Literary Structure of Jonah 1] The first section recounts Jonah's commission and unexpected response (1:1-3). The next section recounts YHWH's storm and the sailor's frantic actions (1:4-16). YHWH creates the storm to thwart Jonah's attempt to flee, but the major portion of the narrative relates how the foreign sailors come to recognize the awesome power of Jonah's God.

---

### Joppa, Tarshish, and Nineveh

The locations of Joppa, Tarshish, and Nineveh play a crucial role in the logic of the story. YHWH commands Jonah to go to Nineveh, several hundred miles east of Israel. Instead, Jonah goes to Joppa, the closest port (1:3). There, he catches a boat going to Tarshish at the far end of the Mediterranean.

**Literary Structure of Jonah 1**

Note the artistically arranged structure.

Narrative introduction (1:1-3): Jonah goes from land to sea after hearing YHWH's command

- A  Narrative and fear motif (1:4, 5aa)
- B     Prayer of sailors (5ab)
- C        Narrative (5bc, 6aa)
- D           Speech of the captain (6ab, b)
- E              Speech of the Sailors 1 (7a)
- F                 Narrative (7b)
- G                    Speech of the sailors 2 (8)
- Center                 Confession of Jonah and fear motif (9, 10aa)
- G'                   Speech of the sailors 2 (10ab, b)
- F'                Narrative (10c)
- E'             Speech of the Sailors 1 (11)
- D'          Speech of Jonah (12)
- C'       Narrative (13)
- B'    Prayer of the sailors (with text) (14)
- A' Narrative and fear motif (15, 16)

Narrative transition (2:1f., 11): Jonah goes from sea to land to hear YHWH's command

For analysis of this structure, see James D. Nogalski, *Redactional Processes in the Book of the Twelve* (Beihefte zur Zeitschrift für die alttestamentliche Wissenschaft 218; Berlin: de Gruyter, 1993) 250–55.

## Jonah's Prophetic Commission and Pathetic Flight, 1:1-3

Jonah 1:1-3 sets the stage for the book with Jonah's prophetic commission (1:1) followed by the response that characterizes Jonah as the anti-hero of the story (1:2-3). The beginning (1:1) narrates YHWH's commission of Jonah using a typical prophetic introductory formula: "And the word of YHWH came to X." The first Hebrew word in this verse typically begins a story—"and so it happened." This is no typical story, however, because it concerns "the word of YHWH" that comes to Jonah. Two vital pieces of information thus convey prophetic connotations at the outset of the narrative: the word of YHWH and the identity of the prophet.

The "word of YHWH" in ancient Judah did not evoke the same images as it does in modern Christian settings. Today, when someone says "the word of God" or "the word of the LORD," they typically mean the Bible. In Old Testament texts, however, this phrase appears in conjunction with God's *prophetic* message—the message of confrontation, warning, invitation, or solace that a prophet speaks from God to the people or its leaders (see discussion of Hos 1:1).

Jonah son of Amittai was a prophetic figure known to the writer of the tale and the writer's contemporaries. Jonah son of Amittai is mentioned in 2 Kings 14:25 as a prophet in Israel who conveyed a message of expansion from YHWH to Jeroboam II (785–745 BCE). The selection of Jonah creates certain ironies from the outset for the attentive postexilic reader. Jonah prophesied during the reign of Jeroboam II at a time, according to the Deuteronomistic Historian, when Israel expanded its borders to their greatest extent. [The Deuteronomistic Historian and Jeroboam's Expansion] This expansion happened despite the fact that Jeroboam II made no attempt to rid Israel of the practices that the historian condemned (2 Kgs 14:24). The prophet Jonah, whom we also learn hailed from Gath-Hepher, was the vehicle through whom YHWH delivered this message of expansion. Ironically, the prophet who delivers a message of expansion to a sinful kingdom (2 Kgs 14:24) is the same prophet who does everything in his power to stop the compassion of YHWH from benefiting foreigners (cf. Jonah 4:2). In the end, Jonah's failure helps God succeed in changing not only the Ninevites but also the sailors.

The name Jonah means "dove," a bird that has both positive and negative characteristics. It is a bird used for sacrifice (e.g., Lev 5:11; 12:8), which suggests a sense of passivity. Doves are also seen as silly or foolish (Hos 7:11; 11:11; Ps 55:7). Their cooing is used as a simile for mourning (Isa 38:14; 59:11; Ezek 7:16; Nah 2:8). "Dove" (*yônâh*) is also used as a term of endearment (Song 2:14; 5:2; 6:9; especially because of the eyes, Song 1:15; 4:1; 5:12).

The New Testament mentions the sign of Jonah ten times, but only in the Gospels (Matt 12:39-41 [4x]; 16:4, 17; Luke 11:29-32 [4x]). These references suggest that at the time of Jesus, Jonah was more famous for his miraculous deliverance from the belly of the fish than for the literary purpose of the story, which is to raise theological questions about the extent of God's grace. The miraculous delivery from the fish is also the subject of many extra-biblical legends about Jonah in rabbinic tradition. (See [Jonah in Jewish Tradition].)

Jonah 1:2 provides YHWH's command and its rationale. YHWH tells Jonah to get up and go to the metropolis of Nineveh and preach against it. The reason for the mission is also communicated: the wickedness of the people of Nineveh has come to

---

### The Deuteronomistic Historian and Jeroboam's Expansion

The expansion of territory under Jeroboam II (785–745) presents a theological enigma for the Deuteronomistic Historian (the editor of the books of Joshua, Judges, Samuel, and Kings). On the one hand, the historian condemns Jeroboam for failing to turn Israel from its sin of false worship. On the other hand, if Jeroboam was so evil, why did God reward him with expanded territory, a lengthy reign, and economic prosperity? No texts explain this tension. By the time of Josephus (c. 37–100 CE), traditions about Jonah's role had expanded to include specific commands given by YHWH in order to expanded Israel's territory by working through Jonah the prophet to the king:

In the fifteenth year of the reign of Amaziah, Jeroboam the son of Joash reigned over Israel in Samaria forty years. This king was guilty of contumely against God, and became very wicked in worshipping of idols, and in many undertakings that were absurd and foreign. He was also the cause of ten thousand misfortunes to the people of Israel. Now one Jonah, a prophet, foretold to him that he should make war with the Syrians, and conquer their army, and enlarge the bounds of his kingdom on the northern parts to the city Hamath, and on the southern to the lake Asphaltitis; for the bounds of the Canaanites originally were these, as Joshua their general had determined them. So Jeroboam made an expedition against the Syrians, and overran all their country, as Jonah had foretold. (*Antiquities*, Book 9 §10.1)

The prophet is thus given credit for enlarging the territory in Jeroboam's time according to Josephus, and the king's sins are described in more graphic detail.

**Gath-Hepher**

2 Kgs 14:25 cites Jonah's birthplace as Gath-Hepher, a small town on the eastern edge of the territory of Zebulon.

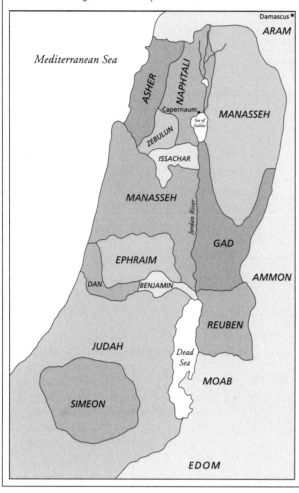

YHWH's attention. The Hebrew term translated as wickedness by the NRSV can be used of concrete acts of injustice (evil), as a state of depravity (wickedness), or as misfortune experienced (calamity). In Jonah 1:2, the word is typically translated as wickedness, but the same Hebrew word appears in 4:2 where Jonah accuses God of being too soft because God is prone "to relent of evil." [YHWH's Repentance]

Nineveh was not just any ancient city. For attentive readers in the postexilic period, Nineveh would have evoked powerful impressions of the Assyrian empire that dominated the ancient Near East as the ruling superpower for much of the eighth to seventh centuries. [Ancient Nineveh] At the time of Jeroboam II, however, Nineveh was not yet the Assyrian capital. It did not become the capital of Assyria until the reign of Sennacherib (704–681 BCE). Nineveh was overthrown in 612 BCE by the Babylonians. The location of the ancient city is not disputed. Its ruins are still standing in places, and the location is encapsulated as part of Mosul in Iraq.

**YHWH's Repentance**

AΩ The NRSV ("ready to relent from punishing") and other English versions translate the word "evil" or "calamity" differently when YHWH is the subject to avoid implying theologically that YHWH is the source of evil. This interpretive translation can mask the extent to which the Hebrew Bible uses the same language for punishment as other texts. See the discussion in [Does God Change God's Mind?] associated with Joel 2:14 and [YHWH Repenting] associated with the first two vision reports of Amos in 7:1-6.

Nineveh, by modern standards, was not very large. It had a 7.75-mile circumference when it was at its largest, a fact that puts it at odds historically with the hyperbole of Jonah 3:3-4. Still, in terms of the reputation it left behind, it was a formidable city. In short, for Judah, Nineveh remained for centuries a powerful symbol of an evil empire. Its destruction did little to staunch the hatred of Assyria in Judah (see discussion of Nah 2:1).

Jonah 1:3 narrates a report of the prophet's response to YHWH's commission. This report contains several humorous elements that heighten the sense of futility in Jonah's flight. Frequently, when God gives a command, Old Testament texts narrate the response to the command in order to remove any doubt about the obedience to that command. Old Testament texts even portray reluctant responses to YHWH's call, but Jonah's great pains to escape the call set his response apart from these patterns. [Reluctant Responses to YHWH's Call]

Jonah was told to get up and go to Nineveh, which lay north and east of Israel, in modern Iraq, but Jonah got up to flee in the opposite direction toward Tarshish, which lay far across the Mediterranean, near modern Spain. Jonah first goes to Joppa where he finds a boat and pays its price to head toward Tarshish. Joppa was a coastal town (modern-day Jaffa, south of Tel-Aviv). [Joppa] With subtle humor, the narrator mentions Tarshish three times in 1:3. The two that speak of Jonah have a directional marker on them (*taršîšâ*), meaning "in the direction of Tarshish." The third instance refers to the ship going to Tarshish. No English translation conveys this variation, but the effect is clear. The narrator distinguishes between the ship going *to* Tarshish and the prophet who is heading *toward* Tarshish (but will never get there). Jonah's flight also involves an exaggeration that again shows the narrator's humorous style. Jonah did not just buy a ticket; he rented the boat. Literally, the text says, "He paid its price." The pronominal suffix relates back to the feminine noun ship (*ŏnîyyâ*).[1]

Finally, the narrator's subtle humor appears in Jonah's reason for flight. According to 1:3, Jonah

**Ancient Nineveh**

The city of Nineveh would become a symbol of brutal military and political power, but only after the time of Jonah. The Lamassu statues that stood at the previous castle of King Ashurnasirpal II at Nimrud were unearthed and are on display in the British Museum. Their impressive size indicates their function as symbols of power guarding the castle.

(Credit: Mujtaba Chohan, http://en.wikipedia.org/wiki/File:BM;_RM6_-_ANE,_Assyrian_Sculpture_14_West_Wall_(M_%2B_N)_%7E_Assyrian_Empire_%2B_-Lamassu,_Gates_at_Balawat,_Relief_Panel_%27s)_%26_Full_Projection.3.JPG)

**Reluctant Responses to YHWH's Call**

It is not uncommon for prophets and other characters in the Old Testament to fail to show immediate joy at the prospects of YHWH calling them to a task, but no other prophet goes to the lengths that Jonah does to try to elude the task. Moses raises a series of verbal objections (Exod 3), but finally goes. Gideon (Judg 6:15) and Saul (1 Sam 9:21) both express their sense of inadequacy when called by God. At the other end of the spectrum, one finds Isaiah who willingly volunteers when YHWH puts out a call (Isa 6:8). Jonah, by contrast, attempts no dialogue with YHWH. He merely flees.

**Joppa**

The name means "beautiful" in Phoenician. Joppa was a Phoenician town, except during those frequent times when it became a vassal to Egypt, Assyria, Persia, or others. In the sixth century, the Persians gave it to the king of Sidon. As a natural harbor, Joppa was a valuable commodity on the political market. It is mentioned as early as the mid-fifteenth century BCE (in a letter from the Egyptian Pharaoh Thutmose III [1479–1429 BCE]). In the Hebrew Bible, Joppa plays a role in the tribal allotments in Joshua (19:46), where it is mentioned as part of the tribal territory of Dan, and in the postexilic narratives of Chronicles and Ezra, where it functions as the port used to receive the cedars of Lebanon for both the first (2 Chr 2:15) and the second temple (Ezra 3:7).

(Credit: Todd Bolen/BiblePlaces.com)

desires to escape from the presence of YHWH. The inadequacy of this desire can be seen in Jonah's response to the sailors in 1:9, as well as in other Old Testament texts (cf. Amos 9:2-4). There is no place one can go to escape the presence of YHWH. Later, the reader will learn Jonah's reason for flight (4:2), but here the narrator simply caricatures Jonah as a prophet who flees rather than accepts YHWH's commission to take a message of judgment to Nineveh.

**YHWH's Storm and the Sailors' Fear, 1:4-16**

Jonah 1:4-16 recounts Jonah's fruitless attempt to flee from YHWH, but does so for theological purposes: to illustrate the extent of God's power and to show that God's redemptive activity is not limited to a special chosen group. These verses present the scene of the storm in a sequence of vignettes that relate the sailor's immediate reaction to the storm (1:4-6), their attempt to determine the reason for the storm (1:7-10), and their effort to figure out how to stop the storm (1:11-16). The narrator skillfully weaves information about the storm and the fear it creates with dialogue involving the sailors, the captain, and Jonah. The weaving of these elements is also a study in contrasts. The violence of the storm comes and goes quickly; the sailors become increasingly fearful while Jonah sleeps; and the sailors become more enlightened about YHWH while Jonah spouts truisms that sound like empty platitudes in his mouth.

In Jonah 1:4-6 YHWH sends a great storm in reaction to Jonah's flight, then the text relates the reaction to the storm from the ship, the sailors, Jonah, and the captain. YHWH hurls a great wind onto the sea because Jonah flees toward Tarshish (1:4). [Wind] Thus, the sea itself experiences a great storm that in turn nearly causes the ship to break apart. The wind begins the storm that stops Jonah's escape. The language of the ship nearly breaking apart utilizes imagery that comes close to personification. The verb *ḥšb* is not used elsewhere in the Old Testament with an inanimate object. The verb means to "think" or "consider," and it could be colloquially translated as, "The ship thought it would break apart."

Next, the narrator contrasts the sailor's frantic actions with Jonah's apathy (1:5). Once the ship seems ready to fall apart, the sailors show fear. [The Sailors' Fear] The sailors do two things: each one cries out to his own god, and the sailors try to lighten the load of the ship. ["Sailors"] The phrase "each cried to his god" implies a multinational group because the sailors worship different gods. Though the narrator never specifically says the sailors were foreigners, the assumption is clearly present. The images convey chaos. The sailors perceive a dramatic threat, cry out in fear, and begin to toss the cargo into the ocean. Meanwhile, Jonah goes down to the belly of the boat to go to sleep. Can there be a greater contrast? The storm rages, and Jonah sleeps.

As a result, the captain tersely confronts Jonah (1:6), "What are you doing sleeping at a time like this? At least get up and pray in the hope that your god will take note of us." The captain's request does not imply that Jonah's god is more powerful than other gods. The captain has run out of ideas and

### Wind

AΩ In Hebrew the word for wind, *rûaḥ*, is the same word as the word for spirit. The gender of *rûaḥ* is feminine in either case. Only the context allows one to decide which is meant. The imagery, however, is instructive for comparing the biblical God to foreign gods in the ancient context. God's spirit does not take human form, nor is it a separate deity. Old Testament texts do not articulate a doctrine of the trinity, though they do contain imagery that forms the background for the development of the doctrine. God's spirit, like the wind, is presented as a mysterious entity that allows God to communicate with humans in a special way (cf. Joel 2:28 [MT 3:1]) or to accomplish a special purpose (Exod 31:3). It is also presumed to be that which dwells within human beings to separate them from the animal world (cf. Gen 6:3 as an interpretation of 2:7) or serves to present God's nurturing presence in the world (Gen 1:2).

### The Sailors' Fear

The motif of the sailors' fear occurs three times in Jonah 1. Each occurrence of the motif heightens the severity of the fear another notch:

1:5—The sailors feared.
1:10—The sailors feared a great fear.
1:16—The sailors feared YHWH a great fear.

Cumulatively, the motif underscores the frantic reactions to the storm but also helps focus the narrator's underlying critique of Jonah by demonstrating that even the foreign sailors came to recognize YHWH as the source of the storm.

---

**"Sailors"**

AΩ The word used for "sailor" (*mâlah*) here comes from the root meaning "to salt" and reflects an ancient Near Eastern idiom that is similar to the English expression "old salt" used to refer to sailors.

---

**Casting Lots**

Casting lots was the ancient equivalent of drawing straws today. The precise way in which lots were cast in Old Testament times is not clear, perhaps because the practice varied from place to place and from time to time. A few texts indicate that the lots were cast into someone's lap (e.g., Prov 16:33), but it is not clear what happened then. What is clear is that the assumption that lies behind the practice is that the deity will control the outcome so that a proper decision can be reached, whether that decision concerns who gets what land (Num 26:55-56), spoils (Obad 11), or prisoners (Nah 3:10).

---

simply asks Jonah to do what everyone else is doing.

Jonah 1:7-10 shifts the focus from the sailors' frenetic activity to their decision to locate the reason for the storm in order to placate the deity responsible for sending it. Behind this shift lie ancient assumptions that severe weather was directly caused by an angry deity. The sailors were just not sure which deity was angry because each one had his own god(s). For this reason, they had to cast lots, and when they did, the lot fell on Jonah. [Casting Lots]

The sailors' reaction in 1:8 displays the narrator's calculated portrayal of the foreign sailors in a rather positive light. They have already stated that the lot would determine the guilty party, so it is surprising that the sailors do not simply throw Jonah overboard as soon as the lot lands on him. Rather, they politely but hurriedly ask Jonah to answer a series of five questions: (1) On whose account has this calamity happened? (2) What is your occupation? (3) From whence do you come? (4) What is your country of origin? (5) From what people are you? The sailors should already know the answer to the first question, and Jonah only answers the final question. The readers know the answer to the three remaining questions, so Jonah's response is not directly recounted. The reader should, however, assume that Jonah's response is only an abbreviated version since 1:10 implies Jonah told them more than is in this short speech (see below).

Jonah responds in 1:9 that he is a Hebrew who worships YHWH, the God of heaven, the God who made the sea and the dry land. [Hebrew] Jonah depicts YHWH as a universal God whose power extends over all creation. The sailors had experienced YHWH's control over the sea, so it is mildly surprising that this piece of information creates even greater fear among them (cf. 1:5, 16). The phrase "God of heaven" is a late phrase. It appears nineteen other times in the Old Testament, with seventeen of those in Daniel, Ezra, or Nehemiah—all postexilic works.

Jonah's doxologic profession marks the structural midpoint of this scene (see [Literary Structure of Jonah 1]). He refers to God as the

Creator using language that specifically recalls the Priestly creation account (cf. Gen 1:9-10). Elsewhere, the combination of the term for "dry land" and "sea" only appears in texts in reference to creation (Gen 1:9, 10) or to the exodus (Exod 14:16, 22, 29; 15:19; Ps 66:6; Neh 9:11; cf. Josh 4:22). Despite the theological significance of Jonah's statement, one can hardly miss the condescension and irony in his speech. [Irony in the Hebrew Bible] Jonah puts the sailors' attempts to call on their own gods in sharp relief. Their gods were powerless to stop the storm, but YHWH created the sea and the dry land. Yet ironically, Jonah, who claims to worship this God, is running because he refuses to do as YHWH has commanded him.

> **Hebrew**
>
> AΩ The term "Hebrew" is an ethnic term. It appears in the OT only in places where it is necessary to distinguish Israelite and Judean peoples from other groups. So it can appear in the mouths of foreigners when referring to Israelites (e.g., Gen 39:14, 17; 40:15; 41:12), it can be used to distinguish one national group from another (Exod 1–10), or it can be used to distinguish Hebrew slaves from those of other nationalities (Exod 21:2; Deut 15:12; Jer 34:9, 14). This fact further illustrates that it is possible to deduce that the sailors were foreigners even though that is never stated explicitly.

The irony continues in Jonah 1:10. It becomes clear to the readers that the sailors do not miss the significance of Jonah's remark. Accordingly, the sailors become even more afraid (cf. 1:5), and *they* confront Jonah with the error of his flight. The men now ask Jonah, "What is this (thing) you have done?" Not, "Have you done something?" Their question implies they know he has done something. The narrator then follows this question with three subordinate clauses that add additional information not present in the dialogue to this point: because (*kî*) the men knew; that (*kî*) he was fleeing from YHWH; because (*kî*) he had told them. Only the second of these clauses contains information already known to the reader. The reader knows Jonah is fleeing from YHWH (1:2), but the reader has not been told that sailors know it. In fact, the logic of their questions in 1:8 would imply they did not yet know. These statements thus function as a parenthetical explanation (whether or not they are the deductions of a later scribal reader).

> **Irony in the Hebrew Bible**
>
> The extent of the use of irony in the Hebrew Bible is not always appreciated, but its presence is well documented (especially by E. M. Good). The rhetorical function of irony continues to be explored. For a recent treatment of the role of irony in Jonah, see Sharp, pages 176–86.
>
> Edwin M. Good, *Irony in the Old Testament* (2d ed.; Sheffield: Sheffield Academic Press, 1981).
>
> Carolyn J. Sharp, *Irony and Meaning in the Hebrew Bible* (Indiana Series in Biblical Literature; Bloomington: Indiana University Press, 2008).

In Jonah 1:11, the sailors ask what they should do to him to make the sea stop raging. The irony of this scene climaxes here. The sailors confront Jonah's behavior, but now they ask him for advice. The sincerity of their question highlights their sense of powerlessness. Even though they know Jonah has attempted to flee from YHWH, they know Jonah still knows more about this god than they do. They essentially ask, "What does this god want from us?"

Jonah's response to the men's question comes in 1:12, where he tells them that they need to throw him into the sea before the sea will settle down and they will be safe. Jonah's admission of his own responsibility ("I know that it is on my account that this great storm has happened to you.") is the closest Jonah comes to an admission of guilt in his dealings with the sailors.

Meanwhile, the ongoing effects of the raging storm are still being felt. This situation is highlighted in two ways: through the use of participles indicating ongoing action and through the use of the verb "to walk." A literal rendering of this passage carries an almost personified quality: the sea was walking and storming. Nevertheless, in spite of Jonah's confirmation that he is responsible for their plight, the sailors do not react as stereotypical foreigners in 1:13. They do not jump at the chance to kill Jonah. Instead, they make another attempt to reach land by "digging" (*ḥtr*) their oars into the water in a concerted but futile effort to reach land. This shows another example of the narrator's efforts to portray the sailors in a positive light. Left with no choice, the sailors must get rid of Jonah the same way they got rid of the cargo in 1:5, but first they offer a prayer to YHWH in their defense. The sailors' prayer narrated in 1:15 asks two things of YHWH: (1) do not let us die; and (2) do not hold us responsible for what you have done. Immediately following the prayer, the sailors throw Jonah into the sea. [Prayer in Jonah 1:14] The narrator tells the reader that the storm ceased as soon as Jonah entered the water.

As if they had not been afraid before (cf. 1:5, 10), the fact that the sea stopped raging so abruptly confirmed to the sailors that they were dealing with a powerful God indeed. Jonah 1:16 brings the sailors' fear motif to its climax. They respectfully offer a sacrifice and make vows to YHWH as a fitting tribute to this God who had threatened them and spared them. The irony is palpable at this point in the narrative. The foreign, pagan sailors offer the appropriate response to the God of heaven, while the obstinate prophet prefers being thrown into the sea to performing the task God had called him to do. However, God is not finished with Jonah.

## Prayer in Jonah 1:14

The excellent studies of P. D. Miller and S. E. Balentine in the 1990s have illuminated the wide variety of forms of prayer in the Hebrew Bible. In terms of form, the sailors' prayer in Jonah 1:14 represents a simple petitionary prayer comprised of three common elements: (1) specific address of the deity (twice YHWH is mentioned specifically); (2) petition (one petition expressed in two ways); (3) motivation (for you . . . have done as you pleased). These elements represent the structural building blocks of the most common type of prayer (Miller, 57). Nevertheless, the common structure should not obscure the fact that the prayer of the sailors in 1:14 is contextual, drawing upon the character and the situation of Jonah 1. This contextual characteristic sets the sailors' prayer apart from Jonah's prayer in 2:2-9, which seems to presuppose a setting quite different from its literary context. Concerning the functionality of contextual prayers, see Balentine, pages 18–19. The function of the two prayers is also noteworthy. Balentine (267) notes that prayer serves two primary functions with regard to characterizing humans: (1) emphasizing essential qualities of faith and (2) providing a lens upon piety by which to judge the characters' actions. In the case of the sailors' prayer, the sailors display a recognition of YHWH's power that motivates their prayer, and their actions are portrayed as consistent with the piety of their prayer. The sailors attempt to avoid harming Jonah before they pray, and after their prayer they make a sacrifice and pay vows (1:16). By contrast, Jonah's prayer in 2:2-9 presents the words of a pious individual who turns to YHWH for help in time of great distress, but the continuation of the narrative casts a negative light on Jonah's piety because he only reluctantly completes his mission, and then spars with YHWH because YHWH has shown compassion on the foreigners. Prayers by foreigners are not common in the Old Testament, so the fact that the sailors pray at all is already unusual. The fact that the sailors serve as a model of piety while Jonah's prayer highlights his petulance as the narrative continues only heightens the contrast between the prophets and the foreign sailors.

Patrick D. Miller, *They Cried to the Lord: The Form and Theology of Biblical Prayer* (Minneapolis: Fortress, 1994).

Samuel E. Balentine, *Prayer in the Hebrew Bible: The Drama of Divine-Human Dialogue* (OBT; Minneapolis: Fortress, 1993).

# CONNECTIONS

The narrator of Jonah does several things with this chapter that play into the purpose of the book. The narrator takes a character from the past, an obscure prophet named Jonah who was credited with great prophetic deeds, and portrays that prophet as a foil for the narrator's dual purpose for the book: to honor God's compassion and to challenge the theology of exclusion. [Theology of Exclusion] The narrator leaves no doubt about who is in control in this story. God commands Jonah, and God controls nature to make sure Jonah does not escape. God's power is used with a purpose, to force Jonah to do as commanded. However, God's power accomplishes more. God's mighty works of controlling the storm's beginning and ending lead to the *de facto* conversion of the sailors. These sailors exhibit fear of YHWH (Jonah 1:10, 16) not because God sends the storm but because God controls nature and because God delivers them. Their fear is grounded in respect, awe, and gratitude. As Proverbs notes repeatedly, the fear of YHWH is the beginning of wisdom, the beginning of meaningful life, and the path to avoiding trouble (Prov 1:7; 1:29; 2:5; 8:13; 9:10; 10:27; 14:26, 27; 15:16, 33; 16:6; 19:23; 22:4; 23:17). The sailors have learned a great

**Theology of Exclusion**

The Hebrew Bible is not of one voice when it comes to its relationship with the nations, though one is more widely represented. A major strand in the Former and Latter Prophets displays a decisively antagonistic stance toward those outside Israel and Judah. Joshua and Judges expect foreigners to be annihilated from the land (e.g., Josh 1:2-5; 12–22; Judg 2:1-5), though the difficulty of doing so is never resolved (see Judg 3:1-5). All four of the Latter Prophets contain collections of oracles directed against foreign nations (Isa 13–23; Jer 46–51; Ezek 25–32; Amos 1–2; Obadiah; Nahum; and Habakkuk). Postexilic narratives (Ezra, Nehemiah, and Chronicles) largely follow this antagonistic strand. One finds this negative attitude illustrated particularly clearly in Ezra and Nehemiah, where acts of exclusion manifest themselves in official policies such as forcing Judean men to divorce their foreign wives (Ezra 10) and correlating loyalty to God with not marrying foreigners (Neh 10:28-31). This theology of exclusion is largely driven by ideas of purity (religious and ethnic) and fear. For further reading, see Miroslav Volf, *Exclusion and Embrace: A Theological Exploration of Identity, Otherness, and Reconciliation* (Nashville: Abingdon, 1996) and Joel S. Kaminsky, *Yet I Loved Jacob: Reclaiming the Biblical Concept of Election* (Nashville: Abingdon, 2007).

lesson about the power of God that starts them on a path of enlightenment and fulfillment.

Subtly, the narrator weaves the sailors' conversion into the story of Jonah's futile attempt to flee from God. In so doing, the narrator already makes the case that the worship of YHWH is not limited to those who live within the confines of Judah and Israel. YHWH is portrayed as a universal God—the creator and controller of the world as we know it. For this reason, God can be experienced by all humanity. Foreigners and "pagans" can come to know God just as surely as Israelite prophets can try to hide from God. Jonah is no hero to be emulated, yet Jonah's resistance to God leads to genuine worship on the part of the foreign sailors. God's power demonstrated in nature and God's compassion in removing the storm create a sense of wonder and gratitude that causes these worshipers of other gods to recognize the true God, to fear that God, and to make vows to this one God.

Jonah 1 presupposes a theological perspective that does not easily coexist with the dominant theological voice of the Hebrew Bible concerning foreigners. But Jonah 1 is not unique in this respect among biblical texts. One finds a different, more tolerant attitude toward the nations expressed or implied in other texts of the Hebrew Bible. Though this strand is less prominent, in terms of the number of texts articulating this tolerance or inclusivity, they are present in significant enough numbers to suggest a debate existed throughout much of Israel's history. Prominent texts that are less interested in excluding foreigners from the land include most of the ancestral narratives in Genesis 12–50 as well as several significant passages in the prophetic corpus. Most of the ancestral narratives, while they might display some tension with foreigners, lack any statements of hostility toward the nations. In fact, in the Joseph cycle (Gen 37–50), Joseph's brothers are the ones who do him harm, whereas the Egyptian pharaoh recognizes his great skill and allows Joseph and his family to reside in Egypt and to prosper. One also finds expression of toleration for one's neighbor and the resident alien expressed alongside texts denouncing anything that is not ritually pure. Leviticus 19:18 and 34 illustrate this tension rather dramatically. Several key passages in prophetic texts also display an openness toward the nations, at least those willing to worship YHWH. To name a few, one can specify the eschatological visions of peace one finds in Isaiah 2:2-4 (= Mic 4:1-3); 11:11-16; 60:1-22; and Zephaniah 3:9-10. The postexilic text that opens Trito-Isaiah (56:1-7) takes direct aim at specific anti-foreigner texts that appear in the Torah.[2] Zechariah 8:20-23 also anticipates the nations turning to Jerusalem and its people for salvation. Malachi 1:10-14 confronts the behavior of the postexilic Jewish community by holding up YHWH's worship among the nations as an example for those in Judah to emulate.

The New Testament exhibits some of the same tension, though perhaps the percentage is reversed. Jesus highlights texts such as Leviticus 19:18, 34 and Isaiah 56:1-7, and frequently associates with the outcasts of society. Paul campaigns among the early church for the need to expand the mission into the nations, and Paul's view ultimately becomes accepted (see Acts 15). Nevertheless, some episodes in the Gospels portray Jesus' ministry as a ministry to Israel alone (e.g., Matt 10:5-6) that Jesus only reluctantly expands (Matt 15:21-28). And Paul articulates profound statements of inclusivity among Christians (e.g., Gal 3:28) but is at times ambivalent toward the fate of Israel (cf. Rom 9:1-18 and 2 Cor 3:12-16). In the end, much of this tension centers on questions of identity. How does one articulate openness to the "other" while at the same time recognizing distinctive qualities for the community of faith? Different generations in different localities have responded to this question in various ways. This tension will not likely go away because it is endemic to the nature of religious identity in communities of faith. Nevertheless, in a pluralistic world where modern technology makes us increasingly aware of the other nations, other religions, and other cultures, finding ways to navigate questions of inclusion and exclusion that demonstrate empathy and respect will continue to challenge communities of faith to seek creative ways to engage others.

## NOTES

1. See fuller discussion in Hans Walter Wolff, *Obadiah and Jonah: A Commentary* (trans. Margaret Kohl; A Continental Commentary; Minneapolis: Augsburg, 1977) 102.

2. See the commentaries by Joseph Blenkinsopp, *Isaiah 56–66* (AB19B; New York: Doubleday, 2003) 134–40; Brevard S. Childs, *Isaiah* (OTL; Louisville: Westminster John Knox, 2001) 457–59.

# JONAH IN THE FISH

## Jonah 1:17–2:10

## COMMENTARY

The next scene (1:17–2:10 [MT 2:1-11]) takes Jonah from the ship to the sea to the belly of a fish and back to dry land. The verses contain a narrative frame (1:17–2:1; 2:10) surrounding a poetic song of thanksgiving (2:2-9). The poetic material exhibits considerable tension with the narrative of Jonah not only because of its poetic character but also because only this poem portrays "Jonah" positively. How one treats this distinction is a matter of no small debate.

The opening portion of the frame (1:17–2:1) narrates YHWH's provision of a fish to swallow Jonah. Jonah is thus saved from drowning only to be swallowed by a fish in whose stomach Jonah remains for three days and three nights before finally praying to God. Jonah's three days in the fish represents a rather common idiom indicating a significant amount of time (see discussion of Hos 6:2). [The Sign of Jonah in the New Testament]

An editor has inserted a song of thanksgiving (2:2-9) to provide Jonah's prayer that was missing in the narrative.

**The Sign of Jonah in the New Testament**

Matthew relates Jonah's time in the belly of the fish to the duration of Jesus' time in the tomb (Matt 12:39-40), but Luke relates the sign of Jonah to the behavior of the people of Nineveh, who, unlike the crowds listening to Jesus, repented at the message of Jonah and were spared by God (Luke 11:29-32).

Scholars debate whether the song was composed independently because of literary tensions with the narrative. [Literary Tension between Jonah 2:2-9 and the Narrative] The cumulative effect of these tensions raises serious doubts whether it was originally composed for Jonah. Recent attempts to explain 2:2-9 as composed for the narrative fail to account adequately for the differences, but these studies go a long way toward explaining the editorial motivation for incorporating the poem. It will thus be necessary to treat the psalm on two levels—its original setting and its setting in the book.

**Fish**

Fourth-century Christian mosaic. Note the portrayal of the fish as a sea monster.

Jonah swallowed by the whale. Early Christian mosaic, 4th C. Basilica Patriarcale, Aquileia, Italy. (Credit: Cameraphoto Arte, Venice/ Art Resource, NY)

The entire tale of the book of Jonah is depicted: God commands Jonah to go to Nineveh, Jonah flees by boat, Jonah is swallowed by a big fish, God gives Jonah a second chance, Jonah preaches in Nineveh, and Jonah sits under a vine as a worm begins to eat it.

Martin Luther (1483–1546). "Episodes from the Life of Jonah." *Die Propheten alle deudsch* (1541). (Credit: Courtesy of the Richard C. Kessler Reformation Collection, Pitts Theology Library, Candler School of Theology, Emory University)

Note that the character of the fish is that of a large fish, no longer the mythic monster.

Waclaw Donay (1744–1796). Fountain sculpture on the Market Square in Skoczów, Poland. 18th C. (Credit: Schweppes, http://commons. wikimedia.org/wiki/File:Skoczow_-_Tryton-Jonasz_2009-04-26.jpg)

By the end of the 19th and 20th centuries, artists tended to depict a whale rather than a large fish, as here where the whale appears twice, including once as Jonah prays.

James Lesesne Wells (1902–1993). *Jonah and the Whale*. n.d. Woodcut. Smithsonian American Art Museum, Washington, DC. (Credit: Smithsonian American Art Museum, Washington, DC/Art Resource, NY)

Depictions of Jonah and the fish appear in paintings, mosaics, and drawings across the centuries. Interestingly, the conceptualization of the fish as a whale is a late development. Through the Middle Ages, two other concepts predominate. Some artists portrayed the fish as a sea monster (perhaps influenced by legends associating the fish with Leviathan; see the top two images). Other artists depicted the fish in less frightening terms merely as an oversized fish (see the image on bottom left). By the end of the nineteenth century, the image of Jonah in a whale begins to dominate (see the image on bottom right).

### Literary Tension between Jonah 2:2-9 and the Narrative

The tension between the thanksgiving song in 2:2-9 and the literary context is difficult to overlook, but explanations of the poem's origins and meaning differ considerably. There are those (e.g., D. Stuart, K. Craig, and J. Magonet) who see the psalm as an integral part of Jonah that was composed by the author of the narrative. Others (e.g., H. W. Wolff) see it as an addition written for the narrative to portray Jonah in a better light, and there are those (e.g., J. D. Nogalski) who see it as a preexisting poem composed independently and inserted here by a later editor to provide the content of Jonah's prayer.

First, Jonah 2:2-9 is poetic while the remainder of the book is narrative prose. Second, the poetic piece can be removed and a coherent narrative exists: "And Jonah prayed to YHWH his God from the belly of the fish. . . . And (then) YHWH spoke to the fish, and it spewed Jonah onto dry land." Admittedly, the narrative lacks detail about the prayer's content, but this deficiency would explain what motivated the poem's addition. Third, only 2:2-9 portrays Jonah in a positive light. In the remainder of the book, Jonah hardly deserves empathy as he flees YHWH, begrudgingly delivers YHWH's message, and gets angry that the Ninevites are spared.

Fourth, while there is some recurring vocabulary between the poem and the surrounding narrative, the poem does not describe the same setting as the narrative. The poem never mentions the fish and accuses YHWH of throwing the psalmist into the heart of the seas (2:3), while the narrative portrays the sailors as the ones who tossed Jonah into the sea (1:15). Moreover, the sea language in the poem is used with parallel expressions (Sheol, the river, the deep, roots of the mountains) to connote images of death and chaos, not simply a large body of water. Finally, the situation that distresses the psalmist is the fact that the psalmist has been expelled from YHWH's temple (2:4, 7), not that he had been caught while trying to flee from YHWH.

Fifth, the thanksgiving genre presumes a setting in which no threat exists any longer. Unlike a complaint song, where a psalmist, in desperation, calls on YHWH for deliverance, the thanksgiving song testifies with gratitude for YHWH's deliverance from danger. Moreover, the thanksgiving song typically exhibits didactic signs that suggest it was sung to a group just prior to the offering of a thanksgiving sacrifice. Presumably, this group normally gathered at the temple. In Jonah 2:2-9, the threat is clearly past (cf. 2:2, 6), and the didactic element, spoken to a group, appears in Jonah 2:8, just prior to the mention of sacrifice and vows (2:9).

For more extensive treatments of these issues, see Hans Walter Wolff, *Obadiah and Jonah: A Commentary* (trans. Margaret Kohl; A Continental Commentary; Minneapolis: Augsburg, 1977) 128–31; Douglas Stuart, *Hosea—Jonah* (WBC 31; Waco: Word, 1987) 438–40, 469–74; James D. Nogalski, *Redactional Processes in the Book of the Twelve* (Beihefte zur Zeitschrift für die alttestamentliche Wissenschaft 218; Berlin–New York: de Gruyter, 1993) 252–55, 265–69; Jonathan Magonet, *Form and Meaning: Studies in Literary Techniques in the Book of Jonah* (Beiträge zur biblischen Exegese und Theologie 2; Bern: Herbert Lang, 1976) 39–50, 59–60; Kenneth M. Craig, "Jonah and the Reading Process," *JSOT* 47 (1990): 103–14 (esp. 106–107, 110–11). For discussion of the genre, see Hermann Gunkel, *Introduction to Psalms: The Genres of the Religious Lyric of Israel* (trans. James D. Nogalski; Mercer Library of Biblical Studies; Macon GA: Mercer University Press, 1998) 199–221.

The structure of 2:2-9 is cohesive, and that cohesion becomes elevated by recognizing that the psalm contains elements typical of thanksgiving songs. [The Structure of Jonah 2:2-9] It displays three parts (2:2-4, 5-7, 8-9). The first two present deliverance motifs in chiastic order. The third part presents a didactic element (2:8-9) that calls hearers to abandon idols and to stay faithful to YHWH. The catchphrase "the temple of your holiness" (2:4, 7) connects the first two sections. In addition to the inherent logic behind the structure, the psalm displays all the marks of a thanksgiving song. [Thanksgiving Song] The most notable element of this genre (and the

**The Structure of Jonah 2:2-9**

The deliverance motifs are chiastically structured in the poem:

A  2:2a The prayer in distress
   B  2:2b The depths of Sheol and the underworld
      C  2:3 The chaotic waters
         D  2:4 I will again see your holy temple
      C' 2:5 The chaotic waters
   B' 2:6 The base of the mountains, bars of the earth, the pit (underworld)
A' 2:7 The prayer reaches YHWH
         D' in your holy temple

Both 2:2-4 and 2:5-7 culminate in a reference to YHWH's holy temple, a strong indication of the location of the thanksgiving service. The didactic element (2:8-9) stands outside this structure.

greatest tension between 2:2-9 and the surrounding narrative) is that the psalmist presumes YHWH's deliverance has already occurred. The psalmist's gratitude for deliverance motivates the thanksgiving song. Unlike a complaint song where the threat is ongoing, the danger is over in a thanksgiving song. A thanksgiving song was sung before a group of worshipers just prior to the presentation of a thanksgiving offering, usually at the temple. Jonah 2:2-9 contains evidence that it was addressed to a group (2:8) prior to the thanksgiving sacrifice (2:9). In Jonah, however, this psalm appears in the narrative while Jonah is still in the belly of the fish, not on dry land. This position leaves one with several choices as to how to understand the psalm's function in the narra-

**Thanksgiving Song**

The consistently appearing elements of the song of thanksgiving have been noted since the time of Hermann Gunkel. Enough of these elements appear in Jonah 2:2-9 so as to leave no real doubt as to how it should be classified. The order and number of these elements varies according to the writer of the song, but the elements themselves are quite consistent in the thanksgiving song. Compare Jonah 2 with Psalm 30, another thanksgiving song:

| Elements (Eng. Verse #s) | Psalm 30 | Jonah 2 |
| --- | --- | --- |
| Call to sing (usually addressed to participants in the celebration, or to YHWH) | 4-5 | |
| Recounting of the danger and deliverance | 3, 6-8 | 3-6 |
| Profession of YHWH as the deliverer from distress | 1-2 | 2,7,9 |
| Announcement of the thanksgiving sacrifice | | 9 |
| Blessing upon the participants | | |
| Hymnic elements or a didactic element (Gunkel, 205) | 5, 9 | 8 |
| A concluding petition | 10-12 | |

For further reading about thanksgiving songs, see Hermann Gunkel, *Introduction to the Psalms*, §7 "Individual Thanksgiving Songs" (trans. James D. Nogalski; Mercer Library of Biblical Studies; Macon GA: Mercer University Press, 1998) 199–221; see also Erhard Gerstenberger, "Psalms," in *Old Testament Form Criticism* (ed. John H. Hayes; San Antonio: Trinity University Press, 1974) 202–205; for an excellent discussion of the thanksgiving song in Jonah, see James Limburg, *Jonah* (OTL; Louisville: Westminster John Knox, 1993) 64–66.

### Poems Inserted into Narratives

The insertion of a poem into a narrative is by no means unique to Jonah in the editorial history of the Hebrew Bible. Some prominent examples include Exod 15, where two songs interrupt the narrative to celebrate the exodus event: the song of Moses (15:1-18) and the much shorter song of Miriam (15:20-22). Another song of Moses appears at the end of Deuteronomy, just prior to Moses' death (Deut 32:1-43). The song of Deborah (Judg 5) memorializes the defeat of Sisera.

David's song of thanksgiving in 2 Sam 22 celebrates the exploits of David's life at the point when "the LORD delivered him from the hand of all his enemies, and from the hand of Saul" (22:1). Hezekiah's psalm recounted in Isa 38:9-20 interrupts the conversation between Isaiah and Hezekiah in 38:1-8, 21. For discussions of these and other psalms in this context, see James W. Watts, *Psalm and Story: Inset Hymns in Hebrew Narrative* (Sheffield: JSOT Press, 1992).

---

tive: (1) to understand the deliverance as the swallowing by the fish, (2) to suspend the chronological elements altogether, (3) to treat the "thanksgiving" as a satirical device to add to the portrayal of Jonah as an antihero who seeks to manipulate YHWH, or (4) to portray Jonah in a more positive light. To interpret this psalm, one must constantly be aware of the differences between the psalm's original setting and its effect when read in its current literary context. These two levels of meaning provide insights into the intentions of the editor who placed the poem here. [Poems Inserted into Narratives]

Jonah 2:2 begins with a narrator's introductory element ("and he said") that transitions into the poetic material. The bulk of this verse functions as a summary motto for the rest of the poem: YHWH saves in times of mortal distress. Structurally, the verse presents two parallel lines, each of which contains three elements: a reference to prayer (I called/cried out), to mortal danger (distress/belly of Sheol), and to YHWH's response (he answered me/you heard my voice). This verse stands at odds with the narrative, since deliverance has not yet happened in the narrative, at least not in a complete sense. In the narrative, the fish has swallowed Jonah (1:17), who has not yet been returned to dry land (2:10). Yet the poem depicts a setting of deliverance that has already occurred.

Jonah 2:3 describes the distress and its cause in images that draw on the chaotic waters of the sea. The psalmist depicts the distress as YHWH's doing ("You cast me . . ."), though in the narrative it was the sailors who threw Jonah into the sea. This verse, to be sure, does draw upon images of the ocean to describe the distress (heart of the seas, breakers, waves), but the use of cosmic terms (the deep, the river) suggests that these terms are used metaphorically in their original context. [Cosmic Terms] Undoubtedly, these terms drew the attention of the editor who incorporated the psalm because the

**Cosmic Terms**

The sea and the river mentioned in Jonah 2:3 evoke ancient Near Eastern mythological images of the chaos battle in which the deity defeats Yam (sea), also called Nahar (river), who represent chaos. In the Baal myth, Baal defeats Yam but later loses to Mot (death):

> And the axe leapt from the hand of Baal,
>     Like an eagle from his fingers.
> It struck the skull of his Highness Yam,
>     Judge Nahar between the eyes.
> Yam collapsed,
>     He fell to the earth.
> His joints quivered,
>     And his pelvis shook.
> Baal wanted to drag away and put Yam down,
>     He wanted to finish off Nahar.

In Enuma Elish, the battle of Marduk and Tiamat pits the great god Marduk against the forces of chaos who fight with Tiamat (from which the Hebrew word for "the great deep," *těhôm*, derives) plays out a similar scene. Tiamat's body is split in two to keep the waters of heaven from the earth. These cosmic images play out in the Old Testament as allusions to YHWH's power over the deep and the sea. In addition to Jonah 2, one sees this language in several Psalms (e.g., 69:14-15; 77:16-18; 107:21-29) and in Hab 3:14-15.

Baal myth adapted from Johannes C. de Moor, *An Anthology of Religious Texts from Ugarit* (Leiden: Brill, 1987) 41.

images they evoke can be understood against the narrative where Jonah has been cast into the sea. This verse also contains linguistic tensions in that it is the only time that the plural term, seas, appears in Jonah. The image is one of the psalmist who is deluged and swamped by the waters of chaos that engulf the writer and threaten the psalmist's life. This water image appears relatively frequently in psalms that recount current or past distress (e.g., Pss 18:3-6, 16; 29:2-10; 69:1-2, 14-15).

Jonah 2:4 describes the psalmist's biggest problem: being removed from YHWH's presence in the temple. The phrase "your holy temple" implies that the psalmist looked at Jerusalem, the site of the temple, as the holy city. However, since Jonah was a prophet of the northern kingdom (2 Kgs 14:25), Jonah would not have worshiped in Jerusalem. The psalmist's dual reference to the temple (see also 2:7) strongly suggests that the psalm has a Judean provenance.[1] Reasons someone would be driven from the temple are numerous, and it is impossible to tell with certainty why this psalmist was expelled. Anyone deemed ritually impure, suffering various maladies, or acting sinfully could have been denied entrance by the priests.[2]

A textual problem complicates the latter half of 2:4. [Textual Problem in Jonah 2:4] It forces one to decide whether the verse is a question (e.g., NRSV) or an affirmation of confidence (e.g., NASB). Nevertheless, the original setting of the thanksgiving song presupposes an occasion in which someone who had been expelled from the temple has now been healed and cleansed, meaning that the person can now reenter the temple for worship. Whoever incorporated the song into the narrative did not focus on the reference to the temple. This editor intended 2:4 to be interpreted as Jonah's thought while he was drowning. Jonah was cut off from YHWH, but Jonah professes his belief that he will return to YHWH's presence.

Jonah 2:5 describes the danger (death) using the language of the chaotic waters that threaten to engulf the psalmist. In the original setting, the metaphorical language for death provides the hook for understanding the psalm within the Jonah narrative. The reference to the waters parallels the reference to the great deep. The waters have engulfed the psalmist up to his *nefeš*, whose range of meanings includes soul, body, life and neck. The word *nefeš* in 2:5 denotes the neck or throat: the waters came up to my neck; the deep surrounded me. This image, while having superficial correspondence to the narrative setting of Jonah being cast into the sea by the sailors, in reality displays significant tension with the details of this narrative context. Jonah 2:5 uses the image of "waters" and "the deep" *rising* around the psalmist (up to the neck) with the implication that they threaten to take his life. By contrast, the narrative portrays the sailors as lifting Jonah and *hurling* him into the sea from the boat—not a situation in which the waters would have gradually surrounded him, but one in which the waters would have immediately been "over his head" as he was hurled into the sea.

> **Textual Problem in Jonah 2:4**
>
> AΩ The MT of 2:4b begins with *'ak: . . . but I* will again look to your holy temple." The NRSV, and other versions, read a variant text from the LXX, presuming that the word *'êk* begins 2:4b, meaning *"How* will I again look to your holy temple?" For reasons of form and *lectio difficilior* ("the more difficult reading" is preferred over the smoother reading), the MT is followed here rather than the variant.

Jonah 2:6 brings a major turning point in the song as the psalmist recounts his descent and deliverance. The psalmist describes the lowest point imaginable, again using the metaphorical language of the underworld (cf. 2:2), by referring to his descent to the roots of the mountain and to the bars of the earth that had closed around him forever. This imagery depicts the psalmist at death's door. He could go no lower. This metaphorical descent to the underworld typifies psalms in which mortal distress is depicted by references to Sheol (Ps 30:3), the pit (88:4; 143:7), or the like. Conveniently, Jonah 2:6 provides the final reference to the verb descend (*yārad*) in Jonah, a verb that played a significant role in the narrative flow of Jonah 1:3, 5. Despite significant tensions between the poem and the narrative, the preexisting thanksgiving song also contains several motifs that allow it to function meaningfully within Jonah. The psalmist reaches the point of no return, but YHWH intervenes to deliver him from death. Jonah 2:6b recounts this deliverance as a testimony directed to God ("You brought up my life from the pit") using a personal epithet ("YHWH my God").

Jonah 2:7 expands on the psalmist's deliverance by stressing that it occurred at the last moment as the result of prayer offered to YHWH. The psalmist literally says, "When my life was fainting away, I remembered YHWH." To "remember YHWH" does not always indicate prayer. It can refer to a lifestyle that keeps God ever in mind (e.g., Deut 8:18), recalls gratefully what YHWH has done (e.g., Judg 8:34), or recollects with sadness what has been lost (e.g., Jer 51:50). Remembering YHWH in Jonah 2:7, however, implies offering a prayer, since the psalmist's prayer went to YHWH in the temple. In the context of Jonah, this prayer functions as a point of repentance even though it contains no explicit confession of wrongdoing. It nevertheless implies (for the reader) a restoration of Jonah's relationship with YHWH.

The tenor and focus of the poem in Jonah 2:8 changes noticeably as the psalmist offers a didactic message to the hearers about a group that has not previously appeared, "those keeping vain idols." Literally, the phrase interpreted as "vain idols" by most English versions actually means "breaths of nothingness." However, the phrase appears in another verse, Psalm 31:6 (MT 31:7), which contrasts the keeping of these elements with trust in YHWH. Most scholars have therefore seen the phrase as a reference to the worship of idols. The fact that the teaching moment comes at this point in the psalm is explained by the setting and the genre of the original poem. Thanksgiving songs often have didactic elements that appear just before the thanksgiving sacrifice is offered (see 2:9). These didactic elements are offered for the enrichment of those attending the thanksgiving service. Undoubtedly, this element offered advice to the original audience of this psalm. If it can be interpreted at all within the Jonah narrative, it functions almost as an admonition, a subtle warning to keep the vows one makes in the throes of danger.

Jonah 2:9 provides another element of the thanksgiving song by announcing the forthcoming sacrifice. The thanksgiving sacrifice climaxed a thanksgiving service, as illustrated in this and other psalms of this genre. The final verse of this song also includes an affirmation to pay the vows and a concluding motto, the latter summarizing the psalmist's profession that "Salvation belongs to YHWH." [Paying Vows] Placed in the mouth of Jonah, when the poem was incorporated into the story, this affirmation softens the character of a now penitent Jonah.

Jonah 2:10 returns to a narrative style and recounts YHWH's reaction to Jonah's prayer. YHWH speaks to the fish, which then inelegantly spews Jonah onto the dry land. The narrator describes the fish's action with the word best translated as "vomit" or "regurgitate." The hyperbole of this image becomes immediately clear when one realizes how far Nineveh was from the Mediterranean Sea (where Jonah had boarded the ship). Nineveh was over 300 miles from the shore of the Mediterranean. Yet by some readings of Jonah 3:4, Jonah reached Nineveh after a day's journey. Oral tradition reflected in the Rabbinic sources solves this problem of distance by one of two paths, either by assuming that the oceans were connected underground to a body of water closer to Nineveh, or by claiming that Jonah became a projectile spewed several hundred miles from the ocean to Assyria. At any rate, Jonah's futile flight has gained Jonah nothing. YHWH has made sure that Jonah will carry out the mission for which he was chosen.

## CONNECTIONS

In a real sense, the book of Jonah was written to address a theological problem: how were Israel and its people supposed to relate to those around them? The Old Testament is not of one voice on this issue. There are texts, represented by the books of Ezra and Nehemiah, that assume that Israel's mission was to keep itself set apart and holy from all those around them, to the point of eliminating virtually all contact with foreign elements. On the other hand, there are texts like Trito-Isaiah (see Isa 56:1-7), Zechariah 8:23, Malachi 1:10-14, and Jonah that depict the role of God's people, in part, as a mission to those outside the borders of Israel.

The thanksgiving song that has been placed in the narrative of Jonah gives the impression of a penitent prophet who turns to God

**Paying Vows**

Vows in the OT represent human responses to distress that essentially bargain with God. In the Hebrew Bible, vows can take place in cultic and non-cultic contexts. In cultic vows, payment usually involved ritual sacrifice from the person who made the vow, and the payment was seen as a kind of repayment for life. Consequently, the amount of the vow was determined by the status of the individual, as illustrated in the following text:

Speak to the people of Israel and say to them: When a person makes an explicit vow to the Lord concerning the equivalent for a human being, the equivalent for a male shall be: from twenty to sixty years of age the equivalent shall be fifty shekels of silver by the sanctuary shekel. If the person is a female, the equivalent is thirty shekels. If the age is from five to twenty years of age, the equivalent is twenty shekels for a male and ten shekels for a female. If the age is from one month to five years, the equivalent for a male is five shekels of silver, and for a female the equivalent is three shekels of silver. And if the person is sixty years old or over, then the equivalent for a male is fifteen shekels, and for a female ten shekels. If any cannot afford the equivalent, they shall be brought before the priest and the priest shall assess them; the priest shall assess them according to what each one making a vow can afford. (Lev 27:2-8)

The payment for vows of a woman could also be nullified by fathers or husbands if they stated their disapproval upon hearing the vow (Num 30:3-15).

Non-cultic vows often take place in battles (e.g, Num 21:1-3), under personal duress (e.g., Gen 28:20-22; see 31:11-13; 35:1-3), or in response to answered prayer (e.g., Absalom's statement of the need to repay a vow in 2 Sam 15:7-8, even though Absalom uses this vow as a ruse to begin his rebellion against David).

at the point when all seems lost. However, foxhole confessions are only as real as the follow-through. In many respects, this song provides all the elements of a dramatic moment of conversion. The poem, placed into the narrative, adds details to God's deliverance of Jonah. It presents the actions of a God who hears cries of distress. It portrays Jonah's gratitude to God for the grace of deliverance, gratitude that would be lacking were it not for the poem. The song provides an image of the softer side of Jonah. The reader of the book now expects a different Jonah to continue the journey. However, what the reader will encounter is a Jonah who does only the bare minimum to fulfill the commission God required of him (see Jonah's five-word sermon in 3:4). Moreover, in chapter 4 Jonah resents the fact that God will show mercy to the Ninevites. How does one account for these opposing pictures of a Jonah whose gratitude to God runs deep for his own deliverance, but whose anger at God for extending compassion to foreigners colors all his actions?

Theologically speaking, Jonah is not the real subject of this tension. Rather, like Jesus' parable of the log and the speck (Matt 7:3), the story of Jonah should cause us to look at ourselves. It is far easier for most of us to see the faults of others than to acknowledge our own shortcomings. The church, like the world at large, still has many Jonahs. These persons can speak at great length about gratitude for what God has done for them, but they have far less interest in what God has done for others. They can tell of dramatic conversion from a life of sin to a life of fulfillment in Christ. Yet they have little compassion for those who remain trapped in similar cycles of destructive behavior or in systems that keep them in poverty. It is far easier to find comfort worshiping with those who are like us than to live and work in ways designed to improve the lives of those who will not be found inside the church walls.

The Bible tells us repeatedly of God's initiative to bring about a saving relationship precisely with those who are least worthy. God redeemed Jacob from his conniving ways, but it took years. God was present with David even after David committed adultery and murder. God made Zacchaeus whole even though Zacchaeus was despised as a tax collector. God appeared to Saul on the road to Damascus, even though Saul was persecuting those who were turning to Jesus. God takes the initiative to redeem those in need, but how often do we stand in the way? Like Jonah, we all need to remember that the purpose of Jesus' ministry was to provide hope and salvation for sinners (Mark 2:17; Matt 9:12-13; Luke 5:31-32).

Jonah's thanksgiving song invites us to look inward and outward. It models the gratitude we owe God for life and salvation. It portrays the sinking despair of one facing premature death before God delivered him. Its larger narrative context, Jonah's mission to the Ninevites, reminds us that lives given to God must participate in God's purpose—improving the lives of those still needing help. It is this lesson that Jonah will have trouble learning.

Finally, what distresses the psalmist most in this thanksgiving song is not the thought of death as such, but the distance from the worshiping community and from God created by the psalmist's plight. The psalmist, as a result of the threat, has been exiled, denied entry to the temple, left without access to the comfort of the sacred place. Surprisingly, the psalmist remembers YHWH and learns a great lesson indeed. The psalmist's prayer reaches YHWH, even though the psalmist has been cut off from the temple. Like Amos (9:2-3) and Obadiah (3-4), Jonah's song of thanksgiving testifies that God is everywhere—which is both a comfort and a threat. Those in need can always find God, but those who try to escape God will not be able to do so when God comes looking for them.

## NOTES

1. If the psalm is viewed as an integral part of the narrative, this implies that the entire book of Jonah as we have it was composed in Judah.

2. For examples, see Gordon J. Wenham, *The Book of Leviticus* (NICOT; Grand Rapids: Eerdmans, 1979) 18–25; or the charts in Jacob Milgrom, *Leviticus 1–16* (AB 3; New York: Doubleday, 1991) 986–89.

# A RELUCTANT PROPHET SPEAKS TO A RECEPTIVE PEOPLE

Jonah 3:1-10

## COMMENTARY

The third scene, Jonah 3:1-10, presents Jonah's reluctant mission to Nineveh and its aftermath. The action of these verses shifts five times: the word of YHWH returns to Jonah (3:1-3); Jonah delivers a brief message to the Ninevites (3:4); they respond (3:5); the king responds (3:6-9); and YHWH shows mercy to Nineveh (3:10).

Jonah 3:1-3 represents a second commissioning of Jonah. Jonah 3:1 restates the report found at the beginning of Jonah (1:1). This report contains two slight variations from the original. Jonah 3:1 does not repeat the name of Jonah's father, since the reader now knows far more about Jonah than in 1:1. Second, Jonah

**Ninevah Repents**
The people of Nineveh repent as Jonah preaches.

David Martin (1639–1721). "Ninevah Repents." *Historie des Ouden en Nieuwen Testaments: verrykt met meer dan vierhonderd printverbeeldingen in koper gesneeden* (1700). (Credit: Courtesy of the Pitts Theology Library, Candler School of Theology, Emory University)

3:1 adds an adverb, "a second time," to make sure the reader recalls that this same message has come to Jonah previously.

YHWH's message also varies slightly from the initial message in 1:2. Jonah 3:2 contains the command to "get up and go to Nineveh, the great city," beginning exactly like the command in 1:2. However, the second portion of 3:2 deviates from the wording of 1:1 in two ways. First, the idiom used for Jonah's task in 3:2 is less intense than 1:2. Jonah 1:2 commanded Jonah to "preach against" the city, while 3:2 calls Jonah to "preach to" the city. Further, 3:2 stresses YHWH's message while 1:2 stresses the wickedness of Nineveh. These subtle changes effectively prepare the reader to take a different attitude toward Jonah (by subtly reminding the reader of his failed attempt to flee) and the Ninevites (by downplaying their wickedness).

Jonah's response to the word of YHWH (3:3) demonstrates a complete turnaround when it portrays Jonah's response as one of obedience rather than flight. In Jonah 3:3, the prophet to responds to YHWH's word by doing as he is told; at least it appears that way on the surface. Jonah was told to get up and go, and this time Jonah got up and went. Briefly, it appears that Jonah has learned his lesson, but readers soon realize that Jonah does only the bare minimum. He remains a reluctant prophet who does his duty and nothing more. Jonah will show his colors as a prophet who hopes for punishment but fears that YHWH will show compassion.

Jonah 3:3b reinforces Nineveh's great importance by hyperbolizing the circumference of the city in grandiose terms. Nineveh is cited as "a great city to God," but most translations (RSV, NRSV, NIV, etc.) change the thrust of this statement by omitting reference to God. The stated size of the city, a three-day journey, does not correspond to the actual size of Nineveh at the time. [The Size of Nineveh] Rather, this description suggests that the author and audience of Jonah come from a time and place quite removed from that of the

## The Size of Nineveh

The last half of 3:3 describes Nineveh in grandiose terms that do not correspond to the historical situation. The archaeological remains of ancient Nineveh have long been excavated. The circumference of the city at the height of its power was around 7.75 miles. Such a city, while not small by ancient standards, would hardly take three days to walk (either going through or around). In addition, the time of the prophet Jonah according to 2 Kgs 14:25 preceded the rise of Nineveh as the capital city of Assyria. Nineveh did not become the capital of Assyria until the reign of Sennacherib (704–681 BCE), some forty years after the reign of Jeroboam II (785–745 BCE), when Jonah ben Amittai was a prophet (2 Kgs 14:25). The exaggerated description of the size of Nineveh adds to the impression that Jonah was composed in a time and place far removed from the setting of the story.

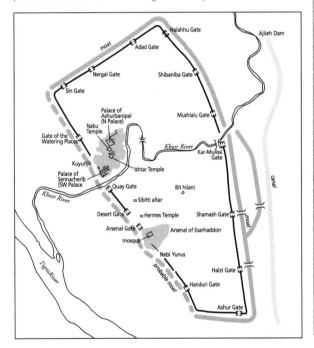

story. In addition, the role of Nineveh as a hated historical enemy is heightened by such a description. (For a sketch of the rise of Assyria in the eighth century, see the introduction to Nahum in James D. Nogalski, *The Book of the Twelve: Micah–Malachi* [Smyth & Helwys Bible Commentary Series].) At the same time, the size of Nineveh heightens the impression of YHWH's great acts. Nineveh is not portrayed as some backwater village, but as a town of immense importance and size in the ancient world, a description it did not have at the time of the prophet Jonah.

Jonah 3:4 recounts Jonah's execution of his task in the briefest possible terms. Jonah, the reader is told, began to enter the city, going a third of the way in, one day's journey. Jonah's message to Nineveh is as terse as any speech recorded in the Bible. It consists of only five words in Hebrew, and it offers no way out for the people. He merely states God's verdict: forty days until Nineveh's overthrow. The prophet offers no call to repentance, no message of hope, and no plea for change. When viewed against chapter 4 (see especially the discussion of Jonah 4:2 and its awareness of Joel 2:12-17), Jonah clearly did not preach to get the people to change their ways. Jonah wanted God to destroy Nineveh. He delivered this message in hopes that the people would do nothing and that God would make good on the threat to destroy the city.

Despite receiving no instructions from YHWH's prophet, the Ninevites intuitively react with fear and contrition. Jonah 3:5 reports the response was immediate, unequivocal, and surprising: "The people of Nineveh believed God. They proclaimed a fast and put on sackcloth from the greatest of them to the least of them." The people put on sackcloth to show remorse. [Sackcloth] They do not question Jonah's message; they presume he speaks the truth. They do not ask Jonah what they can do to avert the disaster; they know they must demonstrate contrition. They do not ask who is to blame; they all take responsibility. Rarely does a biblical text recount such a positive response on the part of anyone, which is then all the more surprising that it is the people of Nineveh, a despised, pagan people, who show such remarkable resolve to change in response to the word of YHWH, no matter how poorly that word was communicated.

To heighten the importance of this response, 3:6-9 narrates that the king followed suit by repenting before proclaiming an official

### Sackcloth

Sackcloth was a piece of clothing to be worn in times of general sorrow (1 Kgs 20:31-32), individual mourning (Gen 37:34), communal mourning (2 Sam 3:31), or repentance (Lam 2:10; Joel 1:8; Esth 4:1-3). Because it was usually made of goat's hair, sackcloth was generally black. People wore it as an outer garment, sometimes specifically over the loins (Amos 8:10).

edict to give the fast his imprimatur. [Kings of Assyria] When he learns of Jonah's message, the king leaves his throne, removes his royal robes, and puts on sackcloth before throwing himself into the dirt in an act of self-abasement and repentance. By his actions, the king divests himself of royal authority. He steps down from the seat of power and sits on an ash heap. He replaces his royal garments with sackcloth. Conversely, these actions cartoonishly present a leader as one who is trying to catch up with those whom he is supposed to lead. The king is the last one to hear the message. He responds first by repenting with great panache, but the king's edict is essentially superfluous. He calls for a fast, but the people have already beaten him to the punch by proclaiming their own fast in 3:5. He demands that everyone wear sackcloth, but they are already doing so (3:5). The only thing the king can add is the requirement that the fast applies to animals as well as humans—hardly actions that would have moved YHWH in their own right. The author of Jonah does things in unexpected ways. Perhaps the author narrated these events to accentuate the complete and total submission of the Ninevites, but it also fits the pattern of the story of Jonah—one in which things happen the opposite way one would expect.

Nevertheless, the king's speech in Jonah 3:8-9 explains what has motivated the people, the nobles, and the king. They are genuinely afraid of YHWH and know that only a radical change of heart and behavior can *possibly* prevent YHWH from executing the pro-

---

### Kings of Assyria

 The eighth-century kings of Assyria are well known because of the extensive records they kept.

| Assyrian Kings | Notes |
| --- | --- |
| Adad-nirari III (811–783 BCE) | |
| Shalmaneser IV (783–773 BCE) | Jeroboam II (king of Israel 786–746 BCE) |
| Ashur-Dan III (773–755 BCE) | |
| Ashur-nirari V (755–745 BCE) | |
| Tiglath-Pileser III (745–727 BCE) | |
| Shalmaneser V (727–722 BCE) | Destruction of Samaria (722 BCE) |
| Sargon II (722–705 BCE; co-regency with Shalmaneser V from 722–709 BCE) | |
| Sennacherib (705–681 BCE) | c. 700 Sennacherib moves capital to Nineveh |

Assyria had four different kings during the reign of Jeroboam II, the king when Jonah was prophet (according to 2 Kgs 14:25). Nineveh was not the capital of Assyria until the time of Sennacherib. During the eighth century, especially beginning with Tiglath-Pileser III, Assyria expanded westward toward the Mediterranean. By the middle of the seventh century, it had conquered territory all the way to Egypt (see discussion in Nah 3:8).

nouncement of doom. The king explains in Jonah 3:8-9, "All shall turn from their evil ways and from the violence that is in their hands. Who knows? God may relent and change his mind; he may turn from his fierce anger so that we do not perish." [Jonah 3:9 and Joel 2:14] Immediately, two things are clear in this text. First, the people of Nineveh realize their behavior threatens their existence. Second, only the God who pronounced the judgment can remove it. The people can do everything in their power to show remorse, but they must ultimately rely on God's mercy if they are to survive. Even the king who commands the people and animals to fast shows considerable deference in recognizing that the ultimate decision belongs to God, not to the king.

For the reader of the Book of the Twelve, this repentance of Nineveh opens new vistas for understanding the message of Nahum. With the incorporation of Jonah into the Twelve, no longer does Nahum's message of judgment on Nineveh come out of the blue. [Jonah and Nahum] Rather, like Israel and Judah, Nineveh, too, had been given a chance to repent of its evil ways. God did not simply decide to destroy the city.

Not surprisingly, God responds positively to the people's actions. God changes God's mind. (For a discussion of this motif, see [Does God Change God's Mind?] and the "Connections" discussions following the five visions of Amos 7–9.) Once God had seen that the people had turned from their wicked ways and approached God in humble submission, "then he had compassion concerning the evil which he spoke of doing to them" (3:10). The Ninevites are spared because they changed their behavior. God responds positively to what they have done. Going through the motions of repentance does not mechanically obligate God to act salvifically, but it is important to note how many times in the Bible God responds to the

### Jonah 3:9 and Joel 2:14

The king here alludes to Joel 2:14, but uses the epithet God rather than YHWH. The allusion creates a parallel and a contrast since the people of Judah in Joel 2:14 are offered a similar chance to repent, but their response is never narrated. The Ninevites in Jonah repent dramatically and God shows compassion (see Jonah 4:2). Jonah 3:9 thus offers a pointed contrast to Joel 2:12-14 in several ways. First, linguistically, the king of Nineveh offers a virtually identical rationale as the prophet in Joel 2:14 ("Who knows whether he will not turn and relent . . . ?"). This combination appears only in these two places. Second, in keeping with the Jonah context, Jonah 3:9 uses the epithet "God" rather than YHWH in the Joel context. Usually, Jonah uses "God" when foreigners speak of the deity. Third, as a point of contrast, Jonah's use of this question leaves no ambiguity of the actions of the people. They had already responded positively to Jonah's sermon (3:5), and the king is taking that a step further (3:6-9). By contrast, Joel never relates the response of the people of Judah, creating the potential for repentance but leaving that open-ended (see [Joel 2:18, Past or Future?]). Remarkably, then, Jonah has the people of Nineveh doing what the people of YHWH have been unable or unwilling to do: turn from evil and violence (Jonah 3:8; cf. Hab 1:2-4).

### Jonah and Nahum

In the Book of the Twelve, Jonah and Nahum both deal with the fate of Assyria, but the message of the two books could hardly be more different. Jonah 3 describes the repentance of Nineveh while Nah 2–3 celebrates Nineveh's destruction. Jonah 4 ends with a rhetorical question, where YHWH confronts Jonah over his lack of compassion for Nineveh. Nah 3 also concludes with a rhetorical question (the only two biblical books to do so), but the question in Nah 3 accuses the Assyrian king of unparalleled cruelty.

responses human beings make. The God of the Bible is not a puppet-master who watches some great cosmic drama unfold before him like a play in which all the lines are already known. In the Bible, God responds to decisions made by humans (as in this text), and to intercession (cf. Amos 7:3, 6; Exod 32:9-14).

Finally, in Jonah 3:10, God responds with pity and with sorrow "concerning the evil about which he spoke of doing." The idea of God doing "evil" (*rāʿâ*) creates a theological problem for many who think of God as a good God. It was less of a problem in the ancient world where all actions were ascribed to God, both positive and negative. However, later Old Testament texts struggled with the idea of God causing evil as well. For example, the Chronicler changes the one responsible for inciting David to take a census. Instead of YHWH (2 Sam 24:1), the Chronicler names Satan (1 Chr 21:1) as the instigator. The idea of *rāʿâ* here does not connote an ontological quality as modern persons often associate with the English word "evil." Rather, the sense is that of "calamity" with the idea of punishment lying behind it.

## CONNECTIONS

Several themes arise from a careful reading of Jonah 3:1-10: God's use of flawed people; the surprising nature of God's salvation; and the nature of God's compassion. Jonah is not a submissive prophet fully attuned to God's purposes. Rather, the character of Jonah is that of a nationalistic bigot who thinks only certain people merit salvation from God. To be sure, God has the power to force Jonah to carry out the task God wants Jonah to do. However, Jonah operates from a paradigm of resistance because he is convinced he knows better than God who is, and is not, worth saving (cf. 4:2). Nevertheless, God's message has the power to change lives. Jonah's vindictive statement of doom (3:4) serves God's purpose, not Jonah's. The people of Nineveh are not delivered because of Jonah, but in spite of him. Jonah delivers a message of doom, but Jonah becomes the agent of God's salvation for those whom Jonah despised.

In the 1960s, Will Campbell, a white civil rights activist and a minister, faced a time of deep personal crisis. At the moment when things seemed darkest to Campbell, after the death of a young nephew, Campbell was consoled by a relative with whom he had argued extensively about civil rights. Looking back on the incident, Campbell writes, "Until the dawn I sat in the redemptive company of a racist Jesus."[1] Moses was a fugitive and a murderer whom God used to lead the people of Israel out of slavery. David was an adulterer and a murderer whom God used to establish a kingdom. Peter denied knowledge of Jesus and denied Gentiles had access to God, but God used Peter to expand the mission of the church to the Gentiles. God does not choose to work through persons who are better than everyone else. Instead, God often accomplishes God's purpose in spite of the messengers chosen to deliver the message.

Given that God uses imperfect messengers, it should come as no surprise that we cannot control whom God delivers. God is concerned with the salvation of all people. People often hasten to make pronouncements about whom God can save or about how God can save. Nevertheless, biblical stories remind us that time and time again God ignores our prejudices so that the spirit can move in unforeseen ways. Jonah would have prevented the Ninevites from hearing God's message, but God's word changed their behavior. The disciples tried to prevent children from "bothering" Jesus, but Jesus brought the children forward (Mark 10:13-16; Matt 19:13-15; Luke 18:15-17). Some in the early church wanted to limit those who could hear the gospel message to Jews, but God used Paul, a converted persecutor of Christians, to convert the Gentiles. God wants the gospel message taken to the entire world, not just those who look like us and sound like us. [Jesus and Hypocritical Religious Leaders] The church still has people who think they know more than God regarding who is worthy of salvation, but God will not be limited by our petty criteria. God's message of salvation and deliverance is open to all. We are well advised not to get in God's way.

God's compassion and judgment also come to us in surprising ways. In Jonah, it is the people of Nineveh who are slated for judgment, yet they receive salvation. God chooses a messenger, but that messenger becomes the focus of God's judgment. That same messenger also receives God's rebuke in chapter 4. In between, that messenger receives God's compassion in the

---

**Jesus and Hypocritical Religious Leaders**

Jesus fought the same attitude among religious leaders of his day as the attitude of Jonah:

> When the Pharisees saw this, they said to his disciples, "Why does your teacher eat with tax collectors and sinners?" But when he heard this, he said, "Those who are well have no need of a physician, but those who are sick. Go and learn what this means, 'I desire mercy, not sacrifice.' For I have come to call not the righteous but sinners." (Matt 9:11-13)

Jonah would surely have sided with the Pharisees.

form of deliverance in chapters 2 and 3. Like the parable of the greedy steward who cannot forgive others, Jonah cannot extend God's mercy to those who are not like him.

Jonah 3 pokes fun at leaders, religious and political, who act as though their power comes from themselves. Jonah does the right thing in this chapter, but just barely. The king does the right thing, but only after everyone in the city has already turned to God. The prophet succeeds in spite of his own desire. The king leads from behind. Jonah is a story that turns normal expectations upside down. Harry Chapin, a songwriter in the 1970s, wrote a song that illustrates the surprising nature of God's activity. The refrain states,

> Have you heard of the Legend of the Lost and Found,
> Tales of a world turning upside down,
> Where all the kings become the clowns,
> And beggars are crowned?
> The Legend of the Lost and Found.[2]

When God takes hold of a situation, all bets are off. God offers compassion to those in need, not those who live in privilege. Jesus was born in a stable, and God turned the world upside down.

## NOTES

1. Will Campbell, *Brother to a Dragonfly* (New York: Seabury Press, 1977) 151.

2. "Legends of the Lost and Found," by Harry Chapin, Elektra Records, 1979.

# JONAH'S PROTESTATIONS AND GOD'S RESPONSE

## Jonah 4:1-11

## COMMENTARY

Jonah 4 presents the book's fourth scene in three movements. Each section involves a divine response to something the prophet does or says: Jonah's petulant prayer and God's response (4:1-4), Jonah's passive-aggressive challenge (4:5-8), and God's final lesson (4:9-11).

### Jonah's Petulant Prayer and God's Response, 4:1-4

Jonah's second prayer (cf. Jonah 2:1f) is narrated not as a typical prophetic prayer but as a confrontational remonstration of God's compassion for a hated enemy (4:1-3). God asks a rhetorical question that challenges Jonah's audacity (4:4).

In 4:1, Jonah considers God's decision to show compassion on Nineveh to be wrong. The extent to which this decision angers Jonah does not come across with the full force of the Hebrew in most English translations. The NRSV uses "displeased" to translate *rā'a* and "to become angry" to translate *ḥārah*. The first verb's basic meaning implies evil or wickedness. The other verb expresses God's wrath and comes from a root meaning "to glow hot." A more idiomatic translation shows the powerful connotations of the combination of these verbs: "Jonah considered it a great evil and his anger burned within him." The Hebrew does not imply that Jonah was merely displeased; Jonah judged God's mercy as a "great evil."

In 4:2, Jonah prays to YHWH. The verb for "pray" is the same verb used in 2:2. Here, however, Jonah offers a prayer of complaint that finally reveals why he fled at the beginning of the book. He did not obey YHWH because Jonah knew God would show compassion (*ḥesed* on Nineveh. Jonah justifies his anger at God's decision by

### Exodus 34:6-7

Jonah 4:2 modifies the confession from Exod 34:6, although the motivation is not easy to discern. The phrasing could simply have been changed to suit the context of Jonah, or it could be calling attention to Joel 2:13, which contains the same variation of Exod 34:6. Exod 34:6 concludes the string of YHWH's characteristics with faithfulness (ʾĕmet), but Jonah 4:2 concludes with "relenting concerning evil," utilizing the phrasing of Jonah 3:10. The same phrase, "relenting of evil," also appears in Joel 2:13. T. B. Dozeman concludes that the interplay between Jonah and Joel shows that the two prophetic texts are interpreting the Torah text from different perspectives: the implications of YHWH's character for Israel (in Joel) and for the nations (in Jonah). Dozeman shows the significant number of connections between Jonah and Joel, and he demonstrates how Jonah expands and compliments Joel. He is less convincing, however, when asserting that the mutual relationship can be read equally in either direction. His contention that the Exodus context already alludes to the questions raised by Jonah rests upon the questionable interpretation of Exod 32:12. He claims the mockery of the nations, if Israel is destroyed, actually concerns how YHWH's punishment of Israel will affect other nations. This citation, however, is not concerned with the effects on the other nations. It is concerned only with YHWH's reputation among the nations if YHWH's people are destroyed. This concern is even more evident in Joel 2:17. In short, Dozeman makes a better case that Jonah is responding to Joel than that Jonah 4:2 could have arisen simply from Exod 34 alone. Dozeman speaks of mutuality, but the case is stronger that Jonah is expanding on Joel by citing Exodus than the other way around. Further, the context of Exod 34:7 may help explain YHWH's response to Jonah in 4:11. The large number of persons in Nineveh (more than 120,000) takes up reference to the "thousands" who are the object of YHWH's ḥesed in 34:7. In sum, Jonah radicalizes Exod 34:6-7 in contradistinction to Joel 2:13.

Exod 34:6-7 recurs as a source for allusions in Joel 2:13; 3:19-20 (MT 3:19-20); Mic 7:18-19 and Nah 1:3. See these locations for more complete discussions of how Exod 34:6-7 function in those contexts. Jonah 4:2 is likely the latest of these to enter the Book of the Twelve. In Jonah 4:2, the allusion to Exod 34:6-7 pointedly critiques, or at least significantly delimits, the ways in which these other passages have used Exod 34:6 and 34:7. In the other four passages the application of Exod 34:6 always relates to God's compassion for God's people while the subject of recompense in 34:7 affirms God's actions toward the nations. By contrast, Jonah 4:2 confronts the prophet with God's compassion for the nations. This expanded theological perspective lies at the heart of the message of Jonah.

See Thomas B. Dozeman, "Inner-Biblical Interpretation of Yahweh's Gracious and Compassionate Character," *JBL* 105 (1989): 222.

---

reformulating the classic confession of Exodus 34:6-7, although the text may be filtered through Joel 2:13. [Exodus 34:6-7]

In 4:3, Jonah asks YHWH to kill him out of frustration with YHWH's compassion on the Ninevites. Jonah offers a real point of contrast with Moses at this point. The Exodus context portrays Moses as interceding on behalf of Israel because of YHWH's compassion. Jonah, by contrast, wants to die *because* YHWH chooses to show compassion upon foreigners. Other biblical figures call on God to take their lives as protest for injustice they perceive at YHWH's hands. [Biblical Figures Call on God to Take Their Lives] Nowhere else, however, does a biblical figure request that God take his life because he is embarrassed by YHWH's compassion.

### Biblical Figures Call on God to Take Their Lives

Other biblical characters who ask God to kill them face far more drastic circumstances than did Jonah. Job, for example, demands that God take his life in response to the loss he has experienced and his inability to get an adequate response from God (6:9-14). In Jer 20:14-18, the prophet laments his life because of the shame he is forced to bear. Samson asks God for strength so that he might die in one final act of vengeance after the Philistines had brutalized him (Judg 16:28-31). By comparison, Jonah's call for God to take his life appears trivial, a petulant and childish response to his momentary discomfort.

In Jonah 4:4, YHWH responds to Jonah's death wish with a rhetorical question: "Is it good for you to be angry?" The question presumes that Jonah knows the answer is "no." The verb used for Jonah's anger is the same as in 4:1 and connotes a burning anger. YHWH chastises Jonah not so much for his bigotry but for the audacity of challenging YHWH's sense of compassion. Ironically, Jonah has himself benefited from YHWH's compassion, but he burns with indignation at the idea of God showing that same compassion to those whom Jonah holds in contempt. The absurdity of Jonah's position is subtly yet powerfully laid bare for all to see.

## Jonah's Passive-aggressive Challenge, 4:5-8

The second section, Jonah 4:5-8, narrates a series of actions by Jonah and God, climaxing with Jonah's cry of anguish. The prophet leaves the city to watch what happens to Nineveh (4:5). God responds with actions to teach Jonah. God first provides a plant for shade and then appoints a worm to kill it. Finally, God sends a scorching wind (4:6-8a) so that the heat is greater than it was at the beginning, prompting Jonah's second request to die (4:8b, 9b). The action in these verses involves Jonah's passive-aggressive behavior in which he goes outside the city to pout. God does not speak to Jonah but uses a plant and a worm to make a point.

In 4:5, Jonah breaks off conversation with YHWH and leaves the city to wait to see what happens to the people. It has often been noted that this verse seems out of place logically. Since the prophet already responded angrily to God's reprieve of Nineveh (4:1), Jonah already knows what will happen. It is thus not clear why he would leave the city to wait to see what will happen. This tension has generated numerous attempts to explain Jonah's response in 4:5, though no real consensus has emerged. [Explaining Jonah's Response in 4:5] However this verse came to its current location, the effect is satirical. Jonah knows God has changed God's mind (3:10; 4:1), so Jonah's decision appears to be little more than a cantankerous protest to demonstrate his displeasure with God. Like a child who takes his ball and goes home, Jonah leaves the city to sulk about the fact that God would not punish Nineveh. Jonah intends to wait God out, since he takes the time to build a booth. The booth, or hut, is a temporary shelter made of twigs, often erected in fields for

### Explaining Jonah's Response in 4:5

J. M. Sasson provides a thorough assessment of the history of interpretation of this verse, along with helpful categories for explaining the problem of the location of the verse: textual corruption, grammatical readjustment, and explanations of the text "as is." Those who see 4:5 as a textual problem generally suggest either omitting the verse (K. Budde, J. Bewer) or relocating it to its "original" position following 3:4 (H. Winckler, E. Bickerman, and P. Trible—although this proposal was first suggested in the Middle Ages). Those who argue for grammatical readjustment (e.g., H. Wolff, P. Weimar) translate the verse as a pluperfect and treat it as a parenthetical flashback. They claim that the scene forces the reader to read the scene as happening simultaneously with the Ninevite reaction to Jonah's preaching. Sasson correctly notes this is highly unusual because of the Hebrew construction. Some treat the text "as is" (e.g., J. Magonet and J. Sasson). Magonet explains the tension from the structural parallel of Jonah's flight to Tarshish in chapter 1. Sasson suggests a purely literary role—to put Jonah east of the city to make him the first one to feel the heat from the east wind.

Jack M. Sasson, *Jonah* (AB 24B; New York: Doubleday, 1990) 287–89; 139.

Karl Budde, "The Book of Jonah," in *Jewish Encyclopedia* (New York: Funk and Wagnall, 1904) 7:227–30.

Julius Bewer, *Jonah* (ICC; Edinburgh: T & T Clark) 58–59.

Hugo Winckler, "Zum Buche Jona," *Altorientalische Forschungen* 2:260–65.

Elias J. Bickerman, "Les Deux Erreurs du prophèt Jonas," *Revue d'histoire et de philosophie religieuses* 45 (1965): 232–64.

Phyllis Trible, "Studies in the Book of Jonah," (Ph.D. diss., Columbia University; Ann Arbor, University Microfilm International, 1963.

Hans Walter Wolff, *Obadiah and Jonah* (trans. Margaret Kohl; Continental Commentary; Minneapolis: Augsburg, 1976) 163, 169.

Peter Weimar, "Jon 4,5. Beobachtungen zur Entstehung der Jonaerzählung," *Biblische Notizen* 18 (1982): 86–109.

Jonathan Magonet, *Form and Meaning: Studies in Literary Techniques in the Book of Jonah* (Beiträge zur biblischen Exegese und Theologie 2; Bern: Herbert Lang, 1976) 5–860.

### The *qîqāyôn* Plant

(Credit: Joaquim Alves Gaspar, http://en.wikipedia.org/wiki/File:Ricinus_March_2010-1.jpg)

Linguistically, Jonah's author may not have intended a castor bean plant (pictured here). The LXX, Syriac, and Vulgate point to other interpretations. The LXX (*kolokuntha*) and Syriac versions interpret the plant as a gourd, while the Vulgate translates it as ivy (*hedera*). The common denominator of all these suggestions is the leafy foliage.

cattle (Gen 33:17), travelers (Lev 23:43), religious pilgrims (Neh 8:15-17), or for those guarding crops (Job 27:18). Its construction conveys the impression that Jonah intends to stay for some time. This is surprising given that Jonah's task is complete. The one who was so reluctant to go is just as set against leaving. His actions become in effect a challenge to God, though he never says a word. God responds in kind—with actions designed to make a point.

In 4:6, God "appoints" something to affect Jonah for the second of four times (see 1:17 [MT 2:1]; 4:7, 8). God appoints a plant specifically to provide shade for Jonah. It is most frequently argued that the *qîqāyôn* plant was probably a castor bean plant because of the large foliage associated with this bush and the speed with which it can grow. In response, Jonah shows genuine joy at the growth of the plant, the only time he displays any positive emotional response. He has thus gone full circle in his emotions in a short space—from great anger to great rejoicing. The joy, however, is short lived.

In 4:7, for the third time, God appoints something to interact with Jonah—this time a worm that destroys the plant over which Jonah rejoiced. The worm arrived at dawn to do its work and the plant withered after the worm struck it. Again, the text comically portrays a situation using hyperbolic images. The image here is that of a tiny creature with a huge appetite. This mighty worm "attacks" a plant large enough to provide shade for a human being. The attack quickly destroys the *qîqāyôn* plant, causing it to wither, thereby removing the shade and making Jonah susceptible to the elements.

In 4:8, for the fourth time (cf. 1:17; 4:6, 7), God appoints something to change Jonah's situation: a searing east wind. Once the sun begins to shine (after the

**Worm**

(Credit: Barclay Burns)

This worm appears in several other OT contexts. It is the same pest that feasts on grapes in Deut 28:39, appears in the rotting manna in Exod 16:20, and consumes human flesh in Isa 14:11; 66:24. The worm, generally thought to be the common fruit grub pictured here (known as *Eupoecilia ambiguella, clysia ambiguella,* or *cochylis ambiguella*), grows only to a length of around 18 mm (*less than 3/4 inch*). The worm is red and served as a base ingredient in old red dyes, thus explaining the use of the same term for "red material" in several texts in the Priestly material of Exodus referring to red elements in the tabernacle (Exod 25:4; 26:1, 31, 36; 27:16; 28:5, 6, 8, 15, 33; 35:6, 23, 25, 35; 36:8, 35, 37; 38:18, 23; 39:1, 2, 3; 39:5. 8, 24, 29).

rising of the dawn), God appoints a sultry east wind. The combination of this dry wind and the heat from the sun makes Jonah's vigil unpleasant. The extent of his discomfort is accentuated with Jonah's comment: "It is better for me to die than to live." Here, Jonah bypasses God. The MT literally reads, "He [Jonah] asked his life to die," while in 4:3 Jonah asks *God* to take his life. The irony of the moment should not be lost. Jonah's life was delivered from drowning by a fish God appointed, only to be baked in the sun and taught a lesson with the aid of the hot desert wind, a plant, and a worm that God had also appointed. Jonah's discomfort becomes the starting point for God's final lesson (4:9-11).

**God's Final Lesson, 4:9-11**

The final subunit, 4:9-11, begins with God repeating the rhetorical question of 4:4 ("Is it right for you to be angry . . . ?"), but this time God asks Jonah about the plant rather than Nineveh. Jonah 4:9 also adds an important element: Jonah responds verbally to God's question, while previously (4:4) he had merely sulked away after God's question. With a rhetorical flourish in 4:10-11, God dispels the claim that Jonah has a right to be angry.

In 4:9, God asks Jonah a second time whether he is angry, but this time God asks Jonah about the plant (cf. 4:4). Jonah's response demonstrates, however, that he is still recalcitrant in his myopic sense of right and wrong. Jonah essentially has the audacity to say to God, "I have every right in the world to be angry even if my anger causes me to perish."

In 4:10-11, YHWH responds to Jonah with a short sermon that ends with a rhetorical question and forces the reader to contemplate the point of the book. YHWH explains the parable of the plant. He reminds Jonah of his pleasure concerning the bush: "You had compassion on the plant." [Compassion] God then elaborates that Jonah did nothing to bring about this plant, since Jonah neither cultivated it nor nurtured it. It simply appeared from one day to the next, and disappeared as quickly as it had come. Despite the transitory nature of the protection, Jonah felt great sadness when it was gone, primarily because its departure had an adverse effect upon him; namely, its disappearance caused Jonah to be more vulnerable to the heat.

Jonah 4:11 concludes the book. The size and fate of Nineveh as depicted in these verses have generated considerable discussion. The size of Nineveh as depicted in 4:11 is huge by ancient standards. Jonah 4:11 indicates that Nineveh had more than 120,000 persons. This number is not impossibly large for later times, but is likely too large for the time in which the prophet Jonah actually lived. By some estimates, ancient Nineveh could have had a population of well over 300,000 at the height of its power in the seventh century. To put this number in perspective, Jerusalem *increased* in size to 24,000 when refugees from Samaria fled to it in the latter eighth century.[1] The parenthetical note at the end of 4:11 further solidifies the impression of God's concern by reminding the readers that in addition to the people, there were large numbers of cattle in the city. According to 3:7-8, these cattle had also fasted and worn

---

**Compassion**

AΩ The Hebrew word *ḥesed* means "to show compassion upon." The NRSV translates the verb here (and in 4:11) as "concerned about," presumably to avoid the idea that one would show emotion toward a plant (see also Sasson, 309). However, the caricature of Jonah's compassion seems to be precisely the point of the text, given that God uses the same verb in 4:11 to imply his "concern" for the living beings of Nineveh.

Jack M. Sasson, *Jonah* (AB 24B; New York: Doubleday, 1990).

sackcloth. So the size of the city as listed, while quite large, should not be understood as astronomical, but it does put Jonah's lack of compassion for the people of Nineveh into stark contrast with God. Jonah could grieve over one plant that had withered, but he could not find any concern for the large numbers of living beings in Nineveh. [The Fate of Nineveh]

Jonah ends with a rhetorical question that both drives home YHWH's point to Jonah and leaves the resolution of the book open to the imagination. [Rhetorical Question] God uses Jonah's compassion about the plant to make a point about the absurdity of Jonah's attempt to limit God's compassion in the case of Nineveh. If Jonah has compassion about the plant, should not God have compassion upon the living beings of Nineveh? Of course. Jonah's compassion about the plant makes quite a caricature when seen against his animosity toward the Ninevites. Jonah sits wallowing in his hatred of Nineveh, though the people and animals had repented before YHWH. In short, YHWH remonstrates Jonah—and indirectly the book's readers—for Jonah's unwillingness to have compassion upon all God's creatures. [God's Compassion on Creation]

### The Fate of Nineveh

The fate of Nineveh created discussion in ancient sources in light of the contradictory statements about Nineveh in the book of Nahum, which pronounces God's judgment upon that city and upon the ultimate overthrow of Nineveh in 612 BCE. Some of these early interpreters treated Jonah as a prophet motivated by his need to protect God. They interpreted Jonah's interest in Nineveh's fate as concern that people would not take God seriously if God did not follow through with his pronouncements of destruction. They treated Jonah as a genuine prophet because Jonah's pronouncement of judgment finally did come true since Nineveh's repentance was only short term. Beate Ego demonstrates that ancient interpreters generally took one of three positions to explain the message of Jonah and Nahum (where the doom of Ninevah is predicted: 1) the interpreters ignored the motif of Nineveh's repentance; 2) they assumed it was only a temporary reprieve because the Ninevites returned to their immoral behavior; or 3) they assumed that the repentance was insincere).

See Beate Ego, "The Repentance of Nineveh in the Story of Jonah and Nahum's Prophecy of the City's Destruction: Aggadic Solutions for an Exegetical Problem in the Book of the Twelve," in *Thematic Threads in the Book of the Twelve* (ed. Aaron Schart and Paul Redditt; Beihefte zur Zeitschrift für die alttestamentliche Wissenschaft 325; Berlin de Gruyter, 2003) 155–64.

## CONNECTIONS

What would happen if God followed our lead? The extent to which the message of the book of Jonah still speaks today represents a sad commentary on our religious development. Too often, we think we know better than God. For some, Jonah's failure rests in his limitation of God's salvific actions to a narrow group of people who look and talk like him. Yet we often want to decide the fate of our enemies and make sure punishment is meted out to those who oppose us. For others,

### Rhetorical Question

In actuality, 4:11 does not contain explicit interrogative markers. It is, however, universally recognized as a rhetorical question because of its close syntactical connection to the previous verse and the manner in which its content would otherwise contradict the point of 4:10. This construction is common in biblical Hebrew. See Wilhelm Gesenius, Emil E. Kautzsch, and Arthur Ernest Cowley, *Gesenius' Hebrew Grammar* (repr. 1970; Oxford; Clarendon, 1910), §150a.

### God's Compassion on Creation

Rüdiger Lux points out that the question with which Jonah ends makes a profound statement about the nature of YHWH's compassion and justice. He says,

God does not base compassion on a human act of piety (confession) or goodness (repentance); nor on religion or morality. God's grace and compassion are the grace of creation (*Schöpfungsgnade*), born from God's uncoerced devotion to God's creatures.

Rüdiger Lux, *Jona: Prophet zwischen 'Verweigerung' und 'Gehorsam'* (Forschungen zur Religion und Literatur des Alten und Neuen Testaments; Göttingen: Vandenhoeck und Ruprecht, 1994) 162 (my translation).

### Jonah as a Joke

For Whedbee, the entire book of Jonah displays a comedic structure based on contradictions between divine and human purpose. Jonah tries to exert his will over God, but God prevails. Jonah tries to act piously but misses the irony. Jonah expresses his anger, but it changes nothing.

See J. William Whedbee, "Jonah as Joke: A Comedy of Contradiction, Caricature, and Compassion," in the *Bible and the Comic Vision* (Cambridge: Cambridge University Press, 1998) 191–220.

Jonah's dereliction lies in his failure to let God be God. Jonah feels the need to protect this God of compassion from God's own compassion. Jonah sees the implications of a God who is too soft on wickedness. Such a God would be open to genuine repentance on the part of anyone, and Jonah must stop this God from forgiving the wrong kind of people.

Jonah, of course, is not the hero of the book in the sense of the character to be emulated. One recent commentator even goes so far as to describe Jonah as a comic "joke." [Jonah as a Joke] The book's author deliberately portrays God's prophet as a cartoonish figure whose petty attempts to thwart God's purpose only make Jonah look more ridiculous. Despite the comedic elements, the book conveys deep theological convictions by exploring the implications of YHWH's sovereignty and depicting an image of God at odds with significant portions of the Old Testament. In Jonah, God is a God of universal power and incomprehensible compassion. YHWH is not just the God of Judah or Israel; YHWH has power over the empire of Assyria, over the creatures of the sea, and over the forces of nature. This portrayal of YHWH's power is taken for granted in much Old Testament literature, but Jonah draws out the implications for the reader in grand terms. God is not limited by geographic boundaries, natural law, or human caprice. God does what God chooses in this book.

God's actions in Jonah are limited, however, by God's compassion. Jonah's God remains ready to respond to genuine acts of repentance. From a human standpoint, this God is a radical God—like the God of the Beatitudes in Matthew 5—a God who is willing and able to forgive our enemies. Jonah knows God will change God's mind about destroying Nineveh if the people provide God with the slightest reason. That's why Jonah runs away (4:2). He is not afraid of the powerful Assyrians. Rather, Jonah fears God's compassion will stop God from pronouncing judgment. Never mind that God shows the same compassion to Jonah repeatedly. The prophet knows God will not destroy the Ninevites because God is patient and merciful to a fault.

Sadly, Jonah's story is still all too real. Unlike God, most of us are too quick to retaliate, too willing to write off people who are not enough like us, and too sure we know how to protect God. Moreover, too few of us strive to be like the radical God of Jonah— the God whose compassion outruns anger and whose patience outlasts indignation. How many times could the God of Israel have opted to wipe Israel off the face of the earth for its stubborn refusal to follow God's commands? About as many times as God could have chosen to abandon the church for its obstinate disregard of the need for compassion and forgiveness. About as many times as we have turned our backs on or have uttered harsh words against "those people." It is far easier to take the road to Joppa than to practice patient *ḥesed*—God's loving-kindness. What would happen if God followed our lead?

## NOTE

1. Jack M. Sasson, *Jonah* (AB 24B; New York: Doubleday, 1990) 312.

# SELECT BIBLIOGRAPHY
# FOR JONAH

Abela, Anthony M. "When the Agenda of an Artistic Composition Is Hidden: Jonah and Intertextual Dialogue with Isaiah 6, The 'Confessions of Jeremiah,' and Other Texts." In *The Elusive Prophet: The Prophet as a Historical Person, Literary Character and Anonymous Artist*, edited by Johannes C. de Moor, 1–30. Leiden: Brill, 2001.

Ackerman, James S. "Satire and Symbolism in the Song of Jonah." In *Traditions in Transformation. Turning Points in Biblical Faith*, edited by B. Halpern and J. D. Levenson, 213–46. Winona Lake: Eisenbrauns, 1981.

Allen, Leslie C. *The Books of Joel, Obadiah, Jonah, and Micah*. New International Commentary on the Old Testament. Grand Rapids: Eerdmans, 1976.

Begg, Christopher T. "Josephus and Nahum Revisited." *Revue des Études Juives* 154 (1995): 5–22.

Bolin, Thomas M. "'Should I Not Also Pity Nineveh?' Divine Freedom in the Book of Jonah." *Journal for the Study of the Old Testament* 67 (1995): 109–20.

Childs, Brevard S. "The Canonical Shape of the Book of Jonah." In *Essays in Honor of William Sanford LaSor*, edited by F. A. Tuttle, 122–28. Grand Rapids: Eerdmans, 1978.

Clements, Ronald E. "The Purpose of the Book of Jonah." *Congress Volume*. Vetus Testamentum Supplement Series 28. Leiden: Brill, 1975. 16–28.

Cooper, Alan. "In Praise of Divine Caprice: The Significance of the Book of Jonah." In *Among the Prophets: Language, Image and Structure in the Prophetic Writings*, edited by Philip R. Davies and David J. A. Clines, 144–63. Journal for the Study of the Old Testament: Supplemental Series 144. Sheffield: JSOT Press, 1993.

Craig, Kenneth M. "Jonah and the Reading Process." *Journal for the Study of the Old Testament* 47 (1990): 103–14.

Cross, Frank Moore. "Studies in the Structure of Hebrew Verse: The Prosody of the Psalm of Jonah." In *The Quest for the Kingdom of God: Studies in Honor of George E. Mendenhall*, edited by H. B. Huffmon et al., 159–67. Winona Lake: Eisenbrauns, 1983.

Dell, Katherine J. "Reinventing the Wheel: The Shaping of the Book of Jonah." In *After the Exile: Essays in Honour of Rex Mason*, edited by John Barton and David J. Reimer, 85–101. Macon GA: Mercer University Press, 1996.

Ellul, Jacques. *The Judgment of Jonah*. Translated by Geoffrey W. Bromiley. Grand Rapids: Eerdmans, 1971.

Emmerson, Grace I. "Another Look at the Book of Jonah." *Expository Times* 88 (1976): 86–88.

Ephros, Abraham Z. "The Book of Jonah as Allegory." *Jewish Bible Quarterly* 27 (1999): 141–51.

Fretheim, Terence E. "Jonah and Theodicy." *Zeitschrift für die alttestamentliche Wissenschaft* 90 (1978): 227–37.

————. *The Message of Jonah: A Theological Commentary*. Minneapolis: Augsburg Publishing House, 1977.

Gitay, Yehoshua. "Jonah: The Prophecy of Antirhetoric." In *Fortunate the Eyes that See*, edited by Astrid Beck et al., 197–206. Grand Rapids: Eerdmans, 1995.

Glasson, T. F. "Nahum and Jonah." *Expository Times* 81 (1969/70): 54–55.

Granot, Hayim. "Jonah and Yom Kippur." *Jewish Bible Quarterly* 26 (1998): 201–202.

Holbert, John C. "'Deliverance Belongs to Yahweh!': Satire in the Book of Jonah." *Journal for the Study of the Old Testament* 21 (1981): 59–81.

Hoop, Raymond de. "The Book of Jonah as Poetry: An Analysis of Jonah 1:1-16." In *Structural Analysis of Biblical and Canaanite Poetry*, edited by Willem van der Meer and Johannes C. de Moor, 156–71. Journal for the Study of the Old Testament: Supplemental Series 74. Sheffield: JSOT Press, 1988.

Houk, Cornelius B. "Linguistic Patterns in Jonah." *Journal for the Study of the Old Testament* 77 (1998): 81–102.

Hunter, Alastair G. "Jonah from the whale: Exodus motifs in Jonah 2." In *The Elusive Prophet: The Prophet as a Historical Person, Literary Character and Anonymous Artist*, edited by Johannes C. de Moor, 142–58. Leiden: Brill, 2001.

Kahn, Pinchas. "The Epilogue to Jonah." *Jewish Bible Quarterly* 28 (2000): 146–55.

Knight, George A. F., and Friedman W. Golka. *Revelation of God: The Song of Songs and Jonah*. International Theological Commentary. Grand Rapids: Eerdmans, 1988.

Kraeling, Emil G. "The Evolution of the Story of Jonah." In *Hommages à André Dupont-Sommer*, edited by Nigel Avigad, 305–18. Paris: Librairie Adrien Maisonneve, 1971.

Landes, George M. "Jonah: A *Mashal*?" In *Israelite Wisdom: Theological and Literary Essays in Honor of Samuel Terrien*, edited by J. G. Gammie, et al., 137–58. Missoula: Scholars Press, 1978.

————. "A Case for the Sixth-Century BCE Dating for the Book of Jonah." In *Realia Dei*, edited by Prescott H. Williams, Jr., and Theodore Hiebert, 100–16. Atlanta: Scholars Pres, 1999.

————. "Textual "Information Gaps" and "Dissonances" in the Interpretation of the Book of Jonah." In *Ki Baruch hu*, edited by Robert Chazan et al., 273–93. Winona Lake: Eisenbrauns, 1999.

Levine, Etan. "Jonah as a Philosophical Book." *Zeitschrift für die alttestamentliche Wissenschaft* 96 (1984): 235–45.

Limburg, James L. *Hosea–Micah*. Interpretation. Atlanta: John Knox, 1988.

Magonet, Jonathan. *Form and Meaning: Studies in Literary Techniques in the Book of Jonah*. Beitrage zur biblischen Exegese und Theologie 2. Bern: Herbert Lang, 1976.

Marcus, David. "Nineveh's "Three Days' Walk" (Jonah 3:3): Another Interpretation." In *On the way to Nineveh*, edited by Megan Bishop Moore, 42–53. Atlanta: Scholars Press, 1999.

Payne, David F. "Jonah from the Perspective of Its Audience." In *"The Place Is Too Small for Us": The Israelite Prophets in Recent Scholarship*, edited by Robert P. Gordon, 263–72. Winona Lake: Eisenbrauns, 1995.

Porten, Bezalel. "Baalshamem and the Date of the Book of Jonah," In *De la Tôrah au Messie. Études d'exégèse et d'Herméneutique Bibliques Offertes á Henri Cazelles pour se 25 années d'Enseignement à l'Institut Catholique de Paris (Octobre 1979)*, edited by Maurice Carrez et al. Paris: Desclée, 1981.

Reed, Jonathan. "The Sign of Jonah (Q 11:29-32) and Other Epic Traditions in Q." In *Reimagining Christian Origins*, 130–43. Valley Forge: Trinity Press International, 1996.

Sasson, Jack M. *Jonah*. Anchor Bible 24B. New York: Doubleday, 1990.

Sherwood, Yvonne. "Rocking the Boat: Jonah and the New Historicism." *Biblical Interpretation* 5 (1997): 364–402.

Snyder, Graydon F. "Sea Monsters in Early Christian Art." *Biblical Research* 44 (1999): 7–21.

Stuart, Douglas. *Hosea–Jonah*. Word Biblical Commentary 31. Waco TX: Word, 1987.

Trible, Phyllis. "Divine Incongruities in the Book of Jonah." In *God in the Fray: A Tribute to Walter Brueggemann*, edited by Tod Linafelt and Timothy K. Beal, 198–208. Minneapolis: Fortress Press, 1998.

Van Wijk-Bos, Johanna W. H. "No Small Thing: The "Overturning" of Nineveh in the Third Chapter of Jonah." In *On the way to Nineveh*, edited by Megan Bishop Moore, 218–37. Atlanta: Scholars Press, 1999.

Walsh, Jerome T. "Jonah 2:3-10: A Rhetorical Critical Study." *Biblica* 63 (1982): 219–29.

Watts, James W. "Song and the Ancient Reader." *Perspectives in Religious Studies* 22 (1995): 135–47.

Watts, John D. W. *The Books of Joel, Obadiah, Jonah, Nahum, Habakkuk and Zephaniah*. Cambridge Bible Commentary. London: Cambridge University Press, 1975.

Wendland, Ernst R. "Recursion and Variation in the "Prophecy" of Jonah: On the Rhetorical Impact of Stylistic Technique in Hebrew Narrative Discourse, with Special Reference to Irony and Enigma." *Andrews University Seminary Studies* 35 (1997): 67–98.

Wolff, Hans Walter. *Obadiah and Jonah. A Commentary*. Translated by Margaret Kohl. Minneapolis: Augsburg, 1977.

Zapff, Burkard M. "The Perspective of the Nations in the Book of Micah as a 'Systematization' of the Nations' Role in Joel, Jonah and Nahum: Reflections on a Context-Oriented Exegesis in the Book of the Twelve." In *Thematic Threads in the Book of the Twelve*, edited by Paul L. Redditt and Aaron Schart, 282–312. Beihefte zur Zeitschrift für die alttestamentliche Wissenschaft 325. Berlin: De Gruyter, 2003.

# INDEX OF MODERN AUTHORS

# INDEX OF SCRIPTURES
# FOR THE INTRODUCTION TO
# THE BOOK OF THE TWELVE

# INDEX OF SCRIPTURES FOR HOSEA

| | | | | | | | |
|---|---|---|---|---|---|---|---|
| 1:12 | 55 | 5:18-19 | 178, 182 | 5:2 | 158 | 3:5, 8, 15 | 169 |
| 1:17 | 54, 186 | 5:21-27 | 123 | 5:4 | 107, 124 | 3:14-20 | 42 |
| 1:17, 19, 20 | 178 | 5:21 | 135 | 5:12 | 68 | | |
| 1:19, 20 | 186 | 5:22, 25 | 147 | 6:1-2 | 74 | **HAGGAI** | |
| 2:1 | 88, 162 | 6:1 | 124 | 6:1, 2, 9 | 74 | 1:6 | 77 |
| 2:3, 22 | 186 | 6:4 | 178, 179 | 6:6-8 | 98, 102, | 1:9-11 | 77 |
| 2:11 | 162 | 6:8 | 107, 124 | | 123, 190 | 1:11 | 54 |
| 2:13 | 74, 99, | 6:12 | 169 | 6:6 | 178, 179 | 2:16-19 | 82 |
| | 104, 161 | 7:1-3, 4-6 | 161 | 6:7 | 179 | 2:16 | 130 |
| 2:14 | 188 | 7:2, 4 | 167 | 6:8 | 74, 99, | 2:19 | 55, 77, |
| 2:15 | 8, 116 | 7:9, 11 | 178, 186 | | 169 | | 186 |
| 2:17, 19 | 172 | 7:10-17 | 125, | 6:8, 11 | 26 | | |
| 2:19 | 54 | | 126, 132 | 6:9-16 | 77 | **ZECHARIAH** | |
| 2:23-25 | 130 | 8:4 | 74 | 6:11 | 169 | 1–8 | 95 |
| 2:24 | 130 | 8:5 | 26, 169 | 6:14 | 77 | 1:2-6 | 95, 123 |
| 2:26 | 77 | 8:7 | 107, 124 | 6:16 | 172 | 1:7–6:14 | 123 |
| 3:16 | 162 | 9:1 | 145 | 7:7 | 133 | 3:10 | 55, 144 |
| 3:18 | 172 | 9:7-10, 11-15 | 31 | 7:9 | 169 | 7:1-7 | 123 |
| 4:16 | 91 | 9:8a, b | 45 | 7:18, 20 | 99, 169 | 7:9 | 99 |
| 4:18 | 186 | 9:11-15 | 44, 131 | 7:18-19 | 161 | 8:9-12 | 82 |
| 4:18, 19 | 178 | 9:11-12 | 30 | | | 8:12 | 77 |
| 4:19 | 186 | | | **NAHUM** | | 8:16 | 74 |
| | | **OBADIAH** | | 1:4 | 161 | 8:17 | 135 |
| **AMOS** | | 10-11 | 167 | 1:14 | 179 | 8:18-19 | 123 |
| 1:1 | 37 | | | 2:2 | 107 | 8:20-23 | 111 |
| 1:2 | 91, 117, | **JONAH** | | 2:11-13 | 91 | 9–14 | 184 |
| | 162 | 2:1 | 96 | | | 9:6 | 107 |
| 1:4 | 124 | 4:2 | 99, 104 | **HABBAKUK** | | 9:14 | 88 |
| 2:2 | 88 | | | 1:2-4 | 102 | 10:2 | 68 |
| 2:4 | 117, 118 | **MICAH** | | 1:5-12 | 42 | 10:11 | 107 |
| 2:8 | 145 | 1:1-9 | 42 | 1:8 | 116 | 13:2-5 | 132 |
| 3:1, 13 | 74 | 1:1 | 37 | 2:1 | 133 | 13:9 | 32 |
| 3:4 | 161, 162 | 1:2-7 | 131, 148 | 2:5 | 185 | | |
| 3:4, 8, 12 | 91 | 1:2 | 74 | 2:18-20 | 80 | **MALACHI** | |
| 3:14 | 145 | 1:5-7 | 98 | 3 | 42 | 1:2 | 32 |
| 3:6 | 88, 116, | 1:5 | 167 | 3:17 | 82 | 1:6-14 | 123 |
| | 162 | 1:7 | 55, 121, | | | 1:6-10 | 98 |
| 3:8 | 91 | | 130 | **ZEPHANIAH** | | 1:6 | 156 |
| 4:1 | 74 | 2:8 | 158 | 1:1 | 37 | 2:9 | 156 |
| 4:4-12 | 126 | 3:1, 8, 9 | 169 | 1:4-18 | 42 | 3:3b-4, 10-12 | 123 |
| 4:4-5 | 123 | 3:1, 9 | 74 | 1:4 | 123, 127 | 3:7-12 | 95 |
| 4:4 | 78 | 3:12 | 55, 148 | 1:16 | 88, 124 | 3:10 | 186 |
| 4:10 | 186 | 4:1-3 | 111 | 2:3 | 169 | 3:11 | 82 |
| 5:1 | 74 | 4:4 | 55, 144 | 2:8 | 172 | 3:16-18 | 95 |
| 5:5 | 78 | 5:2-5 | 30 | 2:10 | 107 | | |
| 5:7, 15, 24 | 169 | | | | | | |

# INDEX OF SCRIPTURES FOR JOEL

# INDEX OF SCRIPTURES FOR AMOS

# INDEX OF SCRIPTURES FOR OBADIAH

# INDEX OF SCRIPTURES FOR JONAH

# INDEX OF SIDEBARS AND ILLUSTRATIONS

# INDEX OF TOPICS